History
of
Welsh
International
Rugby

JOHN BILLOT

Opposite: The providers. Hooker Kevin Phillips, with clubmates Jeremy Pugh and (farther back) Brian Williams ensure the ball is made available against Scotland in 1990.

First published in Wales in 1970
Second Edition 1971

This Edition published in 1999

Roman Way Books
Provincial Printing & Publishing Co. Ltd.
Sanatorium Road, Cardiff CF11 8DG
Wales

Printed in Wales by
Provincial Printing & Publishing Co. Ltd.
Sanatorium Road, Cardiff CF11 8DG
Tel: +44 (0)29 20 228729
Fax: +44 (0)29 22 373494

ACKNOWLEDGEMENTS

It is 27 years since I wrote *History of Welsh International Rugby* and the time is opportune for an update after that unforgettable first victory over South Africa. I am delighted that the great Bleddyn Williams has contributed the Foreword. Obviously, Bleddyn could not include himself in his best Welsh team, but we all know he would be there as captain alongside his soulmate, Jack Matthews, in the centre. They were the dream partnership of their éra. Clive Lewis, a colleague of long standing, permitted me to ransack his collection of brilliant action material that filled so many columns of the *Western Mail and South Wales Echo* over more than three decades. Such was his fame as a cameraman of exceptional vision that many photographers followed him around the touchlines, as if he were the Pied Piper of Hamelin, to be at the scene for the best pictures. *Western Mail and Echo Ltd* allowed me to reproduce many of the photographs and I thank MD Mark Haysom and WM Editor Neil Fowler for their consideration in this respect. Mary St Roas, secretary to a succession of managing directors and the Miss Moneypenny of *Western Mail & Echo Ltd*, also played a key role in making this book possible. Ian Fitzgerald, of *Provincial Printing & Publishing*, contributed his advice and artistic flair, and Muriel Fitzgerald, the legendary Mrs Fitz, read proofs and generally encouraged at every stage. To all who have been of invaluable assistance, I express my wholehearted gratitude.

FOREWORD

By BLEDDYN WILLIAMS

(Cardiff, Wales, British Lions)

We thought 1999 would be forever blessed in our memories for heart-stopping victories in Paris and then over England at Wembley, each by one-point margins; but the cup of good fortune, so long in favouring us, had not yet overflowed. As Welsh rugby continued to clamber from its decline we enjoyed double Test success in Argentina to be followed by the main event: triumph against South Africa. Wales had never defeated the Springboks since the first meeting 93 years earlier; but June 26, 1999 will ever remain a date of overriding significance. Inspired by coach Graham Henry, this revitalised Welsh team were heroes to a man. It was a performance to take the breath away and a fitting occasion for the first match in the impressive new Millennium Stadium. I am sure that everyone who was there will treasure the memory.

Inevitably, in recalling memorable matches – victories as well as disastrous failures – we recollect the famous names who have graced our rugby fields, wearing the scarlet jerseys of our country. I have been asked to select my best Welsh team since the end of World War Two and, as ever, it is an exacting task because in choosing just fifteen there are so many brilliant players omitted.

Some choices are straightforward for me. There has never been a right wing to surpass Gerald Davies for all-round football skill; a wonderful finisher with his dramatic change of direction at top speed and at the very last moment. The streamlined Dewi Bebb must be the automatic selection for the left wing role. Inside that superlative pair I place John Dawes as captain for his fluency and directional ability alongside Dr Jack Matthews, of my era. Jack was the most destructive tackler I have seen, a human battering ram, and my regret is that we played so seldom together for Wales. The ways of selectors are often weird and wonderful!

JPR Williams was far from being the most technically perfect full back and his line-kicking was something of a style of his own; but he has to be first choice for his amazing try-scoring feats and fearless defence. That jump into the air to meet the descending ball was his trademark, now emulated by so many. Half back presents most problems because we have been blessed with such an abundance of truly outstanding performers. Eventually, after long and painful pondering to make the fateful decision, it came down to Gareth Edwards and Cliff Morgan.

To split the Gareth Edwards-Barry John partnership almost amounts to treasonable behaviour. Barry John was dubbed The King in his playing days and no-one denies him his tribute. He flowed through a game, the ultimate laid-back master of proceedings. But for me, Cliff Morgan electrified events as few have done: he was the urgent attacker, the supreme coverer and the complete kicker. Gareth Edwards was the great try-stealer, a scrum half of extraordinary perception and remarkable strength.

There are numerous combinations among the forwards. To start with, my front row is formed by Cliff Davies, an iron scrummager and the fastest loose-head of all time in my rating; the highly-talented Bryn Meredith as a ball-carrying hooker with more running skills than some midfield men; and the magnificent and immovable Graham Price. Roy John has to be first choice as a soaring jumper in the second row and partnering him the man New Zealand's legendary Colin Meads claimed to be the best he ever played against, R H Williams. Mervyn Davies incontestably is the No 8, flanked by ever-alert Dai Morris and rugged RCC Thomas on the open-side.

I realise I will have omitted many fans' favourite players, but there can only be fifteen – and in the great days of Welsh rugby they never needed to send on replacements with 'fresh legs' to bolster the team. We did it our way! So my team is:

JPR Williams; Gerald Davies, Jack Matthews, John Dawes (captain), Dewi Bebb; Cliff Morgan, Gareth Edwards; Cliff Davies, Bryn Meredith, Graham Price, RH Williams, Roy John, Dai Morris, Mervyn Davies, RCC Thomas.

Where is my specialist goal-kicker? Who needs a kicker of goals with all these renowned ball-winners and magical runners? This team is designed to win matches in the classical and romantic manner by scoring tries!

My saddest day in rugby was when it went professional. We were not prepared for it and it has done little for the game. We need time to adapt, to create a recognisable structure that will prove responsible, vibrant and attract back the lost thousands to our club matches. Hopefully, such a display as we witnessed by both sides in that wonderful win in Paris in March 1999, the never-say-die spirit against England at Wembley, the grim determination shown in Argentina and that unbelievable victory over the Springboks will give the game new and exciting impetus.

From Mr Richardson's Field to the Millennium Stadium

Everyone knew Wales would lose their first international match when they met England on Mr Richardson's Field at Blackheath on February 19, 1881. After all, England had lost only two games in 10 years. But the cruel margin of seven goals, one dropped goal and six tries to nil staggered the Welshman in the street. "The Field" said of the match:

"Looked at from whatever point, it is impossible to congratulate the Welsh rugby union team on their first match with England, unless it were on their pluck in coming so far with the prospect of almost certain defeat. It would be difficult to imagine a more easy victory than that gained by the English XV". In those early days of the game there were no points apportioned for goals and tries. By modern scoring values, however, that Welsh defeat would be represented by a total of 82 points. It was indeed a massacre.

Was Welsh rugby really this immature ? The outcry that followed had momentous results. It helped close the ranks of rugby in the Principality, inspired the formation of the Welsh Rugby Union less than a month later, and provided Wales with a challenge that was to carry them to glory on the rugby grounds of Britain by the turn of the century.

It all started with a letter to the editor of the Western Mail and published a few days after the "disgraceful defeat", as it was termed, on Mr Richardson's Field. The letter, signed A Welsh Football Player, read: "Could you or any of your readers inform me whether the members of the Welsh XV who played against England were selected by responsible persons appointed by the committee of the South Wales Football Union? Or was it a private team, got up by Mr Mullock, of Newport, to do battle for Wales?"

A letter of reply was printed from Mr Clarke, honorary secretary of the South Wales Football Union: "I beg to inform your correspondent that the team which represented Wales was not elected by the committee of the South Wales Football Union; neither had they anything to do with it. As your correspondent assumes, Mr Mullock was one of the committee who selected the Welsh team and will, no doubt, be pleased to give any information required".

But no explanation was forthcoming from Mr Mullock and it is quite obvious that this was very much a private team, in no way representative of the true playing strength of the game in the Principality. Indeed, it is recorded that C P Lewis, one of the outstanding sportsmen in Wales was offered the captaincy of this first Welsh international team, but declined because he considered it did not reflect the real power of Welsh rugby. Nevertheless, it was a historic event and the players who took part are credited with caps.

The official statement from the South Wales Football Union showed that they washed their hands of the whole affair. So the "Welsh" team's rout on Mr Richardson's Field could have only one outcome: a responsible and recognised body had to be appointed to control the interests of Wales on the international rugby scene. On Saturday, March 12, 1881 delegates of 11 clubs gathered at the Castle Hotel, Neath. This group of officials met "to consider the question of forming a Welsh Rugby Union."

The Western Mail reports that the clubs represented were Bangor, Brecon, Cardiff, Lampeter, Llandeilo, Llandovery, Llanelli, Merthyr, Newport, Pontypool and Swansea. Mr Richardson, a captain of Swansea, acted as chairman and it needs little imagination to reconstruct the scene. There must have been some hard talking, with Mr Mullock on the receiving end. He was an outstanding organiser, but he could not be permitted to raise private teams in the name of Wales — particularly when they failed so badly! Richard Mullock was in favour of a governing body for Welsh international rugby and promised to disband his private squad of international footballers.

The delegates felt they needed this bold man, who had taken the first step into big rugby. Here was an explorer in the field of sport; and he was undeterred that failure had accompanied his initial mission. The clubs unanimously carried the resolution to form the Welsh Rugby Union, and Richard Mullock was elected the first honorary secretary. He was to hold the post through the first 11 emerging years. Mr C C Chambers, president of Swansea Football Club, was chosen as the first president of the WRU for 1881-2. Out of chaos on Mr Richardson's Field rose a new unity in Welsh rugby. One day Wales would show them all . . . .

The game in Wales was spread principally by students returning from schools and universities in England. That first Welsh XV of 1881 was drawn almost exclusively from players with experience of the game at Oxford and Cambridge Universities and from the powerful Newport and Cardiff clubs. Then, as the Rev Charles Newman, of Newport, and the Swansea half-back, W H Gwynn, introduced passing into the Welsh style, the game assumed an interest for spectators. The South Wales Challenge Cup, however, was the most important single factor in popularising the game.

Larger crowds flocked to the cup ties than watched the early international encounters. Sadly, the competition became too violent: referees were assaulted by irate supporters and players fought on the field. In 1914, following a lapse of nearly 30 years, the cup was reintroduced, but again led to ill-feeling. After the 1914-18 War, discreetly no-one suggested reviving the cup tourney. More than 50 years were to pass before the delegates at the WRU annual general meeting in 1970 voted to bring back the cup, and then there were mixed feelings on the matter.

But the cup had served its purpose in making rugby part of the way of life of Welsh people. It created the initial popularity for the game among spectators. Then the famous players of the early days took the stage and prepared Wales for the Golden Era of supremacy at the start of the Twentieth Century.

First, Wales were to introduce the four threequarter system to the international scene, and that despite the bitter opposition of the greatest Welsh player of the day. Newport's Arthur Gould, who was to captain Wales a record 18 times, protested that, "The four threequarter method won't work." He despised the system and had good cause. When Wales tried the experiment for the first time against Scotland at Cardiff on January 9, 1886, it was reported: "The hardy Scots gave the wearers of the scarlet a fearful thrashing."

Frank Hancock, an Englishman, had perfected the two-centre game with Cardiff. One of 10 rugby playing brothers from Wiveliscombe, Hancock was "deficient in pace, but a corkscrew runner." He was chosen to captain Wales to implement the new formation, but had to send Harry Bowen from full back into the pack to reinforce his eight forwards against Scotland's nine. Gould was switched to full back. Understandably, Gould built a great contempt for what he termed, "the Cardiff game", and in later years Newport were one of the last clubs to adopt the system.

Gould and Hancock differed in many ways. Whereas Gould was an expert drop-kicker, Hancock scorned dropped goals. He refused to allow the Cardiff team to use this as a method of scoring when he captained them in 1885-86. That season Cardiff lost only one match (the final fixture against Moseley at the Arms Park) and scored 70 goals and 61 tries, but not one dropped goal. Hancock sternly rebuked one of his team on one occasion for trying to drop a goal from a mark.

It is interesting how Hancock, who first played as a forward, came to figure in the four threequarter story. On February 9, 1883, Cardiff were short of a threequarter for the match at Cheltenham College. Hancock, a newcomer, was brought in and played so well that Cardiff were reluctant to leave him out of the next match against Gloucester at the Arms Park. The club selectors were anxious not to lose Hancock to another club and at the same time considered it unfair to omit one of the regular threequarters. So Hancock was chosen – as a fourth threequarter. The match with Gloucester was drawn, but everyone thought the formation so successful that it was retained for the remaining four fixtures of the season.

Cardiff had experimented previously with the two-centre style at the suggestion of H D Simpson and W D Phillips, but it was Hancock who brought this method to perfection – despite Arthur Gould's contempt for what he considered an infringement on his freedom to dominate as an individualist in midfield.

After the 1886 failure against Scotland on a semi-frozen pitch, the four threequarter plan was not tried again for nearly two years. Then, significantly, Gould was absent and a Cardiff man was captain when Wales met the Maoris at Swansea in December, 1888. This time the system was a success and Wales never returned to the old formation. In the end, even Gould had to admit its merit as he led Wales to their first Triple Crown by playing eight forwards against the nines of England, Scotland and Ireland in 1893. At long last the two-centre game had been vindicated and the other countries were compelled to adopt the Welsh method.

W H Gwynn, the "father of Welsh halves", and the "Rev Charlie", as Newman was called, were followed in their style of passing the ball out by "Buller" Stadden, a Cardiff forward, who became one of the finest half backs of the early days before he went North to Dewsbury. Previously, half backs had lurked on the skirts of the scrummages ready to scoop up the ball (if it came out) and run as far as they could until they were caught. Half backs often played left and right, sharing the duties of working the scrum, but Wales began to specialise in this direction. Newport found that Fred Parfitt was better suited to work the scrum while the frail Percy "The Sparrow" Phillips was a brilliant dodger as outside half. This pair helped Wales win the Triple Crown for the first time in their specialist roles.

Then came the remarkable brothers Evan and David James, a pair of pocket halves, whose trickery was to become a legend and make Swansea rugby famous. David mostly worked the scrum with Evan as stand-off. When they went to play for Broughton Rangers in Manchester for £200 down and £2 a week it was almost a national disaster. The brothers were branded as professionals, but were reinstated and returned to the Welsh team after a seven-year absence.

Whereas the James brothers, the great initiators of elusive combination, often neglected team work because of their individualism, the Dicky Owen-Dick Jones unit evolved a flawless understanding for the benefit of the team. This Swansea pair were to play for Wales 15 times (a record that stood until Gareth Edwards and Barry John broke it in 1970). Owen is credited with inventing the reverse pass, which he used to launch the try-scoring move in the victory over the 1905 All Blacks. Owen also developed attacking moves with his wing forward, Ivor Morgan, of Swansea and Wales, and was to advance scrum half tactics a stage beyond that reached by any other player.

Wales set examples to other countries in a number of important matters in the emerging years. As well as introducing the successful formula of the two-centre system, they moved the abolition of the mauls in-goal, which so often ended in fights. Wales inaugurated the differential penalty as far back as 1889, when the International Board accepted the proposal that for handling the ball in the scrum or collapsing the scrum a penalty be awarded, but no goal could be kicked from an award of this nature.

The International Board (of which England were not members at the time) also adopted the Welsh suggestion to award points for tries and goals, which had been used in club matches in many parts of the country for several years. This method of scoring came into effect in international rugby in 1890 and Wales beat England by one point (the value then of a try) to nil at Dewsbury on a quagmire ground in a snowstorm. Arthur Gould, the Welsh captain, was so delighted by this first victory over England that, covered with mud, he embraced Welsh secretary Richard Mullock – and the mud-smeared Mr Mullock raised no objection.

But the Welsh plan, at the height of their power in the Golden Era, for an eight backs-seven forwards formation was an experiment that failed. Wales were confident that this new method would revolutionise the game in the manner of the four threequarter innovation, particularly after the 16-3 win over England at Richmond in 1906, and the 22-0 success over England at Swansea in 1907. After Scotland's eight forwards smashed the Welsh seven at Inverleith in 1907, however, Wales discarded their plan. Even pioneers sometimes find the odds too great.

The gates opened on the Welsh Golden Era at Kingsholm, Gloucester, on January 6, 1900. Before that match, Wales had played 46 games and won only 16. Three had been drawn and the other 27 lost. But the Golden Era saw the Red Devils rule almost supreme for 12 years. In that time they won the Triple Crown six times and with it the championship. Wales went through 22 consecutive home matches against England, Scotland, Ireland and France and won them all. In a series of 25 games, the only side to win in Wales were the 1906 Springboks, by eleven points to nil. And Percy Bush, the Welsh outside half in that game, maintained that bad selection was to blame for the defeat.

From that Kingsholm fixture to start 1900, until the final match of 1911, Wales played 43 games, won 35, drew one and lost seven. W J Bancroft, Gwyn Nicholls and Billy Trew were the principal captains of their country in that age of supremacy, though Willie Llewellyn led Wales to the Triple Crown in 1905 and the captaincy was shared around in 1907 and again in 1908, in which year Wales won four games with a different captain in each.

Those captains were fortunate that they had such brilliant teams to lead. Little planning was needed before matches and it is recorded that against England, in his first year of captaincy, Gwyn Nicholls issued instructions on how to neutralise the superior strength of their opponents while the players were waiting for the kick-off.

Tom Graham had introduced theory, pattern and discipline into forward play while captaining Newport from 1889 to 1893, and another famous Newport player, George Boots, was the first man to employ scientific wing forward methods, including corner-flagging. Both these men influenced the development of forward play considerably. George Travers became one of the first specialist hookers in a period when there was no real definition of places in the scrums, though some had favourite positions. It should be remembered also that it was the Welsh system of four threequarters that largely inspired the creation of the wing forward. Ireland's Charles Rooke was known as the prince of wing forwards in the first half of the 1890s.

But not even wing forwards could shackle Wales in their Golden Era. Where Arthur Gould had been the dynamic figure in the three-threequarter days, Gwyn Nicholls was the great player of the two-centre style. Gould and Nicholls played together for Wales on only three occasions in 1896 and 1897, before Gould retired as a result of the bitter dispute over his testimonial. The other countries held that he was professionalised because he had been presented with the deeds of his house after donations from all parts of the world had been made to a fund to recognise his achievements. Fixtures were broken off until Gould announced that he would not play again.

Were those old time players superior to the moderns? The game has changed so much that it is unfair to make comparisons in many respects. But where is there a forward in the mould of Newport's Arthur Boucher? He played 13 games for Wales in the 1890s and, as well as being an automatic choice for the pack, was first reserve for the centre position should either Arthur Gould or Gwyn Nicholls be unfit.

Yet even the old-time heroes played badly, though the passing of time has served to obscure their human failings. When we criticise the modern players, it should be recalled that Arthur Gould, Gwyn Nicholls, W J Bancroft, Trew and Owen were all severely criticised in their playing days.

W J Bancroft (5ft. 6in. and 10 st.) played 33 consecutive games for Wales and was the first to apply lateral spin with the screw kick. But he was far more erratic than his brother Jack, who followed him as the Welsh full back. Jack scored more than any other player for his country with 88 international points. Legends have grown up around the name of WJ, ignoring his many weaknesses and eulogising his unorthodox and risky style of teasing the opposition into chasing him before he kicked to touch. His real claim to fame was as a goal kicker of exceptional skill.

Billy Trew played 29 times for Wales (six on the wing, nine as outside half and 14 in the centre) and, like Owen, was a creative genius. He weighed less than 10 st. and was one of the most closely marked men in the game. Remarkably, he survived some cruel tackles until, at the age of 33, he was badly injured in Paris and his international career came to an end.

The only problem facing Wales during their Golden Era was that they had too many brilliant players. Percy Bush was the most amazing of them all. It was said that he had too much talent for one man and was a veritable team on his own. But he and Owen could not combine as a unit for Wales. The reason for this was that Swansea allowed Owen to control their tactics at scrum half, while Cardiff's strategy was dictated by Bush from the outside half position.

Together their styles did not blend, though they were in partnership to scheme the greatest Welsh victory on a rugby field, when the 1905 All Blacks were beaten 3-0 in Cardiff.

Owen has been credited with perfecting and launching the scoring move, which had been rehearsed carefully. But Bush was the key man in the whole operation. Willie Llewellyn, who played on the wing in that immortal match, explained this to me: "Percy was such a brilliant player on tour in New Zealand with the British team the previous year that when the All Blacks came over in 1905 they were thinking only of stopping him. They really were frightened of Percy because he could run right through a team. So we kept passing the ball out to Percy and the All Blacks concentrated on him. That was what gave us our chance to use the feint attack and win the match."

Then for Wales came the breadline days after World War I. There was a successful season to start in 1920, when only the 5-9 defeat in Scotland prevented them winning the Triple Crown; and in 1922 it was only a 9-9 draw in Scotland that foiled the Red Devils. But the black years crowded in. During 15 consecutive games, from 1923 into 1926, only three victories were recorded. In those seasons, England developed the back row of the scrum as devastating spoilers and Benny Osler, with the 1931 Springboks, brought tactical kicking into vogue from the outside half position. So the adventure faded from back play.

Wales had to wait until the 1930s for new stars to revive the romance of the Golden Era. From 1923 to 1930, in 32 games, Wales won nine, drew two and lost 21. Wick Powell was one of the most spectacular players of that period. A scrum half, big and strong, he played his first game on the wing in Scotland in 1926 as an emergency replacement and made a remarkably successful job of blotting out the flying wing Ian Smith. In his 27 appearances for Wales, Powell played three times on the wing. He was called an erratic adventurer and his long passes often were wildly distributed, but only Owen (35) and Haydn Tanner (25) made more appearances at scrum half for Wales by the start of the 1950s.

Tanner was one of the players who emerged in the thirties to bring glory once again with the magnificent 13-12 victory over the 1935 All Blacks. It was the most spectacular match Wales had played since W J Bancroft won the 1893 tussle with England 12-11 by ignoring his captain's orders. Tanner made his debut against the All Blacks (just as Percy Bush had done) and played a notable part in the victory. He was to become one of the great scrum halves of the game. Tanner was still at school when he played that game against New Zealand. Other Welsh schoolboy caps have been W H Thomas (one of more than 30 international players from Llandovery College), Norman Biggs and Wilf Wooller.

Wooller and Cliff Jones, of course, were two of the most exciting attackers between the war years; and there was Claude Davey, the smiling, sledge-hammer tackler, who captained Wales in succession to line-out expert Watcyn Thomas, the first man to lead a winning Welsh team at

Twickenham in 1933. Cliff Jones remains as one of Wales's greatest outside halves; a dazzling, deceptive runner and superb kicker who was lost to the game because of injuries when only 24 years old.

After a lapse of 39 years, Wales were the Triple Crown winners in 1950, captained by John Gwilliam, who was given the leadership when Bleddyn Williams had to withdraw because of injury. It is an ironic thought for Bleddyn Williams, one of the finest centres of all time, that had he not missed that game he might well have broken Arthur Gould's record of 18 times as captain of Wales. Williams had to wait for three years before he was appointed to captain the national team and in his five appearances as captain led a winning team each time.

Gwilliam had great players in his team to launch Wales on a mini-Golden Era in the 'fifties, during which time 43 matches were played, 29 were won, two drawn and 12 lost. The victories featured the 13-8 success over the All Blacks in 1953. This period included the staggering Murrayfield Massacre, when Wales, as Triple Crown holders and fresh from crushing England 23-5, lost 19-0 to Scotland's team of unknowns. That defeat ranks among the great shocks.

In 1952, with Gwilliam still as their leader, Wales won the Triple Crown again. Ken Jones, the Newport wing, broke the cap record of Dicky Owen by playing 44 times (43 in consecutive matches) and his clubmate Bryn Meredith, a fine hooker, became the most capped forward in 1962, when he played his 34th game. Cliff Morgan and Rex Willis, the Cardiff halves, dominated the 'fifties and Roy John became the most famous line-out forward of all time. Then came Clive Rowlands.

He brought a new concept to Welsh rugby; a new dimension to exploit tactical kicking from the scrum half position. He developed his style to a degree that has never been equalled in scrum half strategy, and never will now that the laws have been changed with prohibition on kicking direct to touch between the 22 lines. Some said he had an obsession for kicking and his methods led to a blaze of controversy. In 1962, Wales had gone throughout the season without scoring a try. Then Rowlands was made captain on his debut. The only previous players to have led Wales on their first appearances had been James Bevan (naturally enough because it was the first game Wales played in 1881), Charles Lewis (in the second game Wales played) and John R Evans, of Newport, in 1934.

Rowlands's first nine games as captain produced only three Welsh victories, but in 1963 he broke the Murrayfield grip after 10 years. Rowlands relied entirely on the power of his pack and his own tactical kicking. There was an outcry against his methods. But he argued that Wales had to win; and that was the way they were best equipped to do so. With line-out domination and Rowlands directing every move to pin-point opposition weaknesses, with the hanging punt to the posts or the corner, Wales won the Triple Crown in 1965. He turned a team of failures into champions.

His 14 successive matches as Welsh captain was a record, but the season after his greatest triumph he was relegated to the role of reserve and never played for Wales again. Alun Pask, an outstanding international No. 8, and David Watkins, a brilliant outside half, were captains who could not lead Wales to further success in the Triple Crown. In a period of 12 games, starting with the first ever defeat by Australia in 1966, Wales managed only three victories.

Then in 1968-69 the ban came on kicking direct to touch between the 22 lines.

Immediately, Wales won the Triple Crown for the 11th time with Brian Price, the Newport line-out expert, captaining the side and Maurice Richards, the Cardiff wing, scoring four tries in the victory over England. Keith Jarrett, the Newport centre, provided the goal points. His debut as full back against England in 1967 had seen him score 19 points to equal the Welsh record by Jack Bancroft in 1910.

Just as Wales had given the lead in many important matters in the early years, so the Principality led the way in the new method of coaching and preparation of their international team. First, Ray Williams was appointed full time coaching organiser in 1966-67, during which season Wales finished bottom of the championship table with only one victory (that astonishing 34-21 success over England in the last match of the season).

At the start of the 1967-68 season, David Nash, the former international forward, was chosen from outside the WRU executive as a selector and later made coach to the national training squad of 25 players. Nash resigned before the start of the 1968-69 season and Clive Rowlands, who had won election as a WRU vice-president less than two months after retiring from the game in April 1968, was appointed as successor. Rowlands helped re-establish Welsh rugby power and the side he coached regained the Triple Crown and were unbeaten champions in 1969. Weekend training sessions were introduced at the Afan Lido, Port Talbot, for the national squad of elite players and clubs were requested not to play squad members in more than one club match a week. A tremendous drive had been started to improve international standards, and the other countries followed the Welsh example.

Under the perceptive command of John Dawes, Wales ushered in the sensational seventies with Barry John and Gareth Edwards cementing their telepathic partnership, which saw them play in harness on 24 occasions after winning their first caps in 1966 and 1967 respectively. Barry was on the winning side in just one of his first seven appearances for Wales; Gareth was marginally more successful with two victories out of seven. Little did we realise we were witnessing a pair of extraordinary apprentices formulating a combination that may never be excelled for its unique style. Barry, alas, did not possess the all-consuming appetite for glory that some enjoyed and decided early retirement was in order. Yet the man dubbed "The King" on tour with the history-making 1971 Lions in New Zealand, lives on in our memories as a supreme master of the laid-back approach. He embraced lassitude of movement where Cliff Morgan, David Watkins and Phil Bennett were human dynamos, crackling with high voltage energy.

In the seventies, great players set standards for all time. Everyone knew without explanation who JPR, TGR and JJ were. JPR Williams was the fearless trampoline full back who frequently caught the ball in mid-air. TGR Davies switched from centre to emerge as probably the most complete right wing of all time: he could twinkle right up to a tackler and then, with a late, late swerve or sidestep, fade past and on his way to another try. JJ was the sleek streak on the left wing; greased lightning and a tip-top footballer into the bargain.

As a unit, Wales have never enjoyed a more impressive and consistent trio than Mervyn Davies and his disciples, breakaways John Taylor and master of the blindside, Dai Morris. Individually, there have been players as talented, or even better, in their positions; except, that is, for Dai Morris. He was one of a special breed: 'Shadow' will always be the greatest. But in unison these men form the most famous Welsh back row of all time. Terry Cobner proved a menacing presence as a speedy, intimidating openside. His terror pack at Pontypool perhaps influenced the making of Jurassic Park! Filmed under the dim floodlights, they could have titled it 'Pontypool Park'.

The experience of playing there certainly put the frighteners on many opposing teams. The Pontypool front row of black belt Tony Faulkner, Bobby Windsor and the superlative Graham Price, the tight head against whom all tight heads are judged, played together for Wales in a wickedly driving scrum while Allan Martin and Geoff Wheel were a magnificent second row who packed together in a record 27 matches. These were the dream tight five. When Gareth Edwards quit the scene there were two outstanding successors in powerful Terry Holmes and smooth-as-silk Robert Jones.

The seventies were launched in a drawn match against South Africa at the Arms Park and ended with yet another victory over England. In 46 full cap games, Wales won 32, drew 3 and lost 11. Of the defeats, only New Zealand (twice) won in Cardiff. Seven defeats in 10 years in the Five Nations were all away from home. Two games were lost in Australia and there was an uncapped fixture with New Zealand in Cardiff that the All Blacks won. Between France succeeding in 1968 until Scotland triumphed in 1982, no Five Nations team won at the Arms Park. That was 27 championship matches with the only blemish a drawn clash with France in 1974. The previous record run of success had been 22 consecutive home victories during the first Golden Era between 1900 and 1912.

The eighties proved a disappointing anti-climax, though the polished Bleddyn Bowen led Wales to the Triple Crown in 1988. Richard Moriarty may have seemed an unlikely captain to many, but the vastly experienced Swansea hard-man led Wales to third place in the inaugural World Cup in 1987 and set a determined example. The nineties saw no great lifeline to Welsh recovery. The first 16 games brought just three successes, and none of those against Five Nations opponents. Namibia (twice) and Argentina were hardly significant victories.

Ieuan Evans was inflicted with the captaincy. Full back and wing are the most difficult positions from which to exert control, but Ieuan, a wing of exceptional skill by any standards, brought dignity to his role. He was the most menacing figure in the Welsh attack and led his side to the championship title outright for the first time for 15 years in 1994. Neil Jenkins arrived on the scene in 1991, a subject of endless debate regarding his style of play. Ignoring the fact that he has become the most famous goal-kicker Welsh rugby has ever seen, with records galore, there were critics who considered the backline was not being released with alacrity and tactical kicking predominated. True, Jenks was not in the mould of the classical Welsh fly half; but too often his talents were given scant credit for a job well done within the limitations of a struggling national team. He became the highest paid player in Wales in 1999 when, after 14 years with Pontypridd, he joined Cardiff. The experiment of playing Jenkins at full back to accommodate the tricky Arwel Thomas at No 10 was a jersey switch too far. Eventually, Jenkins said, never again! It was outside half and nowhere else.

There have been some spine-chilling defeats. New Zealand won 52-3 and 54-9 in 1988; Australia hoisted a 63-6 success in 1991, and 56-25 when Wales ventured Down Under again in 1996. Southern hemisphere superiority could be used as an excuse; but it was difficult to explain the 60-26 demolition at Twickenham in 1998. Or France's 51-0 triumph at Wembley the same season. But Pretoria 1998 was Wales's Wounded Knee: a massacre on an unprecedented scale. South Africa almost reached 100 points: they finished on 96-13. Some may call it the Full Monty Match – Wales were totally exposed.

However, revenge came a year later with a first victory over the Springboks in 93 years, since the first meeting in 1906. It was 29-19 in the opening match at the new Arms Park / Millennium Stadium: a mind-blowing experience for Rob Howley's team. The pack emerged as a new Terrible Eight who tamed the Boks. The Twenty-First Century beckons for Wales to continue to restore the old glory days. That amazing 1999 try by Scott Gibbs to rob England during injury time and the wise ways of New Zealander Graham Henry, a coach who injects ambition and enthusiasm, have captured the headlines. May we witness many more in the years ahead.

WELSH INTERNATIONAL MATCHES

*(*signifies first appearance)*

England won by seven goals, one dropped goal, six tries to nil
(N.B. No points were awarded for goals or tries at this stage)

England played five backs and 10 forwards against the Welsh formation of six backs and nine forwards. Another difference was that whereas England employed one man as full back, Wales used two. James Bevan, the first Welsh captain, was an Australian by birth but lived in the village of Grosmont, near Abergavenny. He was educated at Hereford Cathedral School and then played for Cambridge in the Varsity matches of 1877 and 1880. He almost won the match for Cambridge in 1880 with a dropped goal, but the umpires disallowed it after a dispute and the match was drawn.

As a direct result of Wales's "disgraceful defeat" in this first full international match, the Welsh Rugby Union was formed less than a month later. It was alleged that this first Welsh XV was very far from representative of the real strength of Welsh club rugby and a responsible and recognised authority was needed to select future national teams. Though Wales had done well earlier in the season against Gloucestershire, Somerset and other county sides, Bevan's men were given no chance at all against England, who had lost only two of their games since the very first international 10 years earlier.

Harry Vassall was named to complete the England team after 14 men had been chosen with one place left open. Vassall impressed the selectors playing for Oxford University against Blackheath, and went on to impress again in the Welsh match with three tries on his international debut. Another forward, George Burton, scored four tries. Lennard Stokes, the English captain, who dropped an astonishing goal from 80 yards during this season in the drawn match with Scotland, converted six tries against Wales. It is recorded that Stokes threw a "colossal" pass to Hunt, giving him an easy try against Wales, but the umpires ordered the ball back, their decision being that such a long pass was not football! Had they scored this 14th try it would have been an England record.

The match was refereed by Arthur Guillemard (West Kent), president of the Rugby Union. Those, of course, were the days before neutral referees were appointed. After this overwhelming defeat, Wales were not offered a match with England the following season. Instead, Wales played North of England at Newport on January 16, 1882, but did so well in losing only by a goal to a try, that England readmitted them to full international status for 1882-83.

England: back – T W Fry (Queen's House); threequarters – L Stokes (Blackheath, capt), R Hunt (Preston Grasshoppers and Manchester); half backs – H H Taylor (Blackheath), H T Twynam (Richmond); forwards – H Vassall, A Budd, G W Burton (Blackheath), C W L Fernandes (Leeds), E T Gurdon, C Gurdon (Richmond), W Hewitt (Queen's House), C P Wilson (Marlborough Nomads), H C Rowley (Manchester), H Fowler (Walthamstow).

Wales: backs – C H Newman (Cambridge Univ. and Newport), R H B Summers (Haverfordwest); threequarters – J A Bevan (Cambridge Univ., capt), E Peake (Oxford Univ. and Chepstow); halfbacks – L Watkins (Oxford Univ. and Llandaff), E J Lewis (Cambridge Univ. and Llandovery); forwards – R D Garnons Williams (Cambridge Univ. and Newport), T A Rees (Oxford Univ. and

Llandovery), F Purdon, G F Harding (Newport), B E Girling, B B Mann, W D Phillips (Cardiff), G Darbishire (Bangor), E Treharne (Pontypridd).

For England, George Burton (4), Harry Vassall (3), Bob Hunt, Henry Taylor, 'Jimmy' Budd, Charles Fernandes, Campbell Rowley and Henry Twynam scored tries. Lennard Stokes converted six. Hunt converted one and dropped a goal.

Referee: A G Guillemard (England).

Match 2   **IRELAND v WALES**   Lansdowne Road, Dublin. January 28, 1882

Wales won by two goals, two tries to nil

Wales's second international, and their first with Ireland, brought the first victory. Only four of those who had played against England a year before were included. Newman, Harding, Purdon and Phillips. This time Charles Newman, one of the full backs against England, was at half back, where he had built a reputation for deceptive dodging with Newport.

Reports of this match said that there were "sundry disputes" between the Irish team and the Welsh umpire, Mr. Richard Mullock, who was secretary of the WRU. Two of the Irish players walked off in disgust and two more went off, apparently with injuries. Ireland finished with 11 men and it was such an unsatisfactory game that the fixture was discontinued until 1884.

A week before this victory in Dublin, the Welsh XV, captained by Newman, had gained an outstanding victory over Midland Counties by three goals and three tries to nil at Newport. Bill Evans (Rhymney) scored five of the six tries.

Ireland: back – R E McLean (Dublin Univ.); threequarters – J R Atkinson, St. G McCarthy (Dublin Univ.), W W Fletcher (Kingstown); half backs – G C Bent, E H Greene (Dublin Univ.); forwards – A J Forrest, F Kennedy, W A Wallis, J M Kennedy (Wanderers), H B Morfell, A J Downing (Dublin Univ.), F S Heuston, E McCarthy (Kingstown), R G Thompson (Queen's Coll., Cork).

Wales: backs – *C P Lewis (Llandovery, capt), * S S Clarke (Neath); threequarters – *W B Norton (Cardiff), *W F Evans (Oxford Univ. and Rhymney), G F Harding (Newport); half backs – C H Newman, *R H Bridie (Newport); forwards – F Purdon, *T Baker Jones, * R Gould (Newport), *T J S Clapp (Nantyglo), Tom Williams (Cardiff), W D Phillips (Cardiff), *G L Morris (Swansea), * H C Vincent (Bangor).

For Wales, Tom Baker Jones, Tom Clapp, Bill Evans and Ron Bridie scored tries. Charles Lewis converted two.

Referee: W J Goulding (Ireland).

Match 3   **WALES v ENGLAND**   St. Helen's, Swansea. December 16, 1882

England won by two goals, four tries to nil

One newspaper report said of this first international match played in Wales: "The wonderful passing of the Englishmen proved too much for Wales. The ball could not be followed – so rapid were its movements." Whatever the exaggeration of those remarks, there can be no doubt that Gregory Wade had a devastating effect on the Welsh defence. A fast wing with a powerful hand-off, he scored three tries on his debut. But he would never have played had not Philip Newton, the Blackheath forward, withdrawn. Harry Vassall, one of the greatest names in the history of Rugby Football for his theories of combined passing, suggested playing Wade as an extra threequarter. So that December day at Swansea, England introduced the three

Wales's Terrible Eight: the fearless pack who figured in the 'roughest match of all time' to defeat Ireland 11-3 at Belfast in 1914. Operation Bunch of Fives was planned the night before the match when the teams met at the theatre. It was said that the Rev Alban Jones took no part in the rough house tactics; most of the others did not deprive themselves of some moments of hair-raising how's your father! Standing (left to right): Percy Jones, Edgar Morgan, Harry Uzzell, T J Lloyd, Dai Watts. Seated: Tom Williams, Rev Alban Davies, Walter Rees (WRU Secretary), J Bedwellty Jones.

Not a soccer team! Cardiff's magnificent eleven all played for Wales during the 1947-48 season, 10 of them together in the matches against England, Scotland and France. Standing (left to right): Les Williams, Cliff Davies, Gwyn Evans, Les Manfield, Frank Trott, Maldwyn James. Seated: Billy Cleaver, Haydn Tanner, Bleddyn Williams, Jack Matthews. Inset: Bill Tamplin.

PROMINENT FOOTBALLERS.

R. T. GABE,
CARDIFF.

PROMINENT FOOTBALLERS.

R. M. OWEN,
SWANSEA.

PROMINENT FOOTBALLERS

P. F. BUSH,
CARDIFF.

PROMINENT FOOTBALLERS.

G. BOOTS.
NEWPORT.

PROMINENT FOOTBALLERS.

C. M. PRITCHARD,
NEWPORT.

Football Series No. 42.

A. J. Gould, late of Newport.
Photo by Goldie, Swansea.

Football Series No. 63.

E. Gwyn Nichols, Cardiff.
Photo by Falk, Sydney.

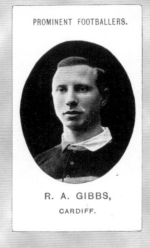

PROMINENT FOOTBALLERS.

R. A. GIBBS,
CARDIFF.

Football Series No. 50.

W. J. Trew, Swansea.
Photo by Goldie, Swansea.

COPE'S
"CLIPS"
CIGARETTES

No. 46—DYKE, L. M.
Cardiff
Noted Footballers

Football Series No. 52.

W. J. Bancroft, Swansea.
Photo by Thiele, London.

J. WETTER

Many of rugby's great players featured on cigarette cards at the turn of the Twentieth Century. Taddy issued Prominent Footballers in 1907 and Wills packed Football Series in Wild Woodbine and Cinderella in 1902. Jack Wetter was given with The Champion boys' paper in 1922.

LLEWELLYN.

F. & J. SMITH'S CIGARETTES

SWANSEA R.F.C.

J. BANCROFT.

LAMBERT & BUTLER'S CIGARETTES

IVOR JONES

(LLANELLY & WALES)

OGDEN'S CIGARETTES.

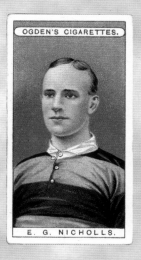

E. G. NICHOLLS.

CHURCHMAN'S CIGARETTES

J. BASSETT

PLAYER'S CIGARETTES.

W. C. POWELL

F. & J. SMITH'S CIGARETTES

CARDIFF, R.F.C.

C. LEWIS,

O.H.M.S.

WILLS'S CIGARETTES.

H. M. BOWCOTT

CHURCHMAN'S CIGARETTES

W. WOOLLER

CHURCHMAN'S CIGARETTES

CLIFF W. JONES

CHURCHMAN'S CIGARETTES

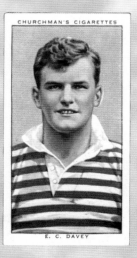

E. C. DAVEY

CHURCHMAN'S CIGARETTES

V. G. J. JENKINS

During the Golden Age of cigarette cards, rugby featured colourfully. This display, starting top left with Willie Llewellyn (issued by Cohen Weenen in 1907) is an example of trade card artwork.

Swansea's famous St. Helen's ground packed to bursting for the Wales v France match of 1952. Wales outside half Alun Thomas prepares to clear to touch. Wales were 9-5 winners to complete another Grand Slam.

The 1950 Wales Grand Slam team, winners for the first time since 1911. Standing (left to right): Ivor Jones (WRU touch-judge), Rex Willis, Don Hayward, Roy John, Bob Evans, Malcolm Thomas, John Robins, Mr M J Dowling (referee). Seated: Ray Cale, Cliff Davies, Jack Matthews, John Gwilliam (capt), Billy Cleaver, Ken Jones, Dai Davies. In front: Gerwyn Williams, Lewis Jones.

threequarter system to their team. They were not the first to adopt this because Scotland used it against Ireland in 1881. Wade played eight times for England, never on the losing side, and was one of the great wings of the early eighties. He later became Premier of New South Wales.

Wales: backs – C P Lewis (Llandovery, capt), *D H Bowen (Llanelli); threequarters – W B Norton, *J Clare (Cardiff), *D Gwynn (Swansea); half backs – C H Newman (Newport), E Treharne (Pontypridd); forwards – *J H Judson (Llandovery and Llanelli), F Purdon, G L Morris (Swansea), T J S Clapp (Nantyglo), *A Cattell (Llanelli), G F Harding, R Gould, T Baker Jones (Newport).

England: back – A S Taylor (Blackheath); threequarters – C G Wade, A M Evanson (Richmond), W N Bolton (Blackheath); half backs – Alan Rotherham (Richmond), J H Payne (Broughton); forwards – E T Gurdon (Richmond, capt), H G Fuller (Bath), W M Tatham (Oxford Univ.), R S Kindersley (Exeter), G T Thomson (Halifax), C S Wooldridge, R S F Henderson, G Standing, H Vassall (Blackheath).

For England, Gregory Wade (3), George Thomson, Robert Henderson and Wilf Bolton scored tries. Arthur Evanson converted two.

Referee: A Herbert (Wales)

Match 4   SCOTLAND v WALES   Raeburn Place, Edinburgh. January 8th, 1883

Scotland won by three goals to one goal

Charles Prydderch Lewis became the first man to play on his own as full back for Wales in a full international. In the first three games Wales had fielded a pair of full backs. The ground was semi-frozen and only 4,000 spectators turned up. Tom Clapp made a couple of rousing runs for Wales. From one he ran threequarters the length of the field and almost scored. Then he knocked over the famous Don Wauchope with another fiery dash and linked with fellow forwards in a move that swept the length of the field for Tom Judson to score a try that C P Lewis converted. This was a Monday match, and Dr. Griffin, of Edinburgh University, played his only game for Wales, possibly to make up a full team, just as two Welsh players did for Ireland when they arrived at Cardiff with only 13 men in 1884.

From this match arose many years later the Bridie mystery. Newspaper reports of the time list him as playing against Scotland in this 1883 fixture. But neither the WRU Handbook nor the official history of Cardiff RFC credit Ron Bridie with a place. The truth may be that Bridie was selected but, as he was a Scotsman, the Scots refused to recognise him as having Welsh qualifications. It was known he came from Glasgow, played for Cardiff until they dropped him and then joined Newport. He always played in running shoes and turned up for matches wearing a frock coat. It was thought that he was the son of a parson "from somewhere in the Monmouthshire hills". Probably George Harding took over as half back because he often played in the backs as well as the pack for Newport.

Scotland: back – D W Kidston (Glasgow Acads.); threequarters – W E Maclagan (Edinburgh Acads., and London Scottish), D J McFarlan (London Scottish) ; half backs – W Sorley Brown (Edinburgh Inst. F.P.), A R Don Wauchope (Edinburgh Wands.); forwards – D Y Cassels (capt.), J G Walker, J Jamieson, A Walker (West of Scotland), J B Brown, W A Walls, J G Mowat (Glasgow Acads.), C Reid (Edinburgh Acads.), D Somerville, T Ainslie (Edinburgh Inst. F.P.).

Wales: back – C P Lewis (Llandovery, capt.); threequarters – C H Newman (Newport), W B Norton (Cardiff); half backs – W F Evans (Oxford Univ. and Rhymney), G F Harding (Newport); forwards – J H Judson (Llandovery and

Llanelli), T J S Clapp, R Gould, T Baker Jones, *H S Lyne (Newport), F Purdon, G L Morris (Swansea), A Cattell (Llanelli), *J A Jones (Cardiff), *Dr. A Griffin (Edinburgh Univ.).

For Scotland, David McFarlan (2) and Andrew 'Bunny' Don Wauchope scored tries. Bill Maclagan converted them.

For Wales, Tom Judson scored a try. Charles Lewis converted.

Referee: G Rowland Hill (England)

Match 5 ENGLAND v WALES St. John's Ground, Leeds. January 5, 1884

England won by one goal, two tries to one goal

Charlie Allen, the Oxford University threequarter from Beaumaris, became the first Welshman to score against England with his try "after a grand dash and kick over the English line." Charles Lewis, the Welsh full back and Llandovery College tutor, converted. W. H. Gwynn made his debut and, although Alan Rotherham, renowned for his passing tactics, was at half back for England, it was stated that Gwynn was the best half back on the field, "passing out in wonderful style." Newman was a staunch tackler at outside half on a wet day. England went on to become the first winners of the Triple Crown.

Charles Gerald Taylor, who made his debut in this match, was the first Welsh international player to be killed in the 1914-18 War. Engineer-Captain Taylor was in the fighting top of HMS Tiger at the Battle of the Dogger Bank on January 24, 1915 when he was struck by gunfire. A naval officer all his life, he was aged 51. During his rugby career he was considered the finest drop-kicker of his era in British rugby. In his day players were warned, "Never fly-kick unless you can do it like C. G. Taylor." He developed this art from his experience as a soccer player before turning to rugby.

England: back – H B Tristram (Durham); threequarters – W N Bolton (Blackheath), C E Chapman (Cambridge Univ.), C G Wade (Richmond); half backs – Alan Rotherham, H T Twynam (Richmond) ; forwards – E T Gurdon (capt.), C Gurdon (Richmond), H G Fuller (Bath), C J B Marriott, C S Wooldridge, R S F Henderson (Blackheath), W M Tatham, E L Strong (Oxford Univ.), J T Hunt (Preston Grasshoppers and Manchester).

Wales: back – C P Lewis (Llandovery); threequarters – *C P Allen (Beaumaris and Oxford Univ.), W B Norton (Cardiff), *C G Taylor (Ruabon and Blackheath); half backs – C H Newman (Newport, capt.), *W H Gwynn (Swansea); forwards – W D Phillips, *J S Smith, *H J Simpson (Cardiff), T J S Clapp, R Gould, H S Lyne (Newport), G L Morris, *F C Andrews (Swansea), *F L Margrave (Llanelli).

For England. Gregory Wade, Alan Rotherham and Henry Twynam scored tries. Wilf Bolton converted one.

For Wales Charlie Allen scored a try. Charles Lewis converted.

Referee: J A Gardner (Scotland)

Match 6 WALES v SCOTLAND Rodney Parade, Newport. January 12, 1884

Scotland won by one dropped goal, one try to nil

Billy Gwynn, later to become WRU secretary, made a sparkling run after selling a dummy. He was looking round for support and did not realise he had crossed the Scottish line. Then he

4

dropped the ball and "a groan of despair rose from the mass of 7,000 spectators." The Welsh players disputed the dropped goal from near halfway by Grant Asher. Then Tom Ainslie's try caused considerable argument among players and referee because it was so near to the corner and not obtained from a clear run in. Protracted arguments with referees were quite common in early international rugby.

> **Wales:** back – C P Lewis (Llandovery); threequarters – C P Allen (Beaumaris and Oxford Univ.), W B Norton (Cardiff), C G Taylor (Ruabon and Blackheath); half backs – C H Newman (Newport, capt.), W H Gwynn (Swansea); forwards – H J Simpson, W D Phillips (Cardiff), R Gould, H S Lyne, T Baker Jones, T J S Clapp (Newport), F L Margrave (Llanelli), G L Morris, F G Andrews (Swansea).

> **Scotland:** back – J P Veitch (Royal HSFP); threequarters – G C Lindsay, D J McFarlan, W E Maclagan (capt., London Scottish); half backs – A R Don Wauchope, A G Grant Asher (Edinburgh Wanderers); forwards – C Reid (Edinburgh Acads.) T Ainslie, D Somerville, R Maitland (Edinburgh Inst. F.P.), J B Brown, W A Walls (Glasgow Acads.), J Jamieson (West of Scotland), J Tod (Watsonians), W A Peterkin (Edinburgh Univ.).

For Scotland, Grant Asher dropped a goal and Tom Ainslie scored a try.

Referee: James S Maclaren (England)

Match 7   WALES v IRELAND   Cardiff Arms Park. April 12, 1884

Wales won by one dropped goal, two tries to nil

Two Welsh players turned out for Ireland in this first international match at the Arms Park. Ireland arrived short, so Frank Purdon (Newport and Swansea), who had played in the pack for Wales against Ireland in 1882, and H. M. Jordan (Newport), a threequarter who was to play for Wales later, gave a helping hand. At least Purdon could claim Irish ancestry! In drizzle, a crowd of 5,000 saw "Buller" Stadden come in as a late replacement to win his first cap and prove the star of the match. He dropped the first goal for Wales in international rugby. Tom Clapp's try came from a clever approach run by Frank Hancock, also making his debut. Ireland did not play Wales during the next two seasons owing to "disagreements".

In order to gain a guide to form before picking their team for this match, the Welsh selectors arranged an East v West trial fixture. But only one of the West XV turned up – Sam Goldsworthy. He was picked. The other players boycotted the trial because they were resentful of selection methods.

> **Wales:** back – *T M Barlow (Cardiff); threequarters – C G Taylor (Ruabon and Blackheath), *F E Hancock, W B Norton (Cardiff); half backs – *W H Stadden (Cardiff), W H Gwynn (Swansea); forwards – T J S Clapp, R Gould, H S Lyne (Newport), *S Goldsworthy (Swansea), *J T Hinton, H J Simpson (capt.), W D Phillips, J S Smith (Cardiff), *W R B Roderick (Llanelli).

> **Ireland:** R W Morrow (Queen's Coll., Belfast); E H Green (Dublin Univ.), J Pedlow (Bessbrook); R G Warren (Lansdowne) H F Spunner (Wanderers); A J Hamilton, H G Cooke (Lansdowne) D F Moore (capt.), F W Moore, J M Kennedy, W S Collis, J Fitzgerald (Wanderers), R O N Hall, L Moyers, W E Johnstone (Dublin Univ.).

The above 15 names are listed as playing for Ireland, but it is known that two of them did not travel and their places were taken by Frank Purdon (Newport and Swansea) and Martyn Jordan (Newport). No record exists of who the missing players were or of how the Irish team lined up in their positions.

For Wales, Bill Stadden dropped a goal and Tom Clapp and Billy Norton scored tries.

Referee: G Rowland Hill (England).

Match 8 WALES v ENGLAND St. Helen's, Swansea, January 3, 1885

England won by one goal, four tries to one goal, one try

Arthur Gould, one of the greatest names in Welsh rugby, played his first game for Wales. He was chosen as full back, though it was as a centre that he became famous, and gained 27 caps in an international career spanning 13 years. His Newport club-mate, Martyn Jordan also made his debut. Described as the smallest man ever to play in international rugby, Jordan scored both the Welsh tries. In cold drizzle, a crowd of 5,000 saw England display smart team work, whereas Wales played purely as individuals, and Gwynn was guilty of reckless passing.

Wales: back – *A J Gould (Newport); threequarters – *H M Jordan (Newport), F E Hancock (Cardiff), C G Taylor (Ruabon and Blackheath) ; half backs – C H Newman (Newport, capt.), W H Gwynn (Swansea); forwards – R Gould, T J S Clapp, H S Lyne, T Baker Jones (Newport), S Goldsworthy, *E S Richards (Swansea), J S Smith, *L C Thomas (Cardiff), *M Rowland (Lampeter).

England: back – H B Tristram (Durham); threequarters – A E Stoddart (Blackheath), J J Hawcridge (Bradford), C G Wade (Richmond); half backs – Alan Rotherham (Richmond), J H Payne (Broughton); forwards – E T Gurdon (capt.), R S Kindersley (Exeter), E D Court, R S F Henderson (Blackheath), H J Ryalls (New Brighton), F Moss (Broughton), A T Kemble (Liverpool), G Harrison (Hull), A Teggin (Broughton Rangers).

For England, Gregory Wade, Dick Kindersley, Henry Ryalls, Alf Teggin and Joe Hawcridge scored tries. John Payne converted one.

For Wales, Martyn Jordan scored two tries. A. J. Gould converted one.

Referee: C P Lewis (Wales)

Match 9 SCOTLAND v WALES Partick, Glasgow. January 10, 1885

Drawn. No score

"Wales have not yet been able to grasp the science of passing" wrote a contemporary Scottish critic. This, perhaps, was an unfair analysis because, with a slippery ball, Charles Newman decided to adopt tight tactics. There were only 3,000 spectators and they saw Wales almost snatch victory with a superb drop-kick by Charles Taylor, which went just under the bar. This was Wales's first drawn match. William Henry Thomas was capped by Wales in this match while still at Llandovery College, aged 19.

Scotland: back – P R Harrower (London Scottish); threequarters – A E Stephens (West of Scotland), W E Maclagan (London Scottish, capt.), G Maitland (Edinburgh Inst. F.P.); half backs – A R Don Wauchope, A G Grant Asher (Edinburgh Wanderers); forwards – C Reid (Edinburgh Acads.), J Tod (Watsonians), T Ainslie, R Maitland (Edinburgh Inst. F.P.), J Jamieson, J G Mitchell (West of Scotland), C W Berry (Fettesian-Lorettonians), W A Peterkin (Edinburgh Univ.), G H Robb (Glasgow Acads).

Wales: back – A J Gould (Newport); threequarters – C G Taylor (Ruabon and Blackheath), F E Hancock (Cardiff), H M Jordan (Newport); half backs – C H Newman (Newport, capt.), W H Gwynn (Swansea); forwards – E P Alexander

(Cambridge Univ.), *A F Hill, L. C. Thomas (Cardiff), *W H Thomas (Llandovery and Cambridge Univ.), S Goldsworthy, *D Morgan (Swansea), T J S Clapp, R Gould, T Baker Jones (Newport).

Referee: G Rowland Hill (England)

Match 10   ENGLAND v WALES   Rectory Field, Blackheath. January 2, 1886

England won by one goal fom a mark and two tries to a goal

Again Stadden came in as a reserve and proved the star behind the Welsh scrum, running from halfway for his try. It was as much of a highlight for the 6,000 crowd as the goal from a mark that Andrew Stoddart scored for England. Charles Elliot claimed the mark at halfway. In those days it was not obligatory for the man making the mark to take the kick. So Stoddart, an expert long-distance goal-kicker, landed the goal. After this game it was decided that Wales would experiment with the four threequarter system that Cardiff had perfected.

England: back – A S Taylor (Blackheath); threequarters – C G Wade (Richmond), R Robertshaw (Bradford), A E Stoddart (Blackheath); half backs – Alan Rotherham (Richmond), F Bonsor (Bradford); forwards – C J B Marriott (capt.), G L Jeffery, R E Inglis, P F Hancock (Blackheath), C Gurdon, W G Clibborn (Richmond), E Wilkinson (Bradford), F Moss (Broughton), C H Elliot (Sunderland).

Wales: back – D H Bowen (Llanelli); threequarters – C G Taylor (Ruabon and Blackheath), A J Gould (Newport), *W M Douglas (Cardiff); half backs – C H Newman (Newport, capt.), W H Stadden (Cardiff); forwards – A F Hill, *D H Lewis, *G A Young (Cardiff), *William Bowen, D Morgan (Swansea), E P Alexander (Cambridge Univ.), R Gould (Newport), W H Thomas (Llandovery and Cambridge Univ.), * E Roberts (Llanelli).

For England, Andrew 'Stoddy' Stoddart kicked a goal from a mark. Gregory Wade and Edgar Wilkinson scored tries.

For Wales, Bill Stadden scored a try. Charles Taylor converted.

Referee: D F Moore (Ireland).

Match 11   WALES v SCOTLAND   Cardiff Arms Park. January 9, 1886

Scotland won by two goals, one try to nil

No international team had ever ventured to field four threequarters. Wales made history in this respect, but the result was a failure and the method was abandoned. In fact, Frank Hancock, the Welsh captain, who had brought the system to a peak of success with Cardiff, had to take drastic steps as the nine Scottish forwards threatened to swamp the Welsh eight. Hancock sent full back Harry Bowen into the pack as a reinforcement, and switched Gould to full back. This experience left a lingering contempt in Gould for the "Cardiff game" and he never really adapted his style to the four threequarter pattern. After this defeat, it was said that the reason for the failure of the experiment was that Wales picked forwards unsuited to playing out to their backs in the manner necessary for the success of the four threequarter scheme.

Wales: back – D H Bowen (Llanelli); threequarters – W M Douglas, F E Hancock (Cardiff capt.), A J Gould (Newport), C G Taylor (Ruabon and Blackheath); half backs – *Rev. A Matthews (Lampeter), W H Stadden (Cardiff); forwards – A F Hill, G A Young, D H Lewis (Cardiff), T J S Clapp (Newport), William Bowen, D Morgan (Swansea), W H Thomas (Llandovery and Cambridge Univ.), E P Alexander (Cambridge Univ.).

Scotland: back – F McIndoe (Glasgow Acads.); threequarters – D J McFarlan (London Scottish), R H Morrison (Edinburgh Univ.), W F Holms (RIE Coll.); half backs – A R Don Wauchope, P H Don Wauchope (Edinburgh Wanderers); forwards – J B Brown (capt.), W A Walls, J French (Glasgow Acads.), C Reid, T W Irvine, A T Clay (Edinburgh Acads.), J Tod (Watsonians), C J B Milne, W M Macleod (Fettesian-Lorettonians).

For Scotland, Andrew 'Bunny' Don Wauchope, Alex Clay and John Tod scored tries. William Macleod converted two.

Referee: D F Moore (Ireland).

Match 12   **WALES v ENGLAND**   Stradey Park, Llanelli. January 8, 1887

Drawn. No score

Arthur Gould demanded that the Welsh selectors revert to the three threequarter formation and, backed by his captain, Charles Newman, got his way. Gould felt his play suffered in the four-line system. As he was the man on whom so much depended behind the scrum, his ultimatum was accepted virtually without question. His decision proved correct, for Wales almost won. Gould himself missed a drop at goal by only a couple of feet. The Welsh forwards were outstanding and had the backs been a little more venturesome, victory could have been gained. The threequarters were criticised for kicking when they should have run. It was a match mainly of "scrimmages", at which Wales were superior. The English side excelled in loose, open play.

Yet the match almost was called off. The English team refused to play on the semi-frozen Stradey turf. In desperation it was suggested playing on the adjoining cricket pitch. The switch was made. This brought loud complaints from ticketholders in the special seats, because the grandstand faced the other way! They had to leave their seats and gather round the ropes – and no money was refunded. A crowd of 8,000 saw a brilliant game, played 40 minutes each way despite the hard ground and the snow and sleet that fell heavily in the second half. One of the cross-bars on the reappointed posts collapsed, and Arthur Gould climbed up to replace it. He had earned the nickname of "Monkey" Gould for his tree-climbing agility as a schoolboy.

Wales: back – D H Bowen (Llanelli); threequarters – C G Taylor (Ruabon and Blackheath), A J Gould (Newport), W M Douglas (Cardiff); half backs – C H Newman (Newport,capt.), *O J Evans (Cardiff); forwards – E P Alexander (Cambridge Univ.), W H Thomas (Llandovery and Cambridge Univ.), D Morgan, William Bowen (Swansea), *A F Bland, *A J Hybart (Cardiff), T J S Clapp, R Gould, * T W Lockwood (Newport).

England: back – S Roberts (Swinton); threequarters –J Le Fleming (Blackheath), R Robertshaw (Bradford), R E Lockwood (Dewsbury); half backs – Alan Rotherham (Richmond capt.), F Bonsor (Bradford); forwards – W G Clibborn, J H Dewhurst (Richmond), N Spurling, G L Jeffrey, C R Cleveland (Blackheath), H C Baker (Clifton), E Wilkinson, J L Hickson (Bradford), R L Seddon (Broughton Rangers).

Referee: G Rowland Hill (England)

Match 13   **SCOTLAND v WALES**   Raeburn Place, Edinburgh. February 26, 1887

Scotland won by four goals, eight tries to nil

George Lindsay came in as a replacement for D. Macfarlane and scored five tries – a record against Wales. The 6,000 crowd saw Wales reduced to 14 men throughout the second half after Jem Evans, the Cardiff half back, was injured. Tom Clapp came out of the pack to deputise. Billy Douglas, the Cardiff captain, was badly hurt after only 12 minutes, but stayed on the field. It was reported: "The Welsh backs completely broke down and seemed almost afraid to tackle the stalwart Scots. A. J. Gould did little or no tackling worth noticing. It is evident that the Scotchmen are far ahead of the Welsh in football. They are a hardier race, much sterner and played with a dash and determination which awed our men. Charles Reid, the 6ft. 4in. Scottish captain, noted for his great strength, was very difficult to hold, and often cleared our backs in grand style."

Scotland: back – A W C Cameron (Watsonians); threequarters – W E Maclagan, G C Lindsay (London Scottish), A N Woodrow (Glasgow Acads.); half backs – C E Orr (West of Scotland), P H Don Wauchope (Edinburgh Wanderers); forwards – C Reid (capt.), T W Irvine, A T Clay, M C McEwan (Edinburgh Acads.), C W Berry (Fettesian-Lorettonians), R G McMillan (London Scottish), D S Morton (West of Scotland), H T Ker, J French (Glasgow Acads.).

Wales: back – *H Hughes (Cardiff); threequarters – D Gwynn (Swansea), A J Gould (Newport), W M Douglas (Cardiff); half backs – *G E Bowen (Swansea), O J Evans (Cardiff); forwards – William Bowen, E S Richards, D Morgan (Swansea), A F Bland, *W E O Williams (Cardiff), W H Thomas (Llandovery and Cambridge Univ.), R Gould (capt.), T W Lockwood, T J S Clapp (Newport).

For Scotland, George Lindsay (5), Patrick Don Wauchope, Charles Orr, Reid, McMillan, McEwan, Maclagan and Morton scored tries. Berry (2) and Woodrow (2) added conversions.

Referee: F I Currey (England)

Match 14   **WALES v IRELAND**   Birkenhead Park. March 12, 1887

Wales won by one dropped goal, one try to three tries

Under modern scoring values, Ireland would have won this game 15-8, but in those days a goal of any kind was equal to three tries. This match of the neutral ground was played at Birkenhead to reduce travelling expenses for Ireland, who were in a parlous financial state. A heavy snow storm on the Friday night threatened the match, but it cleared and, though cold, the Saturday brought an improvement in the weather and "a capital game" for 5,000 spectators. Ireland made a rousing rally that would have won the game had Danny Rambaut been able to convert any of their three tries Arthur Gould dropped the Welsh goal in the first half after 15 minutes from a pass by Stadden, and it was Stadden who sent Morgan in for a try early in the second half. Then Ireland came back with three tries by Bob Montgomery.

Wales: back – S S Clarke (Neath); threequarters – C G Taylor (Ruabon and Blackheath), A J Gould (Newport), G E Bowen (Swansea); half backs – *J Lewis (Llanelli), W H Stadden (Cardiff); forwards – A F Bland, W E O Williams (Cardiff), E P Alexander (Cambridge Univ.), T J S Clapp (capt.), T W Lockwood (Newport), William Bowen, D Morgan, *W H Towers (Swansea), E Roberts (Llanelli).

Ireland: back – D B Walkington (North of Ireland); threequarters – M J Carpendale (Monkstown), D F Rambaut (Dublin Univ.), R Montgomery (Queen's Coll., Belfast); half backs – R G Warren (capt.), P J O'Connor (Lansdowne); forwards – E J Walsh, V C Le Fanu (Lansdowne), J Chambers, T Taggart (Dublin Univ.), H J Neill (North of Ireland), J Johnston, W Davison (Belfast Albion), R Stevenson (Lisburn), J S Dick (Queen's Coll., Cork).

For Wales, A J Gould dropped a goal. Morgan scored a try.

For Ireland, Bob Montgomery scored three tries.

Referee: J A Gardner (Scotland)

Match 15   **WALES v SCOTLAND**   Rodney Parade, Newport. February 4, 1888

Wales won by one try to nil

The giant Charles Reid, captain of Scotland, kicked off and sent the ball straight over the Welsh cross-bar. But it was not to prove a successful omen: the Scots lost to Wales for the first time. Gould played brilliantly and the 7,000 crowd saw Tom Jenkins, making his debut, score the first half try that won the match from a long, clever pass by Stadden.

Incidentally, Charles Reid was the youngest player ever to appear in an international match. He was 17 years and 22 days when he made his debut in 1881.

Wales: back – *E J Roberts (Llanelli); threequarters – G E Bowen (Swansea), A J Gould (Newport), *T J P Jenkins (London Welsh); half backs – O J Evans, W H Stadden (Cardiff); forwards – T J S Clapp (capt.), * R W Powell (Newport), W H Thomas (Llandovery), A F Bland, A F Hill, *Q D Kedzlie (Cardiff), *J Meredith, *T Williams, *W H Howell (Swansea).

Scotland: back – H F T Chambers (Edinburgh Univ.); threequarters – W E Maclagan (London Scottish), H J Stevenson (Edinburgh Acads.), M M Duncan (Fettesian-Lorettonians); half backs – C E Orr (West of Scotland), C F P Fraser (Glasgow Univ.); forwards – C W Berry (Fettesian-Lorettonians), C Reid (capt.), A T Clay, M C McEwan, T W Irvine, T B White (Edinburgh Acads.), A Duke (Royal HSFP), D S Morton (West of Scotland), L E Stevenson (Edinburgh Univ.).

For Wales, Tom Jenkins scored a try.

Referee: J R Chambers (Ireland).

Match 16   **IRELAND v WALES**   Lansdowne Road, Dublin. March 3, 1888

Ireland won by one goal, one dropped goal, one try to nil

After the first win over Scotland it was a disappointment to suffer this first defeat by Ireland. Gould and Stadden, the two best Welsh backs, were unable to travel, and the team were badly affected by seasickness on a rough crossing. Ned Roberts hurt his ankle early in the match and retired. Only 4,000 people watched the match. England did not play any international matches this season. Irish full back Walkington was so shortsighted that he wore a monocle while playing.

Ireland: back – D B Walkington (North of Ireland); threequarters – M J Carpendale (Monkstown), D F Rambaut, C R Tillie (Dublin Univ.); half backs – R G Warren (Lansdowne), J H McLaughlin (Derry); forwards – H J Neil (North of Ireland, capt.), E W Stoker, F O Stoker (Wanderers), W G Rutherford (Tipperary), T Shanahan (Lansdowne), C M Moore (Dublin Univ.) J. Moffatt, R H Mayne (Belfast Albion), W Ekin (Queen's Coll., Belfast).

Wales: back – E J Roberts (Llanelli); threequarters – T J P Jenkins (London Welsh), G E Bowen (Swansea), *C S Arthur (Cardiff); half backs – O J Evans (Cardiff), *C J Thomas (Newport); forwards – T J S Clapp (capt.), R W Powell (Newport), A F Hill, Q D Kedzlie, A F Bland (Cardiff), W H Thomas

(Llandovery), W H Howells, T Williams, J Meredith (Swansea).

For Ireland, Bob Warren and Shanahan scored tries. Max Carpendale dropped a goal and Dan Rambaut converted one try.

Referee: G Rowland Hill (England).

Match 17   WALES v N.Z. NATIVE TEAM (MAORIS)   St Helen's, Swansea. December 22, 1888

Wales won by one goal, two tries to nil

There was so much resentment in the west at the selection of this Welsh team, containing only two men from Swansea and one from Llanelli, that the majority of the St. Helen's crowd seemed to have come to jeer rather than cheer their country. Heavy rain at the start, and the preponderance of players from East Wales, meant a small attendance and only £120 in gate receipts. The Maoris, the first touring team to visit Britain, were upset by Stadden's tactics. They called him, "The champion off-side player in England." The Maoris used the three-threequarter system, but after this defeat adopted the Welsh formation of four against Swansea, Newport and Cardiff.

Norman Biggs made his debut at the age of 18 years and one month, while still at "Cardiff College". His record as the youngest player ever for Wales still stands. Biggs was killed in Northern Nigeria in 1908 in a native ambush, when a wound from a poisoned arrow proved fatal. It was also the first match for the great Jim Hannan, one of the finest forwards ever to play for Newport and Wales.

Wales reintroduced the four threequarter system after nearly two years of playing the orthodox three threequarters.

Doubtless the absence of Arthur Gould from the side enabled this experiment to be revived and it proved successful. Never again were Wales to play only three men in the threequarter line. The Maoris played 107 matches on their tour, including 74 in the British Isles. They defeated Ireland, but lost to England.

Wales: *J E Webb (Newport); *George Thomas (Newport), *R M Garrett (Penarth), C S Arthur, *N Biggs (Cardiff); C J Thomas (Newport), W H Stadden (Cardiff); A F Hill (capt), A F Bland, *S H Nicholls (Cardiff) *J Hannan, *T Harding (Newport), W H Towers, William Bowen (Swansea), *D Griffiths (Llanelli).

Maoris: back – W Warbrick; threequarters – E McCausland, W T Wynyard, D R Gage; half backs – W Elliott, P Keogh, F Warbrick; forwards – T R Ellison, G Wynyard, A Webster, H Lee, G A Williams, A Warbrick, D Stewart, Wi Karauria.

For Wales, George Thomas, Jim Hannan and Will Towers scored tries. Jim Webb converted one.

Referee: S Mortimer (England)

Match 18   SCOTLAND v WALES   Raeburn Place, Edinburgh. February 2, 1889

Scotland won by two tries to nil

This match caused a rupture of fixtures between Cardiff and Llanelli. The trouble began when Norman Biggs said he could not go to Scotland, but would play for Cardiff against Llanelli. Immediately the three Llanelli players chosen for Wales withdrew, saying they could not leave home. The WRU summoned the match committee to select replacements, but only

Mr. W. H. Treatt, of Cardiff, turned up. Biggs, Towers, A. J. Gould and Bishop, plus the three Llanelli men, withdrew. Later Stadden cried off, but Bishop changed his mind. The vacancies were filled mainly by Cardiff men.

Cardiff, now with six men in the Welsh team, told Llanelli that because they were so seriously weakened they would have to postpone the fixture. Llanelli refused to meet them on another date and the clubs needed a cooling off period before friendly relations were restored. Cardiff's Arthur Hill took over the captaincy of what was a Welsh shadow team and they lost in a snow storm. Only 30 minutes each way was played.

In the early days, players occasionally put the interests of their clubs before loyalty to their country. Some matches, particularly cup ties, were considered more important.

Scotland: back – H F T Chambers (Edinburgh Univ.); threequarters – W F Holms, J H Marsh (Edinburgh RIE Coll.), H J Stevenson (Edinburgh Acads.); half backs – C E Orr (West of Scotland), C F P Fraser (Glasgow Univ.); forwards – D S Morton (capt.), J D Boswell, W Auld (West of Scotland), H T Ker (Glasgow Acads.), M C McEwan, T B White (Edinburgh Acads.), A Duke (Royal HSFP), W A McDonald (Glasgow Univ.), A Methuen (London Scottish).

Wales: H Hughes (Cardiff); R M Garrett (Penarth), J E Webb (Newport), * E H Bishop (Swansea), H M Jordan (London Welsh and Newport); C J Thomas (Newport), *Rosser Evans (Cardiff); S H Nicholls, A F Hill (capt.), W E O Williams, *D W Evans (Cardiff), T Harding, J Hannan (Newport), *R L Thomas (London Welsh), William Bowen (Swansea).

For Scotland, Charles Orr and Hugh Ker scored tries.

Referee: E McAllister (Ireland).

Match 19   WALES v IRELAND   St. Helen's, Swansea. March 2, 1889

Ireland won by two tries to nil

Arthur Gould returned to take over the captaincy, but Ireland gained their first victory on Welsh soil. On the morning of the match, the International Board met at the Mackworth Hotel, Swansea, and adopted the Welsh suggestion of employing a system of points for goals and tries. Scotland resisted the proposal. Don Wauchope, who had been a great Scottish player, was chairman of the board and said that in his opinion a goal was the most important thing in the game, worth more than half a dozen tries. The motion was carried by four votes to two and the new scoring system came into force the following season. Of the game, it was reported that the dashing Irish forwards ran through the Welsh pack and "pulverised the Welsh backs".

Wales: E J Roberts (Llanelli); *A C Davies (London Welsh), A J Gould (Newport, capt.), *T Morgan (Llanelli), N Biggs (Cardiff); C J Thomas (Newport), *G Griffiths (Llanelli); William Bowen, D Morgan (Swansea), S H Nicholls, D W Evans (Cardiff), T Harding, J Hannan (Newport), R L Thomas (London Welsh), D Griffiths (Llanelli).

Ireland: back – L J Holmes (Lisburn); threequarters – R A Yeates, R Dunlop (Dublin Univ.), R Pedlow (Beesbrook); half backs R G Warren (Lansdowne, capt.), A C McDonnell (Dublin Univ.); forwards – V C Le Fanu, J S Jameson (Lansdowne), E G Forrest, J Cotton (Wanderers), J Waites (Bective), H W Andrews, J N Lytle (North of Ireland), R Stevenson (Lisburn), H A Richey (Dublin Univ.).

For Ireland, Alaster McDonnell and Cotton scored tries.

Referee: A R Don Wauchope (Scotland).

Scotland won by one goal and two tries (5) to one try (1)
(N.B. A converted try was worth three points, a try one point)

A record Cardiff crowd of 10,000 saw Billy Bancroft make his debut for Wales. He was to become one of the most famous of all Welsh rugby players. Actually, he came into the side as a replacement because Tom England (Newport) was injured, but went on to win 33 consecutive caps. It was his first season in senior rugby. There was bitter criticism of the Welsh selectors for splitting Swansea's brilliant half back unit and playing Evan James without his brother David, but they were not picked together until the final match of the following season.

Wales: *W J Bancroft (Swansea); C J Thomas, A J Gould (Newport), R M Garrett (Penarth), *D P Lloyd (Llanelli); *Evan James (Swansea), W H Stadden (Cardiff); A F Hill (capt.), W E O Williams, A F Bland (Cardiff), William Bowen, J Meredith, *W Rice Evans (Swansea), J Hannan (Newport), *S Thomas (Llanelli).

Scotland: back – G MacGregor (London Scottish); threequarters – W E Maclagan (London Scottish, capt.), H J Stevenson (Edinburgh Acads.), G R Wilson (Royal HSFP); half backs – C E Orr (West of Scotland), D G Anderson (London Scottish); forwards – W Auld, J E Orr, J D Boswell (West of Scotland), R G MacMillan, F W J Goodhue (London Scottish), M C McEwan (Edinburgh Acads.), A Duke (Royal HSFP), A Dalgleish (Gala), I MacIntyre (Edinburgh Wanderers).

For Scotland, D'Arcy Anderson, Matthew McEwan and Bill Maclagan scored tries. McEwan converted one.

For Wales, A J Gould scored a try.

Referee: E McAllister (Ireland).

Wales won by one try (1) to nil
(N.B. A try was worth one point)

A crowd of 5,000 huddled against the wind, snow and sleet that swept in gale force across the ground. Wales had never beaten England. After a lapse of two years in fixtures through dispute, Gould's team were more determined than ever to break England's grip. It was a fast and furious contest, Wales playing eight forwards to England's nine, and four threequarters to the home country's three. Players became so covered in slush that they were unrecognisable. But it was impossible to hide the brilliance of Bancroft, at full back. Gould and Percy Lloyd ran and passed cleverly and Dicky Garrett blotted out the dangerous Stoddart. At half time there was no score, though England had forced Wales to minor on three occasions.

Then, after two minutes of the second half, "Buller" Stadden pounced for his historic try. It was to be the only score. A line-out formed not far from the home line. the Englishmen had expected a long throw, especially as Stadden stretched back with a catapult action, as if preparing to fling the ball far into the back of the line-out. He was a specialist at this and, though a half back, often threw in from touch. A report of the match described what happened: "Quick as lightning, he bounced the ball into play and, while the defence was wondering whether he had the ball or not, he smartly dodged two opponents and scored."

The legend of Welsh subtlety on the rugby field had yet to be born, but Stadden's quick thinking showed the awakening of thought for deception. Stadden was the first Welshman to go North to play for generous expenses in the days before the Rugby League broke away from the Rugby Union over the question of payment for broken time. Stadden joined Dewsbury, so was playing on his home ground.

England: back – W G Mitchell (Richmond); threequarters – P H Morrison (Cambridge Univ.), A E Stoddart (Blackheath, capt.), J Valentine (Swinton); half backs – J Wright (Bradford), F H Fox (Marlborough N.); forwards – A Robinson, P F Hancock, F Evershed, R T D Budworth (Blackheath), J H Dewhurst (Richmond), S M J Woods (Wellington), J H Rogers (Moseley), J L Hickson (Bradford), F Lowrie (Batley).

Wales: W J Bancroft (Swansea); D P Lloyd (Llanelli), A J Gould (Newport, capt.), R M Garrett (Penarth), D Gwynn (Swansea); C J Thomas (Newport), W H Stadden (Cardiff); W E O Williams, A F Bland, D W Evans (Cardiff), J Hannan (Newport), W H Thomas (London Welsh), S Thomas (Llanelli), William Bowen, J Meredith (Swansea).

For Wales, Bill Stadden scored a try.

Referee: R D Rainie (Scotland).

Match 22   IRELAND v WALES   Lansdowne Road, Dublin. March 1, 1890

Drawn. Each side scored one goal (3)
(N.B. A converted try was worth three points)

After two successive defeats by Ireland, Wales looked like going down yet again. But, five minutes from the end, Charlie Thomas, the elusive Newport half back, stole away from a scrum in the home 25 and twisted through the startled defence for a try in a handy position for Bancroft to convert.

Tom Graham made his debut in the Welsh pack. He went on to make 12 international appearances and was considered not only one of the cleverest and fastest forwards ever to play for Newport, but one of their most inspiring captains. After the match, watched by 7,000 spectators, nine of the players were arrested "for too much exuberance of spirits". Eight of them were members of the Irish team. The name of the "riotous" Welsh player was not divulged. Small fines were imposed on a number of the players at Dublin court on Monday morning.

Ireland: back – D B Walkington (North of Ireland); threequarters – R Dunlop, R W Johnston (Dublin Univ.), T Edwards (Lansdowne); half backs – R G Warren (Lansdowne, capt.), A C McDonnell (Dublin Univ.); forwards – J Moffatt, H T Galbraith (Belfast Albion), J Waites, J H O'Conor (Bective), R Stevenson (Lisburn), J Roche (Wanderers), W J N Davis (Bessbrook), E F Doran (Lansdowne), L C Nash (Queen's Coll., Cork).

Wales: W J Bancroft (Swansea); R M Garrett (Penarth), A J Gould (capt.), George Thomas (Newport), D Gwynn (Swansea); C J Thomas (Newport), *H M Ingledew (Cardiff); A F Hill, D W Evans, A F Bland (Cardiff), J Hannan, *T C Graham (Newport), William Bowen (Swansea), W H Thomas, R L Thomas (London Welsh).

For Wales, Charlie Thomas scored a try. W J Bancroft converted.

For Ireland, Bob Dunlop scored a try. Roche converted.

Referee: F W Burnand (England).

Match 23 **WALES v ENGLAND** Rodney Parade, Newport. January 3, 1891

England won by two goals and one try (7) to one goal (3)
(N.B. A converted try was worth three points, a try one point)

Wales were without Arthur Gould this season while he was on business in the West Indies. William Bowen, the Swansea forward, took over the leadership, but there was a complete breakdown of the Welsh halves against superior forwards and Bancroft was so poor in defence that a cry went up to drop him. A crowd of 9,000 saw Tom Pearson make his debut on the wing and score the only Welsh try. Pearson, born at Bombay, played 13 times for Wales. In 1892-93, while captain of Cardiff, he scored 40 tries for the club, a record that stood until Bleddyn Williams scored 41 in 1947-48. Later, Pearson transferred to Newport.

Wales: W J Bancroft (Swansea); *T W Pearson, C S Arthur (Cardiff), D Gwynn (Swansea), D P Lloyd (Llanelli); C J Thomas (Newport), H M Ingledew (Cardiff); William Bowen (capt.), W Rice Evans (Swansea), J Hannan, *H Packer (Newport), *P Bennett (Cardiff Harlequins), *E V Pegge (Neath), R L Thomas (London Welsh), D W Evans (Cardiff).

England: back – W G Mitchell (Richmond); threequarters – R E Lockwood (Dewsbury), F H R Alderson (Hartlepool Rovers, capt.) P Christopherson (Blackheath); half backs – J Berry (Tyldesley), W R M Leake (Harlequins); forwards – S M J Woods (Wellington), E G H North, R T D Budworth (Blackheath), W E Bromet (Tadcaster), J Toothill, J Richards (Bradford), T Kent (Salford), D Jowett (Heckmondwike), R P Wilson (Liverpool OB).

For England, Percy Christopherson (2) and Richard Budworth scored tries. Fred Alderson converted two.

For Wales, Tom Pearson scored a try. W J Bancroft converted.

Referee: R D Rainie (Scotland).

Match 24 **SCOTLAND v WALES** Raeburn Place, Edinburgh. February 7, 1891

Scotland won by one goal, two dropped goals and six tries (15) to nil
(N.B. A converted try was worth three points, a try one point)

The unexpected collapse of what appeared a strong Welsh team was attributed by one critic to, "The visit of the Welsh team a few hours before the game to the dissecting rooms of Edinburgh University Hospital." Whatever upset the visitors Scotland so dominated that it was reported: "So much was play in the Welsh 25 that a flock of sparrows hopped about in the Scottish ground with impunity." Bancroft's tackling was bad. Scotland went on to win the Triple Crown for the first time.

Scotland: back – H J Stevenson (Edinburgh Acads.); threequarters – P R Clauss (Birkenhead Park), G MacGregor, W Neilson (London Scottish); half backs – C E Orr (West of Scotland), D G Anderson (London Scottish); forwards – M C McEwan (Edinburgh Acads. capt.), G T Neilson, J D Boswell, J E Orr (West of Scotland), F W J Goodhue, R G MacMillan (London Scottish), I MacIntyre (Edinburgh Wanderers), H T O Leggatt (Watsonians), A Dalgleish (Gala).

Wales: W J Bancroft (Swansea); R M Garrett (Penarth), D Gwynn (Swansea), George Thomas (Newport), *W McCutcheon (Swansea); *R B Sweet-Escott, H M Ingledew (Cardiff); W H Thomas (capt.), R L Thomas (Llanelli), T C Graham (Newport), P Bennett (Cardiff Harlequins), William Bowen, W Rice Evans (Swansea), *D J Daniel (Llanelli), S H Nicholls (Cardiff).

For Scotland, Paul Clauss (2), C E Orr, Boswell, Legatt, J E Orr and Goodhue scored tries. McEwan converted one. Henry Stevenson and W Neilson each dropped a goal.

Referee: H L Ashmore (England).

Match 25 WALES v IRELAND   Stradey Park, Llanelli. March 7, 1891

Wales won by one goal, one dropped goal (6) to one dropped goal, one try (4)
(N.B. A converted try or dropped goal was worth three points, a try one point)

This first win of the season was a result of Bancroft's return to his sparkling best and the brilliant half back scheming of the brothers Evan and David James, chosen together for Wales for the first time. They were considered a couple of wizards with their combined guile and the originators of half back tactics in Welsh rugby. Later they turned professional, but were reinstated. The Irish team were greeted with ringing cries of; "Home rule for Ireland" from the 10,000 crowd. Bancroft dropped his goal from half-way.

Wales: W J Bancroft (Swansea); R M Garrett (Penarth), C J Thomas (Newport), D P Lloyd (Llanelli), T W Pearson (Cardiff); *David James, Evan James (Swansea); W H Thomas (capt.), R L Thomas, S Thomas, *C B Nicholl (Llanelli), T C Graham (Newport), * J Samuel, *D Samuel, *T Deacon (Swansea).

Ireland: back – D B Walkington (North of Ireland); threequarters – R Dunlop, S Lee (North of Ireland), H G Wells (Bective); half backs – E D Cameron (Bective), R Pedlow (Bessbrook); forwards – R Stevenson (Lisburn, capt.), J Roche, F O Stoker (Wanderers), J S Jameson (Lansdowne), L C Nash, R D Stokes (Queen's Coll., Cork), T Fogarty (Garryowen), C V Rooke (Dublin Univ.), W J N Davis (Bessbrook).

For Wales, David Samuel scored a try. W J Bancroft converted and dropped a goal.

For Ireland, Sam Lee scored a try. Walkington dropped a goal.

Referee: A Rowsell (England).

Match 26 ENGLAND v WALES   Rectory Field, Blackheath. January 2, 1892

England won by three goals, one try (17) to nil
(N.B. A converted try was worth five points, a try two points)

England were Triple Crown winners this season, but the eight Welsh forwards played most effectively against England's nine. It was reported that the Welsh four threequarter system failed because their halves neglected to pass. The brothers James, who had dazzled Ireland in the previous game, were unavailable. Bancroft was excellent and Arthur Boucher made his debut along with another famous Newport forward, Wallace Watts. They were to play together for Wales for five years. Penalty goals allowed for first time in internationals.

England: back – W B Thompson (Blackheath); threequarters – R E Lockwood (Heckmondwike), F H R Alderson (Hartlepool Rovers, capt.), C G Hubbard (Blackheath); half backs – C Emmott, A Briggs (Bradford); forwards F Evershed, A Allport (Blackheath), W Yiend (Hartlepool Rovers), W E Bromet (Tadcaster), W Nicholl (Brighouse Rangers), J Toothill (Bradford), T Kent (Salford), J Pyke (St. Helens Recreation), E Bollough (Wigan).

Wales: W J Bancroft (Swansea); R M Garrett (Penarth), A J Gould (Newport, capt.), W McCutcheon (Swansea), T W Pearson (Cardiff); *P Phillips (Newport), * G R Rowles (Penarth); R L Thomas, C B Nicholl (Llanelli), *F Mills, J Deacon

(Swansea) T C Graham, *A W Boucher, *Wallace Watts, J Hannan (Newport).

For England, William Nicholl, George Hubbard, Fred Alderson and Frank Evershed scored tries. Dicky Lockwood converted two and Alderson one.

Referee: M C McEwan (Scotland).

Match 27   WALES v SCOTLAND   St. Helen's, Swansea. February 6, 1892

Scotland won by one goal, one try (7) to one try (2)
(N.B. A converted try was worth five points, a try two points)

Though Evan James and his brother David returned as the Welsh halves, for once their magic brought no reward. Bancroft also was disappointing in the rain on a heavy pitch and the crowd of 12,000 booed the referee, Mr. Hodgson (London Society), for his handling of a rough game. Angered by several of his decisions, some of the crowd broke past the police and attacked the referee. One newspaper report said: "A mob of cowardly blackguards swept down and set about him." Gould and some other Welsh players went to his rescue and Gould received a blow on the jaw intended for the referee, who was also knocked down.

Wales: W J Bancroft (Swansea); T W Pearson (Cardiff), A J Gould (Newport, capt.), W McCutcheon (Swansea), *J Conway Rees (Llanelli), David James, Evan James (Swansea); C B Nicholl (Llanelli), Wallace Watts, J Hannan, T C Graham, A W Boucher (Newport), F Mills, J Deacon (Swansea), P Bennett (Cardiff Harlequins).

Scotland: back – H J Stevenson (Edinburgh Acads.); threequarters – P R Clauss (Birkenhead Park), G T Campbell, W Neilson (London Scottish); half backs – C E Orr (West of Scotland, capt.), D G Anderson (London Scottish); forwards – F W J Goodhue, R G MacMillan (London Scottish), G T Neilson, J N Millar, J D Boswell, J E Orr (West of Scotland), A Dalgleish (Gala), H T O Leggatt (Watsonians), W R Gibson (Royal HSFP).

For Scotland, D'Arcy Anderson and George Campbell scored tries. John Boswell converted one.

For Wales, Jim Hannan scored a try.

Referee: J R Hodgson (England).

Match 28   IRELAND v WALES   Lansdowne Road, Dublin. March 5, 1892

Ireland won by one goal, two tries (9) to nil
(N.B. A converted try was worth five points, a try two points)

Ireland's victory was gained by sheer strength against lighter Welsh forwards. Only 5,000 spectators saw the match. Arthur Gould was not at his best and Bancroft, though better than against Scotland, was still faulty in defence and a long way below the form he displayed in the England match. For the first time Wales had lost all three matches in a season against the other home country teams, a fate they were not to suffer again until 1923.

Ireland: back – T Peel (Limerick); threequarters – T Edwards (Lansdowne), S Lee (North of Ireland), R Montgomery (Queen's Coll. Belfast); half backs – T Thornhill (Wanderers), F E Davies (Lansdowne); forwards – V C Le Fanu (capt.), E J Walsh, J S Jameson (Lansdowne), C V Rooke (Dublin Univ.), A K Wallis, J Roche (Wanderers), J H O'Connor (Bective), R Stevenson (Lisburn), T J Johnston (Queen's Coll., Belfast).

Wales: W J Bancroft (Swansea); *Bert Gould, A J Gould (Newport, capt.), *F E Nicholls (Cardiff Harlequins), N Biggs (Cardiff); Evan James, David James (Swansea); Wallace Watts, J Hannan, *H T Day, A W Boucher (Newport), P Bennett (Cardiff Harlequins), C B Nicholl (Llanelli), J Deacon, F Mills (Swansea).

For Ireland, Eddie Walsh (2) and Fred Davies scored tries. Roche converted one.

Referee: E B Holmes (England).

Match 29   **WALES v ENGLAND**   Cardiff Arms Park. January 7, 1893

Wales won by one goal, one penalty goal, two tries (12) to one goal, three tries (11)
(N.B. A try was worth two points)

Probably no more colourful and unusual match has been played in Welsh rugby history than this first home victory over England. This was to be Wales's first year of Triple Crown success, and it all started with 18 tons of coal being burned on the pitch at the Arms Park. It was so cold during the week before the game that, though the ground was protected by a thick covering of straw, the frost bit into the turf. The match was in danger of being called off. A newspaper report of the time explained what happened: "The phenomenally successful results which attended the experiment by the groundsman with a small fire were reported to the WRU, and it was immediately determined to carry out this idea on a very large scale.

"From an early hour on Friday morning a large number of men – mostly drawn from the unemployed class – were engaged to lay down and trim more than 500 devils (braziers), extemporised out of buckets pierced with holes and fixed on bricks. Although there was slight snow during the night, the intense heat from the devils softened the ground in a manner far exceeding the most sanguine expectations. When darkness set in, the spectacle was an exceedingly picturesque one and the field was visited by a large number of football enthusiasts." The fire devil squad, who burned the 18 tons of coal, used 30 or 40 boiler plates under the braziers to spread the heat. They worked until 11 a.m. on Saturday and their endeavours produced a superb match with a sensational ending.

A crowd of 15,000 saw England lead by a goal and a try to nil at half time. Fred Lohden scored a try after four minutes. Then Stoddart converted a try by Howard Marshall. England seemed sure of yet another victory, particularly when Marshall added another try. But Wales had what was considered the finest pack they had ever put in the field, five of them from Newport and, though the English nine forwards had swept the Welsh eight before them in the first half, the home pack rallied. They were inspired by a brilliant try by Arthur Gould. Charlie Nicholl broke from a line-out and Jim Hannan sent Gould racing on a corkscrew run from halfway to score between the posts. Bancroft converted.

The Welsh four threequarter system then produced an outflanking try by Norman Biggs from a splendid pass by Conway Rees. It was 9-7 to England, who pulled Sam Woods out of the pack to play at threequarter. Never again did England face Wales with only three threequarters. But skipper Stoddart gambled on sending Woods back into the pack for an all-out forward offensive. It looked to be an inspired move as Harry Bradshaw's dribble enabled Stoddart to send Marshall in for his hat-trick try and an 11-7 lead.

Once again Wales looked to Gould. His speed and skill broke England's defence and his second try put Wales back in the game with the lead cut to 11-9. Wales piled on pressure as time ran out. Then came a penalty award some 30 yards out and near the touch line. Gould instructed Bancroft to place the ball for the attempt. Bancroft refused. "I'm going to drop-kick," he said. A fierce argument developed. Bancroft did not want to risk a faulty placing by

A team group for older readers! Wales v Ireland at Swansea 1949. Standing (left to right): Gwyn Evans, John Gwilliam, Ernie Coleman, Dai Jones, Alun Meredith, Ray Cale, T N Pearce (England) referee. Seated: Terry Cook, Jack Matthews, Bunner Travers, Haydn Tanner (capt), Bleddyn Williams, Rees Stephens, Frank Trott. In front: Ken Jones, Billy Cleaver.

Remember the old Arms Park mudbaths? This Wales v England match of 1959 was typical of the often muddy-aweful conditions. England's Steve Smith is endeavouring to get a pass away.

Rhys Williams finds a wily Irish hand wrapped around his wrist as he soars for a lineout take at the Arms Park in 1959. Ray Prosser also is in lift-off while at the tail they are observed by Danny Harris and John Faull. Wales were lucky 8-6 winners of a thrilling game.

Cliff Morgan, master of the crafty punt, tests South Africa in Cardiff in 1951 with Malcolm Thomas, Rex Willis and Bleddyn Williams anxious onlookers. Cliff was not at his best as kicker this day and the Springboks won 6-3.

the holder of the ball, or a charged kick. Eventually, and with the crowd getting restive, Gould threw the ball down and walked away, furious at Bancroft's rebellious conduct.

Bancroft, completely unruffled by Gould's anger, measured the angle. He dropped the ball, his foot swung and he tells what happens: "Before the ball had travelled 10 yards upon its journey, I shouted to my skipper, now standing in the centre of the field and with his back towards me, "It's there Arthur!" And so it was, though Gould could not bear to watch. One of the rugby correspondents of the day wrote: "Thousands streamed down from the stands and poured out towards the exits in two great cheering mobs. The players were borne away to the Angel Hotel, shoulder high, and the sight and sound of enthusiasm was something to remember. The victory simply sent the population of Cardiff, plus the thousands of visitors, off their blessed chumps. It will take some of us at least a week to get over it."

Some people may have been confused over the final score. This was because at the time the WRU were experimenting in games between Welsh clubs by awarding three points for a try, whereas the other countries valued a try at two points. Had the the Welsh system applied in this international it would have been a draw at 14-14. The International Board did not upgrade the value of a try to three points until the following season.

> **Wales:** W J Bancroft (Swansea); N Biggs (Cardiff), A J Gould (Newport, capt.), J Conway Rees (Llanelli), W McCutcheon (Swansea); P Phillips, *F C Parfitt (Newport); T C Graham, J Hannan, Wallace Watts, H T Day, A W Boucher (Newport), A F Hill (Cardiff), C B Nicholl (Llanelli), F Mills (Swansea).
>
> **England:** back – E Field (Middlesex W.); threequarters – R E Lockwood (Dewsbury), F H R Alderson (Hartlepool Rovers), A E Stoddart (Blackheath, capt.); half backs – H Marshall, R F de Winton (Blackheath); forwards – S M J Woods (Wellington), F Evershed, F C Lohden, P Maud (Blackheath), J Toothill (Bradford), T Broadley (Bingley), H Bradshaw (Bramley), W E Bromet (Tadcaster), J H Greenwell (Rockcliff).

For Wales, A J Gould (2) and Norman Biggs scored tries. W J Bancroft converted one and kicked a penalty goal.

For England, Howard Marshall (3) and Fred Lohden scored tries Andrew Stoddart converted one.

Referee: D S Morton (Scotland).

Match 30   SCOTLAND v WALES   Raeburn Place, Edinburgh. February 4, 1893

Wales won by one penalty goal, three tries (9) to nil
(N.B. A penalty goal was worth three points, a try two points)

The second successful hurdle towards the first Welsh Triple Crown triumph saw Wales gain their initial victory on a Scottish ground. It was considered one of the finest spectacles since rugby was staged at Raeburn Place. Nine Newport men were in the Welsh team. Arthur Gould was not at his best, but at long last he acknowledged the establishment of the four threequarter game. "Our win was beyond my expectations", he said. "I think the moral effect of our victory will be to compel the Scots and English clubs to play the Welsh style. It will probably revolutionise the game, because once a side of players have thoroughly mastered the art, not only are they almost unbeatable by old-style players, but it is a thousand times more interesting to the spectators."

The home defence was so keen that it was considered that Wales could not have scored their three tries without the aid of the fourth threequarter. There was no score at the interval. Billy Bancroft was magnificent and he drop-kicked his penalty goal from a difficult angle. Some newspaper reports gave this Bancroft kick as being a goal from a mark, but the majority assert it was a penalty. Incidentally, it was the first time Wales had scored tries in Scotland.

Scotland: back – A W C Cameron (Watsonians); threequarters – D Robertson (Glasgow Acads.), G MacGregor, J J Gowans (London Scottish); half backs – R C Greig (Glasgow Acads.), W Wotherspoon (West of Scotland); forwards – A Dalgleish (Gala), R G MacMillan (London Scottish, capt.), H T O Leggatt, W B Cownie (Watsonians), G T Neilson, H F Menzies, J N Millar (West of Scotland), W R Gibson (Royal HSFP), T L Hendry (Clydesdale).

Wales: W J Bancroft (Swansea); N Biggs (Cardiff), A J Gould (capt.), Bert Gould (Newport), W McCutcheon (Swansea); P Phillips, F C Parfitt (Newport); H T Day, T C Graham, J Hannan, Wallace Watts, A W Boucher (Newport), F Mills (Swansea), A F Hill (Cardiff), C B Nicholl (Llanelli).

For Wales, Bert Gould, Norman Biggs and William McCutcheon scored tries. W J Bancroft kicked a penalty goal.

Referee: W H Humphreys (England).

Match 31 WALES v IRELAND   Stradey Park, Llanelli. March 11, 1893

Wales won by one try (2) to nil
(N.B. A try was worth two points)

Nearly 20,000 spectators crowded into Stradey Park in gloriously sunny weather to see Wales make rugby history and win the Triple Crown for the first time. The only score, a try, came in the first half. This is how it was described: "A terrific outburst of applause was elicited when it was seen that Percy Phillips (outside half) had baffled the opposing halves, and, by feinting to pass to Bert Gould, had disposed of Sam Lee. The half back threw very trickily to A. J., and the Welsh captain, when his progress was likely to be barred by Dunlop, threw to his brother. Bert only just managed to score with Sparrow on his back and on the extreme verge of the line."

In the second half the Irish, who went into action with the three threequarters system, pulled a forward out of the scrum to help their backs. This player had been playing as a wing forward since Bert Gould's try. Later in the game, Ireland used yet another forward as an extra back, but eventually Sam Lee, their captain, sent them both back in the pack so that nine forwards faced Wales's eight. Lee said afterwards: "I am not convinced of the superiority of the four threequarter system yet. A pack of good forwards will beat four threequarters any day." Wales did not play as well as against Scotland and Arthur Gould's performance deteriorated badly as the game progressed. But it was not realised until afterwards that he had risked playing with a painful shoulder injury.

Wales: W J Bancroft (Swansea); N Biggs (Cardiff), A J Gould (capt.), Bert Gould (Newport), W McCutcheon (Swansea); P Phillips, F C Parfitt (Newport); T C Graham, Wallace Watts, J Hannan, A W Boucher (Newport), D Samuel, F Mills (Swansea), A F Hill (Cardiff), C B Nicholl (Llanelli).

Ireland: back – W Sparrow (Dublin Univ.); threequarters – R Dunlop, S Lee (capt.), W Gardiner (North of Ireland); half backs – F E Davies (Lansdowne), W S Browne (Dublin Univ.); forwards – R Stevenson (Lisburn), C V Rooke, H Lindsay, A D Clinch, B O'Brien (Dublin Univ.), A K Wallis, E G Forrest, R Johnstone, R W Hamilton (Wanderers).

For Wales, Bert Gould scored a try.

Referee: W H Humphreys (England).

Match 32   ENGLAND v WALES   Birkenhead Park. January 6, 1894

England won by four goals, one goal from a mark (24) to one try (3)
(N.B. A goal from a mark was worth four points)

England chose four threequarters for the first time and avenged the defeat of the previous season. After 25 degrees of overnight frost the ground was rock hard. Hurriedly, fire devils were brought into action, but hundreds of ticket-holders went home: they thought the match could never be played on such a surface. Then the sun broke through to help the braziers and the pitch thawed just enough. Fewer than 5,000 people watched what was still called a "veritable fiasco".

England had picked the "bashing type" of Yorkshire forward and they completely unsettled Wales. Arthur Gould played badly, throwing wild passes, running his wings across field and tackling poorly. Bancroft's fielding and defence were often at fault and W. H. Gwynn, the WRU secretary, blamed the Welsh centres for standing too far from their halves.

Frank Hill urged the forwards to keep the ball tight, while Jim Hannan, the pack leader, tried to obey Gould's demand to heel, though the tactics obviously were wrong. This led to a split in the Welsh team and altogether it was a dismal day for the Triple Crown holders.

England: J F Byrne (Mosley); R E Lockwood (Dewsbury, capt.), S Morfitt (West Hartlepool), C A Hooper (Middlesex W.), F Firth (Halifax); C M Wells (Harlequins), E W Taylor (Rockcliff); J Toothill (Bradford), H Bradshaw (Bramley), T Broadley (Bingley), H Speed (Castleford), W E Tucker, A Allport (Blackheath), J Hall (North Durham), F Soane (Bath).

Wales: W J Bancroft (Swansea); N Biggs (Cardiff), A J Gould (Newport, capt.),J Conway Rees (Llanelli), W McCutcheon (Swansea); P Phillips, F C Parfitt (Newport); F Mills (Swansea), A F Hill (Cardiff), D J Daniel, C B Nicholl (Llanelli), Wallace Watts, A W Boucher, T C Graham, J Hannan (Newport).

For England, Sam Morfitt, Dicky Lockwood, Harry Bradshaw and Edward Taylor scored tries. Lockwood converted three. Taylor converted one and kicked a goal from a mark.

For Wales, Fred Parfitt scored a try.

Referee: J Aikman Smith (Scotland).

Match 33   WALES v SCOTLAND   Rodney Parade, Newport. February 3, 1894

Wales won by one dropped goal and one try (7) to nil
(N.B. A dropped goal was worth four points)

Dai Fitzgerald made a brilliant debut for Wales. The Cardiff centre scored a try and dropped a goal to provide all the points. However, selfish centre play prevented Wales from scoring more than the one try. After failing at Birkenhead, Bancroft was back to his best. Pigeons were released to carry the news of victory around Wales.

Wales: W J Bancroft (Swansea); T W Pearson, *D Fitzgerald (Cardiff), A J Gould (capt.), *W Ll Thomas (Newport); P Phillips, F C Parfitt (Newport); F Mills (Swansea), C B Nicholl, D J Daniel (Llanelli), A F Hill (Cardiff), T C Graham, H T Day, J Hannan, Wallace Watts (Newport).

Scotland: J Rogerson (Kelvinside Acads.); J J Gowans, G MacGregor (capt.), G T Campbell, H T S Gedge (London Scottish); W Wotherspoon (West of Scotland), J W Simpson (Royal HSFP); W B Cownie, H B Wright (Watsonians), G T Neilson, H F Menzies (West of Scotland), A Dalgleish (Gala), W M C McEwan (Edinburgh Acads.), R G MacMillan (London Scottish), W R Gibson (Royal HSFP).

For Wales, Dai Fitzgerald dropped a goal and scored a try.

Referee: E B Holmes (England).

Match 34 IRELAND v WALES   Ballynafeigh, Belfast. March 10, 1894

Ireland won by one penalty goal (3) to nil

The day Ireland won the Triple Crown for the first time they described it as the Ballynafeigh Bog match. It was a mud lark in heavy showers with the only score a penalty goal by John Lytle after 10 minutes, while Ireland had the advantage of a stiff wind. Wales were infinitely the better side. Their halves were provided with the ball five times out of six by their forwards, and the Irishmen agreed that they would have lost on a dry day.

The record crowd of nearly 5,000 (exceptional for a strong soccer area such as Belfast) enjoyed watching Charles Rooke and lively Edmund Forrest smash the Welsh backs. These two Irish forwards were among the earliest of specialised flankers.

Ireland had studied Wales's four threequarter system and assigned the speedy, deadly-tackling Rooke and Forrest the special mission of disengaging quickly from the scrums to get among the Welsh backs. Cardiff supplied all four threequarters for the first time.

Ireland: P J Grant (Bective); R Dunlop, S Lee, W Gardiner (North of Ireland), L H Gwynn (Dublin Univ.); B Tuke (Bective), W S Browne (Dublin Univ.); E G Forrest (capt.), T J Crean (Wanderers), C V Rooke, H Lindsay (Dublin Univ.), J H O'Conor (Bective), A T W Bond (Derry), John Lytle, James Lytle (North of Ireland).

Wales: W J Bancroft (Swansea); N Biggs, D Fitzgerald, *J E Elliott, T W Pearson (Cardiff); R B Sweet-Escott (Cardiff), F C Parfitt (Newport); A F Hill (Cardiff, capt.), J Hannan, Wallace Watts, H T Day (Newport), F Mills (Swansea), D J Daniel, *D W Nicholl (Llanelli), *F Hutchinson (Neath).

For Ireland, John Lytle kicked a penalty goal.

Referee: R D Rainie (Scotland).

Match 35 WALES v ENGLAND   St. Helen's, Swansea. January 5, 1895

England won by one goal, three tries (14) to two tries (6)

Arthur Gould, the Welsh captain, summed up the match with the words: "The Englishmen outclassed us." One incident, however, aroused the ire of the Welsh team. In those days tackled players, with the ball held in their possession, could claim a scrum by shouting "Held". Sam Woods, the England captain, was thought to have shouted "Held". When the Welsh tacklers released him he passed to another player, who ran in for a try with the defence offering no resistance because they expected a scrum. The Welsh team protested to the referee, but he said he had not heard Woods shout.

Wales: W J Bancroft (Swansea); T W Pearson (Cardiff), *O Badger (Llanelli), A J Gould (capt.), W Ll Thomas (Newport); *Selwyn Biggs (Cardiff), *B Davies (Llanelli); T C Graham, A W Boucher, Wallace Watts, J Hannan (Newport), *T H Jackson (Swansea), C B Nicholl (Llanelli), *W J Elsey, F Mills (Cardiff).

England: H Ward (Bradford); J H C Fegan, W B Thompson (Blackheath), E M Baker (Moseley), F A Leslie-Jones (Richmond); E W Taylor (Rockcliff), R H B Cattell (Moseley); G M Carey, F Mitchell, W E Tucker, H W Finlinson

(Blackheath), F O Poole (Oxford Univ.), C Thomas (Barnstaple), W E Bromet (Richmond), S M J Woods (Wellington, capt.).

For England, Thomson, Fred Leslie-Jones, Godfrey Carey and Sammy Woods scored tries. Frank Mitchell converted one.

For Wales, Bill Elsey and Tom Graham scored tries.

Referee: J Aikman Smith (Scotland).

Match 36   SCOTLAND v WALES   Raeburn Place, Edinburgh. January 26, 1895

Scotland won by one goal (5) to one goal from a mark (4)

Scotland this season won the Triple Crown for the second time, but had to thank a blunder by Bancroft for their one point victory. Bancroft made a fair catch and dropped a fine goal from the mark to supply the Welsh points. But he gave away a simple try when he allowed Jim Gowans to charge down his delayed clearance and Alan Smith converted. Even so, Wales would have won had not Arthur Gould slipped on the treacherous turf with no-one near him and the line at his mercy.

Inspecting the frozen ground before the match, the Welsh players considered it unplayable. Gould suggested that to avoid the particularly bad area behind the posts at one end, the pitch be shortened by 15 or 20 yards. The Scots at first refused, but when they saw that Wales would not play otherwise, and the referee agreed with Gould's suggestion, the alteration was made. Many of the Welsh team still thought it too dangerous, but this famous game on the short pitch turned out to be surprisingly good.

Despite Bancroft's blunder and Gould's slip Wales could yet have won had a "try" by Frank Mills been allowed. But the shortened end goal-line had been marked by tape and the referee ruled that this tape had been stretched and Mills actually was short of the line, though the ball was just over the tape. It was the first time in a rugby international that one side had been beaten literally "on the tape".

Scotland: A R Smith (London Scottish); J J Gowans, G T Campbell, W Neilson (London Scottish), R Welsh (Watsonians); J W Simpson (Royal HSFP), M Elliot (Hawick); W B Cownie, H O Smith (Watsonians), T M Scott (Hawick), G T Neilson (West of Scotland), W R Gibson (Royal HSFP, capt.), W M C McEwan, J H Dods (Edinburgh Acads.), R G MacMillan (London Scottish).

Wales: W J Bancroft (Swansea); T W Pearson (Cardiff), A J Gould (Newport, capt.), O Badger, *E Lloyd (Llanelli); Selwyn Biggs (Cardiff), F C Parfitt (Newport); T C Graham, A W Boucher, J Hannan, H Packer, *T Pook (Newport), F Mills (Cardiff), C B Nicholl (Llanelli), *E George (Pontypridd).

For Scotland, Jim Gowans scored a try. Allan Smith converted.

For Wales, W. J. Bancroft kicked a goal from a mark.

Referee: E B Holmes (England).

Match 37   WALES v IRELAND   Cardiff Arms Park. March 16, 1895

Wales won by one goal (5) to one try (3)

Tom Pearson's try, from almost halfway, which Bancroft converted to win the match, was spoken of for more than 20 years as one of the greatest in Welsh rugby. This is how a report described it: "The Welsh forwards, although they were badly beaten in the loose rushes, caught the Hibernians napping and sent the ball out in really splendid style. Morgan dexterously scooped it up, feigned to run and then passed to Sweet-Escott. The Cardiff half exercised rare judiciousness in baffling his opponents by aiming to pass to Arthur Gould, and then throwing wide to Llewellyn Thomas.

"He made a dash, as though going for the line, and then transferred in equally good style to Arthur Gould. The veteran, after drawing around him Lee and Gwynn, passed to Badger who, in the nick of time, threw to his wing. All this took place only a few yards beyond the Welsh 25 and, amid boundless enthusiasm, Pearson sprinted round Gardiner, outdistanced Fulton and scored a really magnificent try between the posts". It was revenge for being baulked in the Ballynafeigh Bog the previous season.

Wales: W J Bancroft (Swansea); T W Pearson (Cardiff), O Badger (Llanelli), A J Gould (capt.), W Ll Thomas (Newport); *D Morgan (Llanelli), R B Sweet-Escott (Cardiff); A W Boucher, Wallace Watts, J Hannan, H Packer (Newport), F Mills (Cardiff), C B Nicholl (Llanelli), E George (Pontypridd), *A M Jenkins (Swansea).

Ireland: J Fulton (North of Ireland); W Gardiner, S Lee (North of Ireland), T H Stevenson (Belfast Albion), A P Gwynn (Dublin Univ.); M G Delaney, L M Magee (Bective); C V Rooke (Monkstown), T J Crean, E G Forrest (capt.), A D Clinch (Wanderers), J H Lytle, A Brunker (Lansdowne), H C McCoull (Belfast Albion), E H McIlwaine (North of Ireland).

For Wales, Tom Pearson scored a try. W.J. Bancroft converted.

For Ireland, Tommy Crean scored a try.

Referee: E B Holmes (England).

Match 38   ENGLAND v WALES   Rectory Field, Blackheath. January 4, 1896

England won by two goals, five tries (25) to nil

This was England's first game since the breakaway of the Northern Union over payment for "broken time". It meant that 22 leading clubs in Yorkshire and Lancashire left the RU. Many thought the loss of the powerful Yorkshire forwards would weaken England, as it did, and they were not to win the championship for 16 years. However, in this game the forward weakness was by no means apparent as England ran in seven tries against Gould's team.

Owen Badger played his last game for Wales. Though only 5 ft. 7½ ins. and 10 st. 9 lb., he was an aggressive and determined centre and adopted many of the tricks of the Yorkshire threequarters, including the cross kick. In this game he fractured his collar-bone tackling Valentine after about 15 minutes. Later, he joined Rugby League club Swinton for £75 down and £2 10s. a week. Arthur Boucher, one of the fastest of Newport forwards, took the injured Badger's place.

England: S Houghton (Runcorn); S Morfitt (West Hartlepool), J Valentine (Swinton), E M Baker (Moseley), E F Fookes (Sowerby Bridge); R H B Cattell (Blackheath), E W Taylor (Rockcliff, capt.); G M Carey, F Mitchell, L F Giblin (Blackheath), W Whiteley (Bramley), A Starks, J W Ward, J Rhodes (Castleford), J Pinch (Lancaster).

Wales: W J Bancroft (Swansea); *F H Dauncey, A J Gould (Newport, capt.), O Badger, *C Bowen (Llanelli); B Davies, D Morgan (Llanelli); H Packer, Wallace Watts, A W Boucher (Newport), A M Jenkin (Swansea), E George, F Mills (Cardiff), C B Nicholl (Llanelli), *S H Ramsey (Treorchy).

For England, Sam Morfitt (2), Richard Cattell (2), Ernest Fookes (2) and Frank Mitchell scored tries. Jim Valentine and Edward Taylor each converted one try.

Referee: D Graham Findlay (Scotland).

WALES v SCOTLAND Cardiff Arms Park. January 25, 1896

Wales won by two tries (6) to nil

The great Gwyn Nicholls wore the scarlet jersey for the first time on this day of brilliant Welsh running and passing in quagmire conditions. Nicholls and Gould were magnificent in their midfield partnership to pave the way for victory. But they played only three times together before Gould retired to become a selector. Nicholls, born at Westbury-on-Severn, in Gloucestershire, went on to win 24 caps in a career of 10 glorious years for Wales. Where Gould was the star of the three-threequarter era, Nicholls became the Prince of Centres in the four-threequarter system.

Wales: W J Bancroft (Swansea); C Bowen (Llanelli), *E G Nicholls (Cardiff), A J Gould (capt.), F H Dauncey (Newport); Selwyn Biggs (Cardiff), F C Parfitt (Newport); H Packer (Newport), *J Evans, *W Morris, C B Nicholl (Llanelli), *W Cope, *W Davies (Cardiff), *D Evans (Penygraig), F Hutchinson (Neath).

Scotland: A R Smith (London Scottish); T L Scott (Langholm), G T Campbell (London Scottish), A B Timms (Edinburgh Wanderers), R Welsh (Watsonians); J W Simpson (Royal HSFP), D Patterson (Hawick); G T Neilson (capt.), J H Couper (West of Scotland), A Balfour, H O Smith (Watsonians), J H Dods, W M C McEwan (Edinburgh Acads.), M C Morrison (Royal HSFP), T M Scott (Hawick).

For Wales, Cliff Bowen and A. J. Gould scored tries.

Referee: George Harnett (England).

IRELAND v WALES Lansdowne Road, Dublin. March 14, 1896

Ireland won by one goal, one try (8) to one dropped goal (4)

Gould examined the pitch on the Friday and immediately ordered his team to re-bar their boots ready for the mud-heap of the next day. But Gould's dropped goal was the only Welsh score as they lost for the third successive time in Ireland and the home country went on to win the championship for the second time. Llewellyn Lloyd, aged 19, made his debut at outside half to face the feared wing forward tactics of Rooke and Lindsay. Lloyd, only 5 ft 6 ins., and just over 10 st., was to become one of Newport's immortal names in the game. Gwyn Nicholls said he was the greatest half he ever played with. Praise like that from the 'Prince' sets Llewellyn Lloyd high on the short list of all-time great players.

Ireland: G H McAllan (Royal H.S., Dungannon), T H Stevenson (Belfast Albion), W Gardiner, S Lee (North of Ireland, capt.), L Q Bulger (Lansdowne); L M Magee (Bective), G G Allen (Derry); C V Rooke (Monkstown), T J Crean, A D Clinch (Wanderers), J Sealy (Dublin Univ.), H Lindsay (Armagh), W G Byron, J H Lytle (North of Ireland), J H O'Conor (Bective).

Wales: W J Bancroft (Swansea); C Bowen (Llanelli), E G Nicholls (Cardiff), A J Gould (capt.), F H Dauncey (Newport); *G Ll Lloyd, F C Parfitt (Newport); H Packer, A W Boucher (Newport), J Evans, W Morris, C B Nicholl (Llanelli), D Evans (Penygraig), F Hutchinson (Neath), W H Millar (Mountain Ash).

For Ireland, Tommy Crean and Lytle scored tries. Larry Bulger converted one.

For Wales, A. J. Gould dropped a goal.

Referee: E B Holmes (England).

Wales won by one goal and two tries (11) to nil

Arthur Gould's illustrious career came to an end, appropriately on his home ground, as, in miserable conditions on a soaked ground, he led his side to only their third victory in 14 games with England. Actually, Gould, aged 32 had announced his retirement at the start of the season, but Newport asked him to return to help them. When he did, Wales eagerly asked him to stay as the national captain. His 27 caps represented an international record and his many admirers throughout the world contributed to a testimonial fund that had the support of the WRU.

On Easter Monday, 1897, Sir John Llewellyn, president of the WRU, presented Gould with the title deeds of the house he lived in as a tribute to his greatness and his influence on the game's development. But the other countries considered it an act of professionalism. This was the only international match Wales played this season, because Scotland and Ireland refused to meet them. The Gould dispute was serious. It aroused intense national feeling in Wales. When, in January 1898, the International Board demanded that Wales should give an undertaking that they would never again pick Gould, the WRU indignantly refused. It looked like being the end of international football for Wales for a very long time. But Gould himself saved the situation. He had no wish to be involved in this bitter wrangle. He said he had no desire ever to play for Wales again. It was as simple as that. He would concentrate on his duty as an international selector. The row was over, but Gould's memory lives on. Wales introduced the rugged so-called 'Rhondda type' forwards in this match. Dick Hellings was the most effective of these.

Wales: W J Bancroft (Swansea); C Bowen (Llanelli), E G Nicholls (Cardiff), A J Gould (capt.), T W Pearson (Newport); Selwyn Biggs (Cardiff), *Dan Jones (Aberavon); H Packer, A W Boucher (Newport), W Morris, J Evans (Llanelli), *R Hellings (Llwynypia), *F H Cornish (Cardiff), D Evans, *J Rhapps (Penygraig).

England: J F Byrne (Moseley); E F Fookes (Sowerby Bridge), T Fletcher (Seaton), E M Baker, F A Byrne (Moseley); C M Wells (Harlequins), E W Taylor (Rockcliff, capt.); F Jacob (Cambridge Univ.), R H Mangles, W Ashford, F M Stout (Richmond), P J Ebdon (Wellington), J H Barron (Bingley), R F Oakes (Hartlepool R.), W B Stoddart (Liverpool).

For Wales, Tom Pearson, Arthur Boucher and Dan Jones scored tries. W. J. Bancroft converted one.

Referee: J T Magee (Ireland).

Wales won by one goal, one penalty goal and one try (11) to one penalty goal (3)

Billy Bancroft took over as Wales's new captain in succession to Gould and immediately decided on a gamble. He chose to play up hill and against the strong wind. Wales won through their polished back play and because pack-leader Tom Dobson, who scored a fine try, had rousing support from his forwards. It was the first appearance of George Boots, who was to play 16 times for Wales and become the 'brains' of the pack. He instituted a policy of concentrated back-row covering.

Ireland: J Fulton (North of Ireland); F Purser (Dublin Univ.), F F Smethwick (Monkstown), W Gardiner (North of Ireland, capt.), L Q Bulger (Lansdowne); L M Magee (Bective), A Barr (Methodist Coll., Belfast); W G Byron, J E McIlwaine (North of Ireland), J G Franks (Dublin Univ.), M Ryan, J Ryan (Rockwell Coll.), T Little (Bective), H Lindsay (Armagh), T McCarthy (Cork).

Wales: W J Bancroft (Swansea, capt.); T W Pearson (Newport), E G Nicholls, *W Jones, *H V P Huzzey (Cardiff); J E Elliott, Selwyn Biggs (Cardiff); R Hellings, *W H Alexander (Llwynypia), D J Daniel (Llanelli), *H Davies (Swansea), *G Boots (Newport), *T Dobson, F H Cornish (Cardiff), *J Booth (Pontymister).

For Wales, Tom Dobson and Viv Huzzey scored tries. W. J. Bancroft converted one and kicked a penalty goal.

For Ireland, Larry Bulger kicked a penalty goal.

Referee: A Turnbull (Scotland).

Match 43   ENGLAND v WALES   Rectory Field, Blackheath. April 2, 1898

England won by one goal, three tries (14) to one dropped goal, one try (7)
(N.B. A dropped goal was worth four points)

The playing of this match was delayed until the Gould dispute was settled. So Wales had to wait until April to meet England. Bancroft blamed the defeat on the disappointing form of the Cardiff halves, John Elliott and Selwyn Biggs, and the old failing of a disinclination to vary the passing. During the interval the crowd paraded on the field of play, but on the ringing of a bell they cleared the pitch.

England: J F Byrne (Moseley, capt.); E F Fookes (Sowerby Bridge), P Royds (Blackheath), W L Bunting, P W Stout (Richmond); R O'H Livesay (Blackheath), Arthur Rotherham (Richmond); W Ashford (Exeter), R F Oakes (Hartlepool R.), F Jacob, H W Dudgeon, F M Stout (Richmond), J Davidson (Aspatria), J F Shaw (RNE College, Devon), H E Ramsden (Bingley).

Wales: W J Bancroft (Swansea, capt.); H V P Huzzey, E G Nicholls, W Jones (Cardiff), T W Pearson (Newport); J E Elliott, Selwyn Biggs,(Cardiff); T Dobson, F H Cornish (Cardiff), W H Alexander, R Hellings (Llwynypia), D J Daniel (Llanelli), H Davies (Swansea), G Boots (Newport), D Evans (Penygraig).

For England, Ernest Fookes (2), Frank Stout and Percy Stout scored tries. Fred Byrne converted one.

For Wales, Viv Huzzey scored a try and dropped a goal.

Referee: J T Magee (Ireland).

Match 44   WALES v ENGLAND   St. Helen's, Swansea. January 7, 1899

Wales won by four goals, two tries (26) to one try (3)

After this rousing victory to start the season, it was a bitter disappointment to lose the next two games. A crowd of more than 25,000 saw Willie Llewellyn make a spectacular debut and score a record four tries on the left wing. He was to play 20 times for Wales. It was also the debut match for Jehoida Hodges, who figured in 23 games for Wales and was to score three tries as an emergency wing against England in 1903.

Hodges was one of the great forwards, ranking with the superb George Boots. Both were to captain Newport and exert a notable influence on the play of the Welsh team. Hodges was considered a 25 per cent better performer on the big occasion, as was Alun Pask in the 1960s.

The brothers James returned for Wales after an absence of seven years and upset the English captain, Arthur Rotherham. Evan James (5ft. 7½ in; 9st. 10lb.) and David (5ft. 6in; 10st.) provided the quick possession for the Welsh four-threequarter system to pile up the first big score against England. One report said: "No international team England put in the field had ever been more routed. The English captain wasted a good deal of his energy in empty protests when he found the brothers James too good for him."

Wales: W J Bancroft (Swansea, capt.); H V P Huzzey, E G Nicholls (Cardiff), *R T Skrimshire (Newport), *W M Llewellyn (Llwynypia); Evan James, David James (Swansea); *J Blake, T Dobson (Cardiff), W H Alexander (Llwynypia), *F Scrine (Swansea), *A Brice (Aberavon), D J Daniel (Llanelli), *J J Hodges (Newport), *W Parker (Swansea).

England: H T Gamlin (Devonport Albion); Reggie Forrest (Wellington), P W Stout (Richmond), P M R Royds (Blackheath), G C Robinson (Percy Park); R O'H Livesay (Blackheath), Arthur Rotherham (Richmond, capt.); H W Dudgeon, F Jacob, J Daniell (Richmond), C H Harper (Exeter), W Mortimer (Marlborough Nomads), G R Gibson (Northern), Joe Davidson (Aspatria), R F Oakes (Hartlepool R.).

For Wales, Willie Llewellyn (4) and Viv Huzzey (2) scored tries. W. J. Bancroft converted four.

For England, George Robinson scored a try.

Referee: A Turnbull (Scotland).

Match 45 SCOTLAND v WALES   Inverleith, Edinburgh. March 4, 1899

Scotland won by one goal from a mark, two dropped goals, three tries (21) to two goals (10)

Four times this game had to be postponed because of frozen grounds. It snowed during the first half. Wales led 10-3 at the interval, but the second half was "of the rough-and-tumble kind" and, with Gwyn Nicholls injured and at only half speed, the Welsh defence broke down. The absence of the James brothers was blamed for the defeat

Scotland: H Rottenburg (London Scottish); H T S Gedge, D B Monypenny (London Scottish), G W Lamond (Kelvinside Acads.) T L Scott (Langholm) ; J. W. Simpson (Royal HSFP), R T Neilson (West of Scotland); M C Morrison (Royal HSFP, capt.), W M C McEwan (Edinburgh Acads.), H O Smith (Watsonians), G C Kerr (Durham City), R C Stevenson, A MacKinnon (London Scottish), J M Dykes (Glasgow HSFP), W J Thomson (West of Scotland).

Wales: W J Bancroft (Swansea, capt.); H V P Huzzey, E G Nicholls (Cardiff), R T Skrimshire (Newport), W M Llewellyn (Llwynypia); Selwyn Biggs (Cardiff), G Ll Lloyd (Newport); W H Alexander, R Hellings (Llwynypia), W Parker, F Scrine (Swansea), T. Dobson, J. Blake (Cardiff), A Brice (Aberavon), J J Hodges (Newport).

For Scotland, Henry Gedge, Harry Smith and Douglas Monypenny scored tries. Gedge and George Lamond dropped goals. William Thomson kicked a goal from a mark.

For Wales, Llewellyn Lloyd and Willie Llewellyn scored tries. W J Bancroft converted both.

Referee M G Delaney (Ireland).

Match 46 WALES v IRELAND   Cardiff Arms Park. March 18, 1899

Ireland won by one try (3) to nil

A record crowd of 40,000 at the Arms Park saw Ireland win the Triple Crown for the second time with the only score, a first half try by Gerry Doran. Billy Bancroft was off for threequarters of the match with fractured ribs, after the Ryan brothers had caught him and thrown him into the crowd, and the seven Welsh forwards received a gruelling time. Even so, Wales should have scored when Gwyn Nicholls, who took over as acting captain, broke away, but Reg Skrimshire was hurled down a yard from the line by Louis Magee and a try was lost because he failed to pass to Willie Llewellyn.

This was the match when the crowd broke through the barricades and poured into the ground. The pitch had to be cleared before play could start. Then the game was halted for five minutes when spectators spilled on to the pitch. At half time the crowd swarmed on to the field because there were so many in the uncomfortably crowded ground and the interval lasted 17 minutes. There were two stoppages in the second half, one of five minutes and one of two minutes. There had never been scenes like it before. Alfred Brice, the Aberavon policeman, was sent out of the pack to play at full back in place of Bancroft, and his sturdy defence saved Wales from a heavier defeat.

Wales: W J Bancroft (Swansea, capt.); H V P Huzzey, E G Nicholls (Cardiff), R T Skrimshire (Newport), W M Llewellyn (Llwynypia); Selwyn Biggs (Cardiff), G Ll Lloyd (Newport); W H Alexander, R. Hellings (Llwynypia), J Blake, F H Cornish (Cardiff), D J Daniel (Llanelli), G Boots, J J Hodges (Newport), A Brice (Aberavon).

Ireland: P O'Brien (Monkstown); G P Doran (Lansdowne), G Harman (Dublin Univ.), C Reid (North of Ireland), E F Campbell (Monkstown); L M Magee (Bective, capt.), G G Allen (Derry); W G Byron, J E McIlwaine (North of Ireland), C C H Moriarty (Monkstown), M Ryan, J Ryan (Rockwell Coll.), J. Sealy, A W D Meares (Dublin Univ.), T Little (Bective).

For Ireland, Gerry "Blucher" Doran scored a try.

Referee: A Turnbull (Scotland).

Match 47   ENGLAND v WALES   Kingsholm, Gloucester. January 6, 1900

Wales won by two goals, one penalty goal (13) to one try (3)

The dawn of the Welsh Golden Era broke this day at Gloucester where, during the interval, some of the 15,000 crowd "strolled on the field and mingled with the players, as is general in south country matches". For a period of 12 years Wales were to be almost unchallenged masters of the rugby game and won the Triple Crown six times. One of the men who guided them through those years of destiny and glory made his debut at Gloucester and scored a try in this victory. He was W. J. Trew, a genius by any standards. Billy Trew played on the wing on this occasion, but was rather disappointing. He was best at centre or outside half, in partnership with his Swansea club-mate Dicky Owen. Trew played 29 times for his country in 14 seasons.

Dick Hellings, a superb forward from Llwynypia, scored the other Welsh try, yet played almost throughout the game with a fractured forearm. It was his action in playing a short while before the match with Scotland the previous season that prompted the WRU to institute the rule this season that chosen players could not play during the week before an international match. Bancroft played one of his finest games, diving in to stop the rushes of the English forwards. But selector Arthur Gould was not impressed. "I don't think we are strong enough to beat Scotland," he said.

England: H T Gamlin (Devonport Albion); S F Cooper, G. Gordon-Smith (Blackheath), A T Brettargh (Liverpool O.B.), E T Nicholson (Birkenhead Park); R H B Cattell (Moseley, capt.), G H Marsden (Morley), F J Bell, R W Bell

(Northern), W Cobby (Hull), A Cockerham (Bradford Olicana), J W Jarman (Bristol), S Reynolds (Richmond), C T Scott (Blackheath), J Baxter (Birkenhead Park).

Wales: W J Bancroft (Swansea, capt.); W M Llewellyn (Llwynypia), *Dan Rees, *George Davies, *W J Trew (Swansea); *L A Phillips, G Ll Lloyd (Newport); R Hellings (Llwynpia), A Brice (Aberavon), W H Millar (Mountain Ash), *W H Williams (Pontymister), *Bob Thomas (Swansea), G Boots, J J Hodges (Newport), J Blake (Cardiff).

For Wales, Billy Trew and Dick Hellings scored tries. W J Bancroft converted both and kicked a penalty goal.

For England, Elliot Nicholson scored a try.

Referee: A Turnbull (Scotland).

Match 48 WALES v SCOTLAND   St. Helen's, Swansea. January 27, 1900

Wales won by four tries (12) to one try (3)

There were nearly 40,000 spectators, including 6,000 in a temporary stand that stretched right across the cricket ground end, to see Wales 'whack them', as Billy Bancroft, the Welsh captain, put it. Scottish captain Mark Morrison confessed: "We were beaten in every department. In the second half the Welsh forwards completely overran us." It was reported that, "The vast crowd sang God Save the Queen with fervour because they had just heard the grim news of the withdrawal of General Warren and the loss of his guns at Spion Kop, in one of the bloodiest battles of the Boer War."

Wales: W J Bancroft (Swansea, capt.); W M Llewellyn (Llwynpia), E G Nicholls (Cardiff), George Davies, W J Trew (Swansea); L A Phillips, G Ll Lloyd (Newport); A Brice (Aberavon), W H Millar (Mountain Ash), G. Boots, J J Hodges (Newport), J Blake, *G Dobson (Cardiff), W H Williams (Pontymister), Bob Thomas (Swansea).

Scotland: H Rottenburg (London Scottish); T L Scott (Langholm), A B Timms (Edinburgh Wands) , W H Morrison. J E Crabbie (Edinburgh Acads.); F H Fasson (Edinburgh Univ.), J I Gillespie (Edinburgh Acads.); M C Morrison (Royal HSFP, capt.), W M C McEwan (Edinburgh Acads.), W J Thomson (West of Scotland), J M Dykes, F W Henderson (London Scottish), G C Kerr (Durham City), T M Scott (Hawick), D R Bedell-Sivright (Edinburgh Univ.).

For Wales, Willie Llewellyn (2), Gwyn Nicholls and 'Pontymister' Williams scored tries.

For Scotland, Johnny Dykes scored a try.

Referee: A Hartley (England).

Match 49 IRELAND v WALES   Balmoral, Belfast. March 17, 1900

Wales won by one try (3) to nil

No more gruelling contest is imaginable than this Balmoral battle as Wales won the Triple Crown for the second time by the only score, a second half try which the scorer did not know he had obtained because he was knocked unconscious. Deadly tackling by both sides prevented the game from being a running spectacle and Ireland outshone Wales at half back, "thanks to the wonderful little man, Louis Magee."

But Bancroft proved a master of strategy. Wales took scrums in preference to line-outs, but changed their tactics in this direction in the second half after there had been no score. Just outside the Irish 25, Bancroft called for a line-out. Selwyn Biggs threw in to Alfred Brice, who passed to Lou Phillips. The half back made ground and fed Gwyn Nicholls who beat his man, going at full tilt, and passed to George Davies. The Swansea centre burst strongly, but as he dived over the line he was kicked in the mouth and knocked out. He was carried off to be revived and only then did he realise he had managed to score.

While Wales were registering this victory, fierce fighting was going on for the relief of Mafeking. The Irish crowd spurred their forwards into rushes by shouting reminders of how valiantly the Dublin Fusiliers had fought on the Glencoe Heights. But pack leader Dick Hellings and his Welsh forwards responded magnificently, while Trew at last showed his full potential.

Ireland: J Fulton (North of Ireland); E F Campbell (Monkstown), B R Doran (Lansdowne), J B Allison (Queen's Coll., Belfast), I G Davidson (North of Ireland); L M Magee (Bective, capt.), J H Ferris, (Queen's Coll., Belfast); T Little (Bective), M Ryan, J Ryan (Rockwell Coll.), A W D Meares, P C Nicholson, T A Harvey (Dublin Univ.), C E Allen (Derry), S T Irwin (Queen's Coll., Belfast).

Wales: W J Bancroft (Swansea, capt.); W M Llewellyn (Llwynypia), E G Nicholls (Cardiff), George Davies, W J Trew (Swansea); Selwyn Biggs (Cardiff), L A Phillips (Newport); R Hellings (Llwynypia), J Blake (Cardiff), J J Hodges, G Boots (Newport), A Brice (Aberavon), W H Williams (Pontymister), Bob Thomas (Swansea), W H Millar (Mountain Ash).

For Wales, George Davies scored a try.

Referee: A Turnbull (Scotland).

Match 50 WALES v ENGLAND   Cardiff Arms Park. January 5, 1901

Wales won by two goals, one try (13) to nil

Though the margin of victory was convincing, and Gwyn Nicholls scored a dazzling try with a hand-off, despite having half-a-dozen defenders on top of him, Wales played poorly. Arthur Gould said he had never seen Bancroft play so badly in Wales. The Welsh captain explained his frequent failures to find touch by saying: "It was partly because I have not been able to train owing to a strain of my thighs." Pack leader Hellings grumbled: "We would have done better if every man in the pack had pushed more." John 'Bala' Jones, a 5ft. 5in. scrum half, made his Welsh debut.

Wales: W J Bancroft (Swansea, capt.); W M Llewellyn (Llwynypia), E G Nicholls (Cardiff), George Davies, W J Trew (Swansea); G Ll Lloyd (Newport), *John 'Bala' Jones (Aberavon); R Hellings (Llwynypia), A Brice (Aberavon), W H Millar (Mountain Ash), G Boots, J J Hodges (Newport), J Blake (Cardiff), Bob Thomas (Swansea), W H Williams (Pontymister).

England: J W Sagar (Cambridge Univ.); E W Elliot (Sunderland), J T Taylor (Castleford, capt.), E J Vivyan (Devonport Albion), C Smith (Gloucester); E J Walton (Castleford), R O Schwarz (Richmond); H Alexander (Birkenhead Park), A F C Luxmoore (Richmond), C T Scott (Blackheath), N C Fletcher (OMT), D Graham (Aspatria), C O P Gibson (Northern), E W Roberts, (RNC Dartmouth), A O'Neill (Torquay).

For Wales, Gwyn Nicholls, 'Pontymister' Williams and Jehoida Hodges scored tries. W J Bancroft converted two.

Referee: A Turnbull (Scotland).

SCOTLAND v WALES Inverleith, Edinburgh. February 9, 1901

Scotland won by three goals, one try (18) to one goal, one try (8)

A rousing match ended in an unexpected Welsh rout. Lou Phillips was a passenger after 10 minutes with a recurrence of a knee injury and it was felt that Bancroft should have switched him from half back. Bancroft was severely criticised and it was said: "The Scots demonstrated that forwards who cared to follow on could smash the gallery tactics of the Welsh full back." The 10,000 crowd cheered their side on to what was to become their third season of success as Triple Crown winners.

Scotland: A W Duncan (Edinburgh Univ.); W H Welsh, A B Timms, Phipps Turnbull (Edinburgh Acads.), A N Fell (Edinburgh Univ.); F H Fasson (Edinburgh Univ.), J I Gillespie (Edinburgh Acads.); M C Morrison (Royal HSFP, capt.), J M Dykes (Glasgow HSFP), A B Flett, A Frew (Edinburgh Univ.), J Ross (London Scottish), J A Bell (Clydesdale), R S Stronach (Glasgow Acads.), D R Bedell-Sivright (Edinburgh Univ.).

Wales: W J Bancroft (Swansea, capt.); W M Llewellyn (Llwynypia and London Welsh), E G Nicholls (Cardiff), George Davies, W J Trew (Swansea); L A Phillips, G Ll Lloyd (Newport); R Hellings, W H Alexander (Llwynypia), A Brice (Aberavon), W H Millar (Mountain Ash), G Boots, J J Hodges (Newport), H Davies (Swansea), J Blake (Cardiff).

For Scotland, Johnnie Gillespie (2), Phipps Turnbull and Alf Fell scored tries. Gillespie converted two and Andrew Flett one.

For Wales, Llewellyn Lloyd and George Boots scored tries. W J Bancroft converted one.

Referee: R W Jeffares (Ireland).

WALES v IRELAND St. Helen's, Swansea. March 16, 1901

Wales won by two goals (10) to three tries (9)

A lucky Welsh win by a one-point margin saw the first appearnces of R T Gabe, Dicky Owen and Dick Jones. Gabe came in on the wing because Trew was unfit, and held his place in the team until his career ended 24 caps later, after seven years. Owen went on to win a record 35 caps, a figure not surpassed for more than 50 years. Owen, criticised for being "only moderate," said he injured his shoulder after five minutes and could not pass properly.

"We ought to have won," said Irish captain Louis Magee. "I did not think there was the usual sting in the Welsh backs. The first Welsh try was not a try at all. Mr. George Harnett, the English referee, lost his head and did not see that the man who took the ball was off-side. We ought to have as referees in international matches young men who are as fit as the players themselves." Welsh wing Willie Llewellyn, whose kick on was picked up by Billy Alexander to score the controversial try, admitted that he thought the try was off-side. So Ireland had every reason to feel robbed after scoring three tries to two.

Wales: W J Bancroft (Swansea, capt.); W M Llewellyn (Llwynypia and London Welsh), E G Nicholls (Cardiff), George Davies (Swansea), *R T Gabe (LIanelli and London Welsh); *R Jones, *R M Owen (Swansea); A Brice (Aberavon), W H Millar (Mountain Ash), F Scrine, H Davies (Swansea), G Boots (Newport), J Blake (Cardiff), W H Alexander, *Bob Jones (Llwynypia).

Ireland: C A Boyd (Wanderers); A E Freear, B R Doran (Lansdowne), J B Allison (Queen's Coll., Belfast), I G Davidson (North of Ireland); L M Magee (Bective, capt.), J H Ferris (Queen's Coll., Belfast); M Ryan, J Ryan (Rockwell Coll.), C E

Allen (Derry), F Gardiner (North of Ireland), T A Harvey (Dublin Univ.), P Healey (Limerick), J J Coffey (Lansdowne), S T Irwin (Queen's Coll., Belfast).

For Wales, Billy Alexander scored two tries. W J Bancroft converted both.

For Ireland, Jack Ryan, Arthur Freear and Ian Davidson scored tries.

Referee: George Harnett (England).

Match 53   ENGLAND v WALES   Rectory Field, Blackheath. January 11, 1902

Wales won by one penalty goal, two tries (9) to one goal and one try (8)

Gwyn Nicholls was the new Welsh captain after the retirement of Billy Bancroft, who made 33 consecutive appearances. Bancroft, after playing in every Welsh game for 12 years, was a spectator at a tremendously exciting contest, with England leading 8-3 at halftime. In the mist that hung over the ground Wales rallied in the second half and full back Jack Strand Jones, in his first game, made the best try of the match for Gabe by running around the English forwards when they expected him to kick to touch. Hundreds of forged tickets were on sale outside the ground.

Because he opened a business in Newport, Gwyn Nicholls joined the Rodney Parade club from January until the end of the season and was never on the losing side in his 11 games for Newport. Teddy Morgan, who made his Welsh debut in this match, also appeared on the wing for Newport this season, though London Welsh was his club. He played 16 times for Wales and was to score the historic winning try against the 1905 All Blacks. This was the match where Dicky Owen pretended to pick up the ball at a scrum. Bernard Oughtred dashed round, was off-side and Strand Jones drop-kicked the winning penalty after England led 8-6.

England: H T Gamlin (Devonport Albion); P L Nicholas (Exeter), J E Raphael (OMT), J T Taylor (Castleford), S F Coopper (Blackheath); P D Kendall (Birkenhead Park), B Oughtred (Hartlepool R.); H Alexander (Birkenhead Park, capt.), D D Dobson (Newton Abbot), L R Tosswill (Exeter), S G Williams (Devonport Albion), T H Willcocks (Plymouth), J Jewitt (Hartlepool R.), G. Fraser (Richmond), J J Robinson (Headingley).

Wales: *J Strand Jones (Llanelli); W M Llewellyn (Llwynypia), E G Nicholls, (Newport, capt.), R T Gabe (Llanelli), *E Morgan (London Welsh); R Jones, R M Owen (Swansea); A Brice (Aberavon) J J Hodges, G Boots (Newport), *W Joseph (Swansea), *D Jones (Treherbert), *W T Osborne (Mountain Ash), *A F Harding (Cardiff), *Nathaniel 'Danny' Walters (Llanelli).

For Wales, Rhys Gabe and Bill Osborne scored tries. Jack Strand Jones kicked a penalty goal.

For England, Denys Dobson and John Robinson scored tries. Harry Alexander converted one

Referee: R W Jeffares (Ireland).

Match 54   WALES v SCOTLAND   Cardiff Arms Park. February 1, 1902

Wales won by one goal, three tries (14) to one goal (5)

"I made a mistake," admitted Mark Morrison, the Scottish captain. "When I won the toss I should have played with the strong wind. We were 14-0 down at half time and too tired to fight back. But I'll bet a bob we would win if we played this Welsh team in Edinburgh." This was supposed to be the finest Scottish team ever fielded. They were the Triple Crown holders, a "rare combination of science and robustness." But the Welsh forwards swept them off their feet.

A report of the match said: "People must have wondered what had become of the famous Mark Morrison, the bashing Sivright and the giant Greenlees. They were not to be seen, except as muddled up entities, trying to stem a torrent." The 40,000 crowd paid a record £2,178 in gate receipts.

Wales: J Strand Jones (Llanelli); W M Llewellyn (Llwynypia), E G Nicholls (Newport, capt.) R T Gabe, E Morgan (London Welsh); G Ll Lloyd (Newport), R M Owen (Swansea); A Brice (Aberavon), J J Hodges, G Boots (Newport), W Joseph (Swansea), D Jones (Treherbert), A F Harding (Cardiff), W T Osborne (Mountain Ash), *Harry Jones (Penygraig).

Scotland: A W Duncan (Edinburgh Univ.); W H Welsh, A B Timms (Edinburgh Univ.), Phipps Turnbull (Edinburgh Acads.), A N Fell (Edinburgh Univ.); F H Fasson (Edinburgh Univ.), J I Gillespie (Edinburgh Acads.); M C Morrison (Royal HSFP, capt.), J V Bedell-Sivright, D R Bedell-Sivright (Cambridge Univ.), J R C Greenlees (Kelvinside Acads.) J Ross (London Scottish), J A Bell (Clydesdale), A B Flett (Edinburgh Univ.), W E Kyle (Hawick).

For Wales, Willie Llewellyn (2) and Rhys Gabe (2) scored tries. John Strand Jones converted one.

For Scotland, Willie Welsh scored a try. Gillespie converted.

Referee: P Gilliard (England).

Match 55   IRELAND v WALES   Lansdowne Road, Dublin. March 8, 1902

Wales won by one goal, one dropped goal, two tries (15) to nil

Such was the interest in this match that it was made all ticket for 12,000 spectators, and an agency handled distribution to reduce the risk of profiteers getting their hands on them.

The Irish forwards were more dashing and never really beaten, but the Welsh backs had the polish to outclass the home side. All the scoring was done in the second half after Wales had held out defiantly against the strong wind with Jack Strand Jones a resolute defender and worthy successor to Bancroft.

Wales took the lead with a surprise score. Bertie Doran made a mark, but sliced his kick into the open, where Gwyn Nicholls collected and dropped a left-footed goal. He could drop kick with either foot. Then Dicky Owen sent out a long pass that fell between Nicholls and Willie Llewellyn, but Llewellyn quickly gathered aud darted away for a try. When Llewellyn Lloyd snapped up a quick pass from Owen, the outside half raced in for a corner-try and Brice converted with a fine kick. Finally, Nicholls barged through for a try and the Triple Crown belonged to Wales for the third time.

Ireland: J Fulton (North of Ireland); G P Doran, B R Doran (Lansdowne), J B Allison (Queen's Coll., Belfast), I G Davidson (North of Ireland); L M Magee (Bective, capt.), H H Corley (Wanderers); F Gardiner (North of Ireland), J J Coffey (Lansdowne), A Tedford (Malone), S T Irwin (Queen's Coll., Belfast), T A Harvey (Dublin Univ.), P Healey (Limerick), J C Pringle (RIEC, North of Ireland),G T Hamlet (Old Wesley).

Wales: J Strand Jones (Llanelli); W M Llewellyn (Llwynypia), E G Nicholls (Newport, capt.), R T Gabe, E Morgan (London Welsh); G Ll Lloyd (Newport), R M Owen (Swansea); A Brice (Aberavon), W Joseph (Swansea), J J Hodges, G Boots (Newport), A F Harding (Cardiff), W T Osborne (Mountain Ash), Harry Jones (Penygraig), D Jones (Treherbert).

For Wales, Gwyn Nicholls, Willie Llewellyn and Llewellyn Lloyd scored tries. Alfred Brice converted one. Gwyn Nicholls dropped a goal.

Referee: Crawford Findlay (Scotland).

Match 56 WALES v ENGLAND   St. Helen's, Swansea. January 10, 1903

Wales won by three goals, two tries (21) to one goal (5)

Tom Pearson, the Newport wing, came out of retirement at the age of 31 to help his club, and Wales called him in to captain the side in the absence of Gwyn Nicholls (injured shoulder). But after 25 minutes, Pearson was taken off after being injured in a heavy tackle by Bert Gamlin. Jehoida Hodges switched from the pack to deputise on the wing and scored three remarkable tries.

George Travers made his first appearance. Travers, who played 25 games for Wales, developed his skill in later years as a hooker and became the first specialist in this position. In this match it was feared that Travers would be out of his class because he did not play for one of the major clubs. A terrific downpour, just before the match started, while the band were playing, quickly filled the musical instruments and they had to stop. Despite bad weather, there were 30,000 spectators.

Wales: J Strand Jones (Llanelli); *F Jowett, Dan Rees (Swansea), R T Gabe (Llanelli), T W Pearson (Newport, capt.); G Ll Lloyd (Newport), R M Owen (Swansea); G Boots, J J Hodges (Newport), A Brice (Aberavon), W Joseph (Swansea), A F Harding (Cardiff and London Welsh), D Jones (Treherbert), W T Osborne (Mountain Ash), *G Travers (Pill Harriers).

England: H T Gamlin (Devonport Albion); J H Miles (Leicester), J T Taylor (Castleford), R H Spooner (Liverpool), T Simpson (Rockcliff); B Oughtred (Hartlepool R. capt.), F C Hulme (Birkenhead Park); R Bradley, J Duthie (W. Hartlepool), D D Dobson (Newton Abbot), G Fraser (Richmond), R F A Hobbs (Blackheath), P F Hardwick (Percy Park), R D Wood (Liverpool OB), V H Cartwright (Nottingham).

For Wales, Jehoida Hodges (3), Tom Pearson and Dicky Owen scored tries. Strand Jones converted three.

For England, Denys Dobson scored a try. Jim Taylor converted.

Referee: Robin Welsh (Scotland).

Match 57 SCOTLAND v WALES   Inverleith, Edinburgh. February 7, 1903

Scotland won by one penalty goal, one try (6) to nil

Scotland avenged their shock defeat of the previous season and went on to regain the Triple Crown. This game was played in a tremendous gale. The Welsh forwards were badly beaten and their backs reluctant to fall on the ball in the face of the fiery Scottish forward rushes. The news that Wales were enjoying their Golden Era obviously had not reached as far north as Inverleith. A quarter of an hour before the start, a dozen labourers turned out with brooms to try to sweep away the pools of water on the pitch. Only 9,000 people braved the weather.

Scotland: W T Forrest (Hawick) ; A N Fell, A B Timms (Edinburgh Univ.), H J Orr (London Scottish), J E Crabbie (Edinburgh Acads.); J Knox (Kelvinside Acads.), E D Simson (Edinburgh Univ.); M C Morrison (Royal HSFP., capt.), W E Kyle (Hawick), D R Bedell-Sivright (Cambridge Univ.), A G Cairns

(Watsonians), W P Scott, N Kennedy (West of Scotland), J R C Greenlees (Kelvinside Acads.), L. West (Edinburgh Univ.).

Wales: J Strand Jones (Llanelli); *W Arnold, R T Gabe (Llanelli), Dan Rees, W J Trew (Swansea); G Ll Lloyd (Newport, capt.), R M Owen (Swansea); J J Hodges, G Boots (Newport), A. Brice (Aberavon), A F Harding (Cardiff and London Welsh), W. Joseph (Swansea), D Jones (Treherbert), W T Osborne (Mountain Ash), G Travers (Pill Harriers).

For Scotland. William Kyle scored a try. Alex Timms kicked a penalty goal.

Referee: A E Martelli (Ireland).

Match 58   WALES v IRELAND   Cardiff Arms Park. March 14, 1903

Wales won by six tries (18) to nil

George Boots went off with a broken collar-bone at half time. Actually, he suffered the injury in the first five minutes, but played on until the interval without realising the extent of the damage. Even with 14 men throughout the second half, Wales were superior in a mud-lark match. Irish captain Corley was walking to his hotel shortly after the match when he was approached by a small boy, who did not recognise him. "Buy a memorial card, sir?" he asked. "Death of poor old Ireland." Corley smiled down at him. "No thank you, I'm obliged; but I don't require one. I've been to the funeral." Of the game, Corley said: "We were simply beaten to blazes. The Welsh forwards dribbled skilfully and gave our men a rare dusting up."

Wales: *H B Winfield (Cardiff); W M Llewellyn (London Welsh), E G Nicholls (Cardiff capt.), R T Gabe (Llanelli), E Morgan (London Welsh) ; G Ll Lloyd (Newport), R M Owen (Swansea); A Brice (Aberavon), G Boots, J J Hodges (Newport), G Travers (Pill Harriers), D Jones (Treherbert), W Joseph (Swansea), A F Harding (Cardiff and London Welsh), W T Osborne (Mountain Ash).

Ireland: J Fulton (North of Ireland); G Bradshaw (Belfast Collegians), C Reid (North of Ireland), J C Parke (Dublin Univ.), G P Doran (Lansdowne); L M Magee (Bective), H H Corley (Dublin Univ., capt.); J J Coffey (Lansdowne), P Healy (Garryowen), G Hamlet (Old Wesley) F Gardiner (North of Ireland), C E Allen (Derry), T A Harvey (Monkstown), A Tedford (Malone) Jos Wallace (Wanderers).

For Wales, Willie Llewellyn (2), Teddy Morgan (2), Rhys Gabe and Alfred Brice scored tries.

Referee: P Coles (England).

Match 59   ENGLAND v WALES   Welford Road, Leicester. January 9, 1904

Drawn. England one goal, one penalty goal, two tries (14)
Wales two goals and one goal from a mark (14)

England were leading 14-10 until the last few minutes. Then Will Joseph made a mark and Bert Winfield decided to attempt the kick and try to score a goal from a mark. He was just inside the English half, but put a magnificent kick straight over the bar to force a draw. All the Welsh players were resentful over the methods of Scottish referee Crawford Findlay. It was considered that he disallowed a perfect try by Teddy Morgan that would have won the match in the last minute. The referee ruled a forward pass.

Gwyn Nicholls, the Welsh captain, refused to make any comment on the referee, but in the

Western Mail, the rugby correspondent wrote: "The refereeing of Mr. Findlay was extraordinary. The like of it has never been seen in Wales and there is no desire that it ever should he seen." Certainly it was true that Dicky Owen was penalised so often that eventually he declined to put the ball into the scrums. He simply handed it to England's scrum half to put in. Despite complaint about the refereeing, this was a game packed with good football and excitement. Sam Ramsey, the Treorchy forward, set a remarkable record – that of gaining his second cap eight years after playing his first game for Wales.

England: H T Gamlin (Devonport Albion); E J Vivyan (Devonport Albion), A Brettargh (Liverpool O B), E W Dillon (Blackheath), F W Elliot (Sunderland); P S Hancock (Richmond), W V Butcher (Bristol) ; C J Newbold, B A Hill (Blackheath), G H Keeton (Richmond), P F Hardwick (Percy Park), V H Cartwright (Nottingham), N Moore (Bristol), J G Milton (Bedford Grammar School), F M Stout (Richmond, capt.).

Wales: H B Winfield (Cardiff); W M Llewellyn (Newport), F G Nicholls (capt.), R T Gabe (Cardiff), F Morgan (London Welsh); R Jones, R M Owen (Swansea); A F Harding (London Welsh) G. Boots, J J Hodges (Newport), A Brice (Cardiff), *D J Thomas, W Joseph (Swansea), *J Evans (Blaina), S H Ramsey (Treorchy).

For Wales, Willie Llewellyn and Teddy Morgan scored tries. Bert Winfield converted two and kicked a goal from a mark.

For England, Edgar Elliot (2) and Brettargh scored tries. Frank Stout converted one. Bert Gamlin kicked a penalty goal.

Referee: Crawford Findlay (Scotland).

Match 60   WALES v SCOTLAND   St. Helen's, Swansea. February 6, 1904

Wales won by three goals, one penalty goal, one try (21) to one try (3)

Dick Jones, the Swansea fly half, played excellently. He employed a style of high punting that unsettled Scotland. A surprise was the storming form of the lighter Welsh forwards, and Alfred Brice, a policeman, scored a try. Cliff Pritchard made his debut as replacement for injured Gwyn Nicholls. It was reported that Bedell-Sivright, the Scottish forward, was rebuked by the referee after he had "roughed up" Winfield and then Owen.

Wales: H B Winfield (Cardiff); W M Llewellyn (capt.), *Cliff Pritchard (Newport), R T Gabe (Cardiff), E Morgan (London Welsh); R Jones, R M Owen (Swansea); A F Harding (London Welsh), J J Hodges, *E Thomas (Newport), A Brice, *W O'Neill (Cardiff), W Joseph (Swansea), *D H Davies (Neath), *H Watkins (Llanelli).

Scotland: W T Forrest (Hawick); G E Crabbie (Edinburgh Acads.) H J Orr (London Scottish), L M MacLeod (Cambridge Univ.), J S McDonald (Edinburgh Univ.); A A Bissett (RIE College), E D Simson (Edinburgh Univ.); M C Morrison (Royal HSFP, capt.), W E Kyle (Hawick), W P Scott, G O Turnbull (West of Scotland), D R Bedell-Sivright (Cambridge Univ.), A G Cairns (Watsonians), E J Ross (London Scottish), L H Bell (Edinburgh Acads).

For Wales, Rhys Gabe, Dick Jones, Teddy Morgan and Alfred Brice scored tries. Bert Winfield converted three and kicked a penalty goal.

For Scotland, Hugh Orr scored a try.

Referee: F Nicholls (England).

Ireland won by one goal, three tries (14) to four tries (12)

Once again referee Crawford Findlay upset Wales. He disallowed what would have been a late winning try by Dick Jones. The Irish players admitted that their first try involved a forward pass, while they thought there was nothing wrong with Jones's disallowed score. Wales certainly deserved to win, but their failure balanced that lucky Welsh win of 1901, when everyone agreed that Ireland were robbed.

Only 3,000 spectators attended because of the rival attraction of a soccer international match at nearby Cliftonville. Ireland were six points down at one stage, but produced a glorious rally with only 14 men. In the last few minutes, Joe Wallace, a forward who had replaced the injured Robb on the wing, cross-kicked. Winfield waited for the bounce. Alf Tedford swept in, took the ball 'on the hop', and scored near the posts for Cecil Parke to convert and win the match.

The screw punt that W J Bancroft had introduced through applying lateral spin to the ball, cutting his boot away as he kicked, was further improved by Winfield. In later years, V G J Jenkins also mastered the art of this type of kick.

Ireland: M F Landers (Cork Constitution); H Thrift, J C Parke (Dublin Univ.), G A D. Harvey (Wanderers), C G Robb (Queen's Coll., Belfast); L M Magee (Bective), F A Kennedy (Wanderers); C E Allen (Derry, capt.), A Tedford, R W Edwards (Malone), H J Knox (Dublin Univ.), F Gardiner (North of Ireland), H J Millar (Monkstown), G Hamlet (Old Wesley), Jos Wallace (Wanderers).

Wales: H B Winfield (Cardiff); W M Llewellyn (capt.), Cliff Pritchard (Newport), R T Gabe (Cardiff), E Morgan (London Welsh); R Jones, R M Owen (Swansea); A Brice, W O'Neill (Cardiff), E Thomas, *C M Pritchard (Newport), H Watkins (Llanelli), A F Harding (London Welsh), *S Bevan (Swansea), * Howell Jones (Neath).

For Ireland, Alf Tedford (2), Joe Wallace and Harry Thrift scored tries. Cecil Parke converted one.

For Wales, Teddy Morgan (2), Rhys Gabe and Cliff Pritchard scored tries.

Referee: Crawford Findlay (Scotland).

Wales won by two goals, five tries (25) to nil

A critic of the time wrote: "Nearly 20 years have elapsed since the four threequarter system was adopted as a result of the example set by Wales, and there is no more remarkable phenomenon in the game than the inability of English athletes to adapt themselves to this system of back play. Some of the most worthy men in the councils of English rugby advocate a reversion to the old order of things – nine forwards and three threequarters." Dick Jones again played splendidly, making innumerable openings in a dazzling partnership with Owen. George Davies, previously capped as a centre, was recalled in the new role of full back and proved one of the stars in the overwhelming Welsh victory.

Wales: George Davies (Swansea); W. M Llewellyn (Newport, capt.), Dan Rees (Swansea), R T. Gabe (Cardiff), E. Morgan (London Welsh); R Jones, R M Owen (Swansea) ; W Joseph (Swansea}, G Travers (Pill Harriers), W O'Neill (Cardiff), A F Harding (London Welsh), D Jones (Treherbert), J J Hodges, C M Pritchard (Newport), H Watkins (Llanelli).

England: S H Irvin (Devonport Albion); F H Palmer (Richmond), J E Raphael (OMT), E W Dillon, S F Coopper (Blackheath); W V Butcher (Bristol), F C Hulme (Birkenhead Park); F M Stout (Richmond, capt.), J L Mathias (Bristol), V H Cartwright (Nottingham), B A Hill, W T C Cave, C J Newbold, W L Y Rogers (Blackheath), T A Gibson (Northern).

For Wales ,Teddy Morgan (2), Willie Llewellyn, Harry Watkins, Dick Jones, Rhys Gabe and Arthur Harding scored tries. George Davies converted two.

Referee: C Lefevre (Ireland).

Match 63   SCOTLAND v WALES   Inverleith, Edinburgh. February 4, 1905

Wales won by two tries (6) to one try (3)

Ten minutes from the end, skipper Willie Llewellyn completed a round of passing with a head-down charge through full back 'Watty' Forrest for the winning try and the second leg had been negotiated on the path to the Triple Crown. This was Wales's first victory at Inverleith. Llewellyn said: "Everyone played the game of his life." In the second half it was reported, "There was a terrific fight between the packs and the pace was killing."

Scotland: W T Forrest (Hawick); J E Crabbie (Edinburgh Acads.), L M MacLeod (Cambridge Univ.), J L Forbes (Watsonians), J S McDonald (Edinburgh Univ.); P Munro (London Scottish), E D Simson (Edinburgh Univ.); A W Little, W E Kyle (Hawick), W M Milne, R S Stronach (Glasgow Acads.), A Ross (Royal HSFP), H N Fletcher (Edinburgh Univ.), W P Scott (West of Scotland, capt.), A G Cairns (Watsonians).

Wales: George Davies (Swansea); W M Llewellyn (Newport, capt.), Dan Rees (Swansea), R T Gabe (Cardiff), E Morgan (London Welsh) ; W J Trew, R M Owen (Swansea) ; W. Joseph (Swansea), G. Travers (Pill Harriers), W O'Neill (Cardiff), A F Harding (London Welsh), D Jones (Treherbert), C M Pritchard, J J Hodges (Newport), H Watkins (Llanelli).

For Wales, Willie Llewellyn scored two tries.

For Scotland, Arthur 'Sandy' Little scored a try.

Referee: G H B Kennedy (Ireland).

Match 64   WALES v IRELAND   St. Helen's, Swansea. March 11, 1905

Wales won by two goals (10) to one try (3)

For the first time Wales and Ireland met with either side being able to win the Triple Crown. Ireland took the lead with a try and "despondency crept over the Welsh section, but it was short lived." Wyndham Jones, the Mountain Ash outside half, dummied through to the posts for a daring first try. Then he picked up from the feet of the rushing Irish forwards and sent Teddy Morgan in for the other try. George Davies converted both and Wales had won the crown for the fourth time.

It was reported: "The sides were so evenly balanced that there was no scope for the brilliant experimental tactics which give so much charm to the characteristic Welsh game." On the Saturday morning it was announced that Gwyn Nicholls would come in as replacement for Dan Rees (Swansea), a decision that infuriated Swansea supporters, because the official reserve was another Swansea man, Frank Gordon. It was said that Rees withdrew in order to give Gordon his cap.

Nicholls was pelted with mud and even stones by a section of the crowd when he ran on to the field, but he played magnificently. "I always regretted playing that game," he said many years later. A report of the match said: "Maclear will probably remember Nicholls as long as the Irish centre plays football. He was not allowed to move more than 10 yards at a time, for he and the ball were brought down together by the unerring tackling of the veteran of the Welsh team." But the unlucky Gordon never played for Wales.

Wales: George Davies (Swansea); W M Llewellyn (Newport, capt.), E G Nicholls, R T Gabe (Cardiff), E Morgan (London Welsh); *Wyndham Jones (Mountain Ash), R M Owen (Swansea); W Joseph (Swansea), G Travers (Pill Harriers), W O'Neill (Cardiff), A F Harding, *J F Williams (London Welsh), J J Hodges (Newport) D Jones (Treherbert), H Watkins (Llanelli).

Ireland: M F Landers (Cork Constitution); H Thrift, J C Parke (Dublin Univ.), B Maclear (Monkstown), J E Moffatt (Old Wesley); T H Robinson, E D Caddell (Dublin Univ.); C E Allen (Derry, capt.), J J Coffey (Lansdowne), G. Hamlet (Old Wesley), H G Wilson, A Tedford (Malone), H J Knox (Dublin Univ.), H J Millar (Monkstown), Jos Wallace (Wanderers).

For Wales, Wyndham Jones and Teddy Morgan scored tries. George Davies converted both.

For Ireland, Tom Robinson scored a try.

Referee: W Williams (England).

Match 65   WALES v NEW ZEALAND   Cardiff Arms Park. December 16, 1905

Wales won by one try (3) to nil

Wales had not been beaten at home for six years when the All Blacks, themselves unbeaten, came to the Arms Park with their record of 27 consecutive victories on their sensational tour. What took place has lived on as a legend; the good remembered, the bad forgotten, as it should be. Teddy Morgan's try, and the scheme devised and put into operation to produce it, makes one of the most colourful moments of Welsh rugby history. Also, the match was notable, or notorious, depending which way it is viewed, for the 'try' that was not allowed. New Zealand centre Bob Deans claimed he scored the equalising try, almost at the same spot as Teddy Morgan's score. Some of the Welsh players admitted that they thought Deans had scored. Equally, some of the All Blacks considered Deans did not. The main fact was that referee John Dallas (Scotland) ruled no try, and that was the end of it, on the field, at least.

This most publicised match in the history of the game was played on a dry, but not hard, ground. The sun shone feebly; there was no wind. An hour before the start the gates were closed: inside waited a record 47,000 crowd, who had paid admission worth £2,600. Both teams wore numbers. The scene was described: "Amidst the silence that could almost be felt, the Colonials stood in the centre of the field and sang their weird war-cry. Teddy Morgan acted as conductor while the Welsh team sang their national anthem. The great crowd joined in the chorus. The effect was electrifying."

Then began what one writer called, "a test of physical stamina greater than any I have ever seen on the football field; but it was a greater trial of courage." Another correspondent referred to "much deliberate roughness". Several times Dicky Owen was 'roughed up' and the referee warned New Zealand forwards for their treatment of the little Welsh scrum half. In the Western Mail it was reported: "A New Zealand forward charged at Owen with swinging fist, but the 'Little Wonder' was not only unhurt, but laughing, and the crowd's growls changed to laughs." After this, Wales scored their decisive try, 10 minutes before half time.

Owen had planned the move and it had been practised by the backs before the game at a special training session. The scheme was based on the fear the All Blacks felt for Percy Bush as a brilliant side-stepping runner. Owen kept feeding the ball out to Bush at every opportunity. Cliff Pritchard, the rover back, was not given a single pass. Then a scrum formed down in the middle of the field, halfway between the centre line and the New Zealand 25. As Wales heeled, Bush, Gwyn Nicholls and Willie Llewellyn raced to the right, the three decoys in the famous feint attack. Owen looked as if he were preparing yet another swinging pass out to Bush. Then "with startling speed" he sent one of his reverse passes, of which he was the inventor, catapulting away to the left towards Cliff Pritchard.

It was a long pass and went to ground, but Pritchard scooped it up. It was the first time he had received the ball.

Pritchard deceived the hastily reorganising defence by swerving and then passed to Rhys Gabe. The centre produced another feint inwards, but passed outside to Teddy Morgan. The little wing went round Duncan McGregor and, with his characteristic slight hesitation and swerve, darted past full back George Gillett and "left him agape" to score his historic try in the north stand corner at the Westgate Street end.

So at half time it was 3-0. The crowd sang during the interval to cheer their team. Then it was back to the grim grind of fearless and unfaltering defence against the All Blacks' power forward play. The tourists had become so used to dominating and piling up points that they were bewildered when they could not score. Obviously this was the reason for their over-vigorous methods. "The New Zealanders used their weight without quarter towards the smaller Welsh backs," wrote one correspondent. "Again Owen was badly mauled. Gabe showed unexpected defensive powers, and Owen and Bush were always on their toes. Unable to score by their orthodox methods, the Colonials sort of mixed it up, but they found the Welshmen quite alive and withstanding often decidedly unfair and unduly rough methods without a waver."

Dave Gallaher, the New Zealand captain, was often penalised for spinning the ball on to his hooker's foot, and Wales countered the All Blacks' front row system by keeping a forward waiting on each side of the scrum ready to form down as the outside man in the front row at the last moment to keep the loose head.

Wales had a couple of scoring chances. An interception by Gabe almost brought a try, but Harding could not find the speed to finish the chance. Llewellyn looked all set to score after J F Williams had beaten Billy Wallace from Harding's cross kick. But Llewellyn let the ball slip from his grasp after half-a-dozen strides with no-one in front of him. In the last 10 minutes, Nicholls "made the most magnificent run of the day, which probably would have ended in a sensational score if Harding had been able to steady himself."

Just before this New Zealand had had their great scoring chance. Wallace ran strongly up the wing and swerved inside to slip a pass to Deans. Newspapers of the time say that Deans was brought down by two or three defenders, which seems most likely, because Teddy Morgan said he tackled Deans. Morgan was named as dashing across from his wing to make the tackle. Gabe also claimed he tackled Deans. "I thought he had scored," said Gabe. "Then I felt him wriggling forward to reach the goal-line. So I pulled him back." In the Western Mail it was recorded: "Although the centre made splendid efforts to struggle over, timely reinforcements came to Teddy Morgan and the ball was grounded between three or four feet from the line."

Dave Gallaher said: "It was a real good game, played out to the bitter end with the result that the better team won." Gwyn Nicholls commented: "There really was nothing between the teams. The real difference appeared to be that we took advantage of our only opportunity to score."

So the end came to the game and to the New Zealand record. The crowd burst on to the pitch and carried Teddy Morgan and Bush around the field in triumph. "Other men of the side would have been treated similarly had the crush of the people allowed it," said a report. Afterwards it was found that Owen had displaced a cartilage in his chest. "I was in agony," he said. "I would have gone off the field if it had been any other match than this." In the Western Mail it was stated: "The game was full of incidents that suggested the red maze of war rather than a friendly trial of footer skill. These things are best forgotten and forgiven by the players." They were, but this match lives on as a legend so long as the game is played.

Wales: H B Winfield (Cardiff); W M Llewellyn (Penygraig), E G Nicholls (capt.), R T Gabe (Cardiff), E Morgan (London Welsh); Cliff Pritchard (Pontypool) extra back; *P F Bush (Cardiff), R M Owen (Swansea); D Jones (Aberdare), G Travers (Pill Harriers), J J Hodges, C M Pritchard (Newport), W Joseph (Swansea), A F Harding, J F Williams (London Welsh).

New Zealand: G A Gillett; threequarters – D McGregor, R G Deans, W J Wallace; five-eighths – H J Mynott (second), J Hunter (first); halfback – F Roberts; wing forward – D Gallaher (capt.); forwards - J J O'Sullivan, G A Tyler, S Casey, F Newton, F T Glasgow, A. McDonald, C E Seeling.

For Wales, Teddy Morgan scored a try.

Referee: J D Dallas (Scotland).

Match 66   ENGLAND v WALES   Richmond. January 13, 1906

Wales won by two goals, two tries (16) to one try (3)

Wales launched their new system of seven forwards and eight backs, but the more important measure was their method of planned packing in the scrums. George Travers was now the recognised hooker, with two props, a three-man front row that was said to have been perfected by Jehoida Hodges. A report of this match said: "Having allotted places in the scrums, the Welshmen formed a more cohesive and, consequently, a more effective pack, and to their carefully thought out and ably carried out plans of scrumming, they no doubt owe their success in possession of the ball and shoving of their eight opponents." However, there was criticism that the extra back, Cliff Pritchard, only crowded the midfield attack.

England: E J Jackett (Falmouth); A E Hind (Leicester), J A Raphael (OMT), H E Shewring (Bristol), A Hudson (Gloucester); R A Jago (Devonport Albion), D R Gent (Gloucester); V H Cartwright (capt.), H A Hodges (Nottingham), C E L Hammond (Harlequins), A L Kewney (Rockcliff), T S Kelly (Exeter), W A Mills, G E Dobbs (Devonport Albion), E W Roberts (RNC Dartmouth).

Wales: H B Winfield (Cardiff); *H T Maddock (London Welsh), E G Nicholls (capt.), R T Gabe (Cardiff), E Morgan (London Welsh); P F Bush (Cardiff), R M Owen (Swansea); Cliff Pritchard (Pontypool) rover; W Joseph (Swansea), G Travers (Pill Harriers), H Watkins (Llanelli), A F Harding (London Welsh), D Jones (Aberdare), J J Hodges, C M Pritchard (Newport).

For Wales, C. M. (Charlie) Pritchard, Jehoida Hodges, Hopkin Maddock and Teddy Morgan scored tries. Bert Winfield converted two.

For England, Arthur Hudson scored a try.

Referee: A Jardine (Scotland).

Match 67   WALES v SCOTLAND   Cardiff Arms Park. February 3, 1906

Wales won by three tries (9) to one penalty goal (3)

Wales kept their seven-forward formation and were beaten from beginning to end by

Scotland's eight. Advocates of the new system pleaded for a longer trial. In the Western Mail it said: "It was hard to believe that this was the same Welsh pack that had played so well against New Zealand." Trew, one of two outside halves, was considered not to have justified his selection, but the other fly half, new cap Reggie Gibbs, was the best Welsh back. Gibbs was to become a prolific scorer for Wales with 17 tries in 16 games, mostly as a wing.

Wales: H B Winfield (Cardiff); H T Maddock (London Welsh), E G Nicholls (Cardiff, capt.), Cliff Pritchard (Pontypool), E Morgan (London Welsh); outside halves – W J Trew (Swansea) and *R A Gibbs (Cardiff); inside half– R M Owen (Swansea); forwards – W Joseph (Swansea), G Travers (Pill Harriers), D Jones (Aberdare), A F Harding, J F Williams (London Welsh), C M Pritchard, J J Hodges (Newport).

Scotland: J G Scoular (Cambridge Univ.); W C Church, T Sloan (Glasgow Acads.), K G MacLeod (Cambridge Univ.), A L Purves (London Scottish) ; P Munro (London Scottish), E D Simson (Edinburgh Univ.); L West (Edinburgh Univ., capt.), W E Kyle (Hawick), W P Scott (West of Scotland), W L Russell (Glasgow Acads.), H G Monteith (Cambridge Univ.), D R Bedell-Sivright (Edinburgh Univ.), A G Cairns, J C McCallum (Watsonians).

For Wales, Cliff Pritchard, Hopkin Maddock and Jehoida Hodges scored tries.

For Scotland, Kenneth MacLeod kicked a penalty goal.

Referee: J W Allen (Ireland).

Match 68   **IRELAND v WALES**   Balmoral, Belfast. March 10, 1906

Ireland won by one goal, two tries (11) to two tries (6)

With Wales on the threshold of the Triple Crown for the fifth time, it was decided to revert to eight forwards and Trew was dropped. But Wales were completely outmanoeuvred and outplayed. Even the reliable Rhys Gabe was faulty in defence. Referee Simpson disallowed a Welsh try by Gibbs, though he admitted afterwards that he had erred in his decision. It was reported that, "four or five Welsh forwards cracked up terribly." Gibbs never looked the part of an outside half and Maddock moved from the wing to replace him in the second half. Ireland finished with 13 men. 'Tommy' Caddell broke his ankle and Brooke Purdon so badly damaged knee ligaments that he never played big match rugby again. With both their halves off the field, forwards Joe Wallace (scrum) and Fred Gardiner took over in a great win for Ireland over the Triple Crown holders.

Ireland: G J Henebrey (Garryowen); B Maclear (Monkstown), J C Parke, F Casement, H Thrift (Dublin Univ.); W B Purdon (Queen's Coll., Belfast), E D Caddell (Dublin Univ.); F Gardiner (North of Ireland), C E Allen (Derry, capt.), H J Knox, J J Coffey (Lansdowne), H G Wilson, A Tedford (Malone), M White (Queen's Coll., Cork), Jos Wallace (Wanderers).

Wales: H B Winfield (Cardiff); E Morgan (London Welsh), E G Nicholls (capt.), R T Gabe (Cardiff), H T Maddock (London Welsh) ; R A Gibbs (Cardiff), R M Owen (Swansea); W Joseph (Swansea), G Travers (Pill Harriers), *J Powell, *D Westacott (Cardiff), J J Hodges, C M Pritchard (Newport), *Tom Evans (Llanelli), A F Harding (London Welsh).

For Ireland, Harry Thrift, Joe Wallace and Basil Maclear scored tries. Fred Gardiner converted one.

For Wales, Teddy Morgan and Rhys Gabe scored tries.

Referee: Dr. J W Simpson (Scotland).

South Africa won by one goal, two tries (11) to nil

It was reported that this first Welsh defeat at Swansea for 11 years, "Will be remembered as one of the darkest days in Welsh rugby." There was an unaccountable lack of spirit among the home forwards in the poorest performance by Wales for 10 seasons. The polished passing and fearless dash of the Springboks smashed Gwyn Nicholls's team. The Welsh forwards were badly beaten and Owen and Bush completely failed to function as a half back unit. It was recognised that their styles did not blend and they never played together for Wales again.

"What hurt more than the defeat was that the South Africans never saw even a glimpse of the best that Wales can produce," lamented the rugby correspondent of the Western Mail. Gabe, Nicholls and Teddy Morgan tackled resolutely, but had little chance to attack. Arthur Marsberg, the Lion of the Plains, was magnificent at full back for South Africa, "overflowing with power," and he and skipper Paul Roos were carried shoulder high off the field by admiring Welsh supporters who hid their disappointment with a fine show of sportsmanship. A crowd of more than 40,000 paid record gate receipts of £2,880.

"We had never hoped for such a win," said Roos. "We went on the field not knowing what the result would be, but determined to put up the best that was in us and leave the result to the gods." It was the final appearance of Gwyn Nicholls for Wales, and a sad day as captain. He was injured at one stage and did not attend the after-match dinner. He said he was suffering too much pain. Perhaps it was a broken heart.

Wales: *J C M Dyke (Penarth); E. Morgan (London Welsh), E G Nicholls (capt.), R T Gabe, *J L Williams (Cardiff); P F Bush (Cardiff), R M Owen (Swansea); W Joseph (Swansea), G Travers (Pill Harriers), D Jones (Treherbert), A F Harding, *J C Jenkins, J F Williams (London Welsh), C M Pritchard (Newport), *Dick Thomas (Mountain Ash).

South Africa: A F W Marsberg; S Joubert, H A de Villiers, J D Krige, J A Loubser; D C Jackson, F J Dobbin; P Roos (capt.), W A Burger, H J Daneel, P A le Roux, D J Brink, W C Martheze, J W E Raaff, W S Morkel.

For South Africa, Steve Joubert, Bob Loubser and "Klondyke" Raaff scored tries. Joubert converted one.

Referee: A O Jones (England).

Wales won by two goals, four tries (22) to nil

Wales resumed their seven forwards-eight backs plan and played brilliantly after the knock to national pride by the Springboks. Gabe was back to his best and Trew ran circles around the defence. Gibbs again was the extra back and the wings each scored two tries. This brought Wales level with 11 victories each and two drawn matches. The 12,000 crowd was reported to be the smallest in Wales for 12 years. Dicky Owen captained Wales for the first time in succession to Gwyn Nicholls.

Wales: *D Bailey Davies (Llanelli); J L Williams, R T Gabe (Cardiff), *J H Evans (Pontypool), H T Maddock (London Welsh); R A Gibbs (Cardiff) extra back; W J Trew, R M Owen (capt., Swansea); G Travers (Pill Harriers), W O'Neill, *J Brown (Cardiff), Tom Evans, J Watts (Llanelli), C M Pritchard, *W Dowell (Newport).

England: E J Jackett (Falmouth); S F Coopper (Blackheath), J G G Birkett

(Harlequins), H E Shewring, F S Scott (Bristol) A D Stoop (Harlequins), R Jago (Devonport Albion); B A Hill (capt.), F J V Hopley (Blackheath), C H Shaw (Moseley), L A N Slocock (Liverpool), W A Mills (Devonport Albion), T S Kelly (Exeter), W M Nanson (Carlisle), J Green (Skipton).

For Wales, Johnnie Williams (2), Hopkin Maddock (2), Reg Gibbs and Jack Brown scored tries. Gibbs converted two.

Referee: J I Gillespie (Scotland).

Match 71   SCOTLAND v WALES   Inverleith, Edinburgh. February 2, 1907

Scotland won by two tries (6) to one penalty goal (3)

This was regarded as the decisive test for Wales's system of seven forwards. It resulted in the first defeat for Wales since adopting their new formation, which it was thought was going to revolutionise rugby in the same way as the introduction of the four threequarters. Scotland went on to win the Triple Crown. Winfield's penalty goal gave Wales a 3-0 interval lead, but the full back was off for the last 25 minutes with a back injury and Gibbs deputised. Trew was captain for the first time, and Jim Webb, the great Abertillery scrummager, made the first of his 20 appearances for Wales. Reg Gibbs had a try disallowed, and even Scots players said a mistake had been made.

Scotland: T Sloan (Glasgow Acads.); K G MacLeod (Cambridge Univ.), A L Purves, M W Walter (London Scottish), D G McGregor (Pontypridd); L L Greig (United Services, capt.), E D Simson (London Scottish); D R Bedell-Sivright (Edinburgh Univ.), H G Monteith (United Hospitals), J C McCallum, L M Spiers (Watsonians), I C Geddes (London Scottish), G M Frew (Glasgow HSFP), W P Scott (West of Scotland), G A Sanderson (Royal HSFP).

Wales: H B Winfield (Cardiff); J L Williams, R T Gabe (Cardiff), J H Evans (Pontypool), H T Maddock (London Welsh); R A Gibbs (Cardiff) extra back; W J Trew (capt.), R M Owen (Swansea); *J Webb (Abertillery), G Travers (Pill Harriers), J Watts, Tom Evans (Llanelli), C M Pritchard, W Dowell (Newport), J Brown (Cardiff).

For Scotland, Alex Purves and Hugh Monteith scored tries.

For Wales, Bert Winfield kicked a penalty goal.

Referee: C Lefevre (Ireland).

Match 72   WALES v IRELAND   Cardiff Arms Park. March 9, 1907

Wales won by two goals, one penalty goal, one dropped goal, four tries (29) to nil

Rhys Gabe, the new Welsh captain, was given powers to play Arthur Harding, a forward, in the pack or among the backs, as he felt the need. Gabe preferred Harding in the pack and Wales swept to an overwhelming victory. Percy Bush came in as replacement for Trew and played brilliantly. Bush had a hand in almost every one of the six tries and dropped a goal. Of the try he scored it was said: "His single-handed try was sheer impudence of one man beating the whole of the Irish backs."

Trew, who had captained Wales in the previous match, refused to play. It was said that he withdrew because his Swansea club-mate, Fred Scrine, had been suspended by the WRU, "for using improper language to a referee." Trew felt the suspension was harsh.

Wales: H B Winfield (Cardiff); *D. P Jones, J H Evans (Pontypool), R T Gabe (capt.), J L Williams (Cardiff); P F Bush, *R J David (Cardiff); G Travers (Pill Harriers), W O'Neill, J. Brown (Cardiff), Tom Evans, J Watts (Llanelli), W Dowell, C M Pritchard (Newport), A F Harding (London Welsh).

Ireland: W P Hinton (Old Wesley); B Maclear (Monkstown), TJ Greeves (North of Ireland), J C Parke, H Thrift (Dublin Univ.); T H Robinson, F M Harvey (Wanderers); C E Allen (Derry, capt.), A Tedford, H. G. Wilson (Malone), J A Sweeny (Blackrock Coll.), F Gardiner (North of Ireland), G Hamlet (Old Wesley), M White (Queen's Coll., Cork), H J Knox (Lansdowne).

For Wales, Johnnie Williams (3), Percy Bush, David 'Ponty' Jones and Rhys Gabe scored tries. Bert Winfield converted two and kicked a penalty goal. Bush dropped a goal.

Referee: F W Marsh (England).

Match 73   ENGLAND v WALES   Bristol City AFC Ground. January 18, 1908

Wales won by three goals, one dropped goal, one penalty goal, two tries (28)
to three goals, one try (18)

The phantom football match, as this was called, brought an aggregate of 46 points in a thrilling tussle with elusive and thrustful running by both sides. Reports spoke of "phantom figures flitting to and fro in the thick fog that shrouded the ground". Never before had a match been played and so little seen of it. Yet the 25,000 spectators revelled in the novelty of the occasion and the quality of play that was within their view. Once again Bush was the Welsh genius with his incomparable individualism. Tommy Vile, gaining his first cap, was the perfect scrum half partner. Wales took the lead for the first time in the series at 12 matches to 11 with two drawn. Jim Peters was the first coloured player for England.

England: A E Wood (Gloucester); D Lambert, J G G Birkett (Harlequins, capt.), W N Lapage (United Services), A Hudson (Gloucester); J Peters (Plymouth), R H Williamson (Oxford Univ.); K Gilbert, W Mills (Devonport Albion), F Boylen, H Havelock (Hartlepool R.), L A N Slocock (Liverpool), C E L Hammond, G D Roberts (Harlequins), R Dibble (Bridgwater A.).

Wales: H B Winfield (Cardiff); J L Williams, R T Gabe (Cardiff), W J Trew (Swansea), R A Gibbs (Cardiff); P F Bush (Cardiff), *T H Vile (Newport); J Webb (Abertillery), G Travers (Pill Harriers), W O'Neill, J Brown (Cardiff), J Watts (Llanelli), C M Pritchard (Newport), W Dowell (Pontypool), A F Harding (London Welsh, capt.).

For Wales, Rhys Gabe (2), Percy Bush, Billy Trew and Reg Gibbs scored tries. Bert Winfield converted two and kicked a penalty goal. Bush dropped a goal and converted one try.

For England, John Birkett (2), Walter Lapage and Rupert Williamson scored tries. Alan Wood converted two and Geoff 'Khaki' Roberts converted one.

Referee: J T Tulloch (Scotland).

Match 74   WALES v SCOTLAND   St. Helen's, Swansea. February 1, 1908

Wales won by two tries (6) to one goal (5)

Wales were glad to hear the final whistle and win by one point to move to the last hurdle for the Triple Crown. There was a tense wait for the referee's decision in the last minute as Geddes dived over the Welsh line. But referee W. Williams (England) ruled, as had been the case with Bob Deans in the N.Z. game of 1905, that Ian Geddes had grounded the ball inches short of the line and wriggled forward while being held.

Wales: H B Winfield (Cardiff); J L Williams, R T Gabe (Cardiff), W J Trew (Swansea), R A Gibbs (Cardiff); P F Bush (Cardiff), T H Vile (Newport); *G Hayward (Swansea), G Travers (Pill Harriers, capt.), W O'Neill, J Brown (Cardiff), W Dowell (Pontypool), A F Harding (London Welsh), J Watts (Llanelli), J Webb (Abertillery).

Scotland: D G Schulze (London Scottish); A L Purves, M W Walter, T Sloan (London Scottish), H Martin (Edinburgh Acads.); L L Greig (United Services, capt.), G Cunningham (London Scottish) D R Bedell-Sivright (Edinburgh Univ.), J C McCallum, L M Spiers (Watsonians), I C Geddes, G C Gowlland (London Scottish), J M B Scott (Edinburgh Acads.), J A Brown (Glasgow Acads.), G M Frew (Glasgow HSFP).

For Wales, Billy Trew and Johnnie Williams scored tries.

For Scotland, Alex Purves scored a try. Ian Geddes converted.

Referee: W Williams (England).

Match 75   WALES v FRANCE   Cardiff Arms Park. March 2, 1908

Wales won by three goals, one penalty goal, six tries (36) to one dropped goal (4)

Reggie Gibbs, the Cardiff wing, should have set a Welsh try scoring record in this first game with France. He had scored four tries to equal the record set by Willie Llewellyn in 1899 against England at Swansea, when he went racing away for what looked an easy fifth try. It was so simple, in fact, that when Gibbs crossed the goal-line, although he was in a favourable position for a successful conversion kick, he decided he would plant the ball between the posts. But an enthusiastic French chaser "legged" him with a desperate dive and, as Gibbs lost balance and stumbled, he dropped the ball. Wales still managed nine tries.

Wales: H B Winfield (Cardiff); R A Gibbs (Cardiff), W J Trew (Swansea), R T Gabe (Cardiff), E Morgan (London Welsh, capt.); R Jones, R M Owen (Swansea); J Webb (Abertillery), G Travers (Pill Harriers), Dick Thomas (Mountain Ash), W O'Neill, J Brown (Cardiff), J Watts (Llanelli), G Hayward (Swansea), W Dowell (Pontypool).

France: H Martin (Stade Bordelais); E Lesieur, C Vareilles, (Stade Francais), G. Lane (Racing Club), M Leuvielle (Stade Bordelais); A Mayssonnie (Toulouse), A Hubert (ASF); M Communeau (capt.), A Duval (Stade Francais), P. Mauriat (Lyons), R de Malmann, A. Branlat, P. Guillemin (Racing Club), J. Dufourcq, A. Masse (Stade Bordelais).

For Wales, Reg Gibbs (4), Billy Trew (2), Teddy Morgan (2) and Dick Jones scored tries. Bert Winfield converted two and kicked a penalty goal. Gibbs converted one.

For France, Charles Vareilles dropped a goal.

Referee: W Williams (England).

Match 76   IRELAND v WALES   Balmoral, Belfast. March 14, 1908

Wales won by one goal, two tries (11) to one goal (5)

It was only 10 minutes from the end that Wales looked like a winning team with a burst of sensational scoring to snatch the Triple Crown for the fifth time. On a bitterly cold day and heavy ground the Irish forwards were on top for long periods. The Western Mail said: "Owen never had a more anxious time at the base of the scrum, and never has he displayed finer courage or greater resource. It was as well for Wales that he retained his place in the national side and he was carried shoulder high to the dressing room."

Owen earned the nickname of 'The Bullet' for the speed of his pass. He was also a fearless tackler and his record of 35 appearances for Wales was not beaten for 47 years. New record-breaker Ken Jones, the Newport wing, went on to collect 44 caps. Dick Jones's career ended prematurely in 1910 after an accident, but he deserves to be remembered as a fine outside half.

At 5-5, Ireland looked like at least making it a draw. Then the 15,000 crowd saw Dick Jones make a brilliant opening from a pick up in broken play, and Trew and Gabe linked to send Gibbs in at the corner. Two minutes later, Tom Evans set his backs moving with a serve from a line-out and again Trew and Gabe combined to open the scoring route for J. L. Williams. It was a triumph not so much for organised effort, as superb opportunism in developing their two chances.

Ireland: W P Hinton (Old Wesley); C Thompson (Belfast Collegians), J C Parke (Monkstown, capt.), G P Beckett, H Thrift (Dublin Univ.); H R Aston (Dublin Univ.), E D Caddell (Wanderers); B A Solomons, T G Harpur (Dublin Univ.), T Smyth, A Tedford, H G Wilson (Malone), G Hamlet (Old Wesley), F Gardiner (North of Ireland), J J Coffey (Lansdowne).

Wales: H B Winfield (Cardiff, capt.); R A Gibbs (Cardiff), W J Trew (Swansea), R T Gabe, J L Williams (Cardiff); R Jones, R M Owen (Swansea); W O'Neill (Cardiff), G Travers (Pill Harriers), W Dowell (Pontypool), J Watts, Tom Evans (Llanelli), J. Webb (Abertillery), G Hayward (Swansea), Dick Thomas (Mountain Ash).

For Wales, Johnnie Williams (2) and Reg Gibbs scored tries. Bert Winfield converted one.

For Ireland, Herbert Aston scored a try. Cecil Parke converted.

Referee: J D Dallas (Scotland).

Match 77   WALES v AUSTRALIA   Cardiff Arms Park. December 12, 1908

Wales won by one penalty goal, two tries (9) to two tries (6)

The first Australians to play Wales in front of 30,000 spectators scored try for try with the home team and in the final count it was Bert Winfield's penalty goal that gave Wales victory. It was recorded: "There was nearly an ugly incident when Trew was kicked on the forehead by Burge, and Travers ran up with clenched fist, believing the act to be deliberate." Trew was carried off, badly shaken, but returned to inspire his side.

"It was a very gruelling game," admitted Australian captain Dr. Herbert Moran. "But it was not as rough as many games I have played in. The Welsh forwards broke up very quickly from the scrums, which is the game we have always played, and I think the Welsh team is the only side I have found to do it over us. There was not the same devil in our play as the Welshmen showed."

Wales led when Owen sent Dick Jones away to link with Trew, and the captain made a typically clever run right to the line, where a short pass enabled Travers to score. An interception while Wales were attacking gave Richards an equalising try to make it 3-3 at half time. Then Tom Evans dribbled away and Phil Hopkins pounced for a try before Winfield popped over his decisive penalty goal. Russell scored a breakaway try for the Wallabies, who won their other international of the tour against England 9-3.

Wales: H B Winfield (Cardiff); *P Hopkins (Swansea), W J Trew (Swansea, capt.), *J P Jones (Newport), J L Williams (Cardiff); R Jones, R M Owen (Swansea); J

Webb (Abertillery), G Travers (Pill Harriers), *P D Waller (Newport), Tom Evans, J Watts (Llanelli), G Hayward, D J Thomas, *Ivor Morgan (Swansea).

Australia: P Carmichael; C Russell, J Hickey, E Mandible, D B Carroll; Ward Prentice (five eighth); C H McKivatt (halfback); Dr. H M Moran (capt.), T Richards, R Craig, P McCue, A B Burge, C A Hammond, T Griffin, J E T Barnett.

For Wales, Phil Hopkins and George Travers scored tries. Bert Winfield kicked a penalty goal.

For Australia, Tom Richards and Charlie Russell scored tries.

Referee: Gil Evans (England).

Match 78   WALES v ENGLAND   Cardiff Arms Park. January 16, 1909

Wales won by one goal, one try (8) to nil

Jack Bancroft made his debut at full back when Bert Winfield withdrew with a dislocated thumb. So Jack won his cap as a reserve in exactly the same way as his famous brother W. J., and went on to become another outstanding name in Welsh rugby history with 18 caps and Welsh scoring record of 19 points in a match. Only 25,000 people saw Wales gain this fifth consecutive win over England, but Welsh forward play was disappointing with "passengers in the pack."

England were under indictment by Scotland for infringing the amateur laws by paying one guinea a week expenses to the 1905 All Blacks and the same to the currently touring Australians. This was being paid in addition to the 3s. per day pocket money allowance. Scotland refused to play the Wallabies and cancelled their match with England, though the English match was rearranged after settlement of the dispute.

Wales: *Jack Bancroft (Swansea); J L Williams (Cardiff), J P Jones (Newport), W J Trew (capt.), P Hopkins (Swansea); R Jones, R M Owen (Swansea); Tom Evans (Llanelli), G Travers (Pill Harriers), P D Waller (Newport), J Brown (Cardiff), J Webb, *J Blackmore (Abertillery), G Hayward, Ivor Morgan (Swansea).

England: E J Jackett (Leicester); B B Bennetts (Penzance), F N Tarr (Leicester), E R Mobbs (Northampton); E W Assinder (Old Edwardians); T G Wedge (St. Ives), J Davey (Redruth); R Dibble (Bridgwater, capt.), A L Kewney (Leicester), J G Cooper (Moseley), A D Warrington Morris (United Sercices), W Johns (Gloucester), E D Ibbitson (Headingley), F G Handford (Manchester), H. Archer (Guy's Hospital).

For Wales, Phil Hopkins and Johnnie Williams scored tries. Jack Bancroft converted one.

Referee: J D Dallas (Scotland).

Match 79   SCOTLAND v WALES   Inverleith, Edinburgh. February 6, 1909

Wales won by one goal (5) to one penalty goal (3)

Scotland could have won by one point right at the end, when referee Rupert Jeffares (Ireland) penalised Jack Bancroft for not playing the ball. What the referee did not realise was that Bancroft lay on the ball unconscious, having been kicked on the head making a courageous dive to stop Jim Tennent's foot-rush. George Cunningham, who had kicked an earlier penalty goal, missed this chance of victory "by less than a foot". So Wales scraped to success by a two points margin with a late try as J. P. 'Jack' Jones made a grand burst and sent Trew racing in for

Jack Bancroft to convert. It was reported: "Immediately the final tootle was given, the Welshmen were simply frantic with joy and threw up their hats and sticks and leeks and everything else that was detachable into the air."

Scotland: D G Schulze (London Scottish) H Martin (Edinburgh Acads.), C M Gilray (London Scottish), A W Angus, T J Simson (Watsonians); J. McW Tennent (West of Scotland), G Cunningham (London Scottish); J M B Scott (Edinburgh Acads., capt.), W E Kyle (Hawick), G M Frew (Glasgow HSFP), G C Gowlland, J S Wilson (London Scottish), J M Mackenzie (Edinburgh Univ.), J C McCallum (Watsonians), A Ross (Royal HSFP).

Wales: Jack Bancroft (Swansea); *A M Baker, J P Jones (Newport), W J Trew (Swansea, capt.), J L Williams (Cardiff); R Jones, R M Owen (Swansea); J Webb (Abertillery), G Travers (Pill Harriers), Tom Evans, J Watts (Llanelli), Dick Thomas (Mountain Ash), P D Waller, E Thomas (Newport), Ivor Morgan (Swansea).

For Wales, Billy Trew scored a try. Jack Bancroft converted.

For Scotland, George Cunningham kicked a penalty goal.

Referee: R W Jeffares (Ireland).

Match 80   FRANCE v WALES   Colombes, Paris. February 23, 1909

Wales won by seven goals, four tries (47) to one goal (5)

The match was summed up in the Western Mail: "Wales could not help winning, the scoring of tries being as easy as shelling peas." Dicky Owen and Dick Jones simply fed the ball out to their threequarters and the 10,000 crowd saw Melville Baker and Trew each score three tries, though Jack Jones was the most dazzling runner. The threequarters scored 10 tries between them. This was a Tuesday match and Wales's first visit to France.

France: E de Jouvencel (Stade Francais); E Lesieur, R Sagot (Stade Francais), T Varvier, G Lane (Racing Club); A Hubert (ASF), A Theuriet (SCUF); P Dupre, G Borchard, R de Malmann (Racing Club), G Fourcade (Bordeaux Etudiants), P Mauriat (Lyons), A Masse (Stade Bordelais), J Icard, M Communeau (Stade Francais, capt.).

Wales: Jack Bancroft (Swansea); A M Baker, J P Jones (Newport), W J Trew (Swansea, capt.), J L Williams (Cardiff); R Jones, R M Owen (Swansea); J Webb (Abertillery), *T C Lloyd (Neath), *R Thomas (Pontypool), P D Waller, E Thomas (Newport), Tom Evans, J Watts (Llanelli), Ivor Morgan (Swansea).

For Wales, Billy Trew (3), Melville Baker (3), Johnnie Williams (2), J. P. (Jack) Jones (2) and Jim Watts scored tries. Jack Bancroft converted six. Trew converted one.

For France, Sagot scored a try. Paul Mauriat converted.

Referee: W Williams (England).

Match 81   WALES v IRELAND   St. Helen's, Swansea. March 13, 1909

Wales won by three goals, one try (18) to one goal (5)

Wales completed a great season of success by winning the Triple Crown for the sixth time. It was the first occasion any country had won the crown for a second successive year. Actually, Wales won all five internationals this season, including the match with the Wallabies, and Billy

Trew was captain in each game. This was Wales's ninth consecutive international victory, but there was a poor attendance of 25,000 to see the most exciting and entertaining game of the season. Wales scored 13 of their points in a spell of eight minutes after there had been no score in the first half.

Wales: Jack Bancroft (Swansea); J L Williams (Cardiff), J P Jones (Newport), W J Trew (capt.), P Hopkins (Swansea); R Jones, R M Owen (Swansea); J Webb (Abertillery), G Travers (Pill Harriers), P D Waller, E Thomas (Newport), Tom Evans, J Watts (Llanelli), R Thomas (Pontypool), Ivor Morgan (Swansea).

Ireland: G J Henebrey (Garryowen); H Thrift (Wanderers), J C Parke (Monkstown), T J Greeves (North of Ireland), C Thompson (Belfast Collegians); G Pinion (Belfast Collegians), F M McCormac (Wanderers); T Halpin (Garryowen), O J S Piper (Cork Constitution) M G Garry (Bective), G Hamlet (Old Wesley, capt.), T Smyth, H G Wilson (Malone), B A Solomons (Dublin Univ.), J C Blackham (Queen's Coll., Cork).

For Wales, Phil Hopkins, J.P. (Jack) Jones, Jim Watts and Billy Trew scored tries. Jack Bancroft converted three.

For Ireland, Charles Thompson scored a try. Cecil Parke converted.

Referee: F C Potter-Irwin (England).

Match 82　**WALES v FRANCE**　　St. Helen's, Swansea. January 1, 1910

Wales won by eight goals, one penalty goal, two tries (49) to one
goal, two penalty goals and one try (14)

As well as the unusual procedure of opening the season with a match against France on New Year's Day, there was an equally odd admission from French captain Gaston Lane the night before the game. "I think Wales will win by 35 points," he said. He was not far from the mark as the Welsh attackers built their record aggregate of 49 points. Jack Bancroft established an individual record of 19 points that remained unchallenged until Keith Jarrett equalled it in 1967 against England. Bancroft converted eight tries and kicked a penalty goal. The Welsh players were criticised for "fooling about and not taking the game seriously." Only about 4,000 spectators attended. This was Wales's 11th consecutive victory, a record never since equalled.

Wales: Jack Bancroft (Swansea); H T Maddock (London Welsh), J P Jones (Newport), W J Trew (Swansea, capt.), R. A. Gibbs (Cardiff); R Jones, R M Owen (Swansea); Tom Evans (Llanelli), *J. Pullman (Neath), J Webb (Abertillery), C M Pritchard, E Thomas, P D Waller (Newport), *B Gronow (Bridgend), Ivor Morgan (Swansea).

France: J Menrath (SCUF); M Bruneau (Stade Bordelais), H Houblain (SCUF), M Burgun, G Lane (Racing Club, capt.); C Martin (Lyons), A Mayssonnie (Toulouse); P Mauriat (Lyons), A Masse, M. Hourdebaigt (Stade Bordelais), P Guillemin (Racing Club), L Lafitte, G Thevenot, R Boudreau, J Anduran (SCUF).

For Wales, Reg Gibbs (3), Ivor Morgan (2), Hopkin Maddock (2), Billy Trew, J. P. (Jack) Jones and Ben Gronow scored tries. Jack Bancroft converted eight and kicked a penalty goal.

For France, Lafitte and Paul Mauriat scored tries. Menrath kicked two penalty goals and one conversion.

Referee: W Williams (England).

Match 83 ENGLAND v WALES   Twickenham. January 15, 1910

England won by one goal, one penalty goal and one try (11) to two tries (6)

England's first success over Wales for 12 years marked the opening of the new international stadium in "the picturesque village of Twickenham." Adrian Stoop captained England and said: "We were very lucky to win and I don't know how we managed to do it." However, Trew, the Welsh captain, was under no illusions about the result. "England deserved to win; they were too good for us," he said.

The 18,000 crowd saw England score a spectacular try direct from the kick-off. Ben Gronow kicked off for Wales. Stoop fielded and set off diagonally on an unexpected run. This caught wing forward Ivor Morgan and fly half Dick Jones by surprise and they were too slow to close in. Stoop passed to Ronnie Poulton, on the left wing, just as Jack Jones tackled the England skipper. Poulton cross-kicked and Berry collected. Briefly there was a mix-up. Then scrum half Dai Gent slipped the ball away to Solomon, who made ground, feinted to pass one way and then fed Fred Chapman. The wing sped away, handed-off Trew and, though tackled, dived over for the famous try at the north end.

Before the game, Welsh critics were agreed that, "England's chances of coming out on top are somewhat remote." But Owen and Dick Jones, the renowned Welsh halves, struggled in the rain and mud and looked 'over the hill'. They were dropped for the rest of the season. The Welsh team arrived at the ground only five minutes before kick-off time because their coach was delayed in West End traffic, and the game started 15 minutes late. "England put eight points on us before we knew where we were," grumbled Dicky Owen. "Just at that time our men did not have a gallop in them. We had our chances to win in the last 10 minutes and missed them."

England: W R Johnston (Bristol); F E Chapman (Westoe), B Solomon (Redruth), J G G Birkett, R W Poulton (Harlequins); A D Stoop (Harlequins, capt.), D R Gent (Gloucester); E L Chambers (Bedford), W Johns, H Berry (Gloucester), L Haigh (Manchester), H J S Morton, C H Pillman (Blackheath), D F Smith (Richmond), L E Barrington-Ward (Edinburgh Univ.).

Wales: Jack Bancroft (Swansea); R A Gibbs (Cardiff), J P Jones (Newport), W J Trew (capt.), P Hopkins (Swansea); R Jones, R M Owen (Swansea); J Webb (Abertillery), *J Pugsley (Cardiff), Tom Evans (Llanelli), B Gronow (Bridgend), C M Pritchard, *H Jarman (Newport), D J Thomas, Ivor Morgan (Swansea).

For England, Fred Chapman and Bert Solomon scored tries. Chapman converted one and kicked a penalty goal.

For Wales, Reg Gibbs and Jim Webb scored tries.

Referee: J D Dallas (Scotland).

Match 84 WALES v SCOTLAND   Cardiff Arms Park. February 5, 1910

Wales won by one goal, three tries (14) to nil

On a field fit only for water-polo, the Welsh forwards were irresistible and Billy Spiller, who was to become the first man to score a century for Glamorgan in first-class cricket, scored a sparkling try on his debut. Scotland lost fly half Jim Tennent just after half time. He was badly hurt by studs and this injury led to important new regulations being introduced for the following season. The old pointed studs were banned and flat-bottomed studs of ¾ in. diameter became standard. Though with only 14 men for most of the second half, Scotland did not use it as an excuse. George Frew, their captain, said: "The mud put us off our game."

Wales: Jack Bancroft (Swansea); R A Gibbs, *W Spiller (Cardiff}), W J Trew (Swansea, capt.), A M Baker (Newport); P F Bush, *W L Morgan (Cardiff); J Webb (Abertillery), J Pugsley (Cardiff), B Gronow (Bridgend), Tom Evans (Llanelli), H Jarman, * E Jenkins (Newport), D J Thomas, Ivor Morgan (Swansea).

Scotland: D G Schulze (London Scottish); W R Sutherland (Hawick), J Pearson, A W Angus, J T Simson (Watsonians); J McW Tennent (West of Scotland), E Milroy (Watsonians); L M Spiers, J C McCallum (Watsonians), J M B Scott (Edinburgh Acads.), G C Gowlland (London Scottish), G M Frew (Glasgow HSFP,capt.), W E Kyle (Hawick),J M Mackenzie (Edinburgh Univ.), C D Stuart (West of Scotland).

For Wales, Joe Pugsley, Billy Spiller, Melville Baker and Ivor Morgan scored tries. Jack Bancroft converted one.

Referee: G H B Kennedy (Ireland).

Match 85   IRELAND v WALES   Lansdowne Road, Dublin. March 12, 1910

Wales won by one dropped goal and five tries (19) to one try (3)

Cardiff players supplied all the points in this Dublin victory, which saw the debut of Louis Dyke to complete an all-Cardiff threequarter line. Johnnie Williams, an outstanding wing, who made 17 appearances for Wales, scored three dashing tries. The Irish forwards cracked in the last 15 minutes after dominating the game.

Ireland: W P Hinton (Old Wesley); C T O'Callaghan (Carlow) A S Taylor (Queen's Coll., Belfast), R K Lyle (Dublin Univ.), C Thompson (Belfast Collegians, capt.); A N McClinton (North of Ireland), F M McCormac (Dublin Wands.); H G Wilson, T Smyth, G McIldowie (Malone), W S Smyth (Belfast Collegians), O J S. Piper (Cork Constitution), B A Solomons, J C Blackham (Wanderers), T Halpin (Garryowen).

Wales: Jack Bancroft (Swansea); R A Gibbs (capt.), *L M Dyke, W Spiller, J L Williams (Cardiff); P F Bush (Cardiff), T H Vile (Newport); J Webb (Abertillery), J Pugsley (Cardiff), B Gronow (Bridgend), Tom Evans (Llanelli), H Jarman, E Jenkins (Newport), D J Thomas, Ivor Morgan (Swansea).

For Wales, Johnnie Williams (3), Louis Dyke and Reg Gibbs scored tries. Percy Bush dropped a goal.

For Ireland, George McIldowie scored a try.

Referee: J D Dallas (Scotland).

Match 86   WALES v ENGLAND   St. Helen's, Swansea. January 21, 1911

Wales won by one penalty goal, four tries (15) to one goal and two tries (11)

Trew, the Welsh captain, said: "The side we have defeated after such a hard struggle is the finest English team that I have ever played against. It was a good job for us that we were so well trained, or we would not have lasted the hot pace right to the end". A critic wrote: "The Welshmen gave the impression that they were so thoroughly demoralised at one stage that time alone could save them." But Trew's team staged a fighting rally and changed their anxious

12-11 lead into a 15-11 victory with a late try by Joe Pugsley to avenge the Twickenham defeat of the previous season.

Wales: Jack Bancroft (Swansea); J L Williams, W Spiller (Cardiff), *F W Birt (Newport), R A Gibbs (Cardiff); W J Trew (capt.), R M Owen (Swansea); J Webb (Abertillery), J Pugsley (Cardiff), *A P Coldrick (Newport), H Jarman (Pontypool), *W Perry (Neath), Tom Evans (Llanelli), D J Thomas, Ivor Morgan (Swansea).

England: S H Williams (Newport); A D Roberts (Northern), J A Scholfield (Preston Grasshoppers), J G G Birkett (capt.), D Lambert (Harlequins); A D Stoop (Harlequins), A L H Gotley (Blackheath); A L Kewney (Leicester), J A King (Headingley), R Dibble (Bridgwater), W E Mann, N A Wodehouse (United Services), L Haigh (Manchester), L G Brown, C H Pillman (Blackheath).

For Wales, Reg Gibbs, Ivor Morgan, Billy Spiller and Joe Pugsley scored tries. Fred Birt kicked a penalty goal.

For England, Alan Roberts, Alf Kewney and John Scholfield scored tries. Douglas 'Danny' Lambert converted one.

Referee: J I Gillespie (Scotland).

Match 87   SCOTLAND v WALES   Inverleith, Edinburgh. February 4, 1911

Wales won by two goals, one dropped goal, six tries (32) to one dropped goal, two tries (10)

This record win over Scotland put Wales in line for the Triple Crown. It was a great achievement by the Welshmen on their bogy ground and a Scottish critic commented: "Prettier football has never been seen." Spiller's dropped goal set Wales on the way to victory, though the score was only 7-4 at half time. Then Trew's team piled on 25 points and seven of the eight tries in the match came from the all-Cardiff threequarter line.

Scotland: D G Schulze (London Scottish); D M Grant (Elstow School), F G Buchanan (Kelvinside Acads.), A W Angus (Watsonians), J M Macdonald (Edinburgh Wands.); P Munro (London Scottish, capt.), F L Osler (Edinburgh Univ.); J M B Scott (Edinburgh Acads.), R Stevenson (St. Andrew's Univ.), F H Turner (Liverpool), R Fraser (Cambridge Univ.), J M MacKenzie, A R Ross (Edinburgh Univ.), L Robertson (London Scottish), C H Abercrombie (United Services).

Wales: F W Birt (Newport); R A Gibbs, W Spiller, L M Dyke, J L Williams (Cardiff); W J Trew (capt.), R M Owen (Swansea); J Webb (Abertillery), G Travers, A P Coldrick (Newport), R Thomas (Pontypool), D J Thomas (Swansea), Tom Evans (Llanelli), *J Birch (Neath), J Pugsley (Cardiff).

For Wales, Reg Gibbs (3), Billy Spiller (2), Johnnie Williams (2) and Rhys Thomas scored tries. Louis Dyke converted two. Spiller dropped a goal.

For Scotland, Fred Turner and 'Jock' Scott scored tries. Pat Munro dropped a goal.

Referee: I G Davidson (Ireland).

Match 88   FRANCE v WALES   Parc des Princes, Paris. February 28, 1911

Wales won by three goals (15) to nil

A record crowd of 45,000 saw Wales score all their points in the drizzle in the second half.

Billy Trew, after leading Wales in 11 games, handed the captaincy over to Cardiff wing Johnnie Williams, who had never had the honour and spoke French. Trew resumed as captain in the next match and in all led Wales 14 times.

France: T Varvier (Racing Club); P Failliot (Racing Club), J Dedet (Stade Francais), C du Souich (SCUF), G Lane (Racing Club); R Duval (Stade Francais, capt.), A Theuriet (SCUF); P Mauriat, J Bavozet (Lyons), R Dufour (Tarbes), P Guillemin (Racing Club), P Mounicq (Toulouse), J Cadenat (SCUF), F Forgues (Bayonne), M Legrain (Stade Francais).

Wales: Jack Bancroft (Swansea); R A Gibbs, W Spiller, L M Dyke, J L Williams (Cardiff, capt.); W J Trew, R M Owen (Swansea); J Webb (Abertillery), G Travers (Newport), J Pugsley (Cardiff), Tom Evans (Llanelli), J Birch (Neath), R Thomas (Pontypool), D J Thomas, Ivor Morgan (Swansea).

For Wales, Ivor Morgan, Johnnie Williams and Dicky Owen scored tries. Jack Bancroft converted three.

Referee: W Williams (England).

Match 89   WALES v IRELAND   Cardiff Arms Park. March 11, 1911

Wales won by two goals, one penalty goal, one try (16) to nil

Once again Wales and Ireland were both bidding for the Triple Crown and it seemed that almost every rugby follower in Wales wanted to see the contest. An hour before the kick-off the gates were closed and mounted police tried to disperse the thousands still clamouring to get in. The crowd attacked the gates and hundreds burst through. Others risked scaling the walls and some fell off the roof of the stand and suffered serious injuries. It was reported that "bolder spirits climbed trees, which appeared as if they were swarming with crows, while those who climbed on the roof of the pavilion clustered as thick as bees." The crowd was a record of more than 40,000.

Wales won the Triple Crown for the seventh time and Dicky Owen equalled W. J. Bancroft's record of 33 caps. But this time it was not Welsh brilliance behind the scrum that won the day: Trew instructed his forwards to carry the scrums, driving through rather than keep serving the halves. As a result, forwards Tom Evans and Jim Webb scored two of the three tries. "It was a hard, grim struggle in which strategy and tactics played an important part" said a Welsh critic. Ireland made the mistake of pulling Campbell out of the scrum to mark the Welsh backs. Trew was quick to turn this to advantage by using his forwards to sweep through in attack.

Wales: Jack Bancroft (Swansea); R A Gibbs, W Spiller, L M Dyke, J L Williams (Cardiff); W J Trew (capt.), R M Owen (Swansea); A P Coldrick, G. Travers (Newport), J Webb (Abertillery), Tom Evans (Llanelli), J. Pugsley (Cardiff), *W G Evans (Brynmawr), D J Thomas, Ivor Morgan (Swansea).

Ireland: W P Hinton (Old Wesley); C T O'Callaghan (Carlow), A R Foster (Derry), A R V Jackson (Wanderers), J P Quinn (Dublin Univ.); R A. Lloyd, H M Read (Dublin Univ.); G T Hamlet (capt.), C Adams (Old Wesley), T Smyth (Malone), H Moore (Queen's Univ., Belfast), T. Halpin (Garryowen), M G Garry (Bective), M R Heffernan (Cork Constitution), S B Campbell (Derry).

For Wales, Tom Evans, Jim Webb and Reg Gibbs scored tries. Jack Bancroft converted two and kicked a penalty goal.

Referee: F C Potter-Irwin (England).

Match 90   ENGLAND v WALES   Twickenham. January 20, 1912

England won by one goal, one try (8) to nil

Dicky Owen was granted the captaincy of Wales to mark his 34th cap. It was one more than Billy Bancroft, who had held the British record for most appearances. But their second visit to Twickenham was another keen disappointment for Wales. Their backs produced little rhythm and it was only the heroic defence of Jack Bancroft that saved them from more decisive defeat. A crowd of 30,000, including the Prince of Wales, saw England give a dazzling display in ideal conditions. They scored their points in the second half. England were captained by Bob Dibble, the Newport forward. So Wales came to the end of their Golden Era. After a glorious sequence of 43 games with only seven defeats, Wales did not win the Triple Crown again for 39 years.

England: W R Johnston (Bristol); F E Chapman (Westoe), R W Poulton, J G G Birkett, H Brougham (Harlequins); A D Stoop (Harlequins), J A Pym (Blackheath); R Dibble (Newport, capt.), N A Wodehouse, A H MacIlwaine (United Services), J A King, J H Eddison (Headingley), R C Stafford (Bedford), D. Holland (Devonport Albion), C H Pillman (Blackheath).

Wales: Jack Bancroft (Swansea); *Ewan Davies, W Spiller (Cardiff), F W Birt (Newport), J P Jones (Pontypool); *J M C Lewis (Cardiff), R M Owen (Swansea, capt.); J Webb (Abertillery), *Howell Davies, *Glyn Stephens (Neath), R Thomas (Pontypool), A P Coldrick, *L Trump, *H Uzzell (Newport), D J Thomas (Swansea).

For England, Henry Brougham and John Pym scored tries. Frank Chapman converted one.

Referee: J T Tulloch (Scotland).

Match 91   WALES v SCOTLAND   St. Helen's, Swansea. February 3, 1912

Wales won by two goals, two dropped goals and one try (21) to two tries (6)

Owen and Trew were carried shoulder high in triumph to the pavilion after this victory. The 30,000 crowd saw Newport wings Reggie Plummer and George Hirst score tries on their first appearances for Wales. Trew and Fred Birt dropped goals from unlikely situations under severe pressure. The unlucky Birt dislocated his shoulder in the last minute.

Wales: Jack Bancroft (Swansea); *R C S Plummer, F W Birt (Newport), *Willie Davies (Aberavon), *G L Hirst (Newport); W J Trew, R M Owen (Swansea, capt.); Glyn Stephens, Howell Davies (Neath), J Webb (Abertillery), A P Coldrick, H. Uzzell, L Trump (Newport), R Thomas (Pontypool), Ivor Morgan (Swansea).

Scotland: W M Dickson (Blackheath); W R Sutherland (Hawick), A W Angus, J Pearson (Watsonians), J G Will (OMT); A W Gunn (Royal HSFP), E Milroy (Watsonians) ; J C McCallum (Watsonians, capt.), L Robertson, W D C L Purves (London Scottish), D D Howie (Kirkcaldy), J M B Scott, D M Bain (Edinburgh Acads.), J Dobson (Glasgow Acads.), F H Turner (Liverpool).

For Wales, George Hirst, Ivor Morgan and Reg Plummer scored tries. Jack Bancroft converted two. Billy Trew and Fred Birt dropped goals.

For Scotland, George Will scored two tries.

Referee: F C Potter-Irwin (England).

Ireland won by one goal, one dropped goal, one try (12) to one goal (5)

After the rousing victory over Scotland this was unbelievable anti-climax. Owen and Trew were absent. A critic of the time wrote that they "declined to face the rough and tumble of this Irish game," though the truth of the matter was that they preferred to play for their club. Walter Martin, the Newport fly half, came in on his debut to partner his club captain, Tommy Vile, but the backs squandered scoring chances and at least half a dozen tries were lost, though Wales led 5-0 at half time. Tom Williams, the Swansea forward, in his first game, broke his left forearm in the last few minutes, but insisted on returning with it bound up to play out time. This was considered the lightest pack Wales had ever put in the field, though it was the backs who let them down.

Ireland: W P Hinton (Old Wesley); J P Quinn (Dublin Univ.), A R Foster (Derry), M Abraham (Bective), C V McIvor (Dublin Univ.); R A Lloyd (capt.), H M Read (Dublin Univ.); G S Brown (Monkstown), G V Killeen (Garryowen), R Hemphill (Dublin Univ.), W J Beatty (North of Ireland), H Moore (Queen's Univ., Belfast), S B Campbell (Derry,), C Adams (Old Wesley), R D'A Patterson (Wanderers).

Wales: Jack Bancroft (Swansea, capt.); R C S Plummer, F W Birt (Newport), Willie Davies (Aberavon}, *Bryn Lewis (Swansea) *W J Martin, T H Vile (Newport); Glyn Stephens (Neath), *G Merry (Pill Harriers), *H Hiams, *T Williams (Swansea), L Trump, H Uzzell (Newport), *F Hawkins (Pontypridd), *W Jenkins (Cardiff).

For Ireland, Charles McIvor and Brown scored tries. Dicky Lloyd converted one and dropped a goal.

For Wales, Willie Davies scored a try. Jack Bancroft converted.

Referee: J D Dallas (Scotland).

Wales won by one goal, three tries (14) to one goal, one try (8)

Owen and Trew withdrew, preferring to go on Swansea's Devon tour. Vile and Martin again deputised, this time on their home ground. The match was played on a Monday, watched by 10,000 spectators, and France sprang a major surprise. They led 8-6 at half time and, despite muddy, unfamiliar conditions, they beat the Welsh forwards in scrums and loose. Their halves were more than a match for Vile and Martin and Wales owed their win entirely to the combined skill of Billy Spiller and his Cardiff wing, Ewan Davies. This completed a record sequence of 13 successive Welsh home victories.

Wales: *Harold Thomas (Llanelli); R C S Plummer (Newport) J P Jones (Pontypool), W Spiller, Ewan Davies (Cardiff); W J Martin, T H Vile (Newport, capt.); Glyn Stephens (Neath), G Merry (Pill Harriers), H Hiams (Swansea), F Hawkins (Pontypridd), W Jenkins (Cardiff), A P Coldrick, L Trump, H Uzzell (Newport).

France: F X Dutour (Toulouse); E Lesieur (Stade Francais) G Lane (Racing Club, capt.), J Sentilles (Tarbes), J Dufau (Biarritz); L Larribeau (Perigueux), G Charpentier (Stade Francais); F Forgues (Bayonne), M Communeau (Stade Francais), M Monniot (Racing Club) A Pascarel (Toulouse), J Forestier, J Cadenat (SCUF), P. Thil (Nantes), M Boyau (Stade Bordelais).

For Wales, Ewan Davies (2) Reg Plummer and J P (Jack) Jones scored tries. Harold Thomas converted one.

For France, Emile Lesieur and Leon Larribeau scored tries. Maurice Boyau converted one.

Referee: A O Jones (England).

Match 94   WALES v SOUTH AFRICA   Cardiff Arms Park. December 14, 1912

South Africa won by one penalty goal (3) to nil

Fred Birt was the best goal-kicker in Wales. He had scored all Newport's points (dropped goal, try and conversion) in his club's brilliant 9-3 win over the 1912 Springboks. But he missed a simple penalty kick that would have saved Wales from this first defeat at Cardiff for 13 years. It was called, "The international of missed opportunities." Each side should have scored at least two tries. The match was decided by the only score, a penalty goal from in front of the posts at close range after 15 minutes by Duggie Morkel, when Rhys Thomas, the Pontypool forward, was "forced in front of the ball at a loose scrummage" and penalised for off-side. There was no doubt that referee Frank Potter-Irwin (London) was correct in his decision, but it was considered that Thomas's act was unintentional.

In a quarter of a century only three previous games had been lost at the Arms Park – two against Scotland and one against Ireland. With nine new caps in their side, Wales can feel proud of their efforts and did not deserve to lose. New fly half Horace Wyndham Thomas won his Cambridge Blue and this international cap in the same week, and he almost won the match for his side by one point with a drop kick that missed "by only six inches." A dropped goal was worth four points in those days. Thomas played one more game for Wales before going to India.

Billy Millar, the Springboks' captain, said: "It was the hardest game I have ever played." The South Africans were "hopeless in the line-out where, with the wonderful height and reach and fine physique of their forwards, they should have been terribly effective." The lighter Welsh forwards played with superhuman keenness in the thick drizzle, but were accused of being "occasionally too impetuous." Wales were praised for their staunch tackling and it was said that, "Vile distinguished himself with his grit and daring in going down to the fierce rushes of the South African giants."

So the match was decided by Morkel's one goal kick. Ironically, up to then he had been the disappointing kicker of the tour, whereas Birt was "notorious for his deadliness" as a goal-getter. "No-one imagined for a moment that he would fail," said a report. "His failure was only one of those incidents which convinced the spectators that Wales were destined not to win. It was a strangely silent and undemonstrative assemblage, no attempt being made to indulge in singing, as has been the custom of Welsh crowds on international days in past years. This was due, doubtless, to the feeling of apprehension which was general that the Springboks would win."

Wales: *R F Williams (Cardiff); W P Geen, F W Birt (Newport), W Spiller (Cardiff), R C S Plummer (Newport); *H W Thomas (Cambridge Univ.), T H Vile (Newport, capt.); Glyn Stephens, *F Perrett (Neath), *H Wetter, *Percy Jones (Newport), *F Andrews, R Thomas (Pontypool), *B Hollingdale (Swansea) *J Morgan (Llanelli).

South Africa: G Morkel; J A Stegmann, R Luyt, J Morkel, E E McHardy; F Luyt, F J Dobbin; W A Millar (capt.), W H 'Boy' Morkel, G Thompson, T van Vuuren, D F T Morkel, A S Knight, J A Francis, J D Luyt.

For South Africa, Duggie Morkel kicked a penalty goal.

Referee: F C Potter-Irwin (England).

Match 95   WALES v ENGLAND   Cardiff Arms Park. January 18, 1913

England won by one goal, one dropped goal, one try (12) to nil

This was England's first victory at the Arms Park. A crowd of 20,000 saw them outclass the home backs and subdue the Welsh pack. Charles Pillman was in devastating form as wing forward to disrupt the Welsh backs. Only the resolute Bobby Williams and Billy Geen, the zig-zagging wing, enhanced their reputations. Vile's captaincy was criticised as Wales suffered their most conclusive defeat for 15 years. England went on to win the Triple Crown and Championship. The great W. J. A. Davies made his international debut against Wales and played the main part in enabling Vince Coates to score England's first try at Cardiff for 20 years.

Wales: R F Williams (Cardiff); R C S Plummer, F W Birt (Newport), W Spiller (Cardiff), W P Geen (Newport); H W Thomas (Swansea), T H Vile (Newport, capt.); Glyn Stephens, F Perrett (Neath), B Hollingdale (Swansea), H Wetter, Percy Jones (Newport), R Thomas, F Andrews (Pontypool), J. Morgan (Llanelli).

England: W R Johnston (Bristol); V H M Coates (Bath), F E Steinthal (Ilkley), R W Poulton (Harlequins), C N Lowe (Blackheath); W J A Davies (United Services), W I Cheesman (OMT); N A Wodehouse (United Services, capt.), J A King (Headingley), L G Brown (Blackheath), J A S Ritson (Northern), S Smart (Gloucester), G Ward (Leicester),J E. Greenwood (Cambridge Univ.), C H Pillman (Blackheath).

For England, Vince Coates and Charles Pillman scored tries. John 'Jenny' Greenwood converted one. Ronnie Poulton dropped a goal.

Referee: S H Crawford (Ireland).

Match 96   SCOTLAND v WALES   Inverleith, Edinburgh. February 1, 1913

Wales won by one goal, one try (8) to nil

Trew was recalled as captain, but none of the other players had ever endured the disconcerting experience of playing in Scotland. It was considered a gamble sending such an inexperienced team. But Glyn Stephens was brilliant in the line-out and always first in the rushes to inspire the pack to a great effort. Harry Uzzell was brought back to play the Pillman type of wing forward game.

Scotland: W M Dickson (Blackheath); W R Sutherland (Hawick), R E Gordon (Army), A W Angus (Watsonians), W A Stewart (London Hosp.); J H Bruce Lockhart (London Scottish), E Milroy (Watsonians); F H Turner (Liverpool, capt.), L. Robertson (London Scottish), C M Usher (Edinburgh Wanderers), D D Howie (Kirkcaldy), C H Abercrombie (U.S.), D M Bain, J M B Scott (Edinburgh Acads.), P C B Blair (Cambridge Univ.).

Wales: R F Williams (Cardiff); G L Hirst (Newport), *James 'Tuan' Jones (Pontypool). W J Trew (capt), *Howell Lewis (Swansea); J M C. Lewis (Cardiff), *R Lloyd (Pontypool); *Rev. Alban Davies (Swansea), *Rees Richards (Aberavon), F Perrett, Glyn Stephens (Neath), W Jenkins (Cardiff), F Andrews (Pontypool), Percy Jones, H Uzzell (Newport).

For Wales, Clem Lewis and 'Tuan' Jones scored tries. Clem Lewis converted one.

Referee: S H Crawford (Ireland).

Wales won by one goal, two tries (11) to one goal, one try (8)

A try in the last five minutes by Clem Lewis gave Wales a lucky victory. Welsh supporters admitted that the referee played 17 minutes over time at the end.   France, 0-8 down, drew level after Trew ruptured a groin muscle making a tackle. He looked ill when he returned home and said he thought he would never play international rugby again. He never did, after winning 29 caps.

After the near-riot that had followed the French match against Scotland, there were 50 police on duty to prevent any invasion of the pitch. A squadron of Gardes Republicaires also stood by, but when they paraded the ground near the end and took up positions on the Welsh goal line, the referee thought this was going too far and refused to continue the game until they had retreated – to the cheers of the 20,000 crowd. This match was played on a Thursday.

France: J Semmartin (SCUF); G Andre (Racing Club), A Francquenelle (S.C. Vaugirard), P Jaureguy (Toulouse), P Failliot (Racing Club); C Bioussa, P Struxiano (Toulouse); F Forgues (Bayonne), P Thil (Nantes), M Boyau, M Leuville (Stade Bordelais, capt.), P Mauriat, G Favre (Lyons), J Podevin, M Communeau (Stade Francais).

Wales: *Glyn Gethin (Neath); *Mark Lewis (Llwynypia), J P Jones (Pontypool), W J Trew (capt.), Howell Lewis (Swansea); J M C. Lewis (Cardiff), R Lloyd (Pontypool); Rev. Alban Davies, T Williams (Swansea), F Perrett, T C Lloyd, Glyn Stephens (Neath), Rees Richards (Aberavon), Percy Jones, H Uzzell (Newport).

For Wales, Clem Lewis, Rev. Alban Davies and Tom Williams scored tries. Clem Lewis converted one.

For France, Pierre Failliot and Georges Andre scored tries. Philippe Struxiano converted one.

Referee: J H Miles (England).

Wales won by two goals, one penalty goal, one try (16) to two goals, one penalty goal (13)

Again Wales were thankful to scrape a narrow victory. They were under such severe pressure at one time that they withdrew the Rev. Alban Davies from the pack to stiffen the defence. Ireland had lost their three previous games of the season, but would have drawn this one had Dicky Lloyd not narrowly missed a magnificent attempt to kick a penalty goal from the centre spot. The ball just dipped under the bar. Bryn Lewis ran from halfway for one of his tries and Jack Bancroft kicked his penalty goal when given a second chance because the Irish defenders charged too soon.

Wales: Jack Bancroft (Swansea); Bryn Lewis (Swansea), W P Geen (Newport), J P Jones (Pontypool, capt.), Howell Lewis (Swansea) J M C Lewis (Cardiff), R Lloyd (Pontypool); Rev. Alban Davies (Swansea), F Andrews (Pontypool), W Jenkins (Cardiff), F Perrett, T C Lloyd, Glyn Stephens (Neath), Rees Richards (Aberavon), H Uzzell (Newport).

Ireland: A W P Todd (Dublin Univ.); G H Wood (Dublin Univ.), A R V Jackson (Wanderers), A L Stewart (North of Ireland), J P Quinn (Dublin Univ.); R A Lloyd (Dublin Univ., capt.), S E Polden (Clontarf); C Adams (Old Wesley), J J Clune (Blackrock Coll.), J E Finlay, W Tyrrell (Queen's Coll., Belfast), G V

Killeen (Garryowen), G McConnell (Derry), R D'A Patterson (Wanderers), P O'Connell (Derry).

For Wales, Bryn Lewis (2) and J P Jones scored tries. Jack Bancroft converted two and kicked a penalty goal.

For Ireland, Pat Quinn and Lewis Stewart scored tries. Dicky Lloyd converted two and kicked a penalty goal.

Referee: J G Cunningham (Scotland).

Match 99   ENGLAND v WALES   Twickenham. January 17, 1914

England won by two goals (10) to one goal, one dropped goal (9)

This time Wales employed the lively Tom Williams as a rover to counter effectively the "guerilla tactics" of wing forward 'Cherry' Pillman, who had had more to do with the previous three defeats of Wales than any other English player. But the alert Pillman had the last laugh. When new cap Willie Watts dropped the ball near the end, with Wales leading 9-5, Pillman pounced for a try that Taylor converted to change impending defeat into a one-point victory. England went on to win the Triple Crown for the second successive season and the fourth time.

England: W R Johnston (Bristol); C N Lowe (Blackheath), F E Chapman (W. Hartlepool), R W Poulton (Harlequins, capt.), J H D Watson (Blackheath}; F M Taylor, G W Wood (Leicester); J E Greenwood, A F Maynard (Cambridge Univ.), S Smart (Gloucester), A G Bull (Northampton), J Brunton (N. Durham), G Ward (Leicester), L G Brown, C H Pillman (Blackheath).

Wales: Jack Bancroft (Swansea); Howell Lewis (Swansea), *W H Evans (Llwynypia), *Willie Watts (Llanelli), G L Hirst (Newport); J M C Lewis (Cardiff), R Lloyd (Pontypool); Rev. Alban Davies (Llanelli, capt.), *D Watts (Maesteg), *J Bedwellty Jones (Abertillery), T C Lloyd (Neath}, Percy Jones (Pontypool), T Williams, *Edgar Morgan (Swansea), H Uzzell (Newport).

For England, Len Brown and Charles Pillman scored tries. Fred Chapman converted two.

For Wales, Willie Watts scored a try. Jack Bancroft converted. George Hirst dropped a goal.

Referee: Dr. J R C Greenlees (Scotland).

Match 100   WALES v SCOTLAND   Cardiff Arms Park. February 7, 1914

Wales won by two goals, two dropped goals, one penalty goal, one try (24) to one goal (5)

"The dirtier team won," was the succinct comment of David Bain, the Scottish captain, when asked for his opinion of the game. A crowd of 35,000 saw Wales gain their seventh consecutive victory over Scotland. Ivor Davies and Jack Wetter scored tries in their first appearances after the Scots had stolen the lead in the first five minutes. The Welsh pack, who had been magnificent against England, again dominated.

Wales: Jack Bancroft (Swansea); G L Hirst, J Wetter (Newport), W H Evans (Llwynypia), *I T Davies (Llanelli); J M C Lewis (Cardiff), R Lloyd (Pontypool) ; Rev. Alban Davies (Llanelli, capt.), D Watts (Maesteg), J Bedwellty Jones (Abertillery), T C Lloyd (Neath), Percy Jones (Pontypool). T Williams, Edgar Morgan (Swansea), H Uzzell (Newport).

Scotland: W M Wallace (London Scottish) ; J G Will (OMT), W R Sutherland (Hawick), R M Scobie (London Scottish), W A Stewart (London Hospital); A S

Hamilton (Headingley), A T Sloan (Edinburgh Acads.); A M Stewart, D M Bain (capt.), G H H Maxwell (Edinburgh Acads.), A W Symington (Cambridge Univ.), A. Wemyss (Gala), A D Laing (Royal HSFP), A R Ross (Edinburgh Univ.), D G Donald (Oxford Univ.).

For Wales, Ivor Davies, Jack Wetter and George Hirst scored tries. Jack Bancroft converted two and kicked a penalty goal. Hirst and Clem Lewis each dropped a goal.

For Scotland, W. A. Stewart scored a try. 'Podger' Laing converted.

Referee: V Drennon (Ireland).

Match 101   WALES v FRANCE   St. Helen's, Swansea. March 2, 1914

Wales won by five goals, two tries (31) to nil

When Maurice Leuvielle, the French captain, was asked what he thought of his team's endeavours, he muttered the French equivalent of "Rotten". He had done the work of four men trying to inspire his forwards, but admitted: "We have town teams in France who could have beaten us on today's form." It was in marked contrast to the previous two close tussles with the Tricolours. This match was played on a Monday.

Wales: Jack Bancroft (Swansea); G L Hirst, J Wetter (Newport), W H Evans (Llwynypia), I T Davies (Llanelli) ; J M C Lewis (Cardiff), R Lloyd (Pontypool) ; Rev Alban Davies (Llanelli, capt.), D Watts (Maesteg), J Bedwellty Jones (Abertillery), T C Lloyd (Neath), Percy Jones (Pontypool), T Williams, Edgar Morgan (Swansea), H Uzzell (Newport).

France: J Caujolle (Tarbes); G Andre (Racing Club), G Pierrot (Paloise), L Besset (SCUF), R Lacoste (Tarbes); F Poydebasque, M Hedembaight, (Bayonne); F Faure (Tarbes), R Desvouges (Stade Francais), J M Arnal (Racing Club), P Lavaud (Carcassonne), M F Lubin-Lebrere (Toulouse), M Legrain, M Leuvielle (capt.), J C de Beyssac (Stade Bordelais).

For Wales, Jack Wetter (2), Harry Uzzell (2), George Hirst, W. H. Evans and the Rev. Alban Davies scored tries. Jack Bancroft converted five.

Referee: J H Miles (England).

Match 102   IRELAND v WALES   Balmoral, Belfast. March 14, 1914

Wales won by one goal, two tries (11) to one try (3)

This tremendous forward battle on the Balmoral swamp in heavy rain has lived on as the day of the Welsh Terrible Eight. A report of the game said: "At the start the Irish forwards adopted robust, bustling tactics, designed to upset the Welsh team. It looked like succeeding as the Irishmen took the lead with a try by Foster." Quite obviously, the Welsh forwards were not prepared to be on the receiving end of a hammering, and the way they fought back in one of the most fiery forward combats of all time made the headlines in the Sunday newspapers.

The Rev. Alban Davies, the Welsh captain, said he had no comment to make about reports of rough play. "I did not hear any complaints from the Irish players," he said. This was true: the battered Irish forwards had handed it out, and they never squealed when the Welsh handed it back. Hostilities were arranged on the Friday night, when Dr. William Tyrrell, the Irish pack leader, and a number of his team-mates strolled into the hotel where the Welsh team were staying. "Hello there, Percy Jones. I'll have a go at you tomorrow," joked Tyrrell. Percy Jones smiled his response that he was quite prepared for a little confrontation. The Welsh pack had already earned the title of The Terrible Eight before this match, and there was quite a bit of banter between the parties before they parted on that Friday night.

The storm broke on the morrow. The private tussle between Tyrrell and Percy Jones, designed primarily and without malice to test each other's strength and endurance, spread, though not all the forwards were involved. Sometimes matters did get a little out of hand and players fought when the ball was nowhere near them. Half a dozen players could have been sent off, but the Scottish referee simply ignored it all, as if he had been advised of what was going to happen, accepted the inevitable and got on with the game.

But with the final whistle the battle atmosphere disappeared. Percy Jones said that Tyrrell told him he was the best Welshman he had ever come across. Years later Tyrrell said: "Our bit of a barney founded a life-long friendship between us." In 1951, when Sir William Tyrrell was president of the Irish R.U. Percy Jones sat with him during the match with Wales at Cardiff. The 1914 match became notorious as "the roughest ever," but the forwards who fought so fiercely all became good friends.

Bedwellty Jones played the game of his life and it was fitting that he should score a try. Dicky Lloyd, the Irish captain, was photographed with his team before the kick-off, but while punting the ball during the warm-up, he slipped and strained a tendon. He could not play and Harry Jack came in as replacement. This was Wales's last match before World War One. For the first time Wales's pack had remained unchanged throughout the season.

Ireland: F P Montgomery; (Queen's Univ. Belafst) ; J T Brett (Monkstown), M Abraham (Bective), A R V Jackson (Wanderers), A R Foster (Derry, capt.); H W Jack, V McNamara (Univ. Coll., Cork); W P Collopy (Bective), S Parr (Wanderers), P O'Connoll (Derry), W Tyrrell (Queen's Univ., Belfast), G V Killeen (Garryowen), J C Dowse (Monkstown), J Taylor (Belfast Collegians1, J J Clune (Blackrock Coll.).

Wales: R F Williams (Cardiff); G L Hirst, J Wetter (Newport), W H Evans (Llwynypia), I T Davies (Llanelli) ; J M C Lewis (Cardiff), R Lloyd (Pontypool); Rev. Alban Davies (Llanelli, capt.), D Watts (Maesteg), J Bedwellty Jones (Abertillery), T C Lloyd (Neath), Percy Jones (Pontypool), T Williams, Edgar Morgan (Swansea), H Uzzell (Newport).

For Wales, Bedwellty Jones, Ivor Davies and Jack Wetter scored tries. Clem Lewis converted one.

For Ireland, Alec Foster scored a try.

Referee: J Tulloch (Scotland).

Uncapped Match   **WALES v BARBARIANS**   Cardiff Arms Park. April 17, 1915

Barbarians won by four goals, two tries (26) to one dropped goal, two tries (10)

Termed at the time a military international between Wales and 'England', it was in fact Wales against a team raised under the banner of the Barbarians, who had two Irishmen and one London Welsh player in their side. The Baa-Baas played the novel formation of seven forwards and five threequarters for the simple reason that five of their team were regular threequarters and all expressed the wish to play there! The match was arranged to boost recruitment for the Welsh Guards, who were seeking 1,000 recruits. During the interval, stirring speeches were made to the spectators to join the Forces. It was stated that only about 60 men were enlisted on the Saturday and 17 on the Sunday. But, having had the weekend to give the matter some thought, about 100 more joined the colours on Monday. Over £200 was raised from gate receipts for local military charities.

In the Western Mail it was reported : "The result of the match seemed almost an amazing one in view of the fact that the Welsh team were thoroughly representative of the Principality and consisted of no fewer than 13 internationals." Clem Lewis was the best of the Welsh team, who were captained by the Rev. Alban Davies, an Army chaplain. The only uncapped players in the Welsh side were Tom Parker, who was to gain 14 caps after the war, and Dan Callan, of Cardiff RFC and the Munster Fusiliers, who came in as a late replacement for Swansea international Tom Williams.

Wales: R F Williams (Cardiff); I T Davies (Llanelli), W H Evans (Llwynypia), J. Wetter (Newport), Bryn Lewis (Swansea); J M C Lewis (Cardiff), T H Vile (Newport); T C Lloyd (Neath), Rev. Alban Davies (Llanelli, capt.), D Callan, W J Jenkins (Cardiff), Percy Jones (Pontypool), D Watts (Maesteg), Edgar Morgan, Tom Parker (Swansea).

Barbarians: G E C Wood; threequarters - E G Butcher, J G G Birkett, E R Mobbs (capt.), J B Minch, J P Quinn; halves - A K Horan, H L Higgins; forwards - G D Roberts, J E C Partridge, A G Bull, A J Osbourn, G E Kidman, M P Atkinson, R Lennox Davies.

For the Barbarians, Quinn (2), Bull, Minch, Horan and Birkett scored tries. Butcher and Roberts each converted two.

For Wales, Bryn Lewis and Ivor Davies scored tries. Clem Lewis dropped a goal.

Referee: W M Douglas (Cardiff).

Match 103 WALES v NEW ZEALAND ARMY TEAM St. Helen's, Swansea. April 21, 1919

New Zealand Army Team won by two penalty goals (6) to one penalty goal (3)

Walter Martin and Glyn Stephens were the only pre-war international players chosen for this first big match after World War 1, but it was a game of poor quality for the eager 30,000 crowd and the only scores were penalty goals. Jerry Shea kicked Wales into the lead. Then Jack Stohr won the match for the tourists with his two penalties, one from half-way. With this kick, "no charge" was whistled because Welsh defenders charged too soon, but as the goal was scored anyway, there was no need of another shot. When Martin was carried off with a bad scalp wound, the referee examined the New Zealanders' boot studs, but found nothing wrong. Martin returned after treatment. Though this was the only international match the N.Z. Army Team played in Britain, it was recognised by the WRU as an official game and caps were awarded.

Wales: *Evan Davies (Maesteg); *J Shea (Pill), *Melbourne Thomas (Bridgend), *E B Rees (Swansea), *T J Nicholas (Cardiff); W J Martin (Newport), *I Fowler (Llanelli); Glyn Stephens (Neath, capt.), *Jim Jones (Aberavon), *Rev. W T Havard, *Gwyn Francis (Llanelli), *J Whitfield (Pill), *Aaron Rees (Maesteg), *W Morris (Abertillery), * T Parker (Swansea).

New Zealand Army Team: C H Capper; W A Ford, L B Stohr, P W Storey; J Ryan (capt.), W R Fea; C Brown; M Cain, E W Hasell, J Kissick, J E Moffitt, A Wilson, A H West, R Fogarty, A P Singe.

For New Zealand Army Team, Jack Stohr kicked two penalty goals.

For Wales, Jerry Shea kicked a penalty goal.

Referee: R Charman (England).

Wales won by one goal, two dropped goals, one penalty goal, one try (19) to one goal (5)
(N.B. A dropped goal was worth four points)

Jerry Shea's achievement in this match was one of the most colourful in Welsh rugby history. But was he a hero or villain? Though he supplied 16 of the 19 points, his critics accused him of selfish play and disrupting the smooth flow of the backs as combined attackers. Certainly, Shea loved the satisfaction of selling the dummy and did ignore his fellow attackers. It was a blemish on his style of play that most people found unforgivable. Yet he had his moment of glory as he dropped two goals, kicked a penalty goal drop-style and converted his own try. The only other Welsh score was a try by wing Wickham Powell. Shea, a powerful figure, had a curious lurching stride, in contrast to the graceful running of co-centre Albert Jenkins, who was making his debut. Jenkins went on to play 14 times for Wales, but Shea made only four appearances. Shea and Joe Rees were carried from the field in triumph by some of the 40,000 crowd.

W. M. Lowry (Birkenhead Park) was chosen on the wing and actually photographed with the England team just before the kick-off. But when England ran out for the game, Harold Day had taken his place. Apparently, the selectors decided on a last-minute change, thinking Day better suited to the heavy conditions. Actually, Day scored their try to help take a 5-3 lead at the interval. Lowry later gained his only cap against France. Wales were captained by Harry Uzzell, who was 37 years of age.

Wales: *Joe Rees (Swansea); *W J Powell (Cardiff), J Shea (Newport), *A Jenkins, *Bryn E Evans (Llanelli); *Ben Beynon (Swansea), J Wetter (Newport) ; *Jack Williams (Blaina), H Uzzell (capt.), J Whitfield (Newport), *S Morris (Cross Keys), *G Oliver (Pontypool), T Parker (Swansea), Jim Jones (Aberavon), *Charles W Jones (Bridgend).

England: B S Cumberlege (Blackheath); H L V Day (Leicester), E D G Hammett (Newport), J A Krige (Guy's Hosp.), C N Lowe (Blackheath); H Coverdale (Blackheath), C A Kershaw (United Services); G Holford, S Smart (Gloucester), J R Morgan (Hawick), W H G Wright (Plymouth), L P B Merriam, F W Mellish (Blackheath), W W Wakefield (Harlequins), J E Greenwood (Cambridge Univ., capt.).

For Wales, Jerry Shea and Wickham Powell scored tries. Shea converted one, dropped two goals and kicked a penalty goal.

For England, Harold Day scored a try and converted.

Referee: J T Tulloch (Scotland).

Scotland won by two penalty goals, one try (9) to one goal (5)

This completely unexpected defeat cost Wales the Triple Crown, for Uzzell's men went on to beat Ireland. Jerry Shea was accused of neglecting to link and trying to drop goals repeatedly and was selected on the wing for the next match. Still, Wales led 5-0 and never thought Scotland would gain their first win for 13 years. Wales had won their previous seven games against the Scots. Fly half Ben Beynon, dropped after this game, joined Swansea Town as a professional soccer player. Uzzell and Jim Jones went off injured near the end and Wales finished with 13 men.

Scotland: G L Pattullo (Panmure); G B Crole (Edinburgh Acads.) A W Angus

(Watsonians, capt.), E C Fahmy (Abertillery and Edinburgh Univ.), E B MacKay (Glasgow Acads.); A T Sloan (Edinburgh Acads.), J A R Selby (Watsonians); G H H Maxwell (Edinburgh Acads.), A D Laing (Royal HSFP), F Kennedy (Stewart's Coll. FP), N C Macpherson (Newport), G Thom (Kirkcaldy), C M Usher (London Scottish), D D Duncan (Oxford Univ.), R A Gallie (Glasgow Acads.).

Wales: Joe Rees (Swansea); W J Powell (Cardiff), J. Shea (Newport), A Jenkins, *Bryn Williams (Llanelli); Ben Beynon (Swansea), J Wetter (Newport); Jack Williams (Blaina), S Morris (Cross Keys), H Uzzell (capt.), J Whitfield (Newport), G Oliver (Pontypool), T Parker (Swansea), Jim Jones (Aberavon), Charles W Jones (Bridgend).

For Scotland, Allen Sloan scored a try. Finlay Kennedy kicked two penalty goals.

For Wales, Albert Jenkins scored a try and converted.

Referee: S H Crawford (Ireland).

Match 106   FRANCE v WALES   Colombes, Paris. February 17, 1920

Wales won by two tries (6) to one goal (5)

France claimed they won. Their captain, Struxiano, said: "The try I scored in the corner in the second half was valid. The linesman deprived us of victory." The referee, Col. Craven (Blackheath), awarded the try and then saw the Welsh touch judge standing with his flag raised. After inquiring, the referee disallowed the try. It appeared that the ball crossed the touch line before Joe Rees caught it and therefore it was a Welsh throw in. So Struxiano's quick throw in, before he took a return pass to score, was illegal. It was reported: "At times play was almost too keen and once the referee took the unusual course of putting the ball into the scrum himself." Jack Wetter, normally a scrum half, played at outside half. Shea, picked on the wing, could not travel because he had a professional boxing engagement.

France: T Cambre (Oloron); A Jaureguy (Racing Club), R Lavigne (Dax), R Crabos, A Chilo (Racing Club); E Billac (Bayonne), P Struxiano (Toulouse, capt.); M Biraben, P Pons, M F Lubin-Lebrere (Toulouse), A Cassayet (Tarbes), R Thierry (Racing Club.), G Constant (Perpignan), R Marchand (Stade Poitevin), J Laurent (Bayonne).

Wales: Joe Rees (Swansea); W J Powell (Cardiff), J P Jones (Pontypool), A Jenkins, Bryn Williams (Llanelli); J Wetter (Newport), *F Reeves (Cross Keys); Jack Williams (Blaina), S Morris (Cross Keys), W Morris (Abertillery), H Uzzell (capt.), J Whitfield (Newport), G Oliver (Pontypool), *R Huxtable (Swansea), Charles W Jones (Bridgend).

For Wales, Bryn Williams and Wickham Powell scored tries.

For France, Adolphe Jaureguy scored a try. Phillipe Struxiano converted.

Referee: Col. W S D Craven (England).

Match 107   WALES v IRELAND   Cardiff Arms Park. March 13, 1920

Wales won by three goals, one dropped goal, three tries (28) to one dropped goal (4)

On a waterlogged pitch, Wales were back to their brilliant best. Yet conditions were so bad that referee Frank Potter-Irwin (England) said the match should never have been played. It was Wales's 20th victory over Ireland, who were captained by the Cardiff centre, Dr. Tom Wallace.

Welsh skipper Harry Uzzell said: "I did not consider the Irish forwards as good as they were in the old days." The crowd of 35,000 paid record receipts of £3,900.

Wales: Joe Rees (Swansea); W J Powell (Cardiff), J P Jones (Pontypool), A Jenkins, Bryn Williams (Llanelli) ; J Wetter (Newport), F Reeves (Cross Keys); Jack Williams (Blaina), S Morris (Cross Keys), G Oliver (Pontypool), H Uzzell (capt.), J Whitfield (Newport), R Huxtable, T Parker (Swansea), *Edgar Morgan (Llanelli).

Ireland: W E Crawford (Lansdowne); J A N Dickson (Dublin Univ.), T Wallace (Cardiff capt.), W Duggan (Univ. Coll., Cork), B A T McFarland (Derry); W Cunningham (Lansdowne), A K Horan (Blackheath); M J Bradley (Dolphin), H H Coulter, A W Courtney, J E Finlay (Queen's Univ., Belfast), R Y Crichton (Dublin Univ.), W D Doherty (Guy's Hosp.), H N Potterton (Wanderers), P J Stokes (Garryowen).

For Wales, Bryn Williams (3), Albert Jenkins, Jack Whitfield and Tom Parker scored tries. Albert Jenkins converted two and dropped a goal. Jack Wetter converted one.

For Ireland, Basil McFarland dropped a goal.

Referee: Frank Potter-Irwin (England).

Match 108   ENGLAND v WALES   Twickenham. January 15, 1921

England won by one goal, one dropped goal, three tries (1 8) to one try (3)

The Welsh jumbo pack played "as if under a spell". All the critics had been calling this the greatest Welsh pack of modern times. But England made a devastating start with 12 points in as many minutes and Wales crashed to their heaviest defeat since 1896. Welsh skipper and outside half Jack Wetter displaced a cartilage in his right knee after 20 minutes and was little more than a passenger. Tom Johnson badly hurt his arm and Jack Jones fractured his collarbone five minutes before half time.

Jones played on bravely to the end, despite great pain. It was his 14th and last match for Wales at the age of nearly 34. He had first played for Pontypool on the wing when he was 14 years old. Jack was one of three brothers who played for Wales. The other brothers were James 'Tuan' and David.

W. J. A. Davies and Kershaw were brilliant at half for England. Davies, the England captain, was born at Pembroke Dock. "Until I left Wales I knew nothing about rugby," he said. "We owed our great victory to our magnificent forwards." England went on to win the Triple Crown for the fifth time and led Wales by 16 wins to 15, with two drawn.

England: B S Cumberlege (Blackheath); A M Smallwood (Leicester), E Myers (Bradford), E D G Hammett (Newport), C N Lowe (Blackheath); W J A Davies (capt.), C A Kershaw (United Services); R Edwards (Newport), E R Gardner (Devonport Services), L G Brown, F W Mellish (Blackheath), T Woods (RN), A F Blakiston (Northampton), W W Wakefield (Harlequins), A T Voyce (Gloucester).

Wales: Joe Rees (Swansea); *J Ring (Aberavon), J P Jones (Pontypool), J Shea (Newport), *T Johnson (Cardiff); J Wetter (Newport, capt.), F Reeves (Cross Keys); *L Attewell, J Whitfield (Newport), T Parker (Swansea), *S Winmill (Cross Keys), *Dai Edwards (Glynneath), *W Hodder (Pontypool), *Marsden Jones (Cardiff), E Morgan (Llanelli).

For England, Alistair Smallwood (2), Cecil Kershaw and Cyril Lowe scored tries. Ernie Hammett converted one. W J A Davies dropped a goal.

For Wales, Johnny Ring scored a try.

Referee: J C Sturrock (Scotland).

Match 109 **WALES v SCOTLAND**   St. Helen's, Swansea. February 5, 1921

Scotland won by one goal, one penalty goal, two tries (14) to two dropped goals (8)

"Our own crowd beat us," said skipper Tommy Vile bitterly after Scotland's first win in Wales for 29 years. Some of the near 50,000 spectators broke through the barriers in front of the cricket pavilion. Then thousands spread round the touch lines from the tanner bank. A squad of mounted police cleared the pitch when the crowd encroached shortly after the start and the players were forced to leave the field. After Scotland led 11-0 at half time, Albert Jenkins dropped two goals, the second from the touch-line near half-way.

It put Wales back in the game, only 8-11 behind, with Scotland struggling against intense pressure and longing for some respite. It came for them, but only because the excited crowd spilled back on to the field. For some 12 minutes the Scots were allowed to rest as police, officials and players tried to clear the ground. John Hume, the Scottish captain, threatened to march his team off. Referee John Baxter managed to get the match restarted, but the fire had ebbed from Wales. Albert Jenkins was carried off with a twisted knee and Allen Sloan snatched a try to make victory sure for the Scots.

Wales: Joe Rees (Swansea); *Frank Evans, A Jenkins (Llanelli), *P Baker Jones (Newport), Melbourne G Thomas (St. Bart's Hosp. and Ogmore Vale); *W Bowen (Swansea), T H Vile (Newport, capt.); Jack Williams (Blaina), S Winmill (Cross Keys), *Tom Roberts (Risca), W. Hodder (Pontypool), L Attewell (Newport), T Parker (Swansea), Jim Jones (Aberavon), E Morgan (Llanelli).

Scotland: H H Forsayth (Oxford Univ.); J H Carmichael (Watsonians), A L Gracie (Harlequins), A E Thomson (United Services), A T Sloan (Edinburgh Acads.); J Hume (Royal HSFP, capt.), R L H Donald (Glasgow HSFP); J M Bannerman (Glasgow HSFP), J N Shaw, G H H Maxwell (Edinburgh Acads.), J C R Buchanan (Stewart's Coll. FP), R A Gallie (Glasgow Acads.), R S Cumming (Aberdeen Univ.), G Douglas (Jedforest), C M Usher (Edinburgh Wands.).

For Scotland, 'Tommy' Thomson, Rankin Buchanan and Allen Sloan scored tries. George Maxwell converted one and kicked a penalty goal.

For Wales, Albert Jenkins dropped two goals.

Referee: J Baxter (England).

Match 110 **WALES v FRANCE**   Cardiff Arms Park. February 26, 1921

Wales won by two penalty goals, two tries (12) to one dropped goal (4)

"We want to borrow five of your forwards, put whiskers on them and play them against England," said French skipper Rene Crabos after an impressive performance by the home pack under their new captain, Tom Parker. Full back Ossie Male made his debut as last-minute deputy for Joe Rees. A crowd of nearly 50,000 paid record gate receipts of over £5,000.

Wales: *B O Male (Cross Keys); T Johnson (Cardiff), *Graham Davies, A Jenkins (Llanelli), Melbourne G Thomas (St. Bart's Hosp.,and Ogmore Vale); W Bowen, *Tudor Williams (Swansea) ; L Attewell (Newport), Tom Roberts (Risca), Jack Williams (Blaina), S Winmill (Cross Keys), T Parker (Swansea, capt.), W Hodder (Pontypool), Jim Jones (Aberavon), E Morgan (Llanelli).

France: J Clement (Racing Club); R Got (Perpignan), R. Crabos (capt.), F. Borde, J Lobies (Racing Club); E Billac (Bayonne), R Piteu (Paloise); G Coscoll (Beziers), P Pons (Toulouse), M Biraben (Dax) A Cassayet (Tarbes), P Moureu (Beziers), F Vaquer (Perpignan), J Larrieu (Tarbes), R Lasserre (Bayonne).

For Wales, Jack Williams and Wilf Hodder scored tries. Albert Jenkins kicked two penalty goals.

For France, Rene Lasserre dropped a goal.

Referee: Capt. P M R Royds (England).

Match 111   IRELAND v WALES   Balmoral, Belfast. March 12, 1921

Wales won by one penalty goal, one try (6) to nil

Melbourne Thomas handed-off Irish full back Ernie Crawford so powerfully as the Welsh wing stormed in for his thrilling try in the last five minutes, that Crawford had to have stitches in his jaw. Wales were in complete command, though their only scores were that late try and a penalty goal in the first five minutes by Tom Johnson. Clem Lewis was outstanding at fly half.

Ireland: W E Crawford (Lansdowne); D J Cussen (Dublin Univ.), A R Foster (Derry), G V Stephenson (Queen's Univ., Belfast); H S T Cormac (Clontarf); W Cunningham (Lansdowne), H W Jack (Univ. Coll., Cork); J J Bermingham (Blackrock Coll.), W P Collopy (Bective), A W Courtney (Univ. Coll., Dublin) W D Doherty (Guy's Hosp., capt.), C F Hallaran (United Services), T A McClelland (Queen's Univ., Belfast), N M Purcell (Lansdowne), J K S Thompson (Dublin Univ.).

Wales: Joe Rees (Swansea); T Johnson (Cardiff), Graham Davies (Llanelli), *D Davies (Bridgend), Melbourne G Thomas (St. Bart's Hosp., and Ogmore Vale); J M C Lewis (Cardiff), *Archie Brown (Newport); Jack Williams (Blaina), W Morris (Abertillery), *Jack Prosser (Cardiff), S Winmill (Cross Keys), T Parker (Swansea, capt.), *Ambrose Baker (Neath), Tom Roberts (Risca), Jim Jones (Aberavon).

For Wales, Melbourne Thomas scored a try. Tom Johnson kicked a penalty goal.

Referee: J M Tennent (Scotland).

Match 112   WALES v ENGLAND   Cardiff Arms Park. January 21, 1922

Wales won by two goals, six tries (28) to two tries (6)

Wales employed two wing forwards instead of the customary one. Dai Hiddlestone and Tom Jones were detailed to these duties and destroyed England's plan of playing Harlequin-style open rugby in the mud. It put an end to England's winning sequence of seven games and 35,000 spectators saw Wales score eight sparkling tries. Hiddlestone, making his debut at the age of 32, was brilliant and scored a rousing try. Welsh skipper Tom Parker said: "The policy of the selectors in playing two wing forwards justified itself. The two men had to shove in the scrums as well as break away quickly."

England captain L. G. Brown commented: "The mud levelled up matters and we could not use our superior speed because the Welsh forwards broke up too quickly for us." All five Swansea players in the Welsh team scored. England switched V. G. Davies from fly half to centre in the second half and tried Myers at outside half; but still the relentless Tom Jones and Hiddlestone hunted down the English backs. So it was 16 victories each in the series, with two matches drawn. Players of both sides wore numbers for the first time in a championship match.

Wales: Joe Rees (Swansea); * Cliff Richards (Pontypool), Bryn E Evans (Llanelli), *Islwyn Evans, *Frank Palmer (Swansea); W Bowen (Swansea), *W J Delahay (Bridgend); T Parker (Swansea, capt.), J Whitfield, *Tom Jones (Newport), S Morris (Cross Keys), Tom Roberts (Risca), *Rev. J G Stephens (Llanelli), *W Cummins (Treorchy), *D Hiddlestone (Neath).

England: B S Cumberlege (Blackheath); H L V Day (Leicester), E Myers (Bradford), E D G Hammett, C N Lowe (Blackheath); V G Davies (Harlequins), C A Kershaw (United Services); L G Brown (Blackheath, capt.), J S Tucker (Bristol), E R Gardner (Devonport Services), R Edwards (Newport), G S Conway (Rugby), A F Blakiston (Northampton), W W Wakefield (Harlequins) A T Voyce (Gloucester).

For Wales, Jack Whitfield, Billy Bowen, Dai Hiddlestone, Bobby Delahay, Frank Palmer, Cliff Richards, Tom Parker and Islwyn Evans scored tries. Joe Rees converted two.

For England, Cyril 'Kid' Lowe and Harold Day scored tries.

Referee: J M Tennent (Scotland).

Match 113   **SCOTLAND v WALES**   Inverleith, Edinburgh. February 4, 1922

Drawn. Scotland one penalty goal, two tries (9) Wales one goal, one dropped goal (9)

Two minutes from the end, when Wales seemed doomed to defeat, Swansea centre Islwyn Evans checked in a passing move, took quick aim, and dropped a goal from 20 yards. The score, worth four points, enabled Wales to draw. This shock goal was received "in stony silence" by the 25,000 Scottish spectators who saw their team deprived of victory in sensational fashion.

Scotland: H H Forsayth (Oxford Univ.); E H Liddell (Edinburgh Univ.), A L Gracie (Harlequins), R C Warren (Glasgow Acads.), A Browning (Glasgow HSFP); G P S Macpherson (Oxford Univ.), W E Bryce (Selkirk); C M Usher (Edinburgh Wands., capt.), D S Davies (Hawick), J M Bannerman (Glasgow HSFP), D M Bertram (Watsonians), A Wemyss (Edinburgh Wands.), J R Lawrie (Melrose), W G Dobson (Heriot's FP), J C R Buchanan (Stewart's Coll., F.P.).

Wales: *Fred Samuel (Mountain Ash); Frank Palmer, Islwyn Evans (Swansea), Bryn E Evans (Llanelli), Cliff Richards (Pontypool); W Bowen (Swansea), W J Delahay (Bridgend); T Parker (Swansea, capt.), J Whitfield, Tom Jones (Newport), S Morris (Cross Keys), Tom Roberts (Risca), Rev. J G Stephens (Llanelli), W Cummins (Treorchy), D Hiddlestone (Neath).

For Scotland, Arthur Browning scored two tries and kicked a penalty goal.

For Wales, Billy Bowen scored a try. Fred Samuel converted. Islwyn Evans dropped a goal.

Referee: R A Lloyd (Ireland).

Match 114   **WALES v IRELAND**   St. Helen's, Swansea. March 11, 1922

Wales won by one goal, two tries (11) to one goal (5)

Though the Welsh backs failed, Tom Parker and his fiery pack made sure of success. Jack Whitfield, a magnificent forward, who played 12 times for Wales, scored two tries. "Had the Irish backs been behind the Welsh pack it would have been a cricket score," wrote the Western Mail rugby correspondent. Some 40,000 people watched the match.

Wales: Fred Samuel (Mountain Ash); Frank Palmer, Islwyn Evans (Swansea), Bryn E Evans (Llanelli), Cliff Richards (Pontypool); W Bowen (Swansea), W J Delahay (Bridgend); T Parker (Swansea, capt.), J Whitfield, Tom Jones (Newport}, S Morris (Cross Keys), Tom Roberts (Risca), Rev. J G Stephens (Llanelli), W Cummins (Treorchy), D Hiddlestone (Neath).

Ireland: B A T McFarland (Derry); T G Wallis (Wanderers), D B Sullivan (Univ. Coll., Dublin), G V Stephenson (Queen's Univ., Belfast), H W V Stephenson (United Services); J R Wheeler (Queen's Univ. Belfast), J A Clarke (Bective); J C Gillespie (Dublin Univ.), M J Bradley (Dolphin), C F Hallaran (United Services), W P Collopy (Bective, capt.), S McVicker, T A McClelland (Queen's Univ., Belfast), I Popham (Cork Constitution), P Stokes (Garryowen).

For Wales, Jack Whitfield (2) and Islwyn Evans scored tries. Fred Samuel converted one.

For Ireland, Pat Stokes scored a try. Tommy Wallis converted.

Referee: J C Sturrock (Scotland).

Match 115 FRANCE v WALES   Colombes, Paris. March 23, 1922

Wales won by one goal, two tries (11) to one try (3)

A crowd of 35,000 at this Thursday game saw Wales win the championship and remain unbeaten in the Five Nations' Tournament. Shortly before the kick-off the Welsh selectors restored Islwyn Evans and Cliff Richards, who had been dropped, and decided not to play Harold Davies (Newport) and Frank Palmer (Swansea). Davies must have thought he would not win a cap as a result and had to wait two years before he was to play his one game against Scotland. The reasons for the late changes appear to be the hard, fast state of the ground after snow and frost. It was felt that Evans and Richards were better suited to the conditions. The Welsh pack had gone through the championship matches without change.

France: J Clement (Racing Club); A Jaureguy, F Borde (Toulouse), R Crabos (Racing Club,capt.), R Got (Perpignan); E Billac (Bayonne), R Piteu (Paloise), M F Lubin-Lebrere (Toulouse), A Gonnet (Albi), E Soulie (CASG), A Cassayet (Tarbes), P Moreu (Beziers), J Boubee (Biarritz), F Vaquer (Perpignan), R Lasserre (Cognac).

Wales: Fred Samuel (Mountain Ash); Cliff Richards (Pontypool), A Jenkins (Llanelli), Islwyn Evans (Swansea), Bryn E Evans (Llanelli); W Bowen (Swansea), W J Delahay (Bridgend); T Parker (Swansea, capt.), J Whitfield, Tom Jones (Newport), S Morris (Cross Keys), Tom Roberts (Risca), Rev. J G Stephens (Llanelli), W Cummins (Treorchy), D Hiddlestone (Neath).

For Wales, Bill Cummins, Jack Whitfield and Islwyn Evans scored tries. Albert Jenkins converted one.

For France, Adolphe Jaureguy scored a try.

Referee: R W Harland (Ireland).

Match 116 ENGLAND v WALES   Twickenham. January 20, 1923

England won by one dropped goal, one try (7) to one try (3)

England scored direct from the kick-off and without a Welshman touching the ball – almost exactly as they had done to beat Wales at Twickenham in 1910. The difference this time was that England kicked off. Wavell Wakefield set the game going and Leo Price, one of the fastest forwards in the game, chased and gathered as the Welsh players misjudged the flight of the ball in the swirling wind. Price decided on a drop at goal and the ball sailed only a yard or two wide of the posts. Apparently the Welsh players thought the ball would roll dead, but the strong wind stopped it and Price sprinted in pursuit to pounce and score. The whole operation was reported to have taken only some 10 seconds.

Geoff Conway missed an easy conversion kick, but England made sure of victory when Len Corbett, finding himself hemmed in, passed back between his legs to wing Smallwood who dropped an astonishing goal from 45 yards. The Welsh try followed an elusive run by Tom 'Codger' Johnson, who raced right up to 39-year-old full back Gilbert before putting Gwilym Michael over. There were some 9,000 Welshmen in the crowd of 40,000 and they saw the Welsh players in the wars. D. G. Davies had an ugly gash under the left eye that had to be stitched; Thomson had three front teeth knocked out; Ambrose Baker suffered badly bruised ribs and Johnson was laid out by a kick on the head. England went on to win the Triple Crown for the sixth time. It was the last time for the great W J A Davies to play against Wales. In his 22 games for England he was on the losing side only once – against the 1913 Springboks.

England: F Gilbert (Devonport Services); C N Lowe (Blackheath), L J Corbett (Bristol), E Myers (Bradford), A M Smallwood (Leicester); W J A. Davies (capt.), C A Kershaw (United Services); R Edwards (Newport), E R Gardner (Devonport Services), W E G Luddington (Devonport Services), R Cove-Smith (OMT), W W Wakefield (Cambridge Univ.), H L Price (Leicester), G S Conway (Rugby), A T Voyce (Gloucester).

Wales: Joe Rees (Swansea); T Johnson, *R A Cornish (Cardiff), A Jenkins (Llanelli), *W R Harding (Swansea); J M C Lewis (Cardiff, capt.), W J Delahay (Bridgend); T Parker (Swansea), Tom Roberts (Newport), *D G Davies (Cardiff), *Gethin Thomas (Llanelli), Ambrose Baker (Neath), S Morris, *J Thompson (Cross Keys), *G Michael (Swansea).

For England, Leo Price scored a try. Alistair Smallwood dropped a goal.

For Wales, Gwilym Michael scored a try.

Referee: J M B Scott (Scotland).

Match 117 **WALES v SCOTLAND** Cardiff Arms Park. February 3, 1923

Scotland won by one goal, two tries (11) to one goal, one penalty goal (8)

Welsh supporters swarmed on to the field at the end of this match to carry the hero off in triumph, though he was the captain of the team who had beaten Wales. Archibald Leslie Gracie, the Harlequins' centre, was hoisted high and marched from the field after scoring a brilliant try two minutes from the end to snatch a memorable victory. It enabled Scotland to win at Cardiff for the first time since 1890. In scoring this try at the Westgate Street end, Les Gracie almost ran over the dead ball line while trying to get near the posts. A small boy, sitting near the spot, was struck in the mouth by Gracie's boot and lost some teeth. But the youngster said he did not mind – he was a Scottish lad!

Gracie said: "It was the most wonderful crowd I have ever seen in the whole world. Whoever did a good thing was applauded, no matter which side he belonged to." The crowd of more than 40,000 paid record receipts for a match in Wales of over £5,800. The gates were closed before the start and fans were locked out. They made an attempt to rush the gates but were repulsed by police.

Wales: B O Male (Pontypool); T Johnson, R A Cornish (Cardiff), A Jenkins (Llanelli), W R Harding (Swansea); J M C Lewis (Cardiff, capt.), W J Delahay

(Bridgend); Ambrose Baker (Neath), S Morris (Cross Keys), D G Davies (Cardiff), T Parker, G Michael (Swansea), Gethin Thomas (Llanelli), *L Jenkins (Aberavon), Tom Roberts (Newport).

Scotland: D Drysdale (Heriot's FP); E H Liddell (Edinburgh Univ.), A L Gracie (Harlequins, capt.), E McLaren (Royal HSFP), A Browning (Glasgow HSFP); S B McQueen (Waterloo), W E Bryce (Selkirk); J M Bannerman, L M Stuart (Glasgow HSFP), J C R Buchanan (Stewart's Coll. FP), D S Davies (Hawick), J R Lawrie (Melrose), D M Bertram (Watsonians), D S Kerr (Heriot's FP), A K Stevenson (Glasgow Acads.).

For Scotland, Eric Liddell, Ludovic Stuart and Leslie Gracie scored tries. Dan Drysdale converted one.

For Wales, Clem Lewis scored a try. Albert Jenkins converted and kicked a penalty goal.

Referee: J W Baxter (England).

Match 118   WALES v FRANCE   St. Helen's, Swansea. February 24, 1923

Wales won by two goals, one penaly goal, one try (16) to one goal, one try (8)

This was Wales's only victory of the season and marked the official opening of the new St. Helen's grandstand. But it was a disappointing match. The lighter French forwards were praised for their abundance of pluck. None of them hesitated to 'mix it' in the vigorous melees which took up the greater part of the match. When it became particularly violent at one time, the referee called the French secretary on to the field to translate his final words of warning to the French forwards.

Wales: Joe Rees (Swansea); T Johnson (Cardiff), Melbourne G Thomas (St. Bart's Hosp.), A Jenkins (Llanelli), W R Harding (Swansea); *D E John (Llanelli), W J Delahay (Bridgend); T Parker (capt.), G Michael (Swansea), Ambrose Baker (Neath), Gethin Thomas (Llanelli), S Morris (Cross Keys), L Jenkins (Aberavon), *Mapson Williams (Newport), *D Pascoe (Bridgend).

France: J Clement (Valence); M Lalande, H. Behoteguy (Racing Club), R Ramis (Perpignan), A. Jaureguy (Toulouse); C Lacazedieu (Dax), C Dupont (Lourdes); L Beguet (Racing Club), J Castets (Toulon), J Bayard, J Larrieu (Toulouse), A Cassayet (Tarbes), J Castets (Toulon), J Etcheberry (Rochefort), R Lasserre (Cognac, capt).

For Wales, Rowe Harding, Melbourne Thomas and Ambrose Baker scored tries. Albert Jenkins converted two. Joe Rees kicked a penalty goal.

For France, Max Lalande and Rene Lasserre scored tries. Louis Beguet converted one.

Referee: J B McGowan (Ireland).

Match 119   IRELAND v WALES   Lansdowne Road, Dublin. March 10, 1923

Ireland won by one goal (5) to one dropped goal (4)

Jack Powell's left-footed dropped goal on his debut failed to save Wales from a one-point defeat and Ireland gained their first win over the Welshmen since 1912. It left Wales with the wooden spoon and was only the second time in their history for them to lose to all three home country rivals in one season. The previous occasion had been in 1892. With 'the Troubles' in

Ireland, it was hardly a surprise that each member of the Welsh party was insured for £1,000. Several members of the WRU committee were stopped by the military and searched in Sackville Street, Dublin on the Friday, but the only 'concealed weapon' found was a toothpick. On a sightseeing tour of the city there were 'sinister signs of warfare' and the team had a scare when they were told that rebel snipers were operating from a roof near their hotel.

Ireland: W E Crawford (Lansdowne); D J Cussen (Dublin Univ.), G V Stephenson (Queen's Univ., Belfast), J B Gardiner (North of Ireland), R O McClenahan (Instonians); W H Hall (Instonians), W Cunningham (Lansdowne); M J Bradley (Dolphin), R Collopy, W P Collopy (Bective), D M Cunningham (North of Ireland), T A McClelland (Queen's Univ., Belfast), J K S Thompson (capt.), R Y Crichton, J D Clinch (Dublin Univ.).

Wales: Joe Rees (Swansea) ; W R Harding (Swansea), A Jenkins (Llanelli, capt.), *T Collins (Mountain Ash), *Jack Powell (Cardiff); D E John (Llanelli), W J Delahay (Bridgend); *Stan Davies (Treherbert), Gethin Thomas (Llanelli), Ambrose Baker (Neath), S Morris (Cross Keys), D Pascoe (Bridgend), *J H Davies (Aberavon), *T. L. Richards (Maesteg), *W J Radford (Newport).

For Ireland, Denis Cussen scored a try. Ernie Crawford converted.

For Wales, Jack Powell dropped a goal.

Referee: J M Tennent (Scotland).

Match 120   **WALES v ENGLAND**   St Helen's, Swansea. January 19, 1924

England won by one goal, four tries (17) to three tries (9)

With their backs outpaced and their centres unsteady in defence, Wales suffered their first defeat at Swansea by England for 29 years. It was England's first win on Welsh territory since 1913 and they went on to gain the Triple Crown for the seventh time to equal Wales's record in this achievement. A crowd of 35,000 saw Ivor Jones make his debut. The Llanelli player became one of the world's finest wing forwards and played 16 times for Wales. He was to be president of the WRU in 1968-69 and his record of 256 points in a season for Llanelli stood until wing Andy Hill broke it with 259 in 1968-69. Tom Voyce, England's wing forward, played throughout the second half with a broken rib.

Wales: Joe Rees (Swansea, capt.); T Johnson, R A Cornish (Cardiff), *D Hunt Davies (Aberavon), Melbourne G Thomas (St. Bart's Hosp.); *Albert Owen (Swansea), *Eddie Watkins (Neath); S Morris (Cross Keys), *Ifor Thomas (Bryncethin), Tom Jones (Newport), *W J Ould (Cardiff), *C Pugh (Maesteg), *Arthur C Evans (Pontypool), *Ivor Morris (Swansea), *Ivor Jones (Llanelli).

England: B S Chantrill (Bristol); H C Catcheside (Percy Park), L J Corbett (Bristol), H M Locke (Birkenhead Park), H P Jacob (Oxford Univ.); E Myers (Bradford), A T Young (Cambridge Univ.); W E G Luddington (Devonport Services), A Robson (Northern), R Edwards (Newport),W W Wakefield (Leicester, capt), R. Cove-Smith (OMT), A F Blakiston (Liverpool), G S Conway (Rugby), A T Voyce (Gloucester).

For England, Carston Catcheside (2), Eddie Myers, Bert Jacob and Harold Locke scored tries. Geoff Conway converted one.

For Wales, Tom Johnson, Albert Owen and Tom Jones scored tries.

Referee: A W Angus (Scotland).

Match 121   SCOTLAND v WALES   Inverleith, Edinburgh. February 2, 1924

Scotland won by four goals, one penalty goal, four tries (35) to two goals (10)

Not since the eighties had a Welsh team suffered such an overwhelming defeat. Wing Ian Smith, the 'Flying Scot', scored three of the eight tries as one of the all-Oxford University threequarter line. But Smith was to prove even more of a scoring scourge the following season. Said one of the Welsh team on the Sunday coach trip to view the Forth Bridge: "Take a good look, boys. This is the last time we will see it at the expense of the WRU."

Scotland: D Drysdale (Heriot's FP); I S Smith, G P S Macpherson, G G Aitken, A C Wallace (Oxford Univ.); H Waddell (Glasgow Acads.), W E Bryce (Selkirk); J C R Buchanan (Stewart's Coll., FP., capt.), J M Bannerman (Glasgow HSFP), D M Bertram, A C Gillies (Watsonians), K G P Hendrie (Heriot's FP.), R A Howie (Kirkcaldy), J R Lawrie (Leicester), A Ross (Kilmarnock).

Wales: B O Male (Cardiff) ; *J Elwyn Evans (Llanelli), *Harold J Davies (Newport), *M A Rosser (Penarth), T Johnson (Cardiff); V M Griffiths (Newport), Eddie Watkins (Neath); J Whitfield (Newport, capt.), S Morris (Cross Keys), Ivor Morris (Swansea), Tom Jones (Newport), C Pugh (Maesteg), Ivor Jones (Llanelli), W J Ould (Cardiff), Gwyn Francis (Llanelli).

For Scotland, Ian Smith (3), Willie Bryce, 'Tubby' Bertram, Johnnie Wallace, Phil Macpherson and Herbert Waddell scored tries. Dan Drysdale converted four and kicked a penalty goal.

For Wales, Vincent Griffiths and Ivor Jones scored tries. Ossie Male converted both.

Referee: J B McGowan (Ireland).

Match 122   WALES v IRELAND   Cardiff Arms Park. March 8, 1924

Ireland won by two goals, one try (13) to one dropped goal, two tries (10)

Tom Hewitt and his 17-year-old brother, Frank, each scored thrilling tries to help Ireland to their first win in Wales for 25 years. Frank, the youngest man ever to play for Ireland (he was still at school), sold two beautiful dummies for his try. The Prince of Wales and Duke of York were among the 35,000 spectators to watch the match in ideal conditions. Jack Wetter, the Welsh captain, was 34 years old. For the second successive year Wales had lost to England, Scotland and Ireland.

Wales: B O Male (Cardiff); Cliff Richards (Pontypool), J Wetter (Newport, capt.), *Tom Evans, W R Harding (Swansea); V M Griffiths (Newport), Eddie Watkins (Neath); *D Parker (Swansea), *G Hathway, J Whitfield (Newport), Arthur C Evans (Pontypool), *R Randall (Aberavon), *W J Jones (Llanelli), *J Gore (Blaina), C Pugh (Maesteg).

Ireland: W E Crawford (Lansdowne, capt.); T Hewitt, G V Stephenson (Queen's Univ., Belfast), J B Gardiner (North of Ireland), H W V. Stephenson (United Services); F S Hewitt (Instonians), J A Clarke (Bective); C F Hallaran (United Services), W P Collopy, R Collopy (Bective), R Y Crichton, T A McClelland (Queen's Univ., Belfast), J M McVicker (Belfast Collegians), W R F Collis (Wanderers), J D Clinch (Dublin Univ.).

For Ireland, Tom Hewitt, Frank Hewitt and George Stephenson scored tries. Ernie Crawford converted two.

For Wales, Cliff Richards and Charlie Pugh scored tries. Eddie Watkins dropped a goal.

Referee: J T Tulloch (Scotland).

Match 123 FRANCE v WALES   Colombes, Paris. March 27, 1924

Wales won by one dropped goal, two tries (10) to two tries (6)

While the South Wales Express roared towards Paddington a special meeting of the WRU executive was taking place in an atmosphere of high drama. The sensational outcome was that full back Ossie Male, who had played faultlessly against Ireland in the previous game, was sent home under suspension. It was an amazing disciplinary measure, taken because Male had violated the rule of playing within the week before the date of an international match. He turned out for Cardiff at Birkenhead Park. Cardiff were later censured for playing Male. Melville Rosser, chosen originally on the wing, was switched as emergency full back and Joe Jones came in to make his debut in the threequarter line. The match provided Wales with their only win of the season. It was played on a Thursday before a crowd of nearly 30,000 in rain on a quagmire pitch in icy conditions and Jaureguy and another French player needed medical treatment for frost-bite.

France: E Bonnes (Narbonne); R Got (Perpignan), A Behoteguy (Bayonne), A Dupouy (Bordelais), A Jaureguy (Toulouse); H Galau (Toulouse), C Dupont (Rouen); M F Lubin-Lebrere, J Bayard, A Bioussa (Toulouse), A Cassayet (Narbonne, capt.), P Moureu, F Clauzel (Beziers), J Etcheberry (Rochefort), E Piquiral (Racing Club).

Wales: M A Rosser (Penarth); *E Finch (Llanelli), *A R Stock (Newport), *Joe Jones, W R Harding (Swansea, capt.); V M Griffiths (Newport), Eddie Watkins (Neath); D Parker (Swansea), G Hathway (Newport), S Morris (Cross Keys), *A Rickards (Cardiff), R Randall (Aberavon), J Gore (Blaina), C Pugh (Maesteg), Arthur C Evans (Pontypool).

For Wales, Ernie Finch and Arnold Rickards scored tries. Vincent Griffiths dropped a goal.

For France, Andre Behoteguy and Lubin-Lebrere scored tries.

Referee: R A Roberts (England).

Match 124 WALES v NEW ZEALAND   St. Helen's, Swansea. November 29, 1924

New Zealand won by two goals, one penalty goal, two tries (19) to nil

When the All Blacks finished their traditional haka before the kick-off, Dai Hiddlestone, the little wing-forward, led the Welsh team in an unexpected war-dance of their own to amuse the crowd. It was to be a better team effort by Wales than anything they accomplished during the following 80 minutes of the match. New Zealand avenged their 1905 defeat, outclassed Wales in what was mostly a dull game, and went on to complete their tour with an unbeaten record.

At 2.15 the gates were closed with more than 50,000 spectators in the ground. Bert Cooke's aggressive defence quickly upset the Welsh midfield runners and, with their rhythm destroyed and their forwards overpowered, defeat was inevitable. Often the tussle became rough, as it had been in 1905. Jack Wetter, playing his final game for Wales, and captaining the side, was laid out in a collision with George Nepia. Wetter was taken off and when he resumed after the interval he went into the pack as little more than a limping passenger, and Hiddlestone moved out as the extra back. Wetter said afterwards: "I am rather too shaken to make any comments. It struck me as a hard game!"

Wales were well beaten before Wetter's injury. New Zealand led 11-0 at halftime after Mark Nicholls had kicked a penalty goal and converted one of the two scrambling tries by Maurice Brownlie and Bill Irvine. In the second half, wing Karl Svenson added a try before Irvine bullocked his way over again and Nicholls converted.

There was a sensational start to the match. Wetter rejected the ball because it was over-inflated. He refused the next. The referee agreed that a third ball was unsuitable and both captains waved away the fourth ball. From somewhere, a fifth ball was procured and proved acceptable to everyone. But the result was the most acceptable thing for New Zealand.

Wales: T Johnson (Cardiff); W R Harding (Swansea), A Stock (Newport), A Jenkins, E Finch (Llanelli); J Wetter (Newport, capt.), *Eddie Williams (Neath), W J Delahay (Cardiff); D Parker (Swansea) J Gore (Blaina), Marsden Jones (Cardiff and London Welsh), *C Williams (Llanelli), S. Morris (Cross Keys) C H Pugh (Maesteg). D. Hiddlestone (Neath).

New Zealand: G Nepia; threequarters – J Steel, A E Cooke, K S Svenson; five-eighths – M F Nicholls (first), N P McGregor (second); half back – J J Mill; wing forward – J H Parker; forwards – W Irvine, Q Donald, M J Brownlie, R R Masters, J Richardson (capt.), C J Brownlie, L F Cupples.

For New Zealand, Bill Irvine (2), Maurice Brownlie and Karl Svenson scored tries. Mark Nicholls converted two and kicked a penalty goal.

Referee: Col. J S Brunton (England).

Match 125 ENGLAND v WALES   Twickenham. January 17, 1925

England won by one penalty goal, and three tries (12) to two tries (6)

Wales attacked for threequarters of the game, but just could not find the polish necessary to finish off their efforts. England deserved their success with right wing Hamilton-Wickes as their star. He scored one superb try and made another. Tom 'Codger' Johnson, a spirited wing for his club, was tried at full back and proved a great success to mark his appointment as captain. The Prince of Wales was among the 40,000 spectators.

England: J W Brough (Silloth); R H Hamilton-Wickes (Harlequins), H M Locke (Birkenhead Park), L J Corbett (Bristol), J C Gibbs (Harlequins); H J Kittermaster (Oxford Univ.), E J Massey (Leicester); W E G Luddington (Devonport Services), J S Tucker (Bristol) R Armstrong (Northern), R Cove-Smith (OMT), W W Wakefield (Harlequins, capt.), H G Periton (Waterloo) , A F Blakiston (Liverpool), A T Voyce (Gloucester).

Wales: T Johnson (Cardiff, capt.); *W P James, *Evan Williams (Aberavon), R A Cornish (Cardiff), *Cyril Thomas (Bridgend); *W. J. Hopkins (Aberavon), W J Delahay (Cardiff); S Morris (Cross Keys), Cliff Williams (Llanelli), *Bryn Phillips (Aberavon), C Pugh (Maesteg), *Idris Richards (Cardiff), J Gore (Blaina), D Parker (Swansea), *W Idris Jones (Llanelli).

For England, Harry Kittermaster, Tom Voyce and Dicky Hamilton-Wickes scored tries. Bob Armstrong kicked a penalty goal.

For Wales, Cyril Thomas and Will James scored tries.

Referee: A A Lawrie (Scotland).

Match 126 WALES v SCOTLAND   St. Helen's, Swansea. February 7, 1925

Scotland won by one goal, one dropped goal, five tries (24)
to one goal, one penalty goal, two tries (14)

Ian Smith, the brilliant Scottish wing, raced in for four colourful tries, two of them after 60-

yard sprints, in a grand match described as: "Deserving to rank with the greatest encounters between the countries." There were 40,000 people on a beautiful spring day to see Scotland build a 21-0 lead. Everything pointed to a complete rout for the Welshmen. But somehow they produced a rally that staggered the Scots and brought 14 points in the last 15 minutes. "A shame it could not have gone on for another 15 minutes," said a Welsh official. But Scotland were worthy winners through the pace and penetration of their all-Oxford University threequarter line and went on to win the Triple Crown for the sixth time.

Wales: T Johnson (Cardiff); W P James, Evan Williams (Aberavon), R A Cornish (Cardiff), Cyril Thomas (Bridgend); W J Hopkins (Aberavon), W J Delahay (Cardiff); C Pugh (Maesteg), S.Morris (capt.), *R. C. Herrera (Cross Keys), Bryn Phillips (Aberavon) W Idris Jones (Llanelli), D Parker (Swansea), Idris Richards (Cardiff), * S Lawrence (Bridgend).

Scotland: D Drysdale (Heriot's FP); I S Smith, G P S Macpherson (capt.), G G Aitken, A C Wallace (Oxford Univ.); J C Dykes, J B Nelson (Glasgow Acads.); J M Bannerman, J C H Ireland (Glasgow HSFP), D S Davies (Hawick), J R Paterson (Birkenhead Park), J W Scott (Stewart's Coll., FP), A C Gillies (Watsonians), R A Howie (Kirkcaldy), D J MacMyn (London Scottish).

For Scotland, Ian Smith (4) and 'Johnnie' Wallace (2) scored tries. Dan Drysdale converted one and dropped a goal.

For Wales, Willie John Hopkins, Idris Jones and Arthur Cornish scored tries. Dai Parker converted one and kicked a penalty goal.

Referee: J W Baxter (England).

Match 127 **WALES v FRANCE**   Cardiff Arms Park. February 28, 1925

Wales won by one goal, two tries (11) to one goal (5)

In Wales's only win of the season, play rarely reached even ordinary club standard and the crowd of 28,000 was the smallest for a match in Wales for very many years. The rugged home forwards controlled the game, but most of the backs, as well as being disjointed in attack, preferred to fly-kick than fall on the ball in the mud.

In these days of Welsh rugby depression during the 1920s, Bobby Delahay was a fine player, mostly at scrum half for the national team, though able to play at stand-off and in the centre. He was a particularly clever attacker. Jack Wetter was another player of this era who figured at scrum half, fly half and centre for Wales.

Wales: T Johnson (Cardiff); E Finch, Graham Davies (Llanelli), R A Cornish (Cardiff capt.), W R Harding (Swansea); Eddie Williams (Neath), W J Delahay (Cardiff); S Morris, R C Herrera (Cross Keys), D Parker (Swansea), Idris Richards (Cardiff), W Idris Jones, *W Lewis (Llanelli), Bryn Phillips (Aberavon), *E. Beynon (Swansea).

France: J. Ducousso (Tarbes); R Halet (Strasbourg), M de Laborderie (Racing Club), C Magnanou (Bayonne), A Bringeon (Biarritz); Yves du Manoir (Racing Club), R Piteu (Toulouse); A Maury (Toulouse), C Marcet (Albi), C Montade (Perpignan), R Levasseur (Stade Francais), A Laurent, E Barthe (Biarritz), , A Cassayet (Narbonne, capt.), F Clauzel (Beziers).

For Wales, Ernie Finch (2) and Bobby Delahay scored tries. Dai Parker converted one.

For France, Marcel de Laborderie scored a try. Jean Ducousso converted.

Referee: R W Harland (Ireland).

Ireland won by two goals, one penalty goal, two tries (19) to one try (3)

For the first time Ireland recorded three successive victories over Wales – a feat they were not to repeat for more than 40 years – and also registered their biggest score against the Principality. It was Wales's first visit to Ireland's new ground at Ravenhill, and the experiment of playing scrum half Bobby Delahay at outside half was a failure. Ron Herrera was injured early in the game and eventually had to go off, but Ireland were already 8-0 up and looked easy winners.

Ireland: W E Crawford (Lansdowne, capt.); H W V Stephenson (United Services), T J Millin (Dublin Univ.), J B. Gardiner (North of Ireland), G V Stephenson (Queen's Univ., Belfast); E O'D Davy (Lansdowne), M Sugden (Dublin Univ.); G R Beamish (Coleraine), M J Bradley (Dolphin), S J Cagney (London Irish), R Collopy (Bective), D M Cunningham (North of Ireland), R Flood (Dublin Univ.), J C McVicker (Belfast Collegians), W F Browne (United Services).

Wales: *D N Rocyn Jones (St. Mary's Hosp., and Newport); W R Harding (Swansea), *B R Turnbull (Cardiff), D Davies (Bridgend), E Finch (Llanelli); W J Delahay (Cardiff), *Arthur John (Llanelli); D Parker (Swansea), W Idris Jones (Llanelli, capt.), S Lawrence (Bridgend), R C Herrera (Cross Keys), *J Brown, *S. Hinam (Cardiff), Bryn Phillips (Aberavon), E Beynon (Swansea).

For Ireland, Terry Millin, George Stephenson, 'Horsey' Browne and Harry Stephenson scored tries. George Stephenson converted two and kicked a penalty goal.

For Wales, Bernard Turnbull scored a try.

Referee: J W Baxter (England).

Drawn. Wales one try (3). England one try (3)

Bobby Delahay's disallowed 'try' in the closing minutes caused a great deal of controversy. England heeled near their own line and when the ball came out of the side of the scrum, Delahay picked up and darted away and over the line. But referee W. H. Acton (Ireland) ordered another scrum. This score would have won the game. As it was, Wavell Wakefield's first half try looked like being a winning score until Welsh wing George Andrews, on his debut, tapped a rolling ball forward with his knee and chased to score 15 minutes from the end.

Pack-leader Bryn Phillips led the Welsh forwards in dashing style and they outplayed England's eight in the second half, though matters became over-heated. The gate at the County Club entrance was stormed by the crowd, who were locked out when the ground was full. They broke through and hundreds climbed the back of the stand to gain precarious vantage points. It was reported that, "The great little Delahay was the outstanding Welsh back." Six of the home pack were policemen.

Wales: *D B Evans (Swansea) *G E Andrews, A Stock (Newport), R A Cornish (Cardiff), W R Harding (Swansea, capt.); *Bobby Jones (Northampton), W J Delahay (Cardiff); *Tom Lewis (Cardiff), *J H John (Swansea), David Jones (Newport), R C Herrera (Cross Keys), S Hinam (Cardiff), *T Hopkins (Swansea), *D M Jenkins (Treorchy), Bryn Phillips (Aberavon).

England: H C Catcheside (Percy Park); H C Burton, A R Aslett (Richmond), T E S Francis (Blackheath), R H Hamilton-Wickes (Harlequins); H J Kittermaster, J R

B Worton (Harlequins); A Robson (Northern), J S Tucker (Bristol), E Stanbury (Plymouth Albion), R J Hanvey (Aspatria), W G E Luddington (Devonport Services), H G Periton (Waterloo), W W Wakefield (Harlequins, capt.), A T Voyce (Gloucester).

For Wales, George Andrews scored a try

For England, Wavell Wakefield scored a try.

Referee: W H Acton (Ireland).

Match 130 **SCOTLAND v WALES**   Murrayfield. February 6, 1926

Scotland won by one goal, one penalty goal (8) to one goal (5)

Scotland were lucky winners in front of nearly 50,000 spectators when Wales visited Murrayfield for the first time. But it was described as, "A glorious failure." The Welsh forwards had Scotland badly rattled and Wick Powell blotted out the dangerous Ian Smith. It was astonishing that Powell, normally a scrum half, should make his debut on the wing and play so effectively. When Rowe Harding dropped out through injury, Arthur Cornish, who took over as captain, suggested the daring experiment of playing Powell as a wing.

It was decided to try it, but an emergency plan was prepared if events went wrong. This involved switching Powell to scrum half and moving the versatile Delahay into midfield. This never had to be put into operation because Powell achieved his mission with remarkable success. Smith, the famous 'Flying Scot', who had scored seven tries in the two previous games with Wales, could not score. With this defeat, Wales could claim only three victories in 15 successive matches, and the only triumphs had been against France. Welsh rugby had been at its lowest ebb, but there were signs that the future looked brighter.

Scotland: D Drysdale (Heriot's FP, capt.); I S Smith (Edinburgh Univ.), R M Kinnear (Heriot's FP), J C Dykes, W M Simmers (Glasgow Acads.); H Waddell, J B Nelson (Glasgow Acads.); J M Bannerman, J C H Ireland (Glasgow HSFP), A C Gillies (Watsonians), D S Davies (Hawick), D J MacMyn (London Scottish), J R Paterson (Birkenhead Park), J W Scott (Stewart's Coll., FP), G M Murray (Glasgow Acads.).

Wales: *W A Everson (Newport); G E Andrews, A Stock (Newport), R A Cornish (Cardiff capt.), *W C Powell (London Welsh); Bobby Jones (Northampton), W J Delahay (Cardiff); S Lawrence (Bridgend), J H John (Swansea), David Jones (Newport), S Hinam (Cardiff), R C Herrera (Cross Keys), T Hopkins (Swansea), D M Jenkins (Treorchy), *E. Watkins (Blaina).

For Scotland, Herbert Waddell scored a try. Dan Drysdale converted. 'Sandy' Gillies kicked a penalty goal.

For Wales, Ron Herrera scored a try. Bill Everson converted.

Referee: D Hellewell (England).

Match 131 **WALES v IRELAND**   St. Helen's, Swansea. March 13, 1926

Wales won by one goal and two tries (11) to one goal and one penalty goal (8)

In the last minute, Tom Hewitt's drop shot curled towards the Welsh posts and a sudden silence fell over the ground. Then the ball swung away – and Ireland had failed in their bid to win the Triple Crown. "Wales would have been very unlucky to lose," admitted Irish skipper

Ernie Crawford. It was the first Welsh win over a rival home country team for four years and the field was stormed by excited partisans at the end.

Nearly 55,000 people watched unbeaten Ireland lead 8-3 at half time, but they could not curb the 19-year-old Windsor Lewis, star of the game, as he ripped through the defence to make a thrilling international debut at outside half. Wick Powell, after playing as wing in the previous game, appeared in his customary role of scrum half. Delahay moved to centre. Though Powell was caught often by Sugden and Clinch, the new scrum half showed his tremendous strength by getting his passes away to Windsor Lewis despite the spoiling.

Wales: *T E Rees (Army); *C F Rowlands (Aberavon), R A Cornish, W J Delahay (Cardiff), W R Harding (Swansea, capt.); *Windsor H Lewis, W C Powell (London Welsh); David Jones (Newport), J H John (Swansea), S Lawrence (Bridgend), S Hinam (Cardiff), R C Herrera (Cross Keys), T Hopkins (Swansea), D M Jenkins (Treorchy), E Watkins (Blaina).

Ireland: W E Crawford (Lansdowne, capt.); D J Cussen (Dublin Univ.), G V Stephenson, T R Hewitt, J H Gage (Queen's Univ., Belfast); E O'D Davy (Lansdowne), M Sugden (Dublin Univ.); M J Bradley (Dolphin), A M Buchanan (Dublin Univ.), W F Browne (United Services), S J Cagney (London Irish), J McVicker (Belfast Collegians), J L Farrell (Bective), C J Hanrahan (Dolphin), J D Clinch (Wanderers).

For Wales, Rowe Harding, Tom Hopkins and Ron Herrera scored tries. Tommy Rees converted one.

For Ireland, Charles Hanrahan scored a try. George Stephenson converted and kicked a penalty goal.

Referee: B S Cumberlege (England).

Match 132   FRANCE v WALES   Colombes, Paris. April 5, 1926

Wales won by one dropped goal, one try (7) to one goal (5)

Guardsman Tommy Rees, from Pontyclun, the new Welsh full back, saved his side from defeat with a magnificent display. He was reported to have "tackled like a demon" to prevent France taking more than a 5-0 lead at half time. Rees was considered to be the outstanding Welsh discovery of the season. Windsor Lewis was unable to play in this 14th successive Welsh win over France.

France: L Destarac (Tarbes); M Besson (CASG, Paris), M Baillette (Perpignan), R Graciet (Bordelais), A Jaureguy (Stade Francais, capt.); V Graule (Perpignan), H Laffont (Narbonne); C Montade, J Sayrou, E Ribere (Perpignan), C A Gonnet (Albi), A Cassayet (Narbonne), A Laurent (Biarritz), E Piquiral (Racing Club), G Gerintes (CASG, Paris).

Wales: T E Rees (Army); E Finch (Llanelli), W J Delahay (capt.), R A Cornish (Cardiff), W R Harding (Swansea); Bobby Jones (Northampton), W C Powell (London Welsh); David Jones (Newport), J H John (Swansea), S Lawrence (Bridgend), S Hinam (Cardiff), R C Herrera (Cross Keys), T Hopkins (Swansea), D M Jenkins (Treorchy), E Watkins (Blaina).

For Wales, Emlyn Watkins scored a try. Arthur Cornish dropped a goal.

For France, Gilbert Gerintes scored a try. Albert Gonnet converted.

Referee: R W Harland (Ireland).

England won by one goal, one goal from a mark, one penalty goal (11)
to one penalty goal, two tries (9)

With only 14 men for most of the game, Wales almost conquered the Twickenham bogy in front of 50,000 spectators. Newport forward Dai Jones went off after 15 minutes with a fractured bone in his shoulder. Then Wick Powell was laid out with a knock that would have sent most players to the dressing room. But this hard-as-nails scrum half recovered and played on doggedly to help in the epic struggle, though his passing often was deplorably wild. Ossie Male, who showed inspiring initiative as a running full back, missed a penalty shot by a fraction. Then, in the last few minutes, John Roberts, on his debut, looked to be through, but a desperate ankle-tap by full back Sellar brought him down. "I think we were very unlucky," said Wales's new captain, 22-year-old Bernard 'Lou' Turnbull. England, led by 30-year-old Len Corbett, were thankful to hear the final whistle and disentangle themselves from the grip of the fiery fourteen.

England: K A Sellar (Royal Navy); R H Hamilton-Wickes (Harlequins), L J Corbett (Bristol, capt.), H M Locke (Birkenhead Park), J C Gibbs (Harlequins); H C C Laird, J R B Worton (Harlequins); R Cove-Smith (OMT), J S Tucker (Bristol), J Hanley, E Stanbury (Plymouth Albion), H G Periton (Waterloo), K J Stark (Old Alleynians), T Coulson (Coventry), G S Conway (Hartlepool Rovers).

Wales: B O Male (Cardiff); G E Andrews (Newport), B R Turnbull (capt.), *J Roberts (Cardiff), W R Harding (Swansea); Windsor H Lewis, W C Powell (London Welsh); Tom Lewis (Cardiff), J H John (Swansea), David Jones (Newport), S Lawrence (Bridgend), R C Herrera (Newport), *Harry Phillips (Newport). *Watcyn Thomas (Llanelli), *W. Williams (Crumlin).

For England, Len Corbett scored a try and kicked a goal from a mark. 'Erb' Stanbury converted and kicked a penalty goal.

For Wales, George Andrews and Rowe Harding scored tries. Ossie Male kicked a penalty goal.

Referee: R L Scott (Scotland).

Scotland won by one goal (5) to nil

A scramble in the mud brought Scotland their fifth successive victory over Wales, who never looked like scoring. The much criticised Scottish pack "belied their evil reputation and stood up to the Welshmen from beginning to end." The Scots swept through the home defence repeatedly, but always a last desperate defender emerged from some spot in the swamp to save the grim situation. The only try came just before half time, when Rowe Harding was caught in possession. Ivor Jones was the outstanding Welshman with superbly controlled foot rushes that half-a-dozen times took him right up to full back Dan Drysdale. This was the last appearance of Bobby Delahay, who played 18 times for Wales at scrum half, fly half and centre. A crowd of 40,000, including the Prince of Wales, watched the match. Windsor Lewis and Wick Powell originally were chosen at half back, but Lewis was injured, so the WRU asked Powell to stand down in order to play club pair of Delahay and Gwyn Richards.

Wales: B O Male (Cardiff, capt.); *J D Bartlett (Llanelli and London Welsh), B R Turnbull, J Roberts (Cardiff), W R Harding (Swansea); *Gwyn Richards, W J Delahay (Cardiff); Tom Lewis (Cardiff), J H John (Swansea), Harry Phillips

(Newport), *T Arthur (Neath), *E M Jenkins (Aberavon), W Williams (Crumlin), Watcyn Thomas, Ivor Jones (Llanelli).

Scotland: D Drysdale (Heriot's FP); E G Taylor (Oxford Univ.) G P S. Macpherson (Edinburgh Acads., capt.), J C Dykes, W M Simmers (Glasgow Acads.); H Waddell, J B Nelson (Glasgow Acads.); D S Kerr (Heriot's FP), J M Bannerman (Glasgow HSFP), D S Davies (Hawick), J Graham (Kelso), J C H Ireland (Glasgow HSFP), J R Paterson (Birkenhead Park), J W Scott (Stewart's Coll., FP), A C Gillies (Watsonians).

For Scotland, David Kerr scored a try. 'Sandy' Gillies converted.

Referee: W H Jackson (England).

Match 135 WALES v FRANCE   St. Helen's, Swansea. February 26, 1927

Wales won by two goals and five tries (25) to one dropped goal and one try (7)

Once again France provided Wales with their only victory of the season. The two young Cambridge University centres, Guy Morgan, making his debut, and John Roberts, ripped the defence to ribbons. Despite a waterlogged ground and rain almost throughout the match, Wales sparkled in attack to collect seven tries. Jim Burns was outstanding in his first game for Wales.

Wales: B O Male (Cardiff); G E Andrews (Newport), *W Guy Morgan (Cambridge Univ.), J Roberts (Cardiff), W R Harding (Swansea); Windsor H Lewis, W C Powell (London Welsh, capt.); Harry Phillips (Newport), J H John (Swansea), *J Burns (Cardiff), T Arthur (Neath), E M Jenkins (Aberavon), W Williams (Crumlin), Watcyn Thomas, Ivor Jones (Llanelli).

France: L Destarac (Stade Tarbais); R Houdet (Stade Francais), M Baillette (Quillan), V Graule (Perpignan), F Raymond (Toulouse); A Verger (Stade Francais), P Carbonne (Perpignan); R Hutin (CASG, Paris), A Gonnet (Racing Club), R Bousquet, A Prevost (Albi), A Cassayet (Narbonne, capt.), E Ribere (Quillan), E Piquiral (Lyons), J Etcheberry (Vienne).

For Wales, Rowe Harding (2), John Roberts (2), Watcyn Thomas, George Andrews and Guy Morgan scored tries. Ossie Male converted two.

For France, Alfred Prevost scored a try. Andre Verger dropped a goal.

Referee: W H Jackson (England).

Match 136 IRELAND v WALES   Lansdowne Road, Dublin. March 12, 192.

Ireland won by two goals, one penalty goal, two tries (19) to one goal, one dropped goal (9)

For the fourth time in five seasons Wales became unwilling holders of rugby's wooden spoon, a symbol of failure that is always felt keenly in Wales as a blow to national prestige. There were 32,000 supporters to see Ireland win without encountering much resistance. Even after losing hooker Allan Buchanan with injury just before half time, the seven remaining Irish forwards outplayed the Welsh eight. The Times summed it up: "The Welsh forwards are cavemen in the age of machine guns."

Ireland: W E Crawford (Lansdowne, capt.); J H Gage (Queen's Univ., Belfast), G V Stephenson (North of Ireland), F S Hewitt (Instonians), J B Ganly (Monkstown); E O'D. Davy (Lansdowne), M Sugden (Wanderers); T O Pike

(Lansdowne), A M Buchanan (Dublin Univ.), W F Browne (Army), H McVicker (Richmond), J L Farrell (Bective), J McVicker (Belfast Colegians), C J Hanrahan, M J Bradley (Dolphin).

Wales: B O Male (Cardiff); G E Andrews (Newport), W Guy Morgan (Cambridge Univ.), J Roberts (Cardiff), W R Harding (Swansea); Windsor H Lewis (Maesteg), W C Powell (London Welsh, capt.); T Arthur (Neath), J H John (Swansea), J. Burns (Cardiff), E M Jenkins (Aberavon), Harry Phillips (Newport), W Williams (Crumlin), Watcyn Thomas, Ivor Jones (Llanelli).

For Ireland, George Stephenson (2) and Jim Ganly (2) scored tries. Stephenson converted two and kicked a penalty goal.

For Wales, Guy Morgan scored a try. Wick Powell converted. Windsor Lewis dropped a goal.

Referee: B S Cumberlege (England).

Match 137 WALES v NEW SOUTH WALES   Cardiff Arms Park. November 26, 1927

New South Wales won by three goals, one try (18) to one goal, one try (8)

Wales were beaten by a side possessing superior tactical ability and greater capacity for working smoothly together. The Waratahs, as the New South Wales touring team were called, also defeated Ireland and France, but lost to England and Scotland. They out-scrummaged Wales, controlled the line-out and proved considerably more accurate and enterprising by handling among the forwards. The home pack had to rely on dribbling and foot rushes to worry the tourists, who had no weak links in their side, whereas Wales looked unevenly balanced and lacking inspiration. In recent years this match was awarded full Australia status.

Rowe Harding, the chosen Welsh captain, withdrew because of injury. Dan Jones replaced him on the wing and Ivor Jones assumed the captaincy. The Waratahs led 5-3 at half time. Ernie Finch scored Wales's first half try and only after the visitors had established an 18-3 advantage did Wales obtain their other points. Windsor Lewis, who kicked too often, this time made the half-break and John Roberts linked to return a pass and the outside half scored a try which Tommy Rees converted.

Wales: T E Rees (Army and London Welsh); E Finch (Llanelli), J Roberts (Cardiff), *Roy Jones (Swansea), *Dan Jones (Neath); Windsor H Lewis (Maesteg), *Tal Harris (Aberavon) ; *F A Bowdler (Cross Keys), *D R Jenkins (Swansea), *A Broughton (Treorchy), Harry Phillips (Newport), E M Jenkins (Aberavon), *T Hollingdale (Neath), *Iorwerth Jones, Ivor Jones (Llanelli, capt.).

New South Wales: A W Ross; E Ford, A C Wallace (capt.), W B J Sheenan, S C King; T Lawton, F W Meagher; H F Woods, J C Blackwood, B Judd, A N Finlay, G P Storey, J W Breckenridge, J A Ford, A J Tancred.

For the Waratahs, 'Johnnie' Wallace (2), Billy Sheehan and Syd King scored tries. Tom Lawton converted three.

For Wales, Ernie Finch and Windsor Lewis scored tries. Tommy Rees converted one.

Referee: D Hellewell (England).

Match 138 WALES v ENGLAND   St. Helen's, Swansea. January 21, 1928

England won by two goals (10) to one goal and one try (8)

Rowe Harding's stumble in the first half cost Wales a vital five points and enabled England

84

to forge on to secure the Triple Crown for a record eighth time. In the wind and rain on a slippery ground, the crowd of 30,000 saw Harding try to turn to tackle Taylor, but the Welsh captain slipped and left the way for Taylor's gift try that was to become a winning five points. It was written after the game: "No modern international has terminated in a triumph for a side less deserving of it than England." But a further comment was added: "Whether Welshmen like it or not they must realise that the advance which has been made in back play in Wales in recent years has not been quite sufficient to overtake the lead which other countries have enjoyed in this particular sphere." Though England's pack cracked in the second half, nothing went right for Wales, and Tom Hollingdale had a try disallowed because he was ruled fractionally off-side after a stirring combined dribble. It was the last game for Tommy Rees in the scarlet jersey of his country because a broken leg in a match at Cross Keys ended his international career.

Wales: T E Rees (London Welsh); J D Bartlett (London Welsh), J Roberts, B R Turnbull (Cardiff), W R Harding (Swansea, capt.); Dai John, Arthur John (Llanelli); F A Bowdler (Cross Keys}, *Cecil Pritchard (Pontypool), Harry Phillips (Newport), E M Jenkins (Aberavon), *A Skym, Iorwerth Jones (Llanelli), T Hollingdale (Neath), Ivor Jones (Llanelli).

England: K A Sellar (United Services); W J Taylor, C D Aarvold (Blackheath), J V Richardson (Birkenhead Park), Sir T G Devitt (Blackheath); H C C Laird (Harlequins), A T Young (Blackheath); E Stanbury (Plymouth Albion), J S Tucker (Bristol), T Coulson (Coventry), K J Stark (Old Alleynians), R. Cove-Smith (OMT, capt.), J Hanley (Plymouth Albion), D Turquand-Young (Richmond), T N Lawson (Workington).

For England, Bill Taylor and Colin Laird scored tries. Vere Richardson converted both.

For Wales, John Bartlett and Dai John scored tries. Ivor Jones converted one.

Referee: R W Harland (Ireland).

Match 139 SCOTLAND v WALES   Murrayfield. February 4, 1928

Wales won by two goals, one try (13) to nil

"From forward to back you whacked us," Scottish captain John Bannerman told the Welsh team after this first victory at Murrayfield. It was also the first Welsh success in Scotland since 1913. Winning the toss decided the match as Wales scored all their points with the strong, rain-laden wind at their backs and the home side exhausted themselves in defence before the interval. Dai John's screw-kicking was directed with masterly judgment as he controlled tactics and spearheaded the attack. Ossie Male was at his best with kicking, catching and stopping the Scots' rushes. "I am told this win will do a lot of good for the game in Wales," said Bannerman. Alas, it was not to be: the dismal days were not yet over.

Scotland: D Drysdale (London Scottish); J Goodfellow (Langholm), G P S Macpherson (Edinburgh Acads.), R F Kelly (Watsonians), W M Simmers (Glasgow Acads.); P S Douty (London Scottish), H D Greenlees (Leicester); J M Bannerman (Glasgow HSFP, capt.), J Graham (Kelso), W G Ferguson (Royal HSFP), J R Paterson (Birkenhead Park), W N Roughead (London Scottish), J W Scott (Stewart's Coll., FP), W B Welsh (Hawick), J H Ferguson (Gala).

Wales: B O Male (Cardiff, capt.); J D Bartlett (London Welsh), J Roberts (Cardiff), A Jenkins (Llanelli), W C Powell (London Welsh); Dai John, Arthur John (Llanelli); F A. Bowdler (Cross Keys), Cecil Pritchard (Pontypool), Harry Phillips (Newport), E M Jenkins (Aberavon), A Skym, Iorwerth Jones (Llanelli), F. Hollingdale (Neath), Ivor Jones (Llanelli).

For Wales, Albert Jenkins, Dai John and John Roberts scored tries. Ossie Male converted two.

Referee: R W Harland (Ireland).

Match 140 **WALES v IRELAND**   Cardiff Arms Park. March 10, 1928

Ireland won by two goals, one try (13) to two goals (10)

"Scrap the lot!" was the cry after this defeat. It was a drastic proposal, but reflected the bitterness of public reaction after the promise of so much from the Murrayfield victory. True enough, the Welsh threequarter line were a "lamentable and pitiful failure," as they muddled chance after chance in front of 42,000 spectators. But the brave-hearted home pack tamed one of the most fiery forward combinations Ireland had put in the field since Dr. Tyrrell's men provoked the Terrible Eight in 1914. Albert Jenkins, one of seven Llanelli men in the side, had been a reminder of those past days of glory in Welsh back play, but this was a disappointing end to his international career. It was as doleful a day for the Welsh captain as it had been for Gwyn Nicholls before him. Even the great are human.

Wales: B O Male (Cardiff); W C Powell (London Welsh), J Roberts (Cardiff), A Jenkins (capt.), F Finch (Llanelli); Dai John, Arthur John (Llanelli); Harry Phillips (Newport), Cecil Pritchard (Pontypool), F A Bowdler (Cross Keys), E M Jenkins (Aberavon), A Skym, Iorwerth Jones (Llanelli), T Hollingdale (Neath), Ivor Jones (Llanelli).

Ireland: W J Stewart (North of Ireland); J E Arigho (Lansdowne), J B Ganly (Monkstown), G V Stephenson (capt.), R M Byers (North of Ireland); F 0'D. Davy (Lansdowne), M. Sugden (Wanderers); G R Beamish (Leicester), J L Farrell (Bective), J P Mullane (Limerick Bohemians), J McVicker (Belfast Collegians), C T Payne (North of Ireland), T O Pike (Lansdowne), S J Cagney (London Irish), J D Clinch (Wanderers).

For Ireland, Jack Arigho (2) and Jim Ganly scored tries. George Stephenson converted two.

For Wales, Dai John and Albert Jenkins scored tries. Ivor Jones converted both.

Referee: T H Warren (Scotland).

Match 141 **FRANCE v WALES**   Colombes, Paris. April 9, 1928

France won by one goal, one try (8) to one try (3)

After winning the first 15 games they had played against France, Wales lost for the first time. France had beaten each of the other home countries in previous years and this overdue success completed their set. In glorious Easter Monday weather, the home side fought magnificently with only 14 men for most of the game after Andre Camel had badly hurt his shoulder. For a time they were reduced to 13 players through injuries. Wales had fielded the same pack throughout the championship tournament.

France: L Pellissier (Racing Club); A. Jaureguy (Stade Francais, capt.), Andre Behoteguy, Henri Behoteguy (Cognac), R Houdet (Stade Francais); A Verger (Stade Francais), C Dupont (Stade Bordelais); H Lacaze (Perigueux), F Camicas (Tarbes), J Sayrou (Perpignan), A Camel (Toulouse), R Majerus (Stade Francais), E Ribere, J Galia (Quillan), A Bioussa (Toulouse).

Wales: B O Male (Cardiff, capt.); *Gwyn Davies, B R. Turnbull (Cardiff), Roy Jones (Swansea), J Roberts (Cardiff); Windsor H Lewis (Maesteg), W C Powell

(London Welsh); F A Bowdler (Cross Keys), Cecil Pritchard (Pontypool). Harry Phillips (Newport), E M Jenkins (Aberavon), A Skym, Iorwerth Jones (Llanelli), T Hollingdale (Neath), Ivor Jones (Llanelli).

For France, Robert Houdet scored two tries. Andre Behoteguy converted one.

For Wales, Wick Powell scored a try.

Referee: R W Harland (Ireland).

Match 142 ENGLAND v WALES   Twickenham. January 19, 1929

England won by one goal, one try (8) to one try (3)

So often there had been valid excuses for Welsh failures at Twickenham that it was almost a relief to record that England thoroughly and unquestionably deserved this eighth consecutive win over Wales at Rugby H.Q. England's backs were endowed with greater gifts, natural and cultivated, and the few glints of brilliance came from them. Jack Bassett, considered a surprise full back choice because there were supposed to be three or four better men for the job, played magnificently on his debut. It was reported that the Welsh forwards "failed to deliver the goods." The Prince of Wales and a crowd of 58,000 saw the match.

England: T W Brown (Bristol); R W Smeddle (Durham), C D Aarvold (Blackheath), G M Sladen (United Services), G S Wilson (Tyldesley); H C C Laird (Harlequins), H Whitley (Northern); E Stanbury (Plymouth Albion), J S Tucker (Bristol), R T Foulds (Waterloo), R Cove-Smith (OMT, capt.), J W R. Swayne (Bridgwater), H G Periton (Waterloo), R H Sparks (Plymouth Albion), H Wilkinson (Halifax).

Wales: *J Bassett (Penarth); Gwyn Davies, J Roberts (Cardiff), W Guy Morgan (Swansea), *J C Morley (Newport); *W Roberts (Cardiff), W C Powell (London Welsh); D R Jenkins (Swansea), Cecil Pritchard (Pontypool), F A Bowdier (Cross Keys), T Arthur, *Harold Jones (Neath), *Robert Jones (London Welsh), Watcyn Thomas (Swansea), Ivor Jones (Llanelli, capt.).

For England, Harry Wilkinson scored two tries. Guy Wilson converted one.

For Wales, Jack Morley scored a try.

Referee: R W Harland (Ireland).

Match 143 WALES v SCOTLAND   St. Helen's, Swansea. February 2, 1929

Wales won by one goal, three tries (14) to one dropped goal, one penalty goal (7)

After seven matches with only one victory, Wales delighted their supporters in this first home success over Scotland since 1914. More important than the victory was the manner in which it was accomplished. For the first time in more than 10 years the Welsh backs really showed evidence of a return to the former days of glory. Three of the four Welsh tries were sparkling examples of skilled, combined play behind the scrum. It was reported: "This is an indication that the art of overcoming stern defences by straight running and accurate hand-to-hand passing, lost to Wales for a couple of decades, has been recaptured." John Roberts marked down Ian Smith ruthlessly and Harry Bowcott combined aggression with polish on his debut on a wet and slippery ground.

Wales: J Bassett (Penarth); J Roberts, *H M Bowcott (Cardiff), W Guy Morgan (Swansea, capt.), J C Morley (Newport); *Frank L Williams (Cardiff), W C Powell

(London Welsh); F A Bowdler (Cross Keys), Cecil Pritchard (Pontypool), *R Barrell (Cardiff), T Arthur, Harold Jones (Neath), *H Peacock (Newport), A E Broughton (Treorchy), Ivor Jones (Llanelii).

Scotland: T G Aitchison (Edinburgh Univ.); I S Smith (Edinburgh Univ.), T Gow Brown (Heriot's FP), J C Dykes, W M Simmers (Glasgow Acads.); A H Brown (Heriot's FP), J B Nelson (Glasgow Acads.); J M Bannerman (Glasgow HSFP, capt.), H S Mackintosh (West of Scotland), J R Paterson (Birkenhead Park), J A Beattie (Hawick), W V Berkley (London Scottish), R T Smith (Kelso), K M Wright (London Scottish), J W Allan (Melrose).

For Wales, John Roberts (2), Guy Morgan and Harry Peacock scored tries. Ivor Jones converted one.

For Scotland, Jimmy Dykes kicked a penalty goal. Alec Brown dropped a goal.

Referee: D Hellewell (England).

Match 144 WALES v FRANCE   Cardiff Arms Park. February 25, 1929

Wales won by one goal, one try (8) to one try (3)

The almost total eclipse of the Welsh backs as an attacking force was an unbelievable experience for the 45,000 spectators after the thrills of the previous game. France's stubborn tackling blotted out the Welsh attack and the visitors looked faster and every bit as effective as the home side. French full back Magnol was carried off the pitch by the crowd as a tribute to his superb performance on the slippery turf.

Wales: J Bassett (Penarth); J Roberts, H M Bowcott (Cardiff), W Guy Morgan (Swansea, capt.), J C Morley (Newport); Frank L Williams (Cardiff), W C Powell (London Welsh); R Barrell (Cardiff), Cecil Pritchard (Pontypool), T Arthur (Neath), F A Bowdler (Cross Keys), E M Jenkins (Aberavon), D Parker (Swansea), H Peacock (Newport), Ivor Jones (Llanelli).

France: L Magnol (Toulouse); A Domec (Carcassonne), A Behoteguy (Cognac, capt.), G Gerald (Racing Club), C Dulaurens (Toulouse); C Magnanou (Bayonne), L Serin (Beziers); R Bousquet (Toulon), F Camicas (Tarbes), J Sayrou (Perpignan), H Lacaze (Perigueux), A Camel, M Camel (Toulouse), J Auge (Dax), A Bioussa (Toulouse).

For Wales, Tom Arthur and Bob Barrell scored tries. Dai Parker converted one.

For France, Andre Camel scored a try.

Referee: H E B Wilkins (England).

Match 145 IRELAND v WALES   Ravenhill, Belfast. March 9, 1929

Drawn. Ireland one goal (5). Wales one goal (5)

"Science for a considerable period was forgotten and in its place came primitive fierceness and a terrific struggle for sheer physical supremacy. Men on both sides rocked and reeled in the course of the battle." That was how the Western Mail described this drawn tussle, which a veteran member of the WRU said was the most desperately fought forward engagement he had ever witnessed. "For those who enjoy the physical aspect it was a game not without a powerful appeal," wrote another correspondent.

George Stephenson had a last-minute chance to win the match for Ireland with a penalty shot from a reasonable position. It was an agonising moment for Arthur Bowdler as he waited for the kick to be taken, and a great relief when it missed. He had been penalised, some said harshly, for a fractional and unintentional off-side infringement, by referee J. McGill (Scotland), who was attired in lounge coat, waistcoat and grey Oxford bags. Four Welsh forwards needed treatment, including Tom Arthur (dislocated thumb) and Arthur Lemon (dislocated finger).

Ireland: W J Stewart (North of Ireland);, R M Byers, G V Stephenson (North of Ireland, capt.), M P Crowe, J E Arigho (Lansdowne); E O'D. Davy (Lansdowne), M Sugden (Wanderers); H C Browne (United Services), C T Payne (North of Ireland), J L Farrell, M Deering (Bective), C J Hanrahan (Dolphin), S J Cagney (London Irish), G R Beamish (RAF), J D Clinch (Wanderers).

Wales: J Bassett (Penarth); J Roberts, H M Bowcott (Cardiff), W Guy Morgan (Swansea, capt.), J C Morley (Newport); Frank L Williams (Cardiff), W C Powell (London Welsh); F A Bowdler (Cross Keys), Cecil Pritchard (Pontypool), D Parker (Swansea), T Arthur (Neath), R Barrell (Cardiff), *A Lemon (Neath), H Peacock (Newport}, Ivor Jones (Llanelli).

For Ireland, Eugene Davy scored a try. George Stephenson converted.

For Wales, Frank Williams scored a try. Dai Parker converted.

Referee: J MacGill (Scotland).

Match 146 **WALES v ENGLAND**   Cardiff Arms Park. January 18, 1930

England won by one goal, one penalty goal, one try (11) to one try (3)

Sam Tucker, flown from Bristol shortly before the start as a replacement for Henry Rew (Exeter), played the game of his life. His experience as hooker enabled England to dominate the scrums. Welsh pack-leader Ivor Jones could not raise any marked degree of enthusiasm from his fellow forwards, who were condemned as being slovenly and careless. Malir and Robson smother-tackled in midfield and the only flashes of attacking skill came from Jack Morley, with his love of the unorthodox. England went on to win the championship.

Wales: J Bassett (Penarth); J C Morley (Newport), H M Bowcott (Cardiff, capt.), *T E Jones-Davies (London Welsh), *A Hickman (Neath); Frank L Williams (Cardiff), *D E A Roberts (Oxford Univ.); T Arthur (Neath), F A Bowdler (Cross Keys), A Skym (Cardiff), D Parker (Swansea), E M Jenkins (Aberavon), *W T Thomas (Abertillery), T Hollingdale (Neath), Ivor Jones (Llanelli).

England: J G Askew (Cambridge Univ.); A L Novis (Blackheath), F W S Malir (Otley), M Robson (Oxford Univ.), J S R Reeve (Harlequins); R S Spong, W H Sobey (Old Millhillians); D A Kendrew (Leicester), J S Tucker (Bristol), A H Bateson (Otley), J W Forrest (United Services), B H Black, W E Tucker (Blackheath), P D Howard (Old Millhillians), H G Periton (Waterloo, capt.).

For England, Jimmy Reeve scored two tries. Brian Black converted one and kicked a penalty goal.

For Wales, Tommy Jones-Davies scored a try.

Referee: R W Jeffares (Ireland).

Match 147 **SCOTLAND v WALES**   Murrayfield. February 1, 1930

Scotland won by one goal, one dropped goal, one try (12) to one goal, one dropped goal (9)

A last-minute dropped goal by fly-half Herbert Waddell pipped Wales just when it looked as if Ivor Jones's team would snatch a 9-8 victory. The crowd of some 60,000 saw the Welsh pack show considerably more zest and purpose, but the centres were too slow and orthodox. Wick Powell produced flashes of his old skill and Wales had chances galore. It could be said that Wales were a better side than Scotland everywhere except in the vital matter of producing scores. Bobby Rowand was pulled out of the scrum to help the hard-pressed Scots' defence in the second half. It was Ivor Jones's last game for Wales after playing in 16 internationals.

Scotland: R C Warren (Glasgow Acads.); I S Smith (London Scottish), G P S Macpherson (Edinburgh Acads., capt.), T M Hart (Glasgow Univ.), W M Simmers (Glasgow Acads.); H Waddell, J B. Nelson (Glasgow Acads.); W B Welsh (Hawick), H S Mackintosh (West of Scotland), J A Beattie, R A Foster (Hawick), R T Smith (Kelso), W C Agnew (Stewart's Coll., FP), R Rowand (Glasgow HSFP), F H Waters (London Scottish).

Wales: J Bassett (Penarth); Gwyn Davies, B R Turnbull, *Graham Jones, *R W Boon (Cardiff); Frank L Williams (Cardiff), W C Powell (London Welsh); T Arthur (Neath), *H C Day (Newport), A Skym (Cardiff), E M Jenkins (Aberavon), *D Thomas (Swansea), A Lemon (Neath), H W Peacock (Newport), Ivor Jones (Llanelli, capt.).

For Scotland, Max Simmers scored two tries. Frank Waters converted one. Herbert Waddell dropped a goal.

For Wales, Graham Jones scored a try and dropped a goal. Ivor Jones converted the try.

Referee: Dr J R Wheeler (Ireland).

Match 148 **WALES v IRELAND**   St. Helen's, Swansea. March 8, 1930

Wales won by one penalty goal, three tries (12) to one dropped goal, one penalty goal (7)

Ireland's hopes were high of winning the Triple Crown for the first time since 1899. Their confidence soared as Eugene Davy dropped a goal from 40 yards after only two minutes. Then the 50,000 watchers saw a tremendous struggle develop with the lead changing hands. Jack Bassett, in his first game as captain, did not make a single mistake. His tackling was devastating and one particularly ferocious tackle smashed down Davy when Ireland looked like scoring. It was said that Bassett saved at least three tries.

George Stephenson, who had played in every match against Wales since 1920, was making his world record 42nd and final appearance. He captained Ireland. After Davy's dropped goal, Archie Skym thundered away on a 40-yard gallop from a line-out for a spectacular Welsh try. Then, after two minutes of the second half, Harry Peacock and Howie Jones dived simultaneously for a try, but Murray's penalty goal put Ireland back in the lead at 7-6. Bassett popped over a penalty to swing Wales into the lead before Wick Powell broke away and made a try for Tom Arthur, who had distinguished himself with his line-out 'flip' during the game.

Wales: J Bassett (Penarth, capt.); J C Morley (Newport), T E Jones-Davies (London Welsh), W Guy Morgan (Guy's Hosp.), *Howie Jones (Swansea); Frank L Williams (Cardiff), W C Powell (London Welsh); T Arthur (Neath), H C Day (Newport), E M Jenkins (Aberavon), A Skym (Cardiff), D Thomas (Swansea), A Lemon (Neath), H W Peacock (Newport), *N Fender (Cardiff).

Ireland: W F Williamson (Dolphin); G V Stephenson (London Hosp., capt.), E O'D. Davy, M P Crowe, J E Arigho (Lansdowne); P F Murray, M Sugden (Wanderers); H O'Neill (Queen's Univ., Belfast), C J Hanrahan (Dolphin), C T Payne (North of Ireland), M J Dunne (Lansdowne), J L Farrell (Bective), N F Murphy (Cork Constitution), G R Beamish (Leicester) , J D Clinch (Wanderers).

For Wales Archie Skym, Tom Arthur and jointly Howie Jones and Harry Peacock scored tries. Jack Bassett kicked a penalty goal.

For Ireland, Eugene Davy dropped a goal. Paul Murray kicked a penalty goal.

Referee: D Hellewell (England).

Match 149 FRANCE v WALES   Colombes, Paris. April 21, 1930

Wales won by two dropped goals, one try (11) to nil

"For sheer wanton brutality and savagery this match can surely never be approached in the annals of rugby football," wrote the Western Mail correspondent. "It was a game that will long be talked about for the ferocious conduct of some of the players." The Welshmen were not slow to retaliate, but were not the instigators of the trouble. Hubert Day, the Newport hooker, was punched in the mouth and carried off to have nine stitches in his lip, which was almost severed from his face. "Fists were flying like flails," said a report, "and there were many cases of injury caused by malice." A week after this Easter Monday match, the French Federation announced they had banned one of their famous forwards from playing again in an international match.

The atmosphere was tense from the start because France would become the international champions for the first time if they won. With this incentive they went in with win-at-all costs methods in one of the most infamous matches in the history of the game. One remarkable incident occurred when referee D Hellewell (England) penalised a Welsh forward for throwing a punch. Immediately, the secretary of the French Federation, Cyril Rutherford, rushed on to the field to inform the referee that the punch was provoked by an equally unsporting act by a French player. Claude Davey made his debut and looked a thrustful centre.

France: M Piquemal (Tarbes); J Taillantou (Paloise), G Gerald (Racing Club), R Graciet (SBUC), R Samatan (Agen); C Maganou (Bayonne), L Serin (Beziers); J Choy (Narbonne), A Ambert (Toulouse), R Bousquet (Albi), R Majerus (Stade Francais), A Camel (Toulouse), E Ribere (capt.), J Gallia (Quillan), A Bioussa (Toulouse).

Wales: *T Scourfield (Torquay); Howie Jones (Swansea), W Guy Morgan (capt.), *E C Davey (Swansea), R W Boon (Cardiff); Frank L Williams (Cardiff), W C Powell (London Welsh); *Edgar Jones (Llanelli), H C Day (Newport), T Arthur (Neath), A Skym (Cardiff), E M Jenkins (Aberavon), A Lemon (Neath), H W Peacock (Newport), N Fender (Cardiff).

For Wales, Archie Skym scored a try. Guy Morgan and Wick Powell dropped goals.

Referee: D Hellewell (England).

Match 150 ENGLAND v WALES   Twickenham. January 17, 1931

Drawn. England one goal, two penalty goals (11).
Wales one goal, one goal from a mark and one try (11)

Wales's ninth visit to Twickenham had every indication of bringing their long-sought first victory as they led 11-8 with only three minutes remaining. Then a blast on the whistle gave a penalty to England for 'feet across' in a scrum. Brian Black kicked at goal from five yards inside the Welsh half and sent the ball sailing over the bar for a draw. The bogy had kept its reputation. Though neither side produced a high standard, Wales looked a little better than the home side.

A controversial incident occurred when Don Burland attempted to convert his own try for

England. Neither touch judge signalled a goal and it was not until half time that referee Dr J R Wheeler (Ireland) had the scoreboard amended to include two points for the conversion kick, for which he over-ruled the touch judges. Those two points were to deprive Wales of the Triple Crown. Also of unusual interest was Jack Powell's goal from a mark. The English players, perhaps, thought he was taking a penalty kick, because no defenders charged the ball when he coolly placed it on the ground and measured his run.

England: L L Bedford (Headingley); J S R Reeve (Harlequins), D W Burland (Bristol), M A McCanlis (Gloucester), C D Aarvold (Headingley); T J M Barrington (Bristol), E B Pope (Blackheath); H Rew (Exeter), J S Tucker (Bristol, capt.), M S Bonaventura, B H Black (Blackheath), J W Forrest (United Services), D H Swayne (Oxford Univ.), P D Howard (Old Millhillians), R F Davey (Leytonstone).

Wales: J Bassett (Penarth capt.); J C Morley (Newport), E C Davey (Swansea), T E Jones-Davies (London Welsh), R W Boon (Cardiff); H M Bowcott (Cardiff), W C Powell (London Welsh); A Skym (Cardiff), H C Day (Newport), T Arthur (Neath), *T Day (Swansea), E M Jenkins (Aberavon), A Lemon (Neath), Watcyn Thomas (Swansea), N Fender (Cardiff).

For England, Don Burland scored a try and converted. Brian Black kicked two penalty goals.

For Wales, Jack Morley and Tommy Jones-Davies scored tries. Jack Bassett converted one. Wick Powell kicked a goal from a mark.

Referee: Dr Jim R Wheeler (Ireland).

Match 151 **WALES v SCOTLAND** Cardiff Arms Park. February 7, 1931

Wales won by two goals, one try (13) to one goal, one try (8)

Watcyn Thomas, the Welsh pack-leader, fractured his collar-bone, but refused to leave the field – and scored a vital try. It was a feat comparable with that by another great Welsh forward, Dick Hellings, of Llwynypia, who scored a try with a broken arm against England at Gloucester in 1900. A try in the last few minutes by Ronnie Boon, converted by Jack Bassett, clinched this victory, which was achieved despite the poor form of the Welsh backs. Wales were a collection of individuals rather than a team. The gates were closed to non-ticket holders almost an hour before the start and more than 50,000 watched the game, which began early to avoid trouble.

Wales: J Bassett (Penarth, capt.); J C Morley (Newport), E C Davey (Swansea), T E Jones-Davies (London Welsh), R W Boon (Cardiff) ; H M Bowcott (Cardiff), W C Powell (London Welsh); A Skym (Cardiff), H C Day (Newport), T Day (Swansea), T Arthur (Neath), E M Jenkins (Aberavon), A Lemon (Neath), Watcyn Thomas (Swansea), N. Fender (Cardiff).

Scotland: R W Langrish (London Scottish); I S Smith (London Scottish), G P S Macpherson (Edinburgh Acads.), W M Simmers (Glasgow Acads.), G Wood (Gala); H Lind (Dunfermline), J B Nelson (Glasgow Acads.); J W Allan (Melrose), W N Roughead (London Scottish, capt.), H S Mackintosh (West of Scotland), A W Walker (Birkenhead Park), J A Beattie, W B Welsh (Hawick), J S Wilson (St. Andrew's Univ.), D Crichton-Miller (Gloucester).

For Wales, Jack Morley, Watcyn Thomas and Ronnie Boon scored tries. Jack Bassett converted two.

For Scotland, Donald Crichton-Miller scored two tries. John Allan converted one.

Referee: J G Bott (England).

Wales won by five goals, one dropped goal, two tries (35) to one try (3)

Hubert Day, the Newport hooker, had been chosen by Wales but was not allowed to play. Day had been sent off at Rodney Parade a week before this match in Newport's 3-0 win over Cardiff. He was involved in an incident at a line-out with Cardiff forward T M Williams, who also was ordered to leave the field. As he was under automatic suspension until his case could be discussed by the WRU disciplinary committee, Day could not take his place in the Welsh team. The selectors decided not to call in another specialist hooker. They switched Tom Day from prop and brought in D R James to pack in the front row.

After the fiery forward play and accusations of "brutality" in their game of the previous year, it was with some apprehension that Wales met France. But the French forwards, who had been lions at Colombes, were lambs in the snow-storm of a bitterly cold day. The collapse of the French pack let Wales sweep in for their biggest win since before the First World War. Arthur Lemon was in grand form as an open-side wing forward and four of the seven tries came as a result of his constructive methods. France were handicapped because centre Clement suffered a dislocated shoulder early in the match, which featured a snow storm shortly after the start.

This was the last game between Wales and France until the countries met in the Victory International series in 1945-46. The home unions cancelled fixtures after 1931, following the breakaway of 12 important clubs from the French Federation.

Wales: J Bassett (Penarth, capt.); J C Morley (Newport), E C Davey (Swansea), Frank L Williams, R W Boon (Cardiff); *A R Ralph (Newport), W C Powell (London Welsh); A Skym (Cardiff), T Day (Swansea), *D R James (Treorchy), T Arthur (Neath), E M Jenkins (Aberavon), A Lemon (Neath), *J Lang (Llanelli), N Fender (Cardiff).

France: M Savy (Montferrand); R Samatan (Agen), P Clement (Racing Club), M Vigerie, L Augras (Agen); L Servole (Toulon), L Serin (Beziers); J Duhau, R Scohy (Bordeaux), M Rodrigo (Mauleon), P Barrere (Toulon), E Camo (Villeneuve), C Petit (Nancy), J Galia (Villeneuve), E Ribere (Quillan, capt.).

For Wales, Raymond Ralph (2), Claude Davey, Norman Fender, Jim Lang, Frank Williams and Tom Arthur scored tries. Jack Bassett converted five. Wick Powell dropped a goal.

For France, Charles Petit scored a try.

Referee: R W Harland (Ireland).

Wales won by one goal, one dropped goal, two tries (15) to one try (3)

Victory for Ireland meant the Triple Crown. Success for Wales would bring the championship for the first time since 1922. So a capacity crowd of 30,000 packed into the Ravenhill ground, a hollow surrounded by wooded hills, and it looked a picture in the brilliant sunshine of a perfect day. With eight tearaway forwards, Ireland were opponents to be dreaded; but when their pack were reduced to seven men throughout the second half they were even more fearsome. It was as well for Wales that their backs showed rare opportunism to win the match.

Even with Morgan Crowe off with concussion after the interval and Noel Murphy having to leave the pack as replacement, Ireland never gave up attacking. Jack Bassett and Claude Davey were compelled to tackle with deadly impact, such as when Bassett crashed into Arigho as the Irishman passed to Murphy, and Davey hit Murphy as he received the ball. Both Irish players were knocked unconscious.

Wales also suffered casualties. Wick Powell was dazed and sprained his ankle. Bassett opened an old wound on his head and Ned Jenkins injured his neck, which caused partial paralysis. But they all stayed on the field to fight off the fiery 'Jammie' Clinch and his predators. At the after-match dinner, Irish president James Musgrave bewailed the fact that it was always Ireland's fate to meet Wales in this last match for the Triple Crown.

Ireland: D P Morris (Bective); E J Lightfoot, E O'D Davy, M P Crowe, J E Arigho (Lansdowne); P F Murray, M Sugden (Wanderers, capt.) ; H H C Withers (North of Ireland), J Russell (Univ. Coll., Cork)), J A E Siggins (Belfast Collegians), V J Pike (Lansdowne), J L Farrell (Bective), N Murphy (Cork Constitution), G R Beamish (RAF), J D Clinch (Wanderers).

Wales: J Bassett (Penarth, capt.); J C Morley (Newport), E C Davey (Swansea),Frank L Williams, R W Boon (Cardiff); A R Ralph (Newport), W C Powell (London Welsh); A Skym (Cardiff), T Day (Swansea), D R James (Treorchy), T Arthur (Neath), E M Jenkins (Aberavon), A Lemon (Neath), J Lang (Llanelli), N Fender (Cardiff).

For Wales, Jack Morley (2) and Claude Davey scored tries. Jack Bassett converted one. Raymond Ralph dropped a goal.

For Ireland. Jack Siggins scored a try.

Referee: M A Allan (Scotland).

Match 154 WALES v SOUTH AFRICA St. Helen's, Swansea. December 5, 1931

South Africa won by one goal, one try (8) to one try (3)

Probably this was the finest performance of his career by Welsh captain and full back Jack Bassett in the deluge that transformed the pitch into a lake. But he made the biggest tactical mistake possible when he permitted his side to keep on passing in attack. Benny Osler, the Springboks' skipper, employed the classical wet weather formula of kick and rush and it won the match. So, for the third time, South Africa beat Wales, and the crowd of some 40,000 watched miserably in the downpour. It was so wet that no attempt was made to play the national anthems before the kick-off.

Osler kicked high punts for his fast-following spoilers to get among the anxiously waiting defenders and it was fortunate for Wales that Bassett was so rock-like in his catching and accurate in clearing. He was easily the outstanding personality of the match. All the tries were obtained from chasing kicks. Swansea wing forward Will Davies scored for Wales on his debut and gave his side a 3-0 lead at half time.

George Daneel scored an equalising try, although Claude Davey thought he had minored the ball first and Wales did not look too happy about this decision. Then Ferdie Bergh charged over for the second Springbok try and Osler converted. The Welsh backs found themselves deeply embedded in the morass and easy targets for the hard-tackling tourists, who were delighted to see Wick Powell throwing out a stream of passes to try to get his attackers running. Years later, the lessons of this defeat were still ignored against South Africa.

Wales: J Bassett (Penarth, capt.); J C Morley (Newport), E C Davey (Swansea), Frank L Williams, R W Boon (Cardiff); A R Ralph (Newport), W C Powell (London Welsh); T Day (Swansea), F A Bowdler (Cross Keys), A Skym (Cardiff), T Arthur (Neath), E M Jenkins (Aberavon), *Will Davies, Watcyn Thomas (Swansea), A Lemon (Neath).

South Africa: G Brand; M Zimerman, B G Gray, J White, F D Venter; B L Osler (capt.), D Craven; P J Mostert, H G Kipling, M M 'Boy' Louw, A van der Merwe, F Bergh, P J Nel, G M Daneel, J A Macdonald.

For South Africa, George Daneel and Ferdie Bergh scored tries. Benny Osler converted one.

For Wales, Will Davies scored a try.

Referee: E Holmes (England).

Match 155 WALES v ENGLAND   St. Helen's, Swansea. January 16, 1932

Wales won by one goal, one dropped goal, one penalty goal (12) to one goal (5)

A remarkable 'spooned' dropped goal from short range by Ronnie Boon, that was described as almost a freak score, helped Wales to this first win over England for 10 years. Boon, the boy from Barry, also scored a try and earned the reputation as the best wing in Britain this season. Arthur Lemon was a masterpiece of destruction as he forced fly half Roger Spong to stand deeper and deeper. The Prince of Wales watched among the disappointingly small crowd of 30,000.

Wales: J Bassett (Penarth, capt.); J C Morley (Newport), E C Davey (Swansea), Frank L Williams, R W Boon (Cardiff); A R Ralph (Newport), W C Powell (London Welsh); T Day (Swansea), F A Bowdler (Cross Keys), A Skym (Cardiff), E M Jenkins (Aberavon), D Thomas, Will Davies, Watcyn Thomas (Swansea), A Lemon (Neath).

England: R J Barr (Leicester); C C Tanner (Gloucester), R A Gerrard (Bath), J A Tallent, C D Aarvold (Blackheath, capt.); R S Spong, W H Sobey (Old Millhillians); G G Gregory (Bristol), D J Norman (Leicester), N L Evans (RNEC, Devonport), R G S Hobbs (Richmond), C S H Webb (Devonport Services), L E Saxby (Gloucester), F Coley (Northampton), J McD Hodgson (Northern).

For Wales, Ronnie Boon scored a try and dropped a goal. Jack Bassett converted the try and kicked a penalty goal.

For England, Charlie Webb scored a try. Bobby Barr converted.

Referee: F J C Moffatt (Scotland).

Match 156 SCOTLAND v WALES   Murrayfield. February 6, 1932

Wales won by one penalty goal, one try (6) to nil

Wales were worthy winners of a "gloriously robust forward battle", and so only Ireland stood between them and the Triple Crown, which Wales had not won for 21 years. A record contingent of 12,000 Welshmen made the trek to Murrayfield to swell the crowd to 65,000. Watcyn Thomas, Archie Skym and Arthur Lemon were outstanding in the Welsh pack, but collective brilliance was missing in a generally untidy game.

'Dick' Ralph was considered one of Newport's finest backs between the wars and won many matches on his own with his loping glide. He was also an outstanding defender and resourceful tactician, but played only six games for Wales as outside half before turning professional with Leeds.

Scotland: T H B Lawther (Old Millhillians); I S Smith (London Scottish), W M Simmers (Glasgow Acads., capt.), D St. J Clair-Ford (United Services), G Wood (Gala); H Lind (Dunfermline), W R Logan (Edinburgh Univ.); J W Allan

(Melrose), W N Roughead (London Scottish), J A Beattie, W B Welsh (Hawick), H S Mackintosh (West of Scotland), M S Stewart (Stewart's Coll., FP), J Graham (Kelso), F H Waters (London Scottish).

Wales: J Bassett (Penarth, capt.); J C Morley (Newport), E C Davey (Swansea), Frank L Williams, R W Boon (Cardiff); A R Ralph (Newport), W C Powell (London Welsh); A Skym (Cardiff), F A Bowdler (Cross Keys), T Day, D Thomas (Swansea), E M Jenkins (Aberavon), Will Davies, Watcyn Thomas (Swansea), A Lemon (Neath).

For Wales, Ronnie Boon scored a try. Jack Bassett kicked a penalty goal.

Referee: T Bell (Ireland).

Match 157   WALES v IRELAND   Cardiff Arms Park. March 12, 1932

Ireland won by four tries (12) to one dropped goal, two tries (10)

Jack Bassett's last game for Wales, and his 15th cap, will be remembered always for his blunders. It is one of the cruel jabs that accompany fame that mistakes are remembered before the brilliant moments. The Welsh captain gave away two tries. First, when Eugene Davy dropped at goal and missed, Bassett called that he would field, but lost the ball and Ned Lightfoot was left with an easy try. Then, with a "trance-like pose", he watched Sean Waide race past him to score after a fantastic 90-yard run.

Even then, Bassett had a chance to at least draw the game and at the same time give Wales the championship with the last kick of the match, the conversion attempt of Raymond 'Dicky' Ralph's try. But Bassett was nowhere near with it and Ireland had stopped Wales winning the Triple Crown. It must have been some satisfaction for the Irish, who had been foiled at the last fence on five occasions by Wales – in 1905, 1911, 1926, 1930 and 1931. All round, Ireland were the better side. Boon and Morley missed their chances and once Dai Thomas was over the Irish line, but lost the ball before he could touch down. But they all blamed Bassett.

Wales: J Bassett (Penarth, capt.); J C Morley (Newport), E C Davey (Swansea), Frank L Williams, R W Boon (Cardiff); A R Ralph (Newport), W C Powell (London Welsh); A Skym (Cardiff), F A Bowdler (Cross Keys), T Day, D Thomas (Swansea), E M Jenkins (Aberavon), Will Davies, Walcyn Thomas (Swansea), A Lemon (Neath).

Ireland: E C Ridgeway (Wanderers); E J Lightfoot, M P Crowe (Lansdowne), E W F de V Hunt, S L Waide (Army); E O'D Davy (Lansdowne), P Murray (Wanderers); J L Farrell (Bective), C J Hanrahan (Dolphin), V J Pike, M J Dunne (Lansdowne), J L Siggins (Befast Collegians), W McC Ross (Queen's Univ., Belfast), G R Beamish (RAF, capt.), N Murphy (Cork Constitution).

For Ireland, 'Mac' Ross (2), Eddie Lightfoot and Shaun Waide scored tries.

For Wales, Claude Davey and Raymond Ralph scored tries. Ralph dropped a goal.

Referee: E Holmes (England).

Match 158   ENGLAND v WALES   Twickenham. January 21, 1933

Wales won by one dropped goal, one try (7) to one try (3)

Ronnie Boon's day of glory in front of a record championship match crowd of 64,000, including the Prince of Wales, brought Wales their historic first win at Twickenham after a 23-

year wait. England led 3-0 at half time following a doubtful try by fly half Elliot, who did not seem to ground the ball when he was tackled. Within a minute of the second half starting, the alert Boon dropped his neat goal from a handy position when the ball came back from a maul. Then Boon was sent racing away and in at the corner and round to the posts for a try. Everyone thought Viv Jenkins had converted as the Welsh touch judge flagged a goal and the points were registered on the score-board. But after the match, referee Tom Bell (Ireland) said he had not allowed the goal.

It was a triumph for resourcefulness, stamina and leadership rather than a reward for brilliant attacking rugby. Watcyn Thomas, in his first game as captain, led a pack which thoroughly tamed England in the loose and line-out. Harry Bowcott proved a dominating Welsh figure, particularly with his touch kicking, placed with unerring accuracy. It broke the spirit of the home side, who had had the better of the first half. This match saw the first appearances by Viv Jenkins and Wilf Wooller. Wooller, aged 20, was still attending Rydal School. He made one superb tackle after chasing and catching Elliot, who seemed to be clear. England lost Ron Gerrard and had to withdraw Bolton from the pack as replacement. Gerrard temporarily lost the sight of one eye when Claude Davey handed him off.

During this season the International Board's recommendation that the principle of first forwards on the spot should be the first forwards down in the scrummage was given a trial. The International Board felt that over-specialisation was harmful to the game. So Wales chose only one recognised wing forward in Iorrie Isaacs.

England: T W Brown (Bristol); L A Booth (Headingley) D W Burland (Bristol), R A Gerrard (Bath), C D Aarvold (Blackheath, capt.); W Elliot (United Services), A Key (Old Cranleighans); N L Evans (RN), G G Gregory (Bristol), R J Longland (Northampton), C S H. Webb (Devonport Services), A D S Roncoroni (Richmond), A Vaughan-Jones (Army), B H Black (Blackheath), R Bolton (Wakefield).

Wales: *V G J Jenkins (Bridgend); R W Boon (Cardiff), E C Davey (Swansea), *W Wooller (Rydall School and Colwyn Bay), *A H Jones (Cardiff); H M Bowcott (London Welsh), *M J Turnbull (Cardiff) ; Edgar Jones, *Bryn Evans (Llanelli), A Skym (Cardiff), *R B Jones (Cambridge Univ.), D Thomas (Swansea), T Arthur (Neath), Watcyn Thomas (Swansea, capt.), *I Isaacs (Cardiff).

For Wales, Ronnie Boon scored a try and dropped a goal.

For England, Wally Elliot scored a try.

Referee: T Bell (Ireland).

Match 159 **WALES v SCOTLAND**　　　　　　St. Helen's, Swansea. February 4, 1933

Scotland won by one goal, one penalty goal, one try (11) to one try (3)

The Scottish team arrived in Wales on the same train as a funeral party, but this was far from an ill-omen for Ian Smith's men. Only the crash tackling of Claude Davey saved Wales from being routed. Gwyn Bayliss replaced Viv Jenkins, who withdrew with a septic arm. The Scottish forwards dominated, though Wales were without Dai Thomas for most of the second half through injury. Scotland went on to win the Triple Crown for the seventh time. Because Maurice Turnbull withdrew with injury, the selectors asked Harry Bowcott to stand down from the fly-half position so that they could bring in the Swansea pair Ron Morris and Bryn Evans to make their debut appearances.

Wales: *G Bayliss (Pontypool); A Hickman (Neath), E C Davey (Swansea), W Wooller (Rydal School and Colwyn Bay), A H Jones (Cardiff); *R R Morris, *Bryn Evans (Swansea); Edgar Jones, Bryn Evans (Llanelli), A Skym (Cardiff), R B Jones

(Cambridge Univ.), D. Thomas (Swansea), T Arthur (Neath), Watcyn Thomas (Swansea, capt.), I Isaacs (Cardiff).

Scotland: D I Brown (Cambridge Univ.); I S Smith (London Scottish, capt.), H D B Lorraine (Oxford Univ.), H Lind (Dunfermline), K C Fyfe (Cambridge Univ.); K L T Jackson (Oxford Univ.), W R Logan (Edinburgh Acads.); J M Ritchie (Watsonians), J McL Henderson (Edinburgh Acads.), M S Stewart (Stewart's (Coll., FP), W B Welsh, J A Beattie (Hawick), J R Thom (Watsonians), R Rowand (Glasgow HSFP), J A Waters (Selkirk).

For Scotland, Ian Smith and 'Kiltie' Jackson scored tries. Ken Fyfe converted one and kicked a penalty goal.

For Wales, Tom Arthur scored a try.

Referee: J G Bott (England).

Match 160 IRELAND v WALES   Ravenhill, Belfast. March 11, 1933

Ireland won by one dropped goal, one penalty goal, one try (10) to one goal (5)

Harry Bowcott scored one of the best individual tries in any international match for a number of years, but his score came in the last few minutes and Wales were a well beaten side. Only Bowcott, who remained cool and calculating, and Viv Jenkins, with a masterly display, looked top-class players. Wooller seemed wasted on the wing. Arthur Bowdler (15 caps), Watcyn Thomas (14) and Arthur Lemon (13) made their final appearances for Wales.

Ireland: R H Pratt (Dublin Univ.); E J Lightfoot, M P Crowe (Lansdowne), R. J. Barnes (Dublin Univ.), S L Waide (North of Ireland); E O'D. Davy (Lansdowne), P F Murray (Wanderers) ; M J Dunne, V J Pike (Lansdowne), H O'Neill, J Russell (UC, Cork), J A E Siggins (Belfast Collegians), C E St. J Beamish (North of Ireland), G R Beamish (Leicester, capt.), W McC. Ross (Queen's Univ., Belfast).

Wales: V G J Jenkins (Bridgend); W Wooller (Rydal School and Colwyn Bay), Frank L Williams, Graham Jones, R W Boon (Cardiff); H M Bowcott (London Welsh), M J Turnbull (Cardiff); Edgar Jones (Llanelli), F A Bowdler (Cross Keys), A Skym (Cardiff), *W J Moore (Bridgend), R Barrell, *Lewis Rees (Cardiff), Watcyn Thomas (Swansea, capt.), A Lemon (Neath).

For Ireland, Bob Barnes scored a try. Eugene Davy dropped a goal. Jack Siggins kicked a penalty goal.

For Wales, Harry Bowcott scored a try. Viv Jenkins converted.

Referee: Malcolm A Alln (Scotland).

Match 161 WALES v ENGLAND   Cardiff Arms Park. January 20, 1934.

England won by three tries (9) to nil

The 82 ft. high north grandstand, with seats for 5,242 and costing the WRU some £20,000, was opened and a record attendance of more than 50,000 paid record receipts of over £9,000. But Welsh supporters saw their forwards routed as the team, with 13 new caps, including fly half Cliff Jones, failed dismally on the slippery turf. Only faulty handling prevented England building a big score. Cliff Jones took a pounding without flinching and his clever screw kicking was one of the few pleasing features for Wales, who failed for the first time in 21 years to score against England. Bernard Gadney's team went on to win the Triple Crown for the ninth time. Bryn Howells replaced the unfit Viv Jenkins.

Wales: *Bryn Howells (Llanelli); *B T V Cowey (Newport and The Welch Regiment), E C Davey, *J Idwal Rees (Swansea), *G R R Jones (London Welsh); *C WJones (Porth and Cambridge Univ.), *Dan Evans (Barry and Cheshire); *Ken Jones (Monmouth and London Welsh), *J R Evans (Newport, capt.), *H Truman (Llanelli),*Gomer Hughes (Penarth), D Thomas (Swansea), *Glyn Prosser (Neath), C R Davies (RAF and London Welsh), *A M Rees (London Welsh).

England: H G Owen-Smith (Oxford Univ.); A L Warr, P Cranmer (Oxford Univ.), R A Gerrard (Bath), G W C Meikle (Waterloo); W Elliot (United Services), B C Gadney (Leicester, capt.); R J Longland (Northampton), G G Gregory (Bristol), H Rew (Exeter), J C Wright (Metropolitan Police), J Dicks (Northampton), J McD Hodgson (Northern), P C Hordern (Gloucester), H A Fry.(Liverpool).

For England, Graham Meikle (2) and Tim Warr scored tries.

Referee: Frank W Haslett (Ireland).

Match 162 **SCOTLAND v WALES**   Murrayfield. February 3, 1934

Wales won by two goals, one try (13) to one penalty goal, one try (6)

Cliff Jones was brilliant in his second game to thrill a contingent of 15,000 Welshmen among the 60,000 crowd. He was the man of the match with his midfield thrusts, sidestepping and swerving through the Scots' defence in irrepressible style. It was a well earned team victory and a much improved performance by Wales, though Scotland fought back from being 10 points down to reach 10–6 at one stage with a worrying rally. Jim Lang and Gomer Hughes shone in the line-out.

Scotland: K W Marshall (Edinburgh Acads.); R W Shaw (Glasgow HSFP), R C S Dick (Cambridge Univ.), H Lind (Dunfermline, capt.), J Park (Royal HSFP); K L T Jackson (Oxford Univ.), W R Logan (Edinburgh Wands.); W A Burnet (West of Scotland), L B Lambie (Glasgow HSFP), J M Ritchie (Watsonians), J D Lowe (Heriot's FP), M S Stewart (Stewart's Coll., FP), D A Thom (London Scottish), R Rowand (Glasgow HSFP), J A Waters (Selkirk).

Wales: V G J Jenkins (Bridgend); B T V Cowey (Newport and The Welch Regiment), E C Davey (capt.), J Idwal Rees (Swansea), G R R Jones (London Welsh); C W Jones (Porth and Cambridge Univ.), *Bert Jones (Llanelli); T Day (Swansea), *Iorwerth Evans (London Welsh), *D R Prosser (Neath), Gomer Hughes (Penarth), *W Ward (Cross Keys), Glyn Prosser (Neath), J Lang (Llanelli), *A. Fear (Newport).

For Wales, 'Bunny' Cowey (2) and Idwal Rees scored tries. Viv Jenkins converted two.

For Scotland, Ross Logan scored a try. Jim Ritchie kicked a penalty goal.

Referee: H L V Day (England).

Match 163 **WALES v IRELAND**   St. Helen's, Swansea. March 10, 1934

Wales won by two goals, one try (13) to nil

In a fantastic finish, Wales scored 13 points in the last six minutes. Full back Viv Jenkins started the scoring burst with a 30-yard run, linking with Idwal Rees and Arthur Bassett, before finishing off the attack himself with a try, which he converted. Never before had a Welsh team full back scored a try in an international match and it was 33 years before the feat was repeated – when Keith Jarrett did it against England at Cardiff on his debut in 1967. Irish full back Dan

Langan broke his collar-bone in the closing stages and their defence cracked after they had played more purposefully than either England or Scotland had done against Wales. Albert Fear's work was an outstanding example of wing forward craft in disrupting the Irish back division.

Wales: V G J Jenkins (Bridgend); B T V Cowey (Newport and The Welch Regiment), E C Davey (capt.), J. Idwal Rees (Swansea), *Arthur Bassett (Aberavon); C W Jones (Cambridge Univ.), Bert Jones (Llanelli); T Day (Swansea), Iorwerth Evans (London Welsh), D R Prosser (Neath), Gomer Hughes (Penarth), W Ward (Cross Keys), Glyn Prosser (Neath), J Lang (Llanelli), A Fear (Newport).

Ireland: D J Langan (Clontarf); D Lane (UC, Cork), N H Lambert, A H Bailey (Lansdowne), J J O'Connor (UC, Cork); J L Reid (Richmond), G J Morgan (Clontarf); N F McGrath (London Irish), V J Pike (Aldershot Services), J Megaw (Instonians), J A E Siggins (Belfast Collegians, capt.), J Russell (UC, Cork), C R Graves (Wanderers), M J Dunne (Lansdowne), C E St. J Beamish (RAF).

For Wales, Albert Fear, 'Bunny' Cowey and Viv Jenkins scored tries. Jenkins converted two.

Referee: W A Burnett (Scotland).

Match 164 **ENGLAND v WALES**   Twickenham. January 19, 1935

Drawn. England one penalty goal (3). Wales one try (3)

Neither set of backs fulfilled expectations before a crowd of 72,000. Wales scored the only try as Cliff Jones wriggled through a half-gap to send Wooller crashing in. Though there were seldom any inviting loopholes in the defence, Cliff Jones never gave up trying to find one or make one. He was the star of a game that featured relentless forward play, though at times the "two sets of physical giants" were rather over-vigorous in their methods. The Welsh pack, despite excellent line-out work by Jim Lang and Dai Thomas, faded in the last 20 minutes. This was not surprising, considering that Edgar Jones had cracked a rib early in the game. He played on courageously. It was the last of Archie Skym's 20 games for Wales.

England: H Boughton (Gloucester); L A. Booth (Headingley), P Cranmer (Oxford Univ.), J Heaton (Liverpool Univ.), R Leyland (Waterloo); P L Candler (Cambridge Univ.), J L Giles (Coventry); R J Longland (Northampton), E S Nicholson, D A Kendrew (Leicester, capt.), A J Clarke (Coventry), J Dicks (Northampton), A G Cridlan (Blackheath), D T Kemp (Blackheath), W. H. Weston (Northampton).

Wales: V G J Jenkins (Bridgend); B T V Cowey (Newport and The Welch Regiment), E C Davey (Swansea, capt.), W Wooller (Cambridge Univ.), Arthur Bassett (Aberavon); C W Jones (Cambridge Univ.), W C Powell (Northampton); Edgar Jones (Llanelli), *S C Murphy (Cross Keys), T Day, D Thomas (Swansea), E Truman (Llanelli), A M Rees (Cambridge Univ.), J Lang (Llanelli), A Skym (Cardiff).

For England, Harold Boughton kicked a penalty goal. For Wales, Wilf Wooller scored a try.

Referee: F W Haslett (Ireland).

Match 165 **WALES v SCOTLAND**   Cardiff Arms Park. February 2, 1935

Wales won by one dropped goal, two tries (10) to two tries (6)

Two thrilling tries and a decisive late dropped goal were Wales's contribution in a match that was said to rank high among the many famous Welsh victories. Cliff Jones's magical running produced the tries. First, he cut through with one of his breathtaking jabs, handed-off Marshall and scored after a run of 40 yards. Then, a similar Jones break and quick link with Davey, put in Wooller for a try. But Scotland fought back to equalise and it was left to Viv Jenkins in the closing minutes to drop his vital goal. Cliff Jones had to leave the field with a badly injured arm (torn muscle and wrenched elbow joint) and Albert Fear was withdrawn from the pack to play on the wing. Idwal Rees moved to fly half. Wales still kept Scotland defending by using the gusty wind to send high kicks deep into the home half, and the success of the 14 Welshmen was hailed as, "A triumph of Welsh brains over Scottish brawn."

Wick Powell, the big, strong scrum half, was a waning power. Critics said he seemed too exhausted to throw an accurate pass in the second half. But he was retained in the side for the next match, though already there was talk of the schoolboy star Haydn Tanner, of Gowerton G.S., who was to succeed Powell before the year was out.

Wales: V G J Jenkins (Bridgend); Arthur Bassett (Aberavon), W Wooller (Cambridge Univ.), E C Davey (capt.), J Idwal Rees (Swansea); C W Jones (Cambridge Univ.), W C Powell (Northampton); *Tom Rees (Newport), S C Murphy (Cross Keys), T Day, D Thomas (Swansea), *Trevor Williams (Cross Keys), A M Rees (Cambridge Univ.), J Lang (Llanelli), A Fear (Newport).

Scotland: K W Marshall (Edinburgh Acads.); W G S Johnston (Cambridge Univ.), R C S Dick (Blackheath), R W Shaw (Glasgow HSFP), K C Fyfe (Cambridge Univ., capt.); C F Grieve (Oxford Univ.), W R Logan (Edinburgh Wands.); R O Murray (Cambridge Univ.), G S Cottington, R M Grieve (Kelso), J A Beattie (Hawick), W A Burnet (West of Scotland), D A Thom (London Scottish), J A Waters (Selkirk), L B Lambie (Glasgow HSFP).

For Wales, Cliff Jones and Wilf Wooller scored tries. Viv Jenkins dropped a goal.

For Scotland, David Thom and Wilson Shaw scored tries.

Referee: F W Haslett (Ireland).

Match 166 IRELAND v WALES   Ravenhill, Belfast. March 9, 1935

Ireland won by two penalty goals, one try (9) to one penalty goal (3)

Ireland became outright champions for the first time since 1899 as Wales gave a thoroughly inept display without any excuses on a bitterly cold day. Nearly 10,000 Welshmen were in the 35,000 capacity crowd. Joe O'Connor fractured his collar-bone when he collided with Wooller, but with 14 men for most of the game Ireland still took all the honours. Wooller never stopped trying to break through and it needed Aiden Bailey's 'fling' tackle from behind to keep him in check. Wick Powell, in the last of his 27 games for Wales, could not settle into a rhythm with Cliff Jones.

Ireland: D P Morris (Bective); J J O'Connor, A H Bailey (UC, Dublin), E C Ridgeway (Wanderers), J I Doyle (Bective); V A Hewitt (Instonians), G J Morgan (Clontarf); C E St. J Beamish (RAF), C R Graves (Wanderers), S Walker (Instonians), J Russell (UC, Cork), S J Deering (Bective), H J M Sayers (Aldershot Services), J A E Siggins (Belfast Collegians, capt.), P J Lawlor (Bective).

Wales: *T O James (Aberavon); G R R Jones (Oxford Univ.), E C Davey (Swansea, capt.), W Wooller (Cambridge Univ.), Arthur Bassett (Aberavon); C W Jones (Cambridge Univ.), W C Powell (Northampton); Tom Rees (Newport), S C Murphy (Cross Keys), T Day, D Thomas (Swansea), Trevor Williams (Cross Keys), A M Rees (Cambridge Univ.), J Lang (Llanelli), A Fear (Newport).

For Ireland, Jack Doyle scored a try. Jack Siggins and Aiden Bailey kicked penalty goals.

For Wales, Tommy Owen James kicked a penalty goal.

Referee: M A Allan (Scotland).

Match 167 **WALES v NEW ZEALAND**   Cardiff Arms Park. December 21, 1935

Wales won by two goals, one try (13) to one goal, one dropped goal, one try (12)

As the mist crept grimly across the Arms Park and Welsh hooker Don Tarr was carried off with a dislocated neck, not many among the 50,000 crowd saw any hope of Wales saving the game against the All Blacks. Time was running out. There were fewer than 10 minutes to play. New Zealand were leading 12-10 against 14 men. Near black despair engulfed the crowd. They had seen their team lead by seven points at one stage. All the luck first had gone Wales's way. Then everything went wrong.

The match had started in bright sunshine on a cold day with Welsh hopes high. The All Blacks almost scored direct from Mike Gilbert's long kick-off, when Viv Jenkins slipped on the frost-bound turf at the river-end in-goal area. It was a scare, but nothing more. Shortly before half time, skipper Claude Davey switched Wooller from wing to centre, changing places with Idwal Rees, but almost immediately New Zealand snatched the lead. Joey Sadler and Jack Griffiths worked the blindside to send Nelson Ball in for a corner-try five minutes before half time.

Wales played safe and kept the ball tight in the first half, with Cliff Jones screw kicking to touch. Tactics changed for the second half. With Wooller in midfield, the plan was to pass and run. Haydn Tanner, the schoolboy making his debut, sent Cliff Jones away from a scrum. The fly half punted. Davey chased, steered the ball, picked up and dived over. Jenkins converted: 5-3. Four minutes later, Cliff Jones was away again. He sent Wooller driving through a half-gap and up to Gilbert. A punt over the full back's head and a desperate chase. The ball bounced sideways, away from Wooller's grasp. But not out of reach for Geoffrey Jones, following dutifully in Wooller's tracks.

Again Jenkins added the goal points: 10-3. Then the smiles began to fade from the terraces. New Zealand teams don't know the meaning of giving up. So, when Cliff Jones's long touch-finder missed its mark, Gilbert collected and dropped a low, 35-yard goal, worth four points. Then Gilbert had another drop-shot. Davey and Geoffrey Jones seemed to leave the catching job to each other Too late they tried to prevent the try near the posts, again by Nelson Ball. Gilbert converted and now New Zealand led 12-10.

Tarr's injury seemed just another note of doom for the Welshmen, who had had what seemed a winning lead snatched from them. Then, six minutes from the end, Tanner fed Cliff Jones from a scrum. Wooller was alongside for the short pass. He darted behind Davey, with a sort of dummy scissors ruse, then slanted through the gap. Defenders closed on him from all sides. The big centre knew they must drag him down if he kept the ball. So up went the punt. Another race. If he reached it there would be a try. But the ball bounced right back over his head. As Wooller crashed into the straw with the sick feeling of failure, he heard the roar from the crowd. Again the following figure of Geoffrey Jones, like a shadow, was seen pattering through the mist in Wooller's wake. His eager arms reached for the bouncing ball and his second try. Who cared that Jenkins missed the conversion? That one point was enough for one of the greatest victories Welsh rugby had ever known.

Thousands stormed on to the field to carry their heroes away in triumph. N.Z. skipper Jack Manchester confessed: "I have never played in such a thrilling game."

Wales: V G J Jenkins (London Welsh); G R R Jones (Oxford Univ.), E C Davey (capt.), J Idwal Rees (Swansea}, W Wooller; C W Jones (Cambridge Univ.), *H.

Tanner (Swansea); *H Payne, *D J Tarr (Swansea), Tom Rees (Newport), Trevor Williams (Cross Keys), *E Watkins (Cardiff), Glyn Prosser (Neath), J Lang (Llanelli), A M Rees (London Welsh).

New Zealand: G D M Gilbert; threequarters - G F Hart, N A. Mitchell, N Ball; five-eighths - J L Griffiths (first), C J Oliver (second); half back - B S Sadler; forwards - A Lambourn, W E Hadley, D Dalton, S T Reid, R R King, J E Manchester (capt.), A Mahoney, H F Mclean.

For Wales, Geoffrey Jones (2) and Claude Davey scored tries. Viv Jenkins converted two.

For New Zealand, Nelson Ball scored two tries. Mike Gilbert converted one and dropped a goal.

Referee: C H Gadney (England).

Match 168 WALES v ENGLAND   St. Helen's, Swansea. January 18, 1936

Drawn. No score

England, fielding the side that had beaten the All Blacks 13-0, including the famous rugby-playing Russian prince, Alexander Obolensky, on the wing, could not break through an unflinching Welsh defence in a match of intensive marking. The potential brilliance of Cliff Jones, Wooller, Cranmer and Obolensky packed in a 50,000 crowd, but they were disappointed. Cliff Jones managed a number of his exciting, swerving runs; but the attackers of both sides were subdued, and eventually obscured, by systematic covering and dour tackling. Barney McCall and Viv Jenkins blotted out any threat from Obolensky. Peter Cranmer hit the post with one of two easy penalty kicks he missed for England.

Wales: V G J. Jenkins (London Welsh); G R R Jones (Oxford Univ.), J Idwal Rees (Swansea, capt), W Wooller (Cambridge Univ.), *B E W McCall (The Welch Regiment and Newport); C W Jones (Cambridge Univ.), H Tanner (Swansea); Tom Rees (Newport), Bryn Evans (Llanelli), Trevor Williams (Cross Keys), *Harold Thomas (Neath), *Griff Williams (Aberavon), A M Rees (London Welsh), J Lang (Llanelli), *Eddie Long (Swansea).

England: H G Owen-Smith (St. Mary's Hosp.); Prince A Obolensky (Oxford Univ.), R A Gerrard (Bath), P Cranmer (Richmond), H S Sever (Sale); P L Candler (St. Bart's Hosp.), B C Gadney (Leicester, capt.); D A Kendrew, E S Nicholson (Leicester), R J Longland (Northampton), C S H Webb (Devonport Services), A J Clarke (Coventry), W H Weston (Northampton), P E Dunkley, E A Hamilton-Hill (Harlequins).

Referee: F W Haslett (Ireland).

Match 169 SCOTLAND v WALES   Murrayfield. February 1, 1936

Wales won by two goals, one try (13) to one try (3)

After the defensive stalemate of the England match it was refreshing to see a colourful game full of thrilling movement. Cliff Jones ran himself almost to a standstill setting up attacks. He made the first try for Wooller and scored the third himself, beating man after man in a dazzling run. Tanner supplied a long, smooth service and his play was a major contribution to success. Idwal Rees was a tireless coverer of his fellow backs. It was a severe test for the Welsh forwards, who played with great determination against a pack of exceptional physique.

Scotland: K W Marshall (Edinburgh Acads.); W C W Murdoch (Hillhead HSFP),

R C S Dick (Guy's Hosp., capt.), H M Murray (Glasgow Univ.), K C Fyfe (Cambridge Univ.); R W Shaw (Glasgow HSFP), W R Logan (Edinburgh Wands.); R M Grieve (Kelso), W A H Druitt (London Scottish), J A Waters (Selkirk), J A Beattie (Hawick), W A Burnet (West of Scotland), M McG Cooper (Oxford Univ.), P L Duff (Glasgow Acads.), G D Shaw (Gala).

Wales: V G J Jenkins (London Welsh); B E W McCall (The Welch Regiment and Newport), W Wooller (Cambridge Univ.), E C Davey (capt.), J Idwal Rees (Swansea); C W Jones (Cambridge Univ.), H Tanner (Swansea); Tom Rees (Newport), Bryn Evans (Llanelli), Trevor Williams (Cross Keys), Harold Thomas (Neath), Griff Williams (Aberavon), A M Rees (London Welsh), J Lang (Llanelli), Eddie Long (Swansea).

For Wales, Wilf Wooller, Claude Davey and Cliff Jones scored tries. Viv Jenkins converted two.

For Scotland, Murray scored a try.

Referee: C H Gadney (England).

Match 170 WALES v IRELAND   Cardiff Arms Park. March 14, 1936

Wales won by one penalty goal (3) to nil

Often the fire brigade had been called to pump water off the notorious swamp-like Arms Park pitch. But this day the call went out for the firemen to turn their hoses on the crowd. The most fantastic scenes in the history of Welsh rugby took place in Westgate Street as the crowd rushed the gates when they were closed two hours before the kick-off. Police were overwhelmed and reinforcements were hurried to the ground as the fire brigade drenched thousands to try to break up the crowd. It was estimated that somewhere near 70,000 packed into the ground, which had a safety capacity of 56,000. The massed 'breaking and entering' operation caused the tightly squeezed crowd on the terraces to spill over the railings. They surged 15-deep along the touchlines. People were trampled underfoot in the stampede and the injured were laid side by side in dressing rooms behind the stand. Dozens were taken to hospital for further treatment.

Five hours before the game the queues had begun to form at the ground. The reason for the tremendous interest was that Ireland were bidding for the Triple Crown, which they had not won for 37 years, while victory for Wales would bring them the championship. Wales had beaten the All Blacks and everyone wanted to see Cliff Jones, Wilf Wooller and the other Welsh wizards in action. But the only score was to be a penalty goal, kicked by Welsh full back Viv Jenkins after some 20 minutes of the first half. Michael Sayers was penalised for not playing the ball following a tackle, but the Irish players thought referee Cyril Gadney (England) harsh in his assessment. They claim that Sayers was not pulled down and was fighting with the ball all the time. Even then, Ireland almost won the match with a drop-kick in the closing minutes by Victor Hewitt, but the wind snatched the ball off course just when it seemed to be sailing between the posts.

Many critics were dubious of Wales's unexpected experiment of bringing in Swansea fly half Willie Davies to win his first cap at centre. Davies, a brilliant attacking outside half, was in complete contrast from the man he had to replace, Claude Davey, whose crash-tackling was expected to be an important factor. Davey withdrew on the Friday because he had injured his leg playing for Sale. But Wooller, doing the work of three men with his tackling, sheltered Willie Davies and there was no need to worry that he would let his country down. Harold Thomas was the outstanding forward as the Welsh pack gave their best display of the season. And thousands of drenched spectators went home to dry out, happy that running the gauntlet of the hosepipes had been worth it.

Wales: V G J Jenkins (London Welsh); J Idwal Rees (capt.), *W T H Davies (Swansea), W Wooller (Cambridge Univ.), B E W McCall (The Welch Regiment and Newport); C W Jones (Cambridge Univ.), H Tanner (Swansea); Tom Rees (Newport), Bryn Evans (Llanelli), Trevor Williams (Cross Keys), Harold Thomas (Neath), Griff Williams (Aberavon), A M Rees (London Welsh), J Lang (Llanelli), Eddie Long (Swansea).

Ireland: G L Malcolmson (North of Ireland); C V Boyle (Dublin Univ.), A H Bailey, L B McMahon (UC, Dublin), J J O'Connor (UC, Cork); V A Hewitt (Instonians), G J Morgan (Clontarf); S Walker (Instonians), C R Graves (Wanderers), C E St J Beamish (North of Ireland), J Russell (UC, Cork), S J Deering (Bective), H J M Sayers (Lansdowne), J A E. Siggins (Belfast Collegians, capt.), R Alexander (North of Ireland).

For Wales, Viv Jenkins kicked a penalty goal.

Referee: C H Gadney (England).

Match 171 ENGLAND v WALES   Twickenham. January 16, 1937

England won by one dropped goal (4) to one try (3)

England, in front of 65,000 spectators, looked a poor side, but Wales were even worse. Hal Sever dropped a 40-yard goal for England from the touchline when Viv Jenkins's penalty kick to touch missed its target and bounced off the shoulder of Robin Prescott straight into Sever's hands. He had never dropped a goal before. Haydn Tanner was carried off injured, but returned to launch the attack that brought the Welsh try. Bill Clement, whose sound defence made him the best of the Welsh backs, slipped a return pass as he was tackled and Wooller grasped the ball and burst over. Eddie Long was excellent with his covering, but the Welsh 'cockleshell pack' were criticised as being too small for the job. Wales's back play was considered unworthy of the occasion. England went on to win the Triple Crown for the 10th time. But it would have been all so different if Prescott had not been in the way!

England: H G Owen-Smith (St. Mary's Hosp., capt.); A G Butler (Harlequins), P L Candler (St. Bart's Hosp.), P. Cranmer (Richmond), H S Sever (Sale); T A Kemp (St. Mary's Hosp.), J L Giles (Coventry); R E Prescott (Harlequins), H B Toft (Waterloo), R J Longland (Northampton), T F Huskisson (OMT), A Wheatley (Coventry), D A Campbell (Cambridge Univ.), D L K Milman (Bedford), W H Weston (Northampton).

Wales: V G J Jenkins (London Welsh); *W H Clement (Llanelli), W Wooller (Cardiff), E C Davey (London Welsh, capt.), J Idwal Rees (Swansea); W T H Davies, H Tanner (Swansea); Tom Rees (Newport), Bryn Evans ,*Emrys Evans (Llanelli), *D L Thomas, Harold Thomas (Neath), A M Rees (London Welsh), J Lang, Eddie Long (Swansea).

For England, Hal Sever dropped a goal.

For Wales, Wilf Wooller scored a try.

Referee: R A Beattie (Scotland).

Match 172 WALES v SCOTLAND   St. Helen's, Swansea. February 6, 1937

Scotland won by two goals, one try (13) to two tries (6)

With seven changes and three of them new caps, including hooker 'Bunner' Travers, Wales lost again. Scotland's forwards were called a "Chinese puzzle" because, with almost complete disregard for specialists in the scrum, they chose four No.8 forwards. It was no surprise that Travers dominated the hooking. With the Scots' pack irrepressible on the move, they had Wales defending desperately and looked a far better disciplined and more fiery unit. Wooller, as the cleverest Welsh attacker, scored both his side's tries. Bill Clement was the one Welsh back of unblemished soundness. The crowd was only 35,000. The rival captains, Idwal Rees and Ross Logan, were both playing for the same club at the time – Edinburgh Wanderers.

Wales: T O James (Aberavon); *W H Hopkin (Newport), J Idwal Rees (Swansea and Edinburgh Wands., capt.), W Wooller (Cardiff), W H Clement (Llanelli); R R Morris (Swansea and Bristol), H Tanner (Swansea); Trevor Williams (Cross Keys), *W Travers, Tom Rees (Newport), *Harry Rees (Cardiff), Harold Thomas (Neath), Eddie Long (Swansea), E Watkins (Cardiff), A M Rees (London Welsh).

Scotland: J M Kerr (Heriot's FP); W G S Johnston (Richmond), R C S Dick (Guy's Hosp.), D J Macrae (St. Andrew's Univ.), R W Shaw (Glasgow HSFP); W A Ross (Hillhead HSFP), W R Logan (Edinburgh Wanderers, capt.); M M Henderson (Dunfermline), G L Gray (Gala), W M Inglis, C L Melville (Army), G B Horsburgh, W B Young (London Scottish), J A Waters (Selkirk), G D Shaw (Gala).

For Scotland, Charles Dick (2) and Wilson Shaw scored tries. Duncan Shaw converted two.

For Wales, Wilf Wooller scored two tries.

Referee: C H Gadney (England).

Match 173 **IRELAND v WALES**   Ravenhill, Belfast. April 3, 1937

Ireland won by one goal (5) to one penalty goal (3)

Snow, lying almost a foot deep in parts on Ravenhill Park, cost three Welsh players caps they were never to gain. Full back Tommy Stone, centre Horace Edwards, both of Cardiff, and forward Charlie Anderson (Maesteg) came into the Welsh team owing to the withdrawals of Viv Jenkins, Claude Davey and Trevor Williams. But the match was postponed from March 13 because of the snowstorm that greeted the Welsh team as they sailed up the lough from Liverpool. When the game was played on April 3, the originally nominated players were all fit and chosen to return. Tommy Stone joined Rugby League club Barrow shortly before the selectors announced that the team would revert to the original selection.

Wales led 3-0 at halftime through a penalty goal by Walter Legge, when George Malcolmson was penalised for deliberately throwing the ball into touch. Then the 20,000 spectators saw Ireland snatch the winning lead after four minutes of the second half. Aiden Bailey's try was converted by Sam Walker. This try caused a considerable amount of controversy. Welsh players said that the ball struck the foot of referee M Allan (Scotland) before Siggins fielded it, and the Welsh defence, expecting the whistle to sound for a scrum, did not try to stop Bailey until it was too late. This was a classic example of the need to play to the whistle. The Welsh backs again disappointed, but the pack were in stirring form, with Eddie Watkins the best.

Ireland: G L Malcolmson (North of Ireland); F G Moran (Clontarf), L B McMahon, A H Bailey (UC, Dublin), C V Boyle (Dublin Univ.); G E Cromey (Queen's Univ., Belfast), G J Morgan (Clontarf, capt.); E Ryan (Dolphin), T S Corken (Belfast Collegians), S Walker (Instonians), C J Reidy (London Irish), R B Mayne (Queen's Univ. Belfast), P J Lawlor (Bective), J A E Siggins (Belfast Collegians), R A Alexander (Royal Ulster Constabulary).

Wales: *W G Legge (Newport); J Idwal Rees (Swansea), E C Davey (London Welsh), W Wooller (Cardiff, capt.), W H Clement (Llanelli); W T H Davies, H Tanner (Swansea); Trevor Williams (Cross Keys), W Travers (Newport), *Ivor Bennett (Aberavon), Harold Thomas (Neath), Harry Rees (Cardiff), *A R Taylor (Cross Keys), E Watkins (Cardiff), A M Rees (London Welsh).

For Ireland, Aiden Bailey scored a try. Sam Walker converted.

For Wales, Walter Legge kicked a penalty goal.

Referee: M A Allan (Scotland).

Match 174 WALES v ENGLAND   Cardiff Arms Park, January 15, 1938

Wales won by one goal, two penalty goals, one try (14) to one goal, one try (8)

This jubilee match between Wales and England, played in a gale before 40,000 spectators, found the Welsh backs in fine form. Had Wooller been fit to play, it might have been a runaway victory over the Triple Crown holders. Claude Davey came in for the injured Wooller. Cliff Jones again spread dismay in the opposition ranks and Tanner mixed his smooth service with thrusting breaks. Three Welsh players had to retire at various times for repairs – Cliff Jones, Bill Clement and Eddie Watkins. The new Welsh No. 8, Walter Vickery, followed his father as an international, though his father was capped by England against Ireland in 1905. Of the 50 matches against Wales, England had won 25, Wales 19 and six had been drawn.

Wales: V G J Jenkins (London Welsh); W H Clement (Llanelli), J Idwal Rees (Swansea), E C. Davev (London Welsh), Arthur Bassett (Cardiff); C. W. Jones (Cardiff capt.), H Tanner (Swansea); Harry Rees (Cardiff), W Travers (Newport), *M E Morgan (Swansea), *F L Morgan (Llanelli), Eddie Watkins (Cardiff), A M Rees (London Welsh), *W Vickery (Aberavon), *A McCarley (Neath).

England: H D Freakes (Harlequins); E J Unwin (Rosslyn Park), P Cranmer (Moseley, capt.), B E Nicholson (Harlequins), H S Sever (Sale); P L Candler (St. Bart's Hosp.), B C Gadney (Headingley) ; R J Longland (Northampton), H B Toft (Waterloo), H F Wheatley, A Wheatley (Coventry), T F Huskisson (OMT), W H Weston (Northampton), D L K Milman (Bedford), R Bolton (Harlequins).

For Wales, Alan McCarley and Idwal Rees scored tries. Viv Jenkins converted one and kicked two penalty goals.

For England, Peter Candler and Hal Sever scored tries. Hubert Freakes converted one.

Referee: R A Beattie (Scotland).

Match 175 SCOTLAND v WALES   Murrayfield. February 5, 1938

Scotland won by one goal, one penalty goal (8) to two tries (6)

A Welsh forward, lying on the ball among a jumble of players, half-concussed, was penalised for not releasing the ball two minutes from the end near his own posts and Scotland kicked the penalty goal to win. This was how referee Cyril Gadney (England) described the event: "I awarded the penalty because the Welshman lettered J (Harry Rees) was lying on the ball in a scrummage. It was a horrible thing to have to do at that time of the game. To me it was almost as bad as taking a man's life."

Harry Rees said: "I was lying on the ground with the ball partly under my ribs and with Haydn Tanner lying under me unconscious. I could not have played the ball, however much I tried." Another Welsh player said that Rees was in a state of near-concussion himself and mumbling something about aeroplanes. Still, Scotland played well enough to deserve victory and went on to win the Triple Crown for the eighth time. Eddie Morgan was badly hurt, but insisted on returning. After 15 minutes he staggered and nearly collapsed. He was taken to hospital and it was found that a fractured rib had grazed his lung. When Wooller also was hurt, Alan McCarley had to be taken out of the scrum to cover him for a while and the six forwards could not hold Scotland's eight. It was a match that most of the 60,000 crowd expected Wales to win. But for that penalty, considered harsh by so many people, Wales would have taken the Triple Crown, because they went on to beat Ireland.

Scotland: G Roberts (Watsonians); A H Drummond (Kelvinside Acads.), R C S Dick (Guy's Hosp.), D J Macrae (St. Andrew's Univ.), J G S Forrest (Cambridge Univ.); R W Shaw (Glasgow HSFP, capt.), T F Dorwood (Gala); J B Borthwick (Stewart's Coll., FP), J D Hastie (Melrose), W M Inglis (Army), G B Horsburgh (London Scottish), A Roy (Waterloo), W B Young (London Scottish), P L Duff (Glasgow Acads.), W H Crawford (United Services).

Wales: V G J Jenkins (London Welsh); W H Clement (Llanelli), J Idwal Rees (Swansea), W Wooller, Arthur Bassett (Cardiff); C W Jones (Cardiff, capt.), H Tanner (Swansea); M E Morgan (Swansea), W Travers (Newport), Harry Rees, Eddie Watkins (Cardiff), F L Morgan (Llanelli), A M Rees (London Welsh), W Vickery (Aberavon), A McCarley (Neath).

For Scotland, Wilfred Crawford scored a try, conversion and penalty goal.

For Wales, Alan McCarley scored two tries.

Referee: C H Gadney (England).

Match 176 **WALES v IRELAND**   St. Helen's, Swansea. March 12, 1938

Wales won by one goal, one penalty goal, one try (11) to one goal (5)

Cliff Jones, in his last game for Wales before retiring at the age of 24, led his team to victory. Ireland, concentrating almost entirely on aggressive defence, stalked the Welsh midfield men ruthlessly and waited for mistakes. Russell Taylor, a big success at wing forward, and Bill Clement, the cleverest wing on the field, scored the Welsh tries. Ireland had only 14 men in the second half after George Cromey went off with concussion. Torrens moved to fly half and O'Loughlin came out of the pack to play on the wing. The game, in brilliant sunshine, was watched by 40,000.

Wales: W. G. Legge (Newport); J Idwal Rees (Swansea), E C Davey (London Welsh), W Wooller (Cardiff), W H Clement (Llanelli); C W Jones (Cardiff, capt.), H Tanner (Swansea); M E Morgan (Swansea), W Travers (Newport), Harry Rees, Eddie Watkins (Cardiff), F L Morgan (Llanelli), A R Taylor (Cross Keys), W Vickery (Aberavon), A McCarley (Neath).

Ireland: R G Craig (Queen's Univ., Belfast); F G Moran (Clontarf), H R McKibbin (Queen's Univ., Belfast), J D Torrens (Bohemians), C V Boyle (Dublin Univ.); G E Cromey (Queen's Univ., Belfast), G J Morgan (Old Belvedere); H Kennedy (Bradford), C R A Graves (Wanderers), C E St. J Beamish (RAF), D Tierney (UC, Cork), R B Mayne (Queen's Univ., Belfast), D O'Loughlin (UC, Cork), S Walker (Instonians, capt.), H J M Sayers (Army).

For Wales, Russell Taylor and Bill Clement scored tries. Walter Legge converted one. Wilf Wooller kicked a penalty goal.

For Ireland, Fred Moran scored a try. Harry McKibbin converted.

Referee: J C H Ireland (Scotland).

England won by one try (3) to nil

"If this side does not win, we never shall win again at Twickenham," said skipper Wilf Wooller before the match. It showed his supreme confidence as well as a complete disregard for the grim record of Welsh teams at Rugby H.Q. Perhaps he should have recognised that this was the13th visit by a Welsh team to Twickenham. If the notoriously unlucky number held no significance for him, it left its mark on the Welsh pack: they were hopelessly outclassed by the superior dash and scrummaging power of Bert Toft's eight. It was an unspectacular game on a muddy pitch for the 70,000 crowd, with the only score a try by Richmond prop Derek Teden, after a combined foot rush in the second half. A drop at goal by Wooller missed by only a foot. With fragmentary possession, the Welsh backs were to be more pitied than blamed. Afterwards, Viv Jenkins announced his retirement from international rugby. He had won 14 caps.

England: H D Freakes (Oxford Univ.); R H Guest (Liverpool Univ.), J Heaton (Waterloo), G E Hancock (Birkenhead Park), R S L Carr (Old Cranleighans); G A Walker (RAF), P Cooke (Richmond); R E Prescott (Harlequins), H B Toft (Waterloo, capt.), D E Teden (Richmond), T F Huskisson (OMT), H F Wheatley (Coventry), J T W Berry (Leicester), R M Marshall (Oxford Univ.), J K Watkins (United Services).

Wales: V G J Jenkins (London Welsh); *F J V Ford (The Welch Regiment), *D Idwal Davies (Swansea and London Welsh), W Wooller (Cardiff, capt.), *Sid Williams (Aberavon); W T H Davies, H Tanner (Swansea); M E. Morgan (Swansea), W Travers (Newport), *W E N Davis, Eddie Watkins (Cardiff), F L Morgan (Llanelli), A R Taylor (Cross Keys), W Vickery (Aberavon), *C Challinor (Neath).

For England, Derek Teden scored a try.

Referee: J C H Ireland (Scotland).

Wales won by one goal, one penalty goal, one try (11) to one penalty goal (3)

With nine changes in their side and their pack showing a vast improvement, Wales well deserved victory in this jubilee match against Scotland, the Triple Crown holders. In a game of devastating tackling, Welsh halves Haydn Tanner and Willie Davies still managed to shine. Tanner injured a nerve in his left arm, which was paralysed for a quarter-of-an-hour, but returned to play as skilfully as ever. Eddie Long came out of the pack to act as emergency scrum half. Les Manfleld, who had declined an England trial offer, was the most alert and intelligent of a rousing Welsh pack. Also making their first appearances for Wales were wing Elvet Jones, who had played for the British Lions in 1938, and the South African, Mickey Davies, who was unfortunate not to win a blue in the centre for Oxford. An unusual selection was Emrys Evans, the Llanelli prop, as blind side wing forward. He had been capped at prop in 1937, and played most effectively in his new role. Of the 50 games between the countries, each had won 24 and two had been drawn.

Wales: *C Howard Davies (Swansea); *Elvet L Jones (Llanelli), *M J Davies (Oxford Univ.), W Wooller (Cardiff capt.), Sid Williams (Aberavon); W T H Davies, H Tanner (Swansea); *Leslie Davies (Swansea), W Travers (Newport), W E N Davis, Eddie Watkins (Cardiff), *R E Price (Weston-super-Mare), Emrys Evans (Llanelli), *L Manfield (Otley and Mountain Ash), Eddie Long (Swansea).

Scotland: G Roberts (Watsonians); J B Craig (Heriot's FP), D J Macrae (St.

109

Andrew's Univ.), J R S Innes (Aberdeen Univ.), W N Renwick (Edinburgh Wands.); R W Shaw (Glasgow HSFP, capt.), W R C Brydon (Heriot's FP); G H Gallie (Edinburgh Acads.), R W F Sampson (London Scottish), W. Purdie (Jedforest), G B Horsburgh (London Scottish), A Roy (Waterloo), W H Crawford (United Services), P L Duff (Glasgow Acads.), W B Young (London Scottish).

For Wales, Mickey Davies and 'Bunner' Travers scored tries. Wilf Wooller converted one and kicked a penalty goal.

For Scotland, Wilfred Crawford kicked a penalty goal.

Referee: A S Bean (England).

Match 179   IRELAND v WALES   Ravenhill, Belfast. March 11, 1939

Wales won by one dropped goal, one try (7) to nil

In the last five minutes, Willie Davies won a place of glory in Welsh rugby history and the match for his side. His 30-yard dropped goal from a wide angle and his smartly-taken try provided all the Welsh scores and meant Ireland had been foiled for the seventh time by Wales when the Triple Crown beckoned. In rain, on a heavy pitch, Ireland fought tenaciously for 75 of the 80 minutes without a point to thrill the 28,000 spectators.

Then Tanner sent back from a scrum. The defence raced in to smother Wooller, who had been trying to drop goals throughout the match. But Wooller had instructed that it was to be Willie Davies's job to try the drop shot this time, because he would be free from the savage marking. So the Swansea fly half popped over the first dropped goal of his career and, incidentally, the last one for Wales that was worth the old fashioned four points. Travers and Manfield were spoken of as giants in a pack of giants. This was the last Welsh match until after World War Two, and four of the team were to gain further caps when rugby resumed – Tanner, Manfield, Travers and full back Howard Davies.

Ireland: C J Murphy (Lansdowne); F G Moran (Clontarf), H R McKibbin (Instonians), J D Torrens (Bohemians), C V Boyle (Lansdowne); G E Cromey (Belfast Collegians), G J Morgan (Old Belvedere, capt.); T A Headon (UC, Dublin), C Teehan (UC, Cork), J G Ryan (UC, Dublin), R B Mayne (Malone), D O'Loughlin (Garryowen), R Alexander (Royal Ulster Constabulary), J W S Irwin (North of Ireland), H J M Sayers (Aldershot Services).

Wales: C Howard Davies (Swansea); *Chris Matthews (Bridgend), M J Davies (Oxford Univ.), W Wooller (Cardiff capt.), Sid Williams (Aberavon); W T H Davies, H Tanner (Swansea); W E N Davis (Cardiff), W Travers, *V J Law (Newport), Leslie Davies (Swansea), R E Price (Weston-super-Mare), Emrys Evans (Llanelli), L Manfield (Otley and Mountain Ash), Eddie Long (Swansea).

For Wales, W T H Davies dropped a goal and scored a try.

Referee: J C H Ireland (Scotland).

Uncapped Match   WALES v 2nd NZEF (Kiwis)   Cardiff Arms Park. January 5, 1946

Kiwis won by one goal, two penalty goals (11) to one penalty goal (3)

The Kiwis, before a crowd of 30,000, gained the first victory at the Arms Park by a New Zealand representative side against Wales. There was no score in the first half. Then Hugh Lloyd-Davies kicked Wales into the lead with a long range penalty goal. But Lloyd-Davies missed a kick to touch and Jim Sherratt, the big, powerful wing, fielded and raced almost 70 yards for a spectacular try. Bob Scott converted and, in the last few minutes, added two 45-yard penalty goals. The Kiwis lost only two matches on their colourful tour – against Scotland and Monmouthshire.

This match was one of the series of Victory internationals to mark the return to regular rugby after the war, but official caps were not awarded. Wales played eight Victory internationals, including the Kiwis' match, and beat France 8-0 (Swansea), England 3-0 (Twickenham) and Ireland 6-4 (Cardiff), but lost to England 13-25 (Cardiff), Scotland 6-25 (Swansea) and 11-13 (Murrayfield) and France 0-12 (Paris).

> **Wales:** R H. Lloyd-Davies (London Welsh); W E Williams (Newport), Les Williams (Llanelli), Bleddyn Williams (capt.), G Hale (Cardiff); W B Cleaver, W J Darch (Cardiff); W G Jones, W Travers (Newport), G Bevan (Llanelli), G Hughes, J R G Stephens, Morlais Thomas (Neath), L Manfield (Cardiff), Les Thomas (Llanelli).

> **Second NZEF (Kiwis):** R W H Scott; threequarters – J R Sherratt, J B Smith, W G Argus; 2nd five-eighth - I Proctor, 1st five-eighth - F R Allen; half back - C K Saxton (capt.); forwards - N J McPhail, F M Haigh, J G Simpson, P K Rhind, S L Young, A W Blake, J Finlay, K D Arnold

For the Kiwis, Jim Sherratt scored a try. Bob Scott converted and kicked two penalty goals.

For Wales, Hugh Lloyd-Davies kicked a penalty goal.

Referee: J B G Whitaker (England).

Match 180 WALES v ENGLAND   Cardiff Arms Park. January 18, 1947

England won by one goal, one dropped goal (9) to two tries (6)
(N.B. A dropped goal was worth four points)

Five great names in Welsh rugby made their initial appearances on the losing side in this first official international match after the war. They were Ken Jones, who was to set a Welsh record with 44 caps, Rees Stephens (32),Bleddyn Williams (22), Jack Matthews (17) and Billy Cleaver (14). Stephens scored the first Welsh try of the post-war era. Bleddyn Williams made his debut at outside half, but looked uncomfortable and never played for Wales in this role again. Though England had to withdraw Micky Steele-Bodger from the pack when Keith Scott was injured, their seven forwards never allowed the Welsh eight to take control. Because of war-time bomb damage, the upper deck of the north stand was not in use and there were only 43,000 spectators.

> **Wales:** C Howard Davies (Llanelli); *K J Jones (Newport), *J Matthews, *W B Cleaver (Cardiff), *Les Williams (Llanelli); *Bleddyn Williams, H Tanner (Cardiff, capt.); *Dai Jones (Swansea), *R E Blakemore (Newport), *G Bevan, *Stan Williams (Llanelli), *G Parsons (Newport), *Ossie Williams (Llanelli), *J R G Stephens (Neath), *Gwyn Evans (Cardiff).

> **England:** A Gray (Otley); R H Guest (Waterloo), N O Bennett, E K Scott (St. Mary's Hosp.), D W Swarbrick (Oxford Univ.); N M Hall, (St. Mary's Hosp.), W K Moore (Devonport Services); G A Kelly (Bedford), A P Henderson (Cambridge Univ.), H Walker (Coventry), J Mycock (Sale, capt.), S V Perry, M R Steele-Bodger (Cambridge Univ.), B H Travers (Oxford Univ.), D F White (Northampton).

For England, Don White scored a try. Arthur Gray converted. Norman 'Nim' Hall dropped a goal.

For Wales, Rees Stephens and Gwyn Evans scored tries.

Referee: R A Beattie (Scotland).

Wales won by two goals, one penalty goal, three tries (22) to one goal, one penalty goal (8)

Glyn Davies, who had played for Wales during the previous season in the Victory series while still at Pontypridd Grammar School, won his first full cap and played brilliantly. His gracefully balanced running helped his team to their biggest victory over Scotland since 1914. Bleddyn Williams switched to centre in place of Jack Matthews so that Glyn Davies could occupy the fly half position. Scotland led 8-6 at the interval, but then the Welsh pack took control. Outstanding were two Cardiff forwards, Bill Tamplin, who played on with a dislocated wrist, and Cliff Davies. Both were playing for the first time and Davies went on to win 16 caps as one of the finest props of the post-war era. There were only 2,000 Welshmen among the 45,000 crowd – a contrast from the 20,000 Welshmen who were to make the Murrayfield trek in later years.

Tanner nursed Glyn Davies carefully and their fluent partnership was a highlight of this biggest Welsh success at Murrayfield. Bleddyn Williams also ran delightfully, while Cleaver covered with typical thoroughness.

Scotland: K I Geddes (London Scottish, capt.); T G H. Jackson (London Scottish), C W Drummond (Melrose), C R Bruce (Glasgow Acads.), D D Mackenzie (Edinburgh Univ.); I J M Lumsden (Watsonians) A W Black (Edinburgh Univ.); J C Henderson (Edinburgh Acads.), R W Sampson, R Aitken (London Scottish), D W Deas (Heriot's FP), F H Coutts (Melrose), J H Orr (Edinburgh City Police), A G W Watt, W D Elliot (Edinburgh Acads.).

Wales: C Howard Davies (Llanelli); K J Jones (Newport), Bleddyn Williams, W B C Cleaver (Cardiff), Les Williams (Llanelli); *Glyn Davies (Pontypridd), H Tanner (Cardiff, capt.); *W J Evans (Pontypool), *W Gore (Newbridge), *Cliff Davies, *W E Tamplin (Cardiff), Stan Williams, Ossie Williams (Llanelli), J R G Stephens (Neath), Gwyn Evans (Cardiff).

For Wales, Ken Jones (2), Bleddyn Williams, Billy Cleaver and Les Williams scored tries. Bill Tamplin converted two and kicked a penalty goal.

For Scotland, Doug Elliot scored a try. Keith Geddes converted and kicked a penalty goal.

Referee: M J Dowling (Ireland).

Wales won by one penalty goal (3) to nil

Welsh team pack leader Bill Tamplin won this hardest match of the season with a tremendous penalty goal from just inside the French half shortly before the interval. In a game charged with fierce tension, Cliff Davies had his little finger bitten to the bone. Tackling by both sides was shattering. Glyn Davies could not play because he had injured his knee in an army game, so Billy Cleaver made his first appearance in his best position of fly half. It was the first match for brilliant Bob Evans, the Newport wing forward, who was to win 10 caps. George Parsons, the Newport second row forward, chosen to play, was sent home when he boarded the train. The WRU had heard rumours that he was negotiating with Rugby League representatives. Parsons protested his innocence, but never played for Wales again and within a year turned professional.

France: A Alvarez (Tyrosse); E Pebeyre (Brive), L Junquas (Bayonne, capt.). M Sorondo (Montauban), J Lassegue (Toulouse); M Terreau (Bourg), Y R Bergougnan (Toulouse); J Prin-Clary (Brive), M Jol (Biarritz), E Buzy (Lourdes),

A Moga (Begles), R Soro (Romans), J Matheu (Castres), G Basquet (Agen), J Prat (Lourdes).

Wales: C Howard Davies (Llanelli); K J Jones (Newport), Bleddyn Williams (Cardiff), Les Williams, *Peter Rees (Llanelli); W B Cleaver, H Tanner (Cardiff capt.); Dai Jones (Swansea), W Gore (Newbridge), Cliff Davies W E Tamplin (Cardiff), Stan Williams (Llanelli), *R T Evans (Newport), J R G Stephens (Neath), Gwyn Evans (Cardiff).

For Wales, Bill Tamplin kicked a penalty goal.

Referee: A S Bean (England).

Match 183 WALES v IRELAND   St. Helen's, Swansea. March 29, 1947

Wales won by one penalty goal, one try (6) to nil

Wing forward Gwyn Evans hunted down Irish fly half Jack Kyle to blot him out and, with their pack eventually winning a stirring tussle, Wales triumphed to stop Ireland taking the Triple Crown. In the mud, before 36,000 spectators, a penalty goal by Bill Tamplin and a try by Bob Evans (from a dummying break by Haydn Tanner and a dash by Billy Cleaver) brought the Welsh scores. It was remembered that Wales would have won the Triple Crown but for that left-footed dropped goal by England fly half 'Nim' Hall. Still, Tanner's team shared the championship title with England. The game, which had been postponed from March 8 because of a frozen ground, started 35 minutes late when the Irish team were held up in a traffic jam.

Wales: C Howard Davies (Llanelli); K J Jones (Newport), Bleddyn Williams (Cardiff), Les Williams, Peter Rees (Llanelli); W B Cleaver, H Tanner (Cardiff capt.); Dai Jones (Swansea), W Gore (Newbridge), Cliff Davies, W E Tamplin (Cardiff), Stan Williams (Llanelli), R T Evans (Newport), J R G Stephens (Neath), Gwyn Evans (Cardiff).

Ireland: J A D Higgins (Civil Service); B O'Hanlon (Dolphin), J D E Monteith (Queen's Univ., Belfast, capt.), M Lane (Univ. Coll., Cork), B Mullan (Clontarf); J W Kyle (NIFC), E Strathdee (Queen's Univ., Belfast); M R Neely (Belfast Collegians), K D Mullen (Old Belvedere), J C Daly (London Irish), C P Callan (Lansdowne), E Keefe (Sundays Well), D Hingerty (Univ. Coll., Dublin), R D Agar (Malone), J W McKay (Queen's Univ., Belfast).

For Wales, Bob Evans scored a try. Bill Tamplin kicked a penalty goal.

Referee: J B G Whittaker (England).

Match 184 WALES v AUSTRALIA   Cardiff Arms Park. December 20, 1947

Wales won by two penalty goals (6) to nil

When Trevor Allan, the Australian captain, risked throwing the ball deliberately into touch under pressure he thought the angle and distance too difficult to make his action a reasonable scoring chance for Wales. But Bill Tamplin put over a magnificent penalty goal from 40 yards and shortly afterwards landed a second penalty goal as the only scores. So the Wallabies lost a thrilling match of hard-tackling. Haydn Tanner, the chosen Welsh captain, withdrew with a chipped elbow and Tamplin took over the captaincy. Handel Greville, who came in as deputy scrum half, played splendidly in his only game for Wales. It was the first appearance for a second row forward who was to gain fame as an outstanding Welsh captain. His name was John

Gwilliam, who played for Newport before going up to Cambridge University. Gwilliam later switched to No.8 and captained Wales in 13 matches, including the Triple Crown victories of 1950 and 1952. Billy Cleaver, after duty at centre and fly half for Wales, switched to full back, but had little to do. Glyn Davies returned at outside half to play excellently. Les Williams, the Llanelli wing, had joined Cardiff, who supplied nine men to the team. A crowd of 45,500 saw the match. The Wallabies had the unique record of not having a try against them in their international matches in Britain as they beat Scotland, Ireland and England and lost to Wales.

Wales: W B Cleaver (Cardiff); K J Jones (Newport), Bleddyn Williams, Jack Matthews, Les Williams (Cardiff); Glyn Davies (Pontypridd), *H Greville (Llanelli); *Emlyn Davies (Aberavon), *Maldwyn James, Cliff Davies, W E Tamplin (Cardiff capt.), *J A Gwilliam (Cambridge Univ.), Ossie Williams (Llanelli), L Manfield, Gwyn Evans (Cardiff).

Australia: B Piper; A E Tonkin, T Allan (capt.), M L Howell, J W T MacBride; N A Emery, C T Burke; R MacMaster, K Kearney, B L Davis, G Cooke, D F Kraefft, D H Keller, A J Buchan, C J Windon.

For Wales, Bill Tamplin kicked two penalty goals.

Referee: A S Bean (England).

Match 185 ENGLAND v WALES   Twickenham. January 17, 1948

Drawn. England one penalty goal (3). Wales one try (3)

Ten Cardiff men were in this team – a record. But they could not inspire Wales to victory on the old bogy ground, though Haydn Tanner's team deserved to win. Jack Matthews, a centre, was brought in to play on the wing when his Cardiff club-mate Les Williams withdrew. Matthews had what seemed a perfectly good try disallowed by referee R A Beattie (Scotland) after clever interpassing with Tanner from a quick throw in at a line-out. Glyn Davies lost the slippery ball in the act of diving to score in the second half.

Bleddyn Williams always considered it a harsh decision in this match to penalise him for playing the ball with his hands after a tackle. Williams alleges he was not tackled. But from the award, in the first minutes, Sid Newman kicked a lovely 45-yard goal. At least Wales scored the only try by Ken Jones to force a draw. England forward 'Jyka' Travers played as emergency full back for the last 13 minutes when Newman cracked a bone in his wrist Attendance: 73,000.

England: S C Newman (Oxford Univ.) ; R H Guest (Waterloo), N O Bennett (United Services), E K Scott (Redruth), D W Swarbrick (Oxford Univ.); T A Kemp (Richmond, capt.), R J P Madge (Exeter); H Walker (Coventry), J H Keeling (Guy's Hosp.), G A Kelly (Bedford), S V Perry (Cambridge Univ.), H F Luya (Headingley), B H Travers (Oxford Univ.), D B Vaughan (Devonport Services), M R Steele-Bodger (Edinburgh Univ.).

Wales: *R F Trott (Cardiff); K J Jones (Newport), W B Cleaver, Bleddyn Williams, J Matthews (Cardiff); Glyn Davies(Pontypridd), H Tanner (Cardiff, capt.); *L Anthony (Neath), M James, Cliff Davies, W E Tamplin (Cardiff), *Des Jones, Ossie Williams (Llanelli), L Manfield, Gwyn Evans (Cardiff).

For England, Sid Newman kicked a penalty goal.

For Wales, Ken Jones scored a try.

Referee: R A Beattie (Scotland).

Greatness is often thrust upon someone. Not Roy John: he was born to be the most famous lineout jumper in Welsh rugby history. Here his fingertips get there first against South Africa in 1951.

Another Welsh bag of tricks. Onllwyn Brace was a scrum half who could bamboozle a tackler with a swivel of his eyeballs! Here he fires out a pass against France in 1960.

Two centres and a streaker. Bleddyn Williams (left) was the last man to captain Wales to victor over New Zealand. That was back in 1953. His famous co-centre was Jack Matthews (top), the Iron Doctor and most ferocious tackler of the post World War Two era. Streaking was not in vogue in their days. This was the first Arms Park streaker, during the match with Scotland in 1982 He was fined £50. Wales lost, as they did when another male bared his body and stopped play at Wembley with South Africa playing in 1998.

Cliff Morgan followed Billy Cleaver as a technically faultless tactical kicker in the Fifties, a busy coverer behind his threequarter line and, of course, established a reputation as a dynamic attacker. Here Cliff clears against Scotland in 1958.

Over to you, Terry Davies. Cliff Morgan, the human corkscrew, twists through to unload a pass to full back Terry against England in 1957. Llanelli's Geoff Howells is on the inside.

Alun Pask, a No 8 before his time. A great innovator, he launched the ploy of picking up from the base of the scrum and causing considerable confusion. Brian Price, David Watkins and Dewi Bebb watch and wonder what the next move is against Scotland in 1964.

Lloyd Williams, big and strong, could play the ninth forward game fearlessly. A scrum half with a longer than usual pass, he was a member of the famous Taffs Well family who provided eight brothers, all top notch players for Cardiff, including, of course, Bleddyn. Lloyd in action against France in 1958.

Wales v Scotland 1960. Standing (left to right): Referee, Kevin Kelleher (Ireland), Ray Prosser, Brian Cresswell, Geoff Whitson, Gareth Payne, Danny Harris, Glyn Davidge, Aneurin Williams (touch judge). Seated: Malcolm Price, Len Cunningham, Bryn Meredith (capt), Norman Morgan, Geoff Windsor Lewis. In front: Onllwyn Brace, Dewi Bebb, Fenton Coles, Cliff Ashton.

Wales v France 1962. Standing (left to right): F G Price (touch judge), Len Cunningham, Kingsley Jones, David Nash, Keith Rowlands, Alun Pask, Glyn Davidge. Seated: Kelvin Coslett, D Ken Jones, Tony O'Connor, Bryn Meredith (capt), Haydn Morgan, Meirion Roberts, Dewi Bebb. In front: Alan Rees, Robert Morgan.

Try-getters. Top: Dewi Bebb, the Swansea Express, dives to score against England in 1961, the first of his two thrilling tries. Cyril Davies is alongside. Middle: John Taylor hurtles in for the fourth and final try against Ireland in 1969. Bottom: Maurice Richards plunges across for the third of his four tries against England in 1969. John Taylor was on hand.

Clive Rowlands was a one-man master-class; the kicking scrum half who has never been equalled. He controlled the entire game plan. The driver and conductor. He drives England back (above) watched by Gary Prothero and Alun Pask in 1965.

On the break? Not really. Clive Rowlands is poised to give the heave-ho to Ireland's hopes of territorial advantage at the Arms Park in 1963

Not just a jumper and mauler. Brian Price shows that a front five man could give as good an imitation of a ball-carrier as anyone against Scotland in 1962.

Haydn Morgan was the classical open-side wing forward; fast to the breakdown, a ruthless hunter of midfield opponents and swift with support at every opportunity. French defenders watch his approach warily in this 1966 match.

Triple Crown winners of 1969. The Wales team that defeated England 30-9. Back row (left to right): D P D'Arcy (referee), Stuart Watkins, Delme Thomas, Mervyn Davies, Brian Thomas, Denzil Williams, Dai Morris, John Lloyd, F B Stephens (touch judge). Middle row: Clive Rowlands (coach), JPR Williams, Jeff Young, Gareth Edwards (capt), Keith Jarrett, Maurice Richards. Front row: John Dawes, John Taylor, Barry John.

Barry John slips smoothly into the famous ghost runner routine, weaving through to score against England in 1969.

TGR Davies. Was there ever a greater right wing for Wales? He could swing off either foot with a lethal last-minute sidestep. Most of his 20 tries for Wales were little gems of perfection. Top: In at the Irish corner in 1971 and looking to get nearer the posts. Below: Over England's line in 1967 with Stuart Watkins outside him and apparently wondering why the ball is not in his hands!

Two bobby dazzlers. There was never a Welsh outside half with such explosive speed off the mark as Newport's David Watkins. He was through a half-gap before it had even opened! Above: Watkins puts a calculated boot to it against England in 1967. Jonathan Davies (below) weaves a way through Romania's baffled defence in 1988 with Mike Hall at his shoulder, wondering in which direction his outside half will disappear next.

They were not so much a half back unit as a pair of conspirators. They are, of course, Gareth Edwards and Barry John, Excitement Incorporated. Edwards was a player of enormous strength for his size and developed a huge catapult pass; a try-scorer of exceptional individualism. John was the cultured craftsman at outside half; an attacker of stealth and subtlety; smooth, almost leisurely, in the manner of creating openings. Gareth was explosive, Barry was sinuous. Top: Barry bothers Ireland in 1971. Below: Gareth fires away a pass against Australia in 1975.

Grand slammers. The 1971 team against Ireland. The dream team of the Seventies. Standing (left to right): Barry Llewelyn, Mervyn Davies, Mike Roberts, Denzil Williams, Delme Thomas, Dai Morris, Clive Rowlands (coach). Seated: JPR Williams, John Bevan, Barry John, John Dawes (capt), John Taylor, Gareth Edwards, TGR Davies. In front: Jeff Young, Arthur Lewis.

Not really an old-fashioned foot-rush. But the Welsh forwards are driving a loose ball through in the 35-12 victory over Scotland in 1972. Geoff Evans is about to swoop for the pick-up. In support race (left, with headband) Mervyn Davies, Barrie Llewelyn, Delme Thomas and (right) John Lloyd.

They called him Merv the Swerve. Actually, Mervyn Davies was a man who took the direct line, as here against France in 1974. The back row of John Taylor, Mervyn Davies and Dai Morris is claimed by many to be the perfect trio, and the best to play for Wales.

Terry Cobner's debut try against Scotland in 1974, with Phil Bennett and Dai Morris in close support. Cobner, a no frills wing forward, was as tough as they make them. He became the first WRU Director of Rugby in January 1996; a man with a mission and with the knowledge to complete it.

JJ Williams, whippy wing and perceptive match analyser for BBC Wales. He scored 12 tries for Wales and famously is remembered for the one disallowed try at Twickenham in 1974 when referee J R West qualified for the award of the White Stick. Here JJ gets a nod of approval from watching prop Glyn Shaw against Ireland in 1977.

Not so much a Maori sidestep as a Pontypool shimmy. Graham Price was the most renowned destroyer of loose-heads ever let loose in a Welsh scrum. He scored a famous try in Paris in 1975 on a long supporting run – and Wales did not win there again for 24 years. Here he gives the French another charge in 1976.

Wales won by one goal, one penalty goal, two tries (14) to nil

With a gale behind them in the first half, Scotland could not break the Welsh defence. The Scots missed penalty chances and could have been 15 points in the lead by the change round. For the second time there were 10 Cardiff men in the Welsh team and the only change from Twickenham was the reintroduction of Stan Williams, in the second row, for his Llanelli team-mate, Des Jones.

Wales: R F Trott (Cardiff); K J Jones (Newport), Bleddyn Williams, W B Cleaver, J Matthews (Cardiff), Glyn Davies (Pontypridd), H Tanner (Cardiff, capt.); L Anthony (Neath), M James, Cliff Davies, W E Tamplin (Cardiff), Stan Williams, Ossie Williams (Llanelli), L Manfield, Gwyn Evans (Cardiff).

Scotland: W C W Murdoch (Hillhead HSFP); T G H Jackson (London Scottish), J R S Innes (Aberdeen GSFP, capt.), A Cameron (Glasgow HSFP), D D Mackenzie (Edinburgh Univ.); D P Hepburn (Woodford), W D Allardice (Aberdeen GSFP); L Currie (Dunfermline), G Lyall (Gala), R M Bruce (Aberdeen GSFP), J Dawson (Glasgow Acads.), W P Black (Glasgow HSFP), W I D Elliot (Edinburgh Acads.), G M Watt (Edinburgh Wands.), J B Lees (Gala).

For Wales, Bleddyn Williams, Jack Matthews and Ken Jones scored tries. Bill Tamplin converted one and kicked a penalty goal.

Referee: T N Pearce (England).

France won by one goal and two tries (11) to one penalty goal (3)

"Don't underrate these Frenchmen," Haydn Tanner warned his team before the start. After the titanic tussle at Colombes the previous year this went without saying; but even so, Wales never expected France to snatch their first win on Welsh soil in such conclusive manner. In arctic conditions, the 38,000 crowd saw the French pack take command with the giant second row pair, Alban Moga and Robert Soro in great form. Les Manfield was the best of a bedraggled home pack. Jack Matthews had an unhappy time, giving away one try and missing his tackles. Only Tanner and Frank Trott looked convincing behind the scrum.

Maurice Terreau made two spectacular interceptions. He scored from one and set up a try for Michel Pomathios with the other. When play became over-vigorous, oranges and bottles were thrown on the field and the crowd, swollen by forged tickets, spilled over the touch lines. Their unruly behaviour held up play for long periods and police, players and referee Alan Bean (England) tried to push the crowd back. Bill Tamplin hurled one spectator from a line-out when the trespasser tried to remonstrate with a French player during a spasm of punching. But Welsh fans chaired Pomathios off the field at the end to show their appreciation of his fine play.

Pomathios played 22 games for France, including five appearances against Wales, and was one of the greatest wings the Tricolours have produced, in the classical style of players such as Ken Jones and Dewi Bebb, of Wales.

Wales: R F Trott (Cardiff); K J Jones (Newport), Bleddyn Williams, W B Cleaver, J Matthews (Cardiff); Glyn Davies (Pontypridd), H Tanner (Cardiff capt.); L Anthony (Neath), M James, Cliff Davies, W E Tamplin (Cardiff), Stan Williams, Ossie Williams (Llanelli), L Manfield, Gwyn Evans (Cardiff).

France: A Alvarez (Tyrosse); M Pomathios (Agen), M Terrean (Bourg), L Junquas (Bayonne, capt.), J Lassegue (Toulouse); L Bordenave (Toulon), Y Bergougnan

(Toulouse); E Buzy (Lourdes), L Martin (Pau), L Caron (Castres), R Soro (Romans), A Moga (Begles), J Matheu (Castres), G Basquet (Agen), J Prat (Lourdes).

For France, Guy Basquet, Maurice Terreau and Michel Pomathios scored tries. Andre Alvarez converted one.

For Wales, Ossie Williams kicked a penalty goal.

Referee: A S Bean (England).

Match 188 IRELAND v WALES   Ravenhill, Belfast. March 13, 1948

Ireland won by two tries (6) to one try (3)

Jack Daly's try is a moment of Irish rugby history never to be forgotten. The crowd tore his jersey to shreds at the end and the pieces are prized souvenirs in the households of many Irish families. Daly chased a kick through from a line-out to score after seven minutes of the second half and Ireland won the Triple Crown for the first time since 1899. The Irish pack were magnificent in front of 32,000 spectators. After 12 minutes, Jackie Kyle went to the blind side and put Barney Mullan over for a try. Wales drew level with a side-stepping run by Bleddyn Williams. But Daly's dash decided the game and he was carried off by the crowd to become a national hero.

John Gwilliam, dropped after his first cap against Australia, was recalled by Wales. Glyn Davies was hounded mercilessly by flankers Bill McKay and Jim McCarthy. This season, Bleddyn Williams scored 41 tries for Cardiff to break the club's scoring record by Tommy Pearson in 1892-93.

Ireland: J A D Higgins (Civil Service); B O'Hanlon (Dolphin), W D McKee (NIFC), P J Reid (Garryowen), B Mullan (Clontarf); J W Kyle (NIFC), E Strathdee (Queen's Univ., Belfast); A A McConnell (Belfast Collegians), K D Mullen (Old Belvedere, capt.), J C Daly (London Irish), C P Callan (Lansdowne), J E Nelson (Malone), J W McKay (Queen's Univ., Belfast), D J O'Brien (London Irish), J S McCarthy (Dolphin).

Wales: R F Trott (Cardiff); K J Jones (Newport), Bleddyn Williams, W B Cleaver, Les Williams (Cardiff); Glyn Davies (Pontypridd), H Tanner (Cardiff, capt.); Emlyn Davies (Aberavon), M James, Cliff Davies (Cardiff), J A Gwilliam (Cambridge Univ.), J R G Stephens (Neath), Ossie Williams (Llanelli), L Manfield, Gwyn Evans (Cardiff).

For Ireland, Barney Mullan and Jack Daly scored tries.

For Wales, Bleddyn Williams scored a try.

Referee: M A Allan (Scotland).

Match 189 WALES v ENGLAND   Cardiff Arms Park. January 15, 1949

Wales won by three tries (9) to one dropped goal (3)

Glyn Davies was the man of the match. His graceful, gliding runs and smooth sidestep spearheaded Wales to victory in the classical manner of fly half play. With Tanner superb at scrum half and Gwilliam and Alun Meredith controlling the line-out, Wales, wearing white shorts for the first time, gave a pleasing all-round display. The 51,000 crowd saw 'Nim' Hall drop his customary goal, but that was the end of England's scoring. Don Hayward and Ray

Cale, two outstanding Newbridge forwards, made their initial appearances for Wales. Hayward, who came in as reserve when Rees Stephens dropped out, played 15 times for Wales, first as second row and later as prop. Hooker "Bunner" Travers had the remarkable distinction of being recalled to international rugby after an absence of 10 years.

Wales: R F Trott (Cardiff); K J Jones (Newport), J Matthews, Bleddyn Williams, Les Williams (Cardiff); Glyn Davies (Cambridge Univ.), H Tanner (Cardiff, capt.); *E Coleman, W Travers (Newport), Dai Jones (Swansea), *Don Hayward (Newbridge), *Alun Meredith (Devonport Services), *W R Cale (Newbridge), J A Gwilliam (Cambridge Univ.), Gwyn Evans (Cardiff).

England: W B Holmes (Cambridge Univ.); J A Gregory (Blackheath), L B Cannell, C B van Ryneveld (Oxford Univ.), T Danby (Harlequins); N M Hall (Huddersfield, Capt.), G Rimmer (Waterloo); T W Price (Cheltenham), A P Henderson (Edinburgh Wands.), M J Berridge (Northampton), H F Luya (Headingley), G D' A Hosking (Devonport Services), E L Horsfall (Harlequins), B Braithwaite-Exley (Headingley), V G Roberts (Penryn).

For Wales, Les Williams (2) and Alun Meredith scored tries.

For England, Norman 'Nim' Hall dropped a goal.

Referee: N H Lambert (Ireland).

Match 190 SCOTLAND v WALES — Murrayfield. February 5, 1949

Scotland won by two tries (6) to one goal (5)

The Keller Plan baffled Wales. Doug Keller, who had played against Wales for the 1947-48 Australians, captained Scotland and ordered his side to destroy and wait for their chances. With a stopper threequarter line and a fine breakaway forward trio, the home team were superbly equipped for these tactics. Sheep farmer Doug Elliot, No. 8 Peter Kininmonth and Keller were the breakaway forwards who smashed the Welsh backs. Ray Cale seemed unlucky to have a try disallowed, but Bleddyn Williams eventually scored a lovely try, which Frank Trott converted. However, tries by Doug Smith and Laurie Gloag pipped Wales by one point. Tanner was severely criticised for not changing his tactics. A lack of flexibility in his tactical approach was the one weakness in his play. The 57,000 spectators wondered if they would see much of the game because of thick fog; but it cleared suddenly and play started only seven minutes late.

So Triple Crown thoughts were ended yet again for Wales as Glyn Davies was subjected to a series of bone-jarring tackles from Dr Keller and the rangy Doug Elliot. They made it their business to ensure that the young Welsh star would wreak no havoc this time.

Scotland: I J M Lumsden (Watsonians); T G H Jackson (London Scottish), L G Gloag (Cambridge Univ.), D P Hepburn (Woodford), D W C Smith (London Scottish); C R Bruce (Glasgow Acads.), W D Allardice (Aberdeen GSFP); J C Dawson (Glasgow Acads.), J G Abercrombie (Edinburgh Univ.), S Coltman (Hawick), L R Currie (Dunfermline), G A Wilson (Oxford Univ.), D H Keller (London Scottish, capt.), P W Kininmonth (Oxford Univ.), W I D Elliot (Edinburgh Acads.).

Wales: R F Trott (Cardiff); K J Jones (Newport), J Matthews, Bleddyn Williams, *T Cook (Cardiff); Glyn Davies (Cambridge Univ.), H Tanner (Cardiff, capt.); E Coleman, W Travers (Newport), Dai Jones (Swansea), J A Gwilliam (Cambridge Univ.), Alun Meredith (Devonport Services), W R Cale (Newbridge), J R G Stephens (Neath), Gwyn Evans (Cardiff).

For Scotland, Doug Smith and Laurie Gloag scored tries.

117

For Wales, Bleddyn Williams scored a try. Frank Trott converted.

Referee: N H Lambert (Ireland).

Match 191 WALES v IRELAND   St. Helen's, Swansea. March 12, 1949

Ireland won by one goal (5) to nil

It was Jim McCarthy's turn to have his green jersey ripped from his back and torn into strips by the souvenir hunters after scoring the Triple Crown winning try against Wales. Nearly everyone, except referee Tom Pearce (England), thought McCarthy off-side when he scored, but the fact remains that Ireland thoroughly deserved to win the Triple Crown for the second successive year and fourth time in their history. The try came from a well practised and smoothly executed move. Jackie Kyle went to the blind side on a feint attack. Then he punted high infield and McCarthy, the speedy flank forward, was waiting to leap for the ball and touch down. George Norton converted. With this 5-0 lead at half time, Ireland concentrated on wearing down the older Welsh pack and spoiled relentlessly to complete their first win at Swansea since 1889. Billy Cleaver, known as "Billy the Kick" because of his tactical kicking skill, replaced Glyn Davies at fly half, but the six Cardiff backs surprisingly failed to combine effectively.

Dai Jones, the Swansea prop, was the most industrious of the home pack, and Ken Jones looked the most resourceful of the backs. Wales almost scored just before half time when Jack Matthews ripped through with the best break of the match, but his pass went astray. Attendance: 40,000.

Wales: R F Trott (Cardiff); K J Jones (Newport), J Matthews, Bleddyn Williams, T Cook (Cardiff); W B Cleaver, H Tanner (Cardiff, capt.); E Coleman, W Travers (Newport), Dai Jones (Swansea), J. A. Gwilliam (Cambridge Univ.), Alun Meredith (Devonport Services), W R Cale (Newbridge), J R G Stephens (Neath), Gwyn Evans (Cardiff).

Ireland: G W Norton (Bective); M Lane (Univ. Coll., Cork), W D McKee (NIFC), N J Henderson (Queen's Univ., Belfast), P O'Hanlon (Dolphin); J W Kyle, E Strathdee (Queen's Univ. Belfast); T Clifford (Young Munster), K D Mullen (Old Belvedere, capt.), L Griffin (Wanderers), R Agar, J E Nelson (Malone), J W McKay (Queen's Univ., Belfast), D J O'Brien (London Irish), J S McCarthy (Dolphin).

For Ireland, Jim McCarthy scored a try. George Norton converted.

Referee: T N Pearce (England).

Match 192 FRANCE v WALES   Colombes, Paris. March 26, 1949

France won by one goal (5) to one try (3)

A season that had started so spectacularly with the victory over England, ended in ruins at Colombes, with Wales holders of that highly undesirable symbol of rugby failure, the wooden spoon. Wales did not play badly, but France showed superior team work. GIyn Davies returned in place of Cleaver as outside half, and the controversey raged about who was the player better suited to the team's need. This was Haydn Tanner's 25th and final international match. Ken Jones scored a good try, but let Lassegue slip him to score the try in the second half which Alvarez converted with the winning kick. Frank Trott defended fearlessly, though laid out several times. Bleddyn Williams withdrew from the team with a muscle strain (suffered while playing in a Sunday charity game at Clifton) and did not play again for Wales for two years.

Clem Thomas and Malcolm Thomas wore the Welsh jersey for the first time. Malcolm was to win 27 caps as a wing, centre and outside half; Clem was to play 26 times as wing forward.

France: N Baudry (Montferrand); M Pomathios (Lyons), P Dizabo (Tyrosse), H Dutrain, J Lassegue (Toulouse); A Alvarez (Tyrosse), G Dufau (Racing Club); E Buzy (Lourdes), M Jol (Biarritz), L Caron (Lyons), A Moga (Begles), R Soro (Romans), J Matheu, (Castres), G Basquet (Agen, capt.), J Prat (Lourdes).

Wales: R F Trott (Cardiff); K J Jones, *M C Thomas (Newport), J Matthews (Cardiff), *W Major (Maesteg); Glyn Davies (Pontypridd), H Tanner (Cardiff, capt.); Cliff Davies (Cardiff), W Travers (Newport), Dai Jones (Swansea), Don Hayward (Newbridge), J A Gwilliam (Cambridge Univ.), *P Stone (Llanelli) , J R G Stephens (Neath), *R C C Thomas (Swansea).

For France, Jean Lassegue scored a try. Andre Alvarez converted.

For Wales, Ken Jones scored a try.

Referee: N H Lambert (Ireland).

Match 193 **ENGLAND v WALES** Twickenham. January 21, 1950

Wales won by one goal, one penalty goal, one try (11) to one goal (5)

Lewis Jones was only 18 years and nine months when he wore the Welsh jersey for the first time. He was the full back who ran when everyone (especially his own team) expected him to kick. One run led to a spectacular try as Wales took their first confident step towards the Triple Crown that had eluded them for 39 years. Lewis Jones fielded a kick on the half way line and set off diagonally across the field. He straightened up and England's defence were bewildered. Malcolm Thomas and Bob Evans linked and at the end of it all, prop Cliff Davies was over for an amazing try. Lewis Jones had started the legend of greatness as the player who always did the unexpected, though not always successfully. His career was all too brief: after 10 games for Wales he went to become an even greater legend in the Rugby League game.

A record Twickenham crowd of 75,500 (numbers have since been limited in the interests of comfort) watched this first official Welsh win at Rugby HQ since 1933 and only the second there in 40 years. The gates were closed an hour before the kick-off with thousands locked outside. Bleddyn Williams, chosen as captain, withdrew because of injury and John Gwilliam led the side for the first time. He was to be captain for 13 matches.

Another unfit star was Rees Stephens. His place was taken by his Neath club-mate Roy John. This lively replacement was to win 19 caps and emerge as one of the finest line-out experts the game has known. Also playing for the first time were scrum half Rex Willis (21 caps) and hooker Dai Davies (17 caps). England led after 10 minutes with a John Smith try when he intercepted and ran half the length of the field. Murray Hofmeyr converted.

England: M B Hofmeyr (Oxford Univ.); J V Smith (Cambridge Univ.), B. Boobbyer, L B Cannell, I J Botting (Oxford Univ.); I Preece (Coventry, capt.), G Rimmer (Waterloo); J M Kendall-Carpenter (Oxford Univ.), E Evans (Sale), W A Holmes (Nuneaton), G R D'A Hosking (Devonport Serices), H A Jones (Barnstable), H D Small (Oxford Univ.), D B Vaughan (Headingley), J J Cain (Waterloo).

Wales: *Lewis Jones (Devonport Services); K J Jones, M C Thomas (Newport), J Matthews (Cardiff), *T J Brewer (Newport); W B Cleaver, *W R Willis (Cardiff); *J D Robins (Birkenhead Park), *D M Davies (Somerset Police), Cliff Davies (Cardiff), Don Hayward (Newbridge), *Roy John (Neath), W R Cale (Pontypool), J A Gwilliam (Edinburgh Wands., capt.), R T Evans (Newport).

For Wales, Cliff Davies and Ray Cale scored tries. Lewis Jones converted one and kicked a penalty goal.

For England, J V Smith scored a try. Murray Hofmeyr converted.

Referee: N H Lambert (Ireland).

Match 194 **WALES v SCOTLAND**   St. Helen's, Swansea. February 4, 1950

Wales won by one dropped goal, one penalty goal, two tries (12) to nil

Scotland fielded the same Elliot-Kininmonth-Keller breakaway unit that had hounded Wales to defeat at Murrayfield the previous year, but this time Welsh tactics were different. Wales played it tight, with Billy Cleaver kicking as the tactical controller. Gwilliam led superbly in a stern forward contest with Bob Evans and Ray Cale destroying the Scottish backs. It was an unspectacular game for the 41,000 spectators. Lewis Jones was uncertain at full back and never played in that position for Wales again. Jack Matthews spearheaded the Welsh attack and one of his powerful bursts paved the way for Malcolm Thomas's try and a 3-0 interval lead. Lewis Jones, with a 35-yard penalty goal, Ken Jones, with a try, and Cleaver, with a dropped goal, completed the scoring in the second stage towards the Triple Crown.

Wales: Lewis Jones (Devonport Services); K J Jones, M C Thomas (Newport), J Matthews (Cardiff), W Major (Maesteg); W B Cleaver, W R Willis (Cardiff); J D Robins (Birkenhead Park), D M Davies (Somerset Police), Cliff Davies (Cardiff), Don Hayward (Newbridge), Roy John (Neath), W R Cale (Pontypool), J A Gwilliam (Edinburgh Wands., capt.), R T Evans (Newport).

Scotland: G Burrell (Gala); D W C Smith (Army), R Macdonald (Edinburgh Univ.), D A Sloan (Edinburgh Acads.), C W Drummond (Melrose); L Bruce Lockhart (London Scottish), A W Black (Edinburgh Univ.); J C Dawson (Glasgow Acads.), J G Abercrombie (Edinburgh Univ.), G M Budge (Edinburgh Wands.), D E Muir (Heriot's FP), R Gemmill (Glasgow HSFP), W I D Elliot (Edinburgh Acads., capt.), P W Kininmonth (Richmond), D H Keller (London Scottish).

For Wales, Malcolm Thomas and Ken Jones scored tries. Billy Cleaver dropped a goal. Lewis Jones kicked a penalty goal.

Referee: M J Dowling (Ireland).

Match 195 **IRELAND v WALES**   Ravenhill, Belfast. March 11, 1950

Wales won by two tries (6) to one penalty goal (3)

Three minutes to go. The score: 3-3. Welsh hopes of the Triple Crown after 39 years were fading. Ireland heeled on their own 25. Jackie Kyle was bound to clear to touch. But Ray Cale pounced round the scrum to harass Carroll. As the scrum half desperately shovelled the ball out to Kyle, Cale went with it. What a fearsome combination for even a fly half of Kyle's quality: a bad pass and a deadly tackler at the same time. The ball rolled loose, but at least Kyle was spared to become a missionary in Africa. Cleaver picked up and fed Lewis Jones: the winning try was taking shape. Lewis Jones, in his new position of centre, drew full back Norton and sent a long pass swinging out to Malcolm Thomas. There were 15 yards to go as the Welsh wing threw back his head and ran for the Triple Crown.

Corner-flaggers streamed across like a cloud of locusts. They hit Thomas as he dived for the corner. Down everyone crashed, corner flag and all. Was it a try? There were agonising hour-long seconds before referee R A Beattie (Scotland) raised his arm and Wales had won. If Irish touch judge Ossie Glasgow had signalled that Thomas had knocked down the flag before grounding the ball there would have been few Welsh protests. It was a marginal decision either way.

There was no score in the first half. Then a Ken Jones try was cancelled out by George Norton's penalty goal. It was a tough baptism for new Welsh full back Gerwyn Williams, but he went on to win 13 caps. The jubilation ended on Sunday morning, when a Tudor V aircraft crashed at Llandow, near Cardiff; and 80 Welsh rugby fans died in the worst civil air disaster in history up to that time. It was a shadow across the first Triple Crown triumph since 1911. So for the eighth time Wales had won the honour.

Ireland: G W Norton (Bective); M Lane (Univ. Coll., Cork), R J H Uprichard (RAF), G C Phipps (Rosslyn Park), L Crowe (Old Belvedere); J W Kyle (Queen's Univ., Belfast), R Carroll (Lansdowne); T Clifford (Young Munster), K D Mullen (Old Belvedere, capt.), D McKibbin (Queen's Univ., Belfast), J E Nelson, R Agar (Malone), J W McKay (Queen's Univ., Belfast), D J O'Brien (London Irish), J S McCarthy (Dolphin).

Wales: *Gerwyn Williams (London Welsh); K J Jones (Newport), Lewis Jones (Devonport Services), J Matthews (Cardiff), M C Thomas (Devonport Services); W B Cleaver, W R Willis (Cardiff); J D Robins (Birkenhead Park), D M Davies (Somerset Police), Cliff Davies (Cardiff), Roy John (Neath), Don Hayward (Newbridge), W R Cale (Pontypool), J A Gwilliam (Edinburgh Wands., capt.), R T Evans (Newport).

For Wales, Ken Jones and Malcolm Thomas scored tries.

For Ireland, George Norton kicked a penalty goal.

Referee: R A Beattie (Scotland).

Match 196 WALES v FRANCE   Cardiff Arms Park. March 25, 1950

Wales won by three goals, one penalty goal, one try (21) to nil

Five uniformed buglers sounded the Last Post as the teams stood to attention and the crowd marked a minute's silence in memory of the victims of the Llandow disaster air crash. Wales led only 5-0 at halftime, but cut loose to win comfortably and take the international championship outright for the first time since 1936. It was the first time since 1911 for Wales to win all four championship games in one season.

Wales: Gerwyn Williams (London Welsh); K J Jones (Newport), J Matthews (Cardiff), Lewis Jones (Devonport Services), M C Thomas (Devonport Services); W B Cleaver, W R Willis (Cardiff); J D Robins (Birkenhead Park), D M Davies (Somerset Police), Cliff Davies (Cardiff), Don Hayward (Newbridge), Roy John (Neath), W R Cale (Pontypool), J A Gwilliam (Edinburgh Wands., capt.), R T Evans (Newport).

France: G Brun (Vienne); M Siman (Castres), P Lauga (Vichy), J Merquey (Toulon), M Pomathios (Lyons); F Fournet (Montferrand), G Dufau (Racing Club); P Pascalin (Stade Montois), R Bienne (Cognac), R Ferrien (Tarbes), P Aristuoy (Pau), F Bonnus (Toulon), J Prat (Lourdes), G Basquet (Agen, capt.), J Matheu (Castres).

For Wales, Ken Jones (2), Roy John and Jack Matthews scored tries. Lewis Jones converted three and kicked a penalty goal.

Referee: M J Dowling (Ireland).

Wales won by four goals, one try (23) to one goal (5)

Where was there a team to stop this Welsh rugby juggernaut? England, with nine new caps, were crushed and the 50,000 crowd had visions of John Gwilliam's men sweeping on to the Triple Crown for the second successive season. In registering their fifth consecutive win, Wales had scored an aggregate of 73 points with 13 against. Who could have dreamed that it was to be the only Welsh victory of the season?

Wales: Gerwyn Williams (Llanelli); K J Jones (Newport) J Matthews (Cardiff), Lewis Jones, M C Thomas (Devonport Services); Glyn Davies (Cambridge Univ.) W R Willis (Cardiff); J D Robins (Birkenhead Park), D M Davies (Somerset Police), Cliff Davies (Cardiff), Roy John (Neath), Don Hayward (Newbridge), R T Evans (Newport), J A Gwilliam (Edinburgh Wands., capt.}, *Peter Evans (Llanelli).

England: E N Hewitt (Coventry); C G Woodruff (Harlequins), L F L Oakley (Bedford), B Boobbyer (Oxford Univ.), V R Tindall (Liverpool Univ.); I Preece (Coventry), G R Rimmer (Waterloo); R V Stirling (Leicester), T Smith (Northampton), W A Holmes (Nuneaton), D T Wilkins (Roundhay), J T Bartlett (Waterloo), V G Roberts (Penryn, capt.), P B C Moore (Blackheath), G C Rittson-Thomas (Oxford Univ.).

For Wales, Jack Matthews (2), Malcolm Thomas (2) and Ken Jones scored tries. Lewis Jones converted four.

For England, Chris Rittson-Thomas scored a try. Edwin Hewitt converted.

Referee: M J Dowling (Ireland).

Scotland won by two goals, one dropped goal, one penalty goal, one try (19) to nil

The "Murrayfield Massacre" match is fascinating, for all its dismal failure by Wales. Welshmen argue interminably about it. Who was to blame? How could a brilliant, invincible Welsh team crash so sensationally? No-one gave Scotland the proverbial snowball's chance against Gwilliam's champions. The turning point was the second score of the match, a dropped goal high between the posts from out near the touch line early in the second half by Scottish skipper and No 8 Peter Kininmonth. It ranks as one of the most magnificent dropped goals in international rugby history.

The truth was that the Welsh pack flopped. Gwilliam, of course, was not the only forward to fail, while fly half Glyn Davies never played for Wales again. Lewis Jones, who was switched to outside half for a time, also was dropped. The selectors were in such a dilemma that when they announced the team to face Ireland, they left five places open while they had second thoughts. Eventually, the vacancies were filled by Bleddyn Williams, Malcolm Thomas, Cliff Morgan, Ben Edwards and Cliff Davies. The Murrayfield attendance of 81,000 (including 20,000 Welshmen) was a record for British rugby.

Scotland: I H M Thomson (Heriot's FP); R A Gordon (Edinburgh Wands), D A Sloan (Edinburgh Acads.), D M Scott (Langholm), D M Rose (Jedforest); A Cameron (Glasgow HSFP), I A Ross (Hillhead HSFP); J C Dawson (Glasgow Acads.), N G R Mair (Edinburgh Univ.), R L Wilson (Gala), R Gemmill (Glasgow HSFP), H M Inglis, W I D Elliot (Edinburgh Acads.), P W Kininmonth (Richmond, capt.), R C Taylor (Kelvinside West).

Wales: Gerwyn Williams (Llanelli) ; K J Jones (Newport), J Matthews (Cardiff), Lewis Jones, M C Thomas (Devonport Services); Glyn Davies (Cambridge Univ.), W R Willis (Cardiff); J D Robins (Birkenhead Park), D M Davies (Somerset Police), Cliff Davies (Cardiff), Roy John (Neath), Don Hayward (Newbridge), *A Forward (Pontypool), J A Gwilliam (Edinburgh Wands., capt.), R T Evans (Newport).

For Scotland, Bob Gordon (2) and Hamish Dawson scored tries. Hamish Inglis converted one. Ian Thomson converted one and kicked a penalty goal. Peter Kininmonth dropped a goal.

Referee: M J Dowling (Ireland).

Match 199 WALES v IRELAND   Cardiff Arms Park. March 10, 1951

Drawn. Wales one penalty goal (3). Ireland one try (3)

Ben Edwards played this one game for Wales and then was never chosen again. Yet he kicked a 45-yard, wide-angled penalty goal that stopped Ireland winning the Triple Crown. Ireland salvaged something from their disappointment, because Jackie Kyle's clever try forced a draw and gave them the championship title for the third time in four years. Cliff Morgan played splendidly on his debut as successor to Glyn Davies at fly half. Roy John played in the unexpected role of blind side wing forward so that Ben Edwards could pack in the second row. Edwards kicked his goal in the first minute and 15 minutes later Kyle cut through with a side-stepping run from 20 yards. Later, Kyle saved a try with a fine cover tackle on Ken Jones only 10 yards from the Irish line.

Wales: Gerwyn Williams (Llanelli); K J Jones (Newport), J Matthews, Bleddyn Williams (Cardiff), M C Thomas (Devonport Services) ; *Cliff Morgan, W R Willis (Cardiff); J D Robins (Birkenhead Park), D M Davies (Somerset Police), Cliff Davies (Cardiff), Don Hayward (Newbridge), *Ben Edwards, R T Evans (Newport), J A Gwilliam (Edinburgh Wands., capt.), Roy John (Neath).

Ireland: A McMorrow (Garryowen); W H J Millar, N J Henderson (Queen's Univ., Belfast), R R Chambers (Instonians), M F Lane (Univ. Coll., Cork); J W Kyle (Queen's Univ., Belfast), J A O'Meara (Univ. Coll., Cork); D. McKibbin (Instonians), K D Mullen (Old Belvedere, capt.), J H Smith (Queen's Univ., Belfast), J R Brady (CIYMS), J E. Nelson (Malone), J W. McKay (Queen's Univ., Belfast), D J O'Brien (Cardiff), J S McCarthy (Dolphin).

For Wales, Ben Edwards kicked a penalty goal.

For Ireland, Jack Kyle scored a try.

Referee: W C W Murdoch (Scotland).

Match 200 FRANCE v WALES   Colombes, Paris. April 7, 1951

France won one goal and one penalty goal (8) to one try (3)

After seven successive games as Welsh captain, John Gwilliam was dropped and Jack Matthews took over the leadership. But Wales flattered to deceive in the first half as they led 3-0 through a Ken Jones try, and France looked faster and more resourceful. Wing Haydn Morris and prop W O 'Billy' Williams played for Wales for the first time. Williams was to win 22 caps as one of his country's finest prop forwards.

France: R Arcalis (Brive); A Porthault (Racing Club), G Brun (Vienne), G

Belletante (Nantes), M Pomathios (Lyons); A J Alvarez (Tyrosse), G Dufau (Racing Club); R Bernard (Bergerac), P Pascalin (Mont de Marsan), P Bertrand (Bourg), L Mias (Mazamet), H Foures (Toulouse), R Bienes (Cognac), G Basquet (Agen, capt.), J Prat (Lourdes).

Wales: Gerwyn Williams (Llanelli); K J Jones, M C Thomas (Newport), J Matthews (capt.), *H Morris (Cardiff); Cliff Morgan, W R Willis (Cardiff) *W O Williams (Swansea), D M Davies (Somerset Police), J D Robins (Birkenhead Park), Don Hayward (Newbridge), Roy John (Neath), R T Evans (Newport), J R G Stephens (Neath), Peter Evans (Llanelli).

For France, Andre Alvarez scored a try and kicked a penalty goal. Jean Prat converted the try.

For Wales, Ken Jones scored a try

Referee: M J Dowling (Ireland).

Match 201 WALES v SOUTH AFRICA Cardiff Arms Park. December 22, 1951

South Africa won by one dropped goal, one try (6) to one try (3)

Cliff Morgan, brilliant for Wales in so many of his 29 appearances, cost his side their chance of victory against Basil Kenyon's Springboks. In his third game for Wales, Morgan kicked too often and mostly put the ball straight into the secure hands of full back Johnny Buchler. Basie van Wyk, the Springboks' flanker, curbed Morgan in a manner that no other wing forward ever accomplished, though Morgan obtained his revenge on tour with the 1955 Lions. With Roy John supreme in the line-out and the home forwards giving a magnificent display as ball-winners, it was disheartening to see Morgan waste so much possession. This was the only defeat Wales were to suffer throughout the season – and a lesson Morgan never forgot.

South Africa were expert at kicking, though 'Okey' Geffin, the famous goal kicker (he scored five penalty goals to beat the All Blacks 15-11 in the Newlands test in 1949) missed three penalty shots. They scored just before half time with a typical corner-try by opportunist wing 'Chum' Ochse, as Hannes Brewis sent 'Tjol' Lategan racing away to put the wing clear. With less than 10 minutes to go, the Springboks made it 6-0 when Brewis lobbed a dropped goal high between the Welsh posts.

Just before the end, Wales snatched a memorable try. Gwilliam fed straight back from a line-out with an under-arm pass to Cliff Morgan. Bleddyn Williams and Malcolm Thomas worked a scissors move and Bleddyn stormed over to score. Such was the demand for tickets for a match billed as being for the world rugby championship, that stand seats were fetching £10 on the black market instead of the 15s. face value. The Springboks lost only one match on the tour; 11-9 to London Counties.

Wales: Gerwyn Williams (Llanelli); K J Jones, M C Thomas (Newport), Bleddyn Williams (Cardiff), Lewis Jones (Llanelli); Cliff Morgan, W R Willis (Cardiff); W O Williams (Swansea), D M Davies (Somerset Police), Don Hayward (Newbridge), Roy John, J R G Stephens (Neath), *L Blyth (Swansea), J A Gwilliam (Edinburgh Wands., capt.), A Forward (Pontypool).

South Africa: J Buchler; P Johnstone, R van Schoor, M T Lategan, J K Ochse; J D Brewis, P A du Toit; A Geffin, W Delport, C Koch, W H M Barnard, J du Rand, S Fry, H Muller (capt.), C J van Wyk.

For South Africa, Johannes 'Chum' Ochse scored a try. Hannes Brewis dropped a goal.

For Wales, Bleddyn Williams scored a try.

Referee: N H Lambert (Ireland).

Wales won by one goal, one try (8) to two tries (6)

Six points down and with Lewis Jones a limping passenger on the wing. That was the situation for Wales, and thoughts of the Triple Crown could not have been further away. But John Gwilliam's team fought back to one of their most notable victories and only their third in official games at Twickenham. Props Billy Williams and Don Hayward – the jumbo front row – were giants in the heroic Welsh pack. Len Blyth was pulled out to play on the wing while Lewis Jones was off for 15 minutes with a torn left thigh muscle Albert Agar's try after 15 minutes was followed with a corner-try by Ted Woodward. Just before half time, Cliff Morgan broke through to send Ken Jones in for a try that Malcolm Thomas converted.

Then the near-crippled Lewis Jones joined an attack, though at little more than hobbling speed. Nevertheless, he made the extra man and it ended with Olympic sprinter Ken Jones racing away for the winning try. Roy John again was the line-out maestro and Rex Willis nursed Cliff Morgan with faultless judgment. Bleddyn Williams withdrew because of influenza and Alun Thomas came in as replacement to win his first cap. Crowds were locked out when the gates were closed with 73,000 in the ground, but many were invited into houses around the ground to watch the match on TV.

England: W G Hook (Gloucester); J E Woodward (Wasps), A E Agar (Harlequins), L B Cannell (St. Mary's Hosp.), C E Winn (Rosslyn Park); N M Hall (Richmond, capt.), G Rimmer (Waterloo); E Woodgate (Paignton), E Evans (Sale}, R V Stirling (Leicester), J R C Matthews (Harlequins), D T Wilkins (United Services), D F White (Northampton), J M Kendall-Carpenter (Penzance-Newlyn), A O Lewis (Bath).

Wales: Gerwyn Williams (Llanelli); K J Jones, M C Thomas (Newport), *Alun Thomas (Cardiff), Lewis Jones (Llanelli); Cliff Morgan, W R Willis (Cardiff); W O Williams (Swansea), D M Davies (Somerset Police), Don Hayward (Newbridge), Roy John, J R G Stephens (Neath), L Blyth (Swansea), J A Gwilliam (Edinburgh Wands., capt.), A Forward (Pontypool).

For Wales, Ken Jones scored two tries. Malcolm Thomas converted one.

For England, Albert Agar and Ted Woodward scored tries.

Referee: N H Lambert (Ireland).

Wales won by one goal, two penalty goals (11) to nil

Revenge for the "Murrayfield Massacre" match came in a disappointing game. A record Welsh crowd of 56,000 saw full back Gerwyn Williams and open-side flanker Allen Forward proved the stars for their team. Rex Willis fractured his jaw early in the second half, but refused to leave the field. Wales led 8-0 at half time as Malcolm Thomas kicked a touch-line penalty goal and converted Ken Jones's try. Later, Thomas scored his second penalty goal. All the 19 points in the first two matches of the season had been scored by the Newport combination of Ken Jones and Malcolm Thomas. The Welsh team gave an appearance of staleness, and even John Gwilliam was slack in his tapping back from the line-out.

Wales: Gerwyn Williams (Llanelli); K J Jones, M C Thomas (Newport), Bleddyn Williams, Alun Thomas (Cardiff); Cliff Morgan, W R Willis (Cardiff); W O Williams (Swansea), D M Davies (Somerset Police), Don Hayward (Newbridge), Roy John, J R G Stephens (Neath), L Blyth (Swansea), J A Gwilliam (Edinburgh Wands., capt.), A Forward (Pontypool).

Scotland: I H M Thomson (Heriot's FP); R Gordon, I F Cordial (Edinburgh Wands.), J L Allan (Melrose), D M Scott (London Scottish); N G Davidson (Edinburgh Univ.), A F Dorward (Gala); J C Dawson (Glasgow Acads.), N M Munnoch (Watsonians), J Fox (Gala), J Johnston (Melrose), D E Muir (Heriot's F P), P W Kininmonth (Richmond, capt.), H M Inglis, W I D Elliot (Edinburgh Acads.).

For Wales, Ken Jones scored a try. Malcolm Thomas converted and kicked two penalty goals.

Referee: M J Dowling (Ireland).

Match 204   IRELAND v WALES   Lansdowne Road, Dublin. March 8, 1952

Wales won by one goal, one penalty goal, two tries (14) to one penalty goal (3)

For the ninth time, and the second occasion in three years, Wales became Triple Crown winners. They experienced surprisingly little difficulty. The Irish pack lacked their traditional fire and Clem Thomas kept a tight curb on Jackie Kyle. Cliff Morgan, with flashes of genius in his running, was soundly served by new scrum half Billy Williams, who replaced the injured Willis. After eight minutes, Lewis Jones kicked a penalty goal. Then Clem Thomas sent Rees Stephens in for a try. Cliff Morgan swept away on a dazzling run past Kyle to make a try for Ken Jones. Although Murphy kicked a home penalty goal early in the second half, Roy John dummied like a threequarter and put Clem Thomas over for a try that Lewis Jones converted. Attendance: 42,000.

Ireland: J G Murphy (Dublin Univ); W H J Millar, N J Henderson (Queen's Univ., Belfast), R R Chambers (Instonians), G C Phipps (Rosslyn Park); J W Kyle (Queen's Univ., Belfast), J A O'Meara (Univ. Coll., Cork); T Clifford (Young Munster), K D Mullen (Old Belvedere), J H Smith (Belfast Collegians), P J Lawlor (Clontarf), A O'Leary (Cork Constitution), M Dargan (Old Belvedere), D J O'Brien (Cardiff, capt.), J S McCarthy (Dolphin).

Wales: Gerwyn Williams (Llanelli); K J Jones, M C Thomas (Newport), Alun Thomas (Cardiff), Lewis Jones (Llanelli); Cliff Morgan (Cardiff), *W A Williams (Newport); W O Williams (Swansea), D M Davies (Somerset Police), Don Hayward (Newbridge), Roy John, J R G Stephens (Neath), R C C Thomas (Swansea), J A Gwilliam (Edinburgh Wands., capt.), A Forward (Pontypool).

For Wales, R C C Thomas, Ken Jones and Rees Stephens scored tries. Lewis Jones converted one and kicked a penalty goal.

For Ireland, Gerry Murphy kicked a penalty goal.

Referee: Dr P F Cooper (England).

Match 205   WALES v FRANCE   St. Helen's, Swansea. March 22, 1952

Wales won by two penalty goals, one dropped goal (9) to one goal (5)

Wales gave a far from convincing performance and failed to score a try, though they completed the grand slam to win the championship outright. A badly pulled calf muscle kept Cliff Morgan out, so Alun Thomas replaced him. Thomas played in three positions for Wales during the season – centre, wing and outside half. He dropped a goal, but never looked comfortable. Lewis Jones put over two penalty goals from eight attempts.

Wales: Gerwyn Williams (Llanelli); K J Jones, M C Thomas (Newport), Lewis

Jones (Llanelli), *H Phillips (Swansea); Alun Thomas (Cardiff), W A Williams (Newport); W O Williams (Swansea), D M Davies (Somerset Police), Don Hayward (Newbridge), Roy John, J R G Stephens (Neath), R C C Thomas (Swansea), J A Gwilliam (Edinburgh Wands., capt.), A Forward (Pontypool).

France: G Brun (Vienne); M Pomathios (Lyons), J Mauran (Castres), M Prat (Lourdes), J Collombier (St. Junien); J Carabignac (Agen), G Dufau (Racing Club); R Bienes (Cognac), R Brejassou (Pau), P Labadie (Bayonne), B Chevallier (Montferrand), L Mias (Mazamet), J R Bordeu (Lourdes), G Basquet (Agen, capt.), J Prat (Lourdes).

For Wales, Lewis Jones kicked two penalty goals. Alun Thomas dropped a goal.

For France, Michel Pomathios scored a try. Jean Prat converted.

Referee: A W C Austin (Scotland).

Match 206 **WALES v ENGLAND**   Cardiff Arms Park. January 17, 1953

England won by one goal, one penalty goal (8) to one penalty goal (3)

The day the Welsh selectors left out Cliff Morgan in order to play the Newport half back pair of Roy Burnett and Billy Williams, almost all the Welsh team were out of form. The result was England's first victory over Wales for six years. Scrum half Rex Willis had fractured his shoulder in Cardiff's trials and the WRU selectors did not think Morgan played so confidently without him. So Burnett came in for his only cap and certainly did not play badly. But the home pack lacked dash, the centres had no real penetration and even Ken Jones caused groans from the 56,000 spectators. Among those making their first appearances for Wales were Gareth Griffiths, Sid Judd and full back Terry Davies, who provided his team's only points with a long range penalty goal.

Wales: *Terry Davies (Swansea); K J Jones, M C Thomas (Newport), Bleddyn Williams, *G M Griffiths (Cardiff); R Burnett, W A Williams (Newport); J D Robins (Bradford), *G. Beckingham (Cardiff), W O Williams (Swansea), Roy John, J R G Stephens (Neath), *S Judd (Cardiff), J A Gwilliam (Gloucester, capt.), *W D Johnson (Swansea).

England: N M Hall (Richmond, capt.); J E Woodward (Wasps), A E Agar (Harlequins), L B Cannell (St. Mary's Hosp.), R Bazley (Waterloo); M Regan (Liverpool), P W Sykes (Wasps); W A Holmes (Nuneaton), N A Lambuschagne (Harlequins), R V Stirling (Leicester), S J Adkins (Coventry), D T Wilkins (RN), D F White (Northampton), J M Kendall-Carpenter, A O Lewis (Bath).

For England, Lewis Cannell scored a try. 'Nim' Hall converted. Ted Woodward kicked a penalty goal.

For Wales, Terry Davies kicked a penalty goal.

Referee: M J Dowling (Ireland).

Match 207 **SCOTLAND v WALES**   Murrayfield. February 7, 1953

Wales won by one penalty goal, three tries (12) to nil

John Gwilliam was dropped. Bleddyn Williams became the new Welsh captain and was to lead a winning team in each of his five games as skipper. To mark his first captaincy he scored two excellent tries on the ground where Wales had crashed to that sensational 19-0 defeat on their previous visit. Rees Stephens was a grand pack-leader and Courtenay Meredith and

Russell Robins looked useful in their first big game. But the unlucky Rex Willis badly hurt his shoulder early in the second half, left the field and did not play again that season. Clem Thomas went on the wing and Cliff Morgan took over as emergency scrum half. Attendance: 70,000.

Scotland: N W Cameron (Glasgow Univ.); R A Gordon (Edinburgh Wands.), K J Dalgleish (Cambridge Univ.), J L Allan (Melrose), D M Rose (Jedforest); N G Davidson (Edinburgh Univ.), A F Dorward (Gala, capt.); B E Thomson (Oxford Univ.), J King (Selkirk), R L Wilson (Gala), J H Henderson (Oxford Univ.), J J Hegarty (Hawick), A R Valentine (RN), D C Macdonald (Edinburgh Univ.), K H D McMillan (Sale).

Wales: Terry Davies (Swansea); K J Jones (Newport), Alun Thomas, Bleddyn Williams (capt.), G M Griffiths (Cardiff); Cliff Morgan, W R Willis (Cardiff); W O Williams (Swansea), G Beckingham (Cardiff), *C C Meredith, J R G Stephens, Roy John (Neath), S Judd (Cardiff), *R Robins (Pontypridd), R C C Thomas (Swansea).

For Wales, Bleddyn Williams (2) and Ken Jones scored tries. Terry Davies kicked a penalty goal.

Referee: Dr P F Cooper (England).

Match 208 WALES v IRELAND   St. Helen's, Swansea. March 14, 1953

Wales won by one goal (5) to one try (3)

Roy John, back to his superb best, dummied away from a line-out and linked with pack-leader Rees Stephens and John Gwilliam before Gareth Griffiths was put racing away for a second half try. Terry Davies converted with what proved the match winning kick. But it was a dour, unspectacular tussle with Clem Thomas and Sid Judd forcing Jack Kyle to kick constantly. Cliff Morgan looked a better outside half than the famous Irishman. Scrum half Trevor Lloyd made his debut for Wales behind a dominating pack. Attendance: 50,000.

Wales: Terry Davies (Swansea); K J Jones (Newport), Alun Thomas, Bleddyn Williams (capt.), G M Griffiths (Cardiff) ; Cliff Morgan (Cardiff), *T Lloyd (Maesteg); J D Robins (Bradford), D M Davies (Somerset Police), W O Williams (Swansea) Roy John, J R G Stephens (Neath), S Judd (Cardiff), J A Gwilliam (Gloucester), R C Thomas (Swansea).

Ireland: R J Gregg (Queen's Univ., Belfast}; S Byrne (Lansdowne), N J Henderson (NIFC), A C Pedlow (Queen's Univ., Belfast), M Mortell (Bective); J W Kyle (NIFC, capt.), J A O'Meara (Univ. Coll., Cork); W A O'Neill (Univ. Coll., Dublin), R Roe (Dublin Univ.), F E Anderson (Queen's Univ, Belfast), J R Brady (CIYMS), T E Reid (Garryowen), G Reidy (Dolphin), R Kavanagh (Univ. Coll., Dublin), W E Bell (Belfast Collegians).

For Wales, Gareth Griffiths scored a try. Terry Davies converted.

For Ireland, Seamus Byrne scored a try.

Referee: Dr P F Cooper (England).

Match 209 FRANCE v WALES   Colombes, Paris. March 28, 1953

Wales won by two tries (6) to one penalty goal (3)

A try in each half by wing Gareth Griffiths, both excellent examples of opportunism, gave

Wales victory and meant that they finished runners-up to England in the championship. Cliff Morgan and Trevor Lloyd were a more compact and confident half back unit than the French pair, while Clem Thomas was a ruthless raider in destroying French hopes of setting up midfield attacks. Attendance: 40,000.

France: M Vannier (Racing Club); M Pomathios (Lyons), M Galy (Perpignan), G Brun (Vienne), L Roge (Beziers); L Bidart (La Rochelle), G Dufau (Racing Club); P Bertrand (Bourg), J Arieta (Stade Francais), R Brejassou (Tarbes), L Mias (Mazamet), B Chevallier (Montferrand), J Prat (capt.), R Domec (Lourdes), M Celaya (Biarritz).

Wales: Terry Davies (Swansea); K J Jones (Newport), Alun Thomas, Bleddyn Williams (capt.), G M Griffiths (Cardiff); Cliff Morgan (Cardiff), T Lloyd (Maesteg); W O Williams (Swansea), D M Davies (Somerset Police), J D Robins (Bradford), Roy John, J R G Stephens (Neath), S Judd (Cardiff), J A Gwilliam (Gloucester), R C C Thomas (Swansea).

For Wales, Gareth Grifliths scored two tries.

For France, Pierre Bertrand kicked a penalty goal.

Referee: O B Glasgow (Ireland).

Match 210 WALES v NEW ZEALAND Cardiff Arms Park. December 19, 1953

Wales won by two goals, one penalty goal (13) to one goal, one penalty goal (8)

One of the most astonishing strokes of inspiration by a forward playing for Wales brought victory yet again over the All Blacks. From the touch line on the south stand side, Clem Thomas, hemmed in by hostile New Zealanders, kicked the ball far across into midfield. It bounced. And there was wing Ken Jones, swooping in, scooping up this gift from the gods and sending a mighty roar to the skies from the 56,000 crowd as he raced over at the river end with the winning try. Gwyn Rowlands, on his debut, converted and there was just enough time left for New Zealand to realise that once again the famed and feared Red Devils had beaten them. First 1905. Then 1935. Now 1953. Was there ever to be an official New Zealand victory at the Arms Park? Yes, indeed. And many of them in the years ahead.

Bob Stuart's team should have won this first Welsh home international to be televised live. The All Blacks beat England, Scotland and Ireland on this tour and smashed the Welsh pack all round the field with a merciless display of power. The tourists led 8-5 at half time. Sid Judd (brought in as deputy when injured Glyn 'Shorty' Davies, of London Welsh, withdrew) had pounced for a Welsh try as Bob Scott was hustled into throwing a wild pass back near his goal line. Gwyn Rowlands converted. But Ron Jarden put over a 35-yard New Zealand penalty goal from near the touch line and Scott cross-kicked to create a try for Bill Clark that Jarden goaled. Just after half time, 'Tiny' White, a great second row forward, charged away and it took four Welshmen to pull him down a few yards short of the line and prevent a try.

Then, 10 minutes into the second half, Gareth Griffiths went off with a badly dislocated shoulder. It looked like the end for seven struggling Welsh forwards, with Clem Thomas as emergency wing. "How we came back to win I have never understood," confessed skipper Bleddyn Williams. Griffiths ignored medical advice not to go back on. His return, with some 15 minutes to go, fired the battered home forwards. They fought back; not, perhaps, with the same fanatical zeal of the Cardiff pack when they beat the All Blacks, but with enough spirit to unsettle New Zealand.

Bill Clark was penalised by referee Peter Cooper (England) for playing the ball while lying on the wrong side of a ruck and Rowlands kicked a goal from a handy position to make it 8-8. Then came Clem Thomas's stroke of genius and Ken Jones's greatest try of any of the 17 he scored for Wales. The All Blacks were beaten for the third time at Cardiff. Welsh rugby followers still talk about Bob Scott as the greatest full back of them all .... but they remember Clem Thomas's kick above everything.

Wales: Gerwyn Williams (London Welsh); K J Jones (Newport),G M Griffiths, Bleddyn Williams (capt.), *G Rowlands (Cardiff); Cliff Morgan, W R Willis (Cardiff); W O Williams (Swansea), D M Davies (Somerset Police), C C Meredith, J R G Stephens, Roy John (Neath), S Judd (Cardiff), J A Gwilliam (Gloucester), R C C Thomas (Swansea).

New Zealand: R W H. Scott; threequarters – A E G Elsom, J M Tanner, R A Jarden; 2nd five-eighth – B B J Fitzpatrick; 1st five-eighth – L S Haig; half back – K Davis; forwards – K L Skinner, R C Hemi, I J Clarke, R A White, G N Dalzell, R C Stuart (capt.), W A McCaw, W H Clark.

For Wales, Sid Judd and Ken Jones scored tries. Gwyn Rowlands converted two and kicked a penalty goal.

For New Zealand, Bill Clark scored a try. Ron Jarden converted and kicked a penalty goal.

Referee: Dr P F Cooper (England).

Match 211 ENGLAND v WALES   Twickenham. January 16, 1954

England won by three tries (9) to one penalty goal, one try (6)

A last-minute corner-try by wing Chris Winn gave England their first victory overWales at Twickenham since 1939. This was the first all-ticket match at Rugby HQ and as a result there were only some 10,000 Welsh supporters. Roy John, Dai Davies and John Gwilliam made their final appearances for Wales. For the third successive time at Twickenham, Bleddyn Williams had to withdraw. He was still suffering from a leg injury received in the victory over the All Blacks. New cap Glyn John, who replaced him, 'bought' his way back into the amateur game after joining the Rugby League. He repaid his signing on fee of £400 to Leigh, for whom he played several games on the wing, and was reinstated because he had become a professional at the age of 17, while still at Garw Secondary School. Gerwyn Williams dislocated his shoulder trying to stop Ted Woodward scoring England's first try. Williams had the injury treated at half time and returned soon afterwards, but retired from rugby as a result of this mishap. Gwyn Rowlands played briefly at full back and Cliff Morgan filled in as emergency scrum half when Rex Willis was injured. England went on to win the Triple Crown for the first time since the war.

England: I King (Harrogate); J E Woodward (Wasps), J P Quinn (New Brighton), J Butterfield (Northampton), C E Winn (Rosslyn Park); M Regan (Liverpool), G Rimmer (Waterloo); R V Stirling (Wasps, capt.), E Evans (Sale), D L Sanders (Harlequins), P D Young (Dublin Wands.), P G Yarranton (Wasps), D S Wilson (Metropolitan Police), J M Kendall-Carpenter (Bath), A R Higgins (Liverpool).

Wales: Gerwyn Williams (London Welsh); K J Jones (Newport), Alun Thomas (Cardiff), *Glyn John (St. Luke's College and Aberavon), G Rowlands, (Cardiff); Cliff Morgan, W R Willis (Cardiff); W O Williams (Swansea), D M Davies (Somerset Police), C C Meredith, Roy John (Neath), J A Gwilliam (Gloucester), S Judd (Cardiff), J R G Stephens (Neath, capt.), R C C Thomas (Swansea).

For England, Ted Woodward (2) and Chris Winn scored tries.

For Wales, Gwyn Rowlands scored a try and kicked a penalty goal.

Referee: M J Dowling (Ireland).

130

Match 212 IRELAND v WALES   Lansdowne Road, Dublin. March 13, 1954

Wales won by three penalty goals, one dropped goal (12) to two penalty goals, one try (9)

Viv Evans, the 34-year-old Neath full back, made a successful debut by kicking three penalty goals, but it was Llanelli centre Denzil Thomas who won the match for Wales with a dropped goal in the last minute. New caps included Bryn Meredith, R H Williams and Brian Sparks, but the Welsh forwards again disappointed. A crowd of 45,000 watched a tense, see-saw battle. Irish scrum half John O'Meara twisted his back while reading a newspaper in bed on the morning of the match. He was taken to hospital and McCracken came in as reserve.

Ireland: P J Berkery (Lansdowne); M Mortell (Bective), N J Henderson (NIFC), R P Godfrey (Univ. Coll., Dublin), J T Gaston (Dublin Univ.); S Kelly (Lansdowne), H McCracken (NIFC); J H Smith (London Irish), R Roe (Dublin Univ.), F E Anderson (Queen's Univ., Belfast), J R Brady (CIYMS), R H Thompson (Instonians), G Reidy (Dolphin), R Kavanagh (Wanderers), J S McCarthy (Dolphin, capt.).

Wales: *Viv Evans (Neath); K J Jones (Newport), *Denzil Thomas (Llaneli), Alun Thomas, G M Griffiths (Cardiff); Cliff Morgan, W R Willis (Cardiff); W O Williams (Swansea), *B V Meredith (Newport), C C Meredith J R G Stephens (Neath, capt.), *R H Williams (Llanelli), R C C Thomas (Swansea), *L Jenkins (Newport), *B Sparks (Neath).

For Wales, Viv Evans kicked three penalty goals. Denzil Thomas dropped a goal.

For Ireland, Joe Gaston scored a try. Noel Henderson and Seamus Kelly each kicked a penalty goal.

Referee: A W C Austin (Scotland).

Match 213 WALES v FRANCE   Cardiff Arms Park. March 27, 1954

Wales won by two goals, three penalty goals (19) to two goals, one penalty goal (13)

Another hat-trick of penalty goals by Viv Evans helped Wales to victory. He also converted one try to contribute 11 of his team's points, and never missed a kick to touch throughout the match. Rees Stephens, chosen as captain, withdrew with a neck injury. Russell Robins replaced him and Rex Willis took over as captain. Sid Judd, as pack leader, was picked in his best position of No. 8 for the first time and gave a rousing performance as Wales dashed France's hopes of winning the championship outright for the first time. Glyn John switched to outside half, because Cliff Morgan was unfit.

Wales: Viv Evans (Neath); K J Jones (Newport), Alun Thomas, G M Griffiths, G Rowlands (Cardiff); Glyn John (St. Luke's Coll. and Aberavon), W R Willis (Cardiff, capt.); W O Williams (Swansea), B V Meredith (Newport), C C Meredith (Neath), R Robins (Pontypridd), R H Williams, *Len Davies (Llanelli), S Judd (Cardiff) R C C Thomas (Swansea).

France: H Claverie (Lourdes); A Boniface (Stade Montois), M Prat R Martine (Lourdes), F Cazenave (Stade Montois); A Labazuy (Lourdes). G Dufau (Racing Club); A Domenech (Vichy), P Labadie (Bayonne), R Biennes (Cognac), L Mias (Mazamet), B Chevallier (Montferrand), J Prat (Lourdes, capt.), R Baulon (Vienne), H Domec (Lourdes).

For Wales, Gareth Griffiths and Courtenay Meredith scored tries. Viv Evans converted one and kicked three penalty goals. Gwyn Rowlands converted one.

131

For France, Roger Martine and Robert Baulon scored tries. Jean Prat converted both and kicked a penalty goal.

Referee: A I Dickie (Scotland).

Match 214 WALES v SCOTLAND   St. Helen's, Swansea. April 10, 1954

Wales won by one penalty goal, four tries (15) to one try (3)

Bright sunshine and ideal conditions favoured the final international match to be played at historic St. Helen's. Because the Arms Park brought considerably more revenue to the WRU with its larger seating capacity, it was rightly, though reluctantly, recognised as the better national venue. Still, it was a sad parting with the ground where Wales had played their first home international in 1882 against England. Ken Jones captained Wales for the only time in his record 44 appearances. The occasion marked his feat of equalling Dicky Owen's Welsh record of 35 caps. Cliff Morgan returned and ran with characteristic elusive skill. Viv Evans finished the season with 23 points from his three games – seven penalty goals and one conversion. This match was postponed from January 30 because of a frozen pitch.

Wales: Viv Evans (Neath); K J Jones (Newport, capt.), G M Griffiths, Bleddyn Williams (Cardiff), *Ray Williams (Llanelli); Cliff Morgan, W R Willis (Cardiff); W O Williams (Swansea), B V Meredith (Newport), C C Meredith (Neath), R Robins (Pontypridd), R H Williams, Len Davies (Llanelli), S Judd (Cardiff), R C C Thomas (Swansea).

Scotland: J C Marshall (London Scottish); J S Swan, M K Elgie (London Scottish), D Cameron (Glasgow HSFP), T G. Weatherstone (Stewart's Coll., FP); G T Ross (Watsonians), L P MacLachlan (Oxford Univ.); T P L McGlashan (Royal HSFP), R K G MacEwen (Cambridge Univ.), H F McLeod (Hawick), E A J Fergusson (Oxford Univ.), J W K Kemp (Glasgow HSFP), W I D Elliot (Edinburgh Acads., capt.), P W Kininmonth, J H Henderson (Richmond).

For Wales, W O 'Billy' Williams, Bryn Meredith, Ray Williams and Cliff Morgan scored tries. Viv Evans kicked a penalty goal.

For Scotland, John 'Chick' Henderson scored a try.

Referee: Dr P F Cooper (England).

Match 215 WALES v ENGLAND   Cardiff Arms Park. January 22, 1955

Wales won by one penalty goal (3) to nil

Newport full back Garfield Owen, chosen to play for Wales for the first time, gashed his knee on snow-covered brambles during the run-out session at Glamorgan Wanderers' ground and had to withdraw. The man who replaced him, Arthur Edwards, had the distinction of winning the game with the only score a penalty goal after 10 minutes from a handy position. Bleddyn Williams, never happy in the deep, clinging mud, played the last of his 22 games for Wales and retired at the end of the season. He gave many brilliant displays of centre craft in the manner of the great players of the Golden Era.

This match was postponed a week because of heavy snow, and even then conditions were deplorable and it was just a mud-slog. Only the unswerving determination of the Welsh pack saved their side. It was the first appearances for Gordon Wells and Glyn 'Shorty' Davies, the flank forward who had missed the All Blacks' match in 1953 because of injury. Ken Jones became the most-capped Welsh player with his 36th consecutive appearance. Attendance 56,000.

Wales: *A B Edwards (London Welsh); K J Jones (Newport), Bleddyn Williams (capt.), *G T Wells (Cardiff), T J Brewer (London Welsh); Cliff Morgan, W R Willis (Cardiff) W O Williams (Swansea), B V Meredith (Newport), C C Meredith, J R G Stephens (Neath), R Robins (Pontypridd), *N G Davies (London Welsh), S Judd (Cardiff), B. Sparks (Neath).

England: N M Hall (Richmond, capt.); J E Woodward (Wasps), J Butterfield (Northampton), W P C Davies (Harlequins), R C Bazley (Waterloo); D G S Baker (OMT), J E Williams (Old Millhillians); G W Hastings (Gloucester), N A Labuschagne (Guy's Hosp.), D St G Hazell (Leicester), P D Young (Dublin Wands.), J H Hancock (Newport), P H Ryan (Richmond), P J Taylor (Northampton), R Higgins (Liverpool).

For Wales, Arthur Edwards kicked a penalty goal.

Referee: O B Glasgow (Ireland).

Match 216 SCOTLAND v WALES   Murrayfield. February 5, 1955

Scotland won by one goal, one dropped goal, one penalty goal, one try(14) to one goal, one try (8)

After 17 consecutive defeats, Scotland sprang another sensation in the manner of the 1951 Murrayfield Massacre. Again there were 20,000 Welshmen in the 60,000 crowd to see their side shocked after they had led 3-0 at half time. The pattern was hauntingly familiar; even to the extent of another decisive dropped goal whistling between the Welsh posts, this time from outside half Docherty. Nothing went right for Cliff Morgan; once he let the ball roll between his legs and scrum half Nichol dived for a gift try.

Arthur Smith, playing the first of his 33 games for Scotland, scored the try that turned the game. He was to score other decisive tries against Wales at Murrayfield in 1957 and 1961 to help Scotland win. A beautifully balanced wing, Smith played for a while with Ebbw Vale.

Scotland: A Cameron (Glasgow HSFP, capt.); A R Smith (Cambridge Univ.), M K Elgie (London Scottish), R G Charters (Hawick) J S Swan (London Scottish); J T Docherty (Glasgow HSFP), J A Nichol (Royal HSFP); H F McLeod (Hawick), W K L Relph (Stewart's Coll., FP), T Elliot (Gala), J. W Y Kemp (Glasgow HSFP), E J S Michie (Aberdeen Univ.), W S Glen (Edinburgh Wands.), J T Greenwood (Dunfermline, capt.), A Robson (Hawick).

Wales: A B Edwards (London Welsh); K J Jones (Newport), G T Wells (Cardiff), Alun Thomas (Llanelli), T J Brewer (London Welsh); Cliff Morgan, W R Willis (Cardiff capt.); W O Williams (Swansea), B V Meredith   (Newport); C C Meredith (Neath), R Robins (Pontypridd), R H Williams (Llanelli), S Judd (Cardiff), J R G Stephens (Neath), R C C Thomas (Swansea).

For Scotland, Arthur Smith and Nichol scored tries. Michael Elgie converted one and kicked a penalty goal. Jim Docherty dropped a goal.

For Wales, Trevor Brewer scored two tries. Rees Stephens converted one.

Referee: M J Dowling (Ireland).

Match 217 WALES v IRELAND   Cardiff Arms Park. March 12, 1955

Wales won by three goals, one penalty goal, one try (21) to one penalty goal (3)

With less than 20 minutes to go, the score was 3-3. Then Wales set their attack rolling irresistibly to score 18 breathtaking points, including four tries. These were obtained by Courtenay Meredith, Gareth Griffiths, Cliff Morgan and Haydn Morris. Three were converted by Garfield Owen, making his delayed debut. Gareth Griffiths could not win a place in the Cardiff team because of the fine form of wing Derek Murphy, but Wales picked him as centre. It was 19-year-old Tony O'Reilly's first game for Ireland. Fifteen years later, in 1970, he returned after an absence of nine years to win his 29th cap at Twickenham.

> **Wales :** *G Owen (Newport); K J Jones (Newport), Alun Thomas (Llanelli), G M Griffiths, H Morris (Cardiff); Cliff Morgan (Bective Rangers), W R Willis (Cardiff); W O Williams (Swansea), B V Meredith (Newport), C C Mererdith (Neath), R Robins (Pontypridd), R H Williams, Len Davies (Llanelli), J R G Stephens (Neath, capt.), R C C Thomas (Swansea).

> **Ireland:** P J Berkery (Lansdowne); A C Pedlow (Queen's Univ., Belfast), N J Henderson (NIFC), A J F O'Reilly (Old Belvedere), J T Gaston (Dublin Univ.); J W Kyle (NIFC), S J McDermott (London Irish); P J O'Donoghue (Bective), R Roe (Lansdowne), F E Anderson (NIFC), M N Madden (Sunday's Well), R H Thompson (Instonians, capt.), M J Cunningham (Univ. Coll., Cork), G R P Ross (CIYMS), P Kavanagh (Wanderers).

For Wales, Courtenay Meredith, Gareth Griffiths, Cliff Morgan and Haydn Morris scored tries. Garfield Owen converted three and kicked a penalty goal.

For Ireland, Noel Henderson kicked a penalty goal.

Referee: A I Dickie (Scotland).

Match 218 FRANCE v WALES   Colombes, Paris. March 26, 1955

Wales won by two goals, two penalty goals (16)
to one goal, one dropped goal, one penalty goal (11)

Unbeaten France, poised to win the championship outright for the first time, failed against the fire and purpose of Rees Stephens and his pack. Stephens was the outstanding pack leader of the season and it was ridiculous when the British Lions did not select him for their South African tour because they put an age limit of 30 years on tour candidates. This match attracted so much interest that for the first time a French home game was made all-ticket for a record crowd of 57,000. Russell Robins was superb, playing a No.8 type of game from the second row and, of course, it was as a No.8 that he grew in stature with the Welsh team before turning professional. When Clem Thomas and Len Davies withdrew, Wales called in Brian Sparks and Derek Williams as deputy wing forwards and they played a rousing part in a success that enabled their side to share the championship with France. Garfield Owen kicked his two penalty goals from 50 yards. It was Rex Willis's last appearance. He had been a magnificent successor to Haydn Tanner. Some players even considered Willis a shade better than Tanner for all-round ability. Certainly the lion-hearted Willis developed an ingenuity that few scrum halves have matched, and took more than his share of bumps while nursing his outside halves.

> **France:** M Vannier (Racing Club); H Rancoule, M Prat, R Martine (Lourdes), J Lepatey (Mazamet); A Haget (Paris Univ.), G Dufau (Racing Club); R Brejassou (Tarbes), P Labadie (Bayonne), A Domenech (Vichy), R Baulon (Vienne), B Chevallier (Montferrand), M Celaya (Biarritz), J Prat (capt.), R Domec (Lourdes).

> **Wales:** G Owen (Newport); K J Jones (Newport), Alun Thomas (Llanelli), G M Griffiths, H Morris (Cardiff); Cliff Morgan (Bective Rangers), W R Willis (Cardiff); W O Williams (Swansea), B V Meredith (Newport), C C Meredith (Neath), R Robins (Pontypridd), R H Williams (Llanelli), B Sparks, J R G Stephens (Neath, capt.), *C D Williams (Cardiff).

For Wales, Alun Thomas and Haydn Morris scored tries. Garfield Owen converted both and kicked two penalty goals.

For France, Robert Baulon scored a try. Michel Vannier converted and kicked a penalty goal. Maurice Prat dropped a goal.

Referee O B Glasgow (Ireland).

Match 219 ENGLAND v WALES   Twickenham. January 21, 1956

Wales won by one goal, one try (8) to one penalty goal (3)

Onllwyn Brace, genius of the Oxford University team, made his debut for Wales, but did not attempt any of the unorthodox attacking methods he introduced into the Oxford side. He was content to try to develop an understanding with Wales's new captain, Cliff Morgan. But these two appeared only five times together and, like the partnership of Dicky Owen and Percy Bush in the Golden Era, never played as brilliantly as was hoped.

C L 'Cowboy' Davies marked his debut on the wing with an unusual "belly-flop" try after a 45-yard dash as he slid for yards on his stomach to reach the corner. Garfield Owen, with a polished performance, was the star Welsh back, but the forwards disappointed. Attendance: 75,000.

England: D F Allison (Coventry); P H Thompson (Headingley), J Butterfield (Northampton), W P C Davies (Harlequins), P B Jackson (Coventry); M J K Smith (Oxford Univ.), R E G. Jeeps (Northampton); D L Sanders (Harlequins), E Evans (Sale, capt.), C R Jacobs (Northampton), R W D Marques (Cambridge Univ.), J D Currie, P G D Robbins (Oxford Univ.), A Ashcroft (Waterloo), V G Roberts (Penryn).

Wales: G Owen (Newport); K J Jones, *Harry Morgan, M C Thomas (Newport), *C L Davies (Cardiff); Cliff Morgan (Cardiff, capt.), *D O Brace (Newport); W O Williams (Swansea), B V Meredith (Newport), C C Meredith (Neath), R H Williams (Llanelli), R Robins (Pontypridd), B Sparks (Neath), L H Jenkins (Newport), R C C Thomas (Swansea).

For Wales, Lynn Davies and Russell Robins scored tries. Garfield Owen converted one.

For England, Fenwick Allison kicked a penalty goal.

Referee: R Mitchell (Ireland).

Match 220 WALES v SCOTLAND   Cardiff Arms Park. February 4, 1956

Wales won by three tries (9) to one penalty goal (3)

Through the night the gangs of fire-tenders kept dozens of braziers burning and the sky glowed red over the frozen Arms Park. The unforgettable scenes of the 1893 match with England at Cardiff were re-enacted to thaw out the pitch. On the morrow the ground, scarred by scorch marks and strewn with straw, looked a sorry mess; blackened and treacherously slippery; still semi-frozen in parts. Victory carried Wales to the threshold of the Triple Crown as Rees Stephens, recalled as pack leader, restored the missing hwyl to the home forwards. Ray Prosser looked a useful newcomer, winning the first of his 22 caps. He was a second row forward for Pontypool, but Wales always played him at prop. Brace and Cliff Morgan played excellently. The new south stand was opened officially. It raised the number of stand seats at the ground to 12,800 with the ground capacity increased to 60,000.

Wales: G Owen (Newport); K J Jones, Harry Morgan, M C Thomas (Newport), C L Davies (Cardiff); Cliff Morgan (Cardiff, capt.), D O Brace (Newport); W O Williams (Swansea), B V Meredith (Newport), *R Prosser (Pontypool), R H Williams (Llanelli), J R G Stephens, B Sparks (Neath), L H Jenkins (Newport), R C C Thomas (Swansea).

Scotland: R W T Chisholm (Melrose); A R Smith (Cambridge Univ.), A Cameron (Glasgow HSFP, capt.), K R Macdonald (Stewart's Coll., FP), J S Swan (Coventry); M L Grant (Harlequins), N M Campbell (London Scottish); H F McLeod (Hawick), R K G MacEwen (London Scottish), T Elliot (Gala), E J S Michie (Aberdeen GSFP), J W Y Kemp (Glasgow HSFP), I A A MacGregor (Llanelli), J T Greenwood (Dunfermline), A Robson (Hawick).

For Wales, Lynn 'Cowboy' Davies, Harry Morgan and Cliff Morgan scored tries.

For Scotland, Angus Cameron kicked a penalty goal.

Referee: L M Boundy (England).

Match 221 IRELAND v WALES   Lansdowne Road, Dublin. March 10, 1956

Ireland won by one goal, one penalty goal and one dropped goal (11) to one penalty goal (3)

A record Dublin crowd of 50,573 saw unbeaten Wales fade in the second half, and there was to be no Triple Crown triumph. Garfield Owen's 40-yard penalty goal gave Wales a 3-0 interval lead; but it was their only score. The rampaging Irish forwards thoroughly unsettled Cliff Morgan's team with their rousing kick-and-rush tactics. Morgan and Brace had a nightmare time behind flagging forwards and only the staunch defence of Garfield Owen staved off a heavier defeat. There were five Newport backs in the Welsh side, but they had no chance to show any team work. Ken Jones equalled Irishman George Stephenson's British record of 42 caps.

Ireland: P J Berkery (Lansdowne); S V J Quinlan (Highfield), N J Henderson (NIFC, capt.), A J F O'Reilly (Old Belvedere), A C Pedlow (Queen's Univ., Belfast); J W Kyle (NIFC), J A O'Meara (Dolphin); P J O'Donoghue (Bective), R Roe (London Irish), B G Wood (Garryowen), R H Thompson (Instonians), J R Brady (CIYMS), M J Cunningham (Cork Constitution), T McGrath (Garryowen), J R Kavanagh (Wanderers).

Wales: G Owen (Newport); K J Jones, Harry Morgan, M C Thomas (Newport), C L Davies (Cardiff); Cliff Morgan (Cardiff, capt.), D O Brace (Newport); W O Williams (Swansea), B V Meredith (Newport), C C Meredith, J R G Stephens (Neath), R H Williams (Llanelli), B Sparks (Neath), L H Jenkins (Newport), R C C Thomas (Swansea).

For Ireland, Marney Cunningham scored a try. Cecil Pedlow converted and kicked a penalty goal. Jack Kyle dropped a goal.

For Wales, Garfield Owen kicked a penalty goal.

Referee: A I Dickie (Scotland).

Match 222 WALES v FRANCE   Cardiff Arms Park. March 24, 1956

Wales won by one goal (5) to one try (3)

A flying touch-down, inches before the ball rolled over the dead-ball line at the river end

136

10 minutes before the final whistle, meant a try and a lucky win for Wales. Wing forward Derek Williams was the scorer of this "try in the Taff". The French thought the ball was out of play when Williams grounded it, but referee Peter Cooper (England) awarded a try and Garfield Owen converted from an easy position with the match winning kick. Welsh skipper Cliff Morgan sympathised with France. "The French always have bad luck at the Arms Park," he said. They were still seeking their initial win there since the first match in 1908. But that elusive victory was to be the reward on their next visit. Ken Jones's 43rd consecutive cap broke the British record of George Stephenson (Ireland) and victory made Wales outright champions.

Wales: G. Owen (Newport); K J Jones, Harry Morgan M C Thomas (Newport), G Rowlands (Cardiff); Cliff Morgan (Cardiff, capt.), D O Brace (Newport); *Rex Richards (Cross Keys), B V Meredith (Newport), R Prosser (Pontypool), L H Jenkins (Newport), J R G Stephens, C D Williams (Neath), R Robins (Pontypridd), *G Whitson (Newport).

France: M Vannier (Racing Club); J Dupuy (Tarbes), M Prat (Lourdes), A Boniface (Stade Montois), L Roge (Beziers); J Bouquet (Vienne), G Dufau (Racing Club, capt.); A Domenech (Brive), R Vigier (Montferrand). R. Bienes (Cognac), B Chevallier (Montferrand), M Celaya (Biarritz), R Baulon (Bayonne), J Barthe, H. Domec (Lourdes).

For Wales, Derek Williams scored a try. Garfield Owen converted.

For France, Robert Baulon scored a try.

Referee: Dr P F Cooper (England).

Match 223 **WALES v ENGLAND**   Cardiff Arms Park. January 19, 1957

England won by one penalty goal (3) to nil

Neath wing Keith Maddocks, in his only game for Wales, wandered off-side almost in front of his goal posts as Peter Thompson, the England wing, threw in at a line-out some 15 yards from the Welsh goal-line. Referee 'Sandy' Dickie (Scotland) spotted Maddocks and the penalty award meant an easy goal by Fenwick Allison after 32 minutes. It was the only score and England, who deserved to win, went on to take the championship with an unbeaten record. It gave them the Triple Crown for the 12th time. It was strange to see a Welsh team take the field without Ken Jones for the first time in post-war years. Terry Davies returned after four years, during which he had recovered from serious shoulder injuries. He replaced Garfield Owen, who had joined the Rugby League. It was stalemate at forward, but with Cliff Morgan and Brace unable to link smoothly, Wales were outclassed behind the scrum. Attendance: 60,000.

Wales: Terry Davies (Llanelli); *G Howells (Llanelli), G M Griffiths (Cardiff), M C Thomas (Newport, capt.), *K Maddocks (Neath); Cliff Morgan (Cardiff), D O Brace (Newport); R Prosser (Pontypool), B V Meredith (London Welsh), C C Meredith, J R G Stephens (Neath), R H Williams (Llanelli), *R O'Connor (Aberavon), R Robins (Pontypridd), R C C Thomas (Swansea).

England: D F Allison (Coventry); P B Jackson (Coventry), J Butterfield (Northampton), L B Cannell (St. Mary's Hosp.), P H Thompson (Headingley); R M Bartlett (Harlequins), R E G Jeeps (Northampton); C R Jacobs (Northampton), E Evans (Sale, capt.), G W Hastings (Gloucester), R W D Marques (Cambridge Univ.), J D Currie, P G D Robbins (Oxford Univ.), A Ashcroft (Waterloo), R Higgins (Liverpool).

For England, Fenwick Allison kicked a penalty goal.

Referee: A I Dickie (Scotland).

Scotland won by one dropped goal, one penalty goal, one try (9) to one penalty goal, one try (6)

For a third time at Murrayfield in post-war years a dropped goal doomed Wales. Scrum half Arthur Dorwood was the man responsible. He fielded Terry Davies's attempted clearance from a mark on the goal line, carefully judged his kick from 45 yards out near the touch line, and put over a drop-shot in the best Kininmonth manner. So Wales had lost the first two championship matches in a season for the first time since 1937. Wales were twice in the lead: first with a 35-yard penalty goal by Terry Davies, and then with a Robin Davies try. It was 6-6 at halftime. Brace was dropped and Cardiff's Lloyd Williams came in for the first of his 13 caps at scrum half, but Cliff Morgan produced only brief glimpses of his best form. Ken Jones was recalled for his 44th and final cap on the right wing.

Kenneth Jeffrey Jones, the lean, lithe sprinter, will always remain one of the greatest names in Welsh rugby, remembered for many spectacular tries. He scored 17 for his country and 146 for Newport and for 11 years he was on the Welsh right wing. Ken sprinted for Britain in the 1948 Olympic Games in London and captained the British team at the European Games at Berne in 1954.

Scotland: K J F Scotland (Heriot's FP); A R Smith (Cambridge Univ.), E McKeating (Heriot's FP), K R Macdonald (Stewart's FP), J S Swan (Coventry); T McClung (Edinburgh Acads.), A F Dorward (Gala); H F McLeod (Hawick), R K G MacEwen (London Scottish), T Elliot (Gala), E J S Michie (London Scottish), J W Y Kemp (Glasgow HSFP), I A A MacGregor (Llanelli), J T Greenwood (Perthshire Acads., capt.), A Robson (Hawick).

Wales: Terry Davies (Llanelli); K J Jones, M C Thomas (Newport, capt.), G M Griffiths (Cardiff), G Howells (Llanelli); Cliff Morgan, *Lloyd Williams (Cardiff); R Prosser (Pontypool), B V Meredith (London Welsh), C C Meredith, J R G Stephens (Neath), R H Williams (Llanelli), *R H Davies (Oxford Univ.), R Robins (Pontypridd), B Sparks (Neath).

For Scotland, Arthur Smith scored a try. Arthur Dorwood dropped a goal. Ken Scotland kicked a penalty goal.

For Wales, Robin Davies scored a try. Terry Davies kicked a penalty goal.

Referee: R C Williams (Ireland).

Wales won by two penalty goals (6) to one goal (5)

The entire Welsh team were ordered off the field by referee Jack Taylor (Scotland), but only to change their jerseys! This happened after 17 minutes of the second half, when the referee could no longer distinguish between the teams in this gruelling mud-lark. Wales returned in clean kit and went on to win their first game of the season in a thrilling, and often fierce, forward contest. Rees Stephens was an inspiring pack leader at the age of 34, but did not know his team had triumphed until he came out of a daze a couple of hours after the match. Stephens suffered slight concussion in the last 10 minutes. Although Wales dominated through their pack, they could not score a try. Terry Davies supplied their points with two penalty goals, the first after 10 minutes, the second only five minutes from the end. Ireland, pinned in their 25 for almost all the second half, stole the one try of the match through Ronnie Kavanagh.

Two new centres played for Wales. Graham Powell, who scored more than 200 points in 1958-59, was the first Ebbw Vale player to win a cap. Cyril Davies, his co-centre, was an attacker of exceptional ability. From Llanelli, he joined Cardiff, but faded from the rugby scene after seven games for Wales, spread over five seasons.

Wales: Terry Davies (Llanelli); G. Howells, *Cyril Davies (Llanelli), *G. Powell (Ebbw Vale), G T Wells (Cardiff); Cliff Morgan, Lloyd Williams (Cardiff); R Prosser (Pontypool), B V Meredith (London Welsh), *Henry Morgan, R H Williams (Llanelli), J R G Stephens (Neath, capt.), R Robins (Pontypridd), *J Faull (Swansea), R H Davies (London Welsh).

Ireland: P J Berkery (Lansdowne); R E Roche (Galwegians), A J F O'Reilly (Old Belvedere), N J Henderson (NIFC, capt.), A C Pedlow (Queen's Univ., Belfast); J W Kyle (NIFC), A A Mulligan (London Irish); J I. Brennan (CIYMS), R Roe (London Irish), B G Wood, T E Reid (Garryowen), J R Brady (CIYMS), J R Kavanagh (Wanderers), P J A O'Sullivan (Galwegians), H S O'Connor (Dublin Univ.).

For Wales, Terry Davies kicked two penalty goals.

For Ireland, Ron Kavanagh scored a try. Cecil Pedlow converted.

Referee: J A S Taylor (Scotland).

Match 226 **FRANCE v WALES**   Colombes, Paris. March 23, 1957

Wales won by two goals, one penalty goal, two tries (19) to two goals, one try (13)

This was to be the last Welsh win in Paris for fourteen years. Rees Stephens, in the last of his 32 games, captained the successful Welsh side, and they were thankful that France were so ragged at finishing many dazzling attacks. Welsh midfield tacklers just could not get to grips with the dashing French runners, but Cliff Morgan covered and tidied up expertly. In attack, however, he was subdued as French spoilers pounced on him ruthlessly. Terry Davies, though below his best, landed one superb 55-yard penalty goal from the touch line to help bring victory. Wales were to win only one of the next eight games with France.

France: M Vannier (Racing Club); J Dupuy (Stade Tarbais) M Prat (Lourdes), A Boniface, C Darrouy (Stade Montois); J Bouquet (Vienne), G Dufau (Racing Club); A. Domenech (Brive), R Vigier (Montferrand), A Sanac (Perpignan), M Celaya (Biarritz,capt.), M Hoche (Paris Univ.), F Moncla (Racing Club), J Barthe (Lourdes), J Carrere (Vichy).

Wales: Terry Davies (Llanelli); Ray Williams (Llanelli}, G Powell (Ebbw Vale), G T Wells (Cardiff), G Howells (Llanelli); Cliff Morgan, Lloyd Williams (Cardiff); R Prosser (Pontypool), B V Meredith (London Welsh), Henry Morgan, R H Williams (Llanelli), J R G Stephens (Neath, capt.), R. Robins (Pontypridd), J Faull (Swansea), R H Davies (London Welsh).

For Wales, Ray Prosser, Geoff Howells, John Faull and Bryn Meredith scored tries. Terry Davies converted two and kicked a penalty goal.

For France, Jean Dupuy, Maurice Prat and Andre Sanac scored tries. Jacques Bouquet converted two.

Referee: Dr P F Cooper (England).

Match 227 **WALES v AUSTRALIA**   Cardiff Arms Park. January 4, 1958

Wales won by one dropped goal, one penalty goal, one try (9) to one try (3)

When Cliff Morgan withdrew through injury, Carwyn James was called in to play at fly half

139

in partnership with his Llanelli clubmate, Wynne Evans, both making their debut. It was the only time James played as outside half; he was picked at centre later in the season for his other cap. Roddy Evans also appeared for the first of his 13 caps as a line-out expert. The Wallabies led 3-0 at halftime in the mud through a try by Tony Miller and Wales had to struggle. Fly half Arthur Summons several times slipped past Clem Thomas and if the tourists had possessed stronger centres they could have built a commanding lead.

The Welsh pack struck back forcefully in the second half and the 55,000 spectators saw the home side score three times in a 15 minute spell. First, Terry Davies put over a penalty goal for not straight in a scrum. Then, combined passing sent wing John Collins diving in for a debut try in the corner. Five minutes later, Carwyn James dropped a goal from short range. Bob Davidson's Wallabies lost 15 matches on tour, including all their international matches. It was the first time a touring team had failed to win a single test.

Wales: Terry Davies (Llanelli); *J. Collins (Aberavon), G. T. Wells (Cardiff), Cyril Davies, Ray Williams (Llanelli); *Carwyn James, *Wynne Evans (Llanelli); R Prosser (Pontypool), B V Meredith (Newport), *D Devereux (Neath), R H Williams (Llanelli), W R Evans (Cardiff), R H Davies (London Welsh), J Faull, R C C Thomas (Swansea, capt.).

Australia: T Curley; R Phelps, J M Potts, J K Lenehan, K J Donald; A Summons, D M Connor; N Shehadie, J V Brown, R A L Davidson (capt.), A R Miller, D Emanuel, J Thornett, N M Hughes, P Fenwicke.

For Wales, John Collins scored a try. Carwyn James dropped a goal. Terry Davies kicked a penalty goal.

For Australia, Tony Miller scored a try.

Referee: A I Dickie (Scotland).

Match 228 **ENGLAND v WALES**   Twickenham. January 18, 1958

Drawn. England one try (3). Wales one penalty goal (3)

Terry Davies's 45-yard penalty goal, which enabled Wales to draw with the strongest team England had fielded since the war, had an amusing and audacious sequel. During the night after the match, a small squad of souvenir hunters returned to Twickenham, clambered over the high railings and sawed down the cross-bar at the north end, over which Davies's penalty kick had sailed. They cut off about 3ft and made away into the darkness with their prize. On the Sunday, at a cafe in the Cotswolds, where they stopped while driving home, the 'raiding party' were delighted when Terry Davies walked in. He autographed a section of the bar, which had been divided into three. Terry, a timber merchant, offered to provide a replacement bar for the Rugby Union to avoid the culprits getting into trouble. But the prank was pardoned; the RFU had a spare bar and the man who led the 'raid', Fred Mathias, of Manorbier, near Tenby, wrote a letter of apology to Col F D Prentice, secretary of the RFU.

Cliff Morgan returned to the Welsh team and gave an excellent display of tactical kicking, probably a performance unsurpassed by any outside half in Britain in post-war rugby. Wing forward Haydn Morgan played soundly in the first of his 27 appearances for Wales. Terry Davies hit the post with a 50-yard penalty shot into the wind, and Don Devereux almost scored a thrilling try. Jeff Butterfield made the break for England's try by Peter Thompson. England captain Eric Evans said: "Clem Thomas and his Red Devils must be congratulated for getting us so worried that we were glad to hear the final whistle." England went on to retain the championship. There was no Prince of Wales Feathers emblem on the Welsh team's jerseys because the wrong kit had been packed and they played in trial match jerseys!

England: D F Allison (Coventry); P B Jackson (Coventry), J Butterfield (Northampton), W P C Davies (Harlequins), P H Thompson (Headingley); J P Horrocks-Taylor (Halifax), R E G Jeeps (Northampton); G W Hastings (Gloucester), E Evans (Sale, capt.), C R Jacobs (Northampton), R W D Marques, J D Currie (Harlequins), P G D Robbins (Coventry), A Ashcroft (Waterloo), R E Syrett (Wasps).

Wales: Terry Davies (Llanelli); J. Collins (Aberavon), M C Thomas (Newport), Cyril Davies (Llanelli), G T Wells (Cardiff); Cliff Morgan, Lloyd Williams (Cardiff); R Prosser (Pontypool), B V Meredith (Newport), D Devereux (Neath), R H Williams (Llanelli), W R Evans (Cardiff), R C C Thomas (capt.), J Faull, (Swansea), *H J Morgan (Abertillery).

For England, Peter Thompson scored a try.

For Wales, Terry Davies kicked a penalty goal.

Referee: R C Williams (Ireland).

Match 229 WALES v SCOTLAND   Cardiff Arms Park. February 1, 1958

Wales won one goal, one try (8) to one penalty goal (3)

Again Cliff Morgan was the Welsh tactical controller; the master of every situation. He needed to be because, though hooker Bryn Meredith stole seven tight heads while conceding only one, the home pack were held suprisingly by the mobile and determined Scots. The Welsh backs proved resourceful attackers with Terry Davies giving another faultless display of full back craft.

Wales: Terry Davies (Llanelli); J Collins (Aberavon), M C Thomas (Newport), Cyril Davies (Llanelli), G T Wells (Cardiff); Cliff Morgan, Lloyd Williams (Cardiff); R Prosser (Pontypool), B V Meredith (Newport), D Devereux (Neath), R H Williams (Llanelli), W R Evans (Cardiff), R C C Thomas (capt.), J Faull (Swansea), H J Morgan (Abertillery).

Scotland: R W T Chisholm (Melrose); A R Smith (Cambridge Univ., capt.), G D Stevenson (Hawick), J T Docherty (Glasgow HSFP), T G Weatherstone (Stewart's Coll., FP); G H Waddell (Devonport Services), J A T Rodd (United Services); H F McLeod (Hawick), R K G MacEwen (Lansdowne), T Elliot (Gala), M W Swan (Oxford Univ.), J W Y Kemp (Glasgow HSFP), G K Smith (Kelso), J T Greenwood (Perthshire Acads.), A Robson (Hawick).

For Wales, Gordon Wells and John Collins scored tries. Terry Davies converted one.

For Scotland, Arthur Smith kicked a penalty goal.

Referee: Dr N McNeill-Parkes (England).

Match 230 IRELAND v WALES   Lansdowne Road, Dublin. March 15, 1958

Wales won by three tries (9) to one penalty goal and one try (6)

Noel Henderson's 60-yard penalty goal at the first scrum shook Wales. It was the first of many jolts and the Irish led 6-0 but lost scrum half O'Meara 15 minutes from the end with an injury before Wales scraped to victory through three attacks on the blind side. First, Lloyd Williams launched an attack on the short side that ended with Bryn Meredith scoring. Then Cliff Morgan twice scurried to the blind side. From the first Morgan dart-away, wing Cyril

Roberts scored. From the second, Haydn Morgan crossed and the match was won. Alun Priday gained his first cap as deputy for unfit Terry Davies.

Ireland: J G M W Murphy (London Irish); S Quinlan (Highfeld), N J Henderson (NIFC, capt.), A J F. O'Reilly (Old Belvedere), A C Pedlow (CIYMS); M A English (Bohemians), J A O'Meara (Dolphin); P J O'Donoghue (Bective), A R Dawson (Wanderers), B G M Wood (Garryowen), J B Stevenson (Instonians), W A Mulcahy (Univ Coll., Dublin), J A Donaldson (Belfast Collegians). J R Kavanagh (Wanderers), N A Murphy (Cork Constitution).

Wales: *A J Priday (Cardiff); *C Roberts (Neath), M C Thomas (Newport), Cyril Davies (Llanelli), *H Nicholls (Cardiff); Cliff Morgan, Lloyd Williams (Cardiff); R Prosser (Pontypool), B V Meredith (Newport), *J D Evans, W R Evans (Cardiff), R H Williams (Llanelli), R C C Thomas (capt.), J Faull (Swansea), H J Morgan (Abertillery).

For Wales, Haydn Morgan, Bryn Meredith and Cvril Roberts scored tries.

For Ireland, John O'Meara scored a try. Noel Henderson kicked a penalty goal.

Referee: Dr N McNeill-Parkes (England).

Match 231   **WALES v FRANCE**   Cardiff Arms Park. March 29, 1958

France won by two goals, two dropped goals (16) to one penalty goal, one try (6)

Cliff Morgan's 29th and final game for Wales coincided with France's historic first win at the Arms Park after 50 years of trying. The French certainly deserved this famous victory on their bogy ground. They showed greater combined speed with their all-Lourdes threequarter line and outside half. Full back Michel Vannier was superb and dropped two goals. Cliff Morgan, below his best, and Terry Davies, who put over a 50-yard penalty goal, often had to clear desperately.

Wales: Terry Davies (Llanelli); C Roberts (Neath), M C Thomas (Newport), Carwyn James (Llanelli), J Collins (Aberavon); Cliff Morgan, Lloyd Williams (Cardiff); R Prosser (Pontypool), G Beckingham, J D Evans, W R Evans (Cardiff), R H Williams (Llanelli), R C C Thomas (capt.), J Faull (Swansea), H J Morgan (Abertillery).

France: M Vannier (Racing Club); H Rancoule, M Prat, R Martine, P Tarricq (Lourdes); A Labazuy (Lourdes), P Danos (Beziers); A Roques (Cahors), R Vigier (Montferrand), A Quaglio, L Mias (Mazamet}, M Celaya (Biarritz, capt.), M Crauste (Racing Club), J Barthe, H Domec (Lourdes).

For France, Pierre Danos and Pierre Tarricq scored tries. Antoine Labazuy converted both. Michel Vannier dropped two goals.

For Wales, John Collins scored a try. Terry Davies kicked a penalty goal.

Referee: A I Dickie (Scotland).

Match 232   **WALES v ENGLAND**   Cardiff Arms Park. January 17, 1959

Wales won by one goal (5) to nil

Left wing Dewi Bebb, after only five first-class matches in South Wales, made his international debut and snatched the decisive score, the first Welsh try against England at Cardiff for 10 years. Terry Davies converted with a fine kick. Following heavy rain the pitch resembled a lake. "No fancy stuff for us," skipper Clem Thomas told his team. With Rhys Williams, Ray Prosser and John Faull outstanding, and scrum half Lloyd Williams a dauntless ninth forward, the Welsh pack were in control. Bebb's first half try began at a line-out 15 yards from England's goal-line. Rhys Williams tapped straight back to Bebb when the wing threw in. He whipped away, side-stepped Peter Jackson and baffled full back Jim Hetherington with a dazzling change of direction. As the game drew to its close, the crowd, sensing victory, sang the Welsh national anthem. Then they poured on to the field to carry Bebb away on proud shoulders through the mud. New laws this season: Pick up ball after tackle without first using the foot. Also short penalty came in. Conversion kicks could be taken without using a placer.

Wales: Terry Davies (Llanelli); J Collins, *Haydn Davies (Aberavon), *M Price (Pontypool), *D I Bebb (Swansea); *C Ashton (Aberavon), Lloyd Williams (Cardiff); R Prosser (Pontypool), B V Meredith (Newport), *D R Main (London Welsh), *I Ford (Newport), R H Williams (Llanelli), R C C Thomas (capt.), J Faull (Swansea), *J Leleu (London Welsh).

England: J G G Hetherington (Northampton); P B Jackson (Coventry), M S Phillips (Oxford Univ.), J Butterfield (Northampton, capt.), P H Thompson (Headingley); A B W Risman (Manchester Univ.), S R Smith (Richmond); L H Webb (Bedford), J A S Wackett (Rosslyn Park), G J Bendon (Wasps), J D Currie, R W D Marques (Harlequins), A J Herbert (Wasps}, B J Wightman (Moseley), R Higgins (Liverpool).

For Wales, Dewi Bebb scored a try. Terry Davies converted.

Referee: R C Williams (Ireland).

Match 233 SCOTLAND v WALES   Murrayfield. February 7, 1959

Scotland won by one penalty goal, one try (6) to one goal (5)

Twickenham used to be Wales's bogy ground: now the chamber of horrors for Welsh rugby was firmly established at Murrayfield. This was the third successive defeat at Scottish HQ as the home side proved faster and more deadly into the tackle and swooped swiftly on to the ball. Cliff Ashton was the best of the Welsh backs and almost won the match in the last minutes with a drop-shot that dipped just under the bar. The Welsh try came from a 50-yard dash by Malcolm Price. Attendance: 70,000.

Scotland: K J F Scotland (Cambridge Univ.); A R Smith (Gosforth), T McClung (Edinburgh Acads.), G D Stevenson (Hawick), T G Weatherstone (Stewart's Coll., FP); G H Waddell (Cambridge Univ.), S Coughtrie (Edinburgh Acads.); H F McLeod (Hawick), N S Bruce (Blackheath), I R Hastie (Kelso), M W Swan (London Scottish), J W Y Kemp (Glasgow HSFP), G K Smith (Kelso), J T Greenwood (Perthshire Acads., capt.), A Robson (Hawick).

Wales: Terry Davies (Llanelli); J Collins, Haydn Davies (Aberavon), M Price (Pontypool), D I Bebb (Swansea); C Ashton (Aberavon), Lloyd Williams (Cardiff); R Prosser (Pontypool), B V Meredith (Newport), D R Main (London Welsh), R H Williams (Llanelli), I Ford (Newport), R C C Thomas (capt.), J Faull (Swansea), J Leleu (London Welsh).

For Scotland, Norman Bruce scored a try. Ken Scotland kicked a penalty goal.

For Wales, Malcolm Price scored a try. Terry Davies converted.

Referee: R C Williams (Ireland).

Wales won by one goal, one try (8) to one penalty goal, one try (6)

All the luck went to Wales in a tremendously thrilling contest. Ireland, who often outclassed the home side in the first half, led 6-0 at the interval. Only the unflinching defence of Terry Davies and Lloyd Williams saved Wales from worse trouble. Ireland nearly scored from the start as Noel Henderson caught Wales off guard. He kicked off the 'wrong' way. Niall Brophy gathered in full stride and fed Noel Murphy, but the wing forward's try was disallowed because he had put a foot over the touch line. It was a sensational start, and Ireland had cause to grumble as Brophy and Gordon Wood had seemingly valid tries disallowed. Wales desperately wriggled their way back into the game 20 minutes from the end with a Cliff Ashton try. Then, as the crowd sang the Welsh anthem to inspire their team, Malcolm Price burst through to score and Terry Davies converted with the match-winning kick seven minutes from the end. Wales scored more points (eight) than Ashton gave passes throughout the match!

Wales: Terry Davies (Llanelli); J Collins (Aberavon), M C Thomas (Newport), M Price (Pontypool), D I Bebb (Swansea); C Ashton (Aberavon), Lloyd Williams (Cardiff); R Prosser (Pontypool), B V Meredith (Newport), D R Main (London Welsh), R H Williams (Llanelli), *D J E Harris (Pontypridd), R C C Thomas (capt.), J Faull (Swansea), H J Morgan (Abertillery).

Ireland: N J Henderson (NIFC); A J F O'Reilly (Old Belvedere), J F Dooley (Galwegians), D Hewitt (Queen's Univ., Belfast), N H Brophy (Univ. Coll., Dublin); W Hewitt (Instonians), A A Mulligan (London Irish); B G M Wood (Garryowen), A R Dawson (Wanderers, capt.), S Millar (Ballymena), W A Mulcahy (Univ. Coll., Dublin), M G Culliton (Wanderers), N A Murphy (Cork Constitution), P J A O'Sullivan (Galwegians), J R Kavanagh (Wanderers).

For Wales, Cliff Ashton and Malcolm Price scored tries. Terry Davies converted one.

For Ireland, Tony O'Reilly scored a try. David Hewitt kicked a penalty goal.

Referee: G Burrell (Scotland).

France won by one goal, one penalty goal, one try (11) to one penalty goal (3)

From the sea of mud that opened the season against England, Wales finished their programme in a Paris heatwave. The temperature was 75 degrees. Skipper Clem Thomas said: "We were completely dried up 10 minutes from the end." France became outright champions for the first time after 49 years of playing against all four home countries, and the 16st. second row forward, Lucien Mias, was carried off in triumph. He was one of France's greatest captains as well as a brilliant player, whose inventive attacking methods improved forward play and were copied throughout the world. Malcolm Thomas switched to outside half to play the last of his 27 matches for Wales in an international career that had spanned 11 seasons. For the first time in post-war years there was not a Cardiff man in the team.

France: P Lacaze (Lourdes); H Rancoule (Lourdes), J Bouquet (Vienne), A Marquesuzaa (Racing Club) J Dupuy (Tarbes); A Labazuy (Lourdes), P Danos (Beziers); A Quaglio (Mazamet), R Vigier (Montferrand), A Roques, B Mommejat (Cahors) L Mias (Mazamet, capt.), M Crauste (Racing Club) J Barthe (Lourdes), F Moncla (Racing Club)

Wales: Terry Davies (Llanelli); J Collins (Aberavon), *J E Hurrell (Newport), M Price (Pontypool), D I Bebb (Swansea); M C Thomas, *W Watkins (Newport); R

Prosser (Pontypool), B V Meredith (Newport), D R Main (London Welsh), R H Williams (Llanelli), D J E Harris (Pontypridd), R C C Thomas (Swansea, capt.), *G D Davidge (Newport), H J Morgan (Abertillery)

For France, Francois Moncla scored two tries. Antoine Labazuy converted one and kicked a penalty goal.

For Wales, Terry Davies kicked a penalty goal.

Referee: Dr N McNeill-Parkes (England).

Match 236 ENGLAND v WALES   Twickenham. January 16, 1960

England won by one goal, two penalty goals, one try (14) to two penalty goals (6)

Richard Sharp came in as replacement fly half for injured Beverley Risman and enjoyed a dazzling debut in the England side. He made wing forward Haydn Morgan look a novice as England scored all their 14 points in the first half, and went on to become Triple Crown holders for the 13th time. Derek Morgan, the Newbridge No. 8, studying dental surgery at Durham University, also made a notable first appearance for England. The only Welsh points were two second half penalty goals by Terry Davies as Wales rallied with plenty of spirit. It was the last match for Rhys Williams after 23 caps.

England: D Rutherford (Percy Park); J R C Young (Harlequins), M S Phillips (Oxford Univ.), M P Weston (Richmond), J Roberts (Old Millhillians); R A W Sharp (Oxford Univ.), R E G Jeeps (Northampton, capt.); P T Wright (Blackheath), S A M Hodgson (Durham City), C R Jacobs (Northampton), R W D Marques, J D Currie (Harlequins), P G D Robbins (Moseley), W G D Morgan (Medicals), R E Syrett (Wasps).

Wales: Terry Davies (Llanelli); J Collins (Aberavon), M Price (Pontypool), *Geoff W Lewis (Richmond), D I Bebb (Swansea); C Ashton (Aberavon), *Colin Evans (Pontypool); R Prosser (Pontypool), B V Meredith (Newport), *L J Cunningham (Aberavon), *G W Payne (Pontypridd), R H Williams (LIanelli, capt.), *B Cresswell (Newport), J Faull (Swansea), H J Morgan (Abertillery).

For England, Jim Roberts scored two tries. Don Rutherford converted one and kicked two penalty goals.

For Wales, Terry Davies kicked two penalty goals.

Referee: J A S Taylor (Scotland).

Match 237 WALES v SCOTLAND   Cardiff Arms Park. February 6, 1960

Wales won by one goal, one penalty goal (8) to nil

Newport supplied the entire Welsh breakaway unit in this victory – open-side Geoff Whitson, Glyn Davidge and blindside Brian Cresswell. Hooker Bryn Meredith took over the captaincy after the Twickenham failure and Brace was recalled at scrum half. It was the first time for Brace and Cliff Ashton to play together for Wales. Strangely, seven years earlier, they had played together for Aberavon, with Ashton then at scrum half and Brace as outside half. Brace transferred to Newport because he wanted to specialise at scrum half. Wales, who dropped Haydn Morgan, established forward mastery against the Scots, though the Welsh backs disappointed and only one try was scored. It was the first appearance of Newport full back Norman Morgan, who scored 951 points between 1955 and 1962 for his club, including a record 167 this 1959-60 season.

Wales: *N Morgan (Newport); *F C Coles, M Price (Pontypool), Geoff W Lewis (Richmond), D I Bebb (Swansea); C Ashton (Aberavon), D O Brace (Llanelli); R Prosser (Pontypool), B V Meredith (Newport, capt.), L J Cunningham (Aberavon), G W Payne (Pontypridd), D J E Harris (Cardiff), B Cresswell, G D Davidge, G Whitson (Newport).

Scotland: K J F. Scotland (Cambridge Univ.); A K Smith (Ebbw Vale, capt.), J J McPartlin (Harlequins), I H P Laughland (London Scottish), G D Stevenson (Hawick); T McClung (Edinburgh Acads.), J A T Rodd (RN); H F McLeod (Hawick), N S Bruce (London Scottish), D M D Rollo (Howe of Fife), F H ten Bos (Oxford Univ.), J W Y Kemp (Glasgow HSFP), G K Smith (Kelso), K R F Bearne (Cambridge Univ.), C E B Stewart (Kelso).

For Wales, Dewi Bebb scored a try. Norman Morgan converted and kicked a penalty goal.

Referee: K D Kellerher (Ireland).

Match 238 IRELAND v WALES   Lansdowne Road, Dublin. March 12, 1960

Wales won by two goals (10) to two penalty goals, one try (9)

Norman Morgan, Newport's successful goal kicker, stole a lucky victory for Wales with as fine a conversion shot as he ever scored from the touch line only 10 minutes from the end. It was a travesty of justice that Ireland were pipped by one point because Wales were outplayed for at least three-fifths of the game. In one frustrating period of less than two minutes, Ireland were denied three scores. Tearaway Tim McGrath and David Hewitt were recalled after crossing the line and then Andy Mulligan was ruled to have lost the ball as he dived over. With Bryn Meredith unfit, Norman Gale deputised as hooker to gain the first of his 25 caps. Brace became captain in Meredith's absence and, 10 minutes from the end, dived in for the try that robbed Ireland as Norman Morgan planted his winning conversion between the posts.

Ireland: T J Kiernan (Univ. Coll., Cork); W W Bornemann (Wanderers), D Hewitt (Queen's Univ., Belfast), A C Pedlow (CIYMS), D C Glass (Belfast Collegians); S Kelly (Lansdowne), A A Mulligan (London Irish, capt.); S Millar (Ballymena), L Butler (Blackrock), B G M Wood (Lansdowne), W A Mulcahy (Univ. Coll., Dublin), M G Culliton, J R Kavanagh (Wanderers), T McGrath (Garryowen), N A Murphy (Cork Constitution).

Wales: N Morgan (Newport); F C Coles, M Price (Pontypool), *B J Jones (Newport), D I Bebb (Swansea); C Ashton (Aberavon), D O Brace (Llanelli, capt.); R Prosser (Pontypool), *N R Gale (Swansea), L J Cunningham (Aberavon), D J E. Harris (Cardiff), G W Payne (Pontypridd), B Cresswell, G D Davidge, G Whitson (Newport).

For Wales, Brian Cresswell and Onllwyn Brace scored tries. Norman Morgan converted both.

For Ireland, Noel Murphy scored a try. Seamus Kelly kicked two penalty goals.

Referee: D A Brown (England).

Match 239 WALES v FRANCE   Cardiff Arms Park. March 26, 1960

France won by two goals, two tries (16) to one goal and one penalty goal (8)

Outside half Bryan Richards, a clever dodger, played his only game for Wales, but behind an outpaced pack he had little chance to shine, and France registered their second successive win at Cardiff. Their score could have been even more convincing, but they still did enough to show that the balance of power had swung from classical back play to use of the forwards as fast and inventive attackers. They made Wales realise that there was an urgent need to revise tactical thinking.

There were great names in this French team, including the amazing Alfred 'the Rock' Roques, a 35-year-old prop. He played soccer until he was 26 and won his first rugby cap at the age of 33. He finished with 23 caps. Other French stars were Michel Crauste (43 caps in his colourful career), Amedee 'The Duke' Domenech (34 caps), Michel Celaya (34), Michel Vannier (30), Jacques Bouquet (28), Jean Dupuy (27), Pierre Albaladejo (24), Guy Boniface (23), Francois Moncla (21) and Pierre Lacroix (20). The remarkable Albaladejo, nick-named Monsieur Drop by his countrymen, scored three dropped goals against Ireland during this season.

Wales: N Morgan (Newport); F C Coles, M Price (Pontypool), B J Jones (Newport), D I Bebb (Swansea); *Bryan Richards(Swansea), D O Brace (Llanelli); R Prosser (Pontypool), B V Meredith (Newport, capt.), L J Cunningham (Aberavon), J Faull (Swansea), D J E Harris (Cardiff), B Cresswell, G D Davidge (Newport), J Leleu (Swansea).

France: M Vannier (Racing Club); S Mericq (Agen), G Boniface (Mont de Marsan), J Bouquet (Vienne), J Dupuy (Tarbes); P Albaladejo (Dax), P Lacroix (Mont de Marson); A Domenech (Brive), J de Gregorio (Grenoble), A Roques (Cahors), J P Saux (Pau), H Larrue (Carmaux), F Moncla (Pau, capt.), M Celaya (Bordeaux), M Crauste (Lourdes).

For France, Celaya, Serge Mericq, Lacroix and Dupuy scored tries. Vannier and Albaladejo each converted one.

For Wales, Brian Cresswell scored a try. Norman Morgan converted and kicked a penalty goal.

Referee: Dr N McNeill-Parkes (England).

Match 240 WALES v SOUTH AFRICA   Cardiff Arms Park. December 3, 1960

South Africa won by one penalty goal (3) to nil

"We'll play against the wind," said Welsh skipper Terry Davies with a large grin when he won the toss. So the game was decided before the teams took one step out into the sea of mud and fierce gale that swept icy, stinging rain across the Arms Park. If ever conditions were against playing a football match it was this game. But it had to go on to complete the tight tour schedule. The teams lined up in midfield wearing track suits and did not take them off until after the three anthems had been played. The crowd of 55,000 watched with a mixture of wet misery and hope. In the end it was just misery. All the hope had gone with the wind that carried Keith Oxlee's penalty goal safely between the Welsh posts.

Terry Davies's gamble seemed justified when at half time Wales turned round only three points down. Surely the Springboks could not hold out against the Red Devils with such a slender lead? But Avril Malan and his pack were as strong as buffaloes in the mud. They broke the hearts of the Welsh forwards, driving them back and killing the ball to stop Wales winning possession. Doug Hopwood was a magnificent No. 8, peeling out of the scrums and making sure that his fellow forwards kept the ball tight. The mud-plastered players were unrecognisable: it was difficult to tell one team from the other. "Do you want to call it all off.?" asked referee Jack Taylor (Scotland), 15 minutes from the end. "We would like to carry on," replied the grim faced and weary Terry Davies.

But his forwards were exhausted. The Springboks, with superior stamina and strength,

147

played wet weather tactics faultlessly once again. Yet Wales almost scored a try when Danny Harris crashed over from a line-out. The referee ruled no try. Ken Richards was just wide with a drop at goal. Terry Davies said sadly afterwards: "We gambled on the toss and rightly so, I feel. We thought at one stage that we would just bring it off". The Springboks were beaten only once on the tour (by the Barbarians 6-0 at Cardiff). On the Sunday after the Welsh match, the River Taff, swollen by flood water, broke its banks at high tide and, as if to hide the shame of Welsh rugby's tactical blunder, buried the pitch beneath two feet of muddy water.

Wales: Terry Davies (Llanelli, capt.), *D P Evans (Llanelli), Cyril Davies, *H M Roberts (Cardiff), D I Bebb (Swansea); *Ken Richards (Bridgend), *A O'Connor (Aberavon); R Prosser (Pontypool), B V Meredith (Newport), *K D Jones, D J E Harris (Cardiff), W R Evans (Bridgend), G D Davidge (Newport), *D Nash (Ebbw Vale), J Leleu (Swansea).

South Africa: L G Wilson; F T Roux, A I Kirkpatrick, J L Gainsford, J P Engelbrecht; K Oxlee, P de W Uys; S P Kuhn, R A Hill, P S du Toit, A S Malan (capt.), J T Claassen, G H van Zyl, D J Hopwood, H J M Pelser.

For South Africa, Keith Oxlee kicked a penalty goal.

Referee: J A S Taylor (Scotland).

Match 241 **WALES v ENGLAND**   Cardiff Arms Park. January 21, 1961

Wales won by two tries (6) to one try (3)

Dewi Bebb scored two thrilling tries and had a third disallowed in a match that restored everyone's belief in the spirit of combined running in attack. Wales lost centre Cyril Davies seven minutes after the interval with a knee injury and this gifted player's all-too-brief career in international rugby came to an end. Haydn Morgan came out of the pack to play as centre, a position he occupied with Abertillery until they converted him to wing forward. Glyn Davidge was a fine pack leader. The crowd, with traditional emotion, roared out the national anthem in the closing minutes to encourage their 14 heroes to hold out.

Wales: Terry Davies (Llanelli, capt.); * P M Rees (Newport), Cyril Davies, H M Roberts (Cardiff), D I Bebb (Swansea); Ken Richards (Bridgend), A O'Connor (Aberavon); *P E J Morgan (Aberavon), B V Meredith (Newport), K D Jones, D J E Harris (Cardiff), W R Evans (Bridgend), G D Davidge (Newport), D Nash (Ebbw Vale), H J Morgan (Abertillery).

England: M N Gavins (Leicester); J R C Young (Harlequins), M S Phillips (Fylde), M P Weston (Richmond), J Roberts (Old Millhillians); A B W Risman (Loughborough Colleges), R E G Jeeps (Northampton, capt.); P T Wright (Blackheath), S A M Hodgson (Durham City), C R Jacobs (Northampton), R W D Marques (Harlequins), R French (St. Helens), P G D Robbins (Moseley), W G D Morgan (Medicals), L I Rimmer (Bath).

For Wales, Dewi Bebb scored two tries.

For England, John Young scored a try.

Referee: K D Kelleher (Ireland).

Match 242 **SCOTLAND v WALES**   Murrayfield. February 11, 1961

Scotland won by one try (3) to nil

It was mournful Murrayfield yet again, as Wales slid to their sixth post-war defeat in eight games there. The only score was an Arthur Smith try after 32 minutes, made when full back Ken Scotland joined an attack. Dewi Bebb had what seemed a good try rejected by referee R C Williams (Ireland). Bebb was crashed into touch at the corner after a 60-yard run. He threw in quickly to centre Meirion Roberts, who returned the ball and Bebb dived over. The referee ruled that the ball had not been thrown in to the five yard mark.

Scotland: K J F Scotland (London Scottish); A R Smith (Edinburgh Wands., capt.), E McKeating (Heriot's FP), G D Stevenson (Hawick), R H Thomson (London Scottish); I H P Laughland (London Scottish), A J Hastie (Melrose); H F McLeod (Hawick), N S Bruce (London Scottish), D M D Rollo (Howe of Fife), F H ten Bos (London Scottish), M J Campbell-Lamerton (Halifax), K I Ross (Boroughmuir FP), J Douglas (Stewart's Coll., FP), G K Smith (Kelso).

Wales: Terry Davies (Llanelli, capt.); P M Rees, *G R Britton (Newport), H M Roberts (Cardiff), D I Bebb (Swansea); Ken Richards (Bridgend), A O'Connor (Aberavon); P E J Morgan (Aberavon), B V Meredith (Newport), K D Jones, D J E Harris (Cardiff), W R Evans (Bridgend), G D Davidge (Newport), D Nash (Ebbw Vale), H J Morgan (Abertillery).

For Scotland, Arthur Smith scored a try.

Referee: R C Williams (Ireland).

Match 243 **WALES v IRELAND**   Cardiff Arms Park. March 11, 1961

Wales won by two penalty goals, one try (9) to nil

Fly half Ken Richards, who scored a total of 289 points this season before joining Rugby League club St. Helens, collected all the Welsh points with two penalty goals and a try. But the match was condemned as one of negative tactics, despite perfect conditions. Both sets of halves kicked continually and the crowd slow-handclapped. Ireland had David Hewitt a passenger on the wing for most of the game, and lost prop Gordon Wood 20 minutes from the end with a gash over the eye. Brian Price came in as a late replacement for Danny Harris to win the first of his 32 caps.

Wales: A J Priday (Cardiff); P M Rees (Newport), *D Thomas (Aberavon), H M Roberts (Cardiff), D I Bebb (Swansea); Ken Richards (Bridgend), D O Brace (Llanelli. capt.); R Prosser (Pontypool), B V Meredith (Newport), K D Jones (Cardiff),W R Evans (Bridgend), *Brian Price, G D Davidge (Newport), D Nash (Ebbw Vale), H J Morgan (Abertillery).

Ireland: T J Kiernan (Univ. Coll., Cork); N H Brophy (Blackrock), D Hewitt (Queen's Univ., Belfast), D C Glass (Belfast Collegians), R J McCarten (London Irish); M A F English (Bohemians), A A Mulligan (London Irish); B G M Wood (Lansdowne), A R Dawson (Wanderers, capt.), S Millar, C J Dick (Ballymena), W A Mulcahy (Univ. Coll., Dublin), M G Culliton, J R Kavanagh (Wanderers), N A Murphy (Garryowen).

For Wales, Ken Richards scored try and kicked two penalty goals.

Referee: D C J McMahon (Scotland).

Match 244 **FRANCE v WALES**   Colombes, Paris. March 25, 1961

France won by one goal, one try (8) to two tries (6)

It was try for try, but Michel Vannier's one successful conversion kick made France unbeaten champions with their fourth successive win over Wales. Alun Pask played his first game and scored a try from the blind side wing forward position. He was to play 26 times for the Red Devils. Haydn Mainwaring, full back hero for the Barbarians when they took the Springboks' unbeaten record, gained his only Welsh cap, playing as centre. This was Terry Davies's 21st and final appearance.

France: M Vannier (Chalon); C Mauduy (Perigueux), J Bouquet (Vienne), G Boniface (Mont de Marsan), H Rancoule (Toulon); P Albaladejo (Dax), P. Lacroix (Agen); A Domenech (Brive), J de Gregorio (Grenoble), A Roques (Cahors), G Bouguyon (Grenoble), J P Saux, F Moncla (Pau, capt.), M Celaya (Bordeaux), M Crauste (Lourdes).

Wales: Terry Davies (Llanelli); J. Collins (Aberavon), H M Roberts (Cardiff), *H J. Mainwaring, D I Bebb (Swansea); Ken Richards (Bridgend), Lloyd Williams (Cardiff; capt.); R Prosser (Pontypool), *W J Thomas (Cardiff), P E J Morgan (Aberavon), W R Evans (Bridgend), Brian Price (Newport), *A E I Pask (Abertillery), D Nash (Ebbw Vale), H J Morgan (Abertillery).

For France, Guy Boniface and Jean-Pierre Saux scored tries. Michel Vannier converted one.

For Wales, Alun Pask and Dewi Bebb scored tries.

Referee: Dr N McNeill-Parkes (England).

Match 245 **ENGLAND v WALES**   Twickenham. January 20, 1962

Drawn. No score

A drab stalemate in the swirling wind sent 72,000 spectators home groaning about the lack of adventure in rugby tactics. Still, justice was served, for neither side deserved to win. Kelvin Coslett, in his first game, missed five penalties for Wales in the difficult conditions. Alan Rees, the Glamorgan cricketer, made his debut at outside half, and Alun Pask was brought in at No.8 when David Nash withdrew on the morning of the match with a cold. This time, Richard Sharp was no phantom for Welsh tacklers.

England: J G Wilcox (Oxford Univ.); A M Underwood (Northampton), M R Wade (Cambridge Univ.), M P Weston (Richmond), J Roberts (Sale); R A W Sharp (Oxford Univ.), R E G Jeeps (Northampton, capt.); P E Judd (Coventry), S A M Hodgson (Durham City), P T Wright (Blackheath), V S J Harding (Sale), J D Currie (Bristol), R E Syrett (Wasps), P J Taylor (Northampton), D P Rogers (Bedford).

Wales: *K Coslett (Aberavon); * D R R Morgan, *D K Jones (Llanelli), M Price (Pontypool), D I Bebb (Swansea); * Alan Rees (Maesteg), Lloyd Williams (Cardiff, capt.); L J Cunningham (Aberavon), B V Meredith (Newport), K D Jones (Cardiff), W R Evans (Bridgend), Brian Price (Newport), R H Davies (London Welsh), A E I Pask, H J Morgan (Abertillery).

Referee: J A S Taylor (Scotland).

Match 246 **WALES v SCOTLAND**   Cardiff Arms Park. February 3, 1962

Scotland won by one goal, one try (8) to one dropped goal (3)

Scotland's first victory in Wales for 25 years in atrocious conditions was well deserved. Ron Glasgow's try was the first by a Scottish player at the Arms Park for 27 years and it was their first success at Cardiff for 35 years. So there was little wonder the Scots were so elated. Their kilted fans chaired off Hughie McLeod at the end to mark his record 38 caps. When he retired he had played 40 times. Wales's only points came from a dropped goal by Alan Rees five minutes from the end.

Wales: K Coslett (Aberavon); D R R Morgan, D K Jones (Llanelli), H M Roberts (Cardiff), D I Bebb (Swansea); Alan Rees (Maesteg), Lloyd Williams (Cardiff, capt.); L J Cunningham (Aberavon), B V Meredith, *D Greenslade, Brian Price (Newport), W R Evans (Bridgend), R H Davies (London Welsh), A E I Pask, H J Morgan (Abertillery).

Scotland: K J F Scotland (Leicester); A R Smith (Edinburgh Wands., capt.), J J McPartlin (Oxford Univ.), I H P Laughland (London Scottish), R C Cowan (Selkirk); G H Waddell (London Scottish), S Coughtrie (Edinburgh Acads.); H F McLeod (Hawick), N S Bruce (London Scottish), D M D Rollo (Howe of Fife), F H ten Bos (London Scottish), M J Cambell-Lamerton (Halifax), R J C Glasgow (Dunfermline), J Douglas (Stewart's Coll., FP), K I Ross (Boroughmuir FP).

For Scotland, Ron Glasgow and Frans ten Bos scored tries. Ken Scotland converted one.

For Wales, Alan Rees dropped a goal.

Referee: Dr N McNeil-Parkes (England).

Match 247 **WALES v FRANCE**   Cardiff Arms Park. March 24, 1962

Wales won by one penalty goal (3) to nil

"It was about time I kicked one," smiled Kelvin Coslett after he put over the 35-yard penalty goal as the only score in Wales's great tactical victory. Coslett had missed five penalty shots against England and three against Scotland. This first success of his ended France's sequence of four victories over Wales, though defeat did not prevent the Tricolours becoming outright champions for the third time in four years. Keith Rowlands marked his first cap with a display that won him a British Lions' tour place to South Africa. Likewise, Alun Pask's unforgettable tackle as he caught wing Henri Rancoule from behind, took him into the Lions' team.

Wales: K Coslett (Aberavon); D R R Morgan, D K Jones (Llanelli), H M Roberts (Cardiff), D I Bebb (Swansea); Alan Rees (Maesteg), A O'Connor (Aberavon); L J Cunningham (Aberavon), B V Meredith (Newport, capt.), K D Jones, *K A Rowlands (Cardiff), D Nash (Ebbw Vale), G D Davidge (Newport), A E I Pask, H J Morgan (Aberlillery).

France: C Lacaze (Lourdes); H Rancoule (Tarbes), A Boniface (Mont de Marsan), J Bouquet (Vienne), J Dupuy (Tarbes); P Albaladejo (Dax), P Lacroix (Agen, capt.); A Domenech (Brive), J de Gregorio (Grenoble), A Roques (Cahors), B Mommejat (Albi), J P Saux (Pau), R Gensanne (Beziers), H Romero (Montauban), M Crauste (Lourdes).

For Wales, Kelvin Coslett kicked a penalty goal.

Referee: K D Kelleher (Ireland).

Match 248 **IRELAND v WALES**   Lansdowne Road, Dublin. November 17, 1962

Drawn. Ireland one dropped goal (3). Wales one penalty goal (3)

This was the hangover match, postponed from March until the start of the following season because of the smallpox outbreak in the Rhondda. Hangover described it perfectly: the players just could not find any enthusiasm. The ground was barely two-thirds full, with few Welsh supporters bothering to make the trip. A biting, gale-force wind chilled everyone. Grahame

Hodgson, in the first of his 15 games for Wales, kicked a second half penalty goal after Mick English had dropped an early goal for Ireland. It was the last of Bryn Meredith's 34 games – the record number for a Welsh forward. Wales had gone through four games without scoring a try.

Ireland: T J Kiernan (Univ.Coll.,Cork); W R Hunter, A C Pedlow (CIYMS), M K Flynn (Wanderers), N H Brophy (London Irish); M A F English (Lansdowne), J C Kelly (Univ. Coll., Dublin); M P O'Callaghan (Sunday's Well), A R Dawson (Wanderers), P J Dwyer (Univ. Coll., Dublin), W J McBride (Ballymena), W A Mulcahy (Bective, capt.), P J A O'Sullivan (Galwegians), C J Dick (Ballymena), M D Kiely (Lansdowne).

Wales: *G. T. R. Hodgson (Neath); D R R Morgan, D K Jones, *Brian Davies (Llanelli), D I Bebb (Swansea); C Ashton, A O'Connor (Aberavon); *J Warlow (Llanelli), B V Meredith (Newport, capt.), L J Cunningham (Aberavon), W R Evans (Bridgend), K A Rowlands (Cardiff), *John Davies (Neath), A E I Pask, H J Morgan (Abertillery).

For Ireland, Mick English dropped a goal.

For Wales, Grahame Hodgson kicked a penalty goal.

Referee: J A S Taylor (Scotland).

Match 249 **WALES v ENGLAND**   Cardiff Arms Park. January 19, 1963

England won by two goals and one dropped goal (13) to one penalty goal and one try (6)

David Watkins, the darting Newport outside half, made his Welsh team debut, gaining the first of his 21 caps before he turned professional with Salford for a record £16,000 in October, 1967. It was also the first appearance for the new Welsh captain and scrum half Clive Rowlands, of Pontypool. He led the national team in 14 consecutive games. Newcomers in the pack included Denzil Williams and Brian Thomas, who were to become among the most famous of hard-core forwards. Wing forward David Hayward scored a try on his debut. It was the first try by Wales for five matches. Clive Rowlands said: "England took their chances. We did not take ours. That was the difference." This was the ice-age winter, when only a few games were played on protected grounds during a nine-week spell. It was so cold for this match that the Welsh players were issued with an underwear set of vests and pants as additional protection. England won the championship, but did not win again in Cardiff for 28 years.

Wales: G T R Hodgson (Neath); D R R Morgan, D K Jones, Brian Davies (Llanelli), D I Bebb (Swansea) ; *David Watkins (Newport), *D C T Rowlands (Pontypool, capt.); K D Jones (Cardiff), N R Gale (Llanelli), *Denzil Williams (Ebbw Vale), *Brian Thomas (Neath), Brian Price (Newport), A E I Pask (Abertillery), *R C B Michaelson (Aberavon), *David Hayward (Cardiff).

England: J G Willcox (Oxford Univ.); P B Jackson (Coventry), M S Phillips (Fylde), M P Weston (Durham City), J Roberts (Sale); R A W Sharp (Wasps, capt.), S J S. Clarke (Cambridge Univ.); B A Dovey (Rosslyn Park), J D Thorne (Bristol), N J Drake-Lee (Cambridge Univ.), A M Davis (Torquay Ath.), J E Owen (Coventry), D C Manley (Exeter), B J Wightman (Coventry), D P Rogers (Bedford).

For England, Malcolm Phillips and John Owen scored tries. Richard Sharp converted two and dropped a goal.

For Wales, David Hayward scored a try. Grahame Hodgson kicked a penalty goal.

Referee: K D Kelleher (Ireland).

Wales won by one dropped goal, one penalty goal (6) to nil

Victory at Murrayfield at last after 10 years. But controversy raged over the Welsh tactics. Clive Rowlands kicked almost every time he received the ball and there were 111 line-outs. Wales never produced one combined passing movement. "It was not an attractive match, and I felt sorry for the backs," admitted Rowlands. "But we were out to win and played to win. The pack did a great job." With Alun Pask leading them, the Welsh forwards established a firm grip. Grahame Hodgson, a polished full back, kicked a wide angled penalty goal from 30 yards after 15 minutes, and in the second half Rowlands dropped an angled goal after being fed from a line-out. There were some 7,000 Welsh supporters among the crowd of 60,000.

Scotland: K J F. Scotland (Heriot's FP, capt.); R H Thomson, J A P Shackleton (London Scottish), D M White (Kelvinside Acads.), G D Stevenson (Hawick); I H P Laughland (London Scottish), S Coughtrie (Edinburgh Acads.); D M D Rollo (Howe of Fife), N S Bruce, A C W Boyle, F H ten Bos (London Scottish), M J Campbell-Lamerton (Halifax), K I Ross (Boroughmuir FP), J Douglas (Stewart's Coll., FP), W R A Watherston (London Scottish).

Wales: G T R Hodgson (Neath); D R R Morgan, Brian Davies (Llanelli), *Ron Evans (Bridgend), *W J Morris (Pontypool); David Watkins (Newport), D C T Rowlands (Pontypool, capt.); Denzil Williams (Ebbw Vale), N R Gale (Llanelli), K D Jones (Cardiff), Brian Price (Newport), Brian Thomas (Neath), *Graham Jones (Ebbw Vale), A E I Pask, H J Morgan (Abertillery).

For Wales, Clive Rowlands dropped a goal. Grahame Hodgson kicked a penalty goal.

Referee: R C Williams (Ireland).

Ireland won by one goal, one dropped goal, two penalty goals (14) to one dropped goal, one try (6)

Ireland's first win at Cardiff for 31 years saw the Welsh forwards badly beaten. Terrible weather kept the crowd down to 45,000. Ireland, who had won only one of their previous 16 matches, embarked on a policy of aggressive tackling. Welsh skipper Clive Rowlands conceded: "I have not been tackled so hard in my life." Referee Arthur Luff (England) awarded two unusual penalties against wing forward Haydn Morgan, and from each of them Tom Kiernan kicked Irish penalty goals. The first was because Morgan added himself to the front row in a scrum; the other was when Morgan tried to hook the ball back from the tunnel, which only front row men could do legally. For the first time since 1937 Wales had failed to win one home match during a season.

Wales: G T R Hodgson (Neath); D R R Morgan (Llanelli), Ron Evans (Bridgend), H M Roberts (Cardiff), W J Morris (Pontypool); David Watkins (Newport), D C T Rowlands (Pontypool, capt.); Denzil Williams (Ebbw Vale), N R Gale (Llanelli), K D Jones, K A Rowlands (Cardiff), Brian Thomas (Neath), Graham Jones (Ebbw Vale), A E I Pask, H J Morgan (Abertillery).

Ireland: T J Kiernan (Univ. Coll., Cork); A J F O'Reilly (Old Belvedere), J C Walsh (Univ. Coll., Cork), P J Casey (Univ. Coll., Dublin), N H Brophy (Blackrock); M A F English (Lansdowne), J C Kelly (Univ. Coll., Dublin); R J McLoughlin (Gosforth), A R Dawson (Wanderers), S Millar, W J McBride (Ballymena), W A Mulcahy (Bective, capt.), M D Kiely (Lansdowne), C J Dick (Ballymena), E P McGuire (Univ. Coll., Galway).

For Ireland, Pat Casey scored a try. Tom Kiernan converted and kicked two penalty goals. Mick English dropped a goal.

For Wales, Graham Jones scored a try. David Watkins dropped a goal.

Referee: A C Luff (England).

Match 252 FRANCE v WALES   Colombes, Paris. March 23, 1963

France won by one goal (5) to one penalty goal (3)

For the first time for 14 years Wales found themselves bottom of the championship table. It was a season of disillusionment for captain Clive Rowlands. But his triumphs were to come. There were only 35,000 on a cold day to see Wales stumble, without smoothness and accuracy in midfield, although the pack improved. Only the determined covering of the breakaway forwards, and the staunch defence of Grahame Hodgson and Robert Morgan, prevented a heavier defeat.

France: C Lacaze (Angouleme); C Darrouy, G Boniface, A Boniface (Mont de Marsan), J Dupuy (Tarbes); P Albaladejo (Dax), P Lacroix (Agen, capt.); F Mas (Beziers), J de Gregorio (Grenoble), A Domenech, R Fite (Brive), B Mommejat (Albi), M Lira (La Voulte), J Fabre (Toulouse), M Crauste (Lourdes).

Wales: G T R Hodgson (Neath); D R R Morgan, D K Jones (Llanelli), Ron Evans (Bridgend), D I Bebb (Swansea); David Watkins (Newport), D C T Rowlands (Pontypool, capt.); Denzil Williams (Ebbw Vale), W J Thomas, *C H Norris (Cardiff), Brian Price (Newport), Brian Thomas (Neath), Graham Jones (Ebbw Vale), A E I Pask, H J Morgan (Abertillery).

For France, Guy Boniface scored a try. Pierre Albaladejo converted.

For Wales, Grahame Hodgson kicked a penalty goal.

Referee: P G Brook (England).

Match 253 WALES v NEW ZEALAND   Cardiff Arms Park. December 21, 1963

New Zealand won by one dropped goal, one penalty goal (6) to nil

The fact that they failed to score a try certainly did not spoil New Zealand's elation at this historic first official victory at the Arms Park. After the defeats of 1905, 1935 and 1953, this was a great occasion for the All Blacks. It was the day of Don Clarke, master goal kicker, who had the remarkable record of scoring 102 points in his first 10 tests for N.Z. He kicked six penalty goals in a test against the British Lions at Dunedin in 1959 for the All Blacks to win 18-17. This time Clarke landed a penalty goal after five minutes and struck the posts with two other shots, one from 60 yards and the other from halfway. The other N.Z. points came after 13 minutes of the second half, when Bruce Watt dropped a straight goal.

Had they possessed better backs, or even a little more adventure in their methods, there is no doubt the New Zealanders could have built a much bigger score, because their forwards mostly outplayed the home pack. Wilson Whineray emerged as one of the finest captains of a touring team and his side suffered only one defeat – by Newport 3-0 through John Uzzell's dropped goal in the third match of the tour. The All Blacks beat England, Ireland and France and drew with Scotland. On a dry, sunny day, the 60,000 crowd saw Wales disappoint. Clive Rowlands was taken off on a stretcher in the closing minutes with a jarred spinal disc after being charged by Colin Meads. The injury caused momentary paralysis. Some such disability seemed to afflict the play of many of the Welsh team!

Wales: G T R. Hodgson (Neath); D R R Morgan, D K Jones (Llanelli), *J Uzzell (Newport), D I Bebb (Swansea); David Watkins (Newport), D C T Rowlands (Pontypool, capt.).: K D Jones (Cardiff) N R Gale (Llanelli), L J Cunningham (Aberavon), Brian Price (Newport), Brian Thomas (Neath), David Hayward (Cardiff), A E I Pask (Abertillery,), *Alan Thomas (Newport).

New Zealand: D B Clarke; threequarters – R W Caulton, P F Little, M J Dick; 2nd five-eighth – D A Arnold; 1st five-eighth – B A Watt; half back – K C Briscoe; forwards – K F Gray, D Young, W J Whineray (capt.), A J Stewart, C E Meads, W J Nathan, D J Graham, K R Tremain.

For New Zealand, Don Clarke kicked a penalty goal. Bruce Watt dropped a goal.

Referee: R C Williams (Ireland).

Match 254 ENGLAND v WALES   Twickenham. January 18, 1964

Drawn. England two tries (6). Wales two tries (6)

Dewi Bebb scored the first Welsh try at Twickenham for eight years to help force a draw after the home side had snatched a 6-0 lead in as many minutes. In fact, Bebb scored both the Welsh tries. Only Newport wing Ken Jones had ever scored two tries at Twickenham in the past. It was also the first time for 11 games for a Welsh back to score a try. With their pack staging a late fight-back, Wales had a chance to win in the closing minutes, but Grahame Hodgson, with a penalty kick, missed what was termed a "sitter".

England: J G Willcox (Harlequins, capt.); M. S Phillips (Fylde), M P Weston (Durham City), R D Sangwin (Hull and East Riding), J M Ranson (Rosslyn Park); J P. Horrocks-Taylor (Middlesbrough), S J S Clarke (Cambridge Univ.); C R Jacobs (Northampton), S A M Hodgson (Durham City), N J Drake-Lee (Cambridge Univ.), A M Davis (Torquay Ath.), R Rowsell (Leicester), P Ford (Gloucester) D G Perry, D P Rogers (Bedford).

Wales: G T R Hodgson (Neath); *D Weaver (Swansea), D K Jones (Llanelli), *K Bradshaw (Bridgend), D I Bebb (Swansea); David Watkins (Newport), D C T Rowlands (Pontypool, capt.); Denzil Williams (Ebbw Vale), N R Gale (Llanelli), L J Cunningham (Aberavon), Brian Thomas (Neath), Brian Price, *J T Mantle (Newport), A E I Pask (Abertillery), Alan Thomas (Newport).

For England, John Ranson and David Perry scored tries.

For Wales, Dewi Bebb scored two tries.

Referee: K D Kelleher (Ireland).

Match 255 WALES v SCOTLAND   Cardiff Arms Park. February 1, 1964

Wales won by one goal, one penalty goal, one try (11) to one try (3)

Wales were the only side to beat Scotland this season, but the Scots were a shadow of the team that had drawn with the All Blacks. The Welsh pack, strong and aggressive, were never challenged and Clive Rowlands varied his tactics intelligently. He worked a delightful dummy scissors with David Watkins to create a try for Keith Bradshaw. Stuart Watkins played his first game for Wales on the right wing.

Wales: G T R Hodgson (Neath); *S J Watkins (Newport), D K Jones (Llanelli), K Bradshaw (Bridgend), D I Bebb (Swansea); David Watkins (Newport), D C T Rowlands (Pontypool, capt.); Denzil Williams (Ebbw Vale), N R Gale (Llanelli),

L J Cunningham (Aberavon), Brian Price (Newport), Brian Thomas (Neath), *G J Prothero (Bridgend), A E I Pask (Abertillery), David Hayward (Cardiff).

Scotland: S Wilson (Oxford Univ.); C Elliot (Langholm), J A P Shackleton, I H P Laughland, R H Thomson (London Scottish); G Sharp (Stewart's Coll., FP), J A T Rodd (London Scottish); D M D Rollo (Howe of Fife), N S Bruce (London Scottish), J B Neill (Edinburgh Acads., capt.), W J Hunter (Hawick), P C Brown (West of Scotland), J W Telfer (Melrose), T O Grant (Hawick), J P Fisher (Royal HSFP).

For Wales, Keith Bradshaw and Brian Thomas scored tries. Bradshaw converted one and kicked a penalty goal.

For Scotland, Iain Laughland scored a try.

Referee: P G Brook (England).

Match 256 IRELAND v WALES   Lansdowne Road, Dublin. March 7, 1964

Wales won by three goals (15) to two penalty goals (6)

Not until the last 10 minutes did Wales break out to snatch victory. Ireland led 6-5 almost to the end of an often fiery match, in which injuries took play to 47 minutes in the second half. David Watkins, with his devastating speed off the mark and sharp twisting runs, was often a brilliant attacker at outside half, and wing forward David Hayward marked down Ireland's Mike Gibson with ruthless efficiency. John Dawes, on debut, scored the try that put Wales ahead at the start of their winning late rally. Dawes came in as replacement for injured Ken Jones.

Ireland: F S Keogh (Bective); P J Casey (Univ. Coll., Dublin), M K Flynn (Wanderers), J C Walsh (Univ, Coll., Cork), K J Houston (Queen's Univ. Belfast); C M H Gibson (NIFC), J C Kelly (Univ. Coll., Dublin); P J Dwyer (Univ. Coll., Dublin), P Lane (Old Crescent), T A Moroney (Univ. Coll., Dublin), W A Mulcahy (Bective, capt.), E P McGuire (Univ. Coll., Galway), M G Culliton (Wanderers), N A Murphy (Cork Constitution).

Wales: G T R Hodgson (Neath); S J Watkins (Newport), *S J Dawes (London Welsh), K Bradshaw (Bridgend), P M Rees (Newport); David Watkins (Newport), D C T Rowlands (Pontypool, capt.); Denzil Williams (Ebbw Vale), N R Gale (Llanelli), L J Cunningham (Aberavon), Brian Price (Newport), Brian Thomas (Neath), G J Prothero (Bridgend), A E I Pask (Abertillery), David Hayward (Cardiff).

For Wales, Stuart Watkins. John Dawes and David Watkins scored tries. Keith Bradshaw converted them.

For Ireland, Fergus Keogh kicked two penalty goals.

Referee: A C Luff (England).

Match 257 WALES v FRANCE   Cardiff Arms Park. March 21, 1964

Drawn. Wales one goal, two penalty goals (11). France one goal, two penalty goals (11)

A try in the last few minutes by Stuart Watkins, which Keith Bradshaw converted with a superb kick from near the touch line, after their poorest performance of the season, earned Wales a draw and a share of the championship with Scotland. On a sticky pitch, France led 11-3 at half time and seemed set for victory. Bradshaw missed six of his eight kicks at goal, but his final effort was a magnificent match-winner as Wales pulled out a spirited rally in the last 10 minutes to save their unbeaten record.

Wales: G T R Hodgson (Neath); S J Watkins (Newport), S J Dawes (London Welsh), K Bradshaw (Bridgend), D I Bebb, (Swansea); David Watkins (Newport), D C T Rowlands (Pontypool, capt.); Denzil Williams (Ebbw Vale), N R Gale (Llanelli), L J Cunningham (Aberavon), Brian Price (Newport), Brian Thomas (Neath), G J Prothero (Bridgend), A E I Pask (Abertillery), David Hayward Cardiff).

France: P Dedieu (Beziers); J Gachassin (Lourdes), J Pique (Pau), A Boniface, C Darrouy (Mont de Marsan); P Albaladejo, J C Lasserre (Dax); J C Berejnoi (Tulle), Y Menthiller (Romans), A Gruarin, A Herrero (Toulon), B Dauga (Mont de Marsan), M Sitjar (Agen), M Lira (La Voulte), M Crauste (Lourdes, capt.).

For Wales, Stuart Watkins scored a try. Keith Bradshaw converted and kicked two penalty goals.

For France, Michel Crauste scored a try. Pierre Albaladejo converted and kicked two penalty goals.

Referee: H B Laidlaw (Scotland).

Match 258 **SOUTH AFRICA v WALES**   King's Park, Durban. May 23, 1964

South Africa won by three goals, one dropped goal, two penalty goals(24) to one penalty goal (3)

The biggest Welsh defeat for 40 years. That was how Wales crashed in the heat at Durban on the first tour they undertook. The Springboks ran them off their feet in the last 20 minutes to register their sixth consecutive win over the Red Devils. Not since the 35-10 hammering from Scotland at Inverleith in 1924 had Wales been so routed. The only score Clive Rowlands and his men could manage was a Keith Bradshaw penalty goal. This goal kept Wales in the game with the score 3-3 at half time. But there was no escape after that.

Wales's decision not to run with the ball was a mistake and, though Norman Gale stole six tight heads while conceding three, and Brian Price jumped well to win line-out possession, they could not match the home forwards' mobility and stamina. The pace wore down the Welsh pack and in one spell of eight minutes, South Africa snatched 13 points. Keith Oxlee kicked 12 points and in his 19 tests for the Springboks he aggregated 88 points.

In their other matches on this short tour, Wales beat East Africa 26-8 at Nairobi, and Boland 17-6 at Wellington, lost to Northern Transvaal 9-22 at Pretoria, and beat Orange Free State 14-6 at Bloemfontein. No caps were awarded for these four games.

South Africa: L G Wilson; J P Engelbrecht, J L Gainsford, D A Stewart, C G Dirksen; K Oxlee, C M Smith; J. L. Myburgh, G F Malan (capt.), J F K Marais, G Carelse, A S Malan, T P Bedford, D J. Hopwood, F C H du Preez.

Wales: G T R Hodgson (Neath); D K Jones (Llanelli), S J Dawes (London Welsh), K Bradshaw (Bridgend,) D I Bebb (Swansea); David Watkins (Newport), D C T Rowlands (Pontypool, capt.); L J Cunningham (Aberavon), N R Gale (Llanelli), Denzil Williams (Ebbw Vale), Brian Price (Newport), Brian Thomas (Neath), A E I Pask (Abertillery), J T Mantle (Newport), David Hayward (Cardiff).

For South Africa, Johannes Marais, Doug Hopwood and Nelie Smith scored tries. Keith Oxlee converted them and kicked two penalty goals. Lionel Wilson dropped a goal.

For Wales, Keith Bradshaw kicked a penalty goal.

Referee: Dr G K Engelbrecht (Transvaal).

Wales won by two goals, one penalty goal, five tries (28) to two goals, four tries (22)

Alun Pask dummying, one-handed, and then diving for a dazzling try. That was one of the many thrilling moments of an unforgettable match, which produced 13 tries, seven by Wales and six by Fiji. To the 50,000 spectators it was a revival meeting rather than a rugby spectacle: this was rugby adventure; a step into the past, to the days of the Golden Era, when everyone ran and attacked and rugby was a handling game. The Fijians stole their way into Welsh hearts with their venturesome approach. They were trailing 9-28 only to smash back in the last 12 minutes and score 13 points And all this with only 14 men because Nalio, their heaviest forward, had dislocated his shoulder in the first 10 minutes.

"We expected them to hit back in the last 10 minutes, but we just could not stop them scoring," said Welsh captain Brian Price. "They have tremendous enthusiasm and speed and never gave up trying or chasing. They gave us a great game." The Fijian captain, Suliasi Cavu, said: "Wales were getting a little tired near the end." Though why Wales with 15 men should be more tired than the gallant 14 Fijians he did not explain It was a remarkable feat for Sevaro Walisoliso, a prop, to score three tries. The match was controlled by French referee Bernard Marie. Terry Price, Maurice Richards, Allan Lewis and John Lloyd were to go on to win full caps.

Wales: T G Price (Llanelli); D Weaver (Swansea), M C R Richards (Cardiff), D Thomas (Aberavon), D I Bebb (Swansea); David Waikins (Newport), Allan Lewis (Abertillery); Denzil Williams (Ebbw Vale), N R Gale (Llanelli), D J Lloyd (Bridgend), Brian Price (capt.), J T Mantle (Newport), G J Prothero (Bridgend), A E I Pask (Abertillery), David Hayward (Cardiff).

Fiji: S Tuisese; S Daunitutu, P Rasiosateki, J Nasova, A Robe; G Barley, J Mucunabitu; S Cavu (capt.), U Tukana, S Walisoliso, Jope Naucabalavu, V Nalio, A Soqosoqo, Joeli Naucabalavu, Sela Toga.

For Wales, Dewi Bebb (2), Dave Thomas (2), Alun Pask, David Weaver and Gary Prothero scored tries. Terry Price converted two. David Watkins kicked a penalty goal.

For Fiji, Sevaro Walisoliso (3), Aca Soqosoqo, Jese Mucunabitu and Aporosa Robe scored tries. Josateki Nasova converted two.

Referee: Bernard Marie (France).

Wales won by one goal, one dropped goal, two tries (14) to one penalty goal (3)

For the first time for six years, Wales won their opening match of the season. In the lashing rain and wind, the Welsh pack were in irrepressible form. They looked the best unit Wales had fielded since the Grand Slam triumphs of 1950 and 1952. Alun Pask and his wing forwards controlled the game and the crowd sang happily long before the end. David Watkins dropped a goal from 30 yards after 17 minutes and the home side led 3-0 at half time. Terry Price, the 19-year-old full back, making his debut, played excellently and converted one of the three Welsh tries. These were obtained by Stuart Watkins (2) and Haydn Morgan. Ron Waldron, the Neath prop, gained his cap after a wait of nearly three years. He had been picked against Ireland in 1962, but the match was postponed because of the South Wales smallpox outbreak, and Kingsley Jones (Cardiff) replaced him when the match was played at the start of the following season.

Playing for the Possibles in the WRU first trial at Pontypool earlier in the season, Terry Price scored 16 points, including two tries from the full back spot. He was still at Llanelli G.S. when he made his debut for Llanelli on the wing against the 1963-64 All Blacks.

Wales: *T G. Price (Llanelli); S J Watkins, J Uzzell (Newport), S J Dawes (London Welsh), D I Bebb (Swansea); David Watkins (Newport), D C T Rowlands (Pontypool, capt.); Denzil Williams (Ebbw Vale), N R Gale (Llanelli), *R Waldron, Brian Thomas (Neath), Brian Price (Newport), G J Prothero (Bridgend), A E I Pask, H J Morgan (Abertillery).

England: D Rutherford (Gloucester); E L Rudd (Oxford Univ.), D W A Rosser, G P Frankcom (Cambridge Univ.), C P Simpson (Harlequins); T J Brophy (Liverpool), J E Williams (Sale); A L Horton (Blackheath), S B Richards (Richmond), N J Drake-Lee, R Rowell (Leicester), J L Owen (Coventry), N A Silk (Harlequins), D G Perry (capt.), D P Rogers (Bedford).

For Wales, Stuart Watkins (2) and Haydn Morgan scored tries. Terry Price converted one. David Watkins dropped a goal.

For England, Don Rutherford kicked a penalty goal.

Referee: K D Kelleher (Ireland).

Match 260 **SCOTLAND v WALES**   Murrayfield. February 6, 1965

Wales won by one goal, two penalty goals, one try (14)
to two dropped goals, two penalty goals (12)

Four times the lead changed hands in a hard, vigorous and absorbing tussle before Norman Gale crashed over for the winning try near the end and, for the second successive visit Wales had won at Murrayfield. The only member of the side that had overpowered England to lose his place was Neath second row forward Brian Thomas, and he did not play again during the season. Bill Morris (Newport) replaced him.

Brian Simmers put Scotland in front with a dropped goal. Terry Price equalised with a penalty shot. Stewart Wilson popped over a penalty for Scotland to go ahead again. Wales regained the lead as Terry Price converted Stuart Watkins's try for an 8-6 advantage at the interval. Terry Price added a penalty goal, but Scotland sensationally snatched the lead at 12-11. They did this through another penalty goal by Wilson and a second dropped goal by Simmers. Was this dropped goal another portent of doom, as when Kininmonth, Doherty and Dorwood had dropped deadly goals on those previous days of Welsh defeat at Murrayfield? Not this time. Gale burst over from a line-out and Wales were through, though by only a two points margin – and hundreds of Welshmen poured on to the field to mob their team.

Scotland: S Wilson (London Scottish); C Elliot (Langholm) I H P Laughland (London Scottish), B C Henderson, D J Whyte (Edinburgh Wands.); B M Simmers (Glasgow Acads.), J A T Rodd (London Scottish); D M D. Rollo (Howe of Fife), F A L Laidlaw (Melrose), N Suddon (Hawick), P K Stagg (Sale}, M J Campbell-Lamerton (capt.), J P Fisher (London Scottish), J W Telfer (Melrose), R J C Glasgow (Dunfermline).

Wales: T G Price (Llanelli) ; S J Watkins, J Uzzell (Newport), S J Dawes (London Welsh), D I Bebb (Swansea); David Watkins (Newport), D C T Rowlands (Pontypool, capt.); Denzil Williams (Ebbw Vale), N R Gale (Llanelli), R Waldron (Neath), Brian Price. *W J Morris (Newport), G J Prothero (Bridgend), A E I Pask, H J Morgan (Abertillery).

For Wales, Stuart Watkins and Norman Gale scored tries. Terry Price converted one and kicked two penalty goals.

For Scotland, Brian Simmers dropped two goals. Stewart Wilson kicked two penalty goals.

Referee: R W Gilliland (Ireland).

Wales won by one goal, one dropped goal, one penalty goal, one try (14)
to one goal, one penalty goal (8)

Wales won the Triple Crown for the 10th time in a match in which Alun Pask, one of the most famous No. 8 forwards to play for Wales, spent 20 minutes as emergency full back. He was moved there when centre John Dawes was injured and went off after only five minutes. "I think Clive Rowlands took a tremendous gamble by playing me there," said Pask. But the Abertillery man did the unaccustomed job reliably until Dawes returned and Terry Price, who had switched to centre, resumed at fullback. "The best thing that could have happened to us was to lose Dawes," said Clive Rowlands. "That really put our backs to the wall: it made us fight all the harder. If Ireland could not crack us then, they never would. It was a risk playing Pask at full back, but I wanted to keep my flank forwards and I needed someone with safe hands. Pask was the obvious man for the job."

There were 58,500 spectators to see this Triple Crown decider, fought in the contemporary tight fashion on a greasy turf and in fine rain. It was the first time since 1911 that both sides had faced each other with the Triple Crown waiting for the winners. Just before the interval, David Watkins scored a Welsh try that Terry Price converted. In the second half, Brian Price tapped back to the wing from a line-out and Dewi Bebb dashed in with a try. Tom Kiernan provided Ireland's first points with a penalty goal, but Terry Price dropped a goal from 45 yards with a magnificent kick. Kevin Flynn scored a try that Kiernan converted before, finally, Terry Price put over a penalty goal from the touch line and the championship as well as Triple Crown belonged to Wales. Only 17 players were called on in 1965.

Wales: T G Price (Llanelli); S J Watkins, J Uzzell (Newport), S J Dawes (London Welsh), D I Bebb (Swansea); David Watkins (Newport), D C T Rowlands (Pontypool, capt.); Denzil Williams (Ebbw Vale}, N R Gale (Llanelli), R Waldron (Neath), Brian Price (Newport), K A Rowlands (Cardiff), G J Prothero (Bridgend), A E I Pask, H. J. Morgan (Abertillery).

Ireland: T J Kiernan (Cork Constitution); D Hewitt (Instonians), M K Flynn (Wanderers), J C Walsh, P McGrath (Univ. Coll., Cork); C M H Gibson (NIFC), R M Young (Queen's Univ., Belfast); S MacHale (Lansdowne), K W Kennedy (Queen's Univ., Belfast) R J McLoughlin (Gosforth, capt.), W J McBride (Ballymena), W A Mulcahy (Bective), M G Doyle (Univ. Coll., Dublin), H Wall (Dolphin), N A Murphy (Cork Constitution).

For Wales, David Watkins and Dewi Bebb scored tries. Terry Price converted one, kicked a penalty goal and dropped a goal.

For Ireland, Kevin Flynn scored a try. Tom Kiernan converted and kicked a penalty goal.

Referee: P G Brook (England).

France won by two goals, one dropped goal, one penalty goal, two tries (22)
to two goals, one try (13)

Wales, already outright champions no matter what the result, found themselves trailing 0-22. It was unbelievable. From the dizzy heights of Triple Crown conquest, they plunged to

160

their heaviest defeat at the hands of France. It was a nightmare final international appearance for skipper Clive Rowlands. He had played 14 consecutive games, all of them as captain to beat the previous best sequence of 11 by full back Billy Bancroft to start off the Golden Era. During Rowlands's reign, Wales had won six, lost six and drawn two. Wales fought back with 13 points in a determined effort in the second half to help make this a fine running spectacle. Referee R W Gilliland (Ireland) burst a blood vessel in his left calf after 32 minutes and had to go off. The replacement was French touch judge Bernard Marie, who had refereed the Wales Fiji match in 1964.

France: P Dedieu (Beziers); J Pique (Pau), G Boniface, A Boniface (Mont de Marsan), A Campaes (Lourdes); J Gachassin Lourdes), J C Lasserre (Dax); A Gruarin (Toulon), J M Cabanier (Montauban), J C Berejnoi (Tulle), B Dauga (Mont de Marsan), W Spanghero (Narbonne), J J Rupert (Tyrosse), A Herrero (Toulon), M Crauste (Lourdes, capt.).

Wales: T G Price (Llanelli); S J Watkins, J Uzzell (Newport), S J Dawes (London Welsh), D I Bebb (Swansea); David Watkins (Newport), D C T Rowlands (Pontypool. capt.); Denzil Williams (Ebbw Vale), N R Gale (Llanelli), R Waldron (Neath), Brian Price (Newport), K A Rowlands (Cardiff), G J Prothero (Bridgend), A E I Pask, H J Morgan (Abertillery).

For France, Guy Boniface (2) and Andre Herrero (2) scored tries. Paul Dedieu converted two and kicked a penalty goal. Jean-Claude Lasserre dropped a goal.

For Wales, John Dawes, Stuart Watkins and Dewi Bebb scored tries. Terry Price converted two.

Referee: R W Gilliland (Ireland). Replaced after 32 minutes by Bernard Marie (France).

Match 263 ENGLAND v WALES   Twickenham. January 15, 1966

Wales won by one goal and two penalty goals (11) to one penalty goal, one try (6)

Clive Rowlands was dropped to position of reserve, and Allan Lewis (Abertillery), who built an impressive reputation as a long, fluent passer, came in as successor at scrum half. Alun Pask took over the captaincy and joined the small band of Welsh skippers who had led winning teams at Twickenham – Watcyn Thomas (1933), John Gwilliam (1950 and 1952) and Cliff Morgan (1956). Terry Price kicked superbly to put over two penalty goals and one conversion. Unfortunately, he could not play in any of the other matches this season because of injury. Brian Thomas (Neath) was recalled to play soundly alongside line-out star Brian Price.

England: D Rutherford (Gloucester); E L Rudd (Liverpool), T G Arthur, D W A Rosser (Wasps), K F Savage (Northampton); T J Brophy (Liverpool), J Spencer (Harlequins); P E Judd (Coventry), J V Pullin (Bristol), D L Powell (Northampton}, C M Payne (Harlequins), A M Davis (Devonport Services), R B Taylor (Northampton), D G Perry, D P Rogers (Bedford, capt.).

Wales: T G Price (Llanelli); S J Watkins (Newport), D K Jones (Cardiff), K Bradshaw, *Lyn Davies (Bridgend); David Watkins (Newport), *Allan Lewis (Abertillery); Denzil Williams (Ebbw Vale), N R Gale (Llanelli), *D J Lloyd (Bridgend), Brian Price (Newport), Brian Thomas (Neath), G J Prothero (Bridgend), A E I Pask (capt,), H J Morgan (Abertillery).

For Wales, Alun Pask scored a try. Terry Price converted and kicked two penalty goals.

For England, David Perry scored a try. Don Rutherford kicked a penalty goal.

Referee: R W Gilliland (Ireland).

Wales won by one goal and one try (8) to one penalty goal (3)

"We expected to win when half time came and Wales led only 3-0," said Scottish skipper Stewart Wilson, who had chosen to play against the wind. But Wales had the edge at forward and deserved their success amid the pools of surface water and mud. Scotland had won only seven away games out of 39 in 19 years of post-war rugby. Fly half David Watkins was the dominating player behind the scrum, with Ken Jones running in classical style in the centre and Grahame Hodgson a faultless deputy for the injured Terry Price at full back. Gary Prothero was a tremendous worker in the home pack. Brian Price badly pulled a hamstring muscle after 32 minutes, but played on with typical determination after a pain-killing injection from Welsh team physiotherapist Gerry Lewis.

Wales: T G R Hodgson (Neath); S J Watkins (Newport), D K Jones (Cardiff), K Bradshaw, Lyn Davies (Bridgend); David Watkins (Newport), Allan Lewis (Abertillery); Denzil Williams (Ebbw Vale), N R Gale (Llanelli), D J Lloyd (Bridgend), Brian Price (Newport), Brian Thomas (Neath), G J Prothero (Bridgend), A E I Pask(capt.), H J Morgan (Abertillery).

Scotland: S Wilson (London Scottish, capt.); A J W Hinshelwood, I H P Laughland (London Scottish), B C Henderson, D J Whyte (Edinburgh Wands.); J W C Turner (Gala), A J Hastie (Melrose) D M D Rollo (Howe of Fife), F A L Laidlaw (Melrose), J D Macdonald, M J Campbell-Lamerton (London Scottish), P K Stagg (Sale), D Grant (Hawick), J W Telfer (Melrose), J P Fisher (London Scottish).

For Wales, Ken Jones scored two tries. Keith Bradshaw converted one.

For Scotland, Stewart Wilson kicked a penalty goal.

Referee: M H Titcomb (England).

Ireland won by one dropped goal, one penalty goal, one try (9) to one penalty goal, one try (6)

This was the day the sky fell on Welsh rugby. Their great team, to whom the winning of the Triple Crown was a mere formality, were beaten by an Irish side that had been hooted off this same pitch two weeks previously by their own crowd after a dismal defeat by Scotland. At the end of this Welsh match the field was black with Irish fans who rushed to chair off Tom Kiernan's magnificent men in green. Alun Pask's team of stars went down to one of the most amazing shock defeats in rugby history, and Ireland deserved every point. The Welsh halves never developed real rhythm against fanatical tackling and harassing.

After 20 minutes, Mike Gibson dropped a goal against the wind. Then he added a penalty goal. A try by Gary Prothero reduced the Irish lead to 6-3 at half time, but Barry Bresnihan slipped in for a try when Welsh passing broke down. Keith Bradshaw kicked a late Welsh penalty goal as his one success in four kicks at goal. Then began the glum retreat from Dublin. The impossible had happened. The sky had fallen on Welsh rugby – and it was going to crash down in the same way in 1970.

Ireland: T J Kiernan (Cork Constitution, capt.); A T A Duggan (Lansdowne), F P K Bresnihan (Univ. Coll., Dublin), J C Walsh (Sunday's Well), P J McGrath (Univ. Coll., Cork); C M H Gibson (NIFC), R M Young (Queen's Univ., Belfast); S MacHale (Lansdowne), K W Kennedy (CIYMS), R J McLoughlin (Gosforth), O Waldron (Oxford Univ.), W J McBride (Ballymena), N A Murphy (Cork Constitution), R A Lamont (Instonians), M G Doyle (Cambridge Univ.).

Wales: G T R Hodgson (Neath); S J Watkins (Newport), D K Jones (Cardiff), K Bradshaw, Lyn Davies (Bridgend); David Watkins (Newport), Allan Lewis (Abertillery) ; Denzil Williams (Ebbw Vale), N R Gale (Llanelli), D J Lloyd (Bridgend), Brian Price (Newport), Brian Thomas (Neath), G J Prothero (Bridgend), A E I Pask (capt.), H J Morgan (Abertillery).

For Ireland, 'Barry' Bresnihan scored a try. Mike Gibson dropped a goal and kicked a penalty goal.

For Wales, Gary Prothero scored a try. Keith Bradshaw kicked a penalty goal.

Referee: R P Burrell (Scotland).

Match 266 **WALES v FRANCE**   Cardiff Arms Park. March 26, 1966

Wales won by two penalty goals, one try (9) to one goal, one try (8)

Stuart Watkins pounding 75 yards. Who can ever forget it? Ten minutes from the end, this famous Newport wing brought off his spectacular interception and with it won a game that had long seemed lost. Even then, France had a chance to snatch victory with the last kick of the match, when Newport forward Bill Morris was penalised for deliberately throwing the ball into touch under pressure near his goal-line. Claude Lacaze took the penalty kick. The strong wind blew the ball over when he teed it up the first time. He replaced it in unnerving silence; took aim, ran in and kicked. The ball curled towards the posts. It looked like being a brilliant winning shot from the touch line. But at the last moment a gust of wind swung the ball just wide of the near post. So Wales won by one point and retained the international championship for the first time for 57 years.

Yet Alun Pask's team were 0-8 down after 12 minutes. Against a team of France's power there should have been no escape. Then Wales had a moment of luck: Lacaze hit a post with a penalty shot. When Keith Bradshaw had his chances he landed two penalty goals to cut the French lead to 6-8 at halftime. But Wales had to face the gusty wind after the interval. So to the last 10 minutes. France were attacking. Jean Gachassin threw a long pass. Stuart Watkins streaked in, pulled down the ball in flight and was away. Then began one of the longest and most spectacular runs of post-war rugby by a Welsh player. He pushed away Lacaze as the full back closed for the tackle. And on, on to the goal-line, every stride a thrill and a memory.

Wales named 10 forwards from whom to make their final choice on the morning of the match, depending on ground conditions. The going was firm, so the selectors decided on Bill Morris and Howard Norris and left out Brian Thomas and Denzil Williams.

Wales: G T R Hodgson (Neath); S J Watkins (Newport), D K Jones (Cardiff), K Bradshaw (Bridgend), D I Bebb (Swansea); David Watkins (Newport), Allan Lewis (Abertillery); C H Norris (Cardiff), N R Gale (Llanelli), D J Lloyd (Bridgend), Brian Price, W J Morris (Newport), G J Prothero (Bridgend), A E I Pask (capt.) H J Morgan (Abertillery).

France: C Lacaze (Angouleme); B Duprat (Bayonne), G Boniface, A Boniface, C Darrouy (Mont de Marsan); J Gachassin (Lourdes), L Camberabero (La Voulte); A Gruarin (Toulon), J M Cabanier (Montauban), J C Berejnoi (Tulle), W Spanghero (Narbonne), B Dauga (Mont de Marsan), J J Rupert (Tyrosse), A Herrero (Toulon), M Crauste (Lourdes, capt.).

For Wales, Stuart Watkins scored a try. Keith Bradshaw kicked two penalty goals.

For France, Bernard Duprat and Jean-Joseph Rupert scored tries. Claude Lacaze converted one.

Referee: K D Kelleher (Ireland).

Australia won by one goal, one dropped goal, one penalty goal, one try (14)
to one goal, one penalty goal, one try (11)

Tears trickled down the face of Wallabies manager Bill McLaughlin at the end of this match. They were tears of joy; emotion for an historic occasion. Australia had beaten Wales for the first time. It was also the first home defeat for the Welsh for three years, since the 1963 All Blacks had triumphed. The 50,000 crowd saw a magnificent running game, though some criticised Pask for abandoning the tight, contemporary style. Wales spoiled good approach work by ragged finishing and Terry Price was well below international form. Haydn Morgan had played 26 previous games for Wales, but this was his first against a touring team. It was the debut appearance of Barry John, chosen in preference to David Watkins.

Haydn Morgan scored a fine try with a dummy when Dewi Bebb passed inside to the wing forward. Australia equalised when Phil Hawthorne dropped a goal. Then Jim Lenehan's penalty goal from 35 yards put the Wallabies in front. Terry Price equalised with a 40 yard penalty. Lenehan joined an attack and the full back scored a corner try. He almost converted, but the ball rebounded from a post. Then wing Alan Cardy crossed for a try that Hawthorne converted. Hawthorne played on courageously after having suffered a depressed fracture of his cheekbone after 30 minutes. Right at the end, John Dawes scored a Welsh try that Terry Price converted.

Wales: T G Price (Llanelli); S J Watkins (Newport), S J Dawes (London Welsh), * Gerald Davies (Cardiff), D I Bebb (Swansea); *Barry John (Llanelli), Allan Lewis (Abertillery); Denzil Williams (Ebbw Vale), N R Gale (Llanelli), D J Lloyd (Bridgend), Brian Price (Newport) , *Delme Thomas (Llanelli), *K J Braddock (Newbridge), A E I Pask (capt.), H J Morgan (Abertillery).

Australia: J K Lenehan; S Boyce, R J Marks, J E Brass, A M Cardy; P F Hawthorne, K W Catchpole (capt.); J M Miller, P G Johnson, A R Miller, R G Teitzel, R J Heming, M P Purcell, J F O'Gorman, G V Davis.

For Australia, Jim Lenehan and Alan Cardy scored tries. Phil Hawthorne converted one and dropped a goal. Lenehan kicked a penalty goal.

For Wales, Haydn Morgan and John Dawes scored tries. Terry Price converted one and kicked a penalty goal.

Referee: K D Kelleher (Ireland).

Scotland won by one goal, one dropped goal, one try (11) to one goal (5)

With six new caps and too tight a tactical plan, Wales failed after leading 5-0 at half time. A crowd of 70,000 saw David Chisholm maintain the Scottish tradition of dropping goals against Wales at Murrayfield. It was the sixth in post-war years there, and the 10th time halves Chisholm and Alex Hastie had played together for their country without being on the losing side. Barry John and new scrum half Billy Hullin kicked too much, while Terry Price struggled at full back. A lack of variation by the Welsh attackers was most disappointing.

Scotland: S Wilson (London Scottish); A J W Hinshelwood (London Scottish), J W C Turner (Gala), B M Simmers (Glasgow Acads.), D J Whyte (Edinburgh Wands.); D H Chisholm, A J Hastie (Melrose); J D Macdonald (London Scottish), F A L Laidlaw (Melrose), D M D Rollo (Howe of Fife), P K Stagg (Sale), W J Hunter, D Grant (Hawick), J W Telfer (Melrose), J P Fisher (London Scottish, capt).

Wales: T G Price (Hendy and Leicester Univ.); S J Watkins (Newport), *W H Raybould (London Welsh), Gerald Davies (Cardiff), D I Bebb (Swansea); Barry John (Llanelli), *W G Hullin (Cardiff); D J Lloyd (Bridgend), *B I Rees (London Welsh), *J P O'Shea (Cardiff), Brian Price (Newport), *W T Mainwaring (Aberavon), K J Braddock (Newbridge), A E I Pask (Abertillery, capt.), *J Taylor (London Welsh).

For Scotland, 'Sandy' Hinshelwood and Jim Telfer scored tries. Stewart Wilson converted one. David Chisholm dropped a goal.

For Wales, Stuart Watkins scored a try. Terry Price converted.

Referee: K D Kelleher (Ireland).

Match 269 **WALES v IRELAND**   Cardiff Arms Park. March 11, 1967

Ireland won by one try (3) to nil

David Watkins took over from Alun Pask as captain and almost saved the game for his side with a daring run. But Irish No.8 Ken Goodall ankle-tapped Watkins with a desperate dive. "I think I would have scored," said Watkins, whose searing speed off the mark was unmatched by any outside half in post-war rugby. The match, played in a gale, was won by Ireland with the only score, a try in the third minute by Alan Duggan, after Jerry Walsh kicked diagonally to the corner.

Wales: G T R Hodgson (Neath); S J Watkins (Newport), W H Raybould (London Welsh), Gerald Davies (Cardiff), D I Bebb (Swansea); David Watkins (Newport, capt.), Allan Lewis (Abertillery); J P O'Shea (Cardiff), B I Rees (London Welsh), D J Lloyd (Bridgend), W T Mainwaring (Aberavon), Brian Price (Newport) K J Braddock (Newbridge), A E I Pask (Abertillery), J Taylor (London Welsh).

Ireland: T J Kiernan (Cork Constitution); A T A Duggan (Lansdowne), F P K Bresnihan (Univ. Coll., Dublin), J C Walsh (Sunday's Well), N H Brophy (Blackrock); C M H. Gibson (NIFC), R M Young (Queen's Univ., Belfast); S McHale (Lansdowne), K W Kennedy (CIYMS), S A Hutton (Malone), W J McBride (Ballymena), M G Molloy (Univ. Coll., Galway), N A Murphy (Cork Constitution, capt.), K G Goodall (Newcastle Univ.), M G Doyle (Edinburgh Acads.).

For Ireland, Alan Duggan scored a try.

Referee: M H Titcomb (England).

Match 270 **FRANCE v WALES**   Colombes, Paris. April 1, 1967

France won by one goal, two dropped goals, one penalty goal, two tries (20)
to one goal, two penalty goals, one dropped goal (14)

Fly half Guy Camberabero, 5ft. 6in. of astonishing kicking accuracy, scored 14 of France's 20 points with one try, two dropped goals, one penalty goal and one conversion. It was an extraordinary season for him as he collected 76 points in five games for the Tricolours – I7 against Australia, 10 against England, 14 against Wales, eight against Ireland and 27 against Italy in a 60-13 victory at Toulon. His points were made up of eight penalty goals, seven dropped goals, 14 conversions and one try. He did not play against Scotland. One penalty shot in the Welsh match turned into five points when it rebounded from a post and Claude Dourthe, following up, pounced for a try which Camberabero converted. It was the first time since 1924-25 for Wales to lose four consecutive matches in one season (including the Australian fixture). Terry Price played his last game, again without much success as he missed six of his nine goal attempts. But he scored 45 points in his eight games for Wales before he joined RL club Bradford Northern for £10,000 in July, 1967. Gareth Edwards made his debut.

France: J Gachassin (Lourdes); M Arnaudet (Lourdes), C Dourthe (Dax), J P Lux (Tyrosse), C Darrouy (Mont de Marsan, capt.); G Camberabero, L Camberabero (La Voulte); A Gruarin (Toulon), J M Cabanier (Montauban), J C Berejnoi (Tulle), F Cester (Toulouse), J Fort, M Sitjar (Agen), B Dauga (Mont de Marsan), C Carrere (Toulon).

Wales: T G Price (London Welsh); S J Watkins (Newport), W H Raybould (London Welsh), Gerald Davies (Cardiff), D I Bebb (Swansea); David Watkins (Newport, capt.), *G O Edwards (Cardiff); Denzil Williams (Ebbw Vale), B I Rees (London Welsh), D J Lloyd (Bridgend), Brian Price (Newport), W T Mainwaring (Aberavon), *Ron Jones (Coventry), *W D Morris (Neath), J Taylor (London Welsh).

For France, Guy Camberabero, Benoit Dauga and Claude Dourthe scored tries. Guy Camberabero converted one, dropped two goals and kicked a penalty goal.

For Wales, Dewi Bebb scored a try. Terry Price converted and kicked two penalty goals. David Watkins dropped a goal.

Referee: D P D'Arcy (Ireland).

Match 271	**WALES v ENGLAND**	Cardiff Arms Park. April 15, 1967

Wales won by five goals, two penalty goals, one dropped goal (34)
to four penalty goals, three tries (21)

Keith Jarrett's astonishing debut saw England lose after scoring 21 points and the game produced an aggregate of 55 points. It was a record Welsh total against England and the biggest win for the Red Devils since their 49-14 triumph over France in 1910. Jarrett, at full back, scored 19 points to equal the Welsh record by full back Jack Bancroft in that 1910 match. The 18-year-old Jarrett had left Monmouth School only four months before this game and shot to fame as a goal kicker with Newport, playing in the centre. Ironically, he would never have won his cap in this game if his club had agreed to the WRU request to play him as an experiment at full back against Newbridge. So the national selectors had to take the gamble of playing him out of position, never having seen how he could manage the strange role. They must have felt particularly uneasy when Newport changed their minds and gave Jarrett a chance to see how it felt as a full back in the Newbridge match only to hurriedly switch him back to centre at halftime. He looked hopelessly out of his class.

But everything went right for Jarrett on the big day. "If that first penalty kick, which hit the post and glanced over had bounced back out, it all might have been different," he confessed. Jarrett even scored a spectacular try – only the second time in Welsh rugby history for an international full back to cross the line. Viv Jenkins had become the first against Ireland at Swansea in 1934. England were only 15-19 behind in the second half when Jarrett, standing deep, ran forward to field the ball as Colin McFadyean kicked for touch towards the north stand side. Jarrett kept running for nearly 50 yards and scored in the corner at the Westgate Street end, near the spot where Teddy Morgan had scored his great try to beat the 1905 All Blacks. The young full back converted his try with a superb kick. In all, he converted five tries and kicked two penalty goals as well as scoring a try. No Welsh player has made such a fairy tale international debut.

Wales: *K S Jarrett (Newport); S J Watkins (Newport), W H Raybould (London Welsh), Gerald Davies (Cardiff), D I Bebb (Swansea); David Watkins (Newport, capt.), G O Edwards (Cardiff); Denzil Williams (Ebbw Vale), N R Gale (Llanelli), D J Lloyd (Bridgend), Brian Price (Newport), W T Mainwaring (Aberavon), Ron Jones (Coventry), W D Morris (Neath), J Taylor (London Welsh).

England: R W Hosen (Bristol); K F Savage (Northampton), R D Hearn (Bedford), C W McFadyean (Moseley), R E Webb (Coventry); J F Finlan (Moseley) R D A Pickering (Bradford); M J Coulman (Moseley), S B Richards (Richmond), P E Judd (capt.), J Barton (Coventry), D E J Watt (Bristol), R B Taylor (Northampton), D M Rollitt (Bristol), D P Rogers (Bedford).

For Wales, Gerald Davies (2), Keith Jarrett, Dave Morris and Dewi Bebb scored tries. Jarrett converted them all and kicked two penalty goals. Billy Raybould dropped a goal.

For England, John Barton (2) and Keith Savage scored tries. Roger Hosen kicked four penalty goals.

Referee: D C J McMahon (Scotland).

Match 272 **WALES v NEW ZEALAND**   Cardiff Arms Park. November 11, 1967

New Zealand won by two goals, one penalty goal (13) to one dropped goal, one penalty goal (6)

Welsh mistakes on a rain-soaked and wind-swept pitch enabled New Zealand to square the series 3-3 with their greatest rugby rivals in the U.K. Hooker Norman Gale, leading Wales for the first time, chose to play against the wind and his side were only 0-8 down at half time. There seemed a good chance for Wales. But early in the second half, after Barry John had dropped a goal to trim back the N.Z. lead, John Jeffery committed his notorious blunder on his debut. He threw the ball behind him under pressure just outside his goal-line when Fergie McCormick's penalty shot dropped wide at the river end. Bill Davis darted in for a simple try by the posts which McCormick converted and, at 3-13 down, Wales were doomed.

McCormick's penalty goal after 11 minutes, when Billy Raybould wandered off-side at a scrum, was followed seven minutes later with a corner try by Bill Birtwistle, from the only complete threequarter attack of the match. McCormick converted with a fine kick. After Barry John's dropped goal at the start of the second half, the All Blacks were presented with their gift of five points and the only other score was a penalty goal by Gale for Wales 10 minutes from the end. Wales fielded six new caps and were without Keith Jarrett, who was injured. His expert goal kicking was badly missed. Second row man Brian Thomas played as a prop for the first time. On this short tour, New Zealand were unbeaten, though they were lucky to draw 3-3 with East Wales at Cardiff. The All Blacks beat England, France and Scotland and had their fixture with Ireland cancelled because of the serious outbreak of foot-and-mouth disease in England and Wales.

Wales: *P J Wheeler (Aberavon); S J Watkins (Newport), W H Raybould (London Welsh), *I Hall (Aberavon), *Keri Jones (Cardiff); Barry John, G O Edwards (Cardiff); Denzil Williams (Ebbw Vale), N R Gale (Llanelli, capt.), Brian Thomas (Neath), *M Wiltshire, W T Mainwaring (Aberavon), *D Hughes (Newbridge), *J J Jeffery (Newport), J Taylor (London Welsh).

New Zealand: W F McCormick; threequarters – W M Birtwistle, I R MacRae, M J Dick; 2nd five-eighth - W L Davis; 1st five-eighth – E W Kirton; half back – C R Laidlaw; forwards – K F Gray, B E McLeod, B L Muller, S C Strahan, C E Meads, K R Tremain, B J Lochore (capt.), G C Williams.

For New Zealand, Bill Birtwistle and Bill Davis scored tries. Fergus McCormick converted both and kicked a penalty goal.

For Wales, Barry John dropped a goal. Norman Gale kicked a penalty goal.

Referee: M H Titcomb (England).

Match 273 ENGLAND v WALES · Twickenham. January 20, 1968

Drawn. England one goal, one penalty goal, one try (11)
Wales one goal, one dropped goal, one try (11)

Keith Jarrett kicked one goal in four attempts for Wales. Yet his two penalty misses led to tries for his team. First Colin McFadenan knocked-on while fielding Jarrett's kick at goal and, from the attacking position gained, Gareth Edwards slipped round the blind side for a diving try. Then Jarrett attempted a desperate 6o-yard penalty shot. This time it was Bob Hiller who knocked-on and, from the scrum-five, Welsh No.8 Bob Wanbon burst over for a try that Jarrett converted. Barry John dropped a goal to level the scores at 11-11. So England lost the 11-3 lead they held early in the second half and could not snatch another score in the last 25 minutes. This season, Wales appointed David Nash, the former international forward, as their first national coach. He also became the first man from outside the WRU to be a Welsh team selector.

England: R B Hiller (Harlequins); D H Prout (Northampton), C W McFadyean (Moseley, capt.), R H Lloyd (Harlequins), K F Savage (Northampton); J F Finlan (Moseley), B W Redwood (Bristol); B Keen (Newcastle Univ.). J V Pullin (Bristol), M J Coulman (Moseley), M J Parsons, P J Larter (Northampton), P J Bell (Blackheath), D J Gay (Bath), B R West (Northampton).

Wales: P J Wheeler (Aberavon); S J Watkins, K S Jarrett (Newport), Gerald Davies, Keri Jones (Cardiff); Barry John, G O Edwards (Cardiff); Denzil Williams (Ebbw Vale), N R Gale (Llanelli, capt.), *B James (Bridgend), M Wiltshire, W T Mainwaring (Aberavon), W D Morris (Neath), *R Wanbon (Aberavon), *A J Gray (London Welsh).

For England, Colin McFadyean and Bill Redwood scored tries. Bob Hiller converted one and kicked a penalty goal.

For Wales, Gareth Edwards and Bobby Wanbon scored tries. Keith Jarrett converted one. Barry John dropped a goal.

Referee: D P D'Arcy (Ireland).

Match 274 WALES v SCOTLAND · Cardiff Arms Park. February 3, 1968

Wales won by one goal (5) to nil

Wales's only victory of the season – and that from a try following a forward pass. This was the story of a disappointing match against Scotland, who had won only nine of their previous 43 away internationals in 22 post-war years. Gareth Edwards took over the leadership from Norman Gale to become the youngest player ever to captain his country at the age of 20 years and seven months. Keith Jarrett, who missed four penalty attempts in the gusty conditions, made the break that led to the Welsh try, but his pass to co-centre Gerald Davies was forward. Wing Keri Jones finished the move with a try that Jarrett converted after 17 minutes.

Wales: *Doug Rees (Swansea); S J Watkins, K S Jarrett(Newport), Gerald Davies, Keri Jones (Cardiff); Barry John, G O Edwards (Cardiff capt.); D J Lloyd, *Jeff Young (Bridgend), J P O'Shea (Cardiff), M Wiltshire (Aberavon), Delme Thomas (Llanelli), W D Morris (Neath), Ron Jones (Coventry), A J Gray (London Welsh).

Scotland: S Wilson (London Scottish); G J Keith (Wasps), J N M Frame (Edinburgh Univ.), J W C Turner (Gala), A J W Hinshelwood (London Scottish); D H Chisholm, A J Hastie (Melrose}; A B Carmichael (West of Scotland), F A L. Laidlaw (Melrose), D M D Rollo (Howe of Fife), P K Stagg (Sale) G W E Mitchell, (Edinburgh Wands.), J P Fisher (capt.), A H W Boyle (London Scottish), T G Elliot (Langholm).

For Wales, Ken Jones scored a try. Keith Jarrett converted.

Referee: G C Lamb (England).

Match 275 IRELAND v WALES   Lansdowne Road, Dublin. March 9, 1968

Ireland won by one dropped goal, one penalty goal, one try (9)
to one dropped goal, one penalty goal (6)

There was a near-riot as irate spectators invaded the field and held up play for five minutes. They threw orange peel, apple cores and bottles and booed and hooted. It was a fierce demonstration against referee Mike Titcomb (Bristol), who signalled a dropped goal as being scored by Welsh scrum half Gareth Edwards, when the ball appeared to pass at least a foot outside the post. The Irish players lined up for a drop-out and were aghast when the referee indicated a goal. At the end, police escorted Mr. Titcomb to safety. "I thought the ball had gone over," he said. "It was just one of those things that could happen to anyone." Fortunately it did not deprive Ireland of the victory they deserved, though it enabled Wales to draw level at 6-6. Tom Kiernan, the home captain, said: "The dropped goal incident was balanced out, because the Welsh players claimed that Mike Gibson's dropped goal was invalidated as it had been touched in flight." The winning score came nine minutes into injury time, when Mick Doyle scored around the blind side of a scrum-five. John Dawes took over the captaincy from Edwards and the match saw the first appearance of wing Maurice Richards.

Ireland: T J Kiernan (Cork Constitution, capt.); A T A Duggan (Lansdowne), L Hunter (Civil Service), F P K Bresnihan (Univ. Coll., Dublin), J C M Moroney (London Irish); C M H Gibson (NIFC), R M Young (Queen's Univ., Belfast); P O'Callaghan (Dolphin), A M Brady (Malone), S Millar, W J McBride (Ballymena), M G Molloy (Univ. Coll., Galway), M G Doyle (Blackrock), K G Goodall (City of Derry), T J Doyle (Wanderers).

Wales: Doug Rees (Swansea); Keri Jones (Cardiff), S J Dawes (capt.), W H Raybould (London Welsh), *M C R Richards (Cardiff); Barry John, G O Edwards (Cardiff); J P O'Shea (Cardiff), Jeff Young, D J Lloyd (Bridgend), *I C Jones (London Welsh), Delme Thomas (Llanelli), W D Morris (Neath), Ron Jones (Coventry), J Taylor (London Welsh).

For Ireland, Mick Doyle scored a try. Mike Gibson dropped a goal. Tom Kiernan kicked a penalty goal.

For Wales, Gareth Edwards dropped a goal. Doug Rees kicked a penalty goal.

Referee: M H Titcomb (England).

Match 276 WALES v FRANCE   Cardiff Arms Park. March 23, 1968

France won by one goal, one dropped goal, one penalty goal, one try(14)
to two penalty goals and one try (9)

For the first time France registered the coveted grand slam of four victories in the Five Nations' Tournament – and that after Wales had grasped a 9-3 lead on the mud-patch. Guy

Camberabero, the 31-year-old shopkeeper, followed his 14 points against Wales the previous season with eight points and he and his scrum half partner and brother Lilian provided 11 of their side's 14 points. Gareth Edwards gave a more accurate service than in previous games, but Barry John kicked poorly and the Welsh midfield players faded.

Wales: Doug Rees (Swansea); Keri Jones (Cardiff), S J Dawes, W H Raybould (London Welsh), M C R Richards (Cardiff); Barry John, G O Edwards (Cardiff capt.); D J Lloyd, Jeff Young (Bridgend), J P O'Shea (Cardiff), Delme Thomas (Llanelli), M Wiltshire (Aberavon), W D Morris (Neath), Ron Jones (Coventry), J Taylor (London Welsh).

France: C Lacaze (Angouleme); J M Bonal (Toulouse), J Maso (Perpignan), C Dourthe (Dax), A Campaes (Lourdes); G Camberabero, L Camberabero (La Voulte); J C Noble (La Voulte), M Yachvili (Tulle), M Lasserre, A Plantefol (Agen), E Cester (Toulouse), W Spanghero (Narbonne), M Greffe (Grenoble), C Carrere (Toulon, capt.).

For France, Lilian Camberabero and Christian Carrere scored tries. Guy Camberabero converted one, dropped a goal and kicked a penalty goal.

For Wales, Keri Jones scored a try. Doug Rees kicked two penalty goals.

Referee : H B Laidlaw (Scotland).

Unofficial Matches   ARGENTINA v WALES   1968

Wales played two uncapped games in Buenos Aires in September, losing the first and drawing the next. None of the 11 players who toured South Africa with the British Lions in the summer of 1968 was chosen for the visit to the Argentine, but it was considered a sufficiently strong team to make a favourable impression. Although John Dawes, the captain, was the only capped back, there were 13 international forwards in the party, with Clive Rowlands as coach. Few imagined the Pumas would win the first match, but the watching 25,000 saw tenacious tackling upset the tourists, who lost 9-5. The Welsh try was highly praised as of exceptional quality. Laurie Daniel launched it from almost his goal-line; JPR linked and sent Glyn Turner over for Dawes to convert. In the second match, Stuart Ferguson scored all the Welsh points. He kicked two penalty goals to put his side 6-0 ahead and added a corner try. Tour manager Glyn Morgan summed up, "We suffered because of our ineptitude. Our side did not prove to be good enough. We are not accustomed to the Argentine type of rugby. They played with a reckless abandon which we found disconcerting. They were physically very strong and hard."

First Unofficial Test   September 14, 1968

Argentina won by two penalty goals, one try (9) to one goal (5)

Wales: JPR Williams (Bridgend); L Daniel (Pontypool), G Ball (Neath), S J Dawes (London Welsh, capt.), A K Morgan (London Welsh); P Bennett (Llanelli), G Turner (Ebbw Vale); D J Lloyd (Bridgend), B I Rees (London Welsh), B Butler (Llanelli), L Baxter (Cardiff), W T Mainwaring (Aberavon), W D Morris (Neath), D Hughes (Newbridge), A J Gray (London Welsh).

For Argentina, Adrian Anthony scored a try. Jorge Seaton kicked two penalty goals.

For Wales, Glyn Turner scored a try. John Dawes converted.

Second Unofficial Test   September 28, 1968

Drawn. Argentina two penalty goals, one try (9). Wales two penalty goals, one try (9)

Wales: JPR Williams; L Daniel, G Ball, S J Dawes (capt), S Ferguson (Swansea); R H Phillips (Newport), G Turner; W Williams (Neath), N R Gale (Llanelli), D J Lloyd, W T Mainwaring, M Wiltshire (Aberavon), W D Morris, D Hughes, A J Gray.

For Argentina, push-over try. Jorge Seaton kicked two penalty goals.

For Wales, Stuart Ferguson scored a try and kicked two penalty goals.

Match 277 **SCOTLAND v WALES**   Murrayfield. February 1, 1969

Wales won by one goal, two penalty goals, two tries (17) to one penalty goal (3)

"We planned to make our own tries, but it turned out that we scored mostly from Scottish mistakes," admitted new skipper Brian Price after the biggest Welsh victory at Murrayfield since 1947. Wales, with Clive Rowlands as their national coach in succession to David Nash, collected together an elite squad that practised at a few weekends at Afan Lido Sports Centre. Two young newcomers from this squad, full back JPR Williams and 'unknown' No. 8 Mervyn Davies, made impressive first appearances for Wales in this first leg towards the Triple Crown. Keith Jarrett kicked two penalty goals in the first half. Then Gareth Edwards dodged away for a try before Maurice Richards pounced for a try following a line-out. Barry John charged a kick, and with a classical dummy, scored a try that Jarrett converted. First match under new restrictive kicking to touch law.

Scotland: C F Blaikie (Heriot's FP); A J W Hinshelwood (London Scottish), J N M Frame (Gala), C W W Rea (West of Scotland), W D Jackson (Hawick); C M Telfer (Hawick), I G McCrae (Gordonians); N Suddon (Hawick), F A L Laidlaw (Melrose), A B Carmichael (West of Scotland), P K Stagg (Sale), A F McHarg (London Scottish), T G Elliot (Langholm), J W Telfer (Melrose, capt.), R J Arneil (Edinburgh Acads.).

Wales: *J P R Williams (London Welsh); S J Watkins, K S Jarrett (Newport), Gerald Davies, M C R Richards (Cardiff); Barry John, G O Edwards (Cardiff); Denzil Williams (Ebbw Vale), Jeff Young, D J Lloyd (Bridgend), Brian Price (Newport, capt.), Brian Thomas, W D Morris (Neath), *Mervyn Davies, J Taylor (London Welsh).

For Wales, Barry John, Gareth Edwards and Maurice Richards scored tries. Keith Jarrett converted one and kicked two penalty goals.

For Scotland, Colin Blaikie kicked a penalty goal.

Referee: K D Kelleher (Ireland).

Match 278 **WALES v IRELAND**   Cardiff Arms Park. March 8, 1969

Wales won by three goals, one dropped goal, one penalty goal, one try(24)
to one goal and two penalty goals (11)

Brian Price swung a right upper-cut at a maul and 29,000 spectators, including the Prince of Wales, saw Noel Murphy, the Irish forward, clutch his face and fall to the ground. For a tense moment it seemed that for the first time a Welsh international player would be sent off and the team's captain at that. But referee Doug McMahon (Scotland) stepped forward coolly, penalised Price and warned of the need for control. Mr. McMahon said: "I've had rougher matches to control. There was a lot at stake in this game and some players got excited." Price explained the reason for his action: "A pair of hands clawed round my head in a maul. They were going for my eyes. I was not standing for that. I did not know who it was. I just turned round and let him have it." In a game of intense physical combat feelings ran high, but there was still a great deal of thrilling attacking play.

The Triple Crown was the prize for Ireland if they won. But their forwards could not secure quality possession. Tom Kiernan's penalty goal put Ireland ahead. Barry John equalised with a dropped goal. Kiernan kicked his second penalty, but Wales took the lead for the first time in unusual fashion. When Ireland were penalised, Jarrett came up as if to take the easy kick. He had not indicated that he would kick at goal and so was not committed to do so. As the Irish players turned to retire, Denzil Williams called to Jarrett for the ball, took the quick pass and raced to score a try that Jarrett converted.

Then Welsh pressure built up and Stuart Watkins, Dave Morris and John Taylor romped away for tries. Jarrett converted two and kicked a penalty goal. The only reply was a Mike Gibson try in a breakaway, which Kiernan goaled. The crowd was limited to 29,000 because the north stand had been demolished during reconstruction work on the ground. It was the 11th time Wales had stopped Ireland on the threshold of the Triple Crown. So the years of disappointment for the Irish have been 1905, 1911, 1926, 1930, 1931, 1936, 1939, 1947, 1951, 1965 and 1969.

Wales: J P R Williams (London Welsh); S J Watkins, K S Jarrett (Newport), Gerald Davies, M C R Richards (Cardiff); Barry John, G O Edwards (Cardiff); Denzil Williams (Ebbw Vale), Jeff Young, D J Lloyd (Bridgend), Brian Price (Newport, capt.), Brian Thomas, W D Morris (Neath), Mervyn Davies, J. Taylor (London Welsh).

Ireland: T J Kiernan (Cork Constitution, capt.); A T A Duggan (Lansdowne), F P K Bresnihan (Univ. Coll., Dublin), C M H Gibson (NIFC), J C M Moroney (London Irish); B J McGann (Lansdowne), R M Young (Queen's Univ., Belfast); P O'Callaghan (Dolphin), K W Kennedy (London Irish), S Millar, W J McBride (Ballymena), M G Molloy (London Irish), J C Davidson (Dungannon), M L Hipwell (Terenure Coll.), N A Murphy (Cork Constitution).

For Wales, Stuart Watkins, Denzil Williams, Dave Morris and John Taylor scored tries. Keith Jarrett converted three and kicked a penalty goal. Barry John dropped a goal.

For Ireland, Mike Gibson scored a try. Tom Kiernan converted and kicked two penalty goals.

Referee: D C J McMahon (Scotland).

Match 279 FRANCE v WALES   Colombes, Paris. March 22, 1969

Drawn. France one goal, one penalty goal (8). Wales one goal and one try (8)

France ended a run of 10 defeats by forcing a draw. It was a deep disappointment for Wales, who had not won in Paris since 1957 and had established an 8-0 lead by half time. Gareth Edwards dodged, twirled and bounced off tacklers in an astonishing solo run to score the first Welsh try. Then Edwards chipped a punt across to the left for wing Maurice Richards to pounce for a try that Keith Jarrett converted.

But other Welsh chances were missed. Wing Stuart Watkins was judged to have put a foot into touch near the corner-flag and his try at the start of the second half was disallowed. Barry

John fired wide with a point-blank drop-shot and Jarrett finally missed a reasonable penalty attempt. Gerald Davies injured his elbow and Phil Bennett came on for the last four minutes. He was the first man to win a Welsh cap as replacement and never touched the ball.

France: P Villepreux (Toulouse); B Moraitis (Toulon), C Dourthe (Dax), J Trillo (Begles), A Campaes (Lourdes); J Maso, G Sutra (Narbonne); J Iracabal (Bayonne), R Benesis (Narbonne), J Azarete (Dax), A Plantefol (Agen), E Cester (Toulouse), J P Biemouret (Agen), W Spanghero (capt.), G Viard (Narbonne).

Wales: J P R Williams (London Welsh); S J Watkins, K S Jarrett (Newport), Gerald Davies, M C R Richards (Cardiff); Barry John, G O Edwards (Cardiff); Denzil Williams (Ebbw Vale), Jeff Young, D J Lloyd (Bridgend), Brian Price (Newport capt), Brian Thomas, W D Morris (Neath), Mervyn Davies (London Welsh). Replacement: *P Bennett (Llanelli) for Gerald Davies

For France, Andre Campaes scored a try. Pierre Villepreux converted and kicked a penalty goal.

For Wales, Gareth Edwards and Maurice Richards scored tries. Keith Jarrett converted one.

Referee: R P Burrell (Scotland).

Match 280 WALES v ENGLAND   Cardiff Arms Park. April 12, 1969

Wales won by three goals, two penalty goals, one dropped goal, two tries (30)
to three penalty goals (9)

Maurice Richards equalled the Welsh scoring record of four tries in a match and helped his team to their 11th Triple Crown title as outright winners of the International Championship for the 15th time. Wales played as their teams did in the Golden Era. The forwards dominated and Gareth Edwards sent out his smooth spin-pass in a ceaseless flow to keep his backs running. Edwards took over the captaincy when Brian Price withdrew through injury. Delme Thomas, who replaced Price, was outstanding in the line-out. The 29,000 crowd saw Bob Hiller kick a penalty goal and Richards score a try to make it 3-3 at half time. Two early penalty goals by Keith Jarrett gave Wales the platform to break out in the second half and Barry John scored a breathtaking try with a zig-zag run. Jarrett converted. Richards scored his second try before Hiller landed another penalty goal. Barry John dropped a left-footed goal and then Jarrett converted two more tries by Richards. Finally, Hiller kicked his third penalty goal. It was great to be going to meet New Zealand as European champions. Everyone felt the brilliant Welsh backs would show the All Blacks a trick or two.

Wales: J P R Williams (London Welsh); S J Watkins, K S Jarrett (Newport), S J Dawes (London Welsh), M C R Richards (Cardiff); Barry John, G O Edwards (Cardiff, capt.); Denzil Williams (Ebbw Vale), Jeff Young, D J Lloyd (Bridgend), Delme Thomas (Llanelli), Brian Thomas, W D Morris (Neath), Mervyn Davies, J Taylor (London Welsh).

England: R B Hiller (Harlequins); K C Plummer (Bristol), J S Spencer (Headingley), D J Duckham, R E Webb (Coventry); J F Finlan (Moseley), T C Wintle (Northampton); K E Fairbrother (Coventry), J V Pullin (Bristol), D L Powell, P J Larter (Northampton), N E Horton (Moseley), R B Taylor (Northampton), D M Rollitt (Bristol), D P Rogers (Bedford, capt.).

For Wales, Maurice Richards (4) and Barry John scored tries. Keith Jarrett converted three and kicked two penalty goals. Barry John dropped a goal.

For England, Bob Hiller kicked three penalty goals.

Referee: D P D'Arcy (Ireland).

New Zealand won by two goals, one penalty goal, two tries (19) to nil

They called it the suicide tour: three tests in seven games the first match four days after an unbroken journey round the world in some 52 hours; and the second match the first test with the All Blacks, who had probably the greatest pack that ever donned rugby jerseys. Had scrum half Gareth Edwards been fit it might have been a help, though not much. Brian Price and his Welsh champions would have needed 20 men to have held Brian Lochore's iron-hard forwards. Welsh coach Clive Rowlands called them the finest pack he had ever seen. So New Zealand took a 4-3 lead in the series between the countries and 55,000 spectators saw the Red Devils crushed.

Welsh hooker Jeff Young had his jaw fractured by a blow from Colin Meads, the giant All Black second row forward, as an act of retaliation for jersey-pulling. Vic Perrins (Newport) was flown out as replacement. Coach Rowlands said: "When we made mistakes we didn't lose six yards, as we did at home – we lost 80!" There were criticisms of referee Pat Murphy for his interpretations of the laws, but the basic reason for the Welsh defeat was the clear superiority of the home forwards. Keith Jarrett missed five kicks at goal.

> **New Zealand:** W F McCormick; threequarters – M J Dick, W L Davis, G S Thorne; 2nd five-eighth – I R MacRae; 1st five-eighth – E W Kirton; half back – S M Going; forwards – K F Gray, B E McLeod, B L Muller, C E Meads, A E Smith, T N Lister, B J Lochore (capt.), I A Kirkpatrick.

> **Wales:** J P R Williams (London Welsh); M C R Richards, Gerald Davies (Cardiff), K S Jarrett, S J Watkins (Newport); Barry John, G O Edwards (Cardiff); Denzil Williams (Ebbw Vale), J Young, D J Lloyd (Bridgend), Brian Price (Newport, capt.), Brian Thomas, W D Morris (Neath), Mervyn Davies, J Taylor (London Welsh). Replacement: N R Gale (Llanelli) for Young.

For New Zealand, Malcolm Dick, Bruce McLeod, Brian Lochore and Ken Gray scored tries. Fergus McCormick converted two and kicked a penalty goal.

Referee: J P Murphy (NZ).

New Zealand won by three goals, five penalty goals, one dropped goal (33) to two penalty goals, two tries (12)

Full back Fergus McCormick set a world record for international rugby with his 24 New Zealand points. The previous record of 22 had been held jointly by Springbok Dietlef Mare, against France at Parc des Princes in 1907, and Douglas (nicknamed Daniel) Lambert, the Harlequins wing, for England against France at Twickenham in 1911. McCormick converted all three New Zealand tries, kicked five penalty goals and dropped a magnificent goal from near the touch line.

Keith Jarrett could not match this goal kicking brilliance, though he helped Wales into a 6-3 lead after 25 minutes with a penalty goal. The crowd of 58,000 saw Maurice Richards score a glorious try with a feint inside turn and then an outside curving run. But the All Blacks were 14-6 ahead at the interval and all Wales could do in the second half was add another Jarrett penalty goal and a try by the same player. So, though they did not lose in their provincial matches in New Zealand, drawing 9-9 with Taranaki and beating Otago 27-9 and Wellington 14-6, the Red Devils were hammered in the tests.

> **New Zealand:** W F McCormick; threequarters – M J Dick, W L Davis, G Skudder; 2nd five-eighth – I R MacRae; 1st five-eighth – E W Kirton; half back – S M Going; forwards – K F Gray, B E McLeod, A E Hopkinson, C E Meads, A E Smith, T N Lister, B J Lochore (capt.), I A Kirkpatrick.

Wales: J P R Williams (London Welsh); M C R Richards (Cardiff), S J Dawes (London Welsh), K S Jarrett (Newport), Gerald Davies (Cardiff); Barry John, G O Edwards (Cardiff); Denzil Williams (Ebbw Vale), N R Gale (Llanelli), Brian Thomas (Neath), Delme Thomas (Llanelli), Brian Price (Newport, capt.), W D Morris (Neath), Mervyn Davies (London Welsh), D Hughes (Newbridge).

For New Zealand, George Skudder, Ian MacRae and Ian Kirkpatrick scored tries. Fergus McCormick converted three, dropped one goal and kicked five penalty goals.

For Wales, Keith Jarrett and Maurice Richards scored tries. Jarrett kicked two penalty goals.

Referee: J P Murphy (NZ).

Match 283   AUSTRALIA v WALES   Sydney Cricket Ground. June 21, 1969

Wales won by two goals, two penalty goals, one try (19) to two goals, two penalty goals (16)

Gerald Davies, who had made a success of his switch from centre to wing in the second test against New Zealand, continued in his new role and turned the game for his side. Australia were leading 11-0 after 23 minutes. Keith Jarrett began the Welsh scoring with a penalty goal and Gareth Edwards made a try for flank forward Dave Morris. Then Gerald Davies raced away for a classical try which Jarrett converted to level the scores at 11-11. A 50-yard Jarrett penalty goal swung his team into the lead for the first time and Gerald Davies, with another dazzling sprint, set up a try for John Taylor. Again Jarrett converted. Those two dashes by Davies gave Wales a position from which they could hold off the Wallabies final rally.

Yet the home side had a chance to save the match five minutes from the end in most unusual fashion. They scored a try that could have been worth eight points. It happened this way: Arthur McGill, the Wallaby full back, dived for the corner and was awarded a try. Welsh players protested that McGill had been tackled short of the line and wriggled over; so his try should not have been allowed. Referee Craig Ferguson penalised Wales for disputing his decision. This meant that after McGill had converted his try with a fine kick, Australia had a penalty on the centre spot when play restarted. Alan Skinner attempted to kick a goal, but the range was too great out of the churned up mud.

Australia: A N McGill; T R Forman, P V Smith, G Shaw, J W Cole; J P Ballesty, J N B Hipwell; R B Prosser, P Darvenzia, J Roxburgh, P N P Reilly, A Abrahams, H A Rose, A J Skinner, G V Davis (capt.).

Wales: J P R Williams (London Welsh); M C R Richards (Cardiff), S J Dawes (London Welsh), K S Jarrett (Newport), Gerald Davies (Cardiff); Barry John, G O Edwards (Cardiff); Denzil Williams (Ebbw Vale), N R Gale (Llanelli), D J Lloyd (Bridgend), Brian Price (Newport, capt.), Delme Thomas (Llanelli), W D Morris (Neath), Mervyn Davies, J Taylor (London Welsh).

For Wales, Dave Morris, Gerald Davies and John Taylor scored tries. Keith Jarrett converted two and kicked two penalty goals.

For Australia, Arthur McGill and Phil Smith scored tries. McGill converted both and kicked two penalty goals.

Referee: C F Ferguson (Australia).

Uncapped Match   FIJI v WALES   Buckhurst Park, Suva. June 25, 1969

Wales won by five goals, one dropped, one try (31) to one goal, one penalty goal, one try (11)

With Maurice Richards showing why he was one of the most exciting wings in world rugby by scoring one try and making two others, Wales piled up 18 points in the last 20 minutes to overcome Fiji. The home forwards, after a crash course of special tuition from All Blacks' coach Freddy Allen, gave the Welsh pack a keen tussle, but their defence eventually crumbled against the touring team's brilliant backs. Some spectators almost fell out of their palm tree perches as they waved and cheered when Wales cut loose with their irresistible scoring spree. This game repayed the visit Fiji had made to Wales in 1964, when the Red Devils won a memorable match 28-22. The admirable Dennis Hughes snapped up three tries.

Fiji: S Naqelevuki; A Batisbasaga, L Raitilava, A Gutugutuwai, S Nacolai; J Raikuna, S Sikivou; J Qoro, I Volavola, A Turagacoka, N Ravouvou, T Tuisese, P Nasalo, Sela Toga, Epi Bolawaqatabu (capt.).

Wales: J P R Williams (London Welsh); M C R Richards (Cardiff), S J Dawes (London Welsh), K S Jarrett (Newport), Gerald Davies (Cardiff); P Bennett (Llanelli), G O Edwards (Cardiff, capt.); Denzil Williams (Ebbw Vale), V Perrins, D B Llewelyn (Newport), Delme Thomas (Llanelli), Mervyn Davies, J Taylor (London Welsh), D Hughes (Newbridge), W D Morris (Neath).

For Wales, Dennis Hughes (3), John Taylor (2) and Maurice Richards scored tries. Keith Jarrett converted five. JPR Williams dropped a goal.

For Fiji, Turagacoka and Sikivou scored tries. Raitilava converted one and kicked a penalty goal.

Referee: P Sinnott (Suva).

Match 284 WALES v SOUTH AFRICA Cardiff Arms Park. January 24, 1970

Drawn. Wales one penalty goal, one try (6). South Africa one penalty goal, one try (6)

Barbed wire strung above the railings around the Arms Park pitch. Police patrols along the touchlines and outside the ground, with mounted police as reinforcements. This was the atmosphere for the seventh meeting between Wales and South Africa. It was 'Demo' time in Britain, with the Springboks' rugby team as the target of the anti-apartheid demonstrators. But after the ugly scenes at Swansea earlier in the tour, this was a peaceful and uninterrupted match, watched by 42,000 spectators. The police security precautions were unique for a Welsh international match and so was the result of the game.

Never before, in six encounters with South Africa, had Wales avoided defeat. The Red Devils looked doomed to failure again as the Springboks outplayed them tactically, undaunted by the appalling conditions of mud and rain. But Gareth Edwards, a mud-daubed monster in Springbok eyes, darted for the corner in the last minute, dived and slithered over for the try that made the final score 6-6. He could not convert his try and Edwards said: "Wales were not lucky to draw, but rather were South Africa unfortunate not to win."

In a desperately hard battle, 'no prisoners were taken', and the physically superior tourists, who had lost to Scotland and England and drawn with Ireland, went all out in their last chance to win a test on tour. They led with a penalty goal by Henry de Villiers after 20 minutes when Barry John infringed the 10-yard off-side zone at a line-out. Gareth Edwards landed an equalising penalty with a wide-angled kick to make it 3-3 at halftime, but wing Syd Nomis completed the overlap at a blind side attack with a corner try eight minutes into the second half.

It looked good enough to be the winning score. Time wore on. The final whistle must sound at any moment. Then wing Phil Bennett threw a long pass infield from the touch line. Barry John, who had kicked often with careless lack of accuracy, this time punted perfectly across field. Ian Hall rushed in to worry Nomis and from the quick mini-ruck, Barry Llewelyn fed the ball back swiftly to Gareth Edwards. The scrum half gritted his teeth and went for the north stand corner at the Westgate Street end. It was a hair-raising dash, but he dived and slithered over to score and stop the Springboks making it a magnificent seven wins in a row over their Welsh rivals.

It was a unique experience for the Springboks not to win a single international match on a full tour of Britain. Scotland beat them 6-3; England triumphed 11-8 and then it was 8-8 against Ireland. In Wales, too, the South Africans were toppled. Newport beat them 11-6 and Gwent were 14-8 winners at Ebbw Vale with a great display of goal kicking by 19-year-old Robin Williams. He scored three penalty goals and converted a try.

> **Wales:** J P R Williams (London Welsh); P Bennett (Llanelli), S J Dawes (London Welsh), W H Raybould (Newport), I Hall (Aberavon); Barry John, G O Edwards (Cardiff capt.); Denzil Williams (Ebbw Vale), *V Perrins, *D B Llewelyn (Newport), Delme Thomas (Llanelli), *T G Evans (London Welsh), W D Morris (Neath), Mervyn Davies (London Welsh), D Hughes (Newbridge).

> **South Africa:** H O de Villiers; S H Nomis, O A Roux, J P van der Merwe, G Muller; M J. Lawless, D J de Villiers (capt.); J L Myburgh, C H Cockrell, J F K Marais, F C H du Preez, I J de Klerk, P J F Greyling, T P Bedford, J H Ellis.

For Wales, Gareth Edwards scored a try and kicked a penalty goal.

For South Africa, Syd Nomis scored a try. Henry de Villiers kicked a penalty goal.

Referee: G C Lamb (England).

Match 285 **WALES v SCOTLAND**   Cardiff Arms Park. February 7, 1970

Wales won by three goals, one try (18) to one dropped goal, one penalty goal, one try (9)

"If we had changed round 9-0 up instead of only 9-5, we would have won," reflected Scottish skipper Jim Telfer. Gareth Edwards, the Welsh captain, commented: "It was killing playing into the wind in the first half. It was then that our forwards really played their hearts out in a gruelling test of their stamina. The singing of the crowd was tremendous it inspired every one of us." Telfer also had a rueful comment on that singing: "Those 40,000 or so Welsh voices mean a wee bit of help for Wales whenever they play on the Arms Park."

So, though fly half Barry John over-kicked, and Gareth Edwards tried to do too much himself, with a consequent lack of rhythm in midfield attack, Wales launched a formidable offensive through their forwards once they had the gale-force wind behind them. Denzil Williams led his pack with model determination and Dave Morris was the outstanding home forward. Those Welsh choral tactics also helped in considerable measure to turn the game.

> **Wales:** J P R Williams (London Welsh); *L Daniel (Newport) S J Dawes (London Welsh), P Bennett (Llanelli), I Hall (Aberavon); Barry John, G O Edwards (Cardiff, capt.); D B Llewelyn, V Perrins (Newport), Denzil Williams (Ebbw Vale), Delme Thomas (Llanelli), T G Evans (London Welsh), W D Morris (Neath), Mervyn Davies (London Welsh), D Hughes (Newbridge).

> **Scotland:** I S G Smith (London Scottish); M A Smith (London Scottish), J N M Frame (Gala), C W W Rea (West of Scotland), A J W Hinshelwood (London Scottish); I Robertson, R G Young (Watsonians); J McLauchlan (Jordanhill Coll., FP), F A L Laidlaw (Melrose), A B Carmichael (West of Scotland), P K Stagg (Sale}, P C Brown (Gala), W Lauder (Neath), J W Telfer (Melrose, capt.), R J Arneil (Leicester). Replacement: G Brown (West of Scotland) for P C Brown.

For Wales, Laurie Daniel, Barry Llewelyn, John Dawes and Dave Morris scored tries. Gareth Edwards converted two. Daniel converted one.

For Scotland, Ian Robertson scored a try and dropped a goal. Wilson Lauder kicked a penalty goal.

Referee: D P D'Arcy (Ireland).

Wales won by one goal, one dropped goal, three tries (17) to two goals, one penalty goal (13)

He played only the last 20 minutes, coming on as replacement, but he won the match for Wales when it seemed they must lose. His name: Ray Hopkins, known as 'Chicko' to his Maesteg team-mates. It was a dream debut for the chunky scrum half, who bobbed on to the field as replacement after Welsh skipper Gareth Edwards had limped off. Wales were 6-13 down at the time; but this fantastic match was far from finished. Just before the interval, French referee Robert Calmet retired after being hurt in a collision with players. It was found that he had broken a bone in his left leg and dislocated his left shoulder. R F Johnson, the England touch judge and himself an international referee, took over. It was a repeat of the 1965 Welsh match in Paris, when R W Gilliland was injured and could not continue. Hopkins put Wales back in the game when he darted to the blind side of a 10-yard scrum and sent full back J P R Williams crashing through for a try. It was the third time a Welsh full back had scored a try, following Viv Jenkins against Ireland at Swansea in 1934 and Keith Jarrett against England at Cardiff in 1967. In later years, full back tries would become commonplace.

With the score 9-13 to England, Wales needed a converted try to snatch victory. Hopkins made it possible as the Welsh forwards hurled England back. The substitute scrum half pounced on a loose ball at the back of a line-out and it was a try – the first time Wales had ever managed four tries at Twickenham. Everything depended on the conversion kick; and JPR Williams, who had played brilliantly, made no mistake. To seal the success, Barry John dropped a lovely goal for one of Wales's most thrilling victories. Once again, only Ireland stood between Wales and the Triple Crown.

England: R B Hiller (Harlequins, capt.); M J Novak (Harlequins), J S Spencer (Headingley), D J Duckham (Coventry), P M Hale (Moseley); I R Shackleton (Harrogate), N C Starmer-Smith (Harlequins); C B Stevens (Penzance-Newlyn), J V Pullin (Bristol), K E Fairbrother (Coventry), A M Davis (Harlequins), P J Larter, R B Taylor, B R West (Northampton), A L Bucknall (Richmond).

Wales: J P R Williams (London Welsh); S J Watkins (Cardiff), W H Raybould (Newport), S J Dawes (London Welsh), I Hall (Aberavon); Barry John, G O Edwards (Cardiff, capt.); Denzil Williams (Ebbw Vale), J Young (Harrogate), D B Llewelyn (Newport), Delme Thomas (Llanelli), T G Evans (London Welsh), W D Morris (Neath), Mervyn Davies (London Welsh), D Hughes (Newbridge). Replacement: *R Hopkins (Maesteg) for Edwards.

For Wales, Mervyn Davies, Barry John, JPR Williams and Ray Hopkins scored tries. JPR Williams converted one. Barry John dropped a goal.

For England, David Duckham and John Novak scored tries. Bob Hiller converted both and kicked a penalty goal.

Referee: R Calmet (France) replaced by R F Johnson (England).

Ireland won by one goal, one dropped goal, one penalty goal, one try ,(14) to nil

Not since the Murrayfield 'massacre' match of 1951, when Wales lost 19-0, had the Red Devils crashed to such a sensational defeat in the championship. Tom Kiernan, the Irish captain, making his record breaking 47th appearance as the most capped Irishman (including 10 games against Wales) was chaired off the field. He said: "We took our opportunities when Wales made mistakes. When we stretched our lead on them they began to fall to pieces and went from bad to worse." Tactically Wales were at fault in not applying more pressure through their forwards. The turning point came with the first score, a brilliant, high dropped goal by fly half Barry McGann after 16 minutes of the second half. It was the fifth time Ireland had baulked Wales at the final Triple Crown hurdle. This had happened in 1906, 1932, 1956, 1966 and now 1970. Barry John and Gareth Edwards set a record of 16 appearances together at half back, beating the 15 times that Dick Jones and Dicky Owen, Swansea's famous 'Dancing Dicks', played for Wales between 1901 and 1910.

Ireland: T J Kiernan (Cork Constitution, capt.); A T A Duggan (Lansdowne), F P K. Bresnihan (London Irish), C M H Gibson (NIFC), W J Brown (Malone); B J McGann (Cork Constitution), R M Young (Belfast Collegians); P O'Callaghan (Dolphin), K W Kennedy (London Irish), S Millar, W J McBride (Ballymena), M G Molloy (London Irish), R A Lamont (Instonians), K G Goodall (City of Derry), J F Slattery (Univ. Coll., Dublin).

Wales: J P R Williams (London Welsh); S J Watkins (Cardiff), S J Dawes (London Welsh), W H Raybould (Newport), *K Hughes (Cambridge Univ. and New Dock Stars); Barry John, G O Edwards (Cardiff, capt.); Denzil Williams (Ebbw Vale), J Young (Harrogate), D B Llewelyn (Newport), Delme Thomas (Llanelli), T G Evans (London Welsh), W D Morris (Neath), Mervyn Davies (London Welsh), D Hughes (Newbridge).

For Ireland, Alan Duggan and Ken Goodall scored tries. Tom Kiernan converted one and kicked a penalty goal. Barry McGann dropped a goal.

Referee: G C Lamb (England).

Match 288 WALES v FRANCE   Cardiff Arms Park. April 4, 1970

Wales won by one goal, two penalty goals (11) to two tries (6)

Wales earned a share of the championship with France by this first success over the Tricolours for four years. John Dawes took over the captaincy from Gareth Edwards, while Phil Bennett replaced Barry John when the outside half withdrew. Dawes changed tactics in order to play primarily to the strength of his pack, and Stuart Gallacher was a rousing new cap as second row partner to his Llanelli club-mate Delme Thomas, who dominated the line-out. France scored two tries to one by Wales and defeat was a keen disappointment to the record number of 6,000 French supporters among the capacity crowd of 51,000.

Wales: J P R Williams (London Welsh); *J L Shanklin (London Welsh), S J Dawes (London Welsh, capt.), *Arthur Lewis (Ebbw Vale), *Roy Mathias (Llanelli); P Bennett (Llanelli), G O Edwards (Cardlff); D J Lloyd (Bridgend}, J Young (Harrogate), D. B. Llewelyn (Newport), Delme Thomas, *Stuart Gallacher (Llanelli), W D Morris (Neath), Mervyn Davies (London Welsh), J Taylor (London Welsh). Replacement: W H Raybould (Newport) for Shanklin.

France: P Villepreux (Toulouse); J Cantoni (Beziers), A Marot (Brire), J P Lux (Tyrosse), J M Bonal (Toulouse); L Paries (Biarrittz), M Puget (Brive); J Iracabal (Bayonne), R Benesis (Narbonne), J L Azarete (Dax), J P Bastiat (Dax), E Cester (Toulouse Olympic), J P Biemouret (Agen), B Dauga (Mont de Marson), C Carrere (Toulon, capt.).

For Wales, Dave Morris scored a try. J P R Williams converted and kicked two penalty goals.

For France, Jack Cantoni and Jean-Marie Bonal scored tries.

Referee: K D Kelleher (Ireland).

Wales won by two goals, two dropped goals, one penalty goal, one try (22)
to one penalty goal, one try (6)

For the first time since 1912, Wales took the lead in the series against England with 33 victories to 32 with 11 drawn. Brilliant Barry John dropped two goals, which meant he had dropped five goals in four matches against them. In four successive games at Cardiff, Wales had totalled 100 points against England, who had not beaten the Red Devils since 1963. England, celebrating their centenary year, included seven new caps and were crushed by power scrummaging. The home props and second row each weighed more than 16 st. J P R Williams suffered a depressed fracture of his right cheekbone in the first five minutes in collision with Gareth Edwards, but played on. Wales led 16-3 at the interval and then relaxed their pressure. The crowd, emotionally involved in events, sang the Welsh anthem as Peter Rossborough ran in to take a penalty kick at the Welsh goal and he hit the post.

John Bevan, a 20-year-old Rhondda boy studying at Cardiff College of Education, scored a try on his debut and was to score many other thrilling tries as a star in the British Lions' team in New Zealand in the summer of 1971.

> **Wales:** J P R Williams (London Welsh); Gerald Davies. S J Dawes (London Welsh, capt), Arthur Lewis (Ebbw Vale), *J C Bevan (Cardiff); Barry John, G O Edwards (Cardiff); Denzil Williams (Ebbw Vale), J Young (Harrogate), D B Llewelyn, Delme Thomas (Llanelli), *M G Roberts, J Taylor, Mervyn Davies (London Welsh), W D Morris (Neath).

> **England:** P A Rossborough (Coventry); J P Janion (Bedford), C S Wardlow (Northampton), J S Spencer (Headingley), D J Duckham (Coventry); I D Wright (Northampton), J J Page (Bedford); D L Powell (Northampton), J V Pullin (Bristol), K E Fairbrother, B F Ninnes (Coventry), P J Larter (Northampton), A L Bucknall (Richmond, capt.), R C Hannaford (Bristol), A Neary (Broughton Park).

For Wales, Gerald Davies (2) and John Bevan scored tries. John Taylor converted two. Barry John dropped two goals. JPR Williams kicked a penalty goal.

For England, Peter Rossborough kicked a penalty goal. Charlie Hannaford scored a try.

Referee: D P D'Arcy (Ireland).

Wales won by two goals, one penalty goal, two tries (19) to four penalty goals, two tries (18)

John Taylor's left-footed round-the-corner conversion kick, that carried so many hopes and just as many fears, winged its way between Scotland's posts from a daunting angle and Wales snatched an astonishing one-point victory two minutes from the end. Six times the lead changed hands – Scotland 3-0; Wales 8-6; Scotland 12-11; Wales 14-12; Scotland 15-14; Wales 19-18. "We played badly at time," said Welsh skipper John Dawes, who saw his pack unexpectedly pinned down. Arthur Lewis had to withdraw because he pulled a hamstring muscle running to work on the Tuesday, and Ian Hall replaced him in the centre. This was the only change in the team throughout the season.

Peter Brown's penalty goal for Scotland was cancelled out by a Barry John penalty. Brown planted penalty No. 2 between the posts, but full back J P R Williams launched Wales's first try scoring move with a rousing dash, swerve and dummy to send flanker John Taylor storming through with a hand-off to score. Barry John converted and Wales led 8-6 at half time. Then Gareth Edwards stole away for his customary try against the Scots and everyone thought the anticipated Welsh win was taking shape. Or was it? The watchful Carmichael pounced for a try when the ball bounced awkwardly from a line-out, and then skipper Brown's third penalty swung the game to Scotland 12-11.

Wing John Bevan ran strongly to pave the way for a dodging try by Barry John, who then hit the post with the conversion after he had recovered from a tackle. Should he have been allowed to take the kick? He said he wanted to, and skipper Dawes let him have his way. After all, it was his side of the field for the goal shot! Still, Wales had their noses in front 14-12 until Brown's fourth penalty put Scotland up 15-14. Worse followed as Chris Rea scored a try. The conversion would see Scotland 20-14 ahead, with only five minutes left, but Brown hit the post. Wales had had their lucky break, and yet another was to follow.

Delme Thomas, the Welsh line-out expert, moved towards the front at a throw-in, hoping to make the Scots throw deep to avoid him and perhaps give the tall Mervyn Davies a chance to win possession. Skipper Brown shouted for a long throw, but he went unheard, and the ball was lobbed in short for Delme Thomas to jump and palm down and Wales were away on a last desperate attack.

Full back Williams joined the threequarter line yet again in the style that has made him the most exciting man in his position in world rugby. He slipped a pass to Gerald Davies and the right wing was away on the overlap for a try. The corner-flaggers prevented him from getting near the posts, and everything depended on the conversion kick. The Welsh goal kicking plan involved three men; Barry John took all kicks to the left of the posts, round-the-corner right-footed; John Taylor was deputed for kicks to the right of the posts, swinging the ball in left-footed in similar fashion; J P R Williams generally took the straight kicks with an orthodox run up. So it was Taylor's task this time and he made it look easy while everyone watching died a thousand deaths as they waited.

Scotland: I S G Smith (London Scottish); W C C Steele (Bedford), J N M Frame (Gala), C W W Rea (Headingley), A ,G Biggar (London Scottish); J W C Turner, D S Paterson (Gala); J McLauchlan (Jordanhill Coll.), F A L Laidlaw (Melrose), A B Carmichael, G L Brown (West of Scotland), A F McHarg (London Scottish), R J Arneil (Leicester), P C Brown (capt.), N A MacEwan (Gala).

Wales: J P R Williams (London Welsh); Gerald Davies, S J Dawes (London Welsh, capt.), I Hall (Aberavon), J C Bevan (Cardiff); Barry John, G O Edwards (Cardiff); Denzil Williams (Ebbw Vale), J Young (Harrogate), D B Llewelyn, Delme Thomas (Llanelli), M G Roberts, J Taylor, Mervyn Davies (London Welsh), W D Morris (Neath).

For Wales, John Taylor, Gareth Edwards, Barry John and Gerald Davies scored tries. Barry John converted one and kicked a penalty goal. John Taylor converted one.

For Scotland, 'Sandy' Carmichael and Chris Rea scored tries. Peter Brown kicked four penalty goals.

Referee: M H Titcomb (England).

Match 291 WALES v IRELAND   Cardiff Arms Park. March 13, 1971

Wales won by one goal, two penalty goals, one dropped goal, three tries (23)
to three penalty goals (9)

"We are the champions," chanted the capacity 52,000 crowd and they carried Barry John, Gareth Edwards and other members of the team shoulder high from the field after Wales had won the Triple Crown for the 12th time. There were amazing scenes in the second half as delighted fans stormed on to the field after each home score to congratulate the players. Mike Gibson's two penalty shots gave Ireland a 6-0 lead. Gerald Davies swerved to the corner for a try and Barry John dropped a goal and landed a 40-yard penalty to put Wales in front 9-6 at the interval. Then Gareth Edwards pounced for a try and set up Gerald Davies's second try. Gibson found the mark with his third penalty, but Barry John replied with a 50-yard penalty goal and converted Edwards's second try. Pack leader Denzil Williams passed Bryn Meredith's record of 34 to become the most-capped Welsh forward.

Before the final match of the season against France, the British Lions' team to tour Australia and New Zealand was announced. Eleven of this Welsh team were chosen, including the entire back division. The only unlucky men were prop Denzil Williams and flanker Dave Morris. Hooker Jeff Young and prop Barry Llewelyn had said they were unavailable for consideration.

Wales: J P R Williams (London WeIsh); Gerald Davies, S J Dawes (London Welsh, capt.), Arthur Lewis (Ebbw Vale), J C Bevan (Cardiff); Barry John, G O Edwards (Cardiff); Denzil Williams (Ebbw Vale), J Young (Harrogate), D B Llewelyn, Delme Thomas (Llanelli), M G Roberts, J Taylor, Mervyn Davies (London Welsh), W D Morris (Neath)

Ireland: B J O'Driscoll (Manchester); A T A Duggan (Lansdowne), F P K Bresnihan (London Irish), C M H Gibson (NIFC, capt.), E L Grant (CIYMS); B J McGann (Cork Constitution), R M Young (Belfast Collegians); R J McLoughlin (Blackrock Coll), K W Kennedy (London Irish), J F Lynch (St. Mary's Coll.), W J McBride (Ballymena), M G Molloy (London Irish), M L Hipwell (Terenure Coll.), D J Hickie (St. Mary's Coll), J F Slattery (UC., Dublin).

For Wales, Gerald Davies (2) and Gareth Edwards (2) scored tries. Barry John converted one, dropped one goal and kicked two penalty goals.

For Ireland, Mike Gibson kicked three penalty goals.

Referee: R F Johnson (England).

Match 292 FRANCE v WALES   Colombes, Paris. March 27, 1971

Wales won by one penalty goal, two tries (9) to one goal (5)

Wales's first victory in Paris for 14 years to complete their first Grand Slam triumph since 1952 featured a breathtaking interception by full back J P R Williams. He took Roger Bourgarel's pass in the Welsh 25 and raced more than 70 yards before swerving infield to put Gareth Edwards clear for a try. This meant Wales were only 3-5 down at half time. Early in the second half, Barry John popped over a simple penalty goal and later weaved through for a try that enabled him to equal Keith Jarrett's record of 31 points in the four matches of 1968-69. John played superbly in a great display of Welsh tackling. He injured his nose tackling the powerful Benoit Dauga after 30 minutes, but returned after treatment and, considering he was still feeling the effects of concussion from the Scottish match, this was a magnificent effort by the Welsh fly half. "Our tackling saved us," confessed skipper John Dawes. A record crowd of nearly 60,000 saw France lose their only game of the season. Only 16 players called on in 1971.

France: P Villepreux (Toulouse); R Bourgarel (Toulouse), J P Lux (Tyrosse), R Bertranne (Bagneres), J Cantoni (Beziers); J L Berot (Toulouse), M Barrau (Beaumont); J L Iracabal (Bayonne), R Benesis (Narbonne), M Lasserre (Agen), C Spanghero, W Spanghero (Narbonne), P Biemouret (Agen), B Dauga (Mont de Marsan), C Carrere (Toulon, capt.).

Wales: J P R Williams (London Welsh); Gerald Davies, S J Dawes (London Welsh, capt.), Arthur Lewis (Ebbw Vale), J C Bevan (Cardiff); Barry John, G O Edwards (Cardiff); Denzil Williams (Ebbw Vale), J Young (Harrogate), D B Llewelyn, Delme Thomas (Llanelli), M G Roberts, J Taylor, Mervyn Davies (London Welsh), W D Morris (Neath).

For Wales, Gareth Edwards and Barry John scored tries. Barry John kicked a penalty goal.

For France, Benoit Dauga scored a try. Pierre Villepreux converted.

Referee: J Young (Scotland).

Match 293 **ENGLAND v WALES** Twickenham. January 15, 1972

Wales won by one goal, two penalty goals (12) to one penalty goal (3)
(NB A try was worth four points)

After the spectacular Grand Slam of the previous season, this was mainly a colourless struggle with the Welsh pack unable to assert ascendancy until the closing 20 minutes. But coach Clive Rowlands, with a glance into his crystal ball, saw it as the launch to another successful campaign. It was the first occasion since 1911 that Wales had registered six consecutive victories and the biggest margin of success in 26 visits to 'HQ'. The RFU had to return more than £60,000 to unlucky ticket-seekers and the 71,500 crowd included some 16,000 Welsh fans. The game was notable for another Twickenham try by JPR Williams, the full back taking a pass direct from Gareth Edwards on the narrow side of a scrum and bursting over. JPR was the first Wales full back to score two tries in a match. David Duckham saved two tries with his tackling and covering and England, with six new caps, curbed their opponents most effectively. However, Barry John, though sealed off as a runner, kicked three goals in as many attempts and new Welsh skipper John Lloyd showed he would prove an outstanding successor to John Dawes. Dawes had retired from international rugby following his team's Grand Slam triumph and his shrewd leadership of the 1971 Lions to win the Test series in New Zealand.

England: R Hiller (Harlequins, capt.); J P Janion (Bedford), M C Beese (Liverpool), D J Duckham (Coventry), K J Fielding (Moseley); A G B Old (Middlesbrough), J G Webster (Moseley); C B Stevens (Harlequins), J V Pullin (Bristol), M A Burton, A Brinn (Gloucester), C W Ralston (Richmond), P J Dixon (Harlequins), A G Ripley (Rosslyn Park), A Neary (Broughton Park).

Wales: J P R Williams (London Welsh); Gerald Davies (London Welsh), *R Bergiers (Llanelli), Arthur Lewis (Ebbw Vale), J C Bevan (Cardiff); Barry John, G O Edwards (Cardiff); D J Lloyd (Bridgend, capt.), J Young (RAF), D B Llewelyn, Delme Thomas (Llanelli), T G Evans, J Taylor, Mervyn Davies (London Welsh), W D Morris (Neath).

For Wales, J P R Williams scored a try. Barry John converted and kicked two penalty goals.

For England, Bob Hiller kicked a penalty goal.

Referee: J Young (Scotland).

Match 294 **WALES v SCOTLAND** Cardiff Arms Park. February 5, 1972

Wales won by three goals, three penalty goals, two tries (35) to one goal, two penalty goals (12)

Gareth Edwards picked himself out of the red mud in the south corner at Westgate Street and the Arms Park vibrated like 50,000 hysterical harpstrings. What a muddy marvellous try! If there are gods and heroes up there in the Halls of Valhalla, this was the moment when they must have felt humility. Edwards, in his 53 successive games for Wales, scored 20 tries, but this is generally acknowledged as his greatest: the supreme score. He had already crossed the Scottish line in this match with a typical example of his astonishing strength. Yet his second try was pure inspired opportunism. Edwards probed around the short side of a scrum inside his 25, close to touch. He half hesitated; then in a twinkling, accelerated past Rodger Arneil as the flanker made a one-handed lunge. Edwards exploded away down the touch-line and when Arthur Brown barred the way, punted over the full back's head and hurtled in pursuit. Surely it was too much to expect the impossible? Even of Gareth Edwards? But there he was, catapulting on to the ball in the in-goal zone; slithering face first in the mud while the crowd went wild. The epic dash had covered nearly 90 glorious yards.

"That second try by Gareth was the turning point," affirmed John Lloyd, the home captain. Wales were only 16-12 in front at the time, but Edwards's genius convinced Scotland that Max Boyce's "divine intervention" was in irrefutable evidence. The Scots had led twice; and even scored a try while reduced to 14 men following a leg injury to Alastair Biggar early in the second half. Referee Alf Jamieson waved replacement wing Lewis Dick back off the field until it had been reported to him that Biggar had been medically judged unfit to continue. Wales also needed a replacement when JPR Williams was accidentally kicked in the mouth by Willie Steele as the wing tried to jump over the full back. JPR was carried off with a depressed fracture of the upper jaw and listened to the closing stages of the match on a radio at Cardiff Royal Infirmary while awaiting an operation to straighten his teeth. This was Wales's highest score against Scotland and the Welsh team's biggest victory for 41 years – since the 35-3 win over France at Swansea.

> **Wales:** JPR Williams (London Welsh); Gerald Davies (London Welsh), R Bergiers (Llanelli), Arthur Lewis (Ebbw Vale), J C Bevan (Cardiff); Barry John, G O Edwards (Cardiff); D J Lloyd (Bridgend, capt), J Young (RAF), D B Llewelyn, Delme Thomas (Llanelli), T G Evans, J Taylor, Mervyn Davies (London Welsh), W D Morris (Neath). Rep: P Bennett (Llanelli) for J P R Williams.

> **Scotland:** A R Brown (Gala); W C C Steele (Bedford), J N M Frame (Gala), J M Renwick (Hawick), A G Biggar (London Scottish); C M Telfer (Hawick), D S Paterson (Gala); A B Carmichael (West of Scotland), R L Clark (Edinburgh Wands.), J McLauchlan (Jordanhill Coll.), I A Barnes (Hawick), G L Brown (West of Scotland), N A MacEwan (Gala), P C Brown (Gala, capt), R J Arneil (Northampton). Rep: L G Dick (Loughborough Colleges) for Biggar.

For Wales, Gareth Edwards (2), Gerald Davies, Roy Bergiers and John Taylor scored tries. Barry John converted three and kicked three penalty goals.

For Scotland, Bob Clark scored a try. Peter Brown converted and kicked a penalty goal. Jim Renwick kicked a penalty goal.

Referee: G A Jamieson (Ireland).

IRA v WALES   Lansdowne Road. March 11, 1972

The IRA bombers won this "match", depriving Wales of a chance to win the Triple Crown and denying Ireland lucrative gate receipts. Wales, like Scotland before them, declined to visit Dublin following the Aldershot terrorist bomb attack. Ireland refused to switch to a neutral venue and their officials visited Cardiff to make a special plea that the match go on. Though Scotland turned down the Irish approach on the grounds of insufficient guarantee of security, Ireland still felt they could persuade Wales that risks were minimal. However, some Welsh players had made it known they were unavailable for Dublin and others were expected to follow as a result of pressure from their families. Threats in letters from Dublin to the WRU and leading Welsh clubs hardened the WRU attitude, though an IRA spokesman alleged that the warnings were forgeries, probably sent by the Ulster Volunteer Force – a Protestant organisation. The IRA stated, "The Welsh rugby team, or any other rugby team, are of no importance to us at all." The letters advised teams and supporters not to visit Dublin and pointed out, "Some of my former associates are anxious to take reprisal action against you because of the behaviour of the Paratroops, the Gloucesters and the Queen's Own Scottish Borderers." The signature purported to be that of Roy H W Johnston, described as former secretary of the official IRA. Mr Johnston, a former national executive member of Sinn Fein, denied all connection with the letters and said he was never secretary of the IRA. He suggested that this was the work of an agent provocateur and pleaded that the game go ahead. Unfortunately, the terrorist bombers certainly were real . . . .

Match 295   WALES v FRANCE   Cardiff Arms Park. March 25, 1972

Wales won by four penalty goals, two tries (20) to two penalty goals (6)

Derek Quinnell charging down the players' tunnel and pushing policemen aside to thunder on to the field and win his first cap as replacement for injured Mervyn Davies. That was the abiding memory of this fixture. No wonder dashing Derek was in such an almighty hurry – there was only two minutes of injury time left for play. Time enough, nevertheless, for him to produce a storming burst and a rousing tackle. Pierre Villepreux, the French captain, kicked two amazing penalty goals from inside his half of the field; the first from four yards beyond the halfway mark; the second from one yard over the line. And he missed a third shot from six yards inside his territory. Wales had the match-winner in Barry John, whose four penalty goals on his 25th and final appearance for his country made him the highest scorer for Wales with 90 points to pass the aggregate of 88 by Jack Bancroft set in 1914. Barry also became the highest Welsh scorer in a season with 35 points – and that without the Irish fixture. He would have landed a fifth penalty, but the ball rebounded from a post. So Wales were unbeaten champs in this Mini-Championship season.

Wales: J P R Williams (London Welsh); Gerald Davies (London Welsh), R Bergiers (Llanelli), Arthur Lewis (Ebbw Vale), J C Bevan (Cardiff); Barry John, G O Edwards (Cardiff); D J Lloyd (Bridgend, capt), J Young (RAF), D B Llewelyn, Delme Thomas (Llanelli), T G Evans, J Taylor, Mervyn Davies (London Welsh), W D Morris (Neath). Rep: *D L Quinnell (Llanelli) for Mervyn Davies.

France: P Villepreux (Toulouse, capt); B Duprat (Bayonne), J Maso (Narbonne), J P Lux (Dax), J Sillieres (Tarbes); J L Berot (Toulouse), M Barrau (Beamont); J Iracabal (Bayonne), R Benesis (Agen), J L Azarete (St. Jean de Luz), A Esteve (Beziers), C Spanghero (Narbonne), J C Skrela (Toulouse), B Dauga (Mont de Marsan), J P Biemouret (Agen).

For Wales, Gerald Davies and John Bevan scored tries. Barry John kicked four penalty goals.

For France, Pierre Villepreux kicked two penalty goals.

Referee: M H Titcomb (England).

Match 296   WALES v NEW ZEALAND   Cardiff Arms Park. December 2, 1972

New Zealand won by five penalty goals, one try (19) to four penalty goal, one try (16)

It was Wales's turn to cry, "We wuz robbed," turning the 1905 tables on the All Blacks in yet another controversial episode that almost traditionally provides extra piquancy to meetings of these rugby giants. In the end, it was try for try; but full back Joe Karam, the 21-year-old Lebanese salesman from Wellington, on a sparkling Test debut, pipped the home side with five penalty goals, whereas Phil Bennett could only manage four – and missed a last kick of the match chance with yet another penalty that would have earned the draw the tourists admitted Wales deserved. The controversy centred on J P R Williams. The full back looked to have scored a try some 15 minutes from the end; but referee "Johnny" Johnson, who initially appeared to award the score, suddenly swung his arm around and penalised J P R for "rabbiting" over. J P R

185

indignantly claimed, "My try was exactly the same as the one the referee allowed for New Zealand." The All Blacks try-getter, using his momentum, was Keith Murdoch, the prop sent home in disgrace after this match following an incident with a security guard at the Angel Hotel.

Desperate obstruction and late tackles marred the tourists' play as they panicked in the closing stages against a superb Welsh rally. "It was too close for comfort," conceded New Zealand captain Ian Kirkpatrick. "We were lucky to hold out. We seemed to relax mentally in the second half and Wales pushed us back in the scrums. It was a horrible feeling." Just as horrifying for Wales to see Karam slot over those penalty goals, two of them when hooker Jeff Young was guilty of foot-up and one when he failed to bind correctly – technical offences that would not have warranted direct kicks at goal after the changes introduced in 1977-78. Welsh coach Clive Rowlands observed sadly, "We should have won. It is the biggest disappointment I have ever had." Delme Thomas, promoted to captain when Arthur Lewis pulled out with leg trouble, commented, "I thought we did just enough to scrape home." Instead, Wales went down on their own territory for the first time in almost four years and, ironically, had never scored so many points and finished as losers.

Wales: J P R Williams (London Welsh); Gerald Davies, J L Shanklin (London Welsh), R T Bergiers (Llanelli), J C Bevan (Cardiff); P Bennett (Llanelli), G O Edwards (Cardiff); *G Shaw (Neath), J Young (London Welsh), D B Llewelyn, Delme Thomas (capt), D L Quinnell (Llanelli), W D Morris (Neath), Mervyn Davies (Swansea), J Taylor (London Welsh).

New Zealand: J F Karam; threequarters – B G Williams, D A Hales, G B Batty; 2nd five-eighth – R M Parkinson; 1st five-eighth – R E Burgess; half-back – S M Going; forwards – J D Matheson, R W Norton, K Murdoch, H H McDonald, P J Whiting, A J Wyllie, A R Sutherland, I A Kirkpatrick (capt). Rep: A I Scown for Wyllie.

For Wales, John Bevan scored a try. Phil Bennett kicked four penalty goals.

For New Zealand, Keith Murdoch scored a try. Joe Karam kicked five penalty goals.

Referee: R F Johnson (England).

Match 297   WALES v ENGLAND   Cardiff Arms Park. January 20, 1973

Wales won by one goal, one penalty goal, four tries (25) to two penalty goals,
one dropped goal (9)

For the third time in four visits to Cardiff, England were swamped by a five-try onslaught. The Welsh steamroller finish that had staggered the All Blacks, crushed a courageous English pack in which Andy Ripley proved a daring attacker. England, defeated in all four games the previous season for the first time in history, were on their way back to prominence, though not in this match. The return of Arthur Lewis and John Lloyd brought invaluable expertise and with John Bevan, the powerful Cardiff wing, smashing in for two tries, Welsh fans licked their lips in anticipation of another successful year. But things were to go unexpectedly awry and the season culminated in the unique five-way tie, each country winning their two home fixtures.

Wales: J P R Williams (London Welsh); Gerald Davies (London Welsh), Arthur Lewis (Ebbw Vale, capt), R T Bergiers (Llanelli), J C Bevan (Cardiff); P Bennett (Llanelli), G O Edwards (Cardiff); G Shaw (Neath), J Young (London Welsh), D J Lloyd (Bridgend), Delme Thomas, D L Quinnell (Llanelli), W D Morris (Neath), Mervyn Davies (Swansea), J Taylor (London Welsh).

England: S A Doble (Moseley); A J Morley (Bristol), P J Warfield (Rosslyn Park), P S Preece, D J Duckham (Coventry); A R Cowman (Coventry), J G Webster

(Moseley); C B Stevens (Penzance-Newlyn), J V Pullin (Bristol, capt.), F E Cotton (Loughborough Colleges), P J Larter (Northampton), C W Ralston (Richmond), A Neary (Broughton Park), A G Ripley (Rosslyn Park), J A Watkins (Gloucester). Rep: G W Evans (Coventry) for Warfield.

For Wales, John Bevan (2), Gerald Davies, Gareth Edwards and Arthur Lewis scored tries.

For England, Sam Doble kicked two penalty goals. Dick Cowman dropped a goal.

Referee: G Domercq (France).

Match 298   SCOTLAND v WALES   Murrayfield. February 3, 1973

Scotland won by one goal, one try (10) to three penalty goals (9)

It was not often a Welsh pack during the Second Golden Era revealed a weakness as scrummagers. They did against "Mighty Mouse" McLauchlan and his forwards as Scotland gained their first win over Wales for six years. J P R Williams was slow, often caught and failed to find touch with his usual consistency; and only Gerald Davies played up to his reputation as his countrymen could not score a try against Scotland for the first time in 10 years. Arthur Lewis, the loser's captain, remarked ruefully, "We went out at Murrayfield with a definite plan in mind. It did not materialise because we did not play well enough. If you can get enough good ball you can employ any sort of tactics you like. But we could not get the sort of possession we needed."

Scotland: A R Irvine (Heriot's FP); W C C Steele (Bedford), I R McGeechan (Headingley), I W Forsyth (Stewart's College FP), D Shedden (West of Scotland); C M Telfer (Hawick), D W Morgan (Melville College FP); J McLauchlan (Jordanhill Coll., capt), R L Clark (Edinburgh Wands.), A B Carmichael (West of Scotland), A F McHarg (London Scottish), P C Brown, N A McEwan (Gala), G M Strachan (Jordanhill Coll.), J G Millican (Edinburgh Univ.).

Wales: J P R Williams (London Welsh); Gerald Davies (London Welsh), Arthur Lewis (Ebbw Vale, capt), R T Bergiers (Llanelli), J C Bevan (Cardiff); P Bennett (Llanelli), G O Edwards (Cardiff); G Shaw (Neath), J Young (London Welsh), D J Lloyd (Bridgend), Delme Thomas, D L Quinnell (Llanelli), W D Morris (Neath), Mervyn Davies (Swansea), J Taylor (London Welsh).

For Scotland, Colin Telfer and Billy Steele scored tries. Douglas Morgan converted one.

For Wales, Phil Bennett (2) and John Taylor kicked penalty goals.

Referee: F Palmade (France).

Match 299   WALES v IRELAND   Cardiff Arms Park. March 10, 1973

Wales won by one goal, two penalty goals, one try (16) to one goal, two penalty goals (12)

Gareth Edwards, with precision punting and tactical control, and Phil Bennett, the venturesome counter-attacker, guided Wales to this much-needed victory that restored confidence following the cold douche of the Murrayfield flop. Even so, the Welsh side stumbled about during the first half with little authority and it was essential for the forwards to take a grip. They did in the second half and everyone breathed a sigh of relief, recognising that Ireland, captained for the first time by the legendary Bill McBride, called Willie John by many, had proved particularly stubborn adversaries. "We varied play much more than against Scotland," pointed out coach Clive Rowlands. "We were more controlled this time, although Ireland played excellently in all departments and counter-attacked dangerously from situations we did not expect. This was the best game of the season for good tackling – by both sides." Bennett launched a try from inside his 25 in the same audacious fashion as that famous try he initiated for the Barbarians in their great win over the All Blacks six weeks' earlier. Bennett's scintillating side-steps wrenched apart the Irish defence and Jim Shanklin crowned this 90-yard move with a try. Table tennis kept one Welsh player out of the match. Derek Quinnell aggravated a rheumatic elbow condition while wielding his bat on holiday in Majorca.

Wales: J P R Williams (London Welsh); Gerald Davies (London Welsh), Arthur Lewis (Ebbw Vale, capt.), R T Bergiers (Llanelli), J L Shanklin (London Welsh); P Bennett (Llanelli), G O Edwards (Cardiff); G Shaw (Neath), J Young (London Welsh), *P D Llewellyn (Swansea), M G Roberts (London Welsh), Delme Thomas (Llanelli), W D Morris (Neath), Mervyn Davies (Swansea), J Taylor (London Welsh).

Ireland: A H Ensor (Lansdowne); T O Grace (UC, Dublin),R A Milliken (Bangor), C M H Gibson (NIFC), A W McMaster (Ballymena); B J McGann (Cork Constitution), J J Moloney (St. Mary's Coll.); R J McLoughlin (Blackrock Coll.), K W Kennedy (London Irish), J F Lynch (St. Mary's Coll.), W J McBride (Ballymena, capt.), K M A Mays (UC, Dublin), S A McKinney (Dungannon), T A P Moore (Highfield), J F Slattery (Blackrock Coll.).

For Wales, Jim Shanklin and Gareth Edwards scored tries. Phil Bennett converted one and kicked two penalty goals.

For Ireland, Mike Gibson scored a try. Barry McGann converted one and kicked two penalty goals.

Referee: T F E Grierson (Scotland).

Match 300 FRANCE v WALES   Parc Des Princes, Paris. March 24, 1973

France won by three penalty goals, one dropped goal (12) to one dropped goal (3)

What country could make 10 changes and still turn out a team to topple Wales during the Second Golden Era? Only France. They threw out virtually their entire back division, dropping nine men in all and making one positional switch after the defeat by England – and tackled Welsh attackers into depths of despair. "I have never seen a French team tackle like that," sighed Clive Rowlands, and the Welsh coach could not disguise his disappointment at the missed goal kicks. In contrast, France's Jean-Pierre Romeu won the match with a drop-shot and two penalty goals as he aggregated 26 of his team's total of 38 championship points. Arthur Lewis and John Taylor, dropped following the Irish match, were restored because of injuries to Keith Hughes and Derek Quinnell; but Dai Morris was omitted and he and Taylor, a superb hunting pair, who had figured in memorable partnership 20 times for their country, never played together again. This was Taylor's 25th and final match, and his pace, exceptional constructive skill and that Murrayfield conversion kick to win the 1971 game 19-18 in a hair-raising climax, will ever remain fresh. The magnificent Morris, "Shadow" to his team-mates because he was such a wonderful back-up man, was to be recalled and he finished with 34 caps. He and Taylor were rated by many as the greatest pair of flankers in Welsh history. This was the first occasion since 1913 for Wales to play at Parc des Princes, although now it was transformed into a super-stadium that cost the state and city of Paris over £7 million. It had been opened the previous season with all 54,000 spectators seated and under cover.

France: J M Aguirre (Bagneres); J F Philipponneau (Montferrand), C Badin (Chalon), J Maso (Narbonne), J Cantoni (Beziers); J P Romeu (Montferrand), M Pebeyre (Clermont Ferrand); J L Azarete (St. Jean de Luz), R Benesis (Agen), J Iracabal (Bayonne), E Cester (Valance), W Spanghero (Narbonne, capt), J P Biemouret (Agen), O Saisset (Beziers), J C Skrela (Toulouse).

Wales: J P R Williams (London Welsh); Gerald Davies (London Welsh), A J Lewis (Ebbw Vale), R T Bergiers (Llanelli), J L Shanklin (London Welsh); P Bennett (Llanelli), G O Edwards (Cardiff, capt.); G Shaw (Neath), J Young (London Welsh), P D Llewellyn (Swansea), M G Roberts (London Welsh), Delme Thomas, *T P David (Llanelli), Mervyn Davies (Swansea), J Taylor (London Welsh). Rep: *J J Williams (Llanelli) for A J Lewis.

For France, Jean-Pierre Romeu dropped a goal and kicked three penalty goals.

For Wales, Phil Bennett dropped a goal.

Referee: D P D'Arcy (Ireland).

| Uncapped Match | **CANADA v WALES** | Varsity Stadium, Toronto. June 9, 1973 |

Wales won by eight goals, two penalty goals, one try (58) to one goal, two penalty goals, two tries (20)

In the baking heat – 85 degrees Fahrenheit – Wales sweated wearing their regulation WRU thick jerseys while the cool Canadians, in lightweight kit, snatched a 16-13 lead by half time. But Phil Bennett never got hot under the collar: he supplied 24 points and set up a breathtaking try. "Benny" sped back into his 25, collected a kick, turned and shaped to kick clear. The Canadians were made aware that Phil could just about become invisible if he put his mind to it. He dissolved past tacklers as he changed his mind about kicking and went fluttering away with swerve and jink. When eventually he passed the ball, Tom David was on the spot for a try at the posts. It was the final score of a spectacular tour and a suitably impressive memory to leave with 11,300 sun-grilled Canadian rugby followers.

Canada: B Legh (UBC, Vancouver); A Stanton (Ottawa Beavers), T Cummings (Oak Bay Wanderers, Victoria), S Barber (James Bay, Victoria), T Blackwell (Ottawa Irish); G Greig (Castaways, Victoria), F Deacy (St. John's, Newfoundland); H Wyndham (Calgary Canadian Irish), D Docherty (Oak Bay Wanderers, Victoria), G Gudmundseth (Cowichan, BC), R Hindson (Castaways, Victoria), G Ellwand (Irish Canadians, Toronto), L Hillier (UBC, Vancouver), N Browne (St. John's Newfoundland), K Wilkie (Castaways, Victoria, capt). Rep: R McGeein (Brantford Harlequins) for Wyndham.

Wales: J P R Williams (London Welsh); John J Williams (Llanelli), K Hughes (London Welsh), A J Lewis (Ebbw Vale), J C Bevan (Cardiff); P Bennett (Llanelli), G O Edwards (Cardiff, capt); G Shaw (Neath), J Young (London Welsh), P D Llewellyn (Swansea), M G Roberts (London Welsh), Delme Thomas, T P David (Llanelli), Mervyn Davies (Swansea), J Taylor (London Welsh).

For Canada, Hugh Wyndham (2) and David Docherty scored tries. Frank Deacy converted one and kicked a penalty goal. Rob Hindson kicked a penalty goal.

For Wales, Tom David (2), Keith Hughes (2), John Bevan, J J Williams, Phil Bennett, Phil Llewellyn and John Taylor scored tries. Phil Bennett converted seven and kicked two penalty goals. Taylor converted one.

Referee: Dr M Stiles (Alberta).

| Uncapped Match | **WALES v JAPAN** | Cardiff Arms Park. October 6, 1973 |

Wales won by nine goals, two tries (62) to two penalty goals, two tries (14)

Japanese manager Shigeru Konno wanted his team to play against the strongest side Wales could field in order to evaluate his country's place in world rugby. Alas for Shiggy, who had been training as a kamikaze pilot when World War II ended. His men were overwhelmed by a record Welsh score with 11 tries and Phil Bennett piling up 26 points – the most by a Welsh player until his 34 bettered that again against the Japanese on tour in 1975.

Wales were led by John Taylor, who had made his final full cap appearance at the end of the previous season. "For people of their small stature, they were very good indeed," he said of the tourists. "Their scrummaging was superb and we could not shove them around. The channel on to their hooker's foot was the best I have ever seen. Last season we were too rigid with our set plan tactics; now we are trying more variation. We have to take on opposition as well as spinning the ball. This is what we did. The Japanese were wide open to the jink and the switch, but I think this match will do their rugby a great deal of good."

Wales: J P R Williams (London Welsh); Gerald Davies, K Hughes (London Welsh), R T Bergiers, John J Williams (Llanelli); P Bennett (Llanelli), R C Shell (Aberavon); G Shaw (Neath), R W Windsor (Pontypool), P D Llewellyn (Swansea), A J Martin (Aberavon), D L Quinnell, T P David (Llanelli), Mervyn Davies (Swansea), J Taylor (London Welsh, capt.). Rep: I Robinson (Cardiff) for David.

Japan: I Yamamoto; T Itoh, M Fujiwara, A Yokoi (capt), Y Sakata; T Kamohara, H Shukuzawa; S Hara, K Ohigashi, K Yoshino, K Shibata, T Terai, Y Izawa, Y Murata, H Akama. Rep: B Shimazaki for Yamamoto.

For Wales, Phil Bennett (2), Keith Hughes (2), J J Williams, Roy Bergiers, Clive Shell, John Taylor, J P R Williams, Gerald Davies and Bobby Windsor scored tries. Bennett converted nine.

For Japan, Tadayuki Itoh scored two tries. Iwao Yamamoto kicked two penalty goals.

Referee: G Guilhem (France).

Match 301 **WALES v AUSTRALIA** Cardiff Arms Park. November 10, 1973

Wales won by four penalty goals, three tries (24) to nil

Gerald Davies, the only survivor of the Welsh team sensationally defeated by the Wallabies seven years earlier, scored a sparkling try and, for the first time in a home clash with the Australians, Wales outscored them with tries. All Blacks and Springboks are regarded as the glamour teams from overseas, yet it was not generally realised that tussles with the Aussies had always been close. In fact, this was the first occasion in six meetings that the Welsh margin of success had been more than six points. There was a debut try for Pontypool hooker Bobby Windsor with an injury time charge and a popular try by Dai Morris on his recall. Allan Martin marked his first cap with an admirable display of line-out skill and looked the logical successor to stalwart Delme Thomas, though Del was to return to the national side a year later after retiring. During injury time, Gareth Edwards limped off with hamstring trouble and Clive Shell was replacement for the closing two minutes to win his only cap. Phil Bennett went to scrum half until Shell arrived.

Referee Ken Pattinson warned the forwards not to rush together dangerously when the first scrum went down, but the game was never over-vigorous and Welsh fans inspired their team after just three minutes with a roaring chorus of *Cwm Rhondda*. There was criticism that Wales should have scored more profusely and coach Clive Rowlands admitted, "We made silly little mistakes." Following this first victory for 15 years over a major touring side, it was reassuring to note the upsurge of confidence – though the glory days were still a full season away.

Wales: J P R Williams (London Welsh); Gerald Davies, K Hughes (London Welsh), R T Bergiers, John J Williams (Llanelli); P Bennett (Llanelli), G O Edwards (Cardiff, capt); G Shaw (Neath), *R W Windsor (Pontypool), P D

Llewellyn (Swansea), *A J Martin (Aberavon), D L Quinnell, T P David (Llanelli), Mervyn Davies (Swansea), W D Morris (Neath). Rep: *R C Shell (Aberavon) for Edwards.

Australia: R L Fairfax; O Stevens, R D L'Estrange, G A Shaw, J J McLean; G C Richardson, J N B Hipwell; R Graham, M E Freney, J L P Howard, S C Gregory, G Fay, M R Cocks, A A Shaw, P D Sullivan (capt.).

For Wales, Dave Morris, Gerald Davies and Bobby Windsor scored tries. Phil Bennett kicked four penalty goals.

Referee: K A Pattinson (England).

Match 302 **WALES v SCOTLAND**   Cardiff Arms Park. January 19, 1974

Wales won by one goal (6) to nil

It was another Pontypool forward's turn to score a debut try – flanker Terry Cobner, the only newcomer, and on his 28th birthday. He was called in when Tom David reported unfit with shoulder trouble and "Cob" had not even been chosen for the national squad following the final trial. Terry followed the feat of his clubmate, Bobby Windsor, in the previous match with a try, and it proved the decisive score in this 100th full international match to be staged at the Arms Park and brought Wales their only championship success of the season. Gareth Edwards, captaining his country, said, "When Scotland had not scored after 25 minutes of the second half, I knew we had nothing to fear." However, home scrummaging was ineffective as the Scots rolled up the Welsh front row and further disrupted by collapsing and crabbing sideways. The Cobner try came after 23 minutes. Scotland lost a heel on their put-in and Edwards sent Phil Bennett bustling away on the short side. The fly half unloaded to Gerald Davies, who swerved inside; but Gerald the Jink was pulled down attempting to get round full back Andy Irvine. As he fell, the Welsh wing flicked a clever pass up to his flanker. "I thought Terry had dropped it when I heard the crowd roar," recalled Gerald. Thankfully, Cobner grasped the ball and Bennett converted the try. The reason Scotland were the first opponents of the season was because the new rotation of fixtures system came into operation and the traditional "opener" with England was no more.

Wales: J P R Williams (London Welsh); Gerald Davies, K Hughes (London Welsh), I Hall (Aberavon), John J Williams (Llanelli); P Bennett (Llanelli), G O Edwards (Cardiff, capt); G Shaw (Neath), R W Windsor (Pontypool), P D Llewellyn (Swansea), A J Martin (Aberavon), D L Quinnell (Llanelli), W D Morris (Neath), Mervyn Davies (Swansea), *T J Cobner (Pontypool).

Scotland: A R Irvine (Heriot's FP); A D Gill (Gala), J M Renwick (Hawick), I R McGeechan (Headingley), L G Dick (Jordanhill); C M Telfer (Hawick), A J M Lawson (Edinburgh Wands.); J McLauchlan (Jordanhill, capt.), D F Madsen (Gosforth), A B Carmichael, G L Brown (West of Scotland), A F McHarg (London Scottish), W Lauder (Neath), W S Watson (Boroughmuir), N A MacEwan (Highland).

For Wales, Terry Cobner scored a try. Phil Bennett converted.

Referee: R F Johnson (England).

Match 303 **IRELAND v WALES**   Lansdowne Road, Dublin. February 2, 1974

Drawn. Ireland three penalty goals (9). Wales one goal, one penalty goal (9)

A unique warning by the referee to the captains to keep their teams in order straight from the kick-off was one of the few events of note in this boring struggle in a gale. Ken Pattinson called Gareth Edwards and Ireland's McBride together to hear his ulimatum after the forwards had clashed contesting the kick-off ball. It looked like both packs going to ridiculous lengths to get their retaliation in first! Ireland, defeated at home only once since 1967 – and that by Bob Hiller's three penalty goals in England's 1971 success – missed nine penalty shots, but forced a draw as Tony Ensor managed to put over a hat-trick of kicks. The referee awarded 20 kicks against Wales and 10 against the home country and consequently the stop-start nature of the game ruined it. If Barry McGann had been chosen instead of Mick Quinn, there is little doubt the expert goal-kicker would have won the match for Ireland. Wales, winners just once during their previous five visits to Dublin, fielded four new caps, including Geoff Wheel, who demonstrated his amazing strength at ripping the ball from mauls. J P R Williams, surging up from full back, put J J Williams across for the only try in a move launched by Dai Morris following a wheeled close scrum; and Alex Finlayson marked his first cap with a rousing crash tackle on Mike Gibson to prevent the centre scoring the winning try late in the game.

Ireland: A H Ensor (Wanderers); V A Becker (Lansdowne), C M H Gibson (NIFC), R A Milliken (Bangor), P Lavery (London Irish); M A M Quinn (Lansdowne), J J Maloney (St. Mary's Coll.); R J McLoughlin (Blackrock Coll.), K W Kennedy (London Irish), J F Lynch (St Mary's Coll.), W J McBride (Ballymena, capt.), M I Keane (Lansdowne), J F Slattery (Blackrock Coll.), T A P Moore (Highfield), S M Deering (Garryowen).

Wales: J P R Williams (London Welsh); *Clive Rees (London Welsh), I Hall (Aberavon), *A A J Finlayson (Cardiff), John J Williams (Llanelli); P Bennett (Llanelli), G O Edwards (Cardiff, capt.); G Shaw (Neath), R W Windsor (Pontypool), *Walter Williams (Neath), A J Martin (Aberavon), *G Wheel (Swansea), W D Morris (Neath), Mervyn Davies (Swansea), T J Cobner (Pontypool).

For Wales, J J Williams scored a try. Phil Bennett converted and kicked a penalty goal.

For Ireland, Tony Ensor kicked three penalty goals.

Referee: K A Pattinson (England).

Match 304 **WALES v FRANCE**   Cardiff Arms Park. February 16, 1974.

Drawn. Each side scored three penalty goals, one dropped goal, one try (16)

Phil Bennett was in the Welsh team, ruled out, and back in – all within the space of 90 minutes on match morning. He ended up scoring three vital penalty goals before going home to bed to shake off the effects of a heavy cold. Dr. Jack Matthews declared Phil unfit with a temperature of 101, and Aberavon's John Bevan was alerted to play. "But I got up and felt much better after taking a run around the Cardiff club ground," explained Bennett. "So I told the selectors I would play if they wanted me, and I was back in the team." His three kicks made him top penalty goal collector for his country with a total of 16 – a figure he was to advance to 36 before his career finished. Jean-Pierre Romeu repeated his feat of 12 points a year earlier by supplying three penalty goals and then a drop-shot right at the end to foil Welsh hopes. France confused Wales with the long range dummy scissors trick, which looked a potent innovation but was seldom copied because it demands a high degree of proficiency. Jean-Pierre Lux scored from this ploy, which involved a long pass to the outside centre from his fly half instead of, as indicated, the shorter pass to the inside centre, who ran as decoy.

Wales: J P R Williams (London Welsh); Gerald Davies (London Welsh), I Hall (Aberavon), A A J Finlayson (Cardiff), John J Williams (Llanelli); P Bennett (Llanelli), G O Edwards (Cardiff, capt.); G Shaw (Neath), R W Windsor

(Pontypool), Walter Williams (Neath); *I R Robinson (Cardiff), D L Quinnell (Llanelli), W D Morris (Neath), Mervyn Davies (Swansea), T J Cobner (Pontypool).

France: J M Aguirre (Bagneres); R Bertranne (Bagneres), J Pecune (Tarbes), J P Lux (Dax), A Dubertrand (Montferrand); J P Romeu (Montferrand), J Fouroux (La Voulte); J Iracabal (Bayonne), R Benesis (Agen), A Vaquerin, A Esteve (Beziers), E Cester (Valence, capt.), J C Skrela (Toulouse), C Spanghero (Narbonne), V Boffelli (Aurillac).

For Wales, J J Williams scored a try. Gareth Edwards dropped a goal. Phil Bennett kicked three penalty goals.

For France, Jean Pierre Lux scored a try. Jean Pierre Romeu dropped a goal and kicked three penalty goals.

Referee: N R Sanson (Scotland).

Match 305 ENGLAND v WALES   Twickenham. March 16, 1974

England won by one goal, two penalty goals, one try (16) to one goal, two penalty goals (12)

J J Williams's disallowed try and England's decision not to play the Welsh national anthem while the players were on the field caused a storm in this eventful match. A flood of protests, including an official one from the WRU, ensured that *Hen Wlad Fy Nhadau* would be suitably recognised and respected in future Twickenham matches. Unfortunately, there was no way to put right the "lost" try, which enabled England to record their first victory over Wales at Twickers for 14 years. "No-one will ever convince me I didn't score a perfectly legitimate try," groaned the dumbfounded J J. "My hand had touched the ball down." The incident occurred in the 29th minute of the second half with J J and England's David Duckham and Peter Squires sprinting together for the ball over the goal-line. All three hurled themselves on the ball and spectators at the north end of the ground had a clear view of the Welsh wing reaching the ball first. Referee John West, however, said he could not award a try because the diving figures obscured his view of the ball. Jack Young, chairman of the WRU selectors, grumbled, "We were robbed by that disallowed try and when the referee neglected to allow advantage when Phil Bennett was making his break that could have led to a score."

Bennett completed 36 points in the five games of the season to pass Barry John's record of 35 in 1971-72 while another record was Gareth Edwards's 35th consecutive appearance, making him the most capped Welsh scrum half in succession to the legendary Dicky Owen. The only new cap was Roger Blyth, following his father, wing forward Len, as a Welsh international – the eighth instance of a father-son combination playing for Wales. Roger deputised for J P R Williams, who had played 28 successive games, but was in plaster after a knee cartilage injury. Delme Thomas had retired following the Welsh tour of Canada, but returned to help Llanelli on Boxing Day and was immediately recalled to the national team in place of unfit Derek Quinnell. It was Delme's 25th and final cap and the end of the road for a grand sportsman.

The Welsh players, puzzled by the omission of their national anthem, remained at attention for several seconds before play began while outraged Welsh supporters broke into singing around the ground until drowned out by English cheering. "We were shocked and disappointed at the omission," said WRU secretary Bill Clement. However, RFU secretary Bob Weighill explained, "My committee are firmly of the opinion that when countries of the four home unions play at Twickenham we play The Queen only. We are all part of the United Kingdom and the national anthem of the United Kingdom is The Queen." The WRU called for special talks on the issue and the RFU consented to the request that in future the Welsh national anthem be played in addition to The Queen immediately before kick-off. This hardly eased the bitterness of J J and his try that "went West ."

England: W H Hare (Notts.); P J Squires (Harrogate), K Smith (Roundhay), G W Evans, D J Duckham (Coventry); A G B Old (Leicester), J G Webster (Moseley); C B Stevens (Penzance-Newlyn), J V Pullin (Bristol, capt), M A Burton (Gloucester), C W Ralston (Richmond), R M Uttley, P J Dixon (Gosforth), A G Ripley (Rosslyn Park), A Neary (Broughton Park).

Wales: *W R Blyth (Swansea); Gerald Davies (London Welsh), A A J Finlayson (Cardiff), R T Bergiers, John J Williams (Llanelli); P Bennett (Llanelli), G O Edwards (Cardiff, capt); G Shaw (Neath), R W Windsor (Pontypool), P D Llewellyn (Swansea), Delme Thomas (Llanelli), I R Robinson (Cardiff), W D Morris (Neath), Mervyn Davies (Swansea), T J Cobner (Pontypool). Rep: G Wheel (Swansea) for Robinson.

For Wales, Mervyn Davies scored a try. Phil Bennett converted and kicked two penalty goals.

For England, David Duckham and Andy Ripley scored tries. Alan Old converted one and kicked two penalty goals.

Referee: J R West (Ireland).

Uncapped Match	**WALES v TONGA**	Cardiff Arms Park. October 19, 1974

Wales won by two penalty goals, five tries (26) to one penalty goal, one try (7)

Wales, wearing green jerseys because Tonga's national colours are red, rested their 1974 British Lions ready for the clash with the All Blacks a month later. Cardiff's No.2 scrum half Brynmor Williams, to become a 1977 Lion before winning his full cap, was brought in when Clive Shell withdrew. Aberavon outside half John Bevan, however, proved the man of the match with his cool control as he scored a try and engineered two. Obviously he, like Brynmor, was cap material. Llanelli centre Ray Gravell, a powerful attacker, showed signs that were to make him the most exciting discovery of the 1974-75 season. Cardiff's erudite loose head specialist, Gerry Wallace, one of the finest uncapped props, also impressed in front of a crowd of 28,000, who watched the tourists perform their pre-match war dance, waving wooden spears and rattling chains of paanga seeds fastened around their ankles. Some of their fierce tackling kept the Welsh attackers in chains.

Wales: C Bolderson (Pontypridd); Gerald Davies (Cardiff, capt.), R Gravell (Llanelli), S Fenwick (Bridgend), A A J Finlayson (Cardiff); J D Bevan (Aberavon), Brynmor Williams (Cardiff); G B Wallace (Cardiff), Roy Thomas, D B Llewelyn (Llanelli), M G Roberts (London Welsh), A J Martin (Aberavon), Trevor Evans (Swansea), D L Quinnell (Llanelli), T J Cobner (Pontypool). Rep: I Hall (Aberavon) for Gravell.

Tonga: Valita Ma'ake; Samiuela Latu, Tali Kavapalu, Sitafoti 'Aho, Talilotu Ngaluafe; Malakai 'Alatini, Ha'unga Fonua; Siosaia Fifita, Molou Filimoehala, Tevita Pulumufila, Fa'aleo Tupi, Fatai Kefu, Saimone Vaea, Sione Mafi (capt.), Fakahau Valu.

For Wales, Alex Finlayson (2), Steve Fenwick, John Bevan and Terry Cobner scored tries. Allan Martin kicked two penalty goals.

For Tonga, Talilotu Ngaluafe scored a try. Valita Ma'ake kicked a penalty goal.

Referee: R F Johnson (England).

New Zealand won by one goal, two penalty goals (12) to one penalty goal (3)

After four months out of rugby, would the WRU dare pick JPR against the mighty All Blacks for his first match? Actually, he did play one game before this Wednesday unofficial Test. Bronzed JPR flew into London at 7 a.m. after staying on in Durban when the British Lions' tour ended, and turned out as flank forward for London Welsh Sixth XV that Saturday to conform with the WRU request to prove his match fitness. Against the New Zealanders, the full back lacked his customary assurance and judgement with a greasy ball, but only for the first 20 minutes. Then he recaptured his fluency – and one shattering head-on tackle blocked Bryan Williams when the flying wing was hell-bent for a try. Following the controversey and acrimony of the 1972 match against the All Blacks, this proved a warmingly sporting contest and the tourists were obviously superior with their magnificent pack, scheming Sid Going at scrum half and Joe Karam again brilliant at full back. New Welsh coach John Dawes commented, "The Welsh defence, particularly the back row, tackled splendidly, but we must say that New Zealand were the better team." The only try was a clever effort by flanker Ian Kirkpatrick and New Zealand left no doubt that they had recovered from the loss of prestige against the 1971 Lions.

It was feared that Ian Hall would never play again after suffering a compound fracture and dislocation of his right ankle. Gerry Lewis, the Welsh team physiotherapist, said he had never seen a worse injury of it's kind in more than 20 years experience; but the courageous centre was to recover and play superbly once more for South Wales Police. This brief tour was to mark the Irish RFU centenary season and in order that a Wales-New Zealand clash would not in any way diminish the attraction of the principal fixture against Ireland, the Welsh match was designated unofficial.

Wales: J P R Williams (London Welsh); Gerald Davies (Cardiff), R T Bergiers (Llanelli), I Hall (Aberavon), John J Williams (Llanelli); P Bennett (Llanelli), G O Edwards (Cardiff, capt.); A G Faulkner, R W Windsor (Pontypool), D B Llewelyn, D L Quinnell (Llanelli), G Wheel, Trevor Evans, Mervyn Davies (Swansea), T J Cobner (Pontypool). Reps: W R Blyth (Swansea) for Hall, J D Bevan (Aberavon) for Bergiers.

New Zealand: J F Karam; B G Williams, B J Robertson, G B Batty; I A Hurst, D J Robertson; S M Going; K K Lambert, R W Norton, K J Tanner, P J Whiting, H H Macdonald, I A Kirkpatrick, A R Leslie (capt.), K A Eveleigh. Rep: L G Knight for Eveleigh.

For Wales, Phil Bennett kicked a penalty goal.

For New Zealand, Ian Kirkpatrick scored a try. Joe Karam converted and kicked two penalty goals.

Referee: D P D'Arcy (Ireland).

Wales won by one goal, one penalty goal, four tries (25) to two penalty goals, one try (10)

On the day that the famous Pontypool front row played for Wales for the first time, one of their number, tight-head Graham Price, distinguished his debut with a thrilling injury-time try. It was astonishing that a prop could find such stamina for a long run right at the end of a fast-moving tussle; but Price, of course, was an exceptional player, soon to be recognised as the world's No.1 in his position. With him was prop Tony Faulkner, winning his initial cap just before his 34th birthday. Club-mates Windsor, Cobner and Price had scored tries on their first international appearances and though Faulkner did not achieve that feat, he was a try-scorer later in the season against Ireland. There were six new caps on duty for Wales, who had succeeded only once in their last eight visits to Paris, but the Welsh side produced remarkable cohesion. John Bevan, of Aberavon, was the new outside half, selected in preference to Phil Bennett, who was subjected to searching scrutiny despite his brilliance for the invincible 1974 Lions in South Africa. Bevan, playing in contact lenses, had dislocated his right shoulder three times, but an operation to tighten the ligaments in 1972 saved his career. He was, incidentally, the only uncapped player in the Barbarians' team that drew with the 1974 All Blacks and it was the first time for 74 games that Wales fielded a midfield triangle of new caps: Steve Fenwick and Ray Gravell were the centres starting out on distinguished careers. But Bennett was not long to be left on the reserves' bench.

France: M Taffary (Racing Club); J F Gourdon (Racing Club), C Dourthe (Dax), R Bertranne (Bagneres), J P Lux (Dax); J P Romeu (Montferrand), J Fouroux (La Voulte, capt.); A Vaquerin, A Paco (Beziers), J L Azarete (St. Jean de Luz), G Senal, A Esteve, O Saisset (Beziers), J P Bastiat (Dax), V Boffelli (Aurillac). Reps: J Cantoni (Beziers) for Gourdon, J C Skrela (Toulouse) for Saisset.

Wales: J P R Williams (London Welsh); Gerald Davies (Cardiff), *S P Fenwick (Bridgend), *R Gravell, J J Williams (Llanelli); *J D Bevan (Aberavon), G O Edwards (Cardiff); *A G Faulkner, R W Windsor, *G Price (Pontypool), G Wheel (Swansea), A J Martin (Aberavon), T J Cobner (Pontypool), Mervyn Davies (capt.), *Trevor Evans (Swansea).

For Wales, Steve Fenwick, Gerald Davies, Terry Cobner, Gareth Edwards and Graham Price scored tries. Fenwick converted one and kicked a penalty goal.

For France, Jean-Francois Gourdon scored a try. Michel Taffary kicked two penalty goals.

Referee: K A Pattinson (England).

Match 307 WALES v ENGLAND   Cardiff Arms Park. February 15, 1975

Wales won by one goal, two penalty goals, two tries (20) to one try (4)

"We went off the boil," admitted coach John Dawes after Wales led 16-0 at half time, but could add only one try as they lost fluency and the pack failed to maintain their dominance. Cliff Jones, chairman of the selectors, observed, "It was the psychological effect of scoring too many points too early. The game was won and the boys relaxed. They need a challenge to keep them going flat out." Skipper Merv the Swerve pointed out, "This is a relatively inexperienced team and we have not seen the best of it yet. We all know we'll have to flog our backsides off to beat Scotland at Murrayfield, but we'll do it." Alas, confidence is not an infallible guarantee. Gareth Edwards again showed masterly control to answer critics who implied that his flair was on the decline. Before the French game he had asserted, "I am playing as well as ever. I had a good Lions' tour in South Africa because I was playing behind a magnificent pack. I came home a hero. And straight away I'm expected to turn water into wine. I am working like a slave to bring back that sharpness of last summer." We were to witness many more moments of breathtaking brilliance before Edwards was finished with rugby.

Wales: J P R Williams (London Welsh); Gerald Davies (Cardiff), S P Fenwick (Bridgend), R Gravell, J J Williams (Llanelli); J D Bevan (Aberavon), G O Edwards (Cardiff); A G Faulkner, R W Windsor, G Price (Pontypool), A J Martin (Aberavon), G Wheel, T P Evans, Mervyn Davies (Swansea, capt.), T J Cobner (Pontypool). Rep: D L Quinell (Llanelli) for Wheel.

England: A M Jorden (Bedford); P J Squires (Harrogate), K Smith (Roundhay), P S Preece, D J Duckham (Coventry); M J Cooper, J G Webster (Moseley); C B

Stevens (Penzance-Newlyn), P J Wheeler (Leicester), F E Cotton (Coventry, capt.), N E Horton (Moseley), C W Ralston (Richmond), J A Watkins (Gloucester), R M Uttley (Gosforth), A Neary (Broughton Park). Reps: S Smith (Sale) for Webster, J V Pullin (Bristol) for Wheeler.

For Wales, J J Williams, Gerald Davies and Steve Fenwick scored tries. Allan Martin converted one and kicked two penalty goals.

For England, Nigel Horton scored a try.

Referee: A M Hosie (Scotland).

Match 308 **SCOTLAND v WALES** Murrayfield. March 1, 1975

Scotland won by three penalty goals, one dropped goal (12) to two penalty goals, one try (10)

Phil Bennett will never forget the occasion he played the worst game of his life – watched by a world record crowd of 104,000. It was a St. Davids Day of disaster for Wales and especially Phil. He came on when John Bevan dislocated his left shoulder after 26 minutes and nothing went right for 'Benny.' It was unbelievable that such a talented operator could look so inept. However, the Stradey star was to transform his despair into triumph before long; playing another 13 games for his country, leading the 1977 Lions in New Zealand, and captaining his country to the Grand Slam in 1978. Yet on this particularly day he must have wished he could have been one of the thousands who were locked out of the ground. There were chaotic scenes around Murrayfield with thousands unable to gain admission while hundreds inside tried to fight their way out because the crushed conditions prevented them from viewing the match. It was estimated that 40,000 Welshmen were in Edinburgh for the event. Crowds besieged the Scottish RFU offices at the ground demanding their money back and a week later it was announced that future Murrayfield matches would be all-ticket with a capacity of just over 70,000.

Wales would have drawn with the final kick of the match, but Allan Martin was unable to land the conversion from the touch-line after Trevor Evans had charged in for the only try from an over-the-shoulder pass by Gerald Davies as the wing dodged two tacklers. Scotland had given due warning of their intentions. "We'll give Wales hell," vowed skipper Ian McLauchlan after his side had lost by one point in Paris, where the Scots nevertheless won a fierce punch up with the home pack. McLauchlan's promise was made good through the aggression and purpose of his forwards. "Our senior players made too many elementary mistakes," mused coach Dawes. Occasionally even eloquent Mr Dawes was capable of masterly understatement.

Scotland: A R Irvine (Heriot's FP); W C C Steele (London Scottish), J M Renwick (Hawick), D L Bell (Watsonians), L G Dick (Jordanhill); I R McGeechan (Headingley), D W Morgan (Stewart's-Melville FP); J McLauchlan (Jordanhill, capt), D F Madsen (Gosforth), A B Carmichael, G L Brown (West of Scotland), A F McHarg, M A Biggar (London Scottish), D G Leslie (Dundee HSFP), N A McEwan (Highland).

Wales: J P R Williams (London Welsh); Gerald Davies (Cardiff), S P Fenwick (Bridgend), R Gravell, J J Williams (Llanelli); J D Bevan (Aberavon), G O Edwards (Cardiff); A G Faulkner, R W Windsor, G Price (Pontypool), A J Martin (Aberavon), M G Roberts (London Welsh), T P Evans, Mervyn Davies (Swansea, capt.), T J Cobner (Pontypool). Reps: P Bennett (Llanelli) for J D Bevan, W R Blyth (Swansea) for Fenwick.

For Scotland, Douglas Morgan kicked three penalty goals. Ian McGeechan dropped a goal.

For Wales, Trevor Evans scored a try. Steve Fenwick kicked two penalty goals.

Referee: J R West (Ireland).

Wales won by three goals, two penalty goals, two tries (32) to one try (4)

From Murrayfield flop to Arms Park hero in the space of two weeks. That was Phil Bennett in this record victory over Ireland, featuring one of the greatest displays by a Welsh team on a perfect spring day. Three of Ireland's most famous players gave up rugby after this traumatic experience, which brought their country's heaviest championship reverse for 68 years. Skipper Willie John McBride, aged 35, sorrowfully quit after a then world record 63 caps and five British Lions' tours. Ken Kennedy (45 caps) and Ray McLoughlin (40) also called "time" following the massacre; but the 31 year-old Mike Gibson refused to give up and, although no longer able to shoot away like a scalded leprechaun, the "Old One" went on for another three seasons.

Wales, of course, secured the International Championship by this victory, swamping Ireland with a second half onslaught after leading only 9-0 at the interval. Geoff Wheel was an outstanding ripper of the ball - and even ripped off McLoughlin's scrum-cap during a little disagreement. But essentially it was Bennett's match. His reputation was at stake. Phil had to erase memories of his rock-bottom performance in Scotland. With John Bevan still injured, the WRU selectors gave Bennett another chance. He did not let them down. The Llanelli captain walked down the tightrope of his career without a hesitant step and his legion of fans had their prayers answered. We knew Phil could never again be as bad as that black day at Murrayfield.

Tony Faulkner scored his popular try, put over by clubmate Bobby Windsor; and Ireland managed their only score right at the end when No.8 Willie Duggan intercepted a reverse pass from Gareth Edwards and pounded 45 yards.

Wales: J P R Williams (London Welsh); Gerald Davies (Cardiff), R T Bergiers, R Gravell, J J Williams (Llanelli); P Bennett (Llanelli), G O Edwards (Cardiff); A G Faulkner, R W Windsor, G Price (Pontypool), A J Martin (Aberavon), G Wheel, T P Evans, Mervyn Davies (Swansea, capt.), T J Cobner (Pontypool).

Ireland: A H Ensor (Wanderers); T O Grace (St. Mary's Coll.), R A Milliken (Bangor), C M H Gibson (NIFC), A W McMaster (Ballymena); W M McCombe (Bangor), J J Maloney (St. Mary's Coll.); R J McLoughlin (Blackrock Coll.), K W Kennedy (London Irish), R J Clegg (Bangor), W J McBride (Ballymena, capt.), M I Keane, M J A Shery (Lansdowne), W P Duggan, J F Slattery (Blackrock Coll.).

For Wales, Gareth Edwards, Gerald Davies, J J Williams, Tony Faulkner and Roy Bergiers scored tries. Phil Bennett converted three and kicked two penalty goals.

For Ireland, Willie Duggan scored a try.

Referee: J Guilheim (France).

Wales won by five goals, two penalty goals, five tries (56) to four penalty goals (12)

The Welsh team, sucking salt tablets to combat the effects of the hottest September in Japan for more than 70 years, made a magnificent success of this first visit to the Land of the Rising Sun, repaying the tour of 1973. Mervyn Davies captained the side, under the management of Les Spence (Cardiff) with John Dawes as coach. While recording 45 tries in five games (including a fixture in Hong Kong), Wales had only one try against them – by the Japan 'B' XV. Some 15,000 spectators were suitably impressed by Welsh attackers in this first Test as they shrugged off blistering heat of nearly 90 degrees Fahrenheit to add 20 points in the final 20 minutes. But Mervyn Davies was "burned up" in another way – by lime that had been used for pitch markings.

Japan: N Ueyama; M Fujiwara, S Mori, M Yoshida, T Aruga; M Iguchi, R Imazato (capt.); T Takada, T Kurosaka, S Hara, H Ogasawara, T Terai, Y Izawa, I Kobayashi, T Ishizuka.

Wales: J P R Williams (London Welsh); Gerald Davies (Cardiff), R W R Gravell (Llanelli), S P Fenwick (Bridgend), J J Williams (Llanelli); J D Bevan (Aberavon), G O Edwards (Cardiff); A G Faulkner, R W Windsor (Pontypool), D B Llewelyn (Llanelli), A J Martin (Aberavon), G Wheel, T P Evans, T Mervyn Davies (Swansea, capt.), T J Cobner (Pontypool). Rep: R C Shell (Aberavon) for Edwards.

For Japan, Ueyama kicked four penalty goals.

For Wales, JJ Williams (2), Gerald Davies (2), Ray Gravell (2), Trevor Evans (2), Clive Shell and John Bevan scored tries. Steve Fenwick converted five and kicked two penalty goals.

Referee: N R Sanson (Scotland).

Uncapped Match JAPAN v WALES   National Stadium, Tokyo. September 24, 1975

Wales won by 10 goals, two penalty goals, four tries (82) to two penalty goals (6)

Full back J P R Williams romped away for three of the 14 tries Wales collected in assembling this world record score for an international match. Phil Bennett's 34 points was the most a Welsh player had scored at representative level, beating the 26 he obtained against Japan in Cardiff during 1973. The crowd of 40,000 also watched Pontypool's front row make a dashing contribution, Graham Price pouncing for two tries and fellow prop 'Charlie' Faulkner, appropriately a Judo Black Belt, storming over for one. Gareth Edwards pulled a hamstring in the first Test, so Clive Shell took his place to partner Bennett, who replaced John Bevan in order that both outside halves played a Test each.

Japan: N Ueyama; M Fujiwara, S Mori, N Tanaka, K Aruga; S Hoshino, R Imazato (capt.); T Takada, T Kurosaka, M Miyauchi, T Terai, H Ogasawara, H Akama, I Kobayashi, T Ishizuka.

Wales: J P R Williams (London Welsh); Gerald Davies (Cardiff), R W R Gravell (Llanelli), S P Fenwick (Bridgend), J J Williams (Llanelli); P Bennett (Llanelli), R C Shell (Aberavon); A G Faulkner, R H Windsor, G Price (Pontypool), A J Martin (Aberavon), B G Clegg (Swansea), Gareth Jenkins (Llanelli), T Mervyn Davies (Swansea, capt.), T J Cobner (Pontypool).

For Japan, Ueyama kicked two penalty goals.

For Wales, J P R Williams (3), Phil Bennett (2), Gerald Davies (2), Graham Price (2), J J Williams (2), Mervyn Davies, Ray Gravell and "Charlie" Faulkner scored tries. Bennett converted 10 and kicked two penalty goals.

Referee: N R Sansom (Scotland).

Match 310 WALES v AUSTRALIA   Cardiff Arms Park. December 20, 1975

Wales won by three goals, one dropped goal, one penalty goal, one try (28) to one penalty goal (3)

Critics were murmuring that J J Williams had lost his keen edge of speed. The Stradey sprinter gave his answer on this sunny day: a hat-trick of tries to help build a record win over the Wallabies. J J had switched to the right wing after 10 games on the left because Gerald Davies was a hamstring victim. "There were some people who seem to think I should not have been in the team at all," commented J J. "They said I had lost my zip. So I went out there to show them." It was only the second time in post-war rugby for a Welsh player to score three tries in a match, the other occasion having been when Maurice Richards crossed for four against England in 1969. Those J J tries, all in the second half, were scored as follows: 11 minutes – Ray Gravell burst, linked outside with John Bevan and the fly half put J J diving into the corner; 28 minutes – Gareth Edwards punted high, Fenwick jumped to collect, Mervyn Davies and Trevor Evans gave swift support and J J was away; 39 minutes – Trevor Evans charged, handed on to Gravell and then J J punted over the goal-line and chased to score.

Four days earlier, the Australians had trounced Glamorgan 51-18, but the Welsh forwards won a fierce physical contest, during which the referee called the captains together to discuss the problem of persistent scrum collapsing. Gareth Edwards was at his brilliant best; a tactical controller par excellence with tremendous rolling punts.

Phil Bennett pulled out the day before the match with a foot injury and this brought John Bevan back. He dropped a goal, but it was his last game for Wales. As a final assessment, Welsh coach John Dawes observed, "There was a tendency to over-kick by the Welsh backs and we need to find a better balance between kicking and passing."

Wales: J P R Williams (London Welsh); J J Williams, R Gravell (Llanelli), S P Fenwick (Bridgend), Clive Rees (London Welsh); J D Bevan (Aberavon), G O Edwards (Cardiff); A G Faulkner, R W Windsor, G Price (Pontypool), A J Martin (Aberavon), G Wheel (Swansea), T J Cobner (Pontypool), Mervyn Davies (capt.), T P Evans (Swansea).

Australia: P E McLean; P G Batch, R D L'Estrange, G A Shaw, L E Monaghan; J C Hindmarsh, J N B Hipwell (capt.); J E C Meadows, P A Horton, R Graham, R A Smith, G Fay, J K Lambie, G Cornelsen, A A Shaw. Reps: G K Pearce for Lambie, R G Hauser for Hipwell.

For Wales, J J Williams (3) and Gareth Edwards scored tries. Steve Fenwick converted two and kicked a penalty goal. Allan Martin converted one. John Bevan dropped a goal.

For Australia, Paul McLean kicked a penalty goal.

Referee: D P D'Arcy (Ireland).

Match 311   ENGLAND v WALES   Twickenham. January 17, 1976

Wales won by three goals, one penalty goal (21) to three penalty goals (9)

JPR Williams played his greatest game for Wales in this record victory by his country at Twickenham. Face awash with blood and eyes ablaze with battle, the dauntless full back blasted over for two tries on the day that he passed the renowned Billy Bancroft's 33 appearances to become the most-capped Welsh full back. For the first occasion for almost three years, England named an unchanged side, having defeated the Wallabies convincingly; but JPR destroyed English hopes of repeating their 1974 triumph. During three successive visits to Twickers (he missed the 1974 game), JPR had scored an amazing four tries. "It was my turn for everything to go right," he said. "Consequently, I was able to influence the game. That is how it goes in the Welsh team." Later he had seven stitches in his right cheek. The first JPR try was launched from a scrum after 35 minutes. Phil Bennett and Fenwick linked to put J J Williams away. When threatened, the wing swung an in-pass to JPR and he charged across. Then, right at the end, a switch move with Bennett enabled the full back to crash through two tacklers and score.

However, coach John Dawes and captain Mervyn Davies were far from satisfied with their team's performance. "By our high standards, I don't think it was a very good win," asserted Mervyn. "But it is significant that we played badly and still came out on top." Dawes was more emphatic with his criticism. "We must buck up," he declared. "We were far too loose in various situations and I expect more control. We will not win the title if we continue to play like that." Wales did buck up, stung by cutting accusations from their men at the top – and went on to complete their seventh Grand Slam. Bennett controversially had been dropped. John Bevan was first choice with Swansea's David Richards as replacement, which made Bennett incomprehensibly No.3. But injuries to Bevan (elbow) and Richards (hamstring) meant Bennett was needed after all – and he was never dropped again. Incidentally, playing his 18th game, he was on the winning side for the first time in an away fixture. And this was only the second time in three seasons for Wales to win on opposition terrain. Another interesting point was that flanker Mark Keyworth, who played alongside Trevor Evans and Mervyn Davies for Swansea, played against them for England. The new Twickenham crowd limit came into force. Only 67,000 spectators were permitted, which was 5,500 below the former level.

England: A J Hignell (Cambridge Univ.); P J Squires (Harrogate), A W Maxwell (Headingley), D A Cooke (Harlequins), D J Duckham (Coventry); M J Cooper (Moseley), M S Lampkowski (Headingley); F E Cotton (Sale), P J Wheeler (Leicester), M A Burton (Glousester), W B Beaumont (Fylde), R M Wilkinson (Bedford), M Keyworth (Swansea), A G Ripley (Rosslyn Park), A Neary (Broughton Park, capt.). Rep: P S Preece (Coventry) for Squires.

Wales: J P R Williams (London Welsh); Gerald Davies (Cardiff), R Gravell (Llanelli), S P Fenwick (Bridgend), J J Williams (Llanelli); P Bennett (Llanelli), G O Edwards (Cardiff); A G Faulkner, R W Windsor, G Price (Pontypool), G Wheel (Swansea), A J Martin (Aberavon), T J Cobner (Pontypool), Mervyn Davies (capt.), T P Evans (Swansea).

For Wales, J P R Williams (2) and Gareth Edwards scored tries. Steve Fenwick converted three. Allan Martin kicked a penalty goal.

For England, Alastair Hignell kicked three penalty goals.

Referee: G Domercq (France).

Match 312 **WALES v SCOTLAND**   Cardiff Arms Park. February 7, 1976

Wales won by two goals, three penalty goals, one dropped goal, one try (28) to one goal (6)

The Press called this The Great Gag Match. For the first time the Welsh team were banned from giving interviews to newspapermen. It was suggested that the move was a backlash from the WRU selectors, needled by criticism of their omission of Phil Bennett against England. The selectors pointed out they imposed the sanction in players' interests to minimise the effects of modern investigative journalism and its consequent stress upon some players. Undoubtedly, the "gag" represented an infringement on players' freedom as individuals in an amateur game, though the system had become common practice and long been employed by the feudalists of Scotland, who nurture the distinction between superiors and vassals.

Nevertheless, Mervyn Davies approved the silencing of his men. "I feel it was in the best interests of the team," he said. "We were not disturbed by phone calls throughout the week." The truth of the matter, however, is that the principal cause of stress to players was intensive coaching, the demands of the national squad and a rigorous club programme. Team-preparation had been transformed from the free-and-easy run out to near professional requirements.

Phil Bennett's 13 points made him the highest scorer for Wales with 92, passing Barry John's 90, while Gareth Edwards equalled the Welsh record of 17 tries with a remarkable score in the closing stages. Wales won maul ball close to the Scottish line for Bobby Windsor to feed straight out to Bennett. The fly half found Edwards racing up on his left and the crafty Edwards sold a delicate dummy as he burst over. Referee Andre Cuny, the 48-year old doctor from Grenoble, strained his right calf muscle when knocked over after 10 minutes of the second half, but rejected suggestions from the captains and Welsh touch judge Meirion Joseph that he should retire. "As long as I was in a position to observe clearly, I could continue to control play," he explained. But it was refereeing by remote control for much of the time because limping Dr. Cuny was trailing far behind play.

Wales: J P R Williams (London Welsh); Gerald Davies (Cardiff), S P Fenwick (Bridgend), R Gravell, J J Williams (Llanelli); P Bennett (Llanelli), G O Edwards (Cardiff); A G Faulkner, R W Windsor, G Price (Pontypool), G Wheel (Swansea), A J Martin (Aberavon), T J Cobner (Pontypool), Mervyn Davies (capt.), T P Evans (Swansea).

Scotland: A R Irvine (Heriot's FP); W C C Steele (London Scottish), J M Renwick, A G Cranston (Hawick), D Shedden (West of Scotland); I R McGeechan (Headingley), D W Morgan (Stewart's-Melville FP); J McLauchlan (Jordanhill, capt.), C D Fisher (Waterloo), A B Carmichael, G L Brown (West of Scotland), A F McHarg, M A Biggar (London Scottish), G Y Mackie (Highland), D G Leslie (West of Scotland).

For Wales, J J Williams, Gareth Edwards and Trevor Evans scored tries. Phil Bennett converted two and kicked three penalty goals. Steve Fenwick dropped a goal.

For Scotland, Andy Irvine scored a try. Douglas Morgan converted.

Referee: Dr. A Cuny (France).

Match 313 IRELAND v WALES   Lansdowne Road, Dublin. February 21, 1976

Wales won by three goals, four penalty goals, one try (34) to three penalty goals (9)

Despite a death threat to a number of Welsh players in letters posted from Dublin, allegedly from terrorist extremists, and the fact that the Shelbourne Hotel was bombed following the death of IRA bomber Frank Stagg, on hunger strike in a British prison, both teams stayed at this Dublin hotel under heavy security guard. No member of this Welsh side had ever played on a winning team at Lansdowne Road and this first success there for 12 years brought the added prize of the Triple Crown for the 13th occasion. Ireland, with Mike Gibson becoming the world's most-capped back on his 55th appearance, were 10-0 down after 20 minutes, but rallied with typical tenacity and were only 10-9 in arrears at half time. The home forwards held resolutely until the closing stages and subjected Gareth Edwards to relentless pressure. Often there were three green jerseys pouncing on him. Yet he scored. Fed from a ruck, and taking off on the blind-side, he punted on, chased, regathered and dived across. It was his 18th and a record for Wales. He also equalled Teddy Morgan's feat of scoring tries in five successive international matches.

Mervyn Davies's 37th consecutive game made him the most-capped Welsh forward, passing Denzil Williams's tally, while Phil Bennett's 19 points in the match equalled the joint record of Jack Bancroft (1910) and Keith Jarrett (1967). Phil, in one of his finest displays, scored his first try for Wales – and the best of the match with a delightful dummy and in-swerve – and the last three Welsh tries came in a devastating five-minute onslaught worth 18 points – and as record Welsh total against Ireland.

Ireland: A H Ensor (Wanderers); T O Grace (St, Mary's Coll., capt.), P J Lavery (London Irish), C M H Gibson (NIFC), A W McMaster (Ballymena); B J McGann (Cork Constitution), D M Canniffe (Lansdowne); P Orr (Old Wesley), J Cantrell (U C Dublin), P O'Callaghan (Dolphin), M I Keane (Lansdowne), R F Hakin (CIYMS), S McKinney (Dungannon), W P Duggan (Blackrock Coll.), S M Deering (Garryowen). Rep: L Moloney (Garryowen) for Lavery.

Wales: J P R Williams (London Welsh); Gerald Davies (Cardiff), S P Fenwick (Bridgend), R W Gravell, J J Williams (Llanelli); P Bennett (Llanelli), G O

Edwards (Cardiff); A G Faulkner, R W Windsor, G Price (Pontypool), G Wheel (Swansea), A J Martin (Aberavon), T P David (Pontypridd), Mervyn Davies (capt.), T P Evans (Swansea).

For Wales, Gerald Davies (2), Gareth Edwards and Phil Bennett scored tries. Bennett converted three and kicked three penalty goals. Allan Martin kicked one penalty goal.

For Ireland, Barry McGann kicked three penalty goals.

Referee: N R Sanson (Scotland).

Match 314   **WALES v FRANCE**   Cardiff Arms Park. March 6, 1976

Wales won by five penalty goals, one try (19) to one goal, one penalty goal, one try (13)

Mervyn Davies, kicked on the left calf during the opening minutes, refused to go off for treatment; and when the pain was almost intolerable late in the game, found he dare not quit the field because the French rally was at it's peak and threatened to rob Wales of their Grand Slam triumph. "The swelling came up so quickly, I could barely roll my sock down," recalled the Welsh captain. "There was quite a lot of internal bleeding going on; but it was important to the team to stay on. I dare not leave the field because we would have had only 14 men until a replacement arrived and that might have been time enough for France to score." This was typical of Mervyn Davies and a fitting final match for his country, although he never imagined it that way. "My aim is three Grand Slams in a row," he smiled. But three weeks later the man regarded as the world's No.1 in his position, was carried off the Cardiff RFC ground in the 28th minute of the Schweppes Cup semi-final tie between Swansea and Pontypool. Mervyn was fighting for his life, struck by a brain haemorrhage. A weakened blood vessel had ruptured, but the 29-year-old No.8 made a wonderful recovery following brain surgery. It was, however, the end of his playing career. Wales had lost one of their all-time greats.

France scored two tries to Wales's one and it was remarkable that in 10 successive visits to Cardiff, the Tricolours had outscored Wales by 16 tries to 10 – though France won only three of those games. Inspired by 5 ft. 5 in. scrum half Jacques Fouroux, France's "Little Napoleon", the visitors set a storming pace, though some ugly incidents marred events and Graham Price was compelled to go off with a bad eye injury. Mike Knill, the popular Cardiff tight head, came on as a replacement just before half time to win his only cap and play with customary superhuman strength. It was a nail-biting tussle throughout with a tremendous climax as France threw everything at the home defence. A rousing shoulder-charge by JPR Williams (some say it was his greatest tackle for Wales) prevented Gourdon scoring in the corner and Wales again leaned heavily on Phil Bennett, who finished the season with 38 points to better his own record for a season. Wales's aggregate of 102 points was the highest ever in the championship by any country – there seemed no end to these Welsh records, and Gareth Edwards added to them by passing Ken Jones's total of 44 caps. Wales had used only 16 players during this great Grand Slam season.

Wales: J P R Williams (London Welsh); Gerald Davies (Cardiff), S P Fenwick (Bridgend), R W Gravell, J J Williams (Llanelli); P Bennett (Llanelli), G O Edwards (Cardiff); A G Faulkner, R W Windsor, G Price (Pontypool), G Wheel (Swansea), A J Martin (Aberavon), T P David (Pontypridd), Mervyn Davies (capt.), T P Evans (Swansea). Rep: *M Knill (Cardiff) for Price.

France: M Droitecourt (Montferrand); J F Gourdon (Racing Club), R Bertranne (Bagneres), J Pecune (Tarbes), J L Averous (La Voulte); J P Romeu (Montferrand), J Fouroux (La Voulte, capt.): G Cholley (Castres), A Paco (Beziers), R Paparemborde (Pau), J F Imbernon (Perpignan), M Palmie (Beziers), J P Rives (Toulouse), J P Bastiat (Dax), J C Skrela (Toulouse). Rep: J M Aguirre (Bagneres) for Droitecourt.

For Wales, J J Williams scored a try. Phil Bennett (2), Steve Fenwick (2) and Allan Martin kicked penalty goals.

For France, Jean-Francois Gourdon and Jean-Luc Averous scored tries. Jean-Pierre Romeu converted one and kicked a penalty goal.

Referee: J R West (Ireland).

Uncapped Match   **WALES v ARGENTINA**   Cardiff Arms Park. October 16, 1976

Wales won by four penalty goals, two tries (20) to one goal, three penalty goals, one try (19)

The Grand Slam champions desperately wresting victory on their home turf by a one-point margin with the last kick of the match, a penalty goal for a dangerous tackle, was hardly the way 42,000 Welsh fans expected it to be in this tense tussle with rugged Argentina. "I suppose it was rather a lacklustre performance," admitted coach Dawes. "We were probably a yard slower than last season in getting to the ball and with our support work. But we shall put this right." Wales sensationally looked doomed as their 17-6 lead changed into a 17-19 deficit and five minutes of injury time already ticked off. Only the All Blacks had won at the Arms Park since 1968, and now the Pumas, winners against East Wales, Cardiff and Aberavon, were sharpening their claws for the kill. In all probability they would have made it; but giant centre Adolfo Travaglini charged at JPR Williams and almost took the full back's head off with a short-arm tackle. Referee Norman Sanson gave Wales a penalty chance, and Phil Bennett put it over the bar from 40 yards. It was his fourth penalty goal of the match and a kick that saved a nation's pride. Terry Cobner, leading Wales for the first time, summed up: "We all hope the other games won't be so hard."

> **Wales:** J P R Williams (Bridgend); Gerald Davies (Cardiff), R W Gravell, R T Bergiers, J J Williams (Llanelli); P Bennett (Llanelli), G O Edwards (Cardiff); A G Faulkner, R W Windsor, G Price (Pontypool), B Clegg, G Wheel, T P Evans (Swansea), D L Quinnell (Llanelli), T J Cobner (Pontypool, capt.), Rep: J Squire (Newport) for Clegg.

> **Argentina:** M Sansot; D Beccar Varela, A A Travaglini, G Beccar Varela, J M Gauweloose; H Porta, A M Etchegaray (capt.); R L Iraneta, J D Costante, F Insua, E N Branca, J J Ferandez, J Carracedo, R C Mastai, C M Neyra. Rep: J G Braceras for Costante.

For Wales, Gerald Davies and Gareth Edwards scored tries. Phil Bennett kicked four penalty goals.

For Argentina, Jorge Gauweloose and Gonzalo Beccar Varela scored tries. Gonzalo Beccar Varela kicked two penalty goals. Hugo Porta kicked one penalty goal and converted a try.

Referee: N R Sanson (Scotland).

Match 315   **WALES v IRELAND**   Cardiff Arms Park. January 15, 1977

Wales won by two goals, two penalty goals, one dropped goal, one try (25)
to three penalty goals (9)

Regrettably, the Arms Park was the stage for the first sending off in the history of the International Championship. Scottish referee Norman Sanson ordered off Geoff Wheel, the 25-year-old Swansea lock, and Irish No.8 Willie Duggan for punching after 37 minutes of the first half. Wheel, banished in club games in 1972 and 1973, was suspended for four weeks, which put him out of the next fixture, against France; and Duggan received a two-week ban from his

204

union's disciplinary committee. After this sensational episode, France refused to accept Mr. Sanson to control their match with England, commenting that he was "too strict." The way some of the French forwards behaved, it was not surprising the French Federation feared what might happen with a tough referee in charge.

Phil Bennett was the Welsh captain in succession to Mervyn Davies. Terry Cobner, who led the side against Argentina, was unfit and his place at flanker went to new cap Clive Burgess, the tireless Ebbw Vale No.8. Burgess marked his debut with a try. Jeff Squire, another newcomer, filled Mervyn Davies's position while the Pontypool front row was split by the reintroduction of Glyn Shaw, although deposed Faulkner was to rejoin his colleagues for the Grand Slam triumph of 1978. Gareth Edwards was handicapped by hamstring trouble, which developed the previous week helping Cardiff defeat Llanelli in a thrilling Schwepps Cup tie, and this was one of his poorest games for his country. He was not helped by untidy possession from a disappointing pack. However, the Welsh forwards put their game together in the closing stages and, with little more than 10 minutes remaining, turned a 10-9 lead into a convincing margin of success. There were 15 Welsh points in a flurry of late scoring The famous north enclosure no longer was a swaying, singing sea of fans: it had been transformed into a mainly seated area, to the regret of the Beer-can Brigade and the relief of the majority.

Wales: J P R Williams (Bridgend); Gerald Davies (Cardiff), S P Fenwick (Bridgend), *D Burcher (Newport), J J Williams (Llanelli); P Bennett (Llanelli, capt.), G O Edwards (Cardiff); G Shaw (Neath), R W Windsor, G Price (Pontypool), A J Martin (Aberavon), G Wheel, T P Evans (Swansea), *J Squire (Newport), *R C Burgess (Ebbw Vale). Rep: D L Quinnell (Llanelli) for T P Evans.

Ireland: F Wilson (CIYMS); T O Grace (St. Mary's Coll., capt.), A R McKibbin (Instonians), J A McIlrath (Ballymena), D St. J Bowen (Cork Constitution); C M H Gibson (NIFC), R J McGrath (Wanderers); P A Orr (Old Wesley), P C Whelan (Garryowen), T A O Feighery (St, Mary's Coll.), M I Keane (Lansdowne), R F Hakin (CIYMS), S A McKinney (Dungannon), W P Duggan (Blackrock Coll.), S M Deering (Garryowen). Rep: B O Foley (Shannon) for Hakin.

For Wales, Gerald Davies, J P R Williams and Clive Burgess scored tries. Phil Bennett converted two and kicked two penalty goals. Steve Fenwick dropped a goal.

For Ireland, Mike Gibson kicked three penalty goals.

Referee: N R Sanson (Scotland).

Match 316   **FRANCE v WALES**   Parc Des Princes, Paris. February 5, 1977

France won by one goal, two penalty goals, one try (16) to three penalty goals (9)

Wales travelled as underdogs to Paris following their forwards' subdued efforts against Ireland, and this time produced a thoroughly depressing performance as, for the first occasion for 18 full international matches, they failed to score a try. Gareth Edwards again could not make any positive contribution and it seemed the days of this great player were numbered. But he still had some of the old sparks up his jersey – as we were to witness a year later. Many critics rated this French pack as the greatest they had seen with blond bombshell Jean-Pierre Rives and the ruthlessly efficient Jean-Claude Skrela as dynamic flankers, and 6ft. 6in. Jean-Pierre Bastiat a dominating figure at No.8. This was the same pack that had caused Wales so much trouble the previous season, and on their home pitch France took full revenge. Bastiat put Gerald Davies off with concussion in a fierce tackle and promptly repeated the trick and nearly decapitated replacement wing Gareth Evans in the process. Truly, Bastiat was the "Guillotine Tackler." This was France's first game of a season that was to bring them their second Grand Slam – and without a try scored against them.

France: J M Aguirre (Bagneres); D Harize (Toulouse), R Bertranne (Bagneres), F Sangalli (Narbonne), J L Averous (La Voulte); J P Romeu (Montferrand), J Fouroux (Auch, capt.); G Cholley (Castres), A Paco (Beziers), R Paparemborde (Pau), J F Imbernon (Perpignan), M Palmie (Beziers), J P Rives (Toulouse), J P Bastiat (Dax), J C Skrela (Toulouse).

Wales: J P R Williams (Bridgend); Gerald Davies (Cardiff), S P Fenwick (Bridgend), D Burcher (Newport), J J Williams (Llanelli); P Bennett (Llanelli, capt.), G O Edwards (Cardiff); G Shaw (Neath), R W Windsor, G Price (Pontypool), A J Martin (Aberavon), D L Quinnell (Llanelli), R C Burgess (Ebbw Vale), J Squire (Newport), T J Cobner (Pontypool). Rep: *Gareth Evans (Newport) for Gerald Davies.

For France, Jean-Claude Skrela and Dominique Harize scored tries. Jean-Pierre Romeu converted one and kicked two penalty goals.

For Wales, Steve Fenwick kicked three penalty goals.

Referee: A M Hosie (Scotland).

Match 317 WALES v ENGLAND   Cardiff Arms Park. March 5, 1977

Wales won by two penalty goals, two tries (14) to three penalty goals (9)

England's pack that had pulverised Scotland and Ireland, and jolted the giant French eight, came to Cardiff confident they could lick a suspect Welsh forward unit and win the Triple Crown for the first time in 17 years. But Roger Uttley's men met the backlash of Welsh reaction to the biting criticism of their play. It was the finest Welsh performance of the winter with the badly missed Geoff Wheel restored following his month's suspension and Clive Williams, the Aberavon loose head, making a superb debut as deputy for injured "Charlie" Faulkner. Clive was chosen as a British Lion three weeks later. J P R Williams rang up his customary try against England (his fifth) after Allan Martin, playing his best game for his country, served him from a line-out and David Burcher opened the way for the full back to dummy and sweep in. Phil Bennett was a darting runner and highly organised defensive coverer with clever positional anticipation, and although England led 6-0, making a cracking start, they flagged under mounting Welsh pack pressure. "We played badly against Ireland and France," said coach Dawes. "But our possession against England was the best we have obtained. Our scrummaging was the outstanding factor. Success begins and ends at scrummaging." The restoration of Welsh forward power was a pointer to great deeds the following year.

Wales: J P R Williams (Bridgend); Gerald Davies (Cardiff), S P Fenwick (Bridgend), D Burcher (Newport), J J Williams (Llanelli); P Bennett (Llanelli, capt.), G O Edwards (Cardiff); *Clive Williams (Aberavon), R W Windsor, G Price (Pontypool), A J Martin (Aberavon), G Wheel (Swansea), R C Burgess (Ebbw Vale), D L Quinnell (Llanelli), T J Cobner (Pontypool).

England: A J Hignell (Bristol); P J Squires (Harrogate), B J Corless (Moseley), C P Kent (Rosslyn Park), M A C Slemen (Liverpool); M J Cooper (Moseley), M Young (Gosforth); R J Cowling, P J Wheeler (Leicester), F E Cotton (Sale), W B Beaumont (Fylde), N E Horton (Moseley), M Rafter, R M Uttley (capt.), P J Dixon (Gosforth).

For Wales, Gareth Edwards and J P R Williams scored tries. Steve Fenwick kicked two penalty goals.

For England, Alastair Hignell kicked three penalty goals.

Referee: D I H Burnett (Ireland).

Wales won by two goals, two penalty goals (18) to one goal, one dropped goal (9)

Gareth Edwards flew back from the United States, where he competed in the World Superstars contest at Pine Mountain, Georgia, just in time to join the Welsh team as they held their Thursday run-out before travelling to Edinburgh. Edwards had assured the WRU selectors he would be back and was allowed to keep his substantial "appearance" money from the Superstars organizers, although such monetary rewards were later banned as illegal under the amateur code. Wales's stirring victory to achieve the Triple Crown for the 14th occasion, featured a brilliant team try. It was launched when J P R slipped the ball to Fenwick as the full back was tackled, and the Bridgend centre started an attack out of defence. Gerald Davies dodged away, linking with Phil Bennett and Burcher; and Burcher lobbed an in-pass to Fenwick, who flicked the ball on with one hand, into the grasp of Bennett. He side-stepped and raced to the posts. It was typical of the Welsh attacking magic that enthralled thousands during the Second Golden Era. Scotland without Lion lock Gordon Brown, under suspension for 12 weeks following rough play in a club match, recalled "Mighty Mouse" McLauchlan, the 34-year-old loose head, and the home front row gave Wales an uncomfortable tussle.

Scotland: A R Irvine (Heriot's FP); W B B Gammell (Edinburgh Wands.), A G Cranston, J M Renwick (Hawick), D Shedden (West of Scotland); I R McGeechan (Headingley, capt.), D W Morgan (Stewart's-Melville FP); J McLauchlan (Jordanhill), D F Madsen (Gosforth), A B Carmichael (West of Scotland), I A Barnes (Hawick), A F McHarg (London Scottish), W S Watson (Boroughmuir), D S M Macdonald, M A Biggar (London Scottish).

Wales: J P R Williams (Bridgend); Gerald Davies (Cardiff), S P Fenwick (Bridgend), D Burcher (Newport), J J Williams (Llanelli); P Bennett (Llanelli, capt.), G O Edwards (Cardiff); Clive Williams (Aberavon), R W Windsor, G Price (Pontypool), A J Martin (Aberavon), G Wheel (Swansea), R C Burgess (Ebbw Vale), D L Quinnell (Llanelli), T J Cobner (Pontypool).

For Wales, J J Williams and Phil Bennett scored tries. Bennett converted both and kicked two penalty goals.

For Scotland, Andy Irvine scored a try. Irvine converted and Ian McGeechan dropped a goal.

Referee G Domercq (France).

Wales won by three penalty goals (9) to two penalty goals (6)

Gareth Edwards, winning his 50th cap, was ruthlessly marked by England's back row. They fanned swiftly from the scrums and Wales were denied a try at Twickenham for the first time for 16 years. Edwards's long touch-finding was a feature in the rain on a waterlogged pitch. If Hignell had kicked his penalty chances, England could have at least saved the match.

England: A J Hignell (Bristol); P J Squires (Harrogate), B J Corless (Moseley), P W Dodge (Leicester), M A C Slemen (Liverpool); J P Horton (Bath), M Young (Gosforth); B G Nelmes (Cardiff), P J Wheeler (Leicester), M A Burton (Gloucester), W B Beaumont (Fylde, capt.), N E Horton (Toulouse), M Rafter (Bristol), J P Scott, R J Mordell (Rosslyn Park).

Wales: J P R Williams (Bridgend); Gerald Davies (Cardiff), S P Fenwick (Bridgend), R W Gravell, J J Williams (Llanelli); P Bennett (Llanelli, capt.), G O Edwards (Cardiff); A G Faulkner, R W Windsor, G Price (Pontypool), A J Martin

(Aberavon), G Wheel (Swansea), J Squire (Newport), D L Quinnell (Llanelli), T J Cobner (Pontypool).

For Wales, Phil Bennett kicked three penalty goals.

For England, Alastair Hignell kicked two penalty goals.

Referee: N R Sanson (Scotland).

Match 320   WALES v SCOTLAND   Cardiff Arms Park. February 18, 1978

Wales won by one dropped goal, one penalty goal, four tries (22)
to two penalty goals, two tries (14)

Ray Gravell and Derek Quinnell, Llanelli clubmates, scored their first tries for Wales, Quinnell with a rush for the corner-flag, handing off three tacklers en route. His son Scott repeated the feat in spectacular manner against France in 1994. Gareth Edwards snapped up his 20th try with a dummy, hand-off and dynamic burst through a tackle. A few hours after the match the worst blizzard for 30 years hit South Wales and cut off Cardiff. The Welsh team were snowed in at their hotel until Monday. The Scots went out by coach to fight their way through to Birmingham to get a flight home.

Wales: J P R Williams (Bridgend); Gerald Davies (Cardiff), S P Fenwick (Bridgend), R W Gravell, J J Williams (Llanelli); P Bennett (Llanelli, capt.), G O Edwards (Cardiff); A G Faulkner, R W Windsor, G Price (Pontypool), A J Martin (Aberavon), G Wheel (Swansea), J Squire (Newport), D L Quinnell (Llanelli), T J Cobner (Pontypool).

Scotland: B H Hay (Boroughmuir); W B B Gammell (Edinburgh Wands.), J M Renwick (Hawick), A G Cranston (Hawick), D Shedden (West of Scotland); I R McGeechan (Headingley), D W Morgan (Stewart's Melville FP, capt.); J McLauchlan (Jordanhill), C T Deans (Hawick), N E K Pender (Hawick), A F McHarg (London Scottish), A J Tomes (Hawick), M A Biggar (London Scottish), D S M Macdonald (West of Scotland), C B Hegarty (Hawick). Rep: C G Hogg (Boroughmuir) for Shedden.

For Wales, Gareth Edwards, Ray Gravell, Steve Fenwick and Derek Quinell scored tries. Phil Bennett dropped a goal and kicked a penalty goal.

For Scotland, Jim Renwick and Alan Tomes scored tries. Douglas Morgan kicked two penalty goals.

Referee: J R West (Ireland).

Match 321   IRELAND v WALES   Lansdowne Road, Dublin. March 4, 1978

Wales won by four penalty goals, two tries (20)
to three penalty goals, one dropped goal, one try (16)

Never before had a country registered Triple Crown victories in three successive seasons (though England were to improve on the Welsh achievement in the Nineties). But Wales had to battle desperately and it was only a late try by wing J J Williams and a fourth penalty shot by Fenwick that won the prize. Wales, thoroughly unsettled by the fiery visitors, lost a 13-3 lead. Ireland clawed their way back to 13-all as Tony Ward put over two penalty goals and dropped a goal from an indirect free-kick as he first tapped the ball. The Irish try came from a J P R Williams blunder. The full back sliced a clearance under pressure and the ball pitched behind his goal-line for Maloney to pounce and make it all square. However, Bobby Windsor rolled away from a maul-smuggle, flicked to Gareth Edwards and he handed on to Fenwick. The centre's long lobbed pass sent J J sprinting for a memorable try as he was tackled. Then Fenwick kicked his fourth penalty goal. His 16 points came from a try and those four vital penalty shots, the first from almost 60 yards. Ireland's magnificent display brought their highest score against Wales for 51 years. Mike Gibson led Ireland out to mark his then world record 64th cap in front of 51,000 in perfect conditions. JPR was booed repeatedly following his late tackle on Gibson. JPR admitted it was a little late. "But I've done it before and I'll do it again. I had to stop a likely try," he said.

Ireland: A H Ensor (Wanderers); C M H Gibson (NIFC), A R McKibbin (London Irish), P P McNaughton (Greystones), A C McLennan (Wanderers); A J P Ward (Garryowen), J J Maloney (St. Mary's Coll., capt.); P A Orr (Old Wesley), P C Whelan (Garryowen), E M J Byrne (Blackrock Coll.), M I Keane (Lansdowne), H W Steele (Ballymena), S A McKinney (Dungannon), W P Duggan, J F Slattery (Blackrock Coll.).

Wales: J P R Williams (Bridgend); Gerald Davies (Cardiff), S P Fenwick (Bridgend), R W Gravell, J J Williams (Llanelli); P Bennett (Llanelli, capt.), G O Edwards (Cardiff); A G Faulkner, R W Windsor, G Price (Pontypool), A J Martin (Aberavon), G Wheel (Swansea), J Squire (Newport), D L Quinnell (Llanelli), T J Cobner (Pontypool).

For Wales, Steve Fenwick and J J Williams scored tries. Fenwick kicked four penalty goals.

For Ireland, John Maloney scored a try. Tony Ward dropped a goal and kicked three penalty goals.

Referee: G Domercq (France).

Match 322   WALES v FRANCE   Cardiff Arms Park. March 18, 1978

Wales won by one goal, two dropped goals, one try (16) to one dropped goal, one try (7)

The winners would be Grand Slammers. France were title-holders; but Wales were favourites on home ground – and won with Phil Bennett playing his greatest game. He scored two tries – the first time a Welsh fly half had collected two tries in a match since Dickie Ralph 47 years earlier in the 35-3 win over France. It was the first time for 26 years for a Welsh player to obtain two tries in a match against the French – since Gareth Griffiths in 1952. Bennett took his aggregate (166 points), past the then European record for international rugby of 158 by Ireland's Tom Kiernan. In 10 seasons, Wales had been outright champions six times and twice joint first; in the other years they were in second place. They had collected three Grand Slams and five Triple Crowns. Coach John Dawes considered, "This team deserves to be recognised as one of the greatest of all time." Allan Martin, playing his finest game, fed the pass from a wheeled scrum to enable Bennett to burst across for his first try; then J J Williams, pinned on the touchline, hurled the ball inside one-handed for Bennett to snap up and dive over again. Bennett had withdrawn on the Wednesday because of foot trouble, but was persuaded to change his mind. He played with supports built into his boots and protection around his right big toe. Tony Faulkner, the 37-year-old prop, had kept his age a secret for a long time. "It's not how old I am, but how well I play!" he insisted. Another secret revealed was that this was Gareth Edwards's final match for Wales. He made it known in a Sunday newspaper.

Wales: J P R Williams (Bridgend); J J Williams, R W Gravell (Llanelli), S P Fenwick (Bridgend) Gareth Evans (Newport); P Bennett (Llanelli, capt.), G O Edwards (Cardiff); A G Faulkner, R W Windsor, G Price (Pontypool), A J Martin (Aberavon), G Wheel (Swansea), J Squire (Newport), D L Quinnell (Llanelli), T J Cobner (Pontypool).

France: J M Aguirre (Bagneres); D Bustaffa (Carcassonne), R Bertranne (Bagneres), C Belascain (Bayonne), G Noves (Toulouse); B Vivies (Agen), J Gallion (Toulon); G Cholley (Castres), A Paco (Beziers), R Paparemborde (Pau), F Haget (Biarritz), M Palmie (Beziers), J P Rives (Toulouse), J P Bastiat (Dax, capt.), J C Skrela (Toulouse).

For Wales, Phil Bennett scored two tries and converted one. Gareth Edwards and Steve Fenwick dropped goals.

For France, Jean-Claude Skrela scored a try. Bernard Vivies dropped a goal.

Referee: A Welsby (England).

Match 323   **AUSTRALIA v WALES**   Ballymore, Brisbane. June 11, 1978

Australia won by one goal, four penalty goals (18) to two tries (8)

It was disaster Down Under for Wales when the Grand Slam champions visited Australia for a nine-match tour in May-June 1978. Of the nine games, the tourists lost four, including both Tests. Phil Bennett was unavailable for the trip. There was controversy before the first Test, played on a Sunday, when Wales rejected Bob Burnett as referee following his performance in their match with Queensland. The Australian RU refused to change their decision and the Welsh party, equally intransingent, were on the verge of packing their bags to return home without completing the tour when manager Clive Rowlands announced "under protest" that Burnett would be acceptable. Australia had called the bluff! More controversy followed with flying boots and fists and considerable dissension from players. Referee Burnett complained to skipper Terry Cobner that Geoff Wheel had struck him and threatened to send him off. Cobner warned he would take his team off if the referee took that action. Wheel denied he had punched the referee. Burnett then added he thought the blow quite likely was an accident. It was generally agreed that the refereeing was below international standard. Gerald Davies became Wales's most capped threequarter with his 45th appearance.

Australia: L E Monaghan; P G Batch, A Slack, M Knight, P Crowe; P E McLean, R G Hauser, S Finnane, P A Horton, S Pilecki, D W Hillhouse, G Fay, G Cornelsen, M E Loane, A A Shaw (capt.).

Wales: J P R Williams (Bridgend); Gerald Davies (Cardiff), S P Fenwick (Bridgend), R W R Gravell, J J Williams (Llanelli); *W Gareth Davies (Cardiff), *D B Williams (Newport); A G Faulkner, R W Windsor, G Price (Pontypool), A J Martin (Aberavon), G Wheel (Swansea), J Squire (Newport), D L Quinnell (Llanelli), T J Cobner (Pontypool, capt.). Rep: *S Lane (Cardiff) for Squire.

For Australia, Phil Crowe scored a try. Paul McLean kicked four penalty goals and one conversion.

For Wales, Gerald Davies and Brynmor Williams scored tries.

Referee: R T Burnett (Australia).

Match 324   **AUSTRALIA v WALES**   Sydney Sports Ground. June 17, 1978

Australia won by three penalty goals, two dropped goals, one try (19)
to two penalty goals, one dropped goal, two tries (17)

Wales had never scored so many points and lost. Their confidence destroyed by defeats, injuries and 'biased' referees, they had to play full back JPR Williams at flank forward, though he spent the last half-hour in his customary role. Terry Holmes scored a try on debut. Gareth

Awesome! Wales's human scrummaging machine pile-drives into England at the Arms Park in 1975 during the era when Pontypool's terrible trio of Tony Faulkner, Bobby Windsor and the granite-like Graham Price were the most fearsome front row in world rugby. They were forwards who would dog it out until hell froze over if need be!

Super second row pair. Allan Martin and Geoff Wheel played together for Wales in 27 matches, Wheel jumping in the front and Martin in the middle. They set the highest standards also in every department, two of the legends of Welsh rugby. Here in action against Scotland in 1976.

Wales won the Grand Slam on three occasions and the Triple Crown five times during the Seventies. This was the side that defeated England and took the Crown in 1977. Standing (left to right): David Burcher, Steve Fenwick, Graham Price, Geoff Wheel, Allan Martin, Clive Burgess, Clive Williams, Terry Cobner. Seated: JPR Williams, Derek Quinnell, Bobby Windsor, Phil Bennett (capt), Gareth Edwards, Gerald Davies, JJ Williams.

Many avow Phil Bennett was a more accomplished tactical kicker than Barry John. Whatever, Benny was every bit as audacious as a runner. Barry was laid-back; Benny was as vibrant as a harp string. Top: Wales skipper Phil clears before Ireland's Mike Gibson can charge down in 1977. Below: Bennett on the burst against France in 1976.

High stepper. JPR Williams (top) escapes Irish tackler Frank Wilson in 1977. Steve Fenwick runs shotgun to his famous full back, who scored six tries for his country. One of those tries (below) as JPR evades a line of would-be tacklers to cross against the 1977 England team.

Over the top. Gareth Edwards lobs a teaser against England's 1977 team with Derek Quinnell, Clive Burgess, Bobby Windsor and Terry Cobner interested in the possiblities.

Another of his 20 tries. Gareth Edwards lunges across the Scottish line in 1978 to the satisfaction of Ray Gravell and Jeff Squire.

Reach for the sky. Wales have enjoyed many impressive jumpers. Delme Thomas (top left) always played with his sleeves rolled up. Allan Martin (top right) was more sartorially conscious, but performed the same expert role. Geoff Wheel (below), the Swansea Ripper, was a hard-man of many parts. Rummaging about in the maul was his speciality.

Wales, champions in 1979. Standing (left to right): Graham Price, John Richardson, Jeff Squire, Allan Martin, Mike Roberts, Alan Phillips, David Richards, Billy James (rep). Seated: Paul Ringer, Elgan Rees, JJ Williams, JPR Williams (capt), Derek Quinnell, Steve Fenwick, Terry Holmes, Gareth Davies. In front: Brynmor Williams (rep), Clive Griffiths (rep).

Power on the hoof. Phil Davies, once Wales's most-capped forward before Gareth Llewellyn overtook him, blasts a path through Romania in 1988.

Take that! Wales skipper Brian Price retaliates and Ireland's Noel Murphy takes a spectacular dive at the Arms Park in 1969. Referee Doug McMahon penalised Wales. He said, "I've had rougher matches to control. Some players got excited."

Perhaps someone muttered, "You're a cad and a bounder!" Anyway, there was a lively set-to with England's Wade Dooley in prominent action in the 1987 clash at the Arms Park. Disciplinary action followed after the match.

Royal event. The Queen and Duke of Edinburgh are shown to their seats by WRU centenary president Cliff Jones in November 1980 to the watch Wales/England v Scotland/Ireland match. It was the first occasion for the Queen to watch a rugby match in Cardiff and she saw Wales/England win 37-33.

Terry Holmes swings a dive-pass away against France in 1980. Wales were 18-9 winners with Holmes among the try-scorers. Watching events are (from the left) Paul Ringer, Graham Price and Geoff Wheel.

Tough as teak and one of the most knowledgeable players to wear the scarlet jersey. Terry Holmes (left) was truly a juggernaut among scrum halves. He scored eight tries for Wales, four in his first nine games, a strike rate which even Gareth Edwards (scorer of 20 scrum half tries) could not approach.

Holmes was combative to the end. But he could not stop France's wonderman, Serge Blanco, scoring at Cardiff in 1982 (below). Terry also scored in the match, which Wales won 22-12.

Wales lost their final 1988 game to France 10-9 and so failed by one point to claim the Grand Slam. This was the team who just failed. Back row (left to right): Mike Hall, Ian Watkins, David Young, Paul Moriarty, Phil May, Rob Norster, Rowland Phillips, Richie Collins, 'Staff' Jones, Mark Jones, Jonathan Griffiths. Front row: Mark Ring, Jeremy Pugh, Kevin Phillips, Paul Thorburn, Ieuan Evans, Bleddyn Bowen (capt), Adrian Hadley, Jonathan Davies, Robert Jones, Glen Webbe.

That wide miss-out pass. Robert Ackerman uses it fluently against England at Twickenham in 1984. The ball speeds past Bleddyn Bowen and on to full back Howell Davies.

Smooth as silk and with length and accuracy. That was the trademark of Robert Jones with his fluent service. His chip into the box was another precision aspect of his game. Here he fires the ball away against Scotland in 1990.

David Bishop dive-passes against the 1984 Australians. He also scored a spectacular juggling try. Combative, colourful, courageous: Dai Bish was the most dynamic rugby machine of all time – so say his host of admirers.

Full back in a hurry. Not quite feet of flames, but a deadly boot that made him Wales's top scorer until Neil Jenkins came along to rewrite the record pages. Paul Thorburn (left), however, holds the record for the longest penalty goal kicked by a Welsh player. Measured from kick to crossbar, it was reckoned the ball travelled an amazing 70 yards, 8½ inches, although another couple of yards at least could be added for the ball's landfall. The goal stunned Scotland, who lost 22-15 at the Arms Park in 1986.

Allan Bateman (below) looks to make mischief for Scotland in 1990 with Mark Ring ranging alongside. Bateman did everything by the book: Ring wrote his own!

Ieuan Evans scored only one try against England – but what a try that was! It helped bring 10-9 victory in 1993 as he kicked on and chased past a startled and rooted Rory Underwood.

Another typical Ieuan Evans try as he races away to help Llanelli defeat world champions Australia at Stradey Park in November 1992 by 13-9. Ieuan scored a record 33 tries for Wales, captained his country a record 28 times and holds the record of 72 caps.

The Welsh team that defeated England in 1993. Standing (left to right): Alan Reynolds (rep),
Rupert Moon (rep), Richard Webster, Stuart Davies, Tony Copsey, Gareth Llewellyn, Emyr Lewis,
Ricky Evans, Nigel Meek, Hugh Williams-Jones, Paul Kawulok (rep), Anthony Clement (rep),
John D Davies (rep), Andrew Lamerton (rep). Seated: Scott Gibbs, Mike Hall, Wayne Proctor,
Ieuan Evans (capt), Robert Jones, Mike Rayer, Neil Jenkins.

Kevin Phillips and Neath team-mates Brian Williams and Glyn Llewellyn smuggle the ball back
to scrum half Robert Jones against England in 1991. Neath's pack had an impressive reputation
for rucking and smuggling.

Never has there been such a prolific scorer for Wales. Neil Jenkins, Ponytpridd's Red Baron, shoots down the opposition with deadly precision and can sell a crafty dummy. It certainly does not pay defenders to relax their guard. Here he tests Ireland's tacklers in 1994.

Wales's most-capped outside half is Neil Jenkins. He has been capped also in the centre and at full back (but don't remind him of his reluctant full back days for Wales!). Here, happy at fly half, he spins out a pass against France in 1991.

Davies's tactical kicking was superb, but the intimidating home forwards unsettled Wales for long spells. There was an explosive punch-up at the start of the match and Graham Price had his jaw fractured by a sneak punch from Steve Finnane. Gerald Davies captained Wales in his last game before his shock retirement in September 1978. Paul McLean, scorer of 14 vital points in the first Test, was on target again, landing three penalty shots and a drop-goal. He played both Tests with a broken thumb, always in pain. Manager Rowlands, who vigorously attacked dirty play at the after-match dinner in a pointed reference to Finnane, commented, "If I were ashamed at times of being a Welshman at Canberra, where we lost to Capital Territories, I was very proud of the Welsh players today. They were magnificent in defeat."

Australia: L E Monaghan; P G Batch, A Slack, M Knight, P Crowe; P E McLean, R G Hauser; S Finnane, P A Horton, S Pilecki, D W Hillhouse, G Fay, G Cornelsen, M E Loane, A A Shaw (capt.).

Wales: *A Donovan (Swansea); Gerald Davies (Cardiff), S P Fenwick (Bridgend), R W R Gravell, J J Williams (Llanelli); *W Gareth Davies (Cardiff), *Terry Holmes (Cardiff); A G Faulkner, R W Windsor, G Price (Pontypool), A J Martin (Aberavon), G Wheel (Swansea), J P R Williams (Bridgend), *Clive Davis (Newbridge), S Lane (Cardiff). Reps: *J Richardson (Aberavon) for Price, Gareth Evans (Newport) for Donovan.

For Australia, Mark Loane scored a try. Paul McLean kicked three penalty goals and dropped a goal. Larry Monaghan dropped a goal.

For Wales, Gerald Davies and Terry Holmes scored tries. Gareth Davies kicked two penalty goals and dropped a goal.

Referee: R G Byres (Australia).

Match 325 WALES v NEW ZEALAND   Cardiff Arms Park. November 11, 1978

New Zealand won by three penalty goals, one try (13) to four penalty goals (12)

This match goes down in history for its Lineout of Shame. Andy Haden, the middle jumper for NZ, deliberately threw himself out of a lineout in an attempt to make the referee believe he had been barged. But the referee awarded a penalty for a different reason. He claimed Geoff Wheel had climbed on Frank Oliver's shoulder at the front of the line. Oliver had closed in on Wheel, making no real effort to contest the ball, and Wheel was amazed when Roger Quittenton penalised him. In a book revelation later, Haden admitted the All Blacks had such a lineout plan to 'steal' a penalty if events were going against them. Anyway, in the closing minutes that penalty was put between the Welsh posts by Brian McKechnie, his third of the match, angled but at short range. McKechnie had gone on as replacement when Clive Currie had his jaw broken in a flying charge by Fenwick. Clem Thomas, who had played in the last Welsh team that defeated New Zealand 25 years earlier, condemned the tourists in a television interview as 'cheats.' The All Blacks revived after a disappointing first half, during which they fell 12-4 in arrears, but most critics were of the opinion that Wales deserved to win, although they could not score a try. Welsh chances were considered slim after four great players in Phil Bennett, Gerald Davies, Gareth Edwards and Terry Cobner had left rugby for various reasons.

Wales: J P R Williams (Bridgend, capt.); J J Williams (Llanelli), S P Fenwick (Bridgend), R W R Gravell (Llanelli), Clive Rees (London Welsh); W Gareth Davies, Terry Holmes (Cardiff); A J Faulkner, R Windsor, G Price (Pontypool), A J Martin (Aberavon), G Wheel (Swansea), J Squire (Pontypool), D L Quinnell (Llanelli), *P Ringer (Ebbw Vale).

New Zealand: C J Currie; S S Wilson, B J Robertson, W M Osborne, B G Williams; O D Bruce, D S Loveridge; B R Johnstone, A G Dalton, W K Bush, A

M Haden, F J Oliver, R M Rutledge, G A Seear, G N K Mourie (capt.). Rep: B J McKechnie for Currie.

For New Zealand, Stu Wilson scored a try. Brian McKechnie kicked three penalty goals.

For Wales, Gareth Davies kicked three penalty goals. Steve Fenwick kicked one penalty goal.

Referee R C Quittenton (England).

Match 326   SCOTLAND v WALES   Murrayfield. January 20, 1979

Wales won by one goal, three penalty goals, one try (19) to three penalty goals, one try (13)

All the record books of the time showed Terry Holmes as scoring a try, but Holmes revealed some time later that when Wales drove a scrum over the Scottish line, "It was Derek Quinnell's hand that touched it down first." After three succesive defeats against southern hemisphere countries, Wales urgently needed to taste success again. They did, but had to wait until eight minutes from the end when Quinnell's fingers did the job and Fenwick converted. Thousands thought it was the end of the match with that kick and swarmed on to the pitch, but French referee Francois Palmade had the ground cleared for the game to continue for a further two minutes. Elgan Rees, a Lions' Test player of 1977 in NZ, scored on debut – the first time a Welsh back had achieved that distinction at Murrayfield since centre Graham Jones in the all-Cardiff threequarter line of 1930.

Scotland: A R Irvine (Heriot's FP); K W Robertson (Melrose), J M Renwick (Hawick), I R McGeechan (Headingley, capt.), B H Hay (Boroughmuir); J Y Rutherford (Selkirk), A J M Lawson (London Scottish); J McLauchlan (Jordanhill), C T Deans (Hawick), R F Cunningham (Gala), A J Tomes (Hawick), A F McHarg, M A Biggar (London Scottish), I K Lambie (Watsonians), G Dickson (Gala).

Wales: J P R Williams (Bridgend, capt.); *H E Rees (Neath), R W R Gravell (Llanelli), S P Fenwick (Bridgend), J J Williams (Llanelli); W Gareth Davies, Terry Holmes (Cardiff); A J Faulkner, R Windsor, G Price (Pontypool), A J Martin (Aberavon), G Wheel (Swansea), J Squire (Pontypool), D L Quinnell (Llanelli), P Ringer (Ebbw Vale).

For Scotland, Andy Irvine scored a try and kicked three penalty goals.

For Wales, Elgan Rees and Derek Quinnell scored tries. Steve Fenwick converted one and kicked three penalty goals.

Referee: F Palmade (France).

Match 327   WALES v IRELAND   Cardiff Arms Park. February 3, 1979

Wales won by two goals, four penalty goals (24) to two goals, three penalty goals (21)

Coach John Dawes summed up, "We scored 24 points playing badly. But it would be harsh to judge our back division because they were given poor quality ball. One thing you always get from Ireland is fifteen tackling players. Welsh teams of the past have been able to overcome it. This team did not have the same qualities. The players who have replaced our world-class players are not world class yet." This was Ireland's biggest total against Wales and the largest number of points they had ever scored to finish up losers. In scoring try for try, they scored with smart passing or running, whereas Wales had to rely on Irish errors under pressure for their tries. Steve Fenwick repeated his feat of 16 points against Ireland the previous season to win the match.

Wales: J P R Williams (Bridgend, capt.); Elgan Rees (Neath), R W R Gravell (Llanelli), S P Fenwick (Bridgend), J J Williams (Llanelli); W Gareth Davies, Terry Holmes (Cardiff); A J Faulkner, R Windsor, G Price (Pontypool), A J Martin (Aberavon), G A D Wheel (Swansea), P Ringer, D L Quinnell (Llanelli), J Squire (Pontypool). Rep: S Lane (Cardiff) for Wheel.

Ireland: R M Spring (Lansdowne); T J Kennedy (St. Mary's Coll.), A R McKibbin (London Irish), P P McNaughton (Greystones), A C McLennan (Wanderers); A J P Ward (Garryowen), C S Patterson (Instonians); P A Orr (Old Wesley), P C Whelan (Garryowen), G A J McLoughlin (Shannon), M I Keane (Lansdowne), H W Steele (Ballymena), C C Tucker (Shannon), M E Gibson (Lansdowne), J F Slattery (Blackrock Coll., capt.).

For Wales, Allan Martin and Paul Ringer scored tries. Steve Fenwick converted both and kicked four penalty goals.

For Ireland, Alf 'Freddie' McLennan and Colin Patterson scored tries. Tony Ward converted both and kicked three penalty goals.

Referee: A M Hosie (Scotland).

Match 328   FRANCE v WALES   Parc Des Princes, Paris. February 17, 1979

France won by two penalty goals, two tries (14) to three penalty goals, one try (13)

Terry Holmes, the armour-plated 'ninth forward', was man of the match, but Wales were fortunate to keep the margin to one point. Skipper J P R Williams had warned his team, "If we play as we did against Ireland we will lose." Because of a dispute by television technicians in France, there was no live TV for Welsh viewers. It was the Hole in the Stand Match. some concrete shedding had been noticed as extremes of temperature caused slight structural damage during the very cold spell. It was thought the match might have to be switched to the old Stade Colombes. However, on the Thursday the crisis was over and repairs had been carried out.

France: J M Aguirre (Bagneres); J F Gourdon, R Bertranne (Bagneres), C Belascain (Bayonne), G Noves (Toulouse); A Caussade (Lourdes), J Gallion (Toulon); A Vaquerin, A Paco (Beziers), R Paparemborde (Pau), A Maleig (Oloron), F Haget (Biarritz), J L Joinel (Brive), A Guilbert (Toulon), J P Rives (Toulouse, capt.).

Wales: J P R Williams (Bridgend, capt.); Elgan Rees (Neath), *D S Richards (Swansea), S P Fenwick (Bridgend), J J Williams (Llanelli); W Gareth Davies, Terry Holmes (Cardiff); A G Faulkner, R W Windsor, G Price (Pontypool), A J Martin (Aberavon), *Barry Clegg (Swansea), J Squire (Pontypool), D L Quinnell, P Ringer (Llanelli).

For France, Jean-Francois Gourdon scored two tries. Jean-Michel Aguirre kicked two penalty goals.

For Wales, Terry Holmes scored a try. Steve Fenwick kicked three penalty goals.

Referee: D I H Burnett (Ireland).

Match 329   WALES v ENGLAND   Cardiff Arms Park. March 17, 1979

Wales won by two goals, one dropped goal, three tries (27) to one penalty goal (3)

Mike Roberts, aged 33, first capped nine years earlier, was brought back as deputy for injured Geoff Wheel after four years out of the national side. Grey and grizzled Mike – the

Edward G Robinson of the Welsh pack – scored the try from close range that launched a devastating burst of 14 points in a nine-minute spell in the second half and Wales had won the Triple Crown for a fourth consecutive season. This despite the team suffering a spate of injuries before selection. The famous Pontypool front row was no more, Tony Faulkner suffering a knee problem and Bobby Windsor being in hospital with first degree burns on his back from lime markings on the Pontypool pitch the previous Saturday. J P R Williams went off in the second half to have eight stitches in a gashed calf and Clive Griffiths replaced him to win his first cap and set up a thrilling try for Elgan Rees. It was the last game for J J Williams after 30 consecutive appearances. A record £100 was paid for stand tickets and £35 for ground after England skipper Bill Beaumont said they would beat Wales. Some hope!

Wales: J P R Williams (Bridgend, capt.); Elgan Rees (Neath), D S Richards (Swansea), S P Fenwick (Bridgend), J J Williams (Llanelli); W Gareth Davies, T D Holmes (Cardiff); S J Richardson (Aberavon), *A J Phillips (Cardiff), G Price (Pontypool), A J Martin (Aberavon), M G Roberts (London Welsh), J Squire (Pontypool), D L Quinnell, P Ringer (Llanelli), Rep: *Clive Griffiths (Llanelli) for J P R Williams.

England: A J Hignell (Bristol); P J Squires (Harrogate), R M Cardus (Roundhay), P W Dodge (Leicester), M A C Slemen (Liverpool); W N Bennett (London Welsh), P Kingston (Gloucester); C E Smart (Newport), P J Wheeler (Leicester), G S Pearce (Northampton), W B Beaumont (Fylde, capt.), N E Horton (Toulouse), M Rafter (Bristol), J P Scott (Cardiff), A Neary (Broughton Park).

For Wales, David Richards, Mike Roberts, Paul Ringer J J Williams and Elgan Rees scored tries. Allan Martin and Steve Fenwick each converted one. Gareth Davies dropped a goal.

For England, Neil Bennett kicked a penalty goal.

Referee: J P Bonnet (France).

Uncapped Match   WALES v ROMANIA   Cardiff Arms Park. October 6, 1979

Wales won by two dropped goals, one penalty goal, one try (13)
to one goal, two penalty goals (12)

Wales amazingly selected centre Ray Gravell on the wing. "I'm surprised," he admitted, which perhaps was the understatement of the year. Coach John Dawes called it a "calculated risk". Another questionable choice was that of Llanelli fly half or centre Peter Morgan as full back – a role he had occupied on just three occasions. However, a natural footballer, he played superbly on a day of anxiety for his team, who won by a whisker. The unbeaten Romanians (they had defeated Ebbw Vale, Pontypridd, North Wales and West Wales) took a 12-6 lead before Gareth Davies worked a double dummy to his centres and interpassed with Peter Morgan. Then Gareth put Jeff Griffiths racing in to score with a lovely side-step. Gareth Davies settled matters with two dropped goals.

Wales: Peter Morgan (Llanelli); R W R Gravell (Llanelli), S P Fenwick (Bridgend), D S Richards (Swansea), Jeff Griffiths (Llanelli); W Gareth Davies, T D Holmes (Cardiff); Clive Williams (Swansea), R W Windsor, G Price (Pontypool), R Norster (Cardiff), A J Martin (Aberavon), J Squire (Pontypool), D L Quinnell (capt.), P Ringer (Llanelli).

Romania: M Bucos; M Aldea, I Zafiescu, I Constantin, P Motrescu; D Alexandru, M Paraschiv; C Dinu, M Munteanu, C Scarlat, I Pintea, M Ionescu, F Murariu, G Dumitru (capt.), E Stoica.

For Wales, Jeff Griffiths scored a try. Gareth Davies dropped two goals. Steve Fenwick kicked a penalty goal.

For Romania, Marin Ionescu scored a try. Mihai Bucos converted. Ion Constantin kicked two penalty goals.

Referee: F Palmade (France).

Match 330   WALES v FRANCE   Cardiff Arms Park. January 19, 1980

Wales won by one goal, three tries (18) to one goal, one dropped goal (9)

For the first time in 30 years Wales scored four tries against France in Cardiff – since the Grand Slam season of 1950. But Wales began badly, unable to win possession in the bitingly cold wind. Welsh watchers shivered with apprehension. "It was just a case of nerves," explained new captain Jeff Squire. "Once we settled down the spirit of the side came through." Elgan Rees crossed five times, but twice lost the ball and only one try was awarded by referee Alan Hosie. New coach John Lloyd summed up, "Possibly we could have won by 30 points if we had taken all our chances." Two-tier East Terrace was opened, holding 13,250 with a schoolchildren enclosure for 1,600. The £40,000 electronic scoreboard was used for the first time.

Wales; W R Blyth (Swansea); Elgan Rees (Neath), D S Richards (Swansea), S P Fenwick (Bridgend), *L Keen (Aberavon); W Gareth Davies, T D Holmes (Cardiff); Clive Williams (Swansea), A J Phillips (Cardiff), G Price (Pontypool), A J Martin (Aberavon), G Wheel (Swansea), P Ringer (Llanelli), *E T Butler, J Squire (Pontypool, capt.).

France: J M Aguirre (Bagneres); D Bustaffa (Carcassonne), R Bertranne (Bagneres), D Cordorniou (Narbonne), F Costes (Montferrand); A Caussade (Lourdes), J Gallion (Toulon); P Salas (Narbonne), A Paco (Beziers), R Paparemborde (Pau), F Haget (Biarritz), J F Marchal (Lourdes), J P Rives (Toulouse, capt.), A Maleig (Oloron), J L Joinel (Brive).

For Wales, Elgan Rees, Terry Holmes, David Richards and Graham Price scored tries. Gareth Davies converted one.

For France, Jean-Francois Marchal scored a try. Alain Caussade converted and dropped a goal.

Referee: A M Hosie (Scotland).

Match 331   ENGLAND v WALES   Twickenham. February 16, 1980

England won by three penalty goals (9) to two tries (8)

After 14 minutes, referee David Burnett ordered off Paul Ringer for a head high tackle on John Horton. Ringer thrust his hand into Horton's face after the outside half had punted on. The penalty was awarded where the ball pitched and Dusty Hare kicked the first of his three match-winning goals. Ringer was suspended for eight weeks. It had been an exceptionally tense start to the game and the referee called the captains together to instruct them to warn their players to cool down – after only five minutes. The headstrong Ringer undoubtedly cost his team the match, leaving seven heroic forwards to battle on magnificently against Billy Beaumont's pack. England could not score a try against the gallant fourteen and a great Welsh victory appeared likely when Alan Phillips charged down Steve Smith's kick, snapped up the ball and sent Elgan Rees ripping away for a try and an 8-6 lead with barely five minutes left. But Hare kicked his third penalty goal right at the end from a wide angle just outside the 22 metre line under the west stand. Wales missed five penalty shots (shared among four players), so England went on to their first Grand Slam since 1957.

England: W H Hare (Leicester); J Carleton (Orrell), C R Woodward, P Dodge (Leicester), M A C Slemen (Liverpool); J P Horton (Bath), S J Smith (Sale); F E Cotton (Sale), P J Wheeler (Leicester), P J Blakeway (Gloucester), W B Beaumont (Fylde, capt.), M J Colclough (Angouleme), R M Uttley (Wasps), J P Scott (Cardiff), A Neary (Broughton Park). Rep: M Rafter (Bristol) for Uttley.

Wales; W R Blyth (Swansea); Elgan Rees (Neath), D S Richards (Swansea), S P Fenwick (Bridgend), L Keen (Aberavon); W Gareth Davies, T D Holmes (Cardiff); Clive Williams (Swansea), A J Phillips (Cardiff), G Price (Pontypool), A J Martin (Aberavon), G Wheel (Swansea), P Ringer (Llanelli), E T Butler, J Squire (Pontypool, capt.).

For Wales, Jeff Squire and Elgan Rees scored tries.

For England, "Dusty" Hare kicked three penalty goals.

Referee: D I H Burnett (Ireland).

Match 332 WALES v SCOTLAND   Cardiff Arms Park. March 1, 1980

Wales won by one goal, one penalty goal, two tries (17) to one goal (6)

"It was a very difficult game for us to approach after the criticisms of the Twickenham events," conceded Welsh captain Jeff Squire. His players were on their best behaviour and Squire praised them: "I think we came out of this game with Scotland with a lot of credit and I hope it puts the image of rugby right." The match featured creative try-building and David Richards's try from a double switch was a gem of the first magnitude. Steve Fenwick became the most capped Welsh centre, passing the 83 year old record of Newport's Arthur Gould, who had also played twice at full back.

Wales; W R Blyth (Swansea); Elgan Rees (Neath), D S Richards (Swansea), S P Fenwick (Bridgend), L Keen (Aberavon); W Gareth Davies, T D Holmes (Cardiff); Clive Williams (Swansea), A J Phillips (Cardiff), G Price (Pontypool), A J Martin (Aberavon), G Wheel (Swansea), J Squire (capt.), E T Butler (Pontypool), S Lane (Cardiff). Rep: *Peter Morgan (Llanelli) for Gareth Davies.

Scotland: A R Irvine (Heriot's FP); K W Robertson (Melrose), J M Renwick (Hawick), D I Johnston (Watsonians), B H Hay (Boroughmuir); J S Gossman (West of Scotland), R J Laidlaw (Jedforest); J N Burnett (Heriot's FP), K G Lawrie (Gala), N A Rowan (Boroughmuir), A J Tomes (Hawick), D Gray (West of Scotland), M A Biggar (London Scottish, capt.), J R Beattie (Glasgow Acads.). G Dickson (Gala). Rep: A J M Lawson (Heriot's FP) for Laidlaw

For Wales, Terry Holmes, Les Keen and David Richards scored tries. Roger Blyth converted one. Steve Fenwick kicked a penalty goal.

For Scotland. Jim Renwick scored a try. Andy Irvine converted.

Referee: L M Prideaux (England).

Match 333 IRELAND v WALES   Lansdowne Road, Dublin. March 15, 1980

Ireland won by three goals and one penalty goal (21) to one penalty goal, one try (7)

Fergus Slattery led his team to a slashing victory, their first over Wales for 10 years, and only Terry Holmes lived up to his reputation in the battered Welsh team. Three tries against Wales was the most in a championship match since England in 1967 and was the most by Ireland against Wales for 48 years – since they scored four in a 12-10 success in Cardiff in 1932. Wales had registered just five victories in a sequence of 11 games, including two defeats in Australia. The season produced Wales's lowest aggregate in six seasons: only 50 points with 45 against. Those fast and furious Irish forwards had made it a bad start to the Eighties for Wales – and the decade was to bring 29 defeats in 60 full cap games.

Ireland: R C O'Donnell (St. Mary's coll.); T J Kennedy (St. Mary's Coll.), D Irwin (Queen's Univ.), P P McNaughton (Greystones), A C McLennan (Wanderers); S O Campbell (Old Belvedere), C S Patterson (Instonians); P A Orr (Old Wesley), C F Fitzgerald (St. Mary's Coll.), M P Fitzpatrick (Wanderers), B Foley (Shannon), M I Keane (Lansdowne), J B O'Driscoll (London Irish), D E Spring (Dublin Univ.), J F Slattery (Blackrock Coll., capt.).

Wales: W R Blyth (Swansea); Elgan Rees (Neath), D S Richards (Swansea), S P Fenwick (Bridgend), L Keen (Aberavon); Peter Morgan (Llanelli), T D Holmes (Cardiff); Clive Williams (Swansea), A J Phillips (Cardiff), G Price (Pontypool), G Wheel (Swansea), A J Martin (Aberavon), J Squire (capt.), E T Butler (Pontypool), S M Lane (Cardiff).

For Ireland, David Irwin, John O'Driscoll and Ciaran Fitzgerald scored tries. Ollie Campbell converted them and kicked a penalty goal.

For Wales, Roger Blyth scored a try. Steve Fenwick kicked a penalty goal.

Referee: L M Prideaux (England).

Uncapped Match   WALES v OVERSEAS XV   Cardiff Arms Park. September 20, 1980

Wales won by three goals, two penalty goals, two tries (32)
to one goal, five penalty goals, one try (25)

Roger Blyth's Match. In the first fixture of the WRU centenary season celebrations, he scored three tries from full back and fired over three conversions and two penalty goals for 24 points. Then he was left out for the next match against New Zealand. The Overseas team scored their first try in a spectacular example of the flying wedge (a ploy that was to be outlawed in later years), which Swansea coach Stan Addicott had introduced to the Overseas side. Wales led 28-9, but the visitors hammered back with Ion Constantin kicking 17 points. Attendance: 35,000.

Wales: W R Blyth (Swansea); Elgan Rees (Neath), S P Fenwick (Bridgend, capt.), R W R Gravell (Llanelli), Pat Daniels (Cardiff); W Gareth Davies (Cardiff), D B Williams (Swansea); Clive Williams (Swansea), A J Phillips (Cardiff), G Price (Pontypool), G Wheel (Swansea), R Norster (Cardiff), J Squire, E T Butler (Pontypool), P Ringer (Llanelli). Rep: Peter Morgan (Llanelli) for Daniels.

Overseas: G Taylor (Canada); Masaru Fujiwara (Japan), J Piccardo (Argentine), I Constantin (Romania), Hirotaka Ujino (Japan); R Madero (Argentine), Paulo Waisake (Tonga); Jiro Ishiyama (Japan), M Luke (Canada), Soakai Motu'apuaka (Tonga), H de Goede (Canada), J Clark (USA), F Murariu (Romania), G Dumitru (Romania, capt.), G Travaglini (Argentine). Rep: J Fowler (USA) for Clark, Peseti Ma'afu (Tonga) for Paulo Waisake.

For Wales, Roger Blyth (3), Brynmor Williams and Steve Fenwick scored tries. Blyth converted three and kicked two penalty goals.

For Overseas, Soakai Motu'apuaka scored two tries. Ion Constantin converted one and kicked five penalty goals.

Referee: C Norling (Swansea).

New Zealand won by two goals, one penalty goal, two tries (23) to one penalty goal (3)

This was the first time for 20 years for Wales to concede four tries in a home full international (since France in 1960) and there were no tries for Wales who were completely overpowered by dominating forwards. "Speed to the ball was the decisive factor," pointed out NZ manager Ray Harper, who considered it the greatest performance he had ever seen from an All Blacks side. Robert Ackerman made a rousing debut on the left wing while Gareth Williams was the outstanding Welsh forward, also on his first appearance. J P R Williams regained the full back jersey from Roger Blyth after a season in semi-retirement and proved the best Welsh player with two fearless try-saving tackles. The WRU centenary season match was sponsored for £25,000 by Crown Paints. It was the second heaviest home defeat, surpassed by only England's success 98 years earlier.

Wales: J P R Williams (Bridgend); Elgan Rees (Neath), S P Fenwick (Bridgend, capt.), D S Richards (Swansea), *R Ackerman (Newport); W Gareth Davies (Cardiff), T D Holmes (Cardiff); Clive Williams (Swansea), A J Phillips (Cardiff), G Price (Pontypool), D L Quinnell (Llanelli), A J Martin (Aberavon), J Squire (Pontypool), *Gareth Williams (Bridgend), P Ringer (Llanelli). Reps: E T Butler (Pontypool) for Squire, Peter Morgan (Llanelli) for Rees.

New Zealand: D L Rollerson; S S Wilson, B J Robertson, W M Osborne, B G Fraser; N H Allen, D S Loveridge; R C Ketels, H R Reid, G A Knight, A M Haden, G Higginson, M W Shaw, M G Mexted, J N K Mourie (capt.).

For New Zealand, Graham Mourie, Nick Allen, Bernie Fraser and Hika Reid scored tries. Doug Rollerson converted two and kicked a penalty goal.

For Wales, Steve Fenwick kicked a penalty goal.

Referee: J R West (Ireland).

Wales won by one goal, one dropped goal, four penalty goals (21)
to five penalty goals, one try (19)

J P R Williams, who never played on a losing side against England, broke Gareth Edwards's appearance record in this, JPR's 54th game. Dusty Hare became the first England full back to score a try against Wales and provided all his team's points by adding five penalty goals. He could have stolen a win with the last kick of the match when a Welsh boot was brandished too vigorously in a ruck, but missed for the fifth time. The game brought a record for a Five Nations fixture – a total of nine penalty goals. Steve Fenwick put over four, the last after two minutes of injury time when Woodward was off-side in front of his posts with England leading 19-18.

Wales: J P R Williams (Bridgend); R Ackerman (Newport), S P Fenwick (Bridgend, capt.), D S Richards (Swansea), *D L Nicholas (Llanelli); W Gareth Davies (Cardiff), D B Williams (Swansea); *Ian Stephens (Bridgend), A J Phillips (Cardiff), G Price (Pontypool), G Wheel (Swansea), Clive Davis (Newbridge), J Squire (Pontypool), Gareth Williams (Bridgend), *Rhodri Lewis (Cardiff).

England: W H Hare (Leicester); J Carleton (Orrell), C R Woodward, P W Dodge (Leicester), M A C Slemen (Liverpool); J P Horton (Bath), S J Smith (Sale); F E Cotton (Sale), P J Wheeler (Leicester), P J Blakeway (Gloucester), W B Beaumont (Fylde, capt.), M J Colclough (Angouleme), M Rafter (Bristol), J P Scott (Cardiff), D H Cooke (Harlequins). Rep: A Sheppard (Bristol) for Cotton.

For Wales, Clive Davis scored a try. Steve Fenwick converted and kicked four penalty goals. Gareth Davies dropped a goal.

For England, "Dusty" Hare scored a try and kicked five penalty goals.

Referee: J B Anderson (Scotland).

Match 336 SCOTLAND v WALES Murrayfield. February 7, 1981

Scotland won by two goals, one penalty goal (15) to two penalty goals (6)

Wales were favourites against opponents who had managed just one success from their previous 17 games. But instead of winning for what would have been a record third successive time at Scottish HQ, Wales slumped, without a try. They were defeated by a livelier and more cohesive pack. Gwyn Evans, the Maesteg outside half/full back, came on to win his first cap as replacement for injured wing David Nicholas. Andy Irvine, obstructed in a race for the ball over the goal-line by Gareth Davies, was awarded a try by referee David Burnett. It was Irvine's 10th international try and his fourth against Wales. This match was the last for his country by JPR, a legend in his lifetime.

Scotland: A R Irvine (Heriot's FP, capt.); S Munro (Ayr), J M Renwick (Hawick), K W Robertson (Melrose), B H Hay (Boroughmuir); J Y Rutherford (Selkirk), R J Laidlaw (Jedforest); J Aitken (Gala), C T Deans (Hawick), N A Rowan (Boroughmuir), A J Tomes (Hawick), W Cuthbertson (Kilmarnock), J H Calder (Stewart's/Melville), J R Beattie (Heriot's FP), D G Leslie (Gala).

Wales: J P R Williams (Bridgend); R Ackerman (Newport), D S Richards (Swansea), S P Fenwick (Bridgend, capt.), D Nicholas (Llanelli); W Gareth Davies (Cardiff), D B Williams (Swansea); Ian Stephens (Bridgend), A J Phillips (Cardiff), G Price (Pontypool), G Wheel (Swansea), Clive Davis (Newbridge), J Squire (Pontypool), Gareth Williams (Bridgend), Rhodri Lewis (Cardiff). Rep: *Gwyn Evans (Maesteg) for Nicholas.

For Wales, Steve Fenwick kicked two penalty goals.

For Scotland, Alan Tomes scored a try and Andy Irvine was awarded a penalty try. Jim Renwick converted both tries and kicked a penalty goal.

Referee: D I H Burnett (Ireland).

Match 337 WALES v IRELAND Cardiff Arms Park. February 21, 1981

Wales won by two penalty goals, one dropped goal (9) to two tries (8)

Sensationally, JPR Williams, skipper Steve Fenwick and Gareth Davies were dropped as the selectors, shocked after the Murrayfield debacle, made seven changes, plus two positional switches. The shake-up achieved its objective, though there were no tries for Wales. Gwyn Evans, successor to JPR at full back, kicked two penalty goals and, with Ireland leading 8-6 with barely 10 minutes left, Gary Pearce marked his debut with a left-footed drop-shot that brought victory. Pearce was preparing to set his centres running when he spotted the Irish defenders closing fast and instinctively dropped a goal. Thank goodness he did! Pearce had atoned for his error in giving Peter Morgan a hospital pass that put the Llanelli centre out of the game with three fractured ribs. Jeff Squire, restored as captain, played his finest game for Wales and the magnificently combative Clive Burgess, recalled after four years, helped him rekindle the pack's fire. So both home championship games during the centenary season had been won – by fractional margins and a bit of luck.

Wales: Gwyn Evans (Maesteg); D S Richards (Swansea), R W R Gravell, Peter Morgan, D L Nicholas (Llanelli); *G P Pearce, *Gerald Williams (Bridgend); Ian Stephens (Bridgend), A J Phillips (Cardiff), G Price (Pontypool), G Wheel (Swansea), A J Martin (Aberavon), R C Burgess (Ebbw Vale), J Squire (Pontypool, capt.), Rhodri Lewis (Cardiff). Rep: Alun Donovan (Swansea) for Peter Morgan.

Ireland: H P MacNeill (Dublin Univ.); F P Quinn, S O Campbell (Old Belvedere), D G Irwin (Queen's Univ., Belfast), A C McLennan (Wanderers); A J P Ward (Garryowen), J C Robbie (Greystones); P A Orr (Old Wesley), P C Whelan (Garryowen), M P Fitzpatrick (Wanderers), M I Keane, D E Spring (Lansdowne), J B O'Driscoll (London Irish), W P Duggan, J F Slattery (Blackrock Coll., capt.). Rep: M E Gibson (Lansdowne) for Spring.

For Wales, Gwyn Evans kicked two penalty goals. Gary Pearce dropped a goal.

For Ireland, Fergus Slattery and Hugo MacNeill scored tries.

Referee: F Palmade (France).

Match 338 FRANCE v WALES   Parc Des Princes, Paris. March 7, 1981

France won by five penalty goals, one try (19) to one goal, three penalty goals (15)

At last, a try from a Welsh back! David Richards ripped through with a delicious dummy from a close-up scrum as fly half Gary Pearce swung infield as the decoy. But the home pack could not match the authoritative French driving and ball-winning as their captain, Jean-Pierre Rives, performed inspiringly with his face cut open near his right eye. Rives suffered so many gashes that a blood transfusion unit should have accompanied France to all his games! Wales led 15-13 with about 15 minutes left, but two further penalty goals set France up to collect the Grand Slam they deserved at Twickenham. Wales finished with more points against them in the championship (61) than for 57 years – since the 1924 campaign. When Serge Gabernet pounced for his try it meant that the full back of each country had crossed the Welsh line in this centenary season, a unique record. Allan Martin's last game ended a record 27 appearances in the second row with Geoff Wheel.

France: S Gabernet (Toulouse); S Blanco (Biarritz), R Bertranne (Bagneres), D Codorniou (Narbonne), L Pardo (Bayonne); G Laporte (Graulhet), P Berbizier (Lourdes); P Dospital (Bayonne), P Dintrans (Tarbes), R Paparemborde (Pau), D Revallier (Graulhet), J F Imbernon (Perpignan), P Lacans (Beziers), J L Joinel (Brive), J P Rives (Toulouse, capt.). Rep: P Mesny (Grenoble) for Bertranne.

Wales: Gwyn Evans (Maesteg); Clive Rees (London Welsh), R W R Gravell (Llanelli), D S Richards (Swansea), D L Nicholas (Llanelli); G P Pearce, Gerald Williams (Bridgend); Ian Stephens (Bridgend), A J Phillips (Cardiff), G Price (Pontypool), G Wheel (Swansea), A J Martin (Aberavon), R C Burgess (Ebbw Vale), J Squire (Pontypool, capt.), Rhodri Lewis (Cardiff).

For Wales, David Richards scored a try. Gwyn Evans kicked three penalty goals and converted the try.

For France, Serge Gabernet scored a try. Guy Laporte kicked three penalty goals and Gabernet kicked two penalty goals.

Referee: A Welsby (England).

Wales won by one goal, three penalty goals, three tries (27) to two goals, three penalty goals (21)

This sparkling match against the world team closed the WRU centenary celebrations on a high note in front of 40,000 spectators. The return of Terry Holmes and Gareth Davies as half backs revitalised the backline. Holmes, who had missed the Five Nations games following a shoulder operation after crashing into the advertising boards at Old Deer Park when Cardiff played London Welsh, snapped up two storming tries. Colin Donovan, the smooth-running Maesteg wing, was the only uncapped player in the Welsh line-up and sprinted excitingly for his try.

Wales: Gwyn Evans (Maesteg); Colin Donovan (Maesteg), R W R Gravell (Llanelli), D S Richards (Swansea), Clive Rees (London Welsh); W Gareth Davies, T D Holmes (Cardiff); Ian Stephens (Bridgend), A J Phillips (Cardiff), G Price (Pontypool), G Wheel (Swansea), A J Martin (Aberavon), R C Burgess (Ebbw Vale), J Squire (Pontypool, capt.), Rhodri Lewis (Cardiff).

WRU President's XV: Z M J Piennar (SA); B J Moon, A G Slack (Australia), D I Johnston, A R Irvine (Scotland); M G Ella (Australia), D S Loveridge (NZ); P A Orr (Ireland), P J Wheeler (England), M P Fitzpatrick (Ireland), W B Beaumont (England, capt.), A M Haden, M W Shaw (NZ), R J Louw (SA), J P Rives (France). Rep: L C Moolman (SA) for Rives.

For Wales, Terry Holmes (2), Colin Donovan and Gwyn Evans scored tries. Gwyn Evans converted one and kicked three penalty goals.

For the President's XV, Jean-Pierre Rives and Mark Shaw scored tries. Andy Irvine converted them and kicked three penalty goals.

Referee: K Rowlands (Wales).

Wales won by one goal, one dropped goal, three penalty goals (18)
to one goal, one penalty goal, one try (13)

A rip-roaring contest saw Richard Moriarty storm over for a debut try, set up by quick-thinking wing Clive 'Billy Whizz' Rees – the only try against these 1981-82 Wallabies in seven matches in Wales. New captain Gareth Davies directed operations faultlessly and swung the game at a critical stage with a dropped goal. The Australians were leading 13-6 as a result of Welsh lapses, but Wales kicked the essential goals against the country considered world champions having won the series against New Zealand and France. The Wallabies were to avenge this reverse many times over in the years to come!

Wales: Gwyn Evans (Maesteg); R A Ackerman (Newport), *P C T Daniels (Cardiff), A J Donovan (Swansea), Clive Rees (London Welsh); W Gareth Davies (capt), T D Holmes (Cardiff); Ian Stephens (Bridgend), A J Phillips (Cardiff), G Price (Pontypool), *R D Moriarty, G Wheel (Swansea), Gareth Williams (Bridgend), J Squire (Pontypool), *Mark Davies (Swansea).

Australia: R G Gould; M D O'Connor, A G Slack, M J Hawker, B J Moon; Paul McLean, J N B Hipwell; A M Darcy, C M Carberry, D J Curran, A A Shaw (capt.), Peter McLean, G Cornelsen, M E Loane, S P Poidevin. Reps: M C Martin for Hawker, P A Cox for Hipwell.

For Wales, Richard Moriarty scored a try. Gwyn Evans kicked three penalty goals and converted the try. Gareth Davies dropped a goal.

For Australia, Andy Slack and Mitchell Cox scored tries. Paul McLean converted one and kicked a penalty goal.

Referee: J R West (Ireland).

Match 340 IRELAND v WALES Lansdowne Road, Dublin. January 23, 1982

Ireland won by one goal, two penalty goals, two tries (20)
to one goal, one dropped goal, one penalty goal (12)

This match was postponed for a week because blizzards swept across Britain and left football grounds smothered by snowdrifts. Wales failed to dig themselves out of trouble and gave an abject performance, scourged by the Irish forwards. Welsh tackling also was fragile in the extreme. Gary Pearce replaced injured Gareth Davies and dropped a late goal, but events had long been decided. It was a record sixth successive away defeat, surpassing the five failures during 1894-1896. Ireland, for whom Ollie Campbell's narrow side run and dummy to set up a try was a little gem of creative running, registered their first win in seven games and went on to take the Triple Crown for the first time since 1949.

Ireland: H P MacNeill (Dublin Univ.); T M Ringland, D G Irwin (Queen's Univ., Belfast), P M Dean (St. Mary's Coll.), M Finn (Cork Constitution); S O Campbell (Old Belvedere), R J McGrath (Wanderers); P A Orr (Old Wesley), C F Fitzgerald (St. Mary's Coll., capt.), G A J McLoughlin (Shannon), M I Keane (Lansdowne), D G Lenihan (UC, Cork), J B O'Driscoll (London Irish), W P Duggan, J F Slattery (Blackrock Coll.). Reps: M Kiernan (Dolphin) for Irwin, J Murphy (Greystones) for Dean.

Wales: G Evans (Maesteg); R A Ackerman (Newport), P C T Daniels (Cardiff), D S Richards (Swansea), Clive Rees (London Welsh); W Gareth Davies, (capt.), T D Holmes (Cardiff); Ian Stephens (Bridgend), A J Phillips (Cardiff), G Price (Pontypool), R D Moriarty, G Wheel, Mark Davies (Swansea), J Squire (Pontypool), Gareth Williams (Bridgend). Rep: G Pearce (Bridgend) for W Gareth Davies.

For Wales, Terry Holmes scored a try. Gwyn Evans converted and kicked a penalty goal. Gary Pearce dropped a goal.

For Ireland, "Moss" Finn (2) and Trevor Ringland scored tries. Ollie Campbell converted one and kicked two penalty goals.

Referee: J A Short (Scotland).

Match 341 WALES v FRANCE Cardiff Arms Park. February 6, 1982

Wales won by six penalty goals, one try (22) to one goal, two penalty goals (12)

Wales resisted changes after the Dublin disaster and brought in just one newcomer, Pontypool middle-jumper Steve Sutton, who dominated the line-out with classical two-handed catching. The man of the match, however, proved to be Gwyn Evans. The full back's six penalty goals was a first in the Five Nations tourney and equalled the then world record in a Test recorded by Don Clarke (NZ against 1959 Lions) and Gerald Bosch (SA against France 1975). Another record for Gwyn was his fastest 50 points for Wales. He took just six matches. Keith Jarrett had taken seven games. Wales were not to defeat France again at the Arms Park for 12 years.

Wales: G Evans (Maesteg); R A Ackerman (Newport), D S Richards (Swansea) R W R Gravell (Llanelli), Clive Rees (London Welsh); W Gareth Davies (capt.), T D Holmes (Cardiff); Ian Stephens (Bridgend), A J Phillips (Cardiff), G Price,

*S Sutton (Pontypool), R D Moriarty, R C Burgess (Ebbw Vale), J Squire (Pontypool), Rhodri Lewis (Cardiff).

France: M Sallefranque (Dax); S Blanco (Biarritz), P Perrier, C Belascain, L Pardo (Bayonne); J Lescarboura (Dax), G Martinez (Toulouse); M Cremaschi (Lourdes), P Dintrans (Tarbes), R Paparemborde (Pau), A Lorieux (Grenoble), D Revallier (Graulhet), J P Rives (Toulouse, capt.), L Rodriguez (Mont de Marsan), P Lacans (Beziers).

For Wales, Terry Holmes scored a try. Gwyn Evans kicked six penalty goals.

For France, Serge Blanco scored a try. Marc Sellafranque converted and kicked a penalty goal. Gerald Martinez kicked a penalty goal.

Referee: D I H Burnett (Ireland).

Match 342 **ENGLAND v WALES**   Twickenham. March 6, 1982

England won by three penalty goals, two tries (17) to one dropped goal, one try (7)

Dusty Hare's hat-trick of penalty goals meant he had put over 11 penalty shots in three successive games against Wales as, for the first time since 1939, Wales lost on two successive visits to Twickenham. This was a seventh consecutive Welsh away defeat and featured England's biggest winning margin over Wales for 61 years, since 1921. Mike Slemen's diving corner try was England's first against Wales at Twickenham for eight years. Graham Price became most-capped Welsh prop with his 37th successive appearance to pass Denzil Williams's record.

England: W H Hare (Leicester); J Carleton (Orrell), C R Woodward, P W Dodge (Leicester), M A C Slemen (Liverpool); L Cusworth (Leicester), S J Smith (Sale, capt.); C E Smart (Newport), P J Wheeler (Leicester), P J Blakeway (Gloucester), M J Colclough (Angouleme), S Bainbridge (Gosforth), N C Jeavons (Moseley), J P Scott (Cardiff), P J Winterbottom (Headingley).

Wales: G Evans (Maesteg); R A Ackerman (Newport), R W R Gravell (Llanelli), A J Donovan (Swansea), Clive Rees (London Welsh); W Gareth Davies (capt.), T D Holmes (Cardiff); Ian Stephens (Bridgend), A J Phillips (Cardiff), G Price, S Sutton (Pontypool), R D Moriarty (Swansea), R C Burgess (Ebbw Vale), J Squire (Pontypool), Rhodri Lewis (Cardiff).

For England, Mike Slemen and John Carleton scored tries. Dusty Hare kicked three penalty goals.

For Wales, Rhodri Lewis scored a try. Gareth Davies dropped a goal.

Referee: F Palmade (France).

Match 343 **WALES v SCOTLAND**   Cardiff Arms Park. March 20, 1982

Scotland won by four goals, two dropped goals, one try (34) to one goal, four penalty goals (18)

The superlative record of 27 championship matches at the Arms Park without defeat came to an end in astonishing fashion. Scotland, recording their first win in Cardiff for 20 years, crossed for five tries – a feat never achieved on Welsh ground, not even by the All Blacks. For the first time since 1937 Wales had lost to each of the home countries in one season. It was the first championship reverse at the Arms Park since France triumphed in 1968; and thereby Wales's longest spell of invincibility came to a calamitous close. Many considered the match was lost in the selection room. Changes were anticipated after Twickenham. The Big Five, under fire from all quarters, closed ranks. It was heads in the sand, boys, and hope for the best!

The midfield backs showed no penetration whereas Jim Renwick scored a try for the third successive time for Scotland in Cardiff. This was, at the time, the biggest victory by any side at the Arms Park and the eighth Welsh defeat in 13 games.

Wales: G Evans (Maesteg); R A Ackerman (Newport), R W R Gravell (Llanelli), A J Donovan (Swansea), Clive Rees (London Welsh); W Gareth Davies,(capt..),Gerald Williams (Bridgend); Ian Stephens (Bridgend), A J Phillips (Cardiff), G Price, R D Moriarty (Swansea), *R L Norster (Cardiff), R C Burgess (Ebbw Vale), E T Butler (Pontypool), Rhodri Lewis (Cardiff).

Scotland: A R Irvine (Heriot's FP, capt.); J Pollock (Gosforth), J M Renwick (Hawick), D I Johnston (Watsonians), G R T Baird (Kelso); J Y Rutherford (Selkirk), R J Laidlaw (Jedforest); J Aitken (Gala), C T Deans (Hawick), I G Milne (Heriot's FP), W Cuthbertson (Kilmarnock), A J Tomes (Hawick), J H Calder (Stewart's / Melville), I A M Paxton (Selkirk), D B White (Gala). Rep: G Dickson (Gala) for Paxton.

For Scotland, Jim Calder, Jim Renwick, Jim Pollock, Derek White and David Johnston scored tries. Andy Irvine converted four. Renwick and John Rutherford dropped goals.

For Wales, Eddie Butler scored a try. Gwyn Evans converted and kicked four penalty goals.

Referee: J P Bonnet (France).

Uncapped Match WALES v MAORIS Cardiff Arms Park. November 13, 1982

Wales won by one goal, one dropped goal, four penalty goals, one try (25)
to one goal, three penalty goals, one try (19)

Only six of the team that Scotland had blasted apart faced the Maoris in the eerie darkness that shrouded the ground. Eddie Butler was the new captain, playing despite a twisted ankle suffered in the Thursday runout, and he was out of action for several weeks as a result. New full back Mark Wyatt fired in four penalty goals and a conversion. Attendance was only 42,000 because the south stand was in the course of reconstruction.

Wales: M A Wyatt (Swansea); Elgan Rees (Neath), D S Richards (Swansea), R A Ackerman, Clive Rees (London Welsh); M Dacey (Swansea), T D Holmes (Cardiff); Ian Stephens (Bridgend), W J James (Aberavon), G Price, S J Perkins (Pontypool), R D Moriarty (Swansea), J Squire, E T Butler (Pontypol, capt.), Mark Davies (Swansea). Rep: C Dennehy (Ebbw Vale) for Squire.

Maoris: W D McLean; R Kururangi, A M Stone, M Clamp; S T Pokere, T Wyllie; R R Dunn; P T Koteka, F K O'Carroll, S A Crichton, H Rickit, P S Tuoro, P B Quinn (capt.), J H M Love, F N K Shelford.

For Wales, Elgan Rees and Terry Holmes scored tries. Mark Wyatt converted one and kicked four penalty goals. Malcolm Dacey dropped a goal.

For Maoris, Robert Kururangi and Arthur Stone scored tries. Richard Dunn converted one and kicked three penalty goals.

Referee: A Welsby (England).

Match 344 WALES v ENGLAND Cardiff Arms Park. February 5, 1983

Drawn. Wales one dropped goal, two penalty goals, one try (13),
England one dropped goal, two penalty goals, one try (13)

Malcolm Dacey, brought in to set his backs running, mostly kicked. He dropped a goal and might well have won the match in the closing minutes with another drop-shot, but it was desperately charged down by Les Cusworth. There were first full caps for Dacey, Mark Wyatt, Mark Ring, David Pickering and Billy James. England were relieved to put an end to nine successive Welsh home victories over them.

Wales: *M A Wyatt (Swansea); Elgan Rees (Neath), D S Richards (Swansea), *M G Ring (Cardiff), Clive Rees (London Welsh); *M Dacey (Swansea), T D Holmes (Cardiff); C Williams (Swansea), *W J James (Aberavon), G Price (Pontypool), R L Norster (Cardiff), R D Moriarty (Swansea), P J Squire, E T Butler (Pontypool. capt.), *D F Pickering (Llanelli).

England: W H Hare (Leicester); J Carleton (Orrell), G H Davies (Coventry), P W Dodge (Leicester), A H Swift (Swansea); L Cusworth (Leicester), S J Smith (Sale, capt.); C E Smart (Newport), S G F Mills (Gloucester), G S Pearce (Northampton), S B Boyle (Gloucester), S Bainbridge (Gosforth), N C Jeavons (Moseley), J P Scott (Cardiff), P J Winterbottom (Headingley).

For Wales, Jeff Squire scored a try. Malcolm Dacey dropped a goal and Mark Wyatt kicked two penalty goals.

For England, John Carleton scored a try. Les Cusworth dropped a goal and Dusty Hare kicked two penalty goals.

Referee: J R West (Ireland).

Match 345   SCOTLAND v WALES   Murrayfield. February 19, 1983

Wales won by one goal, three penalty goals, one try (19) to one goal, three penalty goals (15)

This was the match of the Angry Men. The team had been scathingly criticised after the lacklustre performance against England and the selectors roundly condemned for not making more positive changes. So the players were stung to hit back in the most positive manner – and did it in grand style. "We went on the field fifteen angry men," admitted skipper Eddie Butler. "It was every man for himself in the last 10 minutes when Scotland threw everything at us." The game will be remembered for the earth-shaking tackle by Terry Holmes to crash second-row giant Bill Cuthbertson back and flat on the pitch. It was unlucky for bearded Bill that he encountered the strongest scrum half ever to play for Wales. No-one ever ran through Mr. Holmes! There was an unexpected outburst from Graham Price when he was dropped after 39 consecutive caps. He publicly blamed Richard Moriarty, dropped with him, for not scrummaging and thereby losing Price his place. Also angry was Jeff Squire, attacking the media for criticising the Welsh team. Clive Rowlands, chairman of the WRU selectors, observed, "I think players can be more humble in success!"

Scotland: P W Dods (Gala); K W Robertson (Melrose), J M Renwick (Hawick), D I Johnston (Watsonians), G R T Baird (Kelso); B M Gossman (West of Scotland), R J Laidlaw (Jedforest, capt.); J Aitken (Gala), C T Deans (Hawick), I G Milne (Heriot's FP), W Cuthbertson (Harlequins), A J Tomes (Hawick), J H Calder (Stewart's / Melville FP), J R Beattie (Glasgow Acads), D G Leslie (Gala).

Wales: M A Wyatt (Swansea); Elgan Rees (Neath), D S Richards (Swansea), R A Ackerman, Clive Rees (London Welsh); M Dacey (Swansea), T D Holmes (Cardiff); *S T Jones (Pontypool), W J James (Aberavon), *I Eidman, R L Norster (Cardiff), *S J Perkins, J Squire, E T Butler (Pontypool, capt.), D F Pickering (Llanelli).

For Wales, Steve 'Staff' Jones and Elgan Rees scored tries. Mark Wyatt converted one and kicked three penalty goals.

For Scotland, Jim Renwick scored a try. Peter Dods converted and kicked three penalty goals.

Referee: R C Quittenton (England).

Match 346 **WALES v IRELAND** Cardiff Arms Park. March 5, 1983

Wales won by one goal, three penalty goals, two tries (23) to three penalty goals (9)

Ireland, as Triple Crown holders, were confident. But 'Dad's Army', as they were called, with a ring of truth, came unstuck. Mark Wyatt scored 15 points, including a try, as Wales launched irresistible second half pressure. Terry Holmes scored his seventh try as the game's key figure. Graham Price was recalled when Ian Eidman failed a fitness test.

Wales: M A Wyatt (Swansea); Elgan Rees (Neath), D S Richards (Swansea), R A Ackerman, Clive Rees (London Welsh); M Dacey (Swansea), T D Holmes (Cardiff); *S T Jones (Pontypool), W J James (Aberavon), G Price (Pontypool), R L Norster (Cardiff), *S J Perkins, J Squire, E T Butler (Pontypool, capt.), D F Pickering (Llanelli).

Ireland: H P MacNeill (Blackrock Coll.); T M Ringland (Ballymena), D G Irwin (Instonians), M J Kiernan (Dolphin), M C Finn (Cork Constitution); S O Campbell (Old Belvedere), R J McGrath (Wanderers); P A Orr (Old Wesley), C F Fitzgerald (St. Mary's Coll., capt.), G A J McLoughlin (Shannon), D G Lenihan (Cork Constitution), M I Keane (Lansdowne), J B O'Driscoll (Manchester), W P Duggan, J F Slattery (Blackrock Coll.).

For Wales, Mark Wyatt, Terry Holmes and Elgan Rees scored tries. Wyatt converted one and kicked three penalty goals.

For Ireland, Ollie Campbell kicked two penalty goals and Hugo MacNeill one penalty goal.

Referee: J A F Trigg (England).

Match 347 **FRANCE v WALES** Parc Des Princes, Paris. March 19, 1983

France won by three penalty goals, one dropped goal, one try (16)
to one goal, one penalty goal (9)

Victory would have made Wales unbeaten champions; but France proved marginally the better side in a contest marred by over-vigorous play. Terry Holmes, battered by relentless marking, was provoked to hurl the ball at Dintrans as the hooker lay on the ground after a particularly fierce tackle on the scrum half. It was uncharacteristic of Holmes and Blanco turned the penalty award into a goal. Jean-Pierre Rives, bleeding freely from a scalp wound, appeared a heroic figure in bloodstained jersey to fire his team to a furious effort and they finished joint champions with Ireland. New Zealand referee Tom Doocey seemed overawed by the hostility on and off the pitch. "France played better than we did. We can only improve," summed up coach John Bevan.

France: S Blanco (Biarritz); P Sella (Agen), C Belascain (Bayonne), D Codorniou, P Esteve (Narbonne); D Camberabero (La Voulte), G Martinez (Toulouse); P Dospital (Bayonne), P Dintrans (Tarbes), R Paparemborde (Pau), J F Imbernon(Perpignan), J Condom (Le Boucou), D Erbani (Agen), J L Joinel (Brive), J P Rives (Racing Club of France, capt.).

Wales: M A Wyatt (Swansea); Elgan Rees (Neath), R A Ackerman (London Welsh), G Evans (Maesteg), Clive Rees (London Welsh); M Dacey (Swansea), T

D Holmes (Cardiff); S T Jones (Pontypool), W J James (Aberavon), G Price (Pontypool), R L Norster (Cardiff), S J Perkins, J Squire, E T Butler (Pontypool, capt.), D F Pickering (Llanelli). Rep: R Donovan (South Wales Police) for Wyatt.

For Wales, Jeff Squire scored a try. Mark Wyatt converted. Gwyn Evans kicked a penalty goal.

For France, Patrick Esteve scored a try. Didier Camberabero dropped a goal. Serge Blanco kicked three penalty goals.

Referee: T F Doocey (New Zealand).

Match 348   ROMANIA v WALES   Bucharest. November 12, 1983

Romania won by one goal, two penalty goals, three tries (24) to two penalty goals (6)

For the first time, Wales awarded caps for a match against opponents from outside International Board countries and slumped to their heaviest defeat for 14 years. It was dismal, without a try, and Eddie Butler's captaincy came in for some hard words. The selectors had not helped him by picking two front jumpers and two openside wing forwards. Romania dominated the lineout, drove through the tail and scored four tries. A crowd of 25,000 watched in a half-full 23rd August Stadium.

Romania: Vasile Ion; Sorin Fuicu, Adrian Lungu, Mihai Marghescu, Marian Aldea; Dumitru Alexandru, Mircea Paraschiv (capt,); Ioan Bucan, Mircea Munteanu, Vasile Pascu, Gheorghe Dumitru, Gheorghe Caragea, Florica Murariu, Stefan Constantin, Alexandru Radulescu.

Wales: Gwyn Evans (Maesteg); *M H Titley (Bridgend), R C Ackerman (London Welsh), *B Bowen (S W Police), *A M Hadley (Cardiff); M Dacey (Swansea), *R Giles (Aberavon); S T Jones (Pontypool), W J James (Aberavon), I H Eidman (Cardiff), S J Perkins (Pontypool), *T W Shaw (Newbridge), *Mark Brown (Pontypool), E T Butler (Pontypool, capt.), D F Pickering (Llanelli). Rep: D S Richards (Swansea) for Dacey.

For Romania, Gheorghe Caragea, Florica Murariu, Marian Aldea and Adrian Lungu scored tries. Dumitru Alexandru converted one and kicked two penalty goals.

For Wales, Gwyn Evans kicked two penalty goals.

Referee: J-C Yche (France).

Uncapped Match   WALES v JAPAN   Cardiff Arms Park. October 22, 1983

Wales won by three goals, one penalty goal, two tries (29)
to one goal, two penalty goals, three tries (24)

Wales were leading 29-10 in the bright autumn sunshine – then Japan stunned them with a slashing rally. The Cherry Blossoms attacked from every scrap of possession. "It was insane on our part to ease off just because we thought we had it sewn up," reflected captain Eddie Butler. The experimental Welsh team lost its way defensively during the closing 20 minutes. Japan stole back 14 points without response.

Wales: M A Wyatt (Swansea); M H Titley (Bridgend), K Hopkins (South Glam Institute), B Bowen (S W Police), A M Hadley (Cardiff); M Dacey (Swansea), R Giles (Aberavon); J Whitefoot (Cardiff), W J James (Aberavon), I H Eidman (Cardiff), S J Perkins (Pontypool), T W Shaw (Newbridge), Mark Davies (Swansea), E T Butler (Pontypool, capt.), Mark Brown (Pontypool).

Japan: N Tanifuji; F Kanaya, H Kobayashi, S Hirao, T Higashida; Y Matsuo (capt.), Y Konishi; J Ishiyama, T Fujita, K Horaguchi, T Hayashi, A Oyagi, H Kawachi, Y Kawase, M Chida. Rep: Y Ideda for Horaguchi.

For Wales, Adrian Hadley, Mark Brown, Malcolm Dacey, Bleddyn Bowen and Ray Giles scored tries. Mark Wyatt converted three and kicked a penalty goal.

For Japan, Yoshimitsu Konishi, Noahisa Tanifuji, Michihito Chida and Tsuyoshi Fujita scored tries. Hideo Kobayashi converted one and kicked two penalty goals.

Referee: J A F Trigg (England).

Match 349   WALES v SCOTLAND   Cardiff Arms Park. January 21, 1984

Scotland won by two goals, one penalty goal (15) to one goal, one penalty goal (9)

For the first time, Scotland won on two successive visits to the Welsh capital. The home side were considered slight favourites, but the Scottish pack, and particularly David Leslie, at the tail of the line, paved the way for victory and they went on to their first Grand Slam for 59 years. Paxton's try came from a palpable forward pass, yet no-one disputed Scotland were deserved winners. The new south stand was completed just in time, increasing the ground capacity to 62,532 with gate receipts a record £305,000. It had taken 15 years and cost £9m to complete the reconstruction of the national stadium. Ken Harris, the WRU treasurer, revealed that on two occasions a decision had been taken to build a new national ground at Island Farm, near Bridgend. The WRU purchased the ground, but could not obtain planning permission for the 90-acre site. The plan finally was abandoned in June 1964.

Wales: *Howell Davies (Bridgend); M H Titley (Bridgend), R A Ackerman (London Welsh), B Bowen (S W Police), A M Hadley (Cardiff); M Dacey (Swansea), *M H J Douglas (Llanelli); S T Jones (Pontypool), W J James (Aberavon), *G R Morgan (Newport), S J Perkins (Pontypool), R L Norster (Cardiff), R D Moriarty (Swansea), E T Butler (Pontypool, capt.), D F Pickering (Llanelli).

Scotland: P W Dods (Gala); S Munro (Ayr), D I Johnston (Watsonians), A E Kennedy (Watsonians), G R T Baird (Kelso); J Y Rutherford (Selkirk), R J Laidlaw (Jedforest), J Aitken (Gala, capt.), C T Deans (Hawick), I G Milne (Heriot's FP), W Cuthbertson (Harlequins), A J Tomes (Hawick), J H Calder (Stewart's / Melville FP), I A M Paxton (Selkirk), D G Leslie (Gala).

For Wales, Mark Titley scored a try. Howell Davies converted and kicked a penalty goal.

For Scotland, Iain Paxton and Jim Aitken scored tries. Peter Dods converted both and kicked a penalty goal.

Referee: E O Doyle (Ireland).

Match 350   IRELAND v WALES   Lansdowne Road, Dublin. February 4, 1984

Wales won by one goal and four penalty goals (18) to three penalty goals (9)

The Welsh team were robbed of nearly £800 by a sneak thief, who climbed down a ventilator shaft into the dressing room while the match was being played. However, the Irish RFU reimbursed everyone. Ireland opened their £4m stand, but the occasion was hardly auspicious: their team gave one of their most abject displays since World War Two. In contrast, Wales were inspired by new captain Mike Watkins, invested with the leadership on his debut. His forwards dominated with sledgehammer scrum drive and lineout authority while Richard Moriarty performed particularly well in the unaccustomed role of narrow side wing forward.

Ackerman was allowed to run through for an amazingly simple try, the only one of the match, which was watched by a record Dublin crowd of 52,000.

Ireland: H P MacNeill (Blackrock Coll.); T M Ringland(Ballymena), R J Moroney (Lansdowne), D G Irwin, K D Crossan (Instonians), S O Campbell (Old Belvedere), R J McGrath (Wanderers); P A Orr (Old Wesley), C F Fitzgerald (St. Mary's Coll., capt.), J McCoy (Dungannon), M I Keane (Lansdowne), D G Lenihan (Cork Constitution), W R Duncan (Malone), W P Duggan (Blackrock Coll.), J B O'Driscoll (London Irish). Rep: H T Harbison (Bective Rangers) for Fitzgerald.

Wales: Howell Davies (Bridgend); M H Titley (Bridgend), R A Ackerman (London Welsh), B Bowen (S W Police), A M Hadley (Cardiff); M Dacey (Swansea), M H J Douglas (Llanelli); I Stephens (Bridgend), *M J Watkins (Newport, capt.), I H Eidman (Cardiff), S J Perkins (Pontypool), R L Norster (Cardiff), R D Moriarty (Swansea), E T Butler (Pontypool,), D F Pickering (Llanelli).

For Wales, Robert Ackerman scored a try. Howell Davies converted and kicked two penalty goals. Bleddyn Bowen kicked two penalty goals.

For Ireland, Ollie Campbell kicked three penalty goals.

Referee: R G Byres (Australia).

| Match 351 | **WALES v FRANCE** | Cardiff Arms Park. February 18, 1984 |

France won by one goal, four penalty goals, one dropped goal (21)
to one goal, one try, two penalty goals (16)

After four times being on the losing side in Cardiff, Jean-Pierre Rives led his team to their first win in the Welsh capital since 1968. France, however, were fortunate to win a remarkable match. Jean-Patrick Lescarboura, the 6ft. 2in. outside half, scored 17 points with four penalty shots, a drop-shot from fully 45 yards, and a conversion of Sella's lovely try. Wales outscored the visitors 2-1 on tries, but Howell Davies missed two comparatively easy penalty attempts, though the full back snapped up a smart try. For the first time for 21 years Wales had lost both home championship games.

Wales: Howell Davies (Bridgend); M H Titley (Bridgend), R A Ackerman (London Welsh), B Bowen (S W Police), A M Hadley (Cardiff); M Dacey (Swansea), M H J Douglas (Llanelli); I Stephens (Bridgend), M J Watkins (Newport, capt.), I H Eidman (Cardiff), S J Perkins (Pontypool), R L Norster (Cardiff), R D Moriarty (Swansea), E T Butler (Pontypool,), D F Pickering (Llanelli).

France: S Blanco (Biarritz); P Lagisquet (Bayonne), P Sella (Agen), D Codorniou, P Esteve (Narbonne); J P Lescarboura (Dax), J Gallion (Toulon); M Cremaschi (Lourdes), P Dintrans (Tarbes) D Dubroca (Agen), A Lorieux (Grenoble), J Condom (Boucou), J P Rives (Racing Club of France, capt.), J L Joinel (Brive), D Erbani (Agen).

For Wales, Eddie Butler and Howell Davies scored tries. Howell Davies converted one and kicked two penalty goals.

For France, Phillipe Sella scored a try. Jean Patrick Lescarboura converted, kicked four penalty goals and dropped a goal.

Referee: R G Byres (Australia).

Wales won by one goal, two dropped goals, four penalty goals (24) to five penalty goals (15)

Floundering England had been destroyed in their previous game 32-18 by France, and now Malcolm Dacey, playing his greatest game for Wales, stunned them with two late dropped goals to ensure victory. Terry Holmes, back after his knee injury in the first Test in NZ in June, played after an eight-month lay-off and just three first team games for Cardiff. His stability was a source of inspiration. Howell Davies completed the season with a Welsh record of 39 championship points, passing the 38 by Phil Bennett (1976) and Steve Fenwick (1979). The only try, by Adrian Hadley, was made with a lovely dummy and break by Bleddyn Bowen, with Eddie Butler as the link. The 24 points were the most Wales had scored at Twickenham.

> **England:** W H Hare (Leicester); J Carleton (Orrell), B Barley (Wakefield), C R Woodward, R Underwood (Leicester); L Cusworth, N G Youngs (Leicester); P A G Rendall (Wasps), P J Wheeler (Leicester, capt.), P J Blakeway (Gloucester), M C Colclough (Wasps), B Bainbridge (Gosforth), A F Dun (Wasps), J P Scott (Cardiff), P J Winterbottom (Headingley).

> **Wales:** Howell Davies (Bridgend); M H Titley (Bridgend), R A Ackerman (London Welsh), B Bowen (S W Police), A M Hadley (Cardiff); M Dacey (Swansea), T D Holmes (Cardiff); I Stephens (Bridgend), M J Watkins (Newport, capt.), I Eidman, R L Norster (Cardiff), S J Perkins (Pontypool), R D Moriarty (Swansea), E T Butler (Pontypool), D F Pickering (Llanelli).

For Wales, Adrian Hadley scored a try. Howell Davies converted and kicked four penalty goals. Malcolm Dacey dropped two goals.

For England, Dusty Hare kicked five penalty goals.

Referee: J B Anderson (Scotland).

Wales won by two goals, five penalty goals (27) to one goal, one penalty goal, two tries (17)

There were 33,000 to see Wales win on penalty goals: Howell Davies kicked three and Bleddyn Bowen two. The match marked the completion of the £9m National Stadium development project. The Anti-apartheid Group staged a demonstration march through the city streets before kick-off, protesting at the WRU decision to invite three South African players to appear for the World XV. Ironically, the game's outstanding forward was the World team's captain, Springbok No.8 Rob Louw.

> **Wales:** Howell Davies (Bridgend); M H Titley (Bridgend), R A Ackerman (London Welsh), B Bowen (S W Police), A M Hadley (Cardiff); M Dacey (Swansea), T D Holmes (Cardiff); I Stephens (Bridgend), M J Watkins (Newport, capt.), I Eidman, R L Norster (Cardiff), S J Perkins (Pontypool), R D Moriarty (Swansea), E T Butler (Pontypool), D F Pickering (Llanelli).

> **WRU President's World XV:** R G Gould (Australia); P C Grigg (Australia), W Cupido (South Africa), S T Pokere (New Zealand), P Esteve (France); J Y Rutherford (Scotland), J Gallion (France); H J van Aswegen (South Africa), C T Deans (Scotland), M A Harding (Australia), G W Whetton (New Zealand), M J Colclough (England), D G Leslie (Scotland), R J Louw (South Africa, capt.) M Rafter (England).

For Wales, Robert Ackerman and Terry Holmes scored tries. Howell Davies converted both and kicked three penalty goals. Bleddyn Bowen kicked two penalty goals.

For the World XV, Steve Pokere (2) and David Leslie scored tries. John Rutherford converted one and kicked a penalty goal.

Referee: C Norling (Wales).

Match 353 WALES v AUSTRALIA Cardiff Arms Park. November 24, 1984

Australia won by three goals, two penalty goals, one try (28) to one goal, one penalty goal (9)

Wales, favourites, were devastated; destroyed by four tries to one, including a push-over try as the crowning indignity. With Terry Holmes recovering from a dislocated shoulder and Richard Moriarty under six weeks suspension for being sent off at Llanelli, Wales missed the services of two key men. Yet new cap David Bishop, the daredevil Pontypool scrum half, played his heart out as the one member of the Welsh team who responded to the challenge in true fighting fashion. He scored a dazzling try; a marvel of juggling to retain a tenuous grip on the ball as he dived across. The Wallabies raced to a record score by any touring team against Wales on Welsh territory. Australia went on to win the Grand Slam of Test victories for the first time, though they lost against Cardiff and Llanelli.

Wales: M A Wyatt (Swansea); M H Titley (Bridgend), R A Ackerman (London Welsh), M G Ring (Cardiff), *Phil Lewis (Llanelli); M Dacey (Swansea), *D J Bishop (Pontypool); I Stephens (Bridgend), M J Watkins (Newport, capt.), I Eidman (Cardiff), S J Perkins (Pontypool) R L Norster (Cardiff), *Alun E Davies (Llanelli), E T Butler (Pontypool), D F Pickering (Llanelli). Rep: *J Whitefoot (Cardiff) for Stephens.

Australia: R G Gould; P C Grigg, A G Slack (capt.), M P Lynagh, D I Campese; M G Ella, N C Farr-Jones; E E Rodriguez, T A Lawton, A J McIntyre, S A Williams, S A G Cutler, S P Poidevin, S N Tuynman, D Codey.

For Wales, David Bishop scored a try. Mark Wyatt converted and kicked a penalty goal.

For Australia, Tom Lawton, Michael Lynagh, Steve Tuynman and Mark Ella scored tries. Roger Gould converted three and kicked two penalty goals.

Referee: E O Doyle (Ireland).

Match 354 SCOTLAND v WALES Murrayfield. March 2, 1985

Wales won by one goal, one dropped goal, four penalty goals, one try (25)
to two goals, two dropped goals, one penalty goal (21)

Wales's first championship match of the season because of postponments against France (frozen Paris pitch) and England (snow in Cardiff), saw the unexpected recall of Gareth Davies and the switch of Richard Moriarty to No.8. The selectors had refused to recognise that Gareth Davies was in better form than Malcolm Dacey or that Moriarty was more suited to No.8 than blindside. Letters to the *Western Mail* implied that the selectors had been given another chance to get it right by "Divine Intervention." This when Eddie Butler announced his retirement from international rugby after being named at No.8, while Dacey damaged knee ligaments the week before this Murrayfield trip. Gareth Davies dropped a goal after just 50 sec to set his team on the way to a memorable success and perhaps inflict a tinge of remorse for neglect among the selectors! David Pickering, the pack leader, shone with two tries in the biggest Welsh score at Murrayfield. Wyatt equalled Gwyn Evans's feat of fastest 50 points for Wales in six games.

Scotland: P W Dods (Gala); P D Steven (Heriot's FP), K T Murray (Hawick), K W Robertson (Melrose), G R T Baird (Kelso); J Y Rutherford, I G Hunter (Selkirk); G M McGuinness (West of Scotland), C T Deans (Hawick), I G Milne (Harlequins), A J Tomes, A J Campbell (Hawick), J H Calder (Stewart's /

231

Melville FP), I A M Paxton (Selkirk), D G Leslie (Gala, capt). Rep: D S Wyllie (Stewart's / Melville FP) for Murray.

Wales: M A Wyatt (Swansea); M H Titley (Bridgend), R A Ackerman (London Welsh), M G Ring (Cardiff), Phil Lewis (Llanelli); W Gareth Davies, T D Holmes (Cardiff, capt.); J Whitefoot (Cardiff), W J James (Aberavon), I H Eidman, R L Norster (Cardiff), S J Perkins (Pontypool), *M Morris (S W Police), R D Moriarty (Swansea), D F Pickering (Llanelli).

For Wales, David Pickering scored two tries. Mark Wyatt converted one and kicked four penalty goals. Gareth Davies dropped a goal.

For Scotland, Iain Paxton scored two tries. Peter Dods converted both and kicked a penalty goal. John Rutherford dropped two goals.

Referee: R Hourquet (France).

Match 355   WALES v IRELAND   Cardiff Arms Park. March 16, 1985

Ireland won by two goals, three penalty goals (21) to one goal, one dropped goal (9)

Wales lost a fourth consecutive home match for the first time, crashing unexpectedly against a relatively untried Irish team that went on to win the Triple Crown. Mark Wyatt missed six penalty shots and for all the territorial dominance and regular possession. The home backs could not evade tenacious tacklers. Who played well for Wales? Almost nobody as Ireland won in Cardiff for the first occasion in 18 years.

Wales: M A Wyatt (Swansea); M H Titley (Bridgend), R A Ackerman (London Welsh), M G Ring (Cardiff), Phil Lewis (Llanelli); W Gareth Davies, T D Holmes (Cardiff, capt.); J Whitefoot (Cardiff), W J James (Aberavon), I H Eidman, R L Norster (Cardiff), S J Perkins (Pontypool), M Morris (S W Police), R D Moriarty (Swansea), D F Pickering (Llanelli).

Ireland: H P MacNeill (Blackrock); T M Ringland (Ballymena), B J Mullin (Dublin Univ.), M J Kiernan (Lansdowne), K D Crossan (Instonians); P M Dean (St. Mary's Coll.), M T Bradley (Cork Constitution); P A Orr (Old Wesley), C F Fitzgerald (St. Mary's Coll., capt), J J McCoy (Dungannon), D G Lenihan (Cork Constitution), W A Anderson (Dungannon), P Matthews (Ards), B J Spillane (Bohemians), N J Carr (Ards).

For Wales, Phil Lewis scored a try. Mark Wyatt converted. Gareth Davies dropped a goal.

For Ireland, Trevor Ringland and Keith Crossan scored tries. Michael Kiernan converted both and kicked three penalty goals.

Referee: K V J Fitzgerald (Australia).

Match 356   FRANCE v WALES   Parc Des Princes, Paris. March 30, 1985

France won by two penalty goals, two tries (14) to one penalty goal (3)

This winning margin of 11 points was at the time the biggest by France against Wales, whose forwards again failed as drilled ball winners. Paul Thorburn played confidently on debut at full back, but the only Welsh score was his penalty goal. France did not concede a try throughout the championship. Serge Blanco sparkled, having a hand in both his team's tries. Mark Ring was the only inventive and penetrative Welsh back.

France: S Blanco (Biarritz); E Bonneval (Toulouse), P Sella (Agen), D Codorniou, P Esteve (Narbonne); J P Lescarboura (Dax), J Gallion (Toulon); P Dospital

(Bayonne), P Dintrans (Tarbes, capt.) J P Garuet (Lourdes), J C Orso (Nice), J Condom (Boucau), J Gratton (Agen), J L Joinel (Brive), L Rodriguez (Mont de Marsan). Rep: D Erbani (Agen) for Rodriguez.

Wales: *P Thorburn (Neath); Phil Lewis (Llanelli), R A Ackerman (London Welsh), M G Ring (Cardiff), A M Hadley (Cardiff; W Gareth Davies, T D Holmes (Cardiff, capt.); J Whitefoot (Cardiff), W J James (Aberavon), *Stuart Evans (Swansea), S J Perkins (Pontypool), R L Norster (Cardiff), M Morris (S W Police), R D Moriarty (Swansea), D F Pickering (Llanelli). Rep: G J Roberts (Cardiff) for Moriarty.

For Wales, Paul Thorburn kicked a penalty goal.

For France, Patrick Esteve and Jerome Gallion scored tries. Jean-Patrick Lescarboura kicked two penalty goals.

Referee: S Strydom (South Africa).

Match 357   WALES v ENGLAND   Cardiff Arms Park. April 20, 1985

Wales won by two goals, one dropped goal, three penalty goals (24)
to one goal, one dropped goal, two penalty goals (15)

After four successive home defeats, Wales put it together at last – just their second home win in eight matches. England, whose last success in Cardiff had been in 1963, four times took the lead. But the home pack controlled the second half and Jonathan Davies crossed for a try. It was the first debut try by a Welsh fly half for 54 years. Pickering and Gareth Roberts proved a dynamic wing forward pair while Rob Norster ruled the lineout. Gareth Davies announced his retirement from international rugby when the selectors, again showing indecision, named A N Other for the No.10 jersey. The great Phil Davies played his first game.

Wales: P Thorburn (Neath); Phil Lewis (Llanelli), R A Ackerman (London Welsh), *Kevin Hopkins (Swansea), A M Hadley (Cardiff); *Jonathan Davies (Neath), T D Holmes (Cardiff, capt.); J Whitefoot (Cardiff), W J James (Aberavon), Stuart Evans (Swansea), S J Perkins (Pontypool), R L Norster (Cardiff), G J Roberts (Cardiff), *Phil Davies (Llanelli), D F Pickering (Llanelli).

England: C R Martin (Bath); S T Smith (Wasps), K G Simms (Liverpool), P W Dodge (Leicester, capt.), R Underwood (Leicester); C R Andrew (Nottingham), N D Melville (Wasps); A Sheppard (Bristol), S E Brain (Coventry), G S Pearce (Northampton), J Orwin (Gloucester), W A Dooley (Preston Grasshoppers), J P Hall (Bath), R Hesford (Bristol), D H Cooke (Harlequins).

For Wales, Jonathan Davies and Gareth Roberts scored tries. Paul Thorburn converted both and kicked three penalty goals. Jonathan Davies dropped a goal.

For England, Simon Smith scored a try. Rob Andrew converted, dropped a goal and kicked two penalty goals.

Referee: F Palmade (France).

Match 358   WALES v FIJI   Cardiff Arms Park. November 9, 1985

Wales won by three goals, two penalty goals, four tries (40) to one penalty goal (3)

Wales destroyed the Fijian scrum, won the lineout and supplied repeated possession from all phases as seven tries were racked up, two of them by impressive No.8 Phil Davies. He and David Pickering were the outstanding performers. Holmes jarred his knee and was replaced by Ray Giles, winning his second cap. The home midfield did not move as fluently as expected.

Wales: P Thorburn (Neath); M H Titley (Swansea), R A Ackerman (London Welsh), B Bowen (S W Police), A M Hadley (Cardiff); Jonathan Davies (Neath), T D Holmes (Cardiff, capt.); J Whitefoot (Cardiff), W J James (Aberavon), I H Eidman (Cardiff), S J Perkins (Pontypool), R L Norster (Cardiff), Mark Davies (Swansea), Phil Davies (Llanelli), D F Pickering (Llanelli). Rep: R Giles (Aberavon) for Holmes.

Fiji: J Damu; M Nabati, S Laulau, T Cama, S Tuvula; A Niuqila, P Nawalu; P Volavola, E Rakai, R Nomoro, K Rakoroi, A Hughes, I Finau, E Teleni (capt.), P Gale. Rep: J Kubu for Tuvula.

For Wales, Phil Davies (2), Terry Holmes, Adrian Hadley, David Pickering, Mark Titley, Billy James scored tries. Paul Thorburn converted three and kicked two penalty goals.

For Fiji, Jimi Damu kicked a penalty goal.

Referee: S R Hilditch (Ireland).

Match 359   ENGLAND v WALES   Twickenham. January 18, 1986

England won by one dropped goal, six penalty goals (21)
to one goal, one dropped goal, three penalty goals (18)

This was Rob Andrew's game. He kicked all England's points with six right-footed penalty goals and then a left-footed drop-shot in the second minute of injury time to complete his country's highest score against Wales at Twickenham. However, the real heroes for the winners were jumpers Wade Dooley (6ft 8in) and Maurice Colclough (6ft 5in). They cleaned the visitors out in the most decisive manner since the Welsh humiliation in Bucharest in 1983. England's backs failed dismally as attackers and Wales scored the only try from Billy James's long throw to the tail before the lineout had formed. Pickering fed Robert Jones for the new scrum half to put Jonathan Davies darting through to send Bleddyn Bowen over. It was debut day for Robert Jones.

England: G H Davies (Wasps); S T Smith (Wasps), S J Halliday (Bath), J L B Salmon (Harlequins), R Underwood (Leicester); C R Andrew (Nottingham), N D Melville (Wasps, capt.); P A G Rendall (Wasps), S E Brain (Coventry), G S Pearce (Northampton), W A Dooley (Preston Grasshoppers), M J Colclough (Swansea), J P Hall (Bath), G L Robbins (Coventry), P J Winterbottom (Headingley).

Wales: P H Thorburn (Neath); Phil Lewis (Llanelli), *J A Devereux (S. Glam. Inst. and Bridgend), B Bowen (S W Police), A M Hadley (Cardiff); Jonathan Davies (Neath), *Robert N Jones (Swansea); J Whitefoot (Cardiff), W J James (Aberavon), I H Eidman (Cardiff), *D R Waters (Newport), S J Perkins, M Brown (Pontypool), Phil Davies (Llanelli), D F Pickering (Llanelli, capt.).

For Wales, Bleddyn Bowen scored a try. Paul Thorburn converted and kicked three penalty goals. Jonathan Davies dropped a goal.

For England, Rob Andrew dropped a goal and kicked six penalty goals.

Referee: R J Fordham (Australia).

Match 360   WALES v SCOTLAND   Cardiff Arms Park. February 1, 1986

Wales won by five penalty goals, one dropped goal, one try (22)
to one penalty goal, three tries (15)

A murmur of astonishment rippled around the National Stadium as Paul Thorburn made ready to kick at goal from a spot more than 70 yards distance from the Scottish posts. "I fancy my chance," he told skipper David Pickering and, helped by a fierce following wind, over it went at the river end to change a tenuous 16-15 lead into 19-15 and provide much needed breathing space. The penalty was awarded for a late tackle by Finlay Calder on Jonathan Davies and the official measurement made after the match was a carry from kick to pitch of 70 yds. 8½ in. It was the longest goal in the 105 years history of Welsh rugby. Thorburn added a goal from 53 yards and his five penalty shots took his tally in five full cap matches to 54 – the fastest 50 points scored for Wales, topping the six matches it took Gwyn Evans and Mark Wyatt. But Wales managed only one try compared to three by Scotland, who were trying for a record third consecutive victory at Cardiff. The Scots gave Wales a lesson in fast rucking with John 'White Shark' Jeffrey the most impressive forward on view. Wales survived 10 minutes of terror in the north corner at the Westgate Street end as Scotland endeavoured to charge across from a nail biting succession of tapped penalties.

Wales: P H Thorburn (Neath); Phil Lewis (Llanelli), J A Devereux (S. Glam. Inst. and Bridgend), B Bowen (S W Police), A M Hadley (Cardiff); Jonathan Davies (Neath), Robert N Jones (Swansea); J Whitefoot (Cardiff), W J James (Aberavon), I H Eidman (Cardiff), D R Waters (Newport), S J Perkins, M Brown (Pontypool), Phil Davies (Llanelli), D F Pickering (Llanelli, capt.).

Scotland: A G Hastings (Watsonians); M D F Duncan (West of Scotland), D I Johnston (Watsonians), S Hastings (Watsonians), G R T Baird (Kelso); J Y Rutherford (Selkirk), R J Laidlaw (Jedforest); D M B Sole (Bath), C T Deans (Hawick, capt.), I G Milne (Harlequins), A J Campbell (Hawick), I A M Paxton (Selkirk), J Jeffrey (Kelso), J R Beattie (Glasgow Acads.), F Calder (Stewart's / Melville FP).

For Wales, Adrian Hadley scored a try. Jonathan Davies dropped a goal. Paul Thorburn kicked five penalty goals.

For Scotland, Matt Duncan, John Jeffrey and Gavin Hastings scored tries. Gavin Hastings kicked a penalty goal.

Referee: R C Francis (New Zealand).

Match 361   IRELAND v WALES   Lansdowne Road, Dublin. February 15, 1986

Wales won by one goal, three penalty goals, one try (19) to one goal, two penalty goals (12)

Wales, trailing 12-4 at half time, appeared to be fading, but David Pickering's pack responded to his clarion call in rousing style. It was a heart-warming display to drive the Irish scrum in disarray and then defy the late and desperate home rally. Paul Moriarty, brother of Richard, was outstanding on his debut at blindside wing forward and restored balance to the back row.

Ireland: H P MacNeill (London Irish); T M Ringland (Ballymena), M J Kiernan (Dolphin), B J Mullin (Dublin Univ.), M C Finn (Cork Constitution); P M Dean (St. Mary's), M T Bradley (Cork Constitution); A P Kennedy (London Irish), C F Fitzgerald (St. Mary's, capt), D C Fitzgerald (Lansdowne), J J Holland (Wanderers), D G Lenihan (Cork Constitution), R Kearney (Wanderers), B J Spillane (Bohemians), N J Carr (Ards).

Wales: P H Thorburn (Neath); Phil Lewis (Llanelli), J A Devereux (S. Glam. Inst. and Bridgend), B Bowen (S W Police), A M Hadley (Cardiff); Jonathan Davies (Neath), Robert N Jones (Swansea); J Whitefoot (Cardiff), W J James (Aberavon), I H Eidman (Cardiff), D R Waters (Newport), S J Perkins (Pontypool), *Paul Moriarty (Swansea), Phil Davies (Llanelli), D F Pickering (Llanelli, capt.).

For Wales, Phil Lewis and Phil Davies scored tries. Paul Thorburn converted one and kicked three penalty goals.

For Ireland, Trevor Ringland scored a try. Michael Kiernan converted and kicked two penalty goals.

Referee: F A Howard (England).

| Match 362 | **WALES v FRANCE** | Cardiff Arms Park. March 1, 1986 |

France won by two goals, one dropped goal and two tries (23) to five penalty goals (15)

For the first time in 24 years Wales failed to score a try against France in Cardiff, whereas the visitors snapped up four in their biggest score against Wales. The home forwards were outplayed and consequently there were few chances for the backs. Had it not been for French indiscipline, Wales would not have collected a point. However, Paul Thorburn fired in five penalty shots to become the first Welsh player to pass 50 championship points in a season. He kicked one goal from 60 yds and aggregated 64 points in a season (including the Fiji game) and totalled 80 points in seven full cap games. The standard of Welsh tackling, as coach Tony Gray said, was "unacceptable."

Wales: P H Thorburn (Neath); M H Titley (Swansea), J A Devereux (S. Glam. Inst. and Bridgend), B Bowen (S W Police), A M Hadley (Cardiff); Jonathan Davies (Neath), Robert N Jones (Swansea); J Whitefoot (Cardiff), W J James (Aberavon), I H Eidman (Cardiff), D R Waters (Newport), S J Perkins (Pontypool), Paul Moriarty (Swansea), Phil Davies (Llanelli), D F Pickering (Llanelli, capt.).

France: S Blanco (Biarritz); J B Lafond (Racing Club), P Sella (Agen), D Charvet (Toulouse), E Bonneval (Toulouse); G Laporte (Graulhet), P Berbizier (Agen); P Marocco (Montferrand), D Dubroca (Agen, capt.), J P Garuet (Lourdes), F Haget (Biarritz), J Condom (Boucau), D Erbani (Agen), J L Joinel (Brive), E Champ (Toulon).

For Wales, Paul Thorburn kicked five penalty goals.

For France, Jean-Baptiste Lafond (2), Philippe Sella and Serge Blanco scored tries. Guy Laporte converted two and dropped a goal.

Referee: J B Anderson (Scotland).

| Match 363 | **FIJI v WALES** | National Stadium, Suva. May 31, 1986 |

Wales won by one goal, one dropped goal, three penalty goals, one try (22)
to two goals, one penalty goal (15)

This first of three Test matches on the Welsh tour of the South Pacific was remarkable for the appearance of the brothers Richard and Paul Moriarty in the pack – the first instance for Wales since David Leyshon Thomas and Harold Thomas, of Neath, against England in 1937. Before them, Glyn and Dai Prosser, also of Neath, had been in the pack against Scotland and Ireland in 1934. The tour had been arranged after New Zealand and Australia said they could not fit in a visit by Wales. The trip was considered essential experience with the 1987 World Cup in mind. Malcolm Dacey, the Swansea outside half, figured experimentally at full back. Pickering suffered serious concussion from a kick and was flown home. A brain-scan showed he had to rest for four months.

Fiji: J Kubu; J Damu, Savenaca Aria, A Niuquila, S Tuvula; Sirilo Lovokuro, P

Nawalu; P Volavola, E Rakai, R Namoro, Rusi Cavukubu, K Rakoroi, I Tawake, E Teleni (capt), Aliferreti Dere. Rep: Rusi Naituku for Volavola.

Wales: M Dacey (Swansea); M H Titley (Swansea), B Bowen (S W Police), J Devereux (S. Glam. Inst. and Bridgend), A M Hadley (Cardiff); Jonathan Davies (Neath), Robert N Jones (Swansea); J Whitefoot (Cardiff), W J James (Aberavon), Stuart Evans (Neath), R D Moriarty (Swansea), R L Norster (Cardiff), Paul Moriarty (Swansea), Phil Davies (Llanelli), D F Pickering (Llanelli, capt.). Rep: M Brown (Pontypool) for Pickering.

For Wales, Jonathan Davies and Adrian Hadley scored tries. Bleddyn Bowen converted one. Malcolm Dacey kicked three penalty goals and Jonathan Davies dropped a goal.

For Fiji, Acura Niuqila and Serupepeli Tuvula scored tries. Jone Kubu converted both and Sirilo Lovokuro kicked a penalty goal.

Referee: D J Bishop (New Zealand).

Match 364   TONGA v WALES   Nuku'Alofa. June 12, 1986

Wales won by one goal, three penalty goals (15) to one penalty goal, one try (7)

Bridgend's Glen Webbe, a thrilling runner and top try scorer in Welsh club rugby during 1985-86, with 38, became the first black player to win a cap for Wales when he went on as replacement for Adrian Hadley. The Cardiff wing had to be stretchered off after being felled in a fierce massed punch-up in the in-goal area. The Tongans' ferocious approach was condemned as disgraceful by the horrified tourists. Huw Richards, the Neath front jumper, also won his first cap as a replacement. Richard Moriarty, who had been banned from Five Nations championship games during 1986 for being ordered off against Llanelli, captained Wales in the absence of injured Pickering.

Tonga: T Eteaki; L Hopoate, P Moala, F Lavemai, S Mohi; T Lovo, T Fifita; T Bloomfield, A Afu, M Moala, O Vitelefi (capt.), M Tu'ungafasi, E Koloto, P Tupou, P Langi.

Wales: M Dacey (Swansea); M H Titley (Swansea), B Bowen (S W Police), J Devereux (S. Glam. Inst. and Bridgend), A M Hadley (Cardiff); Jonathan Davies (Neath), Robert N Jones (Swansea); J Whitefoot (Cardiff), W J James (Aberavon), Stuart Evans (Neath), R D Moriarty (Swansea, capt.), R L Norster (Cardiff), Paul Moriarty (Swansea), Phil Davies (Llanelli), M Brown (Pontypool). Reps: *G Webbe (Bridgend) for Hadley, *Huw Richards (Neath) for Brown.

For Wales, Paul Moriarty scored a try. Malcolm Dacey converted and kicked a penalty goal and Bleddyn Bowen kicked two penalty goals.

For Tonga, Talai Fifita scored a try and Tomasi Lovo kicked a penalty goal.

Referee: B Kinsey (Australia).

Match 365   WESTERN SAMOA v WALES   Apia. June 14, 1986

Wales won by two goals, three penalty goals, one dropped goal, two tries (32)
to two penalty goals, two tries (14)

The most entertaining of the three South Pacific Tests, this encounter was played in the best of spirits after the ugly atmosphere in Tonga. Wales were trailing 14-7 in a temperature of around 90 degrees, but regrouped to win with Rob Norster a decisive influence in the lineout. Jonathan Davies dropped his fifth goal in nine games.

237

Western Samoa: T Aialupo; T Vaega, L Koko, N Palamo, I Tautau; T Fong, T Aleni; M Jones, M Patolo, D Tafua (capt.), F Kelemete, P Alalatoa, S Toomalatai, Ma'atusi, L Sasi.

Wales: M Dacey (Swansea); M H Titley (Swansea), B Bowen (S W Police), J Devereux (S. Glam. Inst. and Bridgend), G Webbe (Bridgend); Jonathan Davies (Neath), Robert N Jones (Swansea); J Whitefoot (Cardiff), W J James (Aberavon), Stuart Evans (Neath), R D Moriarty (Swansea, capt.), R L Norster (Cardiff), Paul Moriarty (Swansea), Phil Davies (Llanelli), M Brown (Pontypool).

For Wales, Bleddyn Bowen, John Devereux, Richard Moriarty and Mark Titley scored tries. Malcolm Dacey converted two and kicked three penalty goals, and Jonathan Davies dropped a goal.

For Western Samoa, Tafua and Palamo scored tries. Tele'a Aialupo kicked two penalty goals.

Referee: R C Francis (New Zealand).

Match 366   FRANCE v WALES   Parc Des Princes, Paris. February 7, 1987

France won by one goal, two penalty goals, one try (16) to three penalty goals (9)

Paul Thorburn provided all the Welsh points for the third successive match against France, again penalties and two of them from two yards inside his half of the field. Then he broke his collarbone and was replaced by Malcolm Dacey. For the first time, France completed a succession of five victories over Wales and went on to their fourth Grand Slam. It was the first appearance of Ieuan Evans. Norster and Steve Sutton (recalled after five years) cleaned France out in the jumping contest.

France: S Blanco (Biarritz); P Berot, P Sella (Agen), D Charvet, E Bonneval (Toulouse); F Mesnel (Racing Club), P Berbizier (Agen); P Ondarts (Biarritz), D Dubroca (Agen, capt.), J P Garuet (Lourdes), A Lorieux (Aix), J Condom (Boucau), D Erbani (Agen), L Rodriguez (Monferrand), E Champ (Toulon).

Wales: P H Thorburn (Neath); G Webbe (Bridgend), K Hopkins (Swansea), J Devereux (S. Glam. Inst. and Bridgend), *Ieuan Evans (Llanelli); Jonathan Davies (Neath), Robert N Jones (Swansea); J Whitefoot (Cardiff), *K Phillips (Neath), Stuart Evans (Neath), Steve Sutton (S W Police), R L Norster (Cardiff), Paul Moriarty (Swansea), Phil Davies (Llanelli), D F Pickering (Llanelli, capt).Rep: M Dacey (Swansea) for Thorburn.

For Wales, Paul Thorburn kicked three penalty goals.

For France, Franck Mesnel and Eric Bonneval scored tries. Phillippe Berot converted one and kicked two penalty goals.

Referee: C J High (England).

Match 367   WALES v ENGLAND   Cardiff Arms Park. March 7, 1987

Wales won by five penalty goals, one try (19) to four penalty goals (12)

"I was ashamed," admitted Wade Dooley, the 6ft 8in Blackpool policeman, after his punch from behind felled Wales No.8 Phil Davies and caused multiple small facial fractures. Davies tried to play on, but left the field after seven minutes. It was the most violent start to a match for years and England's intimidation brought widespread condemnation. Referee Ray Megson endured a difficult time because the unpleasantness lasted virtually throughout the game. England, thoroughly negative, failed to score a try for the third occasion that season and the match was considered one of the most dismal on record. Mark Wyatt, deputising for injured Thorburn, kicked five penalty goals, but missed four others, all within his scope. Steve Sutton had his nose broken right at the start – from the flying arm of his second row partner Norster. Ironically, it had been a retaliatory punch by Norster at Sutton during the Cardiff-S W Police fixture the previous season that had banned Norster from international rugby in 1986.

Wales: M A Wyatt (Swansea); G Webbe (Bridgend), K Hopkins (Swansea), J Devereux (S. Glam. Inst. and Bridgend), Ieuan Evans (Llanelli); Jonathan Davies (Neath), Robert N Jones (Swansea); J Whitefoot (Cardiff), W J James (Aberavon), Stuart Evans (Neath), Steve Sutton (S W Police), R L Norster (Cardiff), Paul Moriarty (Swansea), Phil Davies (Llanelli), D F Pickering (Llanelli, capt).Rep: *R G Collins (S W Police) for Phil Davies.

England: W H M Rose (Harlequins); M E Harrison (Wakefield), K G Simms (Wasps), J L B Salmon (Harlequins), R Underwood (Leicester); C R Andrew (Wasps), R J Hill (Bath, capt.); G J Chilcott, R G R Dawe (Bath), G S Pearce (Northampton), W A Dooley, S Bainbridge (Fylde), P J Winterbottom (Headingley), J P Hall (Bath), G W Rees (Nottingham).

For Wales, Mark Wyatt kicked five penalty goals. Stuart Evans scored a try.

For England, Marcus Rose kicked four penalty goals.

Referee: R J Megson (Scotland).

| Match 368 | **SCOTLAND v WALES** | Murrayfield. March 21, 1987 |

Scotland won by two goals, two penalty goals, one dropped goal (21) to one goal, two penalty goals, one dropped goal (15)

This was the day the Welsh scrum fell apart and Scotland drove through it like a coach and horses. Stuart Evans, the tight head anchorman, had won his fitness fight from a bruised right ankle only to break a bone in his left foot during his run-out test on the morning before the Murrayfield match. Without him, the scrum disintegrated. Remarkably, Wales kept in contention against faster forwards, mainly because Gavin Hastings missed five penalty attempts and John Jeffrey dropped a scoring pass. Only Mark Jones, the Neath No.8, played with any impact and scored his team's try on his debut.

Scotland: A G Hastings (Watsonians); M D F Duncan (West of Scotland), K W Robertson (Melrose), S Hastings (Watsonians), I Tukalo (Selkirk); J Y Rutherford (Selkirk), R J Laidlaw (Jedforest); D M B Sole (Bath), C T Deans (Hawick, capt.), I G Milne (Heriot's FP), D B White (Gala), I A M Paxton (Selkirk), J Jeffrey (Kelso), J R Beattie (Glasgow Acads.), F Calder (Stewart's / Melville FP).

Wales: M A Wyatt (Swansea); G Webbe (Bridgend), K Hopkins (Swansea), J Devereux (S. Glam. Inst. and Bridgend), Ieuan Evans (Llanelli); Jonathan Davies (Neath), Robert N Jones (Swansea); J Whitefoot (Cardiff), W J James (Aberavon), *Peter Francis (Maesteg), Steve Sutton (S W Police), R L Norster (Cardiff), Paul Moriarty (Swansea), *Mark Jones (Neath), D F Pickering (Llanelli, capt).Rep: A M Hadley (Cardiff) for Ieuan Evans.

For Wales, Mark Jones scored a try. Mark Wyatt converted and kicked two penalty goals. Jonathan Davies dropped a goal.

For Scotland, John Beattie and John Jeffrey scored tries. Gavin Hastings converted both and kicked two penalty goals. John Rutherford dropped a goal.

Referee: K Lawrence (NZ).

Ireland won by two goals, one penalty goal (15) to one penalty goal, two tries (11)

For the first 30 minutes, Wales re-enacted a scene from the Super Seventies. They scored two dazzling tries; the first created by Robert Jones's dummy and dart, with Richie Collins in support, before Ieuan Evans sped clear on the overlap. Then, with a 25-yard charge, Robert Norster surged over for his first try in 22 games after a smart under-arm flick from Jonathan Davies, with Paul Moriarty as the link. A mad moment of Welsh stamping was observed by the touch judge, and Michael Kiernan hoisted a high punt from the penalty. In the confusion, Paul Dean slipped through and Kiernan converted. Ireland's solid scrum and unwavering tackling enabled them to win for the first time in two consecutive games on Welsh soil. Hooker Billy James was the first Aberavon player to captain Wales.

Wales: M A Wyatt (Swansea); Ieuan Evans (Llanelli), M G Ring (Cardiff), J A Devereux (S. Glam. Inst. and Bridgend), A M Hadley (Cardiff); Jonathan Davies (Neath), Robert N Jones (Swansea); J Whitefoot (Cardiff), W J James (Aberavon, capt.), *S W Blackmore (Cardiff), Steve Sutton (S W Police), R L Norster (Cardiff), Paul Moriarty (Swansea), Phil Davies (Llanelli), R G Collins (S W Police).

Ireland: H P MacNeill (London Irish); T M Ringland (Ballymena), B J Mullin (Oxford Univ.), M J Kiernan (Dolphin), K D Crossan (Instonians); P M Dean (St. Mary's Coll.), M T Bradley (Cork Constitution); P A Orr (Old Wesley), H T Harbison (Bective Rangers), D C Fitzgerald (Lansdowne), D G Lenihan (Cork Constitution, capt), W A Anderson (Dungannon), P M Matthews (Wanderers), B J Spillane (Bohemians), N J Carr (Ards).

For Wales, Robert Norster and Ieuan Evans scored tries. Mark Wyatt kicked a penalty goal.

For Ireland, Paul Dean and Brendan Mullin scored tries. Michael Kiernan converted them both and kicked a penalty goal.

Referee: G Maurette (France).

WORLD CUP (Pool 1st Game)

Wales won by two dropped goals, one penalty goal, one try (13) to two penalty goals (6)

It was particular satisfaction to avenge the home defeat by Ireland a month earlier and make a sound start to the First World Cup. John Devereux's tackling was a feature and Jonathan Davies flighted over two dropped goals. Thorburn was up with the attackers to send Mark Ring across for his first try for Wales.

Wales: P H Thorburn (Neath); Ieuan Evans (Llanelli), J A Devereux (S. Glam. Inst. and Bridgend), M G Ring, A M Hadley (Cardiff); Jonathan Davies (Neath), Robert N Jones (Swansea); J Whitefoot (Cardiff), K Phillips, Stuart Evans (Neath), R D Moriarty (Swansea, capt), R L Norster, G Roberts (Cardiff), Paul Moriarty (Swansea), R G Collins (S W Police).

Ireland: H P MacNeill (London Irish); T M Ringland (Ballymena), B J Mullin (Oxford Univ.), M J Kiernan (Dolphin), K D Crossan (Instonians); P M Dean (St. Mary's Coll.), M T Bradley (Cork Constitution); P A Orr (Old Wesley), T Kingston (Dolphin), D C Fitzgerald (Lansdowne), D G Lenihan (Cork Constitution, capt), W A Anderson (Dungannon), P M Matthews (Wanderers), B J Spillane (Bohemians), D G McGrath (Cork Constitution). Rep: J J Glennon (Skerries) for Matthews.

For Wales, Mark Ring scored a try. Jonathan Davies dropped two goals and Paul Thorburn kicked a penalty goal.

For Ireland, Michael Kiernan kicked two penalty goals.

Referee: K V J Fitzgerald (Australia).

WORLD CUP (Pool 2nd Game)

Match 371   WALES v TONGA   Showgrounds, Palmerston North. May 29, 1987

Wales won by two goals, two penalty goals, one dropped goal, two tries (29)
to one goal, two penalty goals, one try (16)

After the relief of winning against Ireland, Wales, wearing green jerseys, aimed for an improved performance, but overall it was disappointing. "It left a lot to be desired," conceded skipper Richard Moriarty. Injuries to Stuart Evans and Glenn Webbe meant they had to fly home after the match. Evans fractured a toe while Webbe suffered concussion. Yet the Bridgend wing scored three tries, the third spectacularly from his own half after a head-high tackle by Tali Ete'Aki had left him dazed.

Wales: P H Thorburn (Neath); G Webbe (Bridgend), K Hopkins (Swansea), M G Ring, A M Hadley (Cardiff); M Dacey, Robert N Jones (Swansea); *A Buchanan (Llanelli), K Phillips, Stuart Evans, Huw Richards (Neath), R D Moriarty (capt), Paul Moriarty (Swansea), Phil Davies (Llanelli), G Roberts (Cardiff). Reps: S Blackmore (Cardiff) for Evans, Jonathan Davies (Neath) for Dacey.

Tonga: Tali Ete'Aki; Kutusi Fielea, Samiu Mohi, Talanoa Fuka, Manu Vunipola; Asaeli 'Amone, Talai Fifita; Viliami Lutua, 'Amone Afu Fungavaka, Hakatoa Tupou, Mofuike Tuungafasi, Kasi Fine, Viliami Kakato, Maliu Felise, Fakahau Valu (capt). Reps: Alamoni Liava'a for Asaeli 'Amone, Latu Va'eono for Hakatoa Tupou.

For Wales, Glen Webbe (3), and Adrian Hadley scored tries. Paul Thorburn converted two and kicked two penalty goals. Jonathan Davies dropped a goal.

For Tonga, Kutusi Fielea and Talai Fifita scored tries. Alamoni Liava'a converted one and kicked a penalty goal. Asaeli 'Amone kicked a penalty goal.

Referee: D J Bishop (New Zealand).

WORLD CUP (Pool 3rd Game)

Match 372   WALES v CANADA   Rugby Park, Invercargill. June 3, 1987

Wales won by four goals, four tries (40) to three penalty goals (9)

Jonathan Davies captained Wales and lanced through on seven thrustful breaks, three of them leading to tries. Ieuan Evans crossed for four tries to equal the Welsh record held by Willie Llewellyn, Reggie Gibbs and Maurice Richards. Canada were in front 9-6 at half time watched by a crowd of about 12,000. Gareth Rees, whose father came from Maesteg, landed three penalty goals for Canada – and was to prove even more troublesome to Wales in years to come!

Wales: P H Thorburn (Neath); Ieuan Evans (Llanelli), B Bowen (S W Police), J A Devereux (S Glam Inst and Bridgend), A M Hadley (Cardiff); Jonathan Davies (Neath, capt), R Giles (Aberavon); J Whitefoot, A J Phillips, S Blackmore, R L Norster (Cardiff), S Sutton (S W Police), Paul Moriarty (Swansea), P T Davies (Llanelli), G Roberts (Cardiff). Reps: R D Moriarty (Swansea) for Paul Moriarty, K Hopkins (Swansea) for Bowen.

Canada: M Wyatt; P Palmer, T Woods, S McTavish, S Gray; G Rees, I Stuart;

R McKellar, K Svoboda, B Handson, R Hindson, H de Goede (capt.), D Breen, S Ennis, R Frame. Rep: D Tucker for Stuart.

For Wales, Ieuan Evans (4), Bleddyn Bowen, John Devereux, Adrian Hadley and Alan Phillips scored tries. Paul Thorburn converted four.

For Canada, Gareth Rees kicked three penalty goals.

Referee: D J Bishop (New Zealand).

WORLD CUP (Quarter-final)

Match 373   **WALES v ENGLAND**   Ballymore, Brisbane. June 8, 1987

Wales won by two goals, one try (16) to one penalty goal (3)

Probably this was the most uninspired of all the 1987 World Cup matches. England, having played all their games in Australia, were fully acclimatised whereas Wales had just arrived from the cold, wet deep south of New Zealand. But rain on a heavy pitch unsettled England. Robert Jones was the star Welsh player and steered his side through as the only British team to reach the semi-final stage. Former Australian coach Bob Templeton condemned both teams. "The All Blacks could play Wales and England at the same time and eat them for breakfast," he remarked.

Wales: P H Thorburn (Neath); Ieuan Evans (Llanelli), B Bowen (S W Police), J A Devereux (S Glam. Inst. and Bridgend), A M Hadley (Cardiff); Jonathan Davies (Neath), Robert N Jones (Swansea); A Buchanan (Llanelli), A J Phillips (Cardiff), *D Young (Swansea), R L Norster (Cardiff), R D Moriarty (Swansea, capt), G Roberts (Cardiff), Paul Moriarty (Swansea), R G Collins (S W Police). Rep: Huw Richards (Neath) for Norster.

England: J Webb (Bristol); M E Harrison (Wakefield, capt), K G Simms (Wasps), J L B Salmon (Harlequins), R Underwood (Leicester); P Williams (Orrell), R Harding (Bristol); P Rendall (Wasps), B C Moore (Nottingham), G S Pearce (Northampton), W A Dooley (Fylde), N Redman (Bath), P J Winterbottom (Headingley), D Richards (Leicester), G W Rees (Nottingham). Rep: G J Chilcott (Bath) for Rendall.

For Wales, Robert Jones, Gareth Roberts and John Devereux scored tries. Paul Thorburn converted two.

For England, Jon Webb kicked a penalty goal.

Referee: R Hourquet (France).

WORLD CUP (Semi-final)

Match 374   **WALES v NEW ZEALAND**   Ballymore, Brisbane. June 14, 1987

New Zealand won by seven goals, one penalty goal, one try (49) to one goal (6)

This semi-final flop was one of the blackest days in Welsh rugby history. They crashed to their heaviest defeat against opponents who powered over for eight tries. To add to the agony, Huw Richards was ordered off by Kerry Fitzgerald for throwing punches at Gary Whetton. Richards was suspended for one week. Some 20,000 onlookers saw the Welsh scrum fail again. Robert Norster was absent injured, as was Gareth Roberts, who broke his nose in the England match. Wayne Shelford laid Richards out cold with a haymaker and it was amazing that Shelford was allowed to remain while Richards dipped his toe in the early bath. New Zealand went on to beat France in the final.

Wales: P H Thorburn (Neath); Ieuan Evans (Llanelli), B Bowen (S W Police), J A

Devereux (S Glam Inst and Bridgend), A M Hadley (Cardiff); Jonathan Davies (Neath), Robert N Jones (Swansea); A Buchanan (Llanelli), K Phillips (Neath), D Young (Swansea), Huw Richards (Neath), R D Moriarty (capt), Paul Moriarty (Swansea), P T Davies (Llanelli), R G Collins (S W Police). Rep: S Sutton (S W Police) for Collins.

New Zealand: J Gallagher; J Kirwan, J Stanley, W Taylor, C Green; G Fox, D Kirk (capt); S McDowell, S Fitzpatrick, J Drake, G Whetton, M Pierce, A Whetton, W Shelford, M Brooke-Cowden. Rep: B McCahill for Stanley.

For Wales, John Devereux scored a try. Paul Thorburn converted.

For New Zealand, John Kirwan (2), Wayne Shelford (2), John Drake, Alan Whetton, Joe Stanley and Mark Brooke-Cowden scored tries. Grant Fox converted seven and kicked a penalty goal.

Referee: K V J Fitzgerald (Australia).

WORLD CUP (3rd place play-off)

| Match 375 | **WALES v AUSTRALIA** | Rugby Park, Rotorua. June 18, 1987 |

Wales won by two goals, two penalty goals, one try (22)
to two goals, two penalty goals, one dropped goal (21)

In the fifth minute of injury time, Paul Thorburn put over a magnificent conversion kick from the touchline after Adrian Hadley had crossed. It was, perhaps, his most important kick and won the match by a whisker. The Australians looked as if they would hang on to their 21-16 lead after playing all but the first four minutes of the match with 14 men. David Codey, an abrasive wing forward, had been sent off for wild footwork. He had been warned just before this for aggression against Gareth Roberts. Five times the lead changed and it would have been humiliation had Wales lost to 14 men. They swung the ball about, playing their most illuminating rugby of the tournament and John Devereux produced a devastating hand-off. Richard Webster, the 19-year-old Swansea wing forward, was playing club rugby in Australia during the summer and Wales brought him in for his first cap as deputy for injured Richie Collins.

Wales: P H Thorburn (Neath); Ieuan Evans (Llanelli), J A Devereux (S Glam Inst and Bridgend), M G Ring, A M Hadley (Cardiff); Jonathan Davies (Neath), Robert N Jones (Swansea); A Buchanan (Llanelli), A J Phillips, S Blackmore (Cardiff), S Sutton (S W Police), R D Moriarty (capt), *R Webster, Paul Moriarty (Swansea), G Roberts (Cardiff).

Australia: A Leeds; D Campese, M Burke, A Slack (capt.), P Grigg; M Lynagh, B Smith; A McIntyre, T Lawton, C Lillicrap, S Cutler, T Coker, D Codey, S Tuynman, S Poidevin. Reps: N Farr-Jones for Grigg, E Rodriguez for Lillicrap.

For Wales, Gareth Roberts, Paul Moriarty and Adrian Hadley scored tries. Paul Thorburn converted two and kicked two penalty goals.

For Australia, Matt Burke and Peter Grigg scored tries. Michael Lynagh converted both, dropped a goal and kicked two penalty goals.

Referee: F A Howard (England).

| Match 376 | **WALES v USA** | Cardiff Arms Park. November 7, 1987 |

Wales won by four goals, two penalty goals, four tries (46) to nil

Swansea's Anthony Clement won his first cap as replacement for injured Kevin Hopkins and scored two tries. It was the first occasion for a new player to cross twice in a game since Raymond Ralph against France in 1931. Bleddyn Bowen, leading Wales for the first time and playing at fly half after 16 appearances in the centre, also collected two tries. Wales, in green because the Eagles' jerseys were red, scored eight tries. Some 23,000 spectators attended in ideal conditions.

Wales: P H Thorburn (Neath); G Webbe (Bridgend), M G Ring (Pontypol), K Hopkins (Swansea), A M Hadley (Cardiff); B Bowen (S W Police, capt.), R N Jones (Swansea); *J Pugh, K Phillips (Neath), D Young (Swansea), *S Russell (London Welsh), R L Norster (Cardiff), *R Phillips (Neath), Paul Moriarty (Swansea), R G Collins (S W Police). Rep: *A Clement (Swansea) for Hopkins.

USA: A Montgomery; W Jefferson, K Higgins, C Doherty, G Hein; Mark Williams, M Saunders; B Horwath, P Johnson, F Paoli (capt), K Swords, R Zenker, M Carlson, B Vizard, J Peter. Rep: D Shanagher for G Hein.

For Wales, Bleddyn Bowen (2), Anthony Clement (2), Glen Webbe, Paul Moriarty, Robert Norster and David Young scored tries. Paul Thorburn converted four and kicked two penalty goals.

Referee: C J High (England).

Match 377   ENGLAND v WALES   Twickenham. February 6, 1988

Wales won by one dropped goal, two tries (11) to one penalty goal (3)

Wales sensationally dropped ace goal-kicker Paul Thorburn, scorer of 140 points in 15 games, and brought in Swansea fly half Anthony Clement, who had never occupied the full back role. The game plan was to run and Wales did it quite superbly with two dazzling scoring moves. Adrian Hadley crossed on each ocassion and had quite a bit of work to do to get in. Clement launched the first try, running back Les Cusworth's loose kick. Jonathan Davies triggered the second try with a wide curving run and Mark Ring's huge dummy confused England. Wales selected four outside halves: Ring, Jonathan Davies, Bleddyn Bowen and Clement. Ring was called in when John Devereux broke a bone at the base of his little finger. There was a first cap for 31-year-old Phil May, the Llanelli front jumper, whose omission had been a mystery for years.

England: J M Webb (Bristol); M E Harrison (Wakefield, capt), W D C Carling (Durham Univ and Harlequins), K G Simms (Wasps), R Underwood (Leicester); L Cusworth (Leicester), N D Melville (Wasps); P A G Rendall (Wasps), B C Moore (Nottingham), J A Probyn (Wasps), J Orwin (Bedford), W A Dooley (Fylde), M G Skinner (Harlequins), D Richards (Leicester), P J Winterbottom (Headingley).

Wales: *A Clement (Swansea); Ieuan Evans (Llanelli), M G Ring (Pontypool), B Bowen (S W Police, capt.), A M Hadley (Cardiff); Jonathan Davies (Llanelli), Robert N Jones (Swansea); Staff Jones (Pontypool), K Phillips (Neath), D Young (Swansea), *Phil May (Llanelli), R L Norster (Cardiff), R Phillips (Neath), Paul Moriarty (Swansea), R G Collins (S W Police). Rep: *Ian Watkins (Ebbw Vale) for Kevin Phillips.

For Wales, Adrian Hadley scored two tries. Jonathan Davies dropped a goal.

For England, Jon Webb kicked a penalty goal.

Referee: S R Hilditch (Ireland).

Wales won by two goals, two dropped goals, one penalty goal, one try (25)
to four penalty goals, two tries (20)

Jonathan Davies dropped a goal 10 minutes from the end that swung Wales 22-20 in front and added a second drop-shot just before the end of a thrill-packed contest. It was a game to equal any from the Super Seventies and for the first time since 1979 Wales were 'on' for the Triple Crown. All this after Scotland were 7-0 up after five minutes and took a 20-10 lead right at the start of the second half.. Two dramatic tries kept Wales in the game: Jonathan Davies swooped for the first and Ieuan Evans evaded five tacklers in a hair-raising curling run infield for the second. Paul Thorburn was recalled when Anthony Clement dropped out through injury. So great was the controversey over the dropping of Thorburn that the *Western Mail* conducted a nationwide poll on whether Clement or Thorburn should be the full back. The result was 65% to 35% in favour of Thorburn.

Wales: P Thorburn (Neath); Ieuan Evans (Llanelli), M G Ring (Pontypool), B Bowen (S W Police, capt.), A M Hadley (Cardiff); Jonathan Davies (Llanelli), Robert N Jones (Swansea); Staff Jones (Pontypool), Ian Watkins (Ebbw Vale), D Young (Swansea), Phil May (Llanelli), R L Norster (Cardiff), R Phillips (Neath), W P Moriarty (Swansea), R G Collins (S W Police). Rep: J Pugh (Neath) for Staff Jones.

Scotland: A G Hastings (Watsonians); M D F Duncan (West of Scotland), A V Tait (Kelso), S Hastings (Watsonians), I Tukalo (Selkirk); A B M Ker (Kelso), R J Laidlaw (Jedforest); D M B Sole (Edinburgh Acads.), G J Callander (Kelso, capt.), N A Rowan (Boroughmuir), A J Campbell (Hawick), D F Cronin (Bath), J Jeffrey (Kelso), D B White (Gala), F Calder (Stewart's / Melville FP).

For Wales, Jonathan Davies, Ieuan Evans and Ian Watkins scored tries. Jonathan Davies dropped two goals. Paul Thorburn kicked a penalty goal and converted two tries.

For Scotland, Finlay Calder and Matt Duncan scored tries. Gavin Hastings kicked four penalty goals.

Referee: Y Bressy (France).

Wales won by one goal, one dropped goal, one penalty goal (12) to one goal, one penalty goal (9)

After Welsh runners had won the first two championship games in exciting style, it was back to Paul Thorburn to clinch the Triple Crown for the first time for nine years at windswept Lansdowne Road. He kicked the decisive penalty goal in the fourth minute of injury time. The Irish scrum creaked unhappily, but they spoiled and rushed tirelessly to upset Welsh rhythm in a mainly negative game. Jonathan Davies dropped yet another goal, but his tactical kicking was awry and the midfield unit seldom functioned cohesively in attack. Ireland never looked like scoring after Robert Jones's charged clearance had presented Terry Kingston with a gift try.

Ireland: P P Danaher (Lansdowne); T M Ringland (Ballymena), B J Mullin (Blackrock Coll.), M J Kiernan (Dolphin), K D Crossan (Instonians); P M Dean (St. Mary's Coll.), M T Bradley (Cork Constitution); T Clancy (Lansdowne), T Kingston (Dolphin), D C Fitzgerald (Lansdowne), D G Lenihan (Cork Constitution, capt.), W A Anderson (Dungannon), P M Matthews (Wanderers), M E Gibson (London Irish), D McBride (Malone).

Wales: P Thorburn (Neath); Ieuan Evans (Llanelli), M G Ring (Pontypool), B Bowen (S W Police, capt.), A M Hadley (Cardiff); Jonathan Davies (Llanelli),

Robert N Jones (Swansea); A Buchanan (Llanelli), Ian Watkins (Ebbw Vale), D Young (Swansea), Phil May (Llanelli), R L Norster (Cardiff), R Phillips (Neath), W P Moriarty (Swansea), R G Collins (S W Police).

For Wales, Paul Moriarty scored a try. Paul Thorburn converted and kicked a penalty goal. Jonathan Davies dropped a goal.

For Ireland, Terry Kingston scored a try. Michael Kiernan converted and kicked a penalty goal.

Referee: R J Megson (Scotland).

Match 380 WALES v FRANCE   Cardiff Arms Park. March 19, 1988

France won by two penalty goals, one try (10) to one goal, one penalty goal (9)

France's deadly deputies dashed Welsh aims of a Grand Slam. Jean-Patrick Lescarboura, brought in at fly half when Didier Camberabero was injured, and Jean-Baptiste Lafond, wing deputy for unfit Philippe Berot, scored the vital points: Lescarboura obtained the try, Lafond kicked the goals. Wales lost their grip after dominating the opening half. They took wrong options and half backs Robert Jones and Jonathan Davies suffered a nightmare match: Jones lost his accuracy while Davies's kicking was at fault. Richie Collins was the outstanding forward of the match on a day of Welsh gloom.

Wales: P Thorburn (Neath); Ieuan Evans (Llanelli), M G Ring (Pontypool), B Bowen (S W Police, capt.), A M Hadley (Cardiff); Jonathan Davies (Llanelli), Robert N Jones (Swansea); Staff Jones (Pontypool), Ian Watkins (Ebbw Vale), D Young (Swansea), Phil May (Llanelli), R L Norster (Cardiff), R Phillips (Neath), W P Moriarty (Swansea), R G Collins (S W Police). Rep: G Webbe (Bridgend) for Ieuan Evans.

France: S Blanco (Biarritz); J B Lafond (Racing Club), P Sella (Agen), M Andrieu (Nimes), P Lagisquet (Bayonne); J P Lescarboura (Dax), P Berbizier (Agen); L Armary (Lourdes), D Dubroca (Agen, capt), P Ondarts (Biarritz), A Lorieux (Aix les Bains), J Condom (Biarritz), M Cecillon (Burgoin), L Rodriguez (Dax), A Carminati (Beziers).

For Wales, Ieuan Evans scored a try. Paul Thorburn converted and kicked a penalty goal.

For France, Jean-Patrick Lescarboura scored a try. Jean-Baptiste Lafond kicked two penalty goals.

Referee: F A Howard (England).

Match 381 NEW ZEALAND v WALES   Lancaster Park, Christchurch. May 28, 1988

New Zealand won by six goals, four tries (52) to one penalty goal (3)

This was men against boys. The black avalanche swept Wales to defeat by the biggest margin in history. The previous worst result had been 49-6 in the World Cup semi-final a year earlier. Now the Black Runners never stopped coming. They piled up 10 tries, the most against Wales. Wing John Kirwan, virtually unstoppable, stormed over for four; Wales never looked like getting one. Their only points came with NZ already 30-0 in front. Then Mark Ring kicked an easy penalty goal. With Bleddyn Bowen out of the tour (fractured wrist), Robert Norster led Wales for the first time, but his pack were overwhelmed.

New Zealand: J Gallagher; J Kirwan, J Stanley, W Taylor, T Wright; G Fox, B Deans; S McDowell, S Fitzpatrick, R Loe, M Pierce, G Whetton, A Whetton, W Shelford (capt), M Jones.

Wales: A Clement (Swansea); Ieuan Evans (Llanelli), M G Ring (Pontypool), J A Devereux, G Webbe (Bridgend); Jonathan Davies (Llanelli), Robert N Jones (Swansea); Staff Jones (Pontypool), K H Phillips (Neath), D Young (Swansea), Phil May (Llanelli), R L Norster (Cardiff, capt.), R Phillips (Neath), W P Moriarty (Swansea), *D Bryant (Bridgend). Reps: *T Fauvel (Aberavon) for Moriarty, *M Hall (Bridgend) for Clement.

For New Zealand, John Kirwan (4), Terry Wright (2), Gary Whetton, Bruce Deans, Wayne Shelford, John Gallagher scored tries. Grant Fox converted six.

For Wales, Mark Ring kicked a penalty goal.

Referee: G Maurette (France).

Match 382   NEW ZEALAND v WALES   Eden Park, Auckland. June 11, 1988

New Zealand won by eight goals, two penalty goals (54) to one goal, one penalty goal (9)

The All Blacks amassed another record tally in this second Test. In their three meetings from the World Cup semi-final, New Zealand had outscored Wales by a staggering 26-2 on tries. Grant Fox supplied 22 points, which gave him 51 against Wales. Rob Norster was injured, so Jonathan Davies assumed the captaincy and scored the most spectacular try of the match. Mark Ring launched the move just outside his goal-line and replacement full back Jonathan Mason joined in to sell a delightful little dummy before in-passing to Jonathan Davies. He raced some 65 yards until overhauled by Terry Wright, but the Welsh skipper hurled himself forward and his momentum carried him across. On this NZ tour, Wales won only two of their eight games. They went as Triple Crown holders and joint Five Nations champions with France.

New Zealand: J Gallagher; J Kirwan, J Stanley, W Taylor, T Wright; G Fox, B Deans; S McDowell, S Fitzpatrick, R Loe, M Pierce, G Whetton, A Whetton, W Shelford (capt), M Jones.

Wales: Mark Ring (Pontypool); Ieuan Evans (Llanelli), *Nigel Davies (Llanellil), J A Devereux, Mike Hall (Bridgend); Jonathan Davies (capt), *Jonathan Griffiths Llanelli); Staff Jones (Pontypool), Ian Watkins (Ebbw Vale), D Young (Swansea), Phil May (Llanelli), *Kevin Moseley (Pontypool), *Gary Jones (Llanelli), R Phillips (Neath), D Bryant (Bridgend). Reps: Mark Jones (Neath) for Phillips, *Jonathan Mason (Pontypridd) for Hall.

For New Zealand, Terry Wright (2), John Kirwan (2), Michael Jones, Bruce Deans, Steve McDowell and Warwick Taylor scored tries. Grant Fox converted eight and kicked two penalty goals.

For Wales, Jonathan Davies scored a try. Mark Ring converted and kicked a penalty goal.

Referee: G Maurette (France).

Match 383   WALES v WESTERN SAMOA   Cardiff Arms Park. November 12, 1988

Wales won by four goals, one try (28) to one goal (6)

Inexplicably, the Welsh lineout failed to function, despite the efforts of Robert Norster, probably the finest jumper in the world game. Co-ordination was at fault and this appeared to disorganise the whole team. "We were too loose," complained new coach John Ryan, the first uncapped player to be appointed national coach. The tourists included an excellent second row man, Darryl Williams, who endeavoured to trace his Welsh roots during the visit. Attendance was just under 20,000.

Wales: P H Thorburn (Neath); Mike Hall (Bridgend), B Bowen (Swansea), Nigel Davies, *Carwyn Davies (Llanelli); Jonathan Davies (Llanelli, capt), Robert N Jones (Swansea); *Mike Griffiths, *Wayne Hall (Bridgend), D Young (Cardiff), *J D M Wakeford (S W Police), R L Norster (Cardiff), R Phillips (Neath), Phil Davies (Llanelli), D Bryant (Bridgend). Reps: *R Wintle (London Welsh) for Carwyn Davies, A Clement (Swansea) for Thorburn.

Western Samoa: Aneterea Aoilupo; Lolani Koko (capt), Keneti Sio, Tupo Faamasino, Taueve Ugapo; John Ah Kuoi, Vincent Fepuleai; Peter Fatialofa, Stan Toomalatai, Vili Alalatoa, Saini Lemamea, Darryl Williams, Lafaele Mano, Sepe Tupuola, Malaki Iupeli. Rep: Vaivase Faasua for Malaki Iupeli.

For Wales, Nigel Davies (2), Carwyn Davies, Jonathan Davies and John Wakeford scored tries. Paul Thorburn converted four.

For Western Samoa, Saini Lemamea scored a try. Aneterea Aoilupo converted.

Referee: E O Doyle (Ireland).

Match 384   WALES v ROMANIA   Cardiff Arms Park. December 10, 1988

Romania won by one goal, three penalty goals (15) to one goal, one penalty goal (9)

Romania's greatest rugby moment – their first away victory over an International Board country. They achieved it with dull, 10-man tactics; Gelu Ignat, an outside half with a huge kick, punted high, sinister kicks to the posts, landed three penalty goals and converted their try following a pack surge. Mark Ring was dropped as a disciplinary measure: he turned up late for the Wednesday final run-out. Paul Thorburn, who came on to play as replacement wing for injured Glen Webbe, reached 170 points to pass Phil Bennett's Welsh record tally of 166. There were calls for the selectors to resign and allow coach John Ryan to become sole selector. Wales fielded an all-Bridgend threequarter line.

Wales: A Clement (Swansea); G Webbe, M R Hall, J A Devereux, *R Diplock (Bridgend); Jonathan Davies (Llanelli, capt), Robert N Jones (Swansea); M Griffiths (Bridgend), I J Watkins (Ebbw Vale), D Young (Cardiff), J D M Wakeford (S W Police), K Moseley (Pontypool), D Bryant (Bridgend), Phil Davies (Llanelli), R G Collins (Cardiff). Rep: P H Thorburn (Neath) for Webbe.

Romania: M Toader; N Racean, N Fulina, A Lungu, D Bolder; G Ignat, D Neaga; G Leonte, I Ion, G Dumitrescu, S Ciorascu, H Dumitras, F Murariu (capt.), I Doja, A Radulescu. Rep: T Oroian for Dumitras.

For Wales, John Devereux scored a try. Paul Thorburn converted and kicked a penalty goal.

For Romania, Gheorghe Ion scored a try. Gelu Ignat converted and kicked three penalty goals.

Referee: I M Bullerwell (England).

Match 385   SCOTLAND v WALES   Murrayfield. January 21, 1989

Scotland won by one goal, one dropped goal, two penalty goals, two tries (23)
to one penalty goal, one try (7)

Wales, 19-0 down at half time, might have collapsed, but new captain Paul Thorburn, the 100th player to lead his country in full cap internationals, rallied the side in this Murrayfield Massacre II. It rekindled memories of the notorious 19-0 defeat in 1951. Thorburn failed to score for the first time in 21 games, but Mike Hall collected a superb momentum corner-try.

The Welsh pack conceded a push-over try for the second successive visit to Scottish HQ. "Some of our players panicked," admitted Thorburn.

Scotland: P W Dods (Gala); M D F Duncan (West of Scotland), S Hastings (Watsonians), S R Lineen (Boroughmuir), I Tukalo (Selkirk); C M Chalmers (Melrose), G Armstrong (Jed-Forest); D M B Sole (Edinburgh Acads), K S Milne, I G Milne (Heriot's FP), C A Gray (Nottingham), D F Cronin (Bath), J Jeffrey (Kelso), D B White (Gala), F Calder (Stewart's / Melville FP,capt).

Wales: P H Thorburn (Neath, capt); M R Hall, J A Devereux (Bridgend), Nigel Davies, Carwyn Davies (Llanelli);B Bowen (Swansea), Jonathan Griffiths (Llanelli); M Griffiths (Bridgend), I J Watkins (Ebbw Vale), D Young (Cardiff), P T Davies (Llanelli), K Moseley (Pontypool), R Phillips, Mark Jones (Neath), D Bryant (Bridgend). Rep: *Hugh Williams-Jones (S W Police) for Young.

For Wales, Mike Hall scored a try. Bleddyn Bowen kicked a penalty goal.

For Scotland, Gary Armstrong, Derek White and Craig Chalmers scored tries. Peter Dods converted one and kicked two penalty goals. Chalmers dropped a goal.

Referee: J C Doulcett (France).

Match 386   WALES v IRELAND   Cardiff Arms Park. February 4, 1989

Ireland won by one goal, three penalty goals, one try (19) to three penalty goals, one try (13)

The luck of the Irish was never more apparent than on this grim day for Wales. The visitors won for a record third successive time in Cardiff, snatching both tries from Welsh blunders and the winning score through the most blatant blunder of all – by referee Roger Quittenton. He was unsighted when David Irwin knocked the ball forward as he lunged to spoil Robert Jones's pass. Paul Dean pounced on the bounce to scamper to the nearby posts in the closing stages. Earlier, Noel Mannion had closed so swiftly on Bleddyn Bowen that the outside half's chip went straight into the No.8's grasp for him to pound some 75 yards for a shock try. Wales produced all the creative play, but only when Mike Hall switched to centre to replace injured John Devereux did Wales display penetration. Paul Turner came on to win his first cap as replacement for injured Thorburn near the end. Charging Mark Jones was the most industrious of the home forwards and scored the try.

Wales: P H Thorburn (Neath, capt); Ieuan Evans, Nigel Davies (Llanelli), J A Devereux, M R Hall (Bridgend);B Bowen (Swansea), Robert N Jones (Swansea); M Griffiths (Bridgend), I J Watkins (Ebbw Vale), *L Delaney, P T Davies (Llanelli), K Moseley (Pontypool), R Phillips, Mark Jones (Neath), D Bryant (Bridgend). Reps: Carwyn Davies (Llanelli) for Devereux, *Paul Turner (Newbridge) for Thorburn.

Ireland: F J Dunlea (Lansdowne); M J Kiernan (Dolphin), B J Mullin (London Irish), D G Irwin (Instonians), K D Crossan (Instonians); P M Dean (St. Mary's Coll.), L D P Aherne (Lansdowne); T P J Clancy (Lansdowne), S J Smith (Ballymena), J J McCoy (Bangor), D G Lenihan (Cork Constitution), W A Anderson (Dungannon), P M Matthews (Wanderers, capt), N P Mannion (Corinthians), P J O'Hara (Sunday's Well).

For Wales, Mark Jones scored a try. Paul Thorburn kicked three penalty goals.

For Ireland, Noel Mannion and Paul Dean scored tries. Michael Kiernan converted one and kicked three penalty goals.

Referee: R C Quittenton (England).

France won by three goals, two penalty goals, one dropped goal, one try (31)
to four penalty goals (12)

With full back Serge Blanco as the pathfinder, scoring the first two tries, France racked up their biggest tally against Wales. Although the forwards produced a vastly improved display from the Ireland game, there was too much pressure on the Welsh backs and the only points came from Thorburn's four penalty goals.

France: S Blanco (Biarritz); J B Lafond (Racing Club), P Sella (Agen), M Andrieu (Nimes), P Lagisquet (Bayonne); F Mesnel (Racing Club), P Berbizier (Agen, capt); L Armary (Lourdes), P Dintrans (Tarbes), P Ondarts (Biarritz), J Condom (Biarritz), A Lorieux (Aix les Bains), D Erbani (Agen), A Carminati (Beziers), E Champ (Toulon).

Wales: P H Thorburn (Neath, capt); Ieuan Evans (Llanelli), M R Hall (Bridgend), *David Evans (Cardiff), Carwyn Davies (Llanelli); P Turner (Newbridge), Robert N Jones (Swansea); M Griffiths (Bridgend), I J Watkins (Ebbw Vale), L Delaney, P T Davies (Llanelli), R L Norster (Cardiff), Gary Jones (Llanelli), Mark Jones (Neath), D Bryant (Bridgend).

For Wales, Paul Thorburn kicked four penalty goals.

For France, Serge Blanco (2), Pierre Berbizier and Philippe Dintrans scored tries. Jean-Baptiste Lafond converted three and kicked two penalty goals. Franck Mesnel dropped a goal.

Referee: J Fleming (Scotland).

Wales won by one goal, two penalty goals (12) to one dropped goal, two penalty goals (9)

Unbeaten England were tipped to win at the Arms Park for the first time for 26 years after an impressive 11-0 verdict over France. So Wales faced the ultimate humiliation: defeat on their home ground and a first ever whitewash in the Five Nations. It was backs to the wall for a desperate side that had won just one of eight matches (against Western Samoa). Wales were being dubbed the Tinpot team, but they answered the critics with a rousing performance in the rain. Robert Jones box-kicked repeatedly with slide-rule exactitude and the pack took on and tamed the fearsome England eight. Rob Norster soared to dominate the lineout. England mishandling under pressure let in Mike Hall for a diving fingertip try. It was the day of the underdogs.

Wales: P H Thorburn (Neath, capt); Ieuan Evans (Llanelli), M R Hall (Bridgend), David Evans (Cardiff), *Arthur Emyr (Swansea); P Turner (Newbridge), Robert N Jones (Swansea); M Griffiths (Bridgend), I J Watkins (Ebbw Vale), L Delaney, P T Davies (Llanelli), R L Norster (Cardiff), Gary Jones (Llanelli), Mark Jones (Neath), D Bryant (Bridgend).

England: J M Webb (Bristol); R Underwood (Leicester), W D C Carling (Harlequins, capt), S J Halliday (Bath), C Oti (Wasps); C R Andrew (Wasps), C D Morris (Liverpool St Helens); P A G Rendall (Wasps), B C Moore (Nottingham), G J Chilcott (Bath), P J Ackford (Harlequins), W A Dooley (Preston Grasshoppers), M C Teague (Gloucester), D Richards (Leicester), R A Robinson (Bath). Rep: G W Rees (Nottingham) for Teague.

For Wales, Mike Hall scored a try. Paul Thorburn converted and kicked two penalty goals.

For England, Rob Andrew dropped a goal, and kicked two penalty goals.

Referee: K V J Fitzgerald (Australia).

WALES V NEW ZEALAND   Cardiff Arms Park. November 4, 1989

New Zealand won by three goals, four penalty goals and one try (34) to three penalty goals (9)

After defeating Cardiff, Pontypool, Swansea, Neath and Llanelli, the cream of Welsh clubs, the All Blacks were perfectly tuned to gobble up Wales and did it with four tries. There was no try for the battered home side, just three Thorburn penalty goals. Gareth Llewellyn, who was to become his country's most capped forward eight years on, and Phil Pugh, the stars for Neath against the Blacks, won their first caps. Robert Jones captained Wales for the first time and 55,000 spectators saw NZ relentlessly wear Wales down. The tourists historically had made the ruck their distinguishing mark; but now they abandoned the ruck for the maul. They rolled it, walked it, galloped it and generally used it to keep possession and gain 20, 30 or 40 yards. It was awesome forward power directed superbly by the ruthless Wayne Shelford.

Wales: P H Thorburn (Neath); M R Hall (Bridgend), M G Ring, David Evans (Cardiff), Arthur Emyr (Swansea); A Clement, Robert N Jones (capt. Swansea); M Griffiths (Bridgend), K H Phillips (Neath), D Young (Cardiff), P T Davies (Llanelli), *Gareth Llewellyn, *Phil Pugh, Mark Jones (Neath), Gary Jones (Llanelli).

New Zealand: J A Gallagher; C R Innes, J T Stanley, N J Schuster, T J Wright; G Fox, G T M Bachop; S C McDowell, S B T Fitzpatrick, R W Loe, G W Whetton, M J Pierce, A T Earl, W T Shelford (capt), M R Brewer.

For Wales, Paul Thorburn kicked three penalty goals.

For New Zealand, Craig Innes (2), Graeme Bachop and Terry Wright scored tries. Grant Fox converted three and kicked four penalty goals.

Referee: A R MacNeill (Australia).

WALES v FRANCE   Cardiff Arms Park. January 20, 1990

France won by three goals, one penalty goal, two tries (29)
to four penalty goals, one dropped goal, one try (19)

Kevin Moseley, the Pontypool captain, was ordered from the field after 35 minutes for stamping on wing Marc Andrieu. Referee Fred Howard had no hesitation, though Moseley protested he was going for the ball. He was banned for 33 weeks. Yet the seven home forwards fought on fearlessly and the championship title holders were only 21-19 in front with six minutes remaining. Then Patrice Lagisquet, with an electrifying swerving run, and Laurent Rodriguez, from a close up scrum drive, swooped for tries that ensured success – their eighth in a row against Wales. Only NZ had a better record. Paul Thorburn's two errors cost 12 points, though he kept his side hanging in with four penalty goals. Mark Titley, recalled after more than three years, scored a spectacular try from Robert Jones's quickly tapped penalty and punt-on. The selection of Phil Davies, heaviest forward to play for Wales at 18 st, in the strange role of blindside, was criticised, but he soon found himself back in the second row when Moseley departed for the dreaded early bath.

Wales: P H Thorburn (Neath); M H Titley (Swansea), M G Ring, M R Hall (Cardiff), Arthur Emyr (Swansea); David Evans (Cardiff), Robert N Jones (Swansea, capt); M Griffiths (Cardiff), K H Phillips (Neath), D Young (Cardiff), *A G Allen (Newbridge), K Moseley (Pontypool), P T Davies (Llanelli), Mark Jones (Neath), Gary Jones (Llanelli). Rep: Hugh Williams-Jones (S W Police) for Griffiths.

France: J B Lafond (Racing Club); M Andrieu (Nimes), P Sella (Agen), D Charvet (Toulouse), P Lagisquet (Bayonne); D Camberabero (Beziers), P

Berbizier (Agen, capt); P Ondarts (Biarritz), L Armary (Lourdes), J P Garuet (Lourdes), T Devergie (Nimes), D Erbani (Agen), E Champ (Toulon), O Roumat (Dax), L Rodriguez (Dax).

For Wales, Mark Titley scored a try. David Evans dropped a goal and Paul Thorburn kicked four penalty goals.

For France, Jean-Baptiste Lafond, Didier Camberabero, Philippe Sella, Patrice Lagisquet and Laurent Rodriguez scored tries. Camberabero converted three and kicked a penalty goal.

Referee: F A Howard (England).

Match 391   ENGLAND v WALES   Twickenham. February 17, 1990

England won by three goals, four penalty goals, one try (34) to one goal (6)

A dismal day indeed as England powered to four tries at Twickenham, a feat they had not achieved against Wales since 1921. The total command of the home pack left Wales with few attacking opportunities. The Welsh scrum disintegrated and heeled just three scrums throughout the match! Near the end, Phil Davies stormed to the posts from the tail of the lineout for their only try. "We have to bounce back," said grim-faced skipper Robert Jones. Unfortunately there was not much bounce about Wales at the time.

England: S D Hodgkinson (Nottingham); R Underwood (Leicester), W D C Carling (Harlequins, capt), J C Guscott, S J Halliday (Bath); C R Andrew (Wasps), R J Hill (Bath); P A G Rendall (Wasps), B C Moore (Nottingham), J A Probyn (Wasps), P J Ackford (Harlequins), W A Dooley (Preston Grasshoppers), M G Skinner (Harlequins), M C Teague (Gloucester), P J Winterbottom (Harlequins).

Wales: P H Thorburn (Neath); M H Titley (Swansea), M G Ring, M R Hall (Cardiff), Arthur Emyr (Swansea); David Evans (Cardiff), Robert N Jones (Swansea, capt); M Griffiths (Cardiff), K H Phillips (Neath), L Delaney (Llanelli), A G Allen (Newbridge), Gareth Llewellyn (Neath), P T Davies (Llanelli), Mark Jones (Neath), R G Collins (Cardiff).

For Wales, Phil Davies scored a try. Paul Thorburn converted.

For England, Rory Underwood (2), Will Carling and Richard Hill scored tries. Simon Hodgkinson converted three and kicked four penalty goals.

Referee: D Leslie (Scotland).

Match 392   WALES v SCOTLAND   Cardiff Arms Park. March 3, 1990

Scotland won by three penalty goals, one try (13) to one goal, one penalty goal (9)

Neath team manager Ron Waldron was called in as national coach when John Ryan resigned after the Twickenham rout. Waldron brought in Neath loose-head Brian Williams, a dynamic spearhead runner, and Allan Bateman, also of Neath, as a perceptive centre to restructure the team around the highly successful club side. "Performance is important, but victory is everything," stressed Waldron. His team certainly rekindled the old fire after Twickenham surrender and scored the game's most exciting try by Arthur Emyr. Alas, Scotland won on goal kicks with Craig Chalmers finding the posts three times after Damian Cronin's corner try.

Wales: P H Thorburn (Neath); M R Hall, M G Ring (Cardiff), *A G Bateman (Neath), A Emyr (Swansea); David Evans (Cardiff), Robert N Jones (Swansea, capt); *B R Williams, K H Phillips, J D Pugh, Gareth Llewellyn (Neath), P T Davies, *M A Perego (Llanelli), Mark Jones (Neath), R G Collins (Cardiff). Rep: A Clement (Swansea) for David Evans.

Scotland: A G Hastings (London Scottish); A G Stanger (Hawick), S Hastings (Watsonians), S R P Lineen (Boroughmuir), I Tukalo (Selkirk); C M Chalmers (Melrose), G Armstrong (Jed-Forest); D M B Sole (Edinburgh Acads, capt), K S Milne (Heriot's FP), A P Burnell (London Scottish), C A Gray (Nottingham), D F Cronin (Bath), J Jeffrey (Kelso), D B White (London Scottish), F Calder (Stewart's / Melville FP).

For Wales, Arthur Emyr scored a try. Paul Thorburn converted and kicked a penalty goal.

For Scotland, Damian Cronin scored a try. Craig Chalmers kicked three penalty goals.

Referee: R Hourquet (France).

Match 393   IRELAND v WALES   Lansdowne Road, Dublin. March 24, 1990

Ireland won by one goal, two tries (14) to two tries (8)

For the first time, Wales lost five consecutive games and also endured the humiliation of the first Five Nations whitewash. The figures made them the worst Welsh team of all time with a 90 points aggregate the most points Wales had ever conceded in the championship. When Mike Hall dropped out through a hamstring injury, Cardiff wing Steve Ford was called up for his first cap just two years after having a life ban imposed by the WRU lifted. He had taken part in an unpaid RL trial with Leeds. Martyn Morris was recalled after five years to strengthen the lineout tail. Ireland also had not won a game before this shoot-out for the Wooden Spoon, but they deserved victory in a messy wind-blasted match.

Ireland: K Murphy (Cork Constitution); K J Hooks (Ards), B J Mullin (Blackrock), M J Kiernan (Dolphin), K D Crossan (Instonians); B A Smith (Oxford University), M T Bradley (Cork Constitution); J J Fitzgerald (Young Munster), T J Kingston (Dolphin), D C Fitzgerald (Lansdowne), N P Francis (Blackrock), D G Lenihan (Cork Constitution, capt), W D McBride (Malone), N P Mannion (Corinthians), P J O'Hara (Sunday's Well). Rep: L F Aherne (Lansdowne) for Bradley.

Wales: P H Thorburn (Neath); *S Ford, M G Ring (Cardiff), A G Bateman (Neath), A Emyr (Swansea); David Evans (Cardiff), Robert N Jones (Swansea, capt); B R Williams, K H Phillips (Neath), H Williams-Jones (S W Police), A G Allen (Newbridge), Gareth Llewellyn, M Morris, Mark Jones (Neath), R G Collins (Cardiff). Reps: A Clement (Swansea) for Thorburn, *A Edmunds (Neath) for David Evans.

For Wales, Steve Ford and Gareth Llewellyn scored tries.

For Ireland, Brian Smith, Denis McBride and Terry Kingston scored tries. Michael Kiernan converted one.

Referee: D J Bishop (New Zealand).

Match 394   NAMIBIA v WALES   Windhoek. June 2, 1990

Wales won by two goals, two penalty goals (18) to one goal, one penalty goal (9)

There were 10 withdrawals from the original tour selection, and a number of leading players were unavailable, when Wales played a two-Test event to mark Namibian independence. Six new caps appeared in this first Test, won by Thorburn's goal kicking. He also scored a try in accumulating 14 points. Home full back Andre Stoop was sent off for butting Steve Ford. After only two victories in 14 full cap fixtures, it was a relief to register this success, though against a third world country in rugby terms. Played at South-West Stadium.

Namibia: A Stoop; G Mans (capt.), V du Toit, J Deysel, B Swartz; S McCulley, B Uitendag; C Derks, S Smit, M Grobler, S Losper, A van der Merwe, J Barnard, T Oosthuizen, A Skinner.

Wales: P H Thorburn (Neath); S P Ford, M G Ring (Cardiff), A G Bateman (Neath), A Emyr (Swansea); A Clement (Swansea), *C J Bridges (Neath); M Griffiths (Cardiff), K H Phillips (Neath, capt.), *P Knight (Pontypridd), *Glyn Llewellyn (Neath), *P Arnold (Swansea), *A Reynolds (Swansea), Mark Jones, M Morris (Neath). Rep: *S Parfitt (Swansea) for Emyr.

For Wales, Paul Thorburn and Chris Bridges scored tries. Thorburn converted both and kicked two penalty goals.

For Namibia, Gerhard Mans scored a try. Shaun McCulley converted and kicked a penalty goal.

Referee: F A Howard (England).

Match 395   NAMIBIA v WALES   Windhoek. June 9, 1990

Wales won by three goals, three penalty goals, one dropped goal, one try (34)
to three goals, three penalty goals, one dropped goal (30)

"We will massacre Wales in the second Test," promised coach Henning Snyman with extravagant optimism after complaining that referee Fred Howard had cost his side victory in the opening match. But it did not turn out quite like that, though Namibia jolted the tourists with a steely recovery from 15-30 to finish just four points adrift. Shaun McCulley missed four home goal shots whereas Thorburn kicked 15 points. Bridgend fly half Aled Williams won his cap as a replacement wing. Unflinching defence undoubtedly saved the day for Wales.

Namibia: Jaco Coetzee; G Mans (capt.), V du Toit, J Deysel, B Swartz; S McCulley, B Uitendag; C Derks, S Smit, M Grobler, S Losper, A van der Merwe, J Barnard, T Oosthuizen, A Skinner. Rep: Jasper Coetzee for Barnard.

Wales: P H Thorburn (Neath); S P Ford, M G Ring (Cardiff), A G Bateman (Neath), A Emyr (Swansea); A Clement (Swansea), C J Bridges (Neath); M Griffiths (Cardiff), K H Phillips (Neath, capt.), P Knight (Pontypridd), Glyn Llewellyn (Neath), P Arnold (Swansea), *Owain Williams (Bridgend), Mark Jones, M Morris (Neath). Reps: *Aled Williams (Bridgend) for Ford, Alan Reynolds (Swansea) for Mark Jones.

For Wales, Arthur Emyr (2) and Owain Williams scored tries and a penalty try was awarded. Paul Thorburn converted three tries and kicked three penalty goals. Anthony Clement dropped a goal.

For Namibia, Ben Swartz (2) and Gerhard Mans scored tries. Shaun McCulley converted one try and kicked two penalty goals. Jaco Coetzee converted two tries, dropped a goal and kicked a penalty goal.

Referee: F A Howard (England).

Match 396   WALES v BARBARIANS   Cardiff Arms Park. October 6, 1990

Barbarians won by three goals, three penalty goals, one try (31)
to one goal, five penalty goals, one dropped goal (24)

The WRU awarded full caps in this match to mark the Barbarians' centenary, though a week earlier England had not distinguished their meeting with the Baa-Baas with similar status.

254

There was considerable controversy that the value of a cap was debased by this Welsh decision. Paul Thorburn's 21 points was a record for a capped match, passing the 19 by Jack Bancroft (1910), Keith Jarrett (1967) and Phil Bennett (1976), though those players achieved their feats against Five Nations opponents. The lineout was a total disaster for Wales, who had nine Neath players involved when Adrian Davies went on as replacement centre.

Wales: P H Thorburn (Neath, capt.); S P Ford, M G Ring (Cardiff), S A Parfitt (Swansea), D A Edmunds (Neath); David Evans (Cardiff), C J Bridges (Neath); B R Williams, K H Phillips (Neath), M Griffiths (Cardiff), Glyn Llewellyn (Neath), P Arnold (Swansea), M S Morris, Mark Jones (Neath), R E Webster (Swansea). Reps: *Adrian Davies (Neath) for Ring, Paul Knight (Pontypridd) for Brian Williams.

Barbarians: D I Campese (Australia); J B Lafond (France), J T Stanley (NZ), J C Guscott (England), D Charvet (France); S Barnes (England), N C Farr-Jones (Australia, capt.); P A G Rendall (England), S J Smith (Ireland), R W Loe (NZ), S A G Cutler (Australia), Ian Jones (NZ), M C Teague (England), D Erbani (France) E J Rush (Otahuhu and Auckland).

For Wales, Paul Thorburn scored a try, converted and kicked five penalty goals. David Evans dropped a goal.

For Barbarians, Joe Stanley, Nick Farr-Jones, Eric Rush and Jeremy Guscott scored tries. Stuart Barnes converted three and kicked three penalty goals.

Referee: F A Howard (England).

Match 397   WALES v ENGLAND   Cardiff Arms Park. January 19, 1991

England won by seven penalty goals, one try (25) to two penalty goals (6)

England at last ended their glum sequence of 28 years without victory at the Arms Park, though there was not a glimmer of adventure in their performance. Not that that worried them! Simon Hodgkinson kicked superbly to put over a record seven penalty goals and Mike Teague stormed across for a try in this first win since 1963. Wales failed for the first time in 27 years to score a try against England in Cardiff. It was a nightmare for Thorburn: he missed four reasonable penalty attempts and handed over the duties to newcomer Neil Jenkins. England's players refused to give interviews to the media after the match because the BBC rejected a request from them for a £5,000 interview fee. Later, the RFU stated that players were required to give interviews as part of their selection duties. First games for Neil Jenkins and Scott Gibbs.

Wales: P H Thorburn (Neath, capt); Ieuan Evans (Llanelli), *I S Gibbs (Neath), M G Ring, S Ford (Cardiff); *Neil Jenkins (Pontypridd), Robert N Jones (Swansea); B R Williams, K H Phillips (Neath), P Knight (Pontypridd), Glyn Llewellyn, Gareth Llewelyn (Neath), *A J Carter (Newport), P Arnold (Swansea), *G M George (Newport), Rep: C J Bridges (Neath) for Robert Jones.

England: S D Hodgkinson (Nottingham); N Helsop (Orrell), W D C Carling (Harlequins, capt), J C Guscott, R Underwood (Leicester); C R Andrew (Wasps), R J Hill (Bath); J Leonard, B C Moore (Harlequins), J A Probyn (Wasps), P J Ackford (Harlequins), W A Dooley (Preston Grasshoppers), M C Teague (Gloucester), D Richards, P J Winterbottom (Harlequins).

For Wales, Paul Thorburn and Neil Jenkins each kicked a penalty goal.

For England, Mike Teague scored a try. Simon Hodgkinson kicked seven penalty goals.

Referee: R J Megson (Scotland).

Scotland won by two goals, three penalty goals, one dropped goal, two tries (32)
to one goal, two penalty goals (12)

A decisive victory for Scotland against a desperately disappointing Wales. The Welsh scrum, so defiant against England, crumbled once again and the home pack established total supremacy. It was the 13th defeat in 14 games against International Board countries. Scott Gibbs looked a penetrative midfield runner, but the Welsh backs had little opportunity.

Scotland: A G Hastings (London Scottish); A G Stanger (Hawick), S Hastings (Watsonians), S R P Lineen (Boroughmuir), A Moore (Edinburgh Acads.); C M Chalmers (Melrose), G Armstrong (Jed-Forest); D M B Sole (capt.), J Allan (Edinburgh Acads, A P Burnell (London Scottish), C A Gray (Nottingham), D F Cronin (Bath), D J Turnbull (Hawick), D B White (London Scottish), J Jeffrey (Kelso). Rep: K S Milne (Heriot's FP) for Allan.

Wales: P H Thorburn (Neath, capt); Ieuan Evans (Llanelli), I S Gibbs (Neath), M G Ring, S Ford (Cardiff); Neil Jenkins (Pontypridd), Robert N Jones (Swansea); B R Williams, K H Phillips (Neath), P Knight (Pontypridd), Glyn Llewellyn, Gareth Llewelyn (Neath), A J Carter (Newport), P Arnold (Swansea), G M George (Newport), Rep: A Clement (Swansea) for Thorburn.

For Wales, Steve Ford scored a try. Paul Thorburn converted and kicked two penalty goals.

For Scotland, Derek White (2), Gary Armstrong and Craig Chalmers scored tries. Chalmers converted one, dropped a goal and kicked a penalty goal. Gavin Hastings converted one try and kicked two penalty goals.

Referee: D J Bishop (New Zealand).

Drawn. Wales scored two goals, two penalty goals, one dropped goal (21)
Ireland scored one goal, one dropped goal, three tries (21)

Ireland, winners on their three previous visits to Cardiff, scored four tries to two, but at least Wales halted a run of six championship defeats. Welsh tackling often was slack and Mark Ring gave away a try when his punt was charged down. Wales dropped the legendary Robert Jones. Phil Davies, who proved the outstanding home forward, Martyn Morris and Mike Griffiths were recalled to beef up the pack. It was a thrilling match but still that victory eluded Wales.

Wales: P H Thorburn (Neath, capt); Ieuan Evans (Llanelli), M G Ring (Cardiff) I S Gibbs (Neath), S Ford (Cardiff); Neil Jenkins (Pontypridd), C J Bridges (Neath); M Griffiths (Cardiff), K H Phillips (Neath), *J D Davies, Glyn Llewellyn (Neath), P Arnold (Swansea), *E W Lewis, P T Davies (Llanelli), M S Morris (Neath).

Ireland: J E Staples (London Irish); S P Geoghegan, D M Curtis (London Irish), B J Mullin (Blackrock Coll.), D J Clarke (Dolphin); B A Smith (Leicester), R Saunders (London Irish, capt); J J Fitzgerald (Young Munster), S J Smith (Ballymena), D C Fitzgerald (Lansdowne), M J Galwey (Shannon), B J Rigney (Greystones), P M Matthews (Wanderers), B F Robinson (Ballymena), G F Hamilton (NIFC). Rep: K Murphy (Cork Constitution) for Staples.

For Wales, Paul Arnold and Neil Jenkins scored tries. Paul Thorburn converted both and kicked two penalty goals. Neil Jenkins dropped a goal.

For Ireland, Jim Staples, Brendan Mullin, Jack Clarke and Simon Geoghegan scored tries. Brian Smith converted one and dropped a goal.

Referee: D J Bishop (New Zealand).

Match 400   FRANCE v WALES   Parc Des Princes, Paris. March 2, 1991

France won by three goals, two penalty goals, three tries (36) to one penalty goal (3)

Another depressing season ended without victory and with a record championship defeat in Paris. France raised their highest Five Nations tally with six tries. There was only a penalty goal for battered Wales as, for the first time, they conceded more than a century of points in a championship season: to be precise, 114. Serge Blanco, the French captain and full back, scored a dazzling try after just two minutes, kicking ahead and chasing more than 50 yards. This was France's eighth consecutive win against Wales and on their fourth successive trip to Paris Wales failed to manufacture a try.

France: S Blanco (Biarritz, capt); J B Lafond, F Mesnel (Racing Club), P Sella (Agen), P Saint-Andre (Montferrand); D Camberabero (Beziers), P Berbizier (Agen); G Lascube (Agen), P Marocco (Montferrand), P Ondarts (Biarritz), J F Gourragne (Beziers), O Roumat (Dax), X Blond, C Deslandes, L Cabannes (Racing Club). Rep: E Bonneval (Toulouse) for Sella.

Wales: P H Thorburn (Neath, capt); Ieuan Evans (Llanelli), M G Ring (Cardiff), I S Gibbs (Neath), Arthur Emyr (Swansea); Neil Jenkins (Pontypridd), C J Bridges (Neath); M Griffiths (Cardiff), K H Phillips (Neath), J D Davies, Glyn Llewellyn (Neath), P Arnold (Swansea), E W Lewis, P T Davies (Llanelli), M S Morris (Neath).

For France, Serge Blanco, Philippe Saint-Andre, Franck Mesnel, Olivier Roumat, Philippe Sella, Jean-Baptiste Lafond scored tries. Didier Camberabero converted two and kicked two penalty goals. Blanco converted one try.

For Wales, Paul Thorburn kicked a penalty goal.

Referee: K V J Fitzgerald (Australia).

Match 401   AUSTRALIA v WALES   Ballymore, Brisbane. July 21, 1991

Australia won by six goals, one penalty goal, six tries (63) to one dropped goal, one penalty goal (6)

Welsh rugby died of shame with this horrendous defeat. Coach Ron Waldron stood down on his return with a blood clot on a lung while Paul Thorburn, the tour captain, announced his retirement from international rugby. There had been disgraceful scenes at the after-match dinner with Welsh players scuffling and shouting among themselves. The WRU sent an official apology to the Australian RU and made an investigation into the incident. The defeat was the heaviest since the 1881 match against England, Wales's first fixture. A week earlier, Wales lost to NSW 71-8 with 13 tries and their worst defeat in a representative match, though it was a non-cap game. Wales also lost to Queensland 35-24, but defeated Western Australia 22-6, Australian Capital Territory 7-3 and Queensland Country Origin 35-7.

Australia: M Roebuck; D Campese, J Little, T Horan, R Egerton; M Lynagh, N Farr-Jones (capt.); A Daly, P Kearns, E McKenzie, R McCall, J Eales, W Ofahengaue, T Gavin, J Miller. Rep: P Slattery for Farr-Jones.

Wales: P H Thorburn (Neath, capt); Ieuan Evans (Llanelli), I S Gibbs (Neath), M

R Hall, S Ford (Cardiff), Adrian Davies (Cardiff), C J Bridges (Neath); Mark Davis (Newport), K H Phillips (Neath), H Williams-Jones (S W Police), Glyn Llewellyn (Neath), P Arnold (Swansea), E W Lewis, P T Davies (Llanelli), R G Collins (Cardiff). Reps: Gareth Llewellyn (Neath) for P T Davies, A Clement (Swansea) for Thorburn, D W Evans (Cardiff) for Ford.

For Australia, Michael Lynagh (2), Phil Kearns (2), Tim Gavin (2), Willie Ofahengaue, Tim Horan, Marty Roebuck, David Campese, Rob Egerton, Jason Little scored tries. Lynagh converted six and kicked one penalty goal.

For Wales, Adrian Davies dropped a goal and Paul Thorburn kicked a penalty goal.

Referee: F A Howard (England).

Match 402 WALES v FRANCE   Cardiff Arms Park. September 4, 1991

France won by two goals, two penalty goals, one try (22) to one goal, one penalty goal (9)

This was the Match of the Night Runners: it marked the opening of the £400,000 Arms Park new floodlights with an 8pm kick-off on a Wednesday during the first week of the season. Caretaker coach Alan Davies, the Nottingham RFC coach, set his prime target as improved ball-winning, especially at the lineout. It was achieved with a vastly improved display, though France recorded their 10th successive victory against Wales. Ieuan Evans took over the captaincy and Mark Ring was given the outside half role and told he had a free hand. Robert Jones was recalled at scrum half and his quick tap-penalty close to the line put Richie Collins over for the only Welsh try. Inevitably, Blanco scored a dazzling try, picking up the bounce from his chip-on. It was his 38th try on his 89th appearance. After the calamitous tour in Australia, this was almost a moral victory!

Wales: A Clement (Swansea); Ieuan Evans (Llanelli, capt.), I S Gibbs (Neath), M R Hall (Cardiff), A Emyr (Cardiff); M G Ring (Cardiff), Robert N Jones (Swansea); M Griffiths (Cardiff), *G R Jenkins (Pontypool), L Delaney (Llanelli), K Moseley (Newport), Glyn Llewellyn (Neath), E W Lewis, P T Davies (Llanelli), R G Collins (Cardiff). Reps: D W Evans (Cardiff) for Ring, *Luc Evans (Llanelli) for Ieuan Evans.

France: S Blanco (Biarritz, capt); J B Lafond, F Mesnel (Racing Club), P Sella (Agen), P Saint-Andre (Montferrand); D Camberabero (Beziers), H Sanz (Narbonne); G Lascube (Agen), L Armary (Lourdes), P Ondarts (Biarritz), T Devergie (Nimes), O Roumat (Dax), M Courtoils (Begles), M Cecillion (Bourgoin), L Cabannes (Racing Club). Reps: T Lacroix (Dax) for Sella, J L Sadourny (Colomiers) for Blanco.

For Wales, Richie Collins scored a try. Mark Ring converted and kicked a penalty goal.

For France, Serge Blanco, Didier Camberabero and Philippe Saint-Andre scored tries. Camberabero converted two and kicked two penalty goals.

Referee: J M Fleming (Scotland).

WORLD CUP (Pool 1st Game)

Match 403 WALES v WESTERN SAMOA   Cardiff Arms Park. October 6, 1991

Western Samoa won by one goal, two penalty goals, one try (16)
to one goal, one penalty goal, one try (13)

"Rock Bottom" announced the banner headline in *The Western Mail*, national morning newspaper of Wales, after this sensational defeat in Wales's opening match in the Second World

258

Cup. Ferocious tackling knocked back even the biggest home forwards. "We thought we could match them for strength, but came off second best," said rueful coach Alan Davies. French referee Patrick Robin blundered when he awarded To'o Vaega a try after Robert Jones clearly had minored. But the fact was painfully obvious: the Samoans were superior and worthy winners. Only Emyr Lewis enhanced his reputation in a Welsh team that had to use three replacements. Phil May, aged 35, recalled after three years, dislocated his left shoulder.

Wales: A Clement (Swansea); Ieuan Evans (Llanelli, capt.), I S Gibbs (Neath), M R Hall (Cardiff), A Emyr (Cardiff); M G Ring (Cardiff), Robert N Jones (Swansea); M Griffiths (Cardiff), *K Waters (Newbridge), L Delaney (Llanelli), P May (Llanelli), K Moseley (Newport), E W Lewis, P T Davies (Llanelli), R G Collins (Cardiff). Reps:*M Rayer (Cardiff) for Clement, M Morris (Neath) for May, G R Jenkins (Pontypool) for Collins.

Western Samoa: Anitelea Aiolupo; Brian Lima, To 'O Vaega, Frank Bunce, Timo Tagaloa; Steve Bachop, Matthew Vaea; Peter Fatialofa (capt), Stan Toomalatai, Vila Alalatoa, Mark Birtwistle, M Keenan, Sila Vaifale, Pat Lam, A Perelini.

For Wales, Arthur Emyr and Ieuan Evans scored tries. Mark Ring converted one and kicked a penalty goal.

For Western Samoa, To 'O Vaega and Sila Vailafe scored tries. Matthew Vaea converted one and kicked two penalty goals.

Referee: P Robin (France).

WORLD CUP (Pool 2nd Game)

| Match 404 | **WALES v ARGENTINA** | Cardiff Arms Park. October 9, 1991 |

Wales won by four penalty goals, one try (16) to one penalty goal, one try (7)

At last! After eight consecutive matches at the Arms Park without success, Wales scraped an unimpressive victory. On rain-soaked turf, Wales made no pretence of adventure behind the scrum. Robert Jones box-kicked while Mark Ring, a mixture of good and bad, fired over three penalty goals. The only home try was nicely worked for Paul Arnold. Next up were Australia, the cup favourites, and Wales would have to win to stay in the tournament. Life is full of surprises, but the Wallabies were not anticipating one – and neither was the Welsh nation!

Wales: M Rayer (Cardiff); Ieuan Evans (Llanelli, capt.), I S Gibbs (Neath), M R Hall, A Emyr (Cardiff); M G Ring (Cardiff), Robert N Jones (Swansea); M Griffiths (Cardiff), G R Jenkins (Pontypool), L Delaney (Llanelli), P Arnold (Swansea), K Moseley (Newport), E W Lewis, P T Davies (Llanelli), R Webster (Swansea).

Argentina: G del Castillo; M Teran, E Laborde, H Garcia Simon, D Cuesta Silva; L Arbizu, G Camardon; F Mendez, R le Fort, L Molina, P Sporleder, G Llanes, P Garreton (capt), J Santamarina, M Carreras.

For Wales, Paul Arnold scored a try. Mark Ring (3) and Mike Rayer kicked penalty goals.

For Argentina, Hernan Garcia scored a try. Guillermo del Castillo kicked a penalty goal.

Referee: R Hourquet (France).

WORLD CUP (Pool 3rd Game)

| Match 405 | **WALES v AUSTRALIA** | Cardiff Arms Park. October 12, 1991 |

Australia won by four goals, two penalty goals, two tries (38) to one penalty goal (3)

Wales had to win to go through to the quarter-final, but crashed to their heaviest home defeat in 111 years of international rugby. There were six Wallaby tries – only the second instance of Wales conceding that many in Cardiff. Fiji had crossed for six in losing an epic game 28-22 in 1964. Wales won just two lineouts compared with 28 by the Australians. It was the fall of a once great rugby nation and, like the Roman Empire, it was shattering. No player impressed in the battered home side. The continued selection of an unfit Mark Ring proved a disaster, but the backs were impotent behind a hapless pack.

Wales: A Clement (Swansea); Ieuan Evans (Llanelli, capt.), I S Gibbs (Neath), M R Hall, A Emyr (Cardiff); M G Ring (Cardiff), Robert N Jones (Swansea); M Griffiths (Cardiff), G R Jenkins (Pontypool), L Delaney (Llanelli), P Arnold (Swansea), K Moseley (Newport), E W Lewis, P T Davies (Llanelli), R Webster (Swansea). Reps: D W Evans (Cardiff) for Emyr, M Rayer (Cardiff) for Gibbs.

Australia: M Roebuck; D Campese, J Little, T Horan, R Egerton; M Lynagh (capt), P Slattery; A Daly, P Kearns, E McKenzie, R McCall, J Eales, S Poidevin, V Ofahengaue, J Miller.

For Wales, Mark Ring kicked a penalty goal.

For Australia, Marty Roebuck (2), Tim Horan, David Campese, Peter Slattery and Michael Lynagh scored tries. Lynagh converted four and kicked two penalty goals.

Referee: K H Lawrence (New Zealand).

Match 406   IRELAND v WALES   Lansdowne Road, Dublin. January 18, 1992

Wales won by three penalty goals, one dropped goal, one try (16)
to one goal, three penalty goals (15)

Wales looked doomed to yet another defeat as Ireland led 15-6 early in the second half. Then Neil Jenkins brought it to 15-12 with two more penalty goals before Stuart Davies, the Swansea No.8, smashed over for a debut try. Another new cap, Llanelli fly half Colin Stephens, dropped a goal. So Wales recorded their first championship success since the 12-9 win over England at Cardiff in 1989 and their first away success in the Five Nations for four years. This ended a sequence of eight championship fixtures without victory – the worst period in Welsh history. Ieuan Evans called his team around him on the field before kick-off and, in a tight circle, they sang the national anthem, which was not played officially. Englishman Tony Copsey, with Made in England tattooed on his hind quarters, made his debut for Wales.

Ireland: J E Staples (London Irish); R Wallace (Garryowen), D M Curtis (London Irish), B J Mullin (Blackrock Coll.), K D Crossan (Instonians); R P Keyes (Cork Constitution), R Saunders (London Irish); N Popplewell (Greystones), S J Smith Ballymena), D C Fitzgerald (Palmerston), N L Francis (Blackrock Coll.), D G Lenihan (Cork Constitution), P M Matthews (Wanderers, capt), B F Robinson (Ballymena), M Fitzgibbon (Shannon).

Wales: A Clement (Swansea); Ieuan Evans (Llanelli, capt.), I S Gibbs (Swansea), N R Jenkins (Pontypridd), M R Hall (Cardiff); *C J Stephens (Llanelli), Robert N Jones (Swansea); M Griffiths (Cardiff), G R Jenkins (Pontypool), L Delaney (Llanelli), Gareth Llewellyn (Neath), *A H Copsey), E W Lewis, P T Davies (Llanelli), *Stuart Davies, R Webster (Swansea).

For Wales, Stuart Davies scored a try. Colin Stephens dropped a goal. Neil Jenkins kicked three penalty goals.

For Ireland, Richard Wallace scored a try. Ralph Keyes converted and kicked three penalty goals.

Referee: F A Howard (England).

WALES v FRANCE Cardiff Arms Park. February 1, 1992

France won by one goal, one dropped goal, one penalty goal (12) to three penalty goals (9)

France, scoring the only try, deserved this 11th successive win over Wales, who secured a great deal of possession, but squandered it by continual kicking. The curse of the kicking scrum half afflicted Wales for some time and in this match the backs were never released to threaten danger. An untried, restructured French team were unimpressive, though there was a moment of outstanding ingenuity when scrum half Galthie toe-kicked the ball straight into the hands of his outside half. French flair was never more flamboyantly exhibited. For the first time, the west end of the ground was all seating. Diana, Princess of Wales, attended with her young sons, Princes Harry and William. Sadly, there was not even a Welsh try for them to remember.

Wales: A Clement (Swansea); Ieuan Evans (Llanelli, capt), I S Gibbs (Swansea), N R Jenkins (Pontypridd), M R Hall (Cardiff); C J Stephens (Llanelli), Robert N Jones (Swansea); M Griffiths (Cardiff), G R Jenkins (Swansea), L Delaney (Llanelli), Gareth Llewelyn (Neath), A H Copsey, E W Lewis (Llanelli), Stuart Davies, R E Webster (Swansea).

France: J B Lafond (Racing Club); P Saint-Andre (Montferrand), P Sella (Agen, capt), F Mesnel (Racing Club), S Viars (Brive); A Penaud (Brive), F Galthie (Colomiers); G Lascube (Agen), V Moscato (Begles), P Gimbert, C Mougeot (Begles), J M Cadieu (Toulouse), J F Tordo (Nice), M Cecillon (Bourgoin), L Cabannes (Racing Club). Rep: O Roumat (Dax) for Mougeot.

For Wales, Neil Jenkins kicked three penalty goals.

For France, Philippe Saint-Andre scored a try. Jean-Baptiste Lafond converted. Sebastien Viars kicked a penalty goal. Alain Penaud dropped a goal.

Referee: E O Doyle (Ireland).

ENGLAND v WALES Twickenham. March 7, 1992

England won by three goals, two penalty goals (24) to nil

This saw the first occasion for 22 years (since the 14-0 drubbing in Dublin in 1970) when Wales failed to score a point. England completed a second successive Grand Slam and a record aggregate of 118 points. Had they been sharper they could have doubled their score. Wales surprisingly named an unchanged side. "We planned to move the ball more, but England did not let us have enough ball," explained coach Alan Davies. "We were under a lot of pressure, particularly in the scrum,"

England: J M Webb (Bath); S J Haliday (Harlequins), J C Guscott (Bath), W D C Carling (Harlequins, capt.), R Underwood (Leicester); C R Andrew (Toulouse), C D Morris (Orrell); J Leonard (Harlequins), B C Moore (Harlequins), J A Probyn (Wasps), M C Bayfield (Northampton), W A Dooley (Preston Grasshoppers), M G Skinner (Harlequins), D Richards (Leicester), P J Winterbottom (Harlequins). Rep: N J Heslop (Orrell) for Carling.

Wales: A Clement (Swansea); Ieuan Evans (Llanelli, capt), I S Gibbs (Swansea), N R Jenkins (Pontypridd), M R Hall (Cardiff); C J Stephens (Llanelli), Robert N Jones (Swansea); M Griffiths (Cardiff), G R Jenkins (Swansea), L Delaney (Llanelli), Gareth Llewelyn (Neath), A H Copsey (Llanelli), M Morris (Neath), Stuart Davies, R E Webster (Swansea). Rep: M Rayer (Cardiff) for Clement.

For England, Will Carling, Mick Skinner and Wade Dooley scored tries. Jonathan Webb converted all three and kicked two penalty goals.

Referee: R J Megson (Scotland).

Wales won by one goal, three penalty goals (15) to one dropped goal, three penalty goals (12)

Captain Ieuan Evans, on his 28th birthday, led his side to their first home victory in the Five Nations for three years. "We still have a very long way to go," he admitted. However, the scrum at last exuded authority and the back row generated suitable drive. But no Welsh back scored a try throughout the championship season and a two-try total was less than satisfactory. Scotland were unfortunate to have Iwan Tukalo's try disallowed: the clearance kick was charged down and not knocked-on. Roger Bidgood was capped after a five-year wait. He had been chosen against Ireland in 1987, but the match was postponed because of snow, and Bidgood was not reselected.

Wales: A Clement (Swansea); Ieuan Evans (Llanelli, capt), I S Gibbs (Swansea), *R A Bidgood (Newport), M R Hall (Cardiff); N R Jenkins (Pontypridd), Robert N Jones (Swansea); M Griffiths (Cardiff), G R Jenkins (Swansea), H Williams-Jones (S W Police), Gareth Llewellyn (Neath), A H Copsey, E W Lewis (Llanelli), Stuart Davies, R E Webster (Swansea).

Scotland: A G Hastings (Watsonians); A G Stanger (Hawick), S Hastings (Watsonians), S R P Lineen (Boroughmuir), I Tukalo (Selkirk); C M Chalmers (Melrose), A D Nicol (Dundee HSFP); D M B Sole (Edinburgh Acads, capt), K S Milne (Heriot's FP), A P Burnell (London Scottish), N G B Edwards (Harlequins), G W Weir (Melrose), D J McIvor (Edinburgh Acads), D B White (London Scottish), I R Smith (Gloucester). Rep: Peter Jones (Gloucester) for Burnell.

For Wales, Richard Webster scored a try. Neil Jenkins converted and kicked three penalty goals.

For Scotland, Craig Chalmers dropped a goal and kicked two penalty goals. Gavin Hastings kicked one penalty goal.

Referee: M Desclaux (France).

Wales won by four goals, three tries (43) to one goal, one try (12)
(N.B. Try increased in value to five points)

There were seven tries for the green jerseys of Wales in this first meeting with Italy, but the forwards lost momentum during the second half and possession dwindled disappointingly. The Italians appeared sharper in collective passing. Nevertheless, it was considered a worthwhile workout before taking on Australia six weeks later. The highlight was a dazzling opportunist try by dodging Mike Rayer, a full back brought on as replacement wing in the closing minutes. Attendance: 26,220.

Wales: A Clement (Swansea); Ieuan Evans (Llanelli, capt), R A Bidgood (Newport), I S Gibbs (Swansea), M R Hall (Cardiff); C J Stephens (Llanelli), Robert N Jones (Swansea); M Griffiths (Cardiff), G R Jenkins (Swansea), H Williams-Jones (S W Police), Gareth Llewellyn (Neath), A H Copsey, E W Lewis (Llanelli), Stuart Davies, R E Webster (Swansea). Rep: M A Rayer (Cardiff) for Bidgood.

Italy: P Vaccari; E Venturi, S Barba, S Zori, Marcello Cuttitta; M Bonomi, I Francescato; Massimo Cuttitta, G Pivetta (capt.), G Grespan, M Giacheri, C Checchinato, R Cassina, J Gardner, A Bottacchiari.

For Wales, Anthony Clement, Ieuan Evans, Colin Stephens, Scott Gibbs, Stuart Davies,

Richard Webster, Mike Rayer scored tries. Colin Stephens converted four.

For Italy, Ivan Francescato and Marcello Cuttitta scored tries. Massimo Bonomi converted one.

Referee: F A Howard (England).

Match 410   WALES v AUSTRALIA   Cardiff Arms Park. November 21, 1992

Australia won by one goal, two penalty goals, two tries (23) to two penalty goals (6)

For the third successive meeting, Wales failed to score a try against Australia. A capacity crowd of 51,700 paid a record £765,000 for a game in Wales. There was an improved display by the home forwards, but the attacking plan was never in operation against the world champions, who had suffered sensational defeats by Swansea and Llanelli. Considering they were without their famous half-backs, Nick Farr-Jones (retired) and Michael Lynagh (injured) and the world's best lineout jumper John Eales (injured), the Wallabies were well-pleased with their efforts on a wet day. Bone-shaking tackles shattered Wales and David Campese hammered in the final nail with a 60-yard run at the end for his 52nd Test try.

Wales: M Rayer (Cardiff); Ieuan Evans (Llanelli, capt), I S Gibbs (Swansea), M R Hall (Cardiff), *W T Proctor (Llanelli); C J Stephens (Llanelli), Robert N Jones (Swansea); M Griffiths (Cardiff), G R Jenkins (Swansea), H Williams-Jones (S W Police), A H Copsey (Llanelli), Gareth Llewellyn (Neath), E W Lewis (Llanelli), Stuart Davies, R E Webster (Swansea). Rep: A Reynolds (Swansea) for Lewis.

Australia: M C Roebuck; P V Carozza, J S Little, T J Horan, D I Campese; P Kahl, P J Slattery; D J Crowley, P N Kearns (capt), E J A McKenzie, R J McCall, G Morgan, V Ofahengaue, B T Gavin, D Wilson. Rep: T Coker for Wilson.

For Wales, Colin Stephens kicked two penalty goals.

For Australia, David Wilson, Rod McCall and David Campese scored tries. Marty Roebuck converted one and kicked two penalty goals.

Referee: A J Spreadbury (England).

Match 411   WALES v ENGLAND   Cardiff Arms Park. February 6, 1993

Wales won by one goal, one penalty goal (10) to two penalty goals, one dropped goal (9)

England's hopes of a unique third successive Grand Slam were impaled on heroic tackling. Wales snatched the only try near half-time as Emyr Lewis shrewdly chipped on wide for Ieuan Evans to chase. Rory Underwood inexplicably slowed and allowed the Welsh captain to breeze past, kick on and pursue to score his most memorable try. Neil Jenkins, who had bombarded Jonathan Webb with high kicks, converted for victory. Crickhowell-born Dewi Morris twice almost stole a try for England. Mike Rayer was the outstanding Welsh performer while new caps Ricky Evans and Nigel Meek never buckled in a fierce front row confrontation. Diana, Princess of Wales, saw Webb hit the post with a penalty shot that would have robbed Wales of a fully deserved success in a match of high drama. Revenue was a record £1.92m.

Wales: M A Rayer (Cardiff); Ieuan Evans (Llanelli, capt), M R Hall (Cardiff), I S Gibbs (Swansea), W T Proctor (Llanelli); N R Jenkins (Pontypridd), Robert N Jones (Swansea); *R L Evans (Llanelli), *N Meek (Pontypool), H Williams-Jones (S W Police), A H Copsey (Llanelli), Gareth Llewellyn (Neath), E W Lewis (Llanelli), Stuart Davies, R E Webster (Swansea).

England: J M Webb (Bath); I Hunter (Northampton), W D C Carling

263

(Harlequins, capt), J C Guscott (Bath), R Underwood (Leicester); C R Andrew (Wasps), C D Morris (Orrell); J Leonard, B C Moore (Harlequins), J A Probyn (Wasps), M C Bayfield (Northampton), W A Dooley (Preston Grasshoppers), M C Teague (Moseley), B B Clarke (Bath), P J Winterbottom (Harlequins). Rep: P R de Glanville (Bath) for Hunter.

For Wales, Ieuan Evans scored a try. Neil Jenkins converted and kicked a penalty goal.

For England, Jonathan Webb kicked two penalty goals. Jeremy Guscott dropped a goal.

Referee: J Dume (France).

Match 412   SCOTLAND v WALES   Murrayfield. Feburary 20, 1993

Scotland won by five penalty goals, one try (20) to nil

After the elation of victory over England, this was a depressingly ineffective Welsh performance: a 'massacre' reminiscent of the amazing 1951 rout at Murrayfield. The Welsh pack were destroyed in all departments and Gavin Hastings hoisted five penalty goals between the posts in a gale. French referee Joel Dume waited until all the forwards had peeled of the ground before deciding Derek Turnbull had scored the game's only try.

Scotland: A G Hastings (Watsonians, capt); A G Stanger (Hawick), S Hastings (Watsonians), A G Shiel (Melrose), D A Stark (Boroughmuir); C M Chalmers (Melrose), G Armstrong (Jedforest); P H Wright (Boroughmuir), K S Milne (Heriot's FP), A P Burnell (London Scottish), A I Reed (Bath), D F Cronin (London Scottish), D J Turnbull (Hawick), G W Weir (Melrose), I R Morrison (London Scottish).

Wales: M A Rayer (Cardiff); Ieuan Evans (Llanelli, capt), M R Hall (Cardiff), I S Gibbs (Swansea), W T Proctor (Llanelli); N R Jenkins (Pontypridd), Robert N Jones (Swansea); R L Evans (Llanelli), N Meek (Pontypool), H Williams-Jones (S W Police), A H Copsey (Llanelli), Gareth Llewellyn (Neath), E W Lewis (Llanelli), Stuart Davies, R E Webster (Swansea).

For Scotland, Derek Turnbull scored a try. Gavin Hastings kicked five penalty goals.

Referee: J Dume (France).

Match 413   WALES v IRELAND   Cardiff Arms Park. March 6, 1993

Ireland won by one goal, one dropped goal, three penalty goals (19) to
three penalty goals, one try (14)

"Inept", summed up team manager Robert Norster after this dismal display which gave Ireland their first championship success in 12 attempts. The selectors had spent seven-and-a-half hours considering changes after the Murrayfield flop, and had came up with just one change – on the left wing! Coach Alan Davies's policy of continuity proved a misplaced faith in his players. The forwards again failed to control any area for a sustained period and Neil Jenkins missed seven goal attempts and was cruelly booed by Welsh fans. Nigel Walker, aged 29, Olympic Games 110 metres hurdles semi-finalist in 1984, in his first season of senior rugby, and after just 20 games for Cardiff, won his cap as the fastest wing in the world.

Wales: M A Rayer (Cardiff); Ieuan Evans (Llanelli, capt), M R Hall (Cardiff), I S Gibbs (Swansea), *N Walker (Cardiff); N R Jenkins (Pontypridd), Robert N Jones (Swansea); R L Evans (Llanelli), N Meek (Pontypool), H Williams-Jones (S W Police), A H Copsey (Llanelli), Gareth Llewellyn (Neath), E W Lewis (Llanelli),

Stuart Davies, R E Webster (Swansea). Rep: A Clement (Swansea) for Ieuan Evans.

Ireland: C P Clarke (Tenure Coll); R M Wallace, P P A Danaher (Garryowen), V G J Cunningham (St. Mary's Coll), S P Geoghegan (London Irish); E P Elwood (Lansdowne), M T Bradley (Cork Constitution, capt); N J Popplewell (Greystones), T J Kingston (Dolphin), P M Clohessy (Young Minster), P S Johns (Dungannon), M J Galwey (Shannon), P T O'Hara (Cork Constitution), B F Robinson (London Irish), W D McBride (Malone).

For Wales, Ieuan Evans scored a try. Neil Jenkins kicked three penalty goals.

For Ireland, Brian Robinson scored a try. Eric Elwood converted and kicked three penalty goals. Ciaran Clarke dropped a goal.

Referee: A R MacNeill (Australia).

Match 414 **FRANCE v WALES**   Parc des Princes. March 20, 1993

France won by one goal, three penalty goals, two tries (26) to one goal, one penalty goal (10)

Wales finished with the wooden spoon, beaten in the enervating heat of an early spring day in Paris. New scrum half Rupert Moon, selected a season after he should have been, triggered his runners at every opportunity; but the home side ruled the lineout as their pack dominated. There was a splendid try by Nigel Walker, Wales's first try in Paris for 10 years. A record eight Llanelli players were on duty. France became the first winners of the new Five Nations Championship Cup.

France: J B Lafond (Begles); P Saint-Andre (Montferrand), P Sella (Agen), T Lacroix (Dax), P Hontas (Biarritz); F Mesnel (Racing Club), A Hueber (Toulon); L Armary (Lourdes), J F Tordo (Nice, capt), L Seigne (Merignac), A Benazzi (Agen), O Roumat (Dax), P Benetton (Agen), M Cecillon (Bourgoin), L Cabannes (Racing Club).

Wales: A Clement (Swansea); Ieuan Evans (Llanelli, capt), I S Gibbs (Swansea), Nigel Davies (Llanelli), N Walker (Cardiff); N R Jenkins (Pontypridd), *R H St J B Moon (Llanelli); R L Evans, *A Lamerton (Llanelli), H Williams-Jones (S W Police), Phil Davies (Llanelli), Gareth Llewellyn (Neath), M A Perego, E W Lewis (Llanelli), R E Webster (Swansea). Reps: P Arnold (Swansea) for Perego, John Davies (Neath) for R L Evans.

For Wales, Nigel Walker scored a try. Neil Jenkins converted and kicked a penalty goal.

For France, Philippe Benetton (2) and Jean-Baptiste Lafond scored tries. Lafond converted one. Thierry Lacroix kicked three penalty goals.

Referee: E O Doyle (Ireland).

Match 415 **ZIMBABWE v WALES**   Bulawayo. May 22, 1993

*Wales won by three goals, two penalty goals, one dropped goal, one try (35)
to three penalty goals, one try (14)*

Simon Hill, replacement wing for injured club-mate Nigel Walker before the party left Wales, scored a debut try after seven minutes, but Wales were disappointed they did not operated more cohesively. A new half back pairing of Rupert Moon and Adrian Davies did duty with Neil Jenkins switching to centre.

Zimbabwe: I Noble; D Nash, M Letcher, D Walters (capt), V Olonga; C Brown,

S Day; G Snyder, B Beattie, A Garvey, R Demblon, T Tabvuma, S Landman, R Fargnoli, B Dawson.

Wales: M A Rayer (Cardiff); *S Hill (Cardiff), R Bidgood (Newport), N R Jenkins (Pontypridd), W T Proctor (Llanelli); Adrian Davies (Cardiff), R H St J B Moon (Llanelli); M Griffiths (Cardiff), A Lamerton (Llanelli), H Williams-Jones (S W Police), P T Davies (Llanelli), Gareth Llewellyn (Neath, capt), M A Perego, E W Lewis, *Lyn Jones (Llanelli). Reps: *N Boobyer (Llanelli) for Proctor, Stuart Davies (Swansea) for Lewis.

For Wales, Simon Hill, Rupert Moon, Wayne Proctor and Phil Davies scored tries. Neil Jenkins converted three and kicked two penalty goals. Adrian Davies dropped a goal.

For Zimbabwe, Victor Olonga scored a try. Dave Walters kicked three penalty goals.

Referee: I Rogers (South Africa).

Match 416   ZIMBABWE v WALES   Harare. May 29, 1993

Wales won by three goals, two penalty goals, three tries (42) to one goal, two penalty goals (13)

Stuart Davies marked his appearance in the unusual role of blind-side with an all-action performance at the Police Grounds in this second Test, but slack finishing faulted the attackers and there should have been more than six tries. Neil Jenkins played as emergency full back because of injuries to Mike Rayer and Ian Jones (and was to figure in that role for the Lions in 1997). Skipper Gareth Llewellyn scored two tries and Jenkins supplied 17 points, including a try.

Zimbabwe: I Noble; W Schultz, M Letcher, D Walters (capt), V Olonga; C Brown, E MacMillan; G Snyder, B Beattie, A Garvey, R Demblon, T Tabvuma, S Landman; D Kirkman, B Dawson. Reps: E Chimbima for Schultz, B Chivandire for Landman.

Wales: N R Jenkins (Pontypridd); S Hill (Cardiff), R Bidgood (Newport), N Boobyer, W T Proctor (Llanelli); Adrian Davies (Cardiff), R H St J B Moon (Llanelli); M Griffiths (Cardiff), A Lamerton (Llanelli), J D Davies (Neath), P Arnold (Swansea), Gareth Llewellyn (Neath, capt), Stuart Davies (Swansea), E W Lewis, Lyn Jones (Llanelli).

For Wales, Gareth Llewellyn (2), Roger Bidgood, Stuart Davies, John Davies and Neil Jenkins scored tries. Jenkins converted three and kicked two penalty goals.

For Zimbabwe, Victor Olonga scored a try. Ian Noble converted and kicked two penalty goals.

Referee: I Anderson (South Africa).

Match 417   NAMIBIA v WALES   Windhoek. June 5, 1993

Wales won by two goals, three penalty goals, three tries (38) to two goals, three penalty goals (23)

Wales continued their Zim-Nam six-match tour by surging away in the final quarter after Namibia had led 20-19. Full back Jaco Coetzee contributed 18 points, including a try, in front of some 7,000 onlookers in very hot conditions. Emyr Lewis, outstanding again, snapped up two tries, the second when the ball went forward off Stuart Davies's legs and all the defenders stood still, thinking it was a knock-on.

Namibia: J Coetzee; G Mans (capt), H Snyman, M Marais, E Meyer; M Booysen, B Buitendag; C Derks, S Smith, A van Wyk, D Kotze, B Malgas, J Barnard, K Goosen, H Brink.

Wales: M A Rayer (Cardiff); S Hill (Cardiff), N Boobyer (Llanelli), R Bidgood (Newport), W T Proctor (Llanelli); N R Jenkins (Pontypridd), R H St J B Moon (Llanelli); M Griffiths (Cardiff), A Lamerton (Llanelli), H Williams-Jones (S W Police), P T Davies (Llanelli), Gareth Llewellyn (Neath, capt), Stuart Davies (Swansea), E W Lewis, Lyn Jones (Llanelli). Reps: M A Perego (Llanelli) for Lewis.

For Wales, Emyr Lewis (2), Wayne Proctor, Simon Hill and Rupert Moon scored tries. Neil Jenkins converted two and kicked three penalty goals.

For Namibia, Jaco Coetzee and Dirk Kotze scored tries. Jaco Coetzee converted both and kicked three penalty goal.

Referee: K W McCartney (Scotland).

Match 418   WALES v JAPAN   Cardiff Arms Park. October 16, 1993

Wales won by five goals, four tries (55) to one try (5)

Wales registered their record score in a full-cap match. They had scored 14 tries in the 82-6 victory in Tokyo in 1975, but that was not accorded cap status. This time there were nine tries to pass the 49-14 success against France in 1910. Skipper Ieuan Evans pounced on an error to score the first try just 45 sec after kick-off.

Wales: A Clement (Swansea); Ieuan Evans (Llanelli, capt), I S Gibbs (Swansea), N R Jenkins (Pontypridd), N Walker (Cardiff); Adrian Davies (Cardiff), R H St J B Moon (Llanelli); M Griffiths (Cardiff), A E Lamerton (Llanelli), J D Davies (Neath), A H Copsey (Llanelli), Gareth Llewellyn (Neath), Stuart Davies (Swansea), E W Lewis, Lyn Jones (Llanelli). Reps: M A Rayer (Cardiff) for Walker, R A Bidgood (Newport) for Ieuan Evans.

Japan: T Matsuda; I Williams, M Fujikake, E Kutsuki, Y Yoshida; A Aoki, Y Nagatomo; O Ota, M Kunda (capt), K Takahashi, Y Sakuraba, B Ferguson, S Kaleta, S Latu, H Ouchi.

For Wales, Ieuan Evans (2), Scott Gibbs (2) Neil Jenkins Rupert Moon, Emyr Lewis, Mike Rayer, Anthony Clement scored tries. Neil Jenkins converted five.

For Japan, Ian Williams scored a try.

Referee: E F Morrison (England).

Match 419   WALES v CANADA   Cardiff Arms Park. November 10, 1993

Canada won by two goals, four penalty goals (26) to eight penalty goals (24)

A try in injury time by second rower Al Charron, who lined out wide with his backs as Canada swung the ball fast across field to their overlap, tied the score 24-all. Then, with the final kick of the match, Gareth Rees, whose Welsh parents had emigrated from Llantrisant to British Columbia, slotted the winning conversion. It earned him the man-of-the-match award as he supplied 16 points. Canada obtained two tries, Wales none. Home points came from eight Neil Jenkins penalty goals, a Welsh record. But his side neglected to play an expansive game and were blocked by sustained tackling. Coach Alan Davies admitted, "We have to get to grips with what went wrong and perhaps I need to improve my communication skills with the players." Then he accused the team, "If they had stuck to the patterns of play we had on our summer tour of Africa, we would have been all right." Under the floodlights, it had been a glum experience for some 22,000 Welsh watchers. The start was delayed by 20 minutes to allow late ticket purchasers to take their seats. There was a first cap for Scott Quinnell, whose father Derek had been capped in 1972.

Wales: A Clement (Swansea); Ieuan Evans (Llanelli, capt), I S Gibbs (Swansea), N R Jenkins (Pontypridd), W T Proctor (Llanelli); Adrian Davies (Cardiff), R H St J B Moon (Llanelli); M Griffiths (Cardiff), G R Jenkins (Swansea), J D Davies (Neath), A H Copsey (Llanelli), Gareth Llewellyn (Neath), *L S Quinnell, E W Lewis, Lyn Jones (Llanelli).

Canada: M Williams; R Toews, S Gray, I Stuart (capt), D S Stewart; G Rees, C Tynan; P Szabo, I Kennedy, D Jackart, J Knauer, A J Charron, I Gordon, C McKenzie, J Hutchinson. Rep: I Mackay for Tynan, I Cooper for Knauer.

For Wales, Neil Jenkins kicked eight penalty goals.

For Canada, Ian Stuart and Al Charron scored tries. Gareth Rees converted both and kicked four penalty goals.

Referee: E O Doyle (Ireland).

Match 420   WALES v SCOTLAND   Cardiff Arms Park. January 15, 1994

Wales won by one goal, four penalty goals, two tries (29) to two penalty goals (6)

Two tries by left wing Mike Rayer, on as replacement for injured clubmate Nigel Walker, saw Wales complete a comprehensive victory; their biggest championship success for 15 years, since their 27-3 defeat of England in 1979. Neil Jenkins, with four penalty goals in his 14 points, set the stage for the revival after the slump against Canada. Despite the chilling rain and slippery turf, Wales spread the ball adventurously. Phil Davies, recalled to the second row, was the most impressive forward. Wales chose a one-club back row from Llanelli again. Garin Jenkins misbehaved and an outraged Scottish spectator asked the SW Police to investigate the punching episode. Hooker Jenkins was warned by the Welsh team management as to his future conduct.

Wales: A Clement (Swansea); Ieuan Evans (Llanelli, capt), M R Hall (Cardiff), N G Davies (Llanelli), N Walker (Cardiff); N R Jenkins (Pontypridd), R H St J B Moon (Llanelli); R L Evans (Llanelli), G R Jenkins (Swansea), J D Davies (Neath), P T Davies (Llanelli), Gareth Llewellyn (Neath), E W Lewis, L S Quinnell, M A Perego (Llanelli). Rep: M A Rayer (Cardiff) for Walker.

Scotland: A G Hastings (Watsonians, capt); A G Stanger (Hawick), G P J Townsend (Gala), I C Jardine (Stirling County), K M Logan (Stirling County); C M Chalmers (Melrose), A D Nicol (Dundee HSFP); P H Wright (Boroughmuir), K S Milne (Heriot's FP), A P Burnell (London Scottish), N G B Edwards (Northampton), D S Munro (Glasgow High/Kelvinside), D J Turnbull (Hawick), R I Wainwright (Edinburgh Acads), I R Morrison (London Scottish). Reps: D S Wyllie (Stewart's Melville FP) for Chalmers, G W Weir (Melrose) for Morrison.

For Wales, Mike Rayer (2) and Ieuan Evans scored tries. Neil Jenkins convertd one and kicked four penalty goals.

For Scotland, Gavin Hastings kicked two penalty goals.

Referee: P Robin (France).

Match 421   IRELAND v WALES   Lansdowne Road, Dublin. February 5, 1994

Wales won by four penalty goals, one try (17) to five penalty goals (15)

Pipped on the post! Eric Elwood would have made Ireland 18-17 winners instead of 17-15 losers; but, after kicking five penalty goals, his next shot rebounded from the top of the post eight minutes from the end. So Wales, behind until 10 minutes from full time, snatched a tense victory. Neil Jenkins scored the only try, sent over by a narrow-side pass from Rupert Moon. Jenkins also kicked four penalty goals to provide all the points. Llanelli had a record nine players in the team. Scrum half Robert Jones assumed a new role when he was called on as a replacement and did emergency duty on the wing for the last few minutes. It was escape from Alcatraz for Wales.

Ireland: C O'Shea (Lansdowne); R M Wallace (Garryowen), M McCall (Bangor), P P A Danaher (Garryowen), S P Geoghegan (London Irish); E P Elwood (Lansdowne), M T Bradley (Cork Constitution, capt); N J Popplewell (Greystones), T J Kingston (Dolphin), P M Clohessy (Young Munster), M J Galwey (Shannon), N P J Francis (Old Belvedere), B F Robinson (Ballymena), P S Johns (Dungannon), W D McBride (Malone).

Wales: A Clement (Swansea); Ieuan Evans (Llanelli, capt), M R Hall (Cardiff), N G Davies (Llanelli), W T Proctor (Llanelli); N R Jenkins (Pontypridd), R H St J B Moon (Llanelli); R L Evans (Llanelli), G R Jenkins (Swansea), J D Davies (Neath), P T Davies (Llanelli), Gareth Llewellyn (Neath), E W Lewis, L S Quinnell, M A Perego (Llanelli). Reps: M A Rayer (Cardiff) for Clement, S Hill (Cardiff) for Proctor, Robert N Jones (Swansea) for Nigel Davies.

For Wales, Neil Jenkins scored a try and kicked four penalty goals.

For Ireland, Eric Elwood kicked five penalty goals.

Referee: A Spreadbury (England).

Match 422 WALES v FRANCE   Cardiff Arms Park. February 19, 1994

Wales won by one goal, four penalty goals, one try (24) to one goal, one penalty goal, one try (15)

This first success against France for 12 years was notable for the performance of 21-year-old Scott Quinnell. He broke away from a lineout and slipped three tackles to score a spine-tingling try. Right at the end, he put Nigel Walker racing away for the other try and Wales were set up for the Grand Slam at Twickenham. France came back from 17-3 down with two tries in the space of five minutes. "We were on the verge of cracking," admitted Gareth Llewellyn, leading the side in the absence of injured Ieuan Evans. But the Welsh pack were magnificent and, of course, Neil Jenkins landed the goals again, four penalty shots plus a conversion from the touch line with the last kick of the match.

Wales: M A Rayer (Cardiff); S D Hill, M R Hall (Cardiff), A Clement (Swansea), N Walker (Cardiff); N R Jenkins (Pontypridd), R H St J B Moon (Llanelli); R L Evans (Llanelli), G R Jenkins (Swansea), J D Davies (Neath), P T Davies (Llanelli), Gareth Llewellyn (Neath, capt), E W Lewis, L S Quinnell, M A Perego (Llanelli).

France: J L Sadourny (Colomiers); E Ntamack (Toulouse), P Sella (Agen), T Lacroix (Dax), P Saint-Andre (Montferrand); A Penaud (Brive), F Galthie (Colomiers); L Armary (Lourdes), J M Gonzales (Bayonne), P Gallart (Beziers), O Merle (Grenoble), O Roumat (Dax, capt), P Benetton (Agen), M Cecillon (Bourgoin), A Benazzi (Agen).

For Wales, Scott Quinnell and Nigel Walker scored tries. Neil Jenkins converted one and kicked four penalty goals.

For France, Olivier Roumat and Philippe Sella scored tries. Thierry Lacroix converted one and kicked one penalty goal.

Referee: L McLachlan (New Zealand).

England won by one goal, one penalty goal, one try (15) to one penalty goal, one try (8)

Wales won the Five Nations title outright for the first time since 1979 on the new highest aggregate match points system, but failed to collect the Grand Slam, last achieved 16 years earlier. The Queen presented the trophy to captain Ieuan Evans after England's 15-8 success. The home side needed to score 16 points more than Wales if they were to steal the title and, at 15-3 ahead, it appeared as if this were possible; but Nigel Walker went over for the only Welsh try from Phil Davies's pass after a powerful surge by prop Ricky Evans. Nevertheless, England deserved their victory through forward supremacy. They had failed to register a try during their previous five matches and had been accused of being boring. This time there were two tries for them: a bobby-dazzler from wing Rory Underwood and a soft try when Garin Jenkins's throw-in on his line went straight to Tim Rodber, who had moved up to stand at No. 1. "We still have a long way to go," reflected coach Alan Davies. The Grand Slam had been a match too far.

England: I G Hunter (Northampton); T Underwood (Leicester), P R de Glanville (Bath), W D C Carling (Harlequins, capt), R Underwood (Leicester); C R Andrew (Wasps), C D Morris (Orrell); J Leonard (Harlequins), B C Moore (Harlequins), V E Ubogu (Bath), M O Johnson (Leicester), N C Redman (Bath), T A K Rodber (Northampton), D Richards (Leicester), B B Clarke (Bath). Rep: M Catt (Bath) for Andrew.

Wales: M A Rayer (Cardiff); Ieuan Evans (Llanelli, capt), M R Hall (Cardiff), N G Davies (Llanelli), N Walker (Cardiff); N R Jenkins (Pontypridd), R H St J B Moon (Llanelli); R L Evans (Llanelli), G R Jenkins (Swansea), J D Davies, Gareth Llewellyn (Neath), P T Davies, E W Lewis, L S Quinnell, M A Perego (Llanelli). Rep: A H Copsey (Llanelli) for E W Lewis.

For Wales, Nigel Walker scored a try. Neil Jenkins kicked a penalty goal.

For England, Rory Underwood and Tim Rodber scored tries. Rob Andrew converted one and kicked a penalty goal.

Referee: J M Fleming (Scotland).

Wales won by 11 goals, five tries (102) to two penalty goals, one try (11)

Sprinter Nigel Walker wafted in for four of the sixteen tries as Wales racked up their record tally of 102 points. Ieuan Evans and Mike Hall each added three tries. Robert Jones, recalled after 10 games, scored his first try for Wales for seven years. Tackling by the home side was of the token variety, watched critically by some 2,000 spectators. Neil Jenkins kicked 22 points. Ieuan Evans passed Arthur Gould's record of captaining Wales 18 times (between 1889-1897). Hemi Taylor became the first New Zealander to play for Wales (residential qualifications).

Portugal: J M Villar-Gomez; P Murinello, R Pereira, N Mourao, T Morais; J Queimado (capt), P Netto Fernandes; S Perreira, M Batista, P Domingos, A Pecas, A Andrade, P Arsenio, J Pires, P Eusebio. Reps: A Cunna for Pires, E Macedo for Perreira.

Wales: M A Rayer (Cardiff); Ieuan Evans (capt), N G Davies (Llanelli), M R Hall, N Walker (Cardiff); N R Jenkins (Pontypridd), Robert N Jones (Swansea); R L Evans (Llanelli), G R Jenkins (Swansea), J D Davies, Gareth Llewellyn (Neath), A H Copsey (Llanelli), H Taylor (Cardiff), L S Quinnell, E W Lewis (Llanelli).

For Portugal, Pedro Murinello scored a try. Vilar-Gomez kicked two penalty goals.

For Wales, Nigel Walker (4), Ieuan Evans (3) Mike Hall (3), Robert Jones (2), Hemi Taylor, Scott Quinnell, Gareth Llewellyn scored tries, and there was a penalty try. Neil Jenkins converted 11.

Referee: D Bishop (NZ).

Match 425   SPAIN v WALES (WC Qualifier)   Madrid University. May 21, 1994

Wales won by five goals, three penalty goals, two tries (54) to nil

There was more resistance and physical presence in this second World Cup qualifying game in front of 4,000 watchers. Ieuan Evans whipped away for another try hat-trick. Spain had shocked Wales to 10-7 defeat in the plate section semi-final of the World Sevens Cup at Murrafield in 1993, but the home side were overpowered in the full game on this occasion.

Spain: J Azkargorta; P Martin, A Mino, A Encisco, J Torres; F Puertas, J Hernandez-Gil; J Alvarez, J Aguiar, J Diez, A Malo, J Villau, J Etxeberria, J Lopez, J Gutierrez (capt). Reps: S Espina for Alvarez, F de le Calle for Etxeberria, I de Lazaro for Diez, O Solano for Lazaro.

Wales: A Clement (Swansea); Ieuan Evans (capt), N G Davies (Llanelli), M R Hall, N Walker (Cardiff); N R Jenkins (Pontypridd), R H St J B Moon (Llanelli); R L Evans (Llanelli), G R Jenkins (Swansea), J D Davies, Gareth Llewellyn (Neath), P Arnold (Swansea), E W Lewis, L S Quinnell, M A Perego (Llanelli). Rep: A H Copsey (Llanelli) for Lewis.

For Wales, Ieuan Evans (3), Scott Quinnell, Nigel Walker, Garin Jenkins scored tries, and there was a penalty try. Neil Jenkins converted five and kicked three penalty goals.

Referee: D Bishop (NZ).

Match 426   CANADA v WALES   Fletcher's Field, Toronto. June 11, 1994

Wales won by three goals, four penalty goals (33) to five penalty goals (15)

Fired up by disparaging comments from the Canadians, Wales exacted revenge for the humiliating defeat in Cardiff seven months earlier. The home side had been discussing just how they would carve up the tourists, who were en route to the South Pacific. It was an encouraging start to this voyage of discovery as Wales fought back after trailing by nine points. "We were stuffed," conceded Canadian hero Gareth Rees, whose goal kicking had doomed Wales in 1993.

Canada: D S Stewart; R Toews, S Gray, I Stuart (capt), D Lougheed; G L Rees, J Graf; E Evans, K Svoboda, D Jackart, A J Charron, M James, G MacKinnon, C McKenzie, I Gordon. Rep: G Ennis for McKenzie.

Wales: M A Rayer (Cardiff); Ieuan Evans (capt), N G Davies (Llanelli), M R Hall (Cardiff), W T Proctor (Llanelli); N R Jenkins (Pontypridd), R H St J B Moon (Llanelli); R L Evans (Llanelli), G R Jenkins (Swansea), J D Davies, Gareth Llewellyn (Neath), P T Davies (Llanelli), H Taylor (Cardiff), L S Quinnell (Llanelli), R G Collins (Pontypridd). Rep: A Clement (Swansea) for Ieuan Evans.

For Canada, Gareth Rees kicked five penalty goals.

For Wales, Mike Rayer (2) and Ieuan Evans scored tries. Neil Jenkins converted three and kicked four penalty goals.

Referee: I Rogers (SA).

Wales won by two goals, three penalty goals (23) to one penalty goal, one try (8)

The first of three South Pacific tour matches brought victory and a warning from team manager Robert Norster. "It is going to get harder from now on. We need to improve." Only six first choice players figured in the Welsh team. Both tries came from close-up scrums: first by full back Mike Rayer, then Richie Collins. An all-Llanelli threequarter line did duty.

Fiji: R Bogisa; J Vidiri, J Toloi, E Nauga, P Tuidraki; P Rayasi, J McLennan; R Williams, E Batimala, J Veitayaki, I Tawake (capt), I Savai, S Matalulu, A Moceletu, J Campbell. Rep: M Korovou for Campbell.

Wales: M A Rayer (Cardiff); Ieuan Evans (capt), N G Davies, N Boobyer, W T Proctor (Llanelli); Adrian Davies (Cardiff), R H St J B Moon (Llanelli); R L Evans (Llanelli), *R C McBryde (Swansea), H Williams-Jones, A H Copsey (Llanelli), P Arnold (Swansea), H Taylor (Cardiff), E W Lewis (Llanelli), R G Collins (Pontypridd). Rep: P T Davies (Llanelli) for Lewis.

For Fiji, Jo Veitayaki scored a try. Rasolsolo Bogisa kicked a penalty goal.

For Wales, Mike Rayer and Richie Collins scored tries. Adrian Davies converted two and kicked three penalty goals.

Referee: E Sklar (Argentina).

Wales won by six penalty goals (18) to three penalty goals (9)

Wales had never recorded five consecutive away victories before this, but there were no tries and manager Robert Norster was far from satisfied that they failed to cross the line for the first occasion in nine games. "We made more errors than during the whole of last season," he accused. Neil Jenkins decided the issue with six penalty goals in six attempts in an exceptional display of place-kicking.

Tonga: S Tu'ipulotu; T Va'enuku, F Manukia, P Latu, S Taupeaafu; E Vunipola, M Vunipola; T Lutua, F Vunipola (capt), U Fa, F Mafi, V Taumoepeau, T Loto'ahea, T Vikilani, K Tu'ipulotu. Rep: F Masila for Mafi.

Wales: A Clement (Swansea); Ieuan Evans (capt), N Boobyer (Llanelli), M R Hall, *G Wilkins (Bridgend); N R Jenkins, *P John (Pontypridd); *I Buckett, G R Jenkins (Swansea), H Williams-Jones, A H Copsey (Llanelli), Gareth Llewellyn (Neath), H Taylor (Cardiff), *S M Williams (Neath), R G Collins (Pontypridd). Rep: N G Davies (Llanelli) for Hall.

For Tonga, Sateki Tu'ipulotu kicked three penalty goals.

For Wales, Neil Jenkins kicked six penalty goals.

Referee: E Sklar (Argentina).

Western Samoa won by two goals, five penalty goals, one try (34) to three penalty goals (9)

In the blast furnace heat, Wales shrivelled to their worst defeat in 24 matches; since 38-3 against Australia in Cardiff in the 1991 World Cup. The explosive running of the home side, especially in broken play, demoralised the tourists, who could respond only with three Neil Jenkins penalty goals. This had been a beach too far!

Western Samoa: A Aiolupo; B Lima, T Vaega, F Tuilagi, T Samania; D Kellett, V Vitale; P Fatialofa (capt), T Leiasamaivao, G Latu, M Birtwistle, M Keenan, S Vaifale, P Lam, M Iupeli. Reps: S Kaleta for Keenan, D Mika for Lam.

Wales: M A Rayer (Cardiff); Ieuan Evans (capt), N G Davies (Llanelli), A Clement (Swansea), W T Proctor (Llanelli); N R Jenkins (Pontypridd), R H St J B Moon (Llanelli); R L Evans (Llanelli), G R Jenkins (Swansea), J D Davies, Gareth Llewellyn (Neath), P T Davies, E W Lewis, L S Quinnell (Llanelli), R G Collins (Pontypridd). Reps: H Williams-Jones (Llanelli) for R L Evans, A H Copsey (Llanelli) for P T Davies, H Taylor (Cardiff) for Quinnell.

For Western Samoa, Brian Lima (2) and Pat Lam scored tries. Darren Kellett converted both and kicked five penalty goals.

For Wales, Neil Jenkins kicked three penalty goals.

Referee: B Leask (Australia).

Match 430   ROMANIA v WALES   Bucharest. September 17, 1994

Wales won by one goal, three penalty goals (16) to three penalty goals (9)

Ieuan Evans scored his record 21st full-cap try to pass the Wales best held jointly by Gareth Edwards and Gerald Davies. It proved the decisive score in this World Cup seeding match. Certainly it proved a desperate victory and coach Alan Davies admitted his side were fortunate to win after the giant home pack had completely dominated the lineout. The coach was highly critical of the match being played during intense mid-afternoon heat. Thankfully, Neil Jenkins again was on target in the 23rd August Stadium.

Romania: V Brici; L Colceriu, N Racean, N Fulina, G Solomie; N Nichitean, D Neaga; G Leonte, G Ion, G Vlad, S Ciorascu, C Cojocariu, T Oroian, T Brinza (capt), A Guranescu. Reps: C Gheorge for Leonte, C Draguceanu for Brinza.

Wales: M A Rayer (Cardiff); Ieuan Evans (capt), N G Davies (Llanelli), M R Hall (Cardiff), W T Proctor (Llanelli); N R Jenkins (Pontypridd), R H St J B Moon (Llanelli); R L Evans (Llanelli), G R Jenkins (Swansea), J D Davies, Gareth Llewellyn, (Neath), P T Davies (Llanelli), H Taylor, E W Lewis (Cardiff), R G Collins (Pontypridd).

For Romania, Neculai Nichitean kicked three penalty goals.

For Wales, Ieuan Evans scored a try. Neil Jenkins converted and kicked three penalty goals.

Referee: D McHugh (Ireland).

Match 431   WALES v ITALY   Cardiff Arms Park. October 12, 1994

Wales won by seven penalty goals, one dropped goal, one try (29)
to one goal, four penalty goals (19)

Italy, having set a World Cup record 104-8 over the Czech Republic in their seeding fixture, fancied their chances under the Arms Park floodlights watched by 25,000 spectators, but Neil Jenkins destroyed their hopes with a record-equalling 24 points. He fired in seven penalty goals and a drop-shot and, in the process, became his country's highest scorer with an aggregate of 308 points, four more than Paul Thorburn. Nigel Davies collected Wales's only try, and a sparkling one at that.

Wales: M A Rayer (Cardiff); W T Proctor, N G Davies (Llanelli), M R Hall (Cardiff), A Clement (Swansea); N R Jenkins (Pontypridd), R H St J B Moon (Llanelli); R L Evans (Llanelli), G R Jenkins (Swansea), J D Davies, Gareth Llewellyn (capt, Neath), P T Davies (Llanelli), H Taylor, E W Lewis (Cardiff), R G Collins (Pontypridd). Rep: H Williams-Jones (Llanelli) for Evans (temp).

Italy: P Vaccari; I Francescato, M Bonomi, S Bordon, M Gerosa; D Dominguez, A Troncon; M Cuttitta (capt), C Orlandi, G Grespan, R Favaro, D Scaglia, O Arancio, C Checchinato, A Sgorlon. Rep: M Dal Sie for Grespan.

For Wales, Nigel Davies scored a try. Neil Jenkins dropped a goal and kicked seven penalty goals.

For Italy, Ivan Francescato scored a try. Diego Dominguez converted and kicked four penalty goals.

Referee: K McCartney (Scotland).

Match 432   WALES v SOUTH AFRICA   Cardiff Arms Park. November 26, 1994

South Africa won by one goal, one penalty goal, two tries (20) to four penalty goals (12)

Wales led 12-10 midway through the second half and, with Gareth Llewellyn and new cap Derwyn Jones commanding the lineout and Neil Jenkins lofting the high ball behind the defence, the Springboks often appeared ragged and vulnerable. However, the tourists scored three tries without one in response. They advised Wales, who were without injury victims Ieuan Evans, Mike Rayer, Nigel Davies and Nigel Walker, to introduce more width into their game. Still, it was considered by most to be something of an honourable defeat with the margin so tight. Incidentally, Derwyn Jones was the biggest forward ever to play for his country at 6ft 10in and 18st 7lb. Springbok captain Francois Pienaar said he was worried when Wales nosed in front. "I had to get the guys together and tell them to stop playing as individuals," he explained.

Wales: A Clement (Swansea); W T Proctor (Llanelli), *M Taylor (Pontypool), M R Hall, S D Hill (Cardiff); N R Jenkins (Pontypridd), R H St J B Moon (Llanelli); R L Evans (Llanelli), G R Jenkins (Swansea), J D Davies, Gareth Llewellyn (capt, Neath), Derwyn Jones, H Taylor, E W Lewis (Cardiff), R G Collins (Pontypridd). Rep: R C McBryde (Llanelli) for G R Jenkins (temp).

South Africa: A J Joubert; P Hendriks, P G Muller, J C Mulder, C M Williams; H P le Roux, J H van der Westhuizen; J P du Randt, U L Schmidt, T G Laubscher, M G Andrews, P J W Schutte, J F Pienaar (capt), R A W Straeuli, R J Kruger.

For Wales, Neil Jenkins kicked four penalty goals.

For South Africa, Rudi Straeuli, Andre Joubert, Chester Williams scored tries. Hennie le Roux converted one and kicked a penalty goal.

Referee: D Mene (France).

Match 433   FRANCE v WALES   Parc de Princes, Paris. January 21, 1995

France won by one goal, three penalty goals, one try (21) to three penalty goals (9)

Again no tries for Wales as Diana, Princess of Wales, watched them struggle after a promising start. It was 20 years since the last victory in Paris and the team had been dogged by injuries. Another occurred in this match when prop Ricky Evans was butted by Olivier Merle and, in falling dazed, twisted and broke his leg. Evans took legal action against the culprit and

France dropped hard-man Merle for their next two games. "We don't expect the British to take much initiative in the game," criticised French coach Pierre Berbizier before the game. It summed up the Welsh performance.

France: J L Sadourny (Colomiers); E Ntamack (Toulouse), P Sella (Agen), T Lacroix (Dax), P Saint-Andre (Montferrand, capt); C Deylaud (Toulouse), G Accoceberry (Begles); L Benezech (Racing Club), J M Gonzalez (Bayonne), C Califano (Toulouse), O Merle (Montferrand), O Roumat (Dax), A Benazzi, P Benetton (Agen), L Cabannes (Racing Club).

Wales: A Clement (Swansea); S D Hill, M R Hall (Cardiff), M Taylor (Pontypool), N Walker (Cardiff); N R Jenkins (Pontypridd), Robert N Jones (Swansea); R L Evans (Llanelli), G R Jenkins (Swansea), J D Davies, Gareth Llewellyn (capt, Neath), Derwyn Jones (Cardiff), Stuart Davies (Swansea), P T Davies (Llanelli), R G Collins (Pontypridd). Reps: *M Back (Bridgend) for Hill, M Griffiths (Cardiff) for Evans.

For France, Emile Ntamack, Philippe Saint-Andre scored tries. Thierry Lacroix converted one and kicked three penalty goals.

For Wales, Neil Jenkins kicked three penalty goals.

Referee: J Pearson (England).

Match 434   WALES v ENGLAND   Cardiff Arms Park. February 18, 1995

England won by one goal, two penalty goals, two tries (23) to three penalty goals (9)

Neath tight-head John Davies was ordered from the field for kicking Ben Clarke in the head at a ruck after 23 minutes of the second half; but England, leading 18-9, were already in control through their awsome pack. Referee Didier Mene allowed Wales to bring on Hugh Williams-Jones as replacement prop in the interest of safety in the scrum. Hemi Taylor went off so that Wales would have 14 men as punishment for the sending off. A month later the International Board made the necessary ruling to make this move permissible. Touch judge Patrick Robin drew attention to Davies's rash act. "Anyone who kicks a player in the head deserves to go off," insisted victim Clarke. Davies was banned for 60 days after his appeal failed. Rory Underwood, dubbed 'Blunderwood' after allowing Ieuan Evans to catch him off-guard and steal victory in 1993, became 'Wonderwood' with two tries on the ground where he had never scored previously for his country. This was Robert Jones's 50th appearance. Moon played as wing replacement.

Wales: A Clement (Swansea); Ieuan Evans (capt), N G Davies (Llanelli), M Taylor (Pontypool), N Walker (Cardiff); N R Jenkins (Pontypridd), Robert N Jones (Swansea); M Griffiths (Cardiff), G R Jenkins (Swansea), J D Davies, Gareth Llewellyn (Neath), Derwyn Jones, H Taylor, E W Lewis (Cardiff), R G Collins (Pontypridd). Reps: M Back (Bridgend) for Clement, R H St J B Moon (Llanelli) for Walker, H Williams-Jones (Llanelli) for Taylor.

England: M J Catt (Bath); T Underwood (Leicester), W D C Carling (Harlequins, capt), J C Guscott (Bath), R Underwood (Leicester); C R Andrew (Wasps), K P P Bracken (Bristol; J Leonard, B C Moore (Harlequins), V E Ubogu (Bath), M O Johnson (Leicester), M C Bayfield, T A K Rodber (Northampton), D Richards (Leicester), B B Clarke (Bath).

For Wales, Neil Jenkins kicked three penalty goals.

For England, Rory Underwood (2), Victor Ubogu scored tries. Rob Andrew converted one and kicked two penalty goals.

Referee: D Mene (France).

Scotland won by two goals, four penalty goals (26) to one goal, two penalty goals (13)

A Welsh try at last – and after just two minutes! But it was a third championship defeat of the season and the fifth in a row at Murrayfield. Scotland's dynamic pack proved faster and most of the game was played in Welsh territory. Robert Jones was the try-getter (his first Five Nations try) after a rousing Emyr Lewis charge. Ieuan Evans played his 50th game. Gavin Hastings kicked 16 points to set up a Grand Slam showdown at Twickenham, which England won. At least Wales had a try after only two in their previous seven games.

Scotland: A G Hastings (Watsonians, capt); C A Joiner (Melrose), G P J Townsend (Gala), S Hastings (Watsonians), K M Logan (Stirling County); C M Chalmers, B W Redpath (Melrose); D I W Hilton (Bath), K S Milne (Heriot's FP), P H Wright (Boroughmuir), G Weir (Melrose), S J Campbell (Dundee HSFP), R I Wainwright (West Hartlepool), E W Peters (Bath), I R Morrison (London Scottish).

Wales: M Back (Bridgend); Ieuan Evans (capt), N G Davies (Llanelli), M R Hall (Cardiff), W T Proctor (Llanelli); N R Jenkins (Pontypridd), Robert N Jones (Swansea); M Griffiths (Cardiff), G R Jenkins (Swansea), *S C John (Llanelli), Gareth Llewellyn (Neath), Derwyn Jones, H Taylor, E W Lewis (Cardiff), R G Collins (Pontypridd).

For Scotland, Eric Peters and David Hilton scored tries. Gavin Hastings converted both and kicked four penalty goals.

For Wales, Robert Jones scored a try. Neil Jenkins converted and kicked two penalty goals.

Referee: S Lander (England).

Ireland won by one goal, two penalty goals, one dropped goal (16) to four penalty goals (12)

This was the grim shoot-out for the wooden spoon – and Wales collected the dreaded symbol of ineptitude for the second time in their history: a whitewash in the same humiliating proportions as 1990. There had been just one Five Nations try all season and Ireland did not permit another as they registered their fifth consecutive victory over Wales. The repercussions were significant. Coach Alan Jones admitted his job was on the line. Robert Jones sprang to his defence. "It is the players who have let him down and to drop him before the World Cup would be crazy," railed the scrum half. But on March 27, Davies, assistant coach Gareth Jenkins and team manager Robert Norster asked to meet the full WRU committee. The outcome saw them offer their resignations just 60 days before Wales went to the World Cup in South Africa. The resignations were accepted. On March 31, the WRU appointed Cardiff's Australian coaching supremo Alex Evans as World Cup team coach. JPR Williams resigned as selection adviser because the side was changed after initial approval.

Wales: M Back (Bridgend); Ieuan Evans (capt), N G Davies (Llanelli), M R Hall (Cardiff), W T Proctor (Llanelli); N R Jenkins (Pontypridd), Robert N Jones (Swansea); M Griffiths (Cardiff), G R Jenkins (Swansea), S C John, P T Davies (Llanelli), Gareth Llewellyn (Neath), *A Gibbs (Newbridge), E W Lewis (Cardiff), R G Collins (Pontypridd).

Ireland: J E Staples (Harlequins); R M Wallace, P P A Danaher (Garryowen), B J Mullin (Blackrock Coll), S P Geoghegan (Bath); E P Elwood (Lansdowne), N A Hogan (Terenure); N J Popplewell (Wasps), T J Kingston (Dolphin, capt.), P M Clohessy (Young Munster), D A Tweed (Ballymena), G M Fulcher (Cork Con.),

A G Foley (Shannon), P S Johns (Dungannon), E O Halvey (Shannon). Rep: P Burke (Cork Con) for Elwood.

For Wales, Neil Jenkins kicked four penalty goals.

For Ireland, Brendan Mullin scored a try. Paul Burke converted, dropped a goal and kicked two penalty goals.

Referee: R J Megson (Scotland).

WORLD CUP (1st Pool Game)

Match 437   WALES v JAPAN   Bloemfontein. May 27, 1995

Wales won by five goals, four penalty goals, two tries (57) to two tries (10)

This opening fixture of the third World Cup was the only match Wales won in their pool and they made no progress into the quarter-final stage. Every other Five Nations team qualified. On the bright side, there were seven tries in this match, three of them by Gareth Thomas on his debut, the first time such a feat had been achieved for 96 years, when Willie Llewellyn marked his first cap with four tries while helping defeat England in 1899. Neil Jenkins kicked 22 points. Wales appeared in green jerseys and after five defeats a measure of optimism was abroad. Only next up was new Zealand!

> **Wales:** A Clement (Swansea); Ieuan Evans (Llanelli, capt), M R Hall (Cardiff), N R Jenkins (Pontypridd), *Gareth Thomas (Bridgend); Adrian Davies, *A P Moore (Cardiff); M Griffiths (Cardiff), G R Jenkins (Swansea), J D Davies, Gareth Llewellyn (Neath), Derwyn Jones, H Taylor, E Lewis (Cardiff), Stuart Davies (Swansea). Reps: D W Evans (Treorchy) for Adrian Davies, *S Roy (Cardiff) for Derwyn Jones.

> **Japan:** T Matsuda; L Oto, A Yoshida, Y Motoki, T Masuho; S Hirao, M Horikoshi; O Ota, M Kunda (capt.), K Takahashi, Y Sakuraba, B Ferguson, H Kajihara, Sione Latu, Sinali Latu.

For Wales, Gareth Thomas (3), Ieuan Evans (2), Hemi Taylor, Andy Moore scored tries. Neil Jenkins converted five and kicked four penalty goals.

For Japan, Lopeti Oto scored two tries.

Referee: E J Sklar (Argentina).

WORLD CUP (2nd Pool Game)

Match 438 WALES v NEW ZEALAND   Ellis Park, Johannesburg. May 31, 1995

New Zealand won by two goals, one dropped goal, four penalty goals, one try (34)
to one dropped goal, two penalty goals (9)

"We were all like rabbits caught in the headlights," summed up skipper Mike Hall after his team had been outclassed in losing for the 13th successive time against the All Blacks in this second World Cup tie. Andrew Mehrtens, the new Grant Fox, kicked 19 points and, although Wales kept Jonah Lomu, the 6ft 5in, 18st wing, quiet he stormed away for 50 yards in the closing 10 minutes to set up a try for dynamic Josh Kronfeld. Defeat, of course, did not come as a surprise.

> **Wales:** A Clement (Swansea); Ieuan Evans (Llanelli), M R Hall (Cardiff, capt), Gareth Thomas (Bridgend), W T Proctor (Llanelli); N R Jenkins (Pontypridd), Robert N Jones (Swansea); R L Evans (Llanelli), *J M Humphreys (Cardiff), J D Davies (Neath), Derwyn Jones (Cardiff), *G Prosser (Pontypridd), Gareth Llewellyn (Neath), H Taylor, *M Bennett (Cardiff).

New Zealand: G M Osborne; J T Lomu, F E Bunce, W K Litle, M C G Ellis; A P Mehrtens, G T M Bachop; C W Dowd, S B T Fitzpatrick (capt), O M Brown, I D Jones, B P Larsen, J W Joseph, M R Brewer, J A Kronfeld. Rep: E J Rush for Lomu.

For Wales, Neil Jenkins dropped a goal and kicked two penalty goals.

For NZ, Walter Little, Marc Ellis, Josh Kronfeld scored tries. Andrew Mehrtens converted two, dropped a goal and kicked four penalty goals.

Referee: E Morrison (England).

WORLD CUP (3rd Pool Game)

| Match 439 | **WALES v IRELAND** | Ellis Park, Johannesburg. June 4, 1995 |

*Ireland won by three goals, one penalty goal (24) to
two goals, one dropped goal, two penalty goals (23)*

A quarter-final place beckoned if Ireland could be overcome in this World Cup final pool tie. It was not to be and this performance by Wales is recognised generally as among the most abject of all time by a Welsh team. For woeful Wales it was a visionless game: Ireland's fast and furious tacklers were destroyers of all they hunted; Wales were near-helpless victims. RIP, Wales! Robert Jones played his 54th and final game for Wales. All were at scrum half except against Ireland in 1995, when he went on as a replacement to figure on the wing in the closing minutes.

Wales: A Clement (Swansea); Ieuan Evans (Llanelli), M R Hall (Cardiff, capt), N R Jenkins (Pontypridd), Gareth Thomas (Bridgend); Adrian Davies (Cardiff), Robert N Jones (Swansea); M Griffiths, J M Humphreys (Cardiff), J D Davies, Gareth Llewellyn (Neath), Derwyn Jones, H Taylor, E W Lewis (Cardiff), Stuart Davies (Swansea). Rep: R L Evans (Llanelli) for J D Davies.

Ireland: C M P O'Shea (Lansdowne); R M Wallace (Garryowen), B J Mullin (Blackrock Coll.), J C Bell (Ballymena), S P Geoghegan (Bath); E P Elwood (Lansdowne), N A Hogan (Terenure Coll); N J Popplewell (Wasps), T J Kingston (Dolphin, capt), G F Halpin (London Irish), G M Fulcher (Cork Con), N P J Francis (Old Belvedere), D Corkery (Cork Con), P S Johns (Dungannon), W D McBride (Malone). Rep: E O Halvey (Shannon) for McBride.

For Wales, Jonathan Humphreys, Hemi Taylor scored tries. Neil Jenkins converted both and kicked two penalty goals. Adrian Davies dropped a goal.

·For Ireland, Nick Popplewell, Denis McBride, Eddie Halvey scored tries. Eric Elwood converted them all and kicked a penalty goal.

Referee: I Rogers (South Africa).

| Match 440 | **SOUTH AFRICA v WALES** | Ellis Park, Johannesburg. September 2, 1995 |

*South Africa won by three goals, three penalty goals, two tries (40)
to two penalty goals, one try (11)*

It took less than five minutes for South Africa to strike a decisive blow: in the form of a sneak punch from 'Kobus' Wiese that put Derwyn Jones out of the match. "I didn't really wake up until I was in the dressing room." recalled Jones. "I've been told my jaw could have gone up through my skull. It might have been planned because there was talk they were out to get me." Certainly, the Springboks feared the lineout reach of the giant Cardiff lock after his successes against them in the autumn of 1994. It was a brutal act and Wiese admitted he should not have done it, but pleaded retaliation after being punched. He was suspended for 30 days and fined some £9,000, though he was not sent off. The suspicion was that this was an arranged mission. Swansea hooker Garin Jenkins was sent off for punching Joost van der Westhuizen and also banned for 30 days. Jenkins alleged he was gouged. This was billed as the first professional Test match with home players enjoying contracts worth over £100,000 per season. Welsh players were still negotiating a financial settlement with the WRU. Wales had suffered their eighth defeat in nine matches.

South Africa: A J Joubert; J T Small, J C Mulder, H P le Roux, J Olivier; J T Stransky, J H van der Westhuizen; I S Swart, J Dalton, M H Hurter, J J Wiese, M G Andrews, J F Pienaar (capt), G H Teichmann, R J Kruger.

Wales: *W J L Thomas (Llanelli); Ieuan Evans (Llanelli), *Gareth Jones, Gareth Thomas (Bridgend), S D Hill (Cardiff); N R Jenkins (Pontypridd), A P Moore (Cardiff); *C D Loader (Swansea), J M Humphreys (Cardiff, capt), J D Davies (Neath), Derwyn Jones (Cardiff), P Arnold (Swansea), A Gibbs (Newbridge), H Taylor, M Bennett (Cardiff). Reps: M Taylor (Pontypool) for Gareth Thomas, *A Moore (Swansea) for Derwyn Jones, G R Jenkins (Swansea) for Gibbs.

For South Africa, 'Kobus' Wiese, Francois Pienaar, James Small, Gary Teichmann, Jappie Mulder scored tries. Joel Stransky converted three and kicked three penalty goals.

For Wales, Mark Bennett scored a try. Neil Jenkins kicked two penalty goals.

Referee: J Dume (France).

Match 441   WALES v FIJI   Cardiff Arms Park. November 11, 1995

Wales won by three penalty goals, two tries (19) to one goal, one penalty goal, one try (15)

"You are kicking far too much ball away and it is stifling your game," warned Fijian technical adviser Brad Johnstone, the former NZ prop. He was reiterating what so many had observed before him. Amazingly, the message had not found a repository of acceptance in Wales. Caretaker coach Kevin Bowring, in charge for the first time and soon to be appointed the first WRU full time professional coach, pointed out that his team had been disrupted when Nigel Davies was injured and Neil Jenkins had to switch to centre. Jenkins again saved his side with 14 points, including a cheeky try. Everyone appeared to think he would kick a close range penalty goal and the sandboy was scampering onto the pitch with the material for Jenkins to build his kicking tee when Jenkins suddenly tapped the ball and darted the few yards to the line for a shock try. Ieuan Evans became the most-capped Welsh player, passing the 55 by JPR Williams.

Wales: W J L Thomas (Llanelli); Ieuan Evans (Llanelli), Gareth Thomas (Bridgend), N G Davies, W T Proctor (Llanelli); N R Jenkins (Pontypridd), A P Moore (Cardiff); C D Loader (Swansea), J M Humphreys (capt), *L Mustoe, Derwyn Jones (Cardiff), A Moore (Swansea), *J C Quinnell (Llanelli), H Taylor, A M Bennett (Cardiff). Reps: Garin Jenkins (Swansea) for Humphreys, Aled Williams (Swansea) for N G Davies.

Fiji: F Rayasi; P Bale, S Sorovaki, L Little, M Bari; J Waqa, J Rauluni; J Veitayaki (capt), G Smith, E Natuivau, E Katalau, I Tawake, W Masirewa, D Rouse, T Tamanivalu. Rep: R Bogisa for Waqa.

For Wales, A P Moore, Neil Jenkins scored tries. Neil Jenkins kicked three penalty.

For Fiji, Manasa Bari, Filipe Rayasi scored tries. Jonetano Waqa converted one and kicked a penalty goal.

Referee: P O'Brien (NZ).

Wales won by two goals, four penalty goals, one try (31) to two goals, four penalty goals (26)

Arwel Thomas, the Bristol outside half who had played for Neath and was later to star for Swansea, collected 16 goal points on debut. Although he kicked loosely at times, and more often than he should, he gave every appearance of being a class act. Wales captain Jonathan Humphreys admitted his team felt keenly disappointed with their performance. "We lost our rhythm," he explained. Italy snapped up two tries in the last 20 minutes to threaten at least to save the game.

Wales: W J L Thomas (Llanelli); Ieuan Evans (Llanelli), *L B Davies (Neath), *M E Wintle, W T Proctor (Llanelli); *A C Thomas (Bristol), A P Moore (Cardiff); *A L P Lewis, J M Humphreys (Cardiff, capt), J D Davies, Gareth Llewellyn (Neath), Derwyn Jones, E W Lewis, H Taylor (Cardiff), *R G Jones (Llanelli).

Italy: M Ravazzolo; P Vaccari, I Francescato, T Visentin, F Roselli; D Dominguez, A Troncon; M Cuttitta (capt), C Orlandi, F Properzi, M Giacheri, P Pedroni, O Arancio, A Sgorlon, J Gardner. Reps: M Bonomi for Visetin, G de Carli for Orlandi.

for Wales, Ieuan Evans (2), Justin Thomas scored tries. Arwel Thomas converted two and kicked four penalty goals.

For Italy, Franco Properzi, Andres Sgorlon scored tries. Diego Dominguez converted both and kicked four penalty goals.

Referee: G Black (Ireland).

England won by one goal, three penalty goals, one try (21)
to one goal, one penalty goal, one try (15)

A dramatic blunder by full back Justin Thomas cost Wales heavily. He was just a shade too casual measuring a clearance kick and Jeremy Guscott charged down and chased to score a gift try. Rob Howley marked his debut with a sparkling try from close up and there was a heartening infusion of passion and commitment into the Welsh performance. With Neil Jenkins absent, recovering from a fractured collarbone, Arwel Thomas continued at fly half and, as the smallest and lightest in his position since Phil Bennett, did remarkably well with some tenacious tackling.

England: M J Catt (Bath); J M Sleightholme, J C Guscott (Bath, W D C Carling (Harlequins, capt), R Underwood (Leicester); P J Grayson, M J D Dawson (Northampton); G C Rowntree (Leicester), M P Regan (Bristol), J Leonard (Harlequins), M O Johnson (Leicester), M C Bayfield, T A K Rodber (Northampton), B B Clarke (Bath), L B N Dallaglio (Wasps). Rep: P R de Glanville (Bath) for Carling.

Wales: W J L Thomas (Llanelli); Ieuan Evans (Llanelli), L B Davies (Neath), N G Davies, W T Proctor (Llanelli); A C Thomas (Bristol), *R Howley (Bridgend); A L P Lewis, J M Humphreys (Cardiff, capt), J D Davies, Gareth Llewellyn (Neath), Derwyn Jones, E W Lewis, H Taylor (Cardiff), R G Jones (Llanelli). Reps: S M Williams (Neath) for E W Lewis and G Jones (temp), G R Jenkins (Swansea) for Humphreys.

For England, Rory Underwood, Jeremy Guscott scored tries. Paul Grayson converted one and kicked three penalty goals.

For Wales, Hemi Taylor, Rob Howley scored tries. Arwel Thomas converted one and kicked a penalty goal.

Referee: K W McCartney (Scotland).

Match 444   **WALES v SCOTLAND**   Cardiff Arms Park. February 17, 1996

Scotland won by one goal, three penalty goals (16) to three penalty goals, one try (14)

Arwel Thomas had the chance to save his country with a conversion attempt from out near the touchline in this 100th game between the teams after Wayne Proctor's exciting try in the last few minutes, but the ball faded in flight to miss the target by a couple of feet. So, for the first time, Wales had lost seven Five Nations games in a row. "Wales deserved to draw," reckoned Scottish captain Rob Wainwright. Justin Thomas, whose error had proved fatal at Twickenham, was brilliant at full back in a game of concentrated defence. When back row man Ian Smith chased to overhaul Justin Thomas it was a colourful example of what was called in the days of the Border reivers a successful 'hot trod.' Pursuit often pays off.

Wales: W J L Thomas (Llanelli); Ieuan Evans (Llanelli), L B Davies (Neath), N G Davies, W T Proctor (Llanelli); A C Thomas (Bristol), R Howley (Bridgend); A L P Lewis, J M Humphreys (Cardiff, capt), J D Davies, Gareth Llewellyn (Neath), Derwyn Jones, E W Lewis, H Taylor (Cardiff), R G Jones (Llanelli).

Scotland: R J S Shepherd (Melrose); C A Joiner (Melrose), S Hastings (Watsonians), I C Jardine (Stirling County), M Dods (Northampton); G P J Townsend (Northampton), B W Redpath (Melrose); D I W Hilton (Bath), K D McKenzie (Stirling County), P H Wright (Boroughmuir), S J Campbell (Dundee HSFP), G W Weir (Melrose), R I Wainwright (West Hartlepool, capt), E W Peters (Bath), I R Smith (Gloucester). Rep: K M Logan (Stirling County) for Joiner.

For Wales, Wayne Proctor scored a try. Arwel Thomas kicked three penalty goals.

For Scotland, Gregor Townsend scored a try. Michael Dods converted and kicked three penalty goals.

Referee: J Dume (France).

Match 445   **IRELAND v WALES**   Lansdowne Road, Dublin. March 2, 1996

Ireland won by two goals, two penalty goals, two tries (30) to two goals, one penalty goal (17)

Arwel Thomas's nightmare match saw Wales lose a record eighth successive Five Nations game despite two typically tasty Ieuan Evans tries (his first in an away championship contest) as the teams met for the 100th time. Ireland had lost their previous fixture 45-10 to France, but the Green Gladiators produced a stiring backlash and scored their highest tally against Wales. A reported 27,000 Welsh fans travelled and watched Wales dominate the lineout while Leigh Davies demolished the midfield defence. "We made too many mistakes," bemoaned skipper Jonathan Humphreys. It was the old story.

Ireland: S J P Mason (Orrell); S P Geoghegan (Bath), J C Bell (Northampton), M J Field (Malone), N K P J Woods (Blackrock Coll); D G Humphreys (London Irish), N A Hogan (Terenure Coll, capt); N J Popplewell (Newcastle), A T H Clarke (Northampton), P S Wallace (Blackrock Coll), G M Fulcher (Cork Con), J W Davidson (Dungannon), D S Corkery (Cork Con), V C P Costello (St. Mary's Coll), W D McBride (Malone).

Wales: W J L Thomas (Llanelli); Ieuan Evans (Llanelli), L B Davies (Neath), N G

Davies, W T Proctor (Llanelli); A C Thomas (Bristol), R Howley (Bridgend); A L P Lewis, J M Humphreys (Cardiff, capt), J D Davies, Gareth Llewellyn (Neath), Derwyn Jones, E W Lewis, H Taylor (Cardiff), R G Jones (Llanelli).

For Ireland, Simon Geoghegan, Niall Woods, Gabriel Fulcher, David Corkery scored tries. Simon Mason converted two and kicked two penalty goals.

For Wales, Ieuan Evans scored two tries. Arwel Thomas converted both and kicked a penalty goal.

Referee: D Mene (France).

Match 446 WALES v FRANCE   Cardiff Arms Park. March 16, 1996

Wales won by one goal, three penalty goals (16) to one goal, one penalty goal, one try (15)

Faced with the grim prospect of a second successive Five Nations whitewash, and with France anticipating a tidy score to clinch the title, Wales produced a compact performance with lineout control and stirring rucking. It brought victory by a nail-biting one point with Neil Jenkins, restored to fly half, kicking the vital goals. So ended a record sequence of eight championship reverses and Jenkins marked his return by becoming the most-capped Welsh player in the outside half position, passing Cliff Morgan's 29. Jenkins won the game with his third penalty shot after 73 minutes. Before kick-off, silence was observed for the 16 five-year-olds and their teacher, murdered by a mad gunman in Dunblane.

Wales: W J L Thomas (Llanelli); Ieuan Evans, N G Davies (Llanelli), L B Davies (Neath), Gareth Thomas (Bridgend); N R Jenkins (Pontypridd), R Howley (Bridgend); C D Loader (Swansea), J M Humphreys (Cardiff, capt), J D Davies, Gareth Llewellyn (Neath), Derwyn Jones, E W Lewis, H Taylor (Cardiff), R G Jones (Llanelli).

France: J L Sadourny (Colomiers); E Ntamack (Toulouse), S Glas (Bourgoin), O Campan (Agen), P Saint-Andre (Montferrand, capt); T Castaignede (Toulouse), G Accoceberry (Begles/Bordeaux); C Califano (Toulouse), J M Gonzalez (Bayonne), F Tournaire (Narbonne), A Benazzi (Agen), O Roumat (Dax), R Castel, S Dispagne (Toulouse), L Cabannes (Racing Club). Reps: F Galthie (Colomiers) for Accoceberry, R Ibanez (Dax) for Castel, O Brouzet (Grenoble) for Dispagne.

For Wales, Rob Howley scored a try. Neil Jenkins converted and kicked three penalty goals.

For France, Thomas Castaignede, Emile Ntamack scored tries. Castaignede converted one and kicked a penalty goal.

Referee: B W Stirling (Ireland).

Match 447 AUSTRALIA v WALES   Ballymore, Brisbane. June 8, 1996

Australia won by six goals, three penalty goals, one try (56)
to two goals, two penalty goals, one try (25)

The Wallabies scored the first of their seven tries (four from mistakes) by Joe Roff after only 54 secs. It was noted on this tour that Welsh tackling varied from fragile to farcical; but 27,000 saw the tourists score their three tries in a purple patch during a 12-minute spell. Wales were trailing 42-6 before their first try arrived. Matt Burke kicked 21 Aussie points. This was the first occasion for Wales to play under the new laws that kept the back row in contact with the scrum until the ball was out.

Australia: M C Burke; D I Campese, J W Roff, T J Horan, A R Murdoch; P W Howard, G M Gregan; R L L Harry, M Caputo, E J A McKenzie, G J Morgan, J A Eales (capt), O Finegan, D T Manu, D J Wilson. Rep: M C Brial for Manu.

Wales: W T Proctor (Llanelli); Ieuan Evans, N G Davies,(Llanelli), L B Davies (Neath), Gareth Thomas (Bridgend); N R Jenkins (Pontypridd), R Howley (Bridgend); C D Loader (Swansea), J M Humphreys (Cardiff, capt), J D Davies, Gareth Llewellyn (Neath), Derwyn Jones, H Taylor (Cardiff), S M Williams (Neath), R G Jones (Llanelli). Reps: L Mustoe (Cardiff) for J D Davies, *M Voyle (Newport) for R G Jones and then D Jones.

For Australia, Joe Roff, Marco Caputo, David Wilson, Pat Howard, Alistair Murdoch, Daniel Manu, Garrick Morgan scored tries. Matt Burke converted six and kicked three penalty goals.

For Wales, Wayne Proctor, Ieuan Evans, Gareth Llewellyn scored tries. Neil Jenkins converted two and kicked two penalty goals.

Referee: G K Wahlstrom (NZ).

Match 448 **AUSTRALIA v WALES**   Sydney Football Ground. June 22, 1996

Australia won by three goals, two penalty goals, three tries (42) to one penalty goal (3)

No explosive start this time for the Wallabies in the second Test of the tour. But no tries for shellshocked Wales, who lost five of their seven games Down Under. Tour manager Terry Cobner summed up, "Australia were bigger and more powerful. They play a very physical, confrontational game and we could not compete with that." Gareth Llewellyn, who ruled the lineout with Derwyn Jones, became Wales's most capped forward (47) in succession to Llanelli's Phil Davies. Attendance: 35,784.

Australia: M C Burke; D I Campese, J W Roff, T J Horan, B N Tune; P W Howard, S J Payne; R L L Harry, M Caputo, E J A McKenzie, G J Morgan, J A Eales (capt), O Finegan, M C Brial, D J Wilson. Reps: D J Crowley for McKenzie, M A Foley for Caputo, S Larkham for Burke, D T Manu for Foley.

Wales: W T Proctor (Llanelli); Ieuan Evans, N G Davies (Llanelli), Gareth Thomas (Bridgend), S D Hill (Cardiff); N R Jenkins (Pontypridd), R Howley (Bridgend); C D Loader (Swansea), J M Humphreys (capt), L Mustoe, Derwyn Jones (Cardiff), Gareth Llewellyn (Neath), A Gibbs (Newbridge), H Taylor (Cardiff), S M Williams (Neath). Reps: A L P Lewis (Cardiff) for Loader, *D R James (Bridgend) for N G Davies.

For Australia, Owen Finegan, Matt Burke, Joe Roff, Michael Foley, Garrick Morgan, Tim Horan scored tries. Burke converted two and kicked two penalty goals. John Eales converted one try.

For Wales, Neil Jenkins kicked a penalty goal.

Referee: C J Hawke (NZ).

Match 449 **WALES v BARBARIANS**   Cardiff Arms Park. August 24, 1996

Wales won by three goals, two tries (31) to two tries (10)

For the first occasion in three meetings, Wales were winners against the Baa-Baas, but there was little satisfaction in success. Captain Jonathan Humphreys said he was "disappointed and frustrated." He elaborated, "We learned lessons from our summer tour of Australia, but to get to world class we need to score from the positions we wasted." Pontypridd openside Martyn Williams impressed on debut. Nigel Walker and replacement Richie Collins comprised the Welsh representation in the Barbarians' line-up. Attendance: 19,000.

Wales: W T Proctor (Llanelli); Ieuan Evans, N G Davies (Llanelli), L B Davies (Cardiff), Gareth Thomas (Bridgend); N R Jenkins (Pontypridd), R Howley (Cardiff); C D Loader (Swansea), J M Humphreys (Cardiff, capt), J D Davies (Neath), Derwyn Jones (Cardiff) Gareth Llewellyn (Harlequins), *K P Jones (Ebbw Vale), S M Williams (Neath), *M E Williams (Pontypridd). Reps: W J L Thomas (Cardiff) for N G Davies, P John (Pontypridd) for Howley, P Arnold (Swansea) for D Jones.

Barbarians: D Arrieta (Biarritz); A Bose (Mana), S Glas (France), R Dourthe (France), N K Walker (Wales); P W Howard (Australia), A Pichot (Argentina); A G J Watt (Scotland), J A Hay (Scotland), R Snow (Canada), R J McCall (Australia), D Sims (Gloucester), M Gusuna (Mana), A R B Pene (New Zealand, capt), D S Corkery (Ireland). Rep: R G Collins (Wales) for Gusuna.

For Wales, Nigel Davies (2), Wayne Proctor, Jonathan Humphreys, Rob Howley scored tries. Neil Jenkins converted three.

For Barbarians, Arran Pene, David Corkery scored tries.

Referee: J Fleming (Scotland).

| Match 450 | **WALES v FRANCE** | Cardiff Arms Park. September 25, 1996 |

France won by four goals, four penalty goals (40) to three goals, four penalty goals (33)

Wales led 27-10 at half time and finished with 33 points, the most they had ever scored while losing. There were 25,000 spectators on a Wednesday night for this friendly fixture. "We sat back instead of going for the jugular," mused coach Kevin Bowring. Hooker Barry Williams snapped up a debut try after just two minutes. 'Friendly' was something of a misnomer: Richard Dourthe, who kicked 20 points, was accused of stamping on Leigh Davies and being 'objectionable' to Neil Jenkins!

Wales: W T Proctor (Llanelli); Ieuan Evans, N G Davies (Llanelli, capt), L B Davies (Cardiff), Gareth Thomas (Bridgend); N R Jenkins (Pontypridd), R Howley (Cardiff); C D Loader (Swansea), *Barry Williams, J D Davies (Neath), M J Voyle (Llanelli), Gareth Llewellyn (Harlequins), K P Jones (Ebbw Vale), S M Williams (Neath), M E Williams (Pontypridd). Reps: A C Thomas (Swansea) for Evans, S D Hill (Cardiff) for Thomas.

France: J L Sadourny (Colomiers); E Ntamak (Toulouse), R Dourthe (Dax), S Glas (Bourgoin), P Saint-Andre (Montferrand, capt.); A Penaud, P Carbonneau (Brive); F Tournaire (Narbonne), M de Rougemont (Toulon), J L Jordana (Toulouse), O Merle (Montferrand), F Pelous (Dax), R Castel (Beziers), A Benazzi, P Benetton (Agen). Reps: D Berty (Toulouse) for Saint-Andre, G Accoceberry (Begles/Bordeaux) for Carbonneau, T Lievremont (Perpignan) for Castel.

For Wales, Barry Williams, Ieuan Evans, Gareth Thomas scored tries. Neil Jenkins converted them all and kicked four penalty goals.

For France, Stephane Glas (2), Jean-Luc Sadourny, Abdelatif Benazzi scored tries. Richard Dourthe converted them all and kicked four penalty goals.

Referee: G Gadjovich (Canada).

Wales won by two goals, four penalty goals, one try (31) to one goal, five penalty goals (22)

This was a particularly anxious victory after Diego Dominguez kicked 17 points and Italy stole a sensational 22-21 lead. Fortunately for Wales, on their first visit to the Eternal City, Scott Gibbs, the first Rugby League returnee to regain his place in the Welsh team, produced an explosive charge late in the game to create the springboard for the winning try by Gareth Thomas. The crowd of nearly 10,000 saw Leigh Davies pressed into emergency duty at full back when Wayne Proctor was concussed after a mid-air collision.

Italy: M Ravazzolo; P Vaccari, S Bordon, I Francescato, L Maneri; D Dominguez,A Troncon; M Cuttitta (capt), C Orlandi, F Properzi, P Pedroni, D Scaglia, A Sgorlon, C Checchinato, O Arancio. Reps: J Pertile for Vaccari, A Castellani for Properzi, R Rampazzo for Checchinato.

Wales: WT Proctor (Llanelli); S D Hill (Cardiff), I S Gibbs (Swansea), Gareth Thomas, D R James (Bridgend); N R Jenkins (Pontypridd), R Howley (Cardiff); C D Loader (Swansea), J M Humphreys (Cardiff, capt), J D Davies (Neath), Gareth Llewellyn (Harlequins), Derwyn Jones, H Taylor (Cardiff), S M Williams (Neath), K P Jones (Ebbw Vale). Reps: M E Williams (Pontypridd) for K P Jones, L B Davies (Cardiff) for Proctor.

For Italy, Ivan Francescato scored a try. Diego Dominguez converted and kicked five penalty goals.

For Wales, Gareth Thomas (2) Dafydd James scored tries. Neil Jenkins converted both and kicked four penalty goals.

Referee: C Spannenberg (South Africa).

Australia won by two goals, three penalty goals, one try (28) to one goal, four penalty goals (19)

Gareth Thomas, hurtling pell-mell almost the length of the pitch for a glorious interception try after grasping George Gregan's pass. That was the abiding memory of this, yet another defeat at the hands of Australia. It inspired a brief, gallant fightback from 18-9 down to an astonishing 19-18 lead midway through the second half. Of course, it was too good to last. Although the Wallabies were by no means the all-consuming opponents of the previous 12 years, they still enjoyed too much command for Wales to impose continuity of attack. Jonathan Davies was recalled after eight years at the expense of Neil Jenkins, to the outrage of Pontypridd coach Dennis John, who considered it a 'financial' rather than tactical selection. Certainly, there was renewed interest in ticket sales which brought 44,000 fans to watch. Jenkins went on as replacement full back in the second half for injured Wayne Proctor and was to play in that role on his next five appearances. Australia's 34 year-old David Campese played his 101st and final Test after a record 64 tries.

Wales: W T Proctor (Llanelli); Ieuan Evans (Llanelli), I S Gibbs (Swansea), Gareth Thomas, D R James (Bridgend); Jonathan Davies, R Howley (Cardiff); C D Loader (Swansea), J M Humphreys (capt), D Young, Derwyn Jones (Cardiff), Gareth Llewellyn (Harlequins), H Taylor (Cardiff), S M Williams (Neath), K P Jones (Ebbw Vale). Reps: N R Jenkins (Pontypridd) for Proctor, *C L Charvis (Swansea) for Taylor, J C Quinnell (Richmond) for K P Jones.

Australia: M Burke; J W Roff, J S Little, T J Horan (capt), D I Campese; P W Howard, G M Gregan; D J Crowley, M A Foley, A T Blades, T Gavin, D Giffin, O Finegan, M C Brial, D J Wilson.

For Wales, Gareth Thomas scored a try. Jonathan Davies converted and kicked four penalty goals.

For Australia, Matthew Burke, Michael Brial scored tries. Burke converted both and kicked three penalty goals.

Referee: D I Ramage (Scotland).

Match 453   **WALES v SOUTH AFRICA**   Cardiff Arms Park. December 15, 1996

South Africa won by three goals, two penalty goals, two tries (37),
to five penalty goals, one try (20)

Joost van der Westhuizen became the first scrum half to score three tries in a match on Welsh territory and earn the praise of 45,000 onlookers. The world champions outplayed the home side by five tries to just one by Arwel Thomas, called in as deputy for unfit Jonathan Davies. Neil Jenkins was chosen at full back. "There are two better full backs at Pontypridd in Kevin Morgan and Crispin Cormack. I don't want to play full back," said a ruffled Jenkins. His Ponty team-mates, Mark Rowley and New Zealander Dale McIntosh won their first caps.

Wales: N R Jenkins (Pontypridd); Ieuan Evans (Llanelli), I S Gibbs (Swansea), A G Bateman (Richmond), D R James (Bridgend); A C Thomas (Swansea), R Howley (Cardiff); C D Loader (Swansea), J M Humphreys (capt.), D Young (Cardiff), Gareth Llewellyn (Harlequins), *M Rowley, *D L M McIntosh (Pontypridd), S M Williams (Neath), C L Charvis (Swansea). Rep: *N Thomas (Bath) for McIntosh.

South Africa: A J Joubert; J T Small, J C Moulder, H P le Roux, J Olivier; H W Honiball, J H van der Westuizen; D Theron, J Dalton, A C Garvey, J J Wiese, M G Andrews, R J Kruger, G Teichmann (capt.), A G Venter. Reps: A H Snyman for Olivier, F J van Heerden for Andrews, A van der Linde for Theron.

For Wales, Arwel Thomas scored a try. Neil Jenkins kicked five penalty goals.

For South Africa, Joost van der Westuizen (3), Andre Joubert, Jacques Olivier scored tries. Henry Honiball converted two and kicked two penalty goals. Joubert converted one try.

Referee: S Lander (England).

Match 454   **WALES v USA**   Cardiff Arms Park. January 11, 1997

Wales won by four goals, two penalty goals (34) to three penalty goals, one try (14)

Scott Gibbs assumed the captaincy because Jonathan Humphreys was under suspension after being ordered off the previous Saturday in Cardiff's Heineken Cup tie in Brive. Neil Jenkins was an influenza victim, so Justin Thomas deputised at full back. Ieuan Evans scored two tries and Arwel Thomas kicked superbly to convert all four tries and add two penalty goals. Attendance: 13,500.

Wales: W J L Thomas (Cardiff); Ieuan Evans (Llanelli), I S Gibbs (Swansea, capt), A G Bateman (Richmond), Gareth Thomas (Bridgend); A C Thomas (Swansea), R Howley (Cardiff); C D Loader, G R Jenkins (Swansea), D Young (Cardiff), Gareth Llewellyn (Harlequins), M Rowley (Pontypridd), S M Williams (Neath), L S Quinnell (Richmond), C L Charvis (Swansea). Reps: Jonathan Davies (Cardiff) for Gibbs, P John (Pontypridd) for Howley, J C Quinnell (Richmond) for Rowley, R G Jones (Cardiff) for Charvis.

USA: M Williams; V Anitoni, R Tardits, M Scharrenberg, B Hightower; M Alexander, A Bachelet; R Lehner, T Billups, B LeClerc, C Vogl, A Parker, D Lyle (capt), R Lumkong, J Wilkerson. Reps: C Morrow for Williams, J Walker for Wilkerson.

For Wales, Ieuan Evans (2), Scott Gibbs scored tries, and a penalty try. Arwel Thomas converted all four tries and kicked two penalty goals.

For USA, Andre Bachelet scored a try. Matt Alexander kicked three penalty goals.

Referee: L Mayne (Ireland).

Match 455 SCOTLAND v WALES   Murrayfield. January 18, 1997

Wales won by four goals, two penalty goals (34)
to one goal, one dropped goal, three penalty goals (19)

Three tries in a hurricane spell of barely five minutes during the second half saw Wales, trailing 16-10, shock Scotland to defeat. It was the fastest triple whammy of its kind in the history of the Five Nations and raised hopes that a Welsh revival had dawned. Neil Jenkins equalled the Welsh record for a Five Nations match of 19 points to become only the fifth player to pass 500 points in Test rugby. Scottish aims of a sixth consecutive home win over their visitors ended in confusion after that quick fire 'mugging'. Wales enjoyed two tries from favourable bounces. "We have not had much luck for years," observed happy captain Humphreys.

Scotland: R J S Shepherd (Melrose); A G Stanger (Hawick), S Hastings (Watsonians), G P J Townsend (Northampton), K M Logan (Stirling County); C M Chalmers (Melrose), G Armstrong (Newcastle); D I W Hilton (Bath), D G Ellis (Currie), M J Stewart (Northampton),G W Weir (Newcastle), A I Reed (Wasps), P Walton (Newcastle), R I Wainwright (Watsonians, capt). M I Wallace (GHK). Reps: D S Munro (GHK) for Reed, D A Stark (Melrose) for Chalmers.

Wales: N R Jenkins (Pontypridd); Ieuan Evans (Llanelli), I S Gibbs (Swansea), A G Bateman (Richmond), Gareth Thomas (Bridgend); A C Thomas (Swansea), R Howley (Cardiff); C D Loader (Swansea), J M Humphreys (capt), D Young (Cardiff), Gareth Llewellyn (Harlequins), M Rowley (Pontypridd), S M Williams (Neath), L S Quinnell (Richmond), C L Charvis (Swansea). Reps: J C Quinnell (Richmond) for Rowley, R G Jones (Cardiff) for Charvis, Jonathan Davies (Cardiff) for Gibbs.

For Scotland, Scott Hastings scored a try. Rowen Shepherd converted and kicked three penalty goals. Craig Chalmers dropped a goal.

For Wales, Scott Quinnell, Neil Jenkins, Arwel Thomas, Ieuan Evans scored tries. Neil Jenkins converted all four and kicked two penalty goals.

Referee: H A Smith (Ireland).

Match 456 WALES v IRELAND   Cardiff Arms Park. February 1, 1997

Ireland won by one goal, three penalty goals, two tries (26)
to two goals, two penalty goals, one try (25)

Ireland achieved what no other team had done: seven successive Five Nations matches in Cardiff without defeat. The visitors also raised their highest score on Welsh territory and this after being roused in the small hours before the match when their hotel's alarm system was triggered by an electrical fault. Ieuan Evans stunned Ireland with a try after only 33 seconds, the quickest on record by a Welsh player in international rugby. Neil Jenkins was the victim of the 'unplayable ball'. Eric Elwood's towering punt struck the padding of the post on descent, just above the full back's reaching hand, and rebounded into the grasp of Jonathan Bell for a gift try. Coach Kevin Bowring was annoyed at his team's tactics: they continually charged instead of spreading the ball. "Players must accept more responsibility," he complained. The good times promised at Murrayfield were not back after all – and Ireland were considering early bird calls before all future games!

Wales: N R Jenkins (Pontypridd); Ieuan Evans (Llanelli), I S Gibbs (Swansea), Gareth Thomas, D R James (Bridgend); AC Thomas (Swansea), R Howley (Cardiff); C D Loader (Swansea), J M Humphreys (capt), D Young (Cardiff), Gareth Llewellyn (Harlequins), M Rowley (Pontypridd), S M Williams (Neath), L S Quinnell (Richmond), C L Charvis (Swansea). Reps: J C Quinnell (Richmond) for Rowley, K P Jones (Ebbw Vale) for Charvis.

Ireland: J E Staples (Harlequins, capt); D Hickie (St. Mary's Coll.), J C Bell (Northampton), M J Field (Malone), D J Crotty (Cork Con); E P Elwood (Lansdowne), N A Hogan (Terenure Coll); N J Popplewell, R P Nesdale (Newcastle), P S Wallace, P S Johns (Saracens), J W Davidson (London Irish), D S Corkery (Bristol), E R P Miller (Leicester), W D McBride (Malone). Rep: G M Fulcher (London Irish) for Johns.

For Wales, Ieuan Evans (2), Scott Quinnell scored tries. Neil Jenkins converted two and kicked two penalty goals.

For Ireland, Jonathan Bell, Eric Miller, Dennis Hickie scored tries. Eric Elwood converted one and kicked three penalty goals.

Referee: W Ericson (Australia).

| Match 457 | **FRANCE v WALES** | Parc des Princes, Paris. February 15, 1997 |

France won by two goals, one penalty goal, two tries (27)
to two goals, one penalty goal, one try (22)

France, with something of a skeleton team, were still too strong, for all that Wales gave their most stirring display in Paris since their last success there in 1975. Runners sought space instead of confrontation and produced an enthralling contest with a delightful Rob Howley try in the dazzling sunshine. Featherweight Arwel Thomas hung one on chunky Philippe Carbonneau to flatten the scrum half, who had been obstructing him. Wales had found another Ghost with a Hammer in his hand! France went on to win the Grand Slam.

France: J L Sadourny (Colomiers); L Leflamand, S Glas (Bourgoin), R Dourthe (Dax), D Venditti (Brive); C Lamaison, P Carbonneau (Brive); C Califano (Toulouse), M Dal Maso (Agen), J L Jordana, H Miorin (Toulouse), O Merle (Montferrand), A Benazzi (Agen, capt.), F Pelous (Dax), R Castel (Beziers). Reps: D Aucagne (Pau) for Dourthe, O Magne (Dax) for Miorin.

Wales: N R Jenkins (Pontypridd); Ieuan Evans (Llanelli), A G Bateman (Richmond), I S Gibbs (Swansea), Gareth Thomas (Bridgend); A C Thomas (Swansea), R Howley (Cardiff); C D Loader (Swansea), J M Humphreys (capt), D Young (Cardiff), Gareth Llewellyn (Harlequins), M Rowley (Pontypridd), S M Williams (Neath), L S Quinnell (Richmond), C L Charvis (Swansea). Rep: Jonathan Davies (Cardiff) for Evans.

For France, Laurant Leflamand (2), David Venditti, Olivier Merle scored tries. Richard Dourthe converted one. David Aucagne converted one and kicked a penalty goal.

For Wales, Gareth Thomas, Allan Bateman, Rob Howley scored tries. Neil Jenkins converted two and kicked a penalty goal.

Referee; P Marshall (Australia).

England won by four goals, two penalty goals (34) to one goal, two penalty goals (13)

The final international match on this great pitch of historic memory could not bring victory for Wales. It was goodbye also to Jonathan Davies, Rob Andrew and Will Carling, all making their final appearances on the international stage to end great careers in the game. Andrew was one of nine replacements used in this first season when tactical substitutions were permitted. Neil Jenkins fractured his arm after six minutes. The only home try came during the last few minutes with a skewering run by Rob Howley, the final international try on the much-loved Arms Park before demolition experts moved in and the hallowed turf was auctioned off. This was the ground where New Zealand lost in 1905, 1935 and 1953; where once the mud lay inches deep and where crowds sang as never since; where more stood than sat and Wales often were a team of unmatchable magic. Goodbye, old friend!

Wales N R Jenkins (Pontypridd); S D Hill (Cardiff), N G Davies (Llanelli), A G Bateman (Richmond), Gareth Thomas (Bridgend); Jonathan Davies, R Howley (Cardiff); C D Loader (Swansea), J M Humphreys (capt), D Young (Cardiff), Gareth Llewellyn (Harlequins), M J Voyle (Llanelli), S M Williams (Neath), L S Quinnell (Richmond), K P Jones (Ebbw Vale). Reps: W T Proctor (Llanelli) for Jenkins, S C John (Llanelli) for Loader, J C Quinnell (Richmond) for Voyle, D L M McIntosh (Pontypridd) for Jones.

England: T R G Stimpson (Newcastle); J M Sleightholme, P R de Glanville (Bath,capt), W D C Carling (Harlequins), T Underwood (Newcastle); M J Catt (Bath), A Healy (Leicester); G C Rowntree (Leicester), M P Regan (Bristol), J Leonard (Harlequins), M O Johnson (Leicester), S D Shaw (Bristol), B B Clarke (Richmond), T A K Rodber (Northampton), R A Hill (Saracens). Reps: J C Guscott (Bath) for Sleightholme, C R Andrew (Newcastle) for Catt, D J Garforth (Leicester) for Rowntree, P B T Greening (Gloucester) for Regan, C M A Sheasby (Wasps) for Clarke.

For Wales, Rob Howley scored a try. Jonathan Davies converted and kicked two penalty goals.

For England, Tim Stimpson, Tony Underwood, Richard Hill, Phil de Glanville scored tries. Mike Catt converted all four and kicked two penalty goals.

Referee: J Dume (France).

Wales won by two goals, two penalty goals, two tries (30) to two goals, two penalty goals (20)

Wales were never in control for significant periods during their three-Test tour of North America. Without numerous key players, some of them with the Lions in South Africa, there was never opportunity to play commanding and relaxed rugby. In this opening Test, Arwel Thomas was a bobby-dazzler amid the rolling thunder and lightning flashes: he crackled through for two tries and completed 20 points with goal kicking. "We have to take the hard tackle and recycle quickly," stressed coach Kevin Bowring. Wales won all six tour games, opening with a 94-3 verdict against Southern Reps with Gareth Wyatt scoring four tries and Lee Jarvis 34 points to equal the record by Phil Bennett also in a non-cap match against Japan in Tokyo in 1975.

USA: C Morrow; V Anitoni, T Takau, M Scharrenberg, B Hightower: M Alexander, A Bachelot; C Lippert, T Billups, R Lehner, D Hodges, L Cross, J Walker, D Lyle (capt), J Wilkerson. Reps: A Saulala for Scharrenberg, S Allen for Billups, K Shuman for Morrow, M McLeod for Lyle.

Wales: *K A Morgan (Pontypridd); W T Proctor (Llanelli), Gareth Thomas (Bridgend), L B Davies, N Walker (Cardiff); A C Thomas (Swansea), P John (Pontypridd); C D Loader, G R Jenkins (Swansea), L Mustoe (Cardiff), Gareth Llewellyn (Harlequins), M J Voyle, A Gibbs (Llanelli), S M Williams (Neath), R G Jones (Cardiff, capt). Reps: *C Anthony (Swansea) for Loader, N Thomas (Bath) for Williams).

For USA, Vaea Anitoni, Tomasi Takau scored tries. Matt Alexander converted both and kicked two penalty goals.

For Wales, Arwel Thomas (2), Nigel Walker, Gwyn Jones scored tries. Arwel Thomas converted two and kicked two penalty goals.

Referee: K W McCartney (Scotland).

Match 460   USA v WALES   Balboa Park, San Francisco. July 12, 1997

Wales won by one goal, two penalty goals, three tries (28) to two goals, three penalty goals (23)

This proved a desperate escape for Wales after the Eagles had drawn level at 16-all and then 23-all with 15 minutes remaining. Wayne Proctor was the hero as the wing went in for three tries (the first two set up by impressive full back Kevin Morgan) before cheeky Arwel Thomas settled the issue with a try. "We must improve, otherwise we will be beaten by Canada," warned coach Bowring. This American Patrol, though hardly producing the rhythm of Glenn Miller, at least had not resulted in defeat.

USA: C Morrow; V Anitoni, T Takau, M Scharrenberg, B Hightower: M Alexander, A Bachelot; C Lippert, T Billups, R Lehner, L Gross ,D Hodges, D Lyle (capt), J Walker, J Wilkerson. Reps: A Saulala for Takau, M Sika for Hightower, S Allen for Billups, M McLeod for Walker, S Youngling for Wilkerson.

Wales: K A Morgan (Pontypridd); W T Proctor (Llanelli), Gareth Thomas (Bridgend), L B Davies, N Walker (Cardiff); A C Thomas (Swansea), P John (Pontypridd); I Buckett (Swansea), R McBryde (Llanelli), L Mustoe (Cardiff), Gareth Llewellyn (Harlequins), M J Voyle, A Gibbs (Llanelli), N Thomas (Bath), G R Jones (Cardiff, capt). Reps: C Anthony (Swansea) for Buckett, S M Williams (Neath) for Jones.

For USA, Vaea Anitoni, Jason Walker scored tries. Matt Alexander converted both and kicked three penalty goals.

For Wales, Wayne Proctor (3), Arwel Thomas scored tries. Arwel Thomas converted one and kicked two penalty goals.

Referee: C B Muir (Scotland).

Match 461   CANADA v WALES   Fletcher's Field, Toronto. July 19, 1997

Wales won by two goals, three penalty goals, one try (28)
to two goals, one dropped goal, one penalty goal, one try (25)

Canada, the Pacific Rim champions, had defeated USA more convincingly than Wales; and when Bob Ross dropped a goal from more than 50 yards just 20 seconds after kick-off, the tourists again felt the gnawing pangs of anxiety. With every justification: the home side dominated the first 30 minutes and led 25-21 some 15 minutes from the end. Then Leigh

Davies lanced to the rescue in flamboyant style with his first try for Wales nine minutes from full time and 5,000 spectators had seen the tourists scrape to an invincible tour record.

Canada: R P Ross: W Stanley, D C Lougheed, S Bryan, D S Stewart; G L Rees (capt), J D Graf; E A Evans, K Morgan, R G A Snow, J Tait, M James, A J Charron, M Schmid, J Hutchinson. Reps: M E Cardinal for Morgan, R Bice for Evans.

Wales: K A Morgan (Pontypridd); W T Proctor (Llanelli), Gareth Thomas (Bridgend), L B Davies, N Walker (Cardiff); A C Thomas (Swansea), P John (Pontypridd, capt); I Buckett, G R Jenkins (Swansea), L Mustoe (Cardiff), *S Moore (Swansea), M J Voyle, A Gibbs (Llanelli), SM Williams (Neath),*R C Appleyard (Swansea). Reps: N Thomas (Bath) for Gibbs, C Anthony (Swansea) for Buckett.

For Canada, Mike Schmid (2), Bob Ross scored tries. Gareth Rees converted two and kicked a penalty goal. Ross dropped a goal.

For Wales, Wayne Proctor, Gareth Thomas, Leigh Davies scored tries. Arwel Thomas converted two and kicked three penalty goals.

Referee: S Borsani (Argentina).

Match 462 **WALES v ROMANIA** Wrexham AFC Racecourse Ground. August 30, 1997

Wales won by six goals, one penalty goal, five tries (70)
to one goal, three penalty goals, one try (21)

Wales hoisted their biggest tally on home territory in a match notable for the fact that it was played in North Wales. With the Arms Park demolished, the game went to The Racecourse Ground, home of Wrexham AFC. Also noteworthy was the remarkable fact that there were only eight lineouts throughout the game (compared to 111 when Wales won at Murrayfield in 1963), and Romania won six of those. "We are not yet ready to beat the big boys," affirmed WRU Director of Rugby Terry Cobner. "We made 28 errors and you can't afford to do that at international level." Arwel Thomas supplied 23 points and would have topped that but he was replaced by Lee Jarvis, who converted the final try. There were just over 11,000 watchers as Wales staged a game away from the Arms Park for the first time since they played Scotland at Swansea in 1954.

Wales: K A Morgan (Pontypridd); W T Proctor (Llanelli), A G Bateman (Richmond), L B Davies (Cardiff) Gareth Thomas (Bridgend); A C Thomas (Swansea), P John (Pontypridd); C D Loader (Swansea), Barry Williams (Richmond), D Young (Cardiff), M Rowley (Pontypridd), S Moore (Moseley), R C Appleyard (Swansea), N Thomas (Bath), G R Jones (Cardiff, capt.). Reps: N Walker (Cardiff for Proctor, *L Jarvis (Cardiff) for A C Thomas, L Mustoe (Cardiff) for Young, S M Williams (Cardiff) for Rowley.

Romania: V Maftei; L Colceriu, R Gontineac, G Solomie, I Rotaru; S Guranescu, M Iacob; G Vlad, M Radoi, A A Salageanu, T Brinza (capt), V Nedelcu, F Corodeanu, C Draguceanu, E Septar. Reps: P Mitu for Maftei, C Stan for Salageanu, I Ruxanda for Septar.

For Wales, Leigh Davies (2), Allan Bateman (2), Arwel Thomas (2), Paul John, Kevin Morgan, Barry Williams, Steve Williams, Nigel Walker scored tries. Arwel Thomas converted five and kicked a penalty goal. Lee Jarvis converted one.

For Romania, Rotaru, Draguceanu scored tries. Guranescu converted one and kicked three penalty goals.

Referee: D I Ramage (Scotland).

Wales won by two goals, four penalty goals, four tries (46) to one goal, one try (12)

Neil Jenkins was restored as outside half after Wales had played 11 matches with Jonathan Davies (twice) and Arwel Thomas (nine times) in that position. Gareth Thomas crossed for two tries and helped manufacture two others in front of the smallest home crowd during the twentieth century, just 6,589. Fewer spectators had watched some home games in the 1880s and gate receipts for the NZ Native team, the Maoris, in 1888 amounted to only £120. Wet conditions for this Tongan fixture on a Sunday undoubtedly deterred people and the match was televised live. Gareth Wyatt, normally a wing, scored a delightful debut try from full back in this first game at Swansea for 43 years.

Wales: *G Wyatt (Pontypridd); Gareth Thomas(Bridgend), I S Gibbs (Swansea), L B Davies, N Walker (Cardiff); N R Jenkins, P John (Pontypridd); C D Loader (Swansea), Barry Williams (Richmond), S C John (Cardiff), S Moore (Moseley), M J Voyle (Llanelli), R C Appleyard (Swansea), N Thomas (Bath), R G Jones (Cardiff, capt), Reps: D R James (Bridgend) for Thomas, C Anthony (Swansea) for S C John, R Howley (Cardiff) for P John, J M Humphreys (Cardiff) for Williams, S M Williams (Cardiff) for Moore.

Tonga: G Tonga; D Tiueti, F Tatafu, P Tanginoa, S Faka 'osi'folau; S Taumalolo, S M Tu'ipulotu; D Briggs (capt), V Ma'asi, N Ta'u, S Latu, K Faletau, H Pohiva, K Tu'ipulotu, T Matakaiongo. Reps: S Tai for Tatafu, H Lavaka for Briggs, S Hafoka for Pohiva, M Molitika for Matakaiongo.

For Wales, Gareth Thomas (2), Leigh Davies, Gareth Wyatt, Chris Anthony, Nigel Walker scored tries. Neil Jenkins converted two and kicked four penalty goals.

For Tonga, Fepi'kou Tatafu, Sione Tai scored tries. Gustavo Tonga converted one.

Referee: S Borsani (Argentina).

New Zealand won by four goals, one dropped goal, two penalty goals, one try (42) to one goal (7)

The twin towers stared down stonily as Wales met their inevitable doom and Christian Cullen, the Human Eel, became the first full back to score three tries against them. There were 76,000 onlookers to witness the All Blacks sweep to their 14th successive victory (including the 1974 unofficial Test) against Wales, whose only try was obtained by former Olympic Games 110 metres hurdler Nigel Walker, following Gareth Llewellyn's forceful charge. Walker also saved two tries when he caught speedy Jeff Wilson. Neil Jenkins prevented another try with a tackle on Josh Kronfeld; and Jenkins would have scored, but the ball was jolted from his grasp as he dived over the line. With the last kick of the match, No. 8 Zinzan Brooke decorated the posts with a memorable dropped goal. Gareth Thomas kept a tight rein on dangerous Jonah Lomu. Leigh Davies looked the most menacing of the Welsh attackers when he replaced Scott Gibbs (nine stitches in an eyebrow). Unusually, it was a game of four hookers: Jonathan Humphreys replaced Barry Williams and NZ captain Sean Fitzpatrick went on for Norm Hewitt. The most distinguishing feature of the day was the superb all-round kicking of Andrew Mehrtens.

Wales: K A Morgan (Pontypridd); Gareth Thomas (Bridgend), A G Bateman (Richmond), I S Gibbs (Swansea), N Walker (Cardiff); N R Jenkins (Pontypridd), R Howley (Cardiff); C D Loader (Swansea), Barry Williams (Richmond), D Young (Cardiff), Gareth Llewellyn (Harlequins), M J Voyle (Llanelli), R C Appleyard (Swansea), N Thomas (Bath), R G Jones (Cardiff, capt). Reps: L B

Davies (Cardiff) for Gibbs, S M Williams (Cardiff) for N Thomas, A C Thomas (Swansea) for Bateman, J M Humphreys (Cardiff) for Williams, S C John (Cardiff) for Loader.

New Zealand: C M Cullen; J W Wilson, F E Bunce, W K Little, J T Lomu; A P Mehrtens, J W Marshall (capt); C W Dowd, N J Hewitt, O M Brown, I D Jones, R W Brooke, T C Randell, Z V Brooke, J A Kronfeld. Reps: S B T Fitzpatrick for Hewitt, M Allen for Brown, A F Blowers for Randell.

For Wales, Nigel Walker scored a try. Neil Jenkins converted.

For NZ, Christian Cullen (3), Taine Randell, Justin Marshall scored tries. Andrew Mehrtens converted four and kicked two penalty goals. Zinzan Brooke dropped a goal.

Referee: W J Erickson (Australia)

Match 465   WALES v ITALY   Stradey Park, Llanelli. February 7, 1998

Wales won by two goals, three penalty goals (23) to two goals, two penalty goals (20)

With what was considered the most menacing back division in the Five Nations, Wales managed only two tries in this unimpressive victory: a penalty try after seven successive scrums on the Italian line; and a 77th minute solo try by Gareth Thomas, racing more than half the length of the field, which was becoming a familiar pattern for him. Italy, with recent victories over Ireland and Scotland, had demolished Denmark 102-3 and now scored try for try with Wales. This was the first international match at Stradey since Arthur Gould's team won the Triple Crown for the first time in 1893, defeating Ireland by a try to nil. A capacity crowd of 13,800 saw Rob Howley lead Wales for the first time with Arwel Thomas preferred to Neil Jenkins at outside half. "Arwel brings more variety and a little unpredictability to our game," explained coach Kevin Bowring. This was the great Ieuan Evans's final game after a record 72 caps, record 33 tries and record 28 times as captain.

Wales: N R Jenkins (Pontypridd); Ieuan Evans (Bath), A G Bateman (Richmond), I S Gibbs (Swansea), Gareth Thomas (Cardiff); A C Thomas (Swansea), R Howley (Cardiff, capt); A L P Lewis (Cardiff), Barry Williams (Richmond), D Young (Cardiff), Gareth Llewellyn (Harlequins), M J Voyle (Llanelli), R C Appleyard (Swansea), L S Quinnell (Richmond), M E Williams (Pontypridd). Reps: J M Humphreys (Cardiff) for Barry Williams, C L Charvis (Swansea) for M E Williams.

Italy: C Pilat; P Vaccari, C Stoica, L Martin, Marcello Cuttitta; D Dominguez, A Troncon; Massimo Cuttitta, C Orlandi, A Castellani, W Cristofoletto, G Groci, M Giovanelli (capt), J Gardner, A Sgorlon.

For Wales, Gareth Thomas scored a try and there was a penalty try. Neil Jenkins converted both and kicked three penalty goals.

For Italy, Cristian Stoica, Andrea Sgorlon scored tries. Diego Dominguez converted both and kicked two penalty goals.

Referee: S Lander (England).

Match 466   ENGLAND v WALES   Twickenham. February 21, 1998

England won by seven goals, two penalty goals, one try (60) to three goals, one try (26)

"We let Wales down," sighed a sorrowful Rob Howley after this record Five Nations defeat. Ironically, Wales played their most compelling rugby of the season for the opening 20 minutes, but England's backlash after losing in Paris was awesome. The riposte to a 12-6 lead by Wales brought 21 points in the space of just seven minutes. Never had Wales scored so many points against England and lost. Allan Bateman's two tries seemed to have set his side up for a stirring challenge. Alas, disaster lurked around the corner. It overtook Nigel Walker after only four minutes when he suffered a dislocated right shoulder that ended his rugby career. After seven matches without a win, England's plot fell into place perfectly with their biggest tally against Wales to pass the Five Nations record of 49-14 by Wales against France in 1910. Neil Jenkins exclaimed that he would never play at full back again. Coach Bowring said, "I felt humiliation and anger." WRU Director of Rugby Terry Cobner later fumed, "Every time I go to bed, and whenever I wake up in the morning, it's the first thing on my mind. I hope it's exactly the same for the players!" Skipper Howley glumly admitted, "It has been the worst week in my entire rugby career."

England: M B Perry (Bath); D L Rees (Sale), J C Guscott (Bath), W J H Greenwood, AS Healey (Leicester); P J Grayson (Northampton), K P P Bracken (Saracens); J Leonard (Harlequins), R Cockerill (Leicester), P J Vickery (Gloucester), M O Johnson (Leicester), G S Archer (Newcastle), L B N Dallaglio (Wasps, capt), R A Hill (Saracens), N A Back (Leicester). Reps: M J Catt (Bath) for Grayson, M J S Dawson (Northampton) for Bracken, P R de Glanville (Bath) for Greenwood, A J Diprose (Saracens) for Hill, D J Grewcock (Saracens) for Johnson, D J Garforth (Leicester) for Vickery.

Wales: N R Jenkins (Pontypridd); Gareth Thomas (Cardiff), A G Bateman (Richmond), I S Gibbs (Swansea), N Walker (Cardiff); A C Thomas (Swansea), R Howley (Cardiff, capt); A L P Lewis (Cardiff), Barry Williams (Richmond), D Young (Cardiff), Gareth Llewellyn (Harlequins), M J Voyle (Llanelli), C L Charvis (Swansea), L S Quinnell (Richmond), M E Williams (Pontypridd). Reps: W T Proctor (Llanelli) for Walker, L B Davies (Cardiff) for Bateman, J M Humphreys (Cardiff) for Barry Williams, L Mustoe (Cardiff) for Lewis, R C Appleyard (Swansea) for Quinnell, *C Stephens (Bridgend) for Voyle.

For England, David Rees (2), Neil Back, Kyran Bracken, Lawrence Dallaglio, Austin Healey, Will Greenwood, Matt Dawson scored tries. Paul Grayson converted seven and kicked two penalty goals.

For Wales, Allan Bateman (2), Gareth Thomas, Scott Gibbs scored tries. Neil Jenkins converted three.

Referee: C J Hawke (NZ).

Match 467   WALES v SCOTLAND   Wembley Stadium. March 7, 1998

Wales won by one goal, four penalty goals (19) to one penalty goal, two tries (13)

This first Five Nations match at Wembley was one that Wales had to win. They did, after dumping six of the Team of Shame that crashed at Twickenham. Neil Jenkins was back at fly half, but lasted only 18 minutes. In a clash of heads he suffered blurred vision, so Arwel Thomas replaced him and won the game with three penalty goals and a magnificent conversion from the touchline of the Welsh try by Wayne Proctor. Training sessions had been behind closed doors as coach Bowring locked out the media so his team could grieve in private. Scotland felt they should have been awarded a penalty try when Gareth Thomas impeded Craig Chalmers. Referee Joel Dume gave a penalty, which Chalmers missed. Had a penalty try been awarded, Scotland would have won 20-19. Manager Arthur Hastie insisted his team were robbed. "We did not command the game, but at least we won," said vastly relieved coach Bowring.

Wales: K A Morgan (Pontypridd); W T Proctor (Llanelli), A G Bateman (Richmond), I S Gibbs (Swansea), Gareth Thomas (Cardiff); N R Jenkins (Pontypridd), R Howley (Cardiff, capt); A L P Lewis (Cardiff), G R Jenkins

(Swansea), D Young (Cardiff), M J Voyle (Llanelli), A Moore, R C Appleyard, C L Charvis (Swansea), K P Jones (Ebbw Vale). Reps: A C Thomas (Swansea) for N R Jenkins, L S Quinnell (Richmond) for Appleyard, J M Humphreys (Cardiff) for G R Jenkins.

Scotland: D J Lee (London Scottish); A G Stanger (Hawick), G P J Townsend (Northampton), A V Tait (Newcastle), S L Longstaff (Dundee HSFP); C M Chalmers (Melrose), G Armstrong (Newcastle, capt); D I W Hilton (Bath), G C Bulloch (West of Scotland), M J Stewart (Northampton), D F Cronin (Wasps), G W Weir (Newcastle), R I Wainwright (Dundee HSFP), E W Peters (Bath), A J Roxburgh (Kelso). Reps: R J S Shepherd (Melrose) for Lee, S B Grimes (Watsonians) for Cronin, G Graham (Newcastle) for Stewart.

For Wales, Wayne Proctor scored a try. Arwel Thomas converted and kicked three penalty goals. Neil Jenkins kicked a penalty goal.

For Scotland, Gregor Townsend, Damian Cronin scored tries. Craig Chalmers kicked a penalty goal.

Referee: J Dume (France).

Match 468   IRELAND v WALES   Lansdowne Road, Dublin. March 21, 1998

Wales won by three goals, three penalty goals (30) to one goal, three penalty goals, one try (21)

Desperate coach Kevin Bowring expressed the view, "I'll be happy to win in any old way!" With three rousing tries it brought the old quiet smile back, but it was his tacklers he praised, not the attackers. "Our defence won it," he acknowledged. Ireland produced an amazing shock tactic in the opening minutes when they put almost the entire team into a lineout close to the Welsh line. That kind of original thinking, plus their traditional tearaway style, could be unsettling. But Neil Jenkins steadied his side with 20 points, including a polished final try. Bowring admitted he had forsaken his flair concept and gone for form players and reliability. Skipper Howley called for a spirit of adventure and a quality performance. He was not disappointed – until the next match!

Ireland: C P Clarke (Terenure Coll); R M Wallace (Saracens), K M Maggs (Bristol), R A J Henderson (Wasps), D A Hickie (St Mary's Coll); E P Elwood (Galwegians), C D McGuinness (St Mary's Coll); R Corrigan (Greystones), K G M Wood (Harlequins, capt), P S Wallace, P S Johns (Saracens), M E O'Kelly (London Irish), D S Corkery (Bristol), V C P Costello (St Mary's Coll), A J Ward (Ballinahinch). Reps: P M Clohessy (Young Munster) for P S Wallace, E R P Miller (Leicester) for Ward, R P Nesdale (Newcastle) for Wood.

Wales: K A Morgan (Pontypridd); W T Proctor (Llanelli), A G Bateman (Richmond), L B Davies, Gareth Thomas (Cardiff); N R Jenkins (Pontypridd), R Howley (Cardiff, capt); A L P Lewis (Cardiff), G R Jenkins (Swansea), D Young (Cardiff), M J Voyle (Llanelli), A Moore, A C Appleyard, C L Charvis (Swansea), K P Jones (Ebbw Vale). Reps: J M Humphreys (Cardiff) for G R Jenkins, L Mustoe (Cardiff) for Young, Stuart Davies (Swansea) for K P Jones.

For Ireland, Andy Ward, Vic Costello scored tries. Eric Elwood converted one and kicked three penalty goals.

For Wales, Allan Bateman, Kevin Morgan, Neil Jenkins, scored tries. Neil Jenkins converted them all and kicked three penalty goals.

Referee: E Morrison (England).

France won by five goals, two penalty goals, two tries (51) to nil

This Sunday massacre in London produced another Five Nations record: the biggest winning margin. The best previously had been 40 points by England against Ireland in 1997. France completed their first back-to-back Grand Slam and Wales ended by conceding the highest number of points in the championship, a hefty 145 compared with the 141 by Ireland in 1997. Wales failed to score for the first time in 90 years of matches against France, who won their 12th championship title. Another unusual record was that each of the Welsh back row, all Swansea players, were shown the yellow card. Coach Bowring, under heavy fire to resign, doggedly repeated, "I'll see my contract through." It was not to be.

Wales: K A Morgan (Pontypridd); W T Proctor, N Boobyer (Llanelli), L B Davies (Cardiff), Gareth Thomas (Cardiff); N R Jenkins (Pontypridd), R Howley (Cardiff, capt); A L P Lewis (Cardiff), G R Jenkins (Swansea), D Young (Cardiff), M J Voyle (Llanelli), A P Moore, R L Appleyard, Stuart Davies, C L Charvis (Swansea). Reps: D R James (Pontypridd) for Boobyer, J M Humphreys (Cardiff) for G R Jenkins, K P Jones (Ebbw Vale) for Appleyard, L Mustoe (Cardiff) for Lewis.

France: J LSadourny (Colomiers); P Bernart-Salles (Pau), C Lamaison (Brive), S Glas (Bourgoin), X Garbajosa (Toulouse); T Castaignede (Castres), P Carbonneau (Brive); C Califano (Toulouse), R Ibanez (Dax, capt), F Tournaire (Toulouse), O Brouzet (Begles-Bordeaux), F Pelous (Toulouse), M Lievremont (Stade Francais), T Lievremont (Perpignan), O Magne (Brive). Reps: J M Aue (Castres) for Lamaison, D Aucagne (Pau) for Castaignede, F Galthie (Colomiers) for Carbonneau, C Soulette (Beziers) for Califano, M Dal Maso (Agen) for Ibanez, T Cleda (Pau) for Brouzet, P Benetton (Agen) for T Lievremont.

For France, Jean-Luc Sadourny (2), Xavier Garbajosa (2), Thomas Lievremont, Stephane Glas, Fabien Galthie scored tries. Christophe Lamaison converted five and kicked two penalty goals.

Referee: P Marshall (Australia).

Wales won by three goals, one penalty goal, five tries (49) to two penalty goals, one try (11)

For various reasons, Wales were without 18 leading players when they toured southern Africa. Further disruption was caused by injuries, which meant seven replacements had to be flown out. This encounter with a sub-standard Zimbabwe side provided the visitors with their only success in six games. Byron Hayward, on as replacement full back, scored three tries to mark his international debut. He was only the third Welsh player to obtain a try hat-trick on his first appearance, following wings Willie Llewellyn (four tries in 1899) and Gareth Thomas (1995). Richard Rees also snapped up two tries on his debut and Arwel Thomas included two tries in 19 points. Some 6,000 watched in scorching heat in a stadium that holds 65,000. Dennis John (Pontypridd) was appointed caretaker WRU coach while the world was trawled for a successor to Bowring.

Zimbabwe: V Olonga; R Karimazondo, J Ewing, B French, C Graham; K Tsimba, R Bekker; G Snyder, W Barrett, G Stewart, B Catterall, S Landman, L Greef, B Dawson (capt), M Mwerenga. Reps: D Walters for Karimazondo, D Trivella for Tsimba, I Nelson for Barrett, C McNab for Mwerenga.

Wales: *D Weatherley (Swansea); *R Rees, M Taylor (Swansea), D R James (Pontypridd), WT Proctor (Llanelli); A C Thomas (Swansea), R Howley (Cardiff, capt); *D R Morris (Neath), G R Jenkins (Swansea), J D Davies (Richmond), A P Moore (Swansea), Mark Jones (Ebbw Vale), Nathan Thomas (Bath), L S Quinnell (Richmond), M E Williams (Pontypridd). Reps: *B Hayward (Ebbw Vale) for Weatherley, *J Funnell (Ebbw Vale) for Taylor, P John (Pontypridd) for Howley, Barry Williams (Richmond) for Jenkins, *C P Wyatt (Llanelli) for Jones, C L Charvis (Swansea) for Quinnell.

For Zimbabwe, Ryan Bekker scored a try. Kenny Tsimba kicked two penalty goals.

For Wales, Byron Hayward (3), Richard Rees (2), Arwel Thomas (2), Wayne Proctor scored tries. Arwel Thomas converted three and kicked a penalty goal.

Referee: J Meuwesen (SA).

Match 471   SOUTH AFRICA v WALES   Loftus Versfeld, Pretoria. June 27, 1998

*South Africa won by nine goals, one penalty goal, six tries (96)
to one goal, two penalty goals (13)*

Welsh fears, it appeared, would be realised under the Loftus Versfeld floodlights. They would become the first of the great teams of the game to be defeated by 100 points. It was the equivalent of the decline and fall of the Roman Empire. But South Africa were too impetuous. They fumbled their way into error after error as they swarmed to snap up the last try they needed. So Wales survived, in a sense, grateful it was only 15 tries and 96 points for a record score in a major international. Percy Montgomery supplied 31 points, including two tries from full back. Arwel Thomas scored all the Welsh points, including a try with a delicious cut-through. Wales were captained by three players during the match: Kingsley Jones began in the absence of hamstring victim Rob Howley; Paul John took over when Jones was replaced; and Garin Jenkins led when John left the field of carnage. In all, 14 replacements were used in a merry-go-round of changes. Without so many frontline players this horrendous defeat was inevitable.

South Africa: P Montgomery; S Terblanche, A Snyman, P Muller, P Rossouw; F Smith, J van der Westhuizen; R Kempson, J Dalton, A Garvey, K Otto, M Andrews, J Erasmus, G Teichmann (capt), A Venter. Reps: H Honiball for Muller, B Skinstad for Andrews, W Swanepoel for van der Westhuizen, M Hendricks for Terblanche, A Aitken for Teichmann, O le Roux for Garvey, N Drotske for Dalton.

Wales: B Hayward (Llanelli); D R James (Pontypridd), M Taylor (Swansea), J Funnell (Ebbw Vale), *Garan Evans (Llanelli); AC Thomas (Swansea), P John (Pontypridd); M Griffiths (Pontypridd), Barry Williams, J D Davies (Richmond), *I Gough (Newport), A P Moore (Swansea), Nathan Thomas (Bath), C L Charvis (Swansea), K P Jones (Ebbw Vale, capt). Reps: C P Wyatt (Llanelli) for K P Jones, *Darril Williams (Llanelli) for Hayward, *Stephen Jones (Llanelli) for Funnell, D Morris (Neath) for John Davies, G R Jenkins (Swansea) for Williams, *G Lewis (Pontypridd) for Charvis, *D Llewellyn (Ebbw Vale) for John.

For SA, Pieter Rossouw (3), Percy Montgomery (2), Stefan Terblanche (2), Andre Venter (2), Joost van der Westhuizen, Krynauw Otto, Franco Smith, Johan Erasmus, Bob Skinstad, McNeil Hendricks scored tries, Montgomery converted nine and kicked a penalty goal.

For Wales, Arwel Thomas scored a try, converted and kicked two penalty goals.

Referee: P O'Brien (NZ).

South Africa won by two goals, three penalty goals, one try (28) to five penalty goals, one try (20)

If South Africa had been leading 14-0, no-one would have been particularly surprised. After all, five months earlier, the Springboks had destroyed Wales 96-13 in Pretoria. Sensationally, now Wales are the team in front 14-0. A delightful try by Gareth Thomas and three Neil Jenkins penalty goals saw Wales take the game to the visitors and thrill 55,000 watchers. Could Wales shock the world champions to defeat for the first time? The opportunity was there and, with three minutes remaining, the Boks trailed 20-17 after a further brace of Jenkins penalty shots. Alas for false hopes, Franco Smith equalised when Scott Quinnell was yellow-carded for a loose elbow. Then Joost van der Westhuizen, always too fast on the draw for Wales, slipped through to set up a try for Venter during injury time and Smith popped over a last-kick penalty goal. The old Springbok bogy had struck again. Many considered the penalty try harsh when hooker Jonathan Humphreys stood up as the scrum was driven back to the Welsh line. Others blamed a male streaker for breaking Welsh concentration when he caused a stoppage of some five minutes at a time when the tourists trailed 20-17. This view was more forcibly expressed when it was discovered the naked intruder was a South African! "I am very relieved to have won," breathed Springbok coach Nick Mallett. Welsh spirits quickly revived. "We are not going to be the whipping boys of international rugby any more," promised captain Howley. It was a reassuring start for new coach Graham Henry.

Wales: *S P Howarth (Sale); Gareth Thomas (Cardiff), M Taylor, I S Gibbs (Swansea), D R James (Pontypridd); N R Jenkins (Pontypridd), R Howley (Cardiff, capt.); A L P Lewis, J M Humphreys (Cardiff), C T Anthony (Swansea), J C Quinnell (Richmond), C P Wyatt (Llanelli), C L Charvis (Swansea), L S Quinnell (Llanelli), M E Williams (Pontypridd). Reps: D R Morris (Swansea) for Lewis, *B Evans (Swansea) for Anthony.

South Africa: P C Montgomery; C S Terblanche, A H Snyman, F Smith, P W G Rossouw; H W Honiball, J H van der Westhuizen; R B Kempson, J Dalton, A C Garvey, K Otto, M G Andrews, J Erasmus, G H Teichmann (capt), A G Venter. Reps: O le Roux for Garvey, R Skinstad for Andrews.

For Wales, Gareth Thomas scored a try. Neil Jenkins kicked five penalty goals.

For SA, Joost van der Westhuizen and Andre Venter scored tries and there was a penalty try. Franco Smith converted two and kicked three penalty goals,

Referee: S Dickinson (Australia).

Wales won by four goals, five penalty goals (43) to two goals, two penalty goals, two tries (30)

Argentina's scrum took on an almost mystical quality as it savaged Wales under the floodlights. The Argies put the frighteners on the home side by scoring 19 points during the last 10 minutes of the opening half. For the second successive match, Wales gave away a penalty try under pressure at a scrum, but this hard-earned win came with a reassuring second half performance. Wales led 20-3 until events began to go wrong and the advantage was trimmed to a perilous 26-25. Colin Charvis's second try, from a thundering Scott Gibbs burst, with Martyn Williams as the link, proved the turning point. Coach Graham Henry, enjoying his first success in his new role, said, "I don't think I have ever seen a team scrummage as well as Argentina. It was a concern for us." Neil Jenkins scored a vital 23 points. Attendance was restricted to 10,500 for safety reasons.

Wales: S P Howarth (Sale); Gareth Thomas (Cardiff), I S Gibbs, M Taylor (Swansea), D R James (Pontypridd); N R Jenkins (Pontypridd), R Howley

(Cardiff, capt.); A L P Lewis, J M Humphreys (Cardiff), C T Anthony (Swansea), J C Quinnell (Richmond), C P Wyatt (Llanelli), C L Charvis (Swansea), L S Quinnell (Llanelli), M E Williams (Pontypridd). Reps: M J Voyle (Llanelli) for L S Quinnell, Barry Williams (Richmond) for M E Williams.

Argentina: M Contepomi; I Corleto, J Orengo, L Arbizu, P Soler; F Contepomi, A Pichot; M Reggiardo, F Mendez, O Hasan, P Sporleder (capt), A Allub, M Durand, P Camerlinckx, M Ruiz. Reps: E Simone for Orengo, D Albanese for Soler, M Ledesema for Reggiardo, R Martin for Durand.

For Wales, Colin Charvis (2), Mark Taylor, Dafydd James scored tries. Neil Jenkins converted four and kicked five penalty goals.

For Argentina, Agustin Pichot, Felipe Contepomi, Pedro Sporleder scored tries and there was a penalty try. Felipe Contepomi converted two and kicked two penalty goals.

Referee: A Lewis (Ireland).

Match 474   SCOTLAND v WALES   Murrayfield. February 6, 1999

Scotland won by two goals, three penalty goals, two tries (33) to two goals, two penalty goals (20)

It was claimed to be the fastest try in the history of the Five Nations: just 10 seconds from kick-off to start the game in front of a capacity 67,500 crowd until centre John Leslie touched down unopposed. Scotland's plan was to kick-off the 'wrong' way and catch Wales unaware as well as putting pressure on new cap Matthew Robinson, standing out wide. Shane Howarth, the Welsh full back, was on hand to help out, but he had the ball snatched from under his nose as he went to catch it and the shock score set the scene for a thrilling contest with the lead swinging five times. Wales were expected to win; but with four of their front five forwards plunged into their first experience of Five Nations atmosphere, the pack were overwhelmed by fast-driving, hard-rucking experts. Errors let in Scotland for some easy tries and they snatched the opportunity to run up a record number of points against Wales at Murrayfield. Coach Graham Henry summed up succinctly, "We didn't deserve to win – in fact, we were lucky to get second!" Scotland won the Five Nations title thanks to Wales's amazing victory over England in the final match of the season.

Scotland: G H Metcalfe (Glasgow Caledonians); C A Murray (Edinburgh Reivers), G P Townsend (Brive), J A Leslie (Glasgow Caledonians), K M Logan (Wasps); D W Hodge (Edinburgh Reivers), G Armstrong (Newcastle, capt); T J Smith, G C Bulloch (Glasgow Caledonians), A P Burnell (London Scottish), S Murray (Bedford), G W Weir, P Walton (Newcastle), E W Peters (Bath), M D Leslie (Edinburgh Reivers). Reps: A V Tait (Edinburgh Reivers) for Hodge, D I W Hilton (Bath) for Burnell, S B Grimes (Glasgow Caledonians) for Weir, AC Pountney (Northampton) for M D Leslie.

Wales: S P Howarth (Sale); *M F D Robinson, I S Gibbs (Swansea), A G Bateman (Richmond), D R James (Pontypridd); N R Jenkins (Pontypridd), R Howley (Cardiff, capt.); D R Morris (Swansea), J M Humphreys (Cardiff), C T Anthony (Swansea), I Gough (Pontypridd), C P Wyatt (Llanelli), C L Charvis (Swansea), L S Quinnell (Llanelli), M E Williams (Pontypridd). Reps: Barry Williams (Richmond) for Humphreys, M J Voyle (Llanelli) for Gough.

For Scotland, John Leslie, Gregor Townsend, Alan Tait, Scott Murray scored tries. Kenny Logan converted two and kicked two penalty goals. Duncan Hodge kicked a penalty goal.

For Wales, Dafydd James, Scott Gibbs scored tries. Neil Jenkins converted both and kicked two penalty goals.

Referee: E Morrison (England).

*Ireland won by two goals, two dropped goals, three penalty goals (29)
to two goals, three penalty goals (23)*

It was the Battle of the Baldies: shaven-headed Craig Quinnell throwing punches extravagantly, yellow-carded and then a thundering try-getter; Ireland's equally thinly-thatched Keith Wood, a hooker masquerading as an outside half, standing off wide to take his scrum half's pass, side-step Scott Gibbs and storm to the posts for a score that will live on in history for the men in green. David Humphreys charged down a Neil Jenkins punt to put Maggs in from 40 yards; Humphreys also popped over two drop-shots in his 19 points. "We lacked discipline," reflected coach Graham Henry. "I went over the top," admitted crestfallen Craig Quinnell. A purple patch by Wales for 20 exciting minutes inspired the hopes of a turnaround. It was not to be and the words on Welsh lips were 'wooden spoon'. The two most difficult matches were still to come. Both countries were coached by New Zealanders: Warren Gatland for Ireland, Graham Henry for Wales.

Wales: S P Howarth (Sale); M F D Robinson, M Taylor, I S Gibbs (Swansea), D R James (Pontypridd); N R Jenkins (Pontypridd), R Howley (Cardiff, capt.); D R Morris (Swansea), Barry Williams (Richmond), D Young (Cardiff), J C Quinnell (Richmond), C P Wyatt (Llanelli), C L Charvis (Swansea), L S Quinnell (Llanelli), M E Williams (Pontypridd). Reps: M J Voyle (Llanelli) for M E Williams, G R Jenkins (Swansea) for Barry Williams, C T Anthony (Swansea) for Young.

Ireland: C M P O'Shea (London Irish); J P Bishop (London Irish), K M Maggs (Bath), J C Bell (Dungannon), N K P Woods (London Irish); D G Humphreys (Dungannon), C D McGuinness (St. Mary's Coll); P M Clohessy (Young Munster), K G M Wood (Harlequins), P S Wallace, P S Johns (Saracens, capt), J W Davidson (Castres), D O'Cuinneagain (Sale), E R P Miller (Terenure Coll), A J Ward (Ballynahinch). Reps: M J Galwey (Shannon) for Johns, J Fitzpatrick (Dungannon) for Clohessy, V Costello (St. Mary's Coll) for Miller.

For Wales, Craig Quinnell, Shane Howarth scored tries. Neil Jenkins converted both and kicked three penalty goals.

For Ireland, Kevin Maggs, Keith Wood scored tries. David Humphreys converted both, dropped two goals and kicked three penalty goals.

Referee: S Young (Australia).

*Wales won by two goals, five penalty goals, one try (34)
to two goals, three penalty goals, two tries (33)*

If Thomas Castaignede's injury-time penalty attempt from wide out had curled in instead of fading, Wales still would have been seeking their first success in Paris after 24 years. But a one-point margin was good enough to bring that long-sought victory in one of the great games of modern times. It was so fast and furious that watchers dare not blink for fear of missing something dramatic. On their first visit to the new, towering, futuristic £270m Stade de France, Wales put together a near-complete performance with Neil Jenkins on target with 19 goal points in front of 80,000. Emile Ntamak scored a hat-trick from full back for venturesome France, who were always ready to attack from deep, and even from behind their goal-line.

They levelled at 28-all before stealing into a 33-31 lead. However, Jenkins kicked his fifth and decisive penalty goal with five minutes left and there were tears of joy from some Welsh players. "This was pay back time," smiled skipper Rob Howley, thinking of the catastrophic 51-0 defeat by France a year earlier at Wembley. France, aiming for a unique third successive Grand Slam, were devastated. Wales, dubbed the 20 minutes team, had clocked the full 80. No wonder the French were staggered to see giant lock Craig Quinnell suddenly appear far out on the wing in swift chain passing to arrow across for an unforgettable try. Anything could have happened on this day of undreamed of drama. It was simply intoxicating.

France: E Ntamack (Toulouse); P Bernat-Salles (Biarritz), R Dourthe, F Comba, T Lombard (Stade Francais); T Castaignede (Castres), P Carbonneau (Brive); C Califano (Toulouse), R Ibanez (Perpignan, capt), F Tournaire (Toulouse), O Brouzet (Begles/Bordeaux), F Pelous (Toulouse), P Benetton (Agen), T Lievremont (Perpignan), M Raynaud (Narbonne). Reps: X Garbajosa (Toulouse) for Bernat-Salles, D Aucagne (Pau) for Dourthe, S Marconnet (Stade Francais) for Tournaire, R Castel (Beziers) for Benetton.

Wales: S P Howarth (Sale); M F D Robinson, M Taylor, I S Gibbs (Swansea), D R James (Pontypridd); N R Jenkins (Pontypridd), R Howley (Cardiff, capt.); *P J D Rogers (London Irish), G R Jenkins, B R Evans (Swansea), J C Quinnell (Richmond), C P Wyatt (Llanelli), C L Charvis (Swansea), L S Quinnell (Llanelli), *B D Sinkinson (Neath). Reps: Gareth Thomas (Cardiff) for Robinson, A L P Lewis (Cardiff) for Rogers, D Llewellyn (Ebbw Vale) for Howley.

For France, Emile Ntamack (3), Thomas Castaignede scored tries. Castaignede converted two and kicked three penalty goals.

For Wales, Colin Charvis, Dafydd James, Craig Quinnell scored tries. Neil Jenkins converted two and kicked five penalty goals.

Referee: J Fleming (Scotland).

Match 477 ITALY v WALES Stadio Comunale di Monigo, Treviso. March 20, 1999

Wales won by five goals, five penalty goals, two tries (60)
to one goal, three penalty goals, one try (21)

Gareth Thomas, again the dashing cavalier, romped away for four tries to equal the Welsh record for a match and Neil Jenkins contributed a Welsh record 30 points to stun the Azzurri. They had lost only 23-20 at Stradey in 1998, but this time a second half of breathtaking attack advanced an 18-16 Welsh interval advantage into a total rout. Craig Quinnell scored a try for the third consecutive match. All seven replacements were sent on to savour the atmosphere of another dazzling success, watched by 9,000. Italy, who were to join in and make a new Six Nations Championship in 2000, were astounded as they crumbled to concede seven tries.

Italy: J Pertile; F Roselli, C Stoica, L Martin, D Dallan; D Dominguez, A Troncon; M Cuttitta, A Moscardi, F Properzi, M Giacheri, W Cristofoletto, M Giovanelli (capt), D Scaglia, A Sgorlon. Reps: M Baroni for Stoica, A Castellani for Properzi, S Stocco for Cristofoletto, S Saviozzi for Sgorlon.

Wales: S P Howarth (Sale); Gareth Thomas (Cardiff), M Taylor, I S Gibbs (Swansea), D R James (Pontypridd); N R Jenkins (Pontypridd), R Howley (Cardiff, capt.); P J D Rogers (London Irish), G R Jenkins, B R Evans (Swansea), J C Quinnell (Richmond), C P Wyatt (Llanelli), C L Charvis (Swansea), L S Quinnell (Llanelli), B D Sinkinson (Neath). Reps: N Boobyer (Llanelli) for Taylor, *N J Walne (Richmond) for James, D Llewellyn (Ebbw Vale) for Howley, D Morris (Swansea) for Rogers, Barry Williams (Richmond) for G Jenkins, M J Voyle (Llanelli) for J C Quinnell, G Lewis (Pontypridd) for Charvis.

For Italy, Luca Martin, Andrea Sgorlon scored tries. Diego Dominguez converted one and kicked three penalty goals.

For Wales, Gareth Thomas (4), Craig Quinnell, Rob Howley and Neil Jenkins scored tries. Neil Jenkins converted five and kicked five penalty goals.

Referee: R Dickson (Scotland).

Match 478   **WALES v ENGLAND**   Wembley Stadium. April 11, 1999

Wales won by two goals, six penalty goals (32) to two goals, four penalty goals, one try (31)

Next time a volunteer is required to storm an impregnable fortress, call for Scott Gibbs. He was a one-man Forlorn Hope to breach England's defence on this dramatic Sunday at Wembley Stadium. This was the assault on the Kashmir Gate, Badajoz and the Taku Forts rolled into one. Five tacklers failed to stop this glory boy as he strode down the Valley of Peril with breathtaking swerve and verve. Who will ever forget his try in the second minute of injury time? And then Neil Jenkins, who was to kick eight goals in eight attempts for 22 famous points, drilled the conversion and victory by a point. Wales had never been in the lead until the last fateful kick. Indeed, England were seven points up before the first three minutes had elapsed. Dan Luger went in as tacklers missed him and Jonny Wilkinson converted. What had England to fear? "Our chances of winning are pretty remote," considered Wales coach Graham Henry before the game. Afterwards he commented, "England were the better side. We didn't play very well, giving away so many turn-overs and missing tackles on the fringes. But we hung on in there." And how!

England, going for a 12th Grand Slam and a record fifth successive Triple Crown, were favourites with their fearsome front five and dynamic back row; but they gave away silly penalties, such as when Neil Back walked off with the ball to prevent Wales taking a quick tap. Neil Jenkins punished that with the resultant penalty and England captain Lawrence Dallaglio ruminated, "We let them off the hook." His shattered coach, Clive Woodward, muttered darkly, "I still won't believe we lost this game when I wake up in the morning." Some of his players sank to their knees behind the posts, waiting for 'executioner' Jenkins to land the inevitable conversion and first Welsh success over their opponents for six years. On their knees, England's warriors must have reflected on what had happened: a year earlier they had inflicted a record Five Nations defeat on Wales 60-26. Now the under-dogs in red had stolen the game when they trailed 31-25 and the final whistle was a whisker away. For that decisive score, Wales called a four-man line; Chris Wyatt won the throw and with Scott Quinnell running decoy, Gibbs stormed the ramparts for the final try in the Five Nations before it became the Six Nations championship. Tom Jones sang one of his greatest hits, *Delilah*, with Max Boyce supplying some of his much-loved rugby songs as pre-match entertainment for 78,000 spectators. But it was Gibbs and Jenks, the Chosen Men, who hit the sweetest notes in injury time!

Wales: S P Howarth (Sale); Gareth Thomas (Cardiff), M Taylor, I S Gibbs (Swansea), D R James (Pontypridd); N R Jenkins (Pontypridd), R Howley (Cardiff, capt.); P J D Rogers (London Irish), G R Jenkins, B R Evans (Swansea), J C Quinnell (Richmond), C P Wyatt (Llanelli), C L Charvis (Swansea), L S Quinnell (Llanelli), B D Sinkinson (Neath). Reps: N J Walne (Richmond) for Thomas, A L P Lewis (Cardiff) for Rogers, D Young (Cardiff) for Evans.

England: M B Perry (Bath); D D Luger (Harlequins), J P Wilkinson (Newcastle), B J Mather, S M Hanley (Sale); M J Catt (Bath), M J S Dawson (Northampton); J Leonard (Harlequins), R Cockerill, D J Garforth, M O Johnson (Leicester), T A K Rodber (Northampton), R A Hill (Saracens), L B N Dallaglio (Wasps, capt), N A Back (Leicester). Rep: V E Ubogu (Bath) for Garforth.

For Wales, Shane Howarth, Scott Gibbs scored tries. Neil Jenkins converted both and kicked six penalty goals.

For England, Dan Luger, Steve Hanley, Richard Hill scored tries. Jonny Wilkinson converted two and kicked four penalty goals.

Referee: A Watson (SA).

Match 479   ARGENTINA v WALES   1st Test Buenos Aires. June 5, 1999

Wales won by three goals, one dropped goal, four penalty goals (36)
to two goals, four penalty goals (26)

When Argentina's Galloping Gauchos hustled their way to a 23-0 lead and looked to be riding pell-mell to victory after only 35 minutes, the scene was laid out for Wales to give an exposition of their amazing survival skills. Not for nothing after Scott Gibbs had stunned England were Wales being called the Comeback Kids. They did it again with a breathtaking recovery. It became a bit of a Mexican stand-off as Neil Jenkins's long penalty shot made it 23-all; and Shane Howarth's memorable drop-goal from around 45 yards brought it to 26-all. Then came the bolas blow that produced Chris Wyatt's thunderbolt charge to the posts for a try to put his team in front for the first time with only some six minutes remaining. Jenkins converted and added a penalty goal as Argentina snatched defeat from the jaws of victory! "They tore us apart," said Rob Howley, reflecting on his team's terrible start. "When a team are 23-0 up they should never lose a Test match," opined coach Graham Henry, who emphasised the key to success was the rock solid scrum that defused the explosive Pumas' front row. As legendary Bill McLaren might have said, "They certainly won't be singing on the pampas tonight!"

Argentina: D Albanese; O Bartolucci, E Simone, L Arbizu, E Jurado; G Quesada, A Pichot; R Grau, F Mendez, M Reggiardo, P Sporleder (capt.), A Allub, I Lobbe, P Camerlinckx, R Martin. Reps: O Hasan for Grau, L Ostiglia for Allub, G Longo for Camerlinckx.

Wales: S P Howarth (Sale); M F D Robinson, M Taylor (Swansea), A G Bateman (Northampton), D R James (Pontypridd); N R Jenkins (Pontypridd), R Howley (Cardiff, capt.); P J D Rogers (Newport), G R Jenkins, B R Evans (Swansea), J C Quinnell (Cardiff), C P Wyatt (Llanelli), C L Charvis (Swansea), L S Quinnell (Llanelli), B D Sinkinson (Neath). Reps: A L P Lewis (Cardiff) for Rogers, D Young (Cardiff) for Evans.

For Argentina, Gonzalo Quesada, Octavio Bartolucci scored tries. Quesada converted two and kicked four penalty goals.

For Wales, Dafydd James, Brett Sinkinson, Chris Wyatt scored tries. Neil Jenkins converted three and kicked four penalty goals. Shane Howarth dropped a goal.

Referee: Brian Campsall (England).

Match 480   ARGENTINA v WALES   2nd Test Buenos Aires. June 12, 1999

Wales won by one dropped goal, five penalty goals, one try (23)
to one goal, three penalty goals (16)

"They will throw the kitchen sink at us," warned coach Graham Henry as Wales anticipated a backlash from the angry Pumas, who could not believe how they allowed the tourists to escape from the First Test at the Stadio Ferro Carril Oeste. Back at the same venue, and again in front of 16,000 watchers, it was indeed a 'kitchen sink' job as the home forwards exploded into an ugly brawl that spilled over the touchline and into the Argentine trainers' dugout midway through the opening half. Welsh players joined in with a will; no-one was going to work them over with impunity. The punch-up was a draw, but the match undoubtedly belonged to Wales. Pumas' captain Pedro Sporleder and pugnacious prop Mauricio Reggiardo were yellow carded for their part in the flying fists together with Wales prop Peter Rogers. It proved to be the match of the Jenkinses: magnificently combative hooker Garin scored the Welsh try and dead-shot Neil popped over 18 goal points, including a tasty drop-shot for a fifth consecutive Welsh win. Also it implied important psychological one-upmanship over Argentina, who would face Wales again in the first match of World Cup 1999 in Cardiff. Hopefully, the Argies would leave the 'kitchen sink' at home!

Argentina: D Albanese; O Bartolucci, J Orengo, L Arbizu, G Camardon; F Contepomi, A Pichot; R Grau, F Mendez, M Reggiardo, P Sporleder (capt.), I Lobbe, R Martin, G Longo, M A Ruiz. Reps: J L Cilley for Contepomi, M Ledesma for Mendez, O Hasan for Reggiardo, A Allub for Lobbe, L Ostiglia for Martin.

Wales: S P Howarth (Sale); Gareth Thomas (Cardiff), A G Bateman (Northampton), M Taylor (Swansea) D R James (Pontypridd); N R Jenkins (Pontypridd), R Howley (Cardiff, capt.); P J D Rogers (Newport), G R Jenkins, B R Evans (Swansea), J C Quinnell (Cardiff), C P Wyatt (Llanelli), G Lewis (Pontypridd), L S Quinnell (Llanelli), B D Sinkinson (Neath). Reps: J M Humphreys (Cardiff) for G R Jenkins, A L P Lewis (Cardiff) for Rogers, D Young (Cardiff) for Evans.

For Argentina, Jose Orengo scored a try. Jose Luis Cilley converted. Felipe Contpomi kicked three penalty goals.

For Wales, Garin Jenkins scored a try. Neil Jenkins dropped a goal and kicked five penalty goals.

Referee: Chris White (England).

Match 481   WALES v SOUTH AFRICA   Cardiff Arms Park. June 26, 1999

Wales won by two goals, five penalty goals (29) to three penalty goals, two tries (19)

Ruffle Neil Jenkins's feathers and suffer the consequences. The shocked Springboks did. The world champions made the outside half a target in the opening minutes with a couple of late, bruising body-checks to try to put him off his game, if not off the field. That sealed their fate. We saw Wales win gloriously for the first time in 13 meetings with South Africa to make history in the opening game at the new £121m Millennium Stadium, which is, of course, the Arms Park and always will be. It was two tries each; but Jenkins, unshaken and unstirred, fired over 19 goal points, every one a relished reprisal for those early bone-shakers. This was revenge for that heaviest Welsh defeat 96-13 a year earlier in Pretoria and the only disappointment was that a mere 27,500 witnessed it because the stadium was still under construction. We saw no classic contest: just a furiously-fought encounter. After 15 minutes there was a lively punch-up, initiated by South Africa; and three minutes later, Craig Quinnell left the battlefield with a broken thumb. The Welsh pack were heroes, inspired further as the crowd sang *Bread of Heaven*. Three times waves of menacing Sprinbok forwards assailed the goal line. Surely they must score? But fearless tacklers repulsed them in those moments of terrifying tension. Undeniably, defence won the match. There were yellow cards for Robbie Kempson, who nursed a donk in the eye for his trouble, and then Corne Krige for trying to rearrange a Welsh face on the ground with impressive lack of guile.

Cunning coach Graham Henry confessed he had fooled everyone except his players. "I think our chances are remote," he forecast. "This is a game too far. We would rather not play it." Then he told his team, "We can win this time." They did it with Neil Jenkins a majestic influence. This was the finest of his many fine performances. His line-kicking destroyed the Boks and his overall control was matchless. He kicked seven of his eight attempts, including a superb conversion after putting Gareth Thomas across in the corner. Mark Taylor scored the first try on the new ground with a delicious hand-off as he rounded Pieter Muller. It was all high drama in high summer and stimulating to see Welsh forwards gnawing and battering the South African pack. True, the visitors were without half-a-dozen top players, but this Welsh pack were unconquerable – and Jenkins was going to make the Boks pay! There were a lot of unhappy people in the Old Transvaal.

Wales: S P Howarth (Sale); Gareth Thomas (Cardiff), A G Bateman (Northampton), M Taylor (Swansea), D R James (Pontypridd); N R Jenkins (Pontypridd), R Howley (Cardiff, capt.); P J D Rogers (Newport), G R Jenkins (Swansea), D Young, J C Quinnell (Cardiff), C P Wyatt (Llanelli), C L Charvis (Swansea), L S Quinnell (Llanelli), B D Sinkinson (Neath). Reps: M J Voyle (Llanelli) for J C Quinnell, A L P Lewis (Cardiff) for Rogers, J M Humphreys (Cardiff) for G R Jenkins.

South Africa: P C Montgomery; C S Terblanche, P G Muller, J C Mulder, P W G Rossouw; B van Straaten, W Swanepoel; R B Kempson, A E Drotske, C Visagie, S Boome, K Otto, C P J Krige, G H Teichmann (capt.), J C Erasmus. Reps: G du Toit for van Straaten, D von Hoesslin for Swanepoel, O le Roux for Kempson, A G Venter for Boome.

For Wales, Mark Taylor, Gareth Thomas scored tries. Neil Jenkins converted two and kicked five penalty goals.

For SA, Werner Swanepoel, Percy Montgomery scored tries. Braam van Straaten kicked two penalty goals. Gaffie du Toit kicked one penalty goal.

Referee: Ed Morrison (England).

Match 482   WALES v CANADA   Cardiff Arms Park. August 21, 1999

Wales won by one goal, seven penalty goals, one try (33)
to one goal, one dropped goal, three penalty goals (19)

Like the Mounties, Canadian tacklers had sworn to get their man and they spread wide and fast to block and disrupt. So there were only two Welsh tries in this build-up match before the World Cup in October. Neil Jenkins obtained one of them in his 28 points, which featured another masterly display of goal-kicking for the edification of 47,000 onlookers. Rob Howley became the first Welsh captain to lead seven consecutive winning teams and it was the first occasion for almost 22 years to register seven victories in a row. This was revenge for the shock 26-24 victory Canada snatched on their last Cardiff visit in 1993.

Wales: S P Howarth (Newport); N J Walne, L B Davies (Cardiff), I S Gibbs (Swansea), A G Bateman (Northampton); N R Jenkins, R Howley (Cardiff, capt.); P J D Rogers (Newport), J M Humphreys (Cardiff), B R Evans, A P Moore (Swansea), J C Quinnell (Cardiff), G Lewis (Pontypridd), L S Quinnell (Llanelli), M E Williams (Cardiff). Reps: Stephen Jones (Llanelli) for Gibbs, D Young (Cardiff) for Evans, Gareth Llewellyn (Harlequins) for J C Quinnell, C P Wyatt (Llanelli) for L S Quinnell, A L P Lewis (Cardiff) for Humphreys.

Canada: S Stewart; W Stanley, D Lougheed, S Bryan, C Smith; G Rees (capt.), M Williams; R Snow, M Cardinal, R Bice, J Tait, M James, J Hutchinson, A Charron, D Baugh. Reps: J Thiel for Bice, M Schmid for Tait, R Banks for Hutchinson, B Ross for Rees.

For Wales, Neil Jenkins, Nick Walne scored tries. Jenkins converted one and kicked seven penalty goals.

For Canada, David Lougheed scored a try. Gareth Rees converted, dropped a goal and kicked three penalty goals.

Referee: D McHugh (Ireland).

Wales won by one goal, nine penalty goals (34) to two goals, three penalty goals (23)

Dead-shot Neil Jenkins found the posts with a world record-equalling nine penalty shots in his 29 points to ensure Wales's eighth consecutive victory and first back-to-back success over France since 1976. But coach Graham Henry warned, "We can't afford to play like this in the World Cup." France snapped up two tries to one in front of 63,000 at the almost completed Millennium Stadium in a friendly fixture warm-up before the World Cup. Master-blaster Scott Gibbs produced the only truly thrilling long break before a late attack put Dafydd James across. Victory in the first pool game against Argentina would give Wales a ninth successive win and their longest sequence since the record 11 games from 1907 to 1910.

Wales: S P Howarth (Newport); G Thomas (Cardiff), M Taylor, I S Gibbs (Swansea), D R James (Llanelli); N R Jenkins, R Howley (Cardiff, capt); P J D Rogers (Newport), G R Jenkins (Swansea), D Young, J C Quinnell (Cardiff), C P Wyatt (Llanelli), C L Charvis (Swansea), L S Quinnell (Llanelli), B D Sinkinson (Neath). Rep: M J Voyle (Llanelli) for L S Quinnell.

France: U Mola (Castres); X Garbajosa (Toulouse), R Dourthe (Dax), S Glas (Bourgoin), C Dominici (Stade Francais); T Castaignede (Castres), S Castaignede (Mont-de-Marsan); C Califano (Toulouse), R Ibanez (Perpignan, capt), P de Villiers (Stade Francais), A Benazzi (Agen), F Pelous (Toulouse), M Lievremont (Stade Francais), T Lievremont (Perpignan), O Magne (Montferrand). All seven reps used: P Mignoni (Toulon), C Lamaison, L Mallier (Brive), E Ntamack, C Soulette (Toulouse), D Auradou (Stade Francais), M Dal Maso (Colomiers).

For Wales, Dafydd James scored a try. Neil Jenkins converted and kicked nine penalty goals.

For France, Lionel Mallier, Pierre Mignoni scored tries. Richard Dourthe converted one and kicked two penalty goals. Christophe Lamaison converted one and kicked one penalty goal.

Referee: P Honiss (New Zealand).

Wales won by five goals, one penalty goal, three tries (53) to three goals, one penalty goal (24)

After a trickle of Welsh tries in the three previous Millennium Stadium matches, now there was a cascade with eight in this third and final World Cup build-up fixture. Allan Bateman collected three in his despised role of wing and tricky David Llewellyn wriggled across for two.

Wales: N Boobyer (Llanelli); N J Walne, L B Davies (Cardiff), A Marinos (Newport), A G Bateman (Northampton); Stephen Jones (Llanelli), D Llewellyn (Newport); A L P Lewis, J M Humpheys (Cardiff), B R Evans (Swansea), Gareth Llewellyn (Harlequins), M J Voyle (Llanelli), G Lewis (Pontypridd), H Jenkins (Llanelli), M E Williams (Cardiff, capt). All seven reps used: M Robinson, T Maullin, C Anthony, D Morris, A P Moore, A C Thomas (Swansea), G Cooper (Bath).

USA: K Shuman; S Uiagalili, J Grobler, T Takau, B Hightower; M Williams, K Dalzell; G Sucher, T Billups, R Lehner, L Gross, A Parker, D Hodges, R Lumkong, D Lyle (capt). Reps: R Schurfeld, D Stroble, S Paga, K Khasigian, F Mounga, M L'Huillier.

For Wales, Allan Bateman (3), Neil Boobyer (2), David Llewellyn (2), Geraint Lewis scored tries. Stephen Jones converted five and kicked one penalty goal.

For USA, Juan Grobler, Kurt Shuman, Tomasi Takau scored tries. Mark Williams converted two and kicked one penantly goal. Kevin Dalzell converted one try.

Referee: B Campsall (England).

Wales became champions in 1994 with victory over France. This is the team that did it. Back row (left to right): Ian Jones (rep), Hugh Williams-Jones, John D Davies, Ricky Evans, Phil Davies, Emyr Lewis, Scott Quinnell, Mark Perego, Robin McBryde (rep), Tony Copsey (rep). In front: Robert Jones (rep), Mike Rayer, Nigel Walker, Simon Hill, Mike Hall, Gareth Llewellyn (capt), Rupert Moon, Anthony Clement, Garin Jenkins, Neil Jenkins, Hemi Taylor (rep). Mascot: Huw Tillman.

Try coming up. Scott Quinnell prepares to pop a scoring pass into the ready hands of wing Nigel Walker in the 24-15 win over France in 1994.

Anticipation . . . .
Expectation . . . .
Realisation . . . .

South Wales Echo *cameraman Steve Phillips captures the pulsating build-up and climax of that unforgettable 1999 Wembley try as Scott Gibbs steals the game from England 32-31 in the second minute of injury time.*

THEY PLAYED FOR WALES

*Ieuan
Evans*

Key: E – England, S – Scotland, SA – South Africa, A – Australia, M – Maoris (1888), I – Ireland, F – France, NZ – New Zealand, NSW – New South Wales, R – Romania, FJ – Fiji, T – Tonga, WS – Western Samoa, C – Canada, N – Namibia, B – Barbarians, AR – Argentina, Z – Zimbabwe, J – Japan, P – Portugal, Sp – Spain, It – Italy.
* Denotes Replacement player.

Ackerman, R. *(Newport and London Welsh)* NZ. 1980; E.S.A. 1981; I.F.E.S. 1982; S.I.F.R. 1983; S.I.F.E.A. 1984; S.I.F.E.FJ 1985.

Alexander, E.P. *(Cambridge Univ. and Brecon)* S. 85; E.S. 86; E.I. 87.

Alexander, W.H. *(Llwynypia)* I.E. 98.; E.S.I. 99; S.I. 1901.

Allen, A. *(Newbridge)* F.E.I. 1990.

Allen, C.P. *(Oxford Univ. and Beaumaris)* E.S. 84.

Andrews, F *(Pontypool)* SA. 1912; E.S.I. 1913.

Andrews, F.G. *(Swansea)* E.S. 84.

Andrews, G. *(Newport)* E.S. 1926; E.F.I. 1927.

Anthony, Chris *(Swansea)* USA (1* and 2*).C*. T* 1997; SA.AR. 1998; S.I.* 1999.

Anthony, L. *(Neath)* E.S.F. 1948.

Appleyard, Rob *(Swansea)* C. R.T.NZ. 1997; It.*E.S.I.F. 1998.

Arnold, P. *(Swansea)* N. 1, 2, B. 1990; E.S.I.F.A.AR.A. 1991; F.Z. (2nd) 1993; Sp. FJ. 1994; SA 1995; B* 1996.

Arnold, W. *(Llanelli)* S. 1903.

Arthur, C.S. *(Cardiff)* I.M. 88; E. 91.

Arthur, T. *(Neath)* S.F.I. 1927; E.S.F.I. 1929; E.S.I.F. 1930; E.S.F.I. 1931; SA. 1931; E.S. 1933.

Ashton, C. *(Aberavon)* E.S.I. 1959, 1960; I. 1962.

Attewell, L. *(Newport)* E.S.F. 1921.

Back, M. *(Bridgend)* F*.E*.S.I. 1995.

Badger, O. *(Llanelli)* E.S.I. 95; E. 96.

Baker, A. *(Neath)* I. 1921; E.S.F.I. 1923.

Baker, A.M. *(Newport)* S.F. 1909; S. 1910.

Bancroft, J. *(Swansea)* E.S.F.I. 1909; F.E.S.I. 1910; E.F.I. 1911; E.S.I. 1912; I. 1913; E.S.F. 1914.

Bancroft, W.J. *(Swansea)* S.E.I. 90; E.S.I. 91, 92, 93, 94, 95, 96; E. 97; I.E. 98; E.S.I. 99, 1900, 1901.

Barlow, T.M. *(Cardiff)* I. 84

Barrell, R. *(Cardiff)* S.F.I. 1929; I. 1933.

Bartlett, J.D. *(Llanelli and London Welsh)* S. 1927; E.S. 1928.

Phantom Menace and Jedi Knight

Ieuan Evans is the Phantom Menace of Welsh Rugby: the wing who made opponents feel the Force in sensational manner as he swept to a Wales record 33 tries during his record 72 caps. He also registered a Wales record 14 tries in the Rugby World Cup (including two qualifying matches and two seeding fixtures). Four of those tries came against Canada in the pool match of 1987. The only other World Cup Welsh four-try scorer is Cardiff's Nigel Walker. He snapped up his four in one go against Portugal in Lisbon in 1994. Ieuan Evans holds another record – 28 times as captain of Wales. So, though he may be a Phantom Menace with his sinuous swerves to baffle opposition teams, Ieuan most certainly is a Jedi Knight in Welsh eyes.

Bassett, A. *(Aberavon and Cardiff)* I. 1934; E.S.I. 1935; E.S. 1938.

Bassett, J. *(Penarth)* E.S.F.I. 1929; E.S.I. 1930; E.S.F.I.SA. 1931; E.S.I. 1932.

Bateman, A. *(Neath, Richmond, Northampton)* S.I. N. (1, 2) 1990; SA. 1996; USA.S.F.E. R.NZ. 1997; It. E.S.I. 1998; S.AR (1, 2) SA.C. 1999.

Bayliss, G. *(Pontypool)* S. 1933.

Bebb, D. *(Carmarthen T.C. and Swansea)* E.S.I.F. 1959; E.S.I.F.SA. 1960; E.S.I.F. 1961; E.S.F.I. 1962; E.F.NZ. 1963; E.S.F.SA. 1964; E.I.S.F. 1965; F.A. 1966; S.I.F.E. 1967.

Beckingham, G. *(Cardiff)* E.S. 1953; F. 1958.

Bennett, Ivor *(Aberavon)* I. 1937.

Bennett, M. *(Cardiff)* NZ. SA. FJ. 1995.

Bennett, P. *(Cardiff Harlequins)* E.S. 91; S.I. 92.

Bennett, P. *(Llanelli)* F.* 1969; SA.S.F. 1970; S.* 1972; NZ. 1972; E.S.I.F.A. 1973; S.I.F.E. 1974; S.*I. 1975; E.S.I.F. 1976; I.F.E.S. 1977; E.S.I.F. 1978.

Bergiers, R.T.E. *(Llanelli)* E.S.F.NZ. 1972; E.S.I.F.A. 1973; E. 1974; I. 1975.

Bevan, Griff. *(Llanelli)* E. 1947.

Bevan, J.A. *(Cambridge Univ.)* E. 81.

Bevan, J.C. *(Cardiff)* E.S.I.F. 1971; E.S.F. 1972; NZ. 1972; E.S. 1973.

Bevan, J.D. *(Aberavon)* F.E.S.A. 1975.

Bevan, Sid. *(Swansea)* I. 1904.

Beynon, Ben *(Swansea)* E.S. 1920.

Beynon, E. *(Swansea)* F.I. 1925.

Bidgood, R.A. *(Newport)* S. 1992; Z. (1st and 2nd), N.J.* 1993.

Biggs, N. *(Cardiff)* M. 88; I. 89, 92; E.S.I. 93; E.I. 94.

Biggs, S. *(Cardiff)* E.S. 95; S. 96; E. 97; I.E. 98; S.I. 99; I. 1900.

Birch, J. *(Neath)* S.F. 1911.

Birt, F.W. *(Newport)* E.S. 1911; E.S.I.SA. 1912; E. 1913.

Bishop, D.J. *(Pontypool)* A. 1984.

Bishop, E.H. *(Swansea)* S. 89.

Blackmore, J. *(Abertillery)* E. 1909.

Blackmore, S. *(Cardiff)* I.T.*C.A. 1987.

Blake, J. *(Cardiff)* E.S.I. 99, 1900, 1901.

Blakemore, R.E. *(Newport)* E. 1947.

Bland, A.F. *(Cardiff)* E.S.I. 87; S.I.M. 88; S.E.I. 90.

Blyth, L. *(Swansea)* SA. 1951; E.S. 1952.

Blyth, W.R. *(Swansea)* E. 1974; S.*1975; F.E.S.I. 1980.

Boobyer, N. *(Llanelli)* Z. (1st* and 2nd), N. 1993; F.T. 1994; F. 1998; It.* 1999.

Boon, R. *(Cardiff)* S.F. 1930; E.S.I.F.SA. 1931; E.S.I.1932; E.I. 1933.

Booth, J. *(Pontymister)* I. 98.

Boots, G. *(Newport)* I.E. 98; I. 99; E.S.I 1900, 1901, 1902, 1903; E. 1904.

Boucher, A.W. *(Newport)* E.S.I. 92, 93; E. 94, E.S.I. 95; E.I. 96; E. 97.

Bowcott, H.M. *(Cardiff, Cambridge Univ. and London Welsh)* S.F.I. 1929; E. 1930; E.S. 1931; E.I. 1933.

Bowdler, F.A. *(Cross Keys)* NSW 1927; E.S.I.F. 1928; E.S.F.I. 1929; E. 1930; SA. 1931; E.S.I. 1932; I. 1933.

Bowen, B. *(S. Wales Police and Swansea)* R. 1983; S.I.F.E. 1984; FJ. 1985; E.S.I.F.FJ.T.WS. 1986; C.E.NZ.USA. 1987; E.S.I.F. 1988; S.I. 1989.

Bowen, C. *(Llanelli)* E.S.I. 96; E. 97.

Bowen, D.H. *(Llanelli)* E. 82; E.S.86; E. 87.

Bowen, G.E. *(Swansea)* S.I. 87, 88.

Bowen, W. *(Swansea)* S.F. 1921; E.S.I.F. 1922.

Bowen, Wm. *(Swansea)* E.S. 86; E.S.I. 87; M. 88; S.I. 89; S.E.I. 90; E.S. 91.

Brace, D.O. *(Newport, Oxford Univ. and Llanelli)* E.S.I.F. 1956; E. 1957; S.I.F. 1960; I. 1961.

Braddock, K.J. *(Newbridge)* A. 1966; S.I. 1967.

Bradshaw, K. *(Bridgend)* E.S.I.F.SA. 1964; E.S.I.F. 1966.

Brewer, T.J. *(Newport, Oxford Univ. and London Welsh)* E. 1950; E.S. 1955.

Brice, A. *(Aberavon and Cardiff)* E.S.I. 99, 1900, 1901, 1902, 1903, 1904.

Bridges, C. *(Neath)* N. 1, 2, B. 1990; E.* I.F.A. 1991.

Bridie, R. *(Newport)* I. 82.

Britton, G. *(Newport)* S. 1961.

Broughton, A. *(Treorchy)* NSW. 1927; S. 1929.

Brown, Archie *(Newport)* I. 1921.

Brown, J. *(Cardiff)* E.S.I. 1907; E.S.F. 1908; E. 1909.

Brown, J. *(Cardiff)* I. 1925.

Brown, M. *(Pontypool)* R. 1983; E.S.FJ(R).T.WS. 1986.

Bryant, D. *(Bridgend)* NZ.(1 and 2), WS.R. 1988, S.I.F.E. 1989.

Buchanan, A. *(Llanelli)* T.E.*NZ.A. 1987; I. 1988.

Buckett, I. *(Swansea)* T. 1994; USA.C. 1997.

Burcher, D. *(Newport)* I.F.E.S. 1977.

Burgess, R.C. *(Ebbw Vale)* I.F.E.S. 1977; I.F. 1981; F.E.S. 1982.

Burnett, R. *(Newport)* E. 1953.

Burns, J. *(Cardiff)* F.I. 1927.

Bush, P. *(Cardiff)* NZ. 1905; E. 1906; SA. 1906; I. 1907; E.S. 1908; S.I. 1910.

Butler, E.T. *(Pontypool and Cambridge Univ.)* F.E.S.I.NZ.* 1980; S. 1982; E.S.I.F.R. 1983; S.I.F.E.A. 1984.

Cale, W.R. *(Newbridge and Pontypool)* E.S.I. 1949; E.S.I.F. 1950.

Carter, A.J. *(Newport)* E.S. 1991.

Cattell, A. *(Llanelli)* E. 1882; S. 1883.

Challinor, C. *(Neath)* E. 1939.

Charvis, Colin *(Swansea)* A*.SA. 1996; USA.S.I.F. 1997; It*.E.S.I.F. Z*.SA.SA.AR. 1998; S.I.F.It.E.AR(2).SA.F. 1999.

Clapp, T. *(Newport)* I.E. 82; S. 83; E.S.I. 84; E.S. 85; S. 86; E.S.I. 87; S.I. 88.

Clare, J. *(Cardiff)* E. 82.

Clarke, S.S. *(Neath)* I. 82; I. 87.

Cleaver, W.B. *(Cardiff)* E.S.I.F.A. 1947; E.S.F.I. 1948; I. 1949; E.S.I.F. 1950.

Clegg, B. *(Swansea)* F. 1979.

Clement, A. *(Swansea)* USA. 1987; E.NZ (1), WS(R), R. 1988; NZ. 1989; S(R),I.N. (1, 2) 1990; S*.A*.F.WS.AR.A. 1991; I.F.E.S. 1992; I*.F.J.C. 1993; S.I.F.Sp.C*.T.WS.It.SA. 1994; F.E.J.NZ.I. 1995.

Clement, W.H. *(Llanelli)* E.S.I. 1937, 1938.

Cobner, T.J. *(Pontypool)* S.I.F.E. 1974; F.E.S.I. 1975; A. 1975; E.S. 1976; F.E.S. 1977; E.S.I.F.A.(1) 1978.

Coldrick, A.P. *(Newport)* E.S.I. 1911; E.S.F. 1912.

Coleman, E. *(Newport)* E.S.I. 1949.

Coles, F.C. *(Pontypool)* S.I.F. 1960.

Collins, J. *(Aberavon)* A.E.S.F. 1958; E.S.I.F. 1959; E. 1960; F. 1961.

Longest Goal – and Fastest 50

Paul Thorburn kicked the longest goal for Wales. It happened during the 1986 victory by 22-15 against Scotland at the old Arms Park. The Neath full back (who held the Wales scoring record with 304 points until Neil Jenkins overtook him) had his down-wind kick measured afterwards and from kick to cross-bar it was reckoned to be 70 yards, 8½ inches, though where they found the half-inch from is anyone's guess. A couple of yards probably could be added for the ball to pitch over the bar. From 15 yards inside his half of the field this was indeed a monster of a goal kick. Thorburn still holds the record of fastest 50 points for Wales – in just five games.

Paul Thorburn

Collins, R.G. *(S Wales Police, Cardiff, Pontypridd)* E*.I.I.E.NZ.USA 1987; E.S.I.F.R. 1988; E.S.I. 1990; A.F.WS. 1991; C.FJ.T.WS.R.It.SA. 1994; F.E.S.I. 1995.

Collins, T. *(Mountain Ash)* I. 1923.

Cook, T. *(Cardiff)* S.I. 1949.

Cope, W. *(Cardiff, Cambridge Univ. and Blackheath)* S. 96.

Copsey, A.H. *(Llanelli)* I.F.E.S.A. 1992; E.S.I.J.C. 1993; E*.P.Sp*.FJ.T.WS*. 1994.

Cornish, F.H. *(Cardiff)* E. 97; I.E. 98; I. 99.

Cornish, R.A. *(Cardiff)* E.S. 1923; E. 1924;E.S.F. 1925; E.S.I.F. 1926;

Coslett, K. *(Aberavon)* E.S.F. 1962.

Cowey, B.T.V. *(Newport)* E.S.I. 1934; E. 1935.

Cresswell, B. *(Newport)* E.S.I.F. 1960.

Cummins, W. *(Treorchy)* E.S.I.F. 1922.

Cunningham, L.J. *(Aberavon)* E.S.I.F. 1960; E.S.F. 1962; I. 1962; NZ. 1963; E.S.I.F.SA. 1964.

Dacey, M. *(Swansea)* E.S.I.F.R. 1983; S.I.F.E.A. 1984; FJ.T.WS. 1986; F*.T. 1987.

Daniel, D.J. *(Llanelli)* S. 91; E.S.I. 94; I.E. 98; E.I. 99.

Daniel, L.T.D. *(Newport)* S. 1970.

Daniels, P.C.T. *(Cardiff)* A. 1981; I. 1982.

Darbishire, G. *(Bangor)* E. 81.

Dauncey, F.H. *(Newport)* E.S.I. 96.

Davey, Claude *(Swansea and London Welsh)* F. 1930; E.S.I.F.SA. 1931; E.S.I. 1932; E.S. 1933; E.S.I. 1934, 1935; NZ. 1935; S. 1936; E.I. 1937, 1938.

David, R. *(Cardiff)* I. 1907.

David, T.P. *(Pontypridd and Llanelli)* F.A. 1973; I.F. 1976.

Davidge, G. *(Newport)* F. 1959; S.I.F. 1960; SA. 1960; E.S.I. 1961; F. 1962.

Davies, Adrian *(Neath and Cardiff)* B*. 1990, A. 1991; Z. (1st and 2nd) J.C. 1993; FJ. 1994; J.I. 1995.

Davies, A.C. *(London Welsh)* I. 89.

Davies, A.E. *(Llanelli)* A. 1984.

Davies, Rev. Alban *(Swansea and Llanelli)* S.F.I. 1913; E.S.F.I. 1914.

Davies, B *(Llanelli)* E. 95, 96.

Davies, Bailey *(Oxford and Llanelli)* E. 1907.

Davies, Carwyn *(Llanelli)* WS. 1988, S.I(R).F. 1989.

Davies, C.H.A. *(Llanelli and Cardiff)* I. 1957; A.E.S.I. 1958; SA. 1960; E. 1961.

Davies, C.L. *(Cardiff)* E.S.I. 1956.

Davies, C.R. *(Bedford)* E. 1934.

Davies, Cliff *(Cardiff)* S.F.I.A. 1947; E.S.F.I. 1948; F. 1949; E.S.I.F. 1950; E.S.I. 1951.

Davies, Daph. *(Bridgend)* I. 1921. 1925.

Davies, D. Brian *(Llanelli)* I. 1962; E.S. 1963.

Davies, D.G. *(Cardiff)* E.S. 1923.

Davies, D.H. *(Neath)* S. 1904.

Davies, D. Hunt *(Aberavon)* E. 1924.

Davies, D. Idwal *(Swansea)* E. 1939.

Davies D.J. *(Neath)* I. 1962

Davies, D.M. *(Somerset Police)* E.S.I.F. 1950, 1951; SA. 1951; E.S.I.F. 1952; I.F.N.Z. 1953; E. 1954.

Davies, E. *(Aberavon)* A. 1947; I. 1948.

Davies, Evan *(Maesteg)* NZ. 1919.

Davies, Ewan *(Cardiff)* E.F. 1912.

Davies, Geo. *(Swansea)* E.S.I. 1900, 1901, 1905.

Davies, Glyn *(Pontypridd and Cambridge Univ.)* S.A. 1947; E.S.F.I. 1948; E.S.F. 1949; E.S. 1951.

Davies, Graham *(Llanelli)* F.I. 1921; F. 1925.

Davies, Gwyn *(Cardiff)* F. 1928; E. 1929; S. 1930.

Davies, H. *(Bridgend)* S.I.F.E. 1984.

Davies, H. *(Swansea)* I.E. 98; S.I. 1901.

Davies, H.J. *(Cambridge Univ. and Aberavon)* E.S. 1959.

Davies, Harold *(Newport)* S. 1924.

Davies, Howard *(Swansea and Llanelli)* S.I. 1939; E.S.F.I. 1947.

Davies, Howel *(Neath)* E.S. 1912.

Davies, Jonathan *(Neath,Llanelli and Cardiff)* E.FJ. 1985; E.S.I.F.FJ.T.WS. 1986; F.E.S.I.I.T*.C.E.NZ.A. 1987; F.S.I.F.NZ. (1 and 2). WS.R. 1988; A. 1996; USA*.S*.F*.E. 1997.

Davies, J.D. *(Neath)* I.F. 1991, F*.Z.(2nd), J.C. 1993; S.I.F.E.P.Sp.C.WS.R.It.SA. 1994; F.E.J.NZ.I.SA. 1995; It.E.S.I.F.A.B.F.It. 1996; Z.SA. 1998

Davies, J.H. *(Aberavon)* I. 1923.

Davies, I.T. *(Llanelli)* S.F.I. 1914.

Davies, Leigh *(Neath and Cardiff)* It.E.S.I.F.A.B.F.It*. 1996; USA (1 and 2).C.R.T.NZ*. 1997; E*.I.F. 1998; C. 1999.

Davies, Len *(Llanelli)* F.S. 1954; I. 1955.

Davies, Leslie *(Swansea)* S.I. 1939.

Davies, Lyn *(Bridgend)* E.S.I.1966.

Davies, Mark *(Swansea)* A. 1981; I. 1982; FJ. 1985.

Davies, M.J. *(Oxford)* S.I. 1939.

Davies, N. Glyn *(London Welsh)* E. 1955.

Davies, Nigel *(Llanelli)* NZ. (2nd). WS. 1988; S.I. 1989; F. 1993; S.I.E.P.Sp.C.FJ.T*.WS.R.It. 1994; E.S.I.FJ. 1995; E.S.I.F.A. (1and 2).B.F. 1996; E. 1997.

Davies, P.T. *(Llanelli)* E.FJ. 1985; E.S.I.F.FJ.T. WS. 1986; F.E.It.T.C.NZ. 1987; WS.R. 1988; S.I.F.E.NZ. 1989; F.E.S. 1990; I.F.A.F.WS.AR.A. 1991; F.Z. (1st) N. 1993; S.I.F.E.C.FJ*.WS.R.It. 1994; F.I. 1995.

Davies, R.H. *(Oxford Univ. and London Welsh)* S.I.F. 1957; A. 1958; E.S. 1962.

Davies, Stan *(Treherbert)* I. 1923.

Davies, Stuart *(Swansea)* I.F.E.S.A. 1992; E.S.I.Z. (1st* and 2nd) N.J. 1993; FJ.I. 1995; I*.F. 1998.

Davies, Terry *(Swansea and Llanelli)* E.S.I.F. 1953; E.S.I.F. 1957; A.E.S.F. 1958; E.S.I.F. 1959; E.SA. 1960; E.S.F. 1961.

Davies, T.G.R. *(Cardiff, Cambridge Univ. and London Welsh)* A. 1966; S.I.F.E. 1967; E.S. 1968; S.I.F.NZ.(1 and 2)A. 1969; E.S.I.F. 1971; E.S.F. 1972; NZ. 1972; E.S.I.F.A. 1973; S.F.E. 1974; F.E.S.I. 1975; E.S.I.F. 1976; I.F.E.S. 1977; E.I.S.A.(1 and 2) 1978.

Davies, T.M. *(London Welsh and Swansea)* S.I.F. E.NZ.(1 and 2)A. 1969; SA.S.E.I.F. 1970; E.S.I.F. 1971; E.S.F. 1972; NZ. 1972; E.S.I.F.A. 1973; S.I.F.E. 1974; F.E.S.I. 1975; A. 1975; E.S.I.F. 1976.

Davies, W. *(Cardiff)* S. 96.

Davies, W. *(Swansea)* SA. 1931; E.S.I. 1932.

Davies, W.G. *(Cardiff and Oxford Univ.)* A.(1 and 2)NZ. 1978; S.I.F.E. 1979; F.E.S.NZ. 1980; E.S.A. 1981; I.F.E.S. 1982; S.I.F. 1985.

Davies, W.T.H. *(Swansea)* I. 1936; E.I. 1937; E.S.I. 1939.

Davies, Willie *(Aberavon)* E.S.I. 1912.

Davis, C. *(Newbridge)* A.(2) 1978; E.S. 1981.

Davis, Mark *(Newport)* A. 1991.

Davis, W.E.N. *(Cardiff)* E.S.I. 1939.

Dawes, S.J. *(London Welsh)* I.F.SA. 1964; E.S.I.F. 1965; A. 1966; I.F. 1968; E.NZ.(2)A. 1969; SA.S.E.I.F. 1970; E.S.I.F. 1971.

Day, H. *(Newport)* I. 92; E.S. 93; S.I. 94.

Day, H.C. *(Newport)* S.I.F. 1930; E.S. 1931.

Day, T. *(Swansea)* E.S.I.F.SA. 1931; E.S.I. 1932; S.I. 1934; E.S.I. 1935.

Deacon, T. *(Swansea)* I. 91; E.S.I. 92.

Delahay, W. *(Bridgend and Cardiff)* E.S.I.F. 1922; E.S.I.F. 1923; NZ. 1924; E.S.F.I. 1926; E.S.I.F. 1926; S. 1927.

Delaney, L. *(Llanelli)* I.F.E. 1989; E. 1990; F.WS.AR.A. 1991; I.F.E. 1992.

Devereux, D. *(Neath)* A.E.S. 1958.

Devereux, J. *(S. Glam Inst. and Bridgend)* E.S.I.F.FJ.T.WS. 1986; F.E.S.I.I.C*.E.NZ.A. 1987; NZ.(1 and 2) R. 1988; S.I. 1989.

Diplock, R. *(Bridgend)* R. 1988.

Dobson, G. *(Cardiff)* S. 1900.

Dobson, T. *(Cardiff)* I.E. 98; E.S 99.

Donovan, A. *(Swansea)* A.(2) 1978; I*.A. 1981; E.S. 1982.

Donovan, R. *(S. Wales Constab.)* F*. 1983.

Douglas, M.H.J. *(Llanelli)* S.I.F. 1984.

Douglas, W.M. *(Cardiff)* E.S. 86, 87.

Dowell, W. *(Newport)* E.S.I. 1907; E.S.F.I. 1908.

Dyke, J.C.M. *(Penarth)* SA. 1906.

Dyke, L.M. *(Cardiff)* I. 1910; S.F.I. 1911.

Edmunds, A. *(Neath)* I.(R), B. 1990.

Edwards, A.B. *(London Welsh and Army)* E.S. 1955.

Edwards, B. *(Newport)* I. 1951.

Edwards, D. *(Glynneath)* E. 1921.

Edwards, G.O. *(Cardiff and Cardiff Training College)* F.E. 1967; NZ. 1967; E.S.I.F. 1968; S.I.F.E.NZ.(1 and 2)A. 1969; SA.S.E.I.F. 1970; E.S.I.F. 1971; E.S.F. 1972; NZ. 1972; E.S.I.F.A. 1973; S.I.F.E. 1974; F.E.S.I. 1975; A. 1975; E.S.I.F. 1976; I.F.E.S. 1977; E.S.I.F. 1978.

Eidman, I. *(Cardiff)* S.R. 1983; I.F.E.A. 1984; S.I.FJ. 1985; E.S.I.F. 1986.

Elliott, J.E. *(Cardiff)* I. 94; I.E. 98.

Elsey, W.J. *(Cardiff)* E. 95.

Emyr, A. *(Swansea and Cardiff)* E.NZ. 1989; F.E.S.I.N.(1, 2) 1990; F.F.WS.AR.A. 1991.

Evans, A.C. *(Pontypool)* E.I.F. 1924.

Evans, Ben *(Swansea)* SA.* 1998; F.It.E.AR (1+2) C. 1999.

Evans, Bryn *(Llanelli)* E.S. 1933; E.S.I. 1936; E. 1937.

Evans, Bryn *(Swansea)* S. 1933.

Evans, Bryn S. *(Llanelli)* E. 1920; E.S.I. 1922.

Evans, C. *(Pontypool)* E. 1960.

Evans, David W. *(Cardiff and Treorchy)* F.E.NZ. 1989; F.E.S.I.B. 1990; A.F*.A*. 1991; J*. 1995.

Evans, D. *(Penygraig)* S.I. 96; E. 97; E. 98.

Evans, D.B. *(Swansea)* E. 1926.

Evans, D.D. *(Cheshire and Cardiff Univ.)* E. 1934.

Evans, D.P. *(Llanelli and Oxford Univ.)* SA. 1960.

Evans, D.W. *(Cardiff and Oxford Univ.)* S.I. 89; E.I. 90; E. 91.

Evans, Emrys *(Llanelli)* E. 1937; S.I, 1939.

Evans, Frank *(Llanelli)* S. 1921.

Evans, Garan *(Llanelli)* SA. 1998.

Evans, G. *(Cardiff)* E.S.F.I.A. 1947; E.S.F.I. 1948; E.S.I. 1949.

Evans, G. *(Newport)* F*. 1977; F.A*.(2) 1978.

Evans, Gwyn *(Maesteg)* S*.I.F.A. 1981; I.F.E.S. 1982; F.R. 1983.

Men who 'Marched' for Wales

Upsetting the opposition is all part of the elaborate fabric of the game. But rubbing the referee up the wrong way by illegal use of physical force has its hazards. Then the Order of the Early Bath sends culprits on their way. It began for Wales in 1977, when Geoff Wheel and Willie Duggan exchanged heated disagreement and Norman Sanson decided enough was enough and they followed the dismissive finger to the dressing room in the Wales v Ireland match at Cardiff. Doubtless, both were peeved at the referee intervening in a private brouhaha.

More open to public discernment was Paul Ringer's high challenge on England fly half John Horton at Twickenham after an explosive start to the 1986 match. Referee David Burnett was suitably outraged after he had issued an earlier warning and this left Wales with 14 men – and then they nearly snatched victory.

Others to tread the path to first use of the soap were Huw Richards v New Zealand at Rotorua in the 1987 World Cup; Kevin Moseley against France in Cardiff in 1990; John D Davies for a stray toe-cap against England in Cardiff in 1995; and hooker Garin Jenkins for a bit of the old nonsense in South Africa in 1995.

Paul Ringer

There had only been one sending off in major international matches from the first game in 1871 until 1967. That was when Welsh referee Albert Freethy gave the march to New Zealand's Cyril Brownlie at Twickenham in 1925.

Evans, Ieuan *(Llanelli, Bath)* F.E.S.I.I.C.E.NZ.A. 1987; E.S.I.F.A.F.NZ.(1 and 2) 1988; I.F.E. 1989; E.S.I.F.A.F.WS.AR.A. 1991; I.F.E.S.A. 1992; E.S.I.F.J.C. 1993; S.I.E.P.Sp.C.FJ.T.WS.R. 1994; E.S.I.J.NZ.I.SA.FJ. 1995; It.E.S.I.F.A.(1 and 2).B.F.A.SA. 1996; USA.S.I.F. 1997; It. 1998.

Evans, Iowerth *(London Welsh)* S.I. 1934.

Evans, Islwyn *(Swansea)* E.S.I.F. 1922.

Evans, J. *(Llanelli)* S.I. 96; E. 97.

Evans, J. *(Blaina)* E. 1904.

Evans, J. *(Pontypool)* E.S.I. 1907.

Evans, J.D. *(Cardiff)* I.F. 1958.

Evans, J. Elwyn *(Llanelli)* S. 1924.

Evans, J.R. *(Newport)* E. 1934.

Evans, Luc *(Llanelli)* F*. 1991.

Evans, O.J. *(Cardiff)* E.S. 87; S.I. 88.

Evans, Peter *(Llanelli)* E.F. 1951.

Evans, R. *(Bridgend)* S.I.F. 1963.

Evans, R. *(Cardiff)* S. 89.

Evans, Ricky *(Llanelli)* E.S.I.F. 1993; S.I.F.E.P. Sp.C.FJ.WS.R.It.SA. 1994; F.NZ.I*. 1995.

Evans, R.T. *(Newport)* F.I. 1947; E.S.I.F. 1950, 1951.

Evans, S. *(Neath and Swansea)* F.E. 1985; FJ.T.WS. 1986; F.E.I.T. 1987.

Evans, T.G. *(London Welsh)* SA.S.E.I. 1970; E.S.F. 1972.

Evans, T.P. *(Swansea)* F.E.S.I. 1975. A. 1975; E.S.I.F. 1976; I. 1977.

Evans, Tom *(Llanelli)* I. 1906; E.S.I. 1907; I.A. 1908; E.S.F.I. 1909; F.E.S.I. 1910; E.S.F.I. 1911.

Evans, Tom *(Swansea)* I. 1924.

Evans, V. *(Neath)* I.F.S. 1954.

Evans, W.F. *(Rhymney)* I. 82; S. 83.

Evans, W.G. *(Brynmawr)* I. 1911.

Evans, W.H. *(Llwynypia)* E.S.F.I. 1914.

Evans, W.J. *(Pontypool)* S. 1947.

Evans, W.R. *(Cardiff, Bridgend)* A.E.S.I.F. 1958; SA. 1960; E.S.I.F. 1961; E.S. 1962; I. 1962.

Evans, W. Rice *(Swansea)* S. 90; E.S. 91.

Evans, Wynne *(Llanelll)* A. 1958.

Everson, W. *(Newport)* S. 1926.

Faulkner, A.G. *(Pontypool)* F.E.S.I. 1975; A. 1975; E.S.I.F. 1976; E.S.I.F.A.(1 and 2)NZ. 1978; S.I.F. 1979.

Faull, J. *(Swansea)* I.F. 1957; A.E.S.I.F. 1958; E.S.I. 1959; E.F. 1960.

Fauvel, T. *(Aberavon)* *NZ.(1) 1988.

Fear, A. *(Newport)* S.I. 1934, 1935.

Fender, N. *(Cardiff)* I.F. 1930; E.S.F.I. 1931.

Fenwick, S.P. *(Bridgend)* F.E.S. 1975; A. 1975; E.S.I.F. 1976; I.F.E.S. 1977; E.S.I.F.A.(1 and 2), NZ. 1978; S.I.F.E. 1979; F.E.S.I.NZ. 1980; E.S. 1981.

Finch, E. *(Llanelli)* F.NZ. 1924; F.I. 1925; F. 1926; NSW. 1927; I. 1928.

Finlayson, A.J. *(Cardiff)* I.F.E. 1974.

Fitzgerald, D. *(Cardiff)* S.I. 94.

Ford, F.J.V. *(Welch Regt. and Newport)* E. 1939.

Ford, I *(Newport)* E.S. 1959.

Ford, S. *(Cardiff)* I.N.(1,2), B. 1990; E.S.I.A. 1991.

Forward, A. *(Pontypool and Mon. Police)* S. 1951; SA. 1951; E.S.I.F. 1952.

Fowler, I. *(Llanelli)* NZ. 1919.

Francis, G. *(Llanelli and Oxford Univ)* NZ. 1919; S. 1924.

Francis, P.W. *(Maesteg)* S. 1987.

Funnell, John *(Ebbw Vale)* Z*.SA. 1998.

Gabe, R.T. *(Llanelli and Cardiff)* I. 1901; E.S.I. 1902, 1903, 1904, 1905; NZ. 1905; E.I. 1906; SA. 1906; E.S.I. 1907; E.S.F.I. 1908.

Gale, N.R. *(Swansea and Llanelli)* I. 1960; E.S.I.NZ. 1963; E.S.I.F.SA. 1964; E.S.I.F. 1965; E.S.I.F.A. 1966; E. 1967; NZ. 1967; E. 1968; NZ.(1* and 2)A. 1969.

Gallacher, I.S. *(Llanelli)* F. 1970.

Garrett, R.M. *(Penarth)* M. 88; S. 89; E.S.I. 90; S.I. 91; E. 92.

Geen, W.P. *(Newport)* SA. 1912; E.I. 1913.

George, E. *(Pontypridd & Cardiff)* S.I. 95; E. 96.

George, G.M. *(Newport)* E.S. 1991.

Gethin, Glyn *(Neath)* F. 1913.

Gibbs, Andrew *(Newbridge and Llanelli)* I.SA. 1995; A. 1996; USA (1 and 2).C. 1997.

Gibbs, I.S. *(Neath and Swansea)* E.S.I.F.A.F.WS. AR.A. 1991; I.F.E.S.A. 1992; E.S.I.F.J.C. 1993; It.A.SA. 1996; USA.S.I.F.T.NZ. 1997; It.E.S.SA.AR. 1998; S.I.F.It.E. C.F. 1999.

Gibbs, R.A. *(Cardiff)* S.I. 1906; E.S. 1907; E.S.F.I. 1908; F.E.S.I. 1910; E.S.F.I. 1911.

Giles, S.R. *(Aberavon)* R. 1983; FJ* 1985; C. 1987.

Girling, B.E. *(Cardiff)* E. 81.

Goldsworthy, S. *(Swansea)* I. 84; E.S. 85.

Gore, J. *(Blaina)* I.F.NZ. 1924; E. 1925.

Gore, W. *(Newbridge)* S.F.I. 1947.

Gough, Ian *(Newport and Pontypridd)* SA. 1998; S. 1999.

Gould, A.J. *(Newport)* E.S. 85, 86; E.S.I. 87; S. 88; I. 89; S.E.I. 90; E.S.I. 92, 93; E.S. 94; E.S.I. 95, 96; E. 97.

Gould, B. *(Newport)* I. 92; S.I. 93.

Gould, R. *(Newport)* I.E. 82; S. 83; E.S.I. 84; E.S. 85; E. 86; E.S. 87.

Graham, T.C. *(Newport)* I. 90; S.I. 91; E.S. 92; E.S.I. 93; E.S. 94, 95.

Gravell, R.W.R. *(Llanelli)* F.E.S.I.A. 1975; E.S.I.F. 1976; E.S.I.F.A.(1 and 2)NZ. 1978; S.I. 1979; I.F. 1981; F.E.S. 1982.

Gray, A.J. *(London Welsh)* E.S. 1968.

Greensglade, D. *(Newport)* S. 1962.

Greville, H. *(Llanelli)* A. 1947.

Griffin, Dr.A. *(Edinburgh Univ.)* S. 83.

Griffiths, C. *(Llanelli)* E*. 1979.

Griffiths, D. *(Llanelli)* M. 88; I. 89.

Griffiths, G. *(Llanelli)* I. 89.

Griffiths, Gareth *(Cardiff)* E.S.I.F. 1953; NZ. 1953; I.F.S. 1954; I.F. 1955; E.S. 1957.

Griffiths, J. *(Llanelli)* NZ.(2nd) 1988; S. 1989.

Griffiths, M. *(Bridgend, Cardiff and Pontypirdd)* WS.R. 1988; S.I.F.E.NZ. 1989; F.E.N.(1,2)B. 1990; I.F.F.WS.AR.A. 1991; I.F.E.S.A. 1992; Z.(1st and 2nd)N.J.C. 1993; F*.E.S.I.J.I. 1995; WS.SA. 1998.

Griffiths, V.M. *(Newport)* S.I.F. 1924.

Gronow, B. *(Bridgend)* F.E.S.I. 1910.

Gwilliam, J.A. *(Cambridge Univ., Edinburgh Wanderers and Gloucester)* A. 1947; I. 1948; E.S.I.F. 1949, 1950; E.S.I.SA. 1951; E.S.I.F. 1952; E.I.F. 1953; NZ. 1953; E. 1954.

Gwynn, D. *(Swansea)* E. 82; S. 87; E.I. 90; E.S. 91.

Gwynn, W.H. *(Swansea)* E.S.I. 84; E.S. 85.

Hadley, A.M. *(Cardiff)* R. 1983; S.I.F.E. 1984; F.E.FJ. 1985; E.S.I.F.FJ.T. 1986; S.*I.I.T.C.E.NZ.A.USA. 1987; E.S.I.F. 1988.

Hall, I. *(Aberavon)* NZ. 1967; SA.S.E. 1970; S. 1971; S.I.F. 1974.

Hall, M. *(Bridgend and Cardiff)* *NZ.(1) NZ.(2nd) WS.R. 1988; S.I.F.E.NZ. 1989; F.E.S. 1990; A.F.WS.AR.A. 1991; I.F.E.S.A. 1992; E.S.I. 1993; S.I.F.E.P.Sp.C.T.R.It.SA. 1994; F.S.I.J.NZ.I. 1995.

Hall, W. *(Bridgend)* WS. 1988.

Hancock, F.E. *(Cardiff)* I. 84; E.S. 85; S. 86.

Hannan, J. *(Newport)* M. 88; S.I. 89; S.E.I. 90; E. 91; E.S.I. 92, 93, 94, 95.

Harding, A.F. *(Cardiff and London Welsh)* E.S.I. 1902, 1903, 1904, 1905; NZ. 1905; E.S.I. 1906; SA. 1906; I. 1907; E.S. 1908.

Harding, G.F. *(Newport)* E. 81; I.E. 82; S. 83.

Harding, Rowe *(Swansea)* E.S.F.I. 1923; I.F.NZ. 1924; F.I. 1925; E.I.F. 1926; E.S.F.I. 1927; E. 1928.

Harding, Theo *(Newport)* M. 88; S.I. 89.

Harris, D.J.E. *(Pontypridd and Cardiff)* I.F. 1959; S.I.F. 1960; SA. 1960; E.S. 1961.

Harris, Tal. *(Aberavon)* NSW. 1927.

Hathway, G. *(Newport)* I.F. 1924.

Havard, Rev. W.T. *(Llanelli)* NZ. 1919.

Hawkins, F. *(Pontypridd)* I.F. 1912.

Hayward, Byron *(Ebbw Vale)* Z*.SA. 1998.

Hayward, D. *(Newbridge)* E.F. 1949; E.S.I.F. 1950; E.S.I.F. 1951; SA. 1951; E.S.I.F. 1952.

Hayward, D.J. *(Cardiff)* E. 1963; NZ. 1963; S.I.F.SA. 1964.

Hayward, G. *(Swansea)* S.F.I.A. 1908; E. 1909.

Hellings, R. *(Llwynypia)* E. 97; I.E. 98; S.I. 99; E.I. 1900; E.S. 1901.

Herrera, R. *(Cross Keys)* S.F.I. 1925; E.S.I.F. 1926; E. 1927.

Hiams, H. *(Swansea)* I.F. 1912.

Hickman, Arthur *(Neath)* E. 1930; S. 1933.

Hiddlestone, D. *(Neath)* E.S.I.F. 1922; NZ. 1924.

Hill, A.F. *(Cardiff)* S. 85; E.S. 86; S.I.M. 88; S. 89; S.I. 90; E.S.I. 93, 94.

Hill, Simon *(Cardiff)* Z.(1st and 2nd)N. 1993; I. *F.SA. 1994; F.SA. 1995; A.F*.It. 1996; E. 1997.

Hinam, S. *(Cardiff)* I. 1925; E.S.I.F. 1926.

Hinton, J.T. *(Cardiff)* I. 84.

Hirst, G.L. *(Newport)* S. 1912, 1913; E.S.F.I. 1914.

Hodder, W. *(Pontypool)* E.S.F. 1921.

Hodges, J.J. *(Newport)* E.S.I. 99, 1900; E.S. 1901; E.S.I. 1902, 1903; E.S. 1904; E.S.I. 1905; NZ. 1905; E.S.I. 1906.

Hodgson, G.T.R. *(Neath)* I. 1962; E.S.I.F. 1963; NZ. 1963; E.S.I.F.SA. 1966; S.I.F. 1966; I. 1967.

Hollingdale, B. *(Swansea)* SA. 1912; E. 1913.

Hollingdale, T. *(Neath)* NSW. 1927; E.S.I.F. 1928; E. 1930.

Holmes, T.D. *(Cardiff)* A.(2)NZ. 1978; S.I.F.E. 1979; F.E.S.I.NZ. 1980; A. 1981; I.F.E. 1982; E.S.I.F. 1983; E. 1984; S.I.F.E.FJ. 1985.

Hopkin, W.H. *(Newport)* S. 1937.

Hopkins, K. *(Cardiff and Swansea)* E. 1985; F.E.S.T.C.*USA. 1987.

NZ on Top on Try Count 60-12

Wales have scored just 12 tries in 18 full cap meetings with New Zealand, whereas the All Blacks have piled up 60, including 10 in the first Test at Christchurch in 1988 and eight in the second Test at Auckland. They also raised eight tries in humbling Wales 49-6 at Brisbane in the semi-final of the first World Cup in 1987.

The handful of Welsh try-getters were: Teddy Morgan (1905); Geoffrey Rees Jones (2) and Claude Davey (1935); Sid Judd and Ken Jones (1953); Keith Jarrett and Maurice Richards (1969); John C Bevan (1972); John Devereux (1987); Jonathan Davies (1988) and Nigel Walker (1997). Of these, only one was a forward – Cardiff's Sid Judd. He also scored a try to help Cardiff beat the Blacks in 1953 – a unique double for a forward, though Claude Davey also scored for Swansea in their victory over the 1935 New Zealanders.

Hopkins, Phil *(Swansea)* A. 1908; E.I. 1909; E. 1910.

Hopkins, R. *(Maesteg)* E*. 1970.

Hopkins, T. *(Swansea)* E.S.I.F. 1926.

Hopkins, W.J. *(Aberavon)* E.S. 1925.

Howarth, S.P. *(Sale and Newport)* SA.AR. 1998; S.I.F.It.E.AR (1+2), SA.C.F. 1999.

Howells, Bryn *(Llanelli)* E. 1934.

Howells, G. *(Llanelli)* E.S.I.F. 1957.

Howells, W.H. *(Swansea)* S.I. 88.

Howley, R. *(Bridgend and Cardiff)* E.S.I.F.A.(1 and 2).B.F.It.A.SA. 1996; USA.S.I.F.E.T.*NZ. 1997; It.E.S.I.F.Z.SA.AR. 1998; S.I.F.It.E.Ar (1+2).SA.C.F. 1999

Hughes, D. *(Newbridge)* NZ. 1967; NZ.(2)C.F. 1969; SA.S.E.I. 1970.

Hughes, Gomer *(Penarth)* E.S.I. 1934.

Hughes, H. *(Cardiff)* S. 87, 89.

Hughes, K. *(Cambridge Univ. and London Welsh)* I. 1970. A. 1973; S. 1974.

Hullin, W. *(Cardiff)* S. 1967.

Humphreys, J. *(Cardiff)* NZ.I.SA.FJ. 1995; It.E.S.I.F.A.(1 and 2).B.It.A.SA.1996; S.I.F.E.T*. NZ*. 1997; It*.E*.S*.I*.F*.SA.AR. 1998; S.AR (2*).SA*.C. 1999.

Hurrell, J. *(Newport)* F. 1959.

Hutchinson, F. *(Neath)* I. 94; S.I. 96.

Huxtable, R. *(Swansea)* F.I. 1920.

Huzzey, V. *(Cardiff)* E.I. 98; E.S.I. 99.

Hybart, A.J. *(Cardiff)* E. 87.

Ingledew, H.M. *(Cardiff)* I. 90; E.S. 91.

Isaacs, I. *(Cardiff)* E.S. 1933.

Jackson, T.H. *(Swansea)* E. 95.

James, B. *(Bridgend)* E. 1968.

James, C. *(Llanelli)* A.F. 1958.

James, Dafydd *(Bridgend, Pontypridd and Llanelli)* A*.It. A.SA. 1996; I.T*. 1997; F*.Z.SA.SA.AR. 1998; S.I.F. It.E.AR (1+2). SA.F. 1999.

James, D.R. *(Treorchy)* F.I. 1931.

James, David *(Swansea)* I. 91; S.I. 92; E. 99.

James, Evan *(Swansea)* S. 90, I. 91; S.I. 92; E. 99.

James, Maldwyn *(Cardiff)* A. 1947; E.S.F.I. 1948.

James, T.O. *(Aberavon)* I. 1935; S. 1937.

James, W.J. *(Aberavon)* E.S.I.F.R. 1983; S. 1984; S.I.F.E.FJ. 1985; E.S.I.F.FJ.T.WS. 1986; E.S.I. 1987.

James, W.P. *(Aberavon)* E.S. 1925.

Jarman, H. *(Newport)* E.S.I. 1910; E. 1911.

Jarrett, K.S. *(Newport)* E. 1967; E.S. 1968; S.I.F.E.NZ.(1 and 2)A. 1969.

Jarvis, Lee *(Cardiff)* R*. 1997.

Jeffery, J.J. *(Newport)* NZ. 1967.

Jenkins, Albert *(Llanelli)* E.S.F.I. 1920; S.F. 1921; F. 1922; E.S.F.I. 1923; NZ. 1924; S.I. 1928.

Jenkins, A.M. *(Swansea)* I. 95; E. 96.

Jenkins, D. *(Treorchy)* E.S.I.F. 1926.

Jenkins, D.R. *(Swansea)* NSW. 1927; E. 1929.

Jenkins, E. *(Newport)* S.I. 1910.

Jenkins, E.M. *(Aberavon)* S.F.I. 1927; NSW. 1927; E.S.I.F. 1928; F. 1929; E.S.I.F. 1930; E.S.F.I. 1931; SA. 1931; E.S.I. 1932.

Jenkins, G.R. *(Pontypool and Swansea)* F.WS.*AR.A. 1991; I.F.E.S.A. 1992; C. 1993; S.I.F.E.P. Sp.C.T.WS.R.It.SA. 1994; F.E.S.I.J. *SA. *FJ. 1995 *E. 1996; USA.USA.C. 1997; S.I.F.Z.SA*. 1998; I*.F.It.E.AR (1+2).SA.F. 1999.

Jenkins, J.C. *(London Welsh)* SA. 1906.

Jenkins, L. *(Aberavon)* S.F. 1923.

Jenkins, Leighton *(Newport)* I. 1954; E.S.I.F. 1956.

Jenkins, N.R. *(Pontypridd and Cardiff)* E.S.I.F. 1991; I.F.E.S. 1992; E.S.I.F.Z. (1st and 2nd) N.J.C. 1993; S.I.F.E.P.Sp.C.T.WS.R.It.SA. 1994; F.E.S.I.J. NZ.I.SA.FJ. 1995; F.A. (1 and 2).B.F.It.A*.SA. 1996; S.I.F.E.T.NZ. 1997; It.E.S.I.F.SA.AR. 1998; S.I.F.It.E.AR (1+2).SA. C.F. 1999.

Jenkins, T-Pryce *(London Welsh)* S.I. 88.

Jenkins, V.G. *(Oxford Univ. London Welsh and Bridgend)* E.I. 1933; S.I. 1934; E.S. 1935; NZ. 1935; E.S.I. 1936; E. 1937; E.S. 1938; E. 1939.

Jenkins, W. *(Cardiff)* I.F. 1912; S.I. 1913.

John, A. *(Llanelli)* I. 1925; E.S.I. 1928.

John, B. *(Llanelli and Cardiff)* A. 1966; S. 1967; NZ. 1967; E.S.I.F. 1968; S.I.F.E.NZ.(1 and 2)A. 1969; SA.SE.I. 1970; E.S.I.F. 1971; E.S.F. 1972.

John, D.E. *(Llanelli)* F.I. 1923; E.S.I. 1928.

John, G. *(St. Luke's College, Exeter)* E.F. 1954.

John, J.H. *(Swansea)* E.S.I.F. 1926; E.S.F.I. 1927.

John, Paul. *(Pontypridd)* T. 1994; B*. 1996; USA*.USA (1 and 2).C.R.T. 1997; Z*.SA. 1998.

John, R. *(Neath)* E.S.I.F. 1950, 1951; SA. 1951; E.S.I.F. 1952; E.S.I.F. 1953; NZ. 1953; E. 1954.

John, Spencer *(Llanelli and Cardiff)* S.I. 1995; E*.T.NZ*. 1997.

Johnson, T. *(Cardiff)* E.F.I. 1921; E.S.F. 1923; E.S.NZ. 1924; E.S.F. 1925.

Johnson, W.D. *(Swansea)* E. 1953.

Jones, A.H. *(Cardiff)* E.S. 1933.

Jones, B.J. *(Newport)* I.F. 1960.

Jones, J. Bedwellty *(Abertillery)* E.S.F.I. 1914.

Jones, Bert *(Llanelli)* S.I. 1934.

Jones, Bob *(Llwynypia)* I. 1901.

Jones, C.W. *(Bridgend)* E.S.F. 1920.

Jones, Cliff *(Cambridge Univ. and Cardiff)* E.S.I. 1934, 1935; NZ. 1935; E.S.I. 1936, 1938.

Jones, D. *(Neath)* NSW. 1927.

Jones, Dan *(Aberavon)* E. 97.

Jones, David *(Newport)* E.S.I.F. 1926; E. 1927.

Jones, David *(Swansea)* E.F.I. 1947; E.S.I.F. 1949.

Jones, David *(Treherbert)* E.S.I. 1902, 1903, 1905; NZ. 1905; E.S. 1906; SA. 1906.

Jones, Derwyn *(Cardiff)* SA. 1994; F.E.S.J.NZ.I. SA.FJ. 1995; It.E.S.I.F.A. (1and 2).B.It.A. 1996.

Jones, Desmond *(Llanelli)* E. 1948.

Jones, D.K. *(Llanelli, Cardiff)* E.S.F.I. 1962; E.F.NZ. 1963; E.S.SA. 1964; E.S.I.F. 1966.

Jones, D.N. Rocyn *(St. Mary's Hospital, Cambridge Univ. and Newport)* I. 1925.

Jones, D.P. *(Pontypool)* I. 1907.

Jones, Edgar. *(Llanelli)* F. 1930; E.S.I 1933; E. 1935.

Jones, Elvet *(Llanelli)* S. 1939.

Jones, Gareth *(Bridgend)* SA. 1995.

Jones, Gary *(Llanelli)* NZ.(2nd) 1988; F.E.NZ. 1989; F. 1990.

Jones, Graham *(Cardiff)* S. 1930; I. 1933.

Jones, Graham *(Ebbw Vale)* S.I.F. 1963.

Jones, G.R. Rees *(Oxford and London Welsh)* E.S. 1934; I. 1935; NZ. 1935; E. 1936.

Jones, Gwyn *(Llanelli and Cardiff)* It.E.S.I.F.A. 1996; USA*. S*. USA (1 and 2).R.T.NZ. 1997.

Jones, Harold *(Neath)* E.S. 1929.

Jones, Harry *(Penygraig)* S.I. 1902.

Jones, Howel *(Neath)* I. 1904.

Jones, Howie *(Swansea)* I.F. 1930.

Jones, I.C. *(London Welsh)* I. 1968.

Jones, Iowerth *(Llanelli)* NSW. 1927; E.S.I.F. 1928.

Jones, Ivor *(Llanelli)* E.S. 1924; S.F.I. 1927; NSW. 1927; E.S.F.I. 1928; E.S.F.I. 1929; E.S. 1930.

Jones, J. *(Aberavon)* E. 1901.

Jones, J.A *(Cardiff)* S. 83.

Jones, J.P 'Tuan' *(Pontypool)* S. 1913.

Jones, Jim *(Aberavon)* NZ. 1919; E.S. 1920; S.F.I. 1921.

Jones, Joe *(Swansea)* F. 1924.

Jones, J.P. *(Newport and Pontypool)* A. 1908; E.S.F.I. 1909; F.E. 1910; E.F. 1912; F.I. 1913, 1920; E. 1921.

Jones, J. Strand *(Llanelli and Oxford Univ.)* E.S.I. 1902; E.S. 1903.

Jones, K.D. *(Cardiff)* SA. 1960; E.S.I. 1961; E.F. 1962; E.S.I. 1963; NZ. 1963.

Jones, Ken *(Monmouth and L Welsh)* E. 1934.

Jones, Ken *(Newport)* E.S.F.I.A. 1947; E.S.F.I. 1948; E.S.I.F. 1949, 1950, 1951; SA. 1951; E.S.I.F. 1952, 1953; NZ. 1953; E.I.F.S. 1954; E.S.I.F. 1955, 1956; S. 1957.

Jones, Kingsley *(Ebbw Vale)* B.F.It.A. 1996; I*.E. 1997; S.I.F*.SA. 1998.

Jones, Lewis *(Devonport Services and Llanelli)* E.S.I. 1950; E.S. 1951; SA. 1951; E.I.F. 1952.

Jones, Lyn *(Llanelli)* Z.(1st and 2nd)N.J.C. 1993.

Jones, Mark *(Neath and Ebbw Vale)* S. 1987; NZ.*(2nd) 1988; S.I.E.F.NZ. 1989; F.E.S.I.N.(1,2)B. 1990; Z. 1998.

Jones, Marsden *(Cardiff and London Welsh)* E. 1921; NZ. 1924.

Jones, P. Baker *(Newport)* S. 1921.

Jones, Percy *(Newport and Pontypool)* SA. 1912; E.S.F. 1913; E.S.F.I. 1914.

Jones, R. *(London Welsh)* E. 1929.

Jones, R. *(Swansea)* I. 1901, E. 1902; E.S.I. 1904; E. 1905; F.I.A. 1908; E.S.F.I. 1909; F.E. 1910.

Jones, R.B. *(Cambridge)* E.S. 1933.

Jones, R.E. *(Coventry)* F.E. 1967; S.I.F. 1968.

Jones, Robert *(Northampton)* E.S.F. 1926.

Jones, R.N. *(Swansea)* E.S.I.F.FJ.T.WS. 1986; F.E.S.I.I.T.E.NZ.A.USA. 1987; E.S.I.F.NZ(1). WS.R. 1988; I.F.E.NZ. 1989; F.E.S.I. 1990; E.S.F.WS.AR.A. 1991; I.F.E.S.A. 1992; E.S.I. 1993; I.*P. 1994; F.E.S.I.NZ.I. 1995.

Jones, Roy *(Swansea)* NSW. 1927; F. 1928.

Jones, Stephen *(Llanelli)* SA*. 1998; C*. 1999.

Jones, S.T. *(Pontypool)* S.I.F.R. 1983; S. 1984; E.S.F.NZ.(1 and 2) 1988.

Jones, T.B. *(Newport)* I.E. 82; S. 83; S. 84; E.S 85.

Jones, Tom *(Newport)* E.S.I.F. 1922; E.S. 1924.

Jones, W. *(Cardiff)* I.E. 98.

Jones, W.I. *(Llanelli)* E.S.F.I. 1925.

Jones, W.J. *(Llanelli)* I. 1924.

Jones, W.K. *(Cardiff)* NZ. 1967; E.S.I.F. 1968.

It's a Fallacy

Robert Jones is not the most-capped scrum half for Wales. Though he won 54 caps compared to 53 by Gareth Edwards, one of Robert's appearances was as an emergency wing. He went on as replacement for centre Nigel Davies against Ireland in Dublin in 1994 and in the reshuffle (Rupert Moon continued at scrum half) Robert took up duties on the wing. So Robert Jones and Gareth Edwards share the distinction as Wales's most-capped scrum workers.

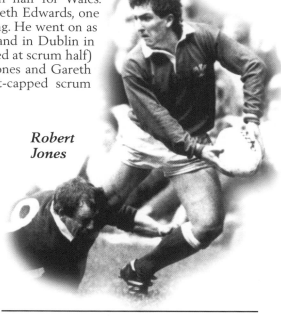

Robert Jones

Jones, Wyndham *(Mountain Ash)* I. 1905.

Jones-Davies, T.E. *(London Welsh)* E.I. 1930; E.S. 1931.

Jordan, H.M. *(Newport)* E.S. 85; S. 89.

Joseph, W. *(Swansea)* E.S.I. 1902, 1903; E.S. 1904; E.S.I.NZ. 1905; E.S.I. 1906; SA. 1906.

Jowett, F. *(Swansea)* E. 1903.

Judd, S. *(Cardiff)* E.S.I.F. 1953; NZ. 1953; E.F.S. 1954; E.S. 1955.

Judson, J.H. *(Llandovery Coll.)* E. 82; S. 83.

Kedzlie, Q.D. *(Cardiff)* S.I. 88.

Keen, L. *(Aberavon)* F.E.S.I. 1980.

Knight, P. *(Pontypridd)* N.(1,2),B.* 1990; E.S. 1991.

Knill, F.M.D. *(Cardiff)* F*. 1976.

Lamerton, A.E. *(Llanelli)* F.Z.(1st and 2nd)N.J. 1993.

Lane, S. *(Cardiff)* A. (1* and 2) 1978; I.* 1979; S.I. 1980.

Lang, J. *(Llanelli and Swansea)* F.I. 1931; S.I. 1934; E.S.I. 1935; NZ. 1935; E.S.I. 1936; E. 1937.

Law, V.J. *(Newport)* I. 1939.

Lawrence, S. *(Bridgend)* S.I. 1925; S.I.F. 1926; E. 1927.

Legge, W.G. *(Newport)* I. 1937, 1938.

Leleu, J. *(London Welsh and Swansea)* E.S. 1959; F. 1960; SA. 1960.

Lemon, A. *(Neath)* I. 1929; S.I.F. 1930; E.S.F.I.SA. 1931; E.S.I. 1932; I. 1933.

Lewis, A.J.L. *(Ebbw Vale)* F. 1970; E.I.F. 1971; E.S.F. 1972; E.S.I. 1973.

Lewis, Andrew *(Cardiff)* It.E.S.I.A*. 1996; It.E.S. I.F.SA.AR. 1998; F*.E*.AR (1*+2*).SA*.C*. 1999.

Lewis, A.R. *(Abertillery)* E.S.I.F. 1966; A. 1966; I. 1967.

Lewis, Bryn *(Swansea)* I. 1912, 1913.

Lewis, Clem *(Cardiff)* E. 1912; S.F.I. 1913; E.S.F.I. 1914; I. 1921; E.S. 1923.

Lewis, C.P. *(Llandovery)* I.E. 82; S. 83; E.S. 84.

Lewis, D.H. *(Cardiff)* E.S. 86.

Lewis, Emyr *(Llanelli and Cardiff)* I.F.A.F.WS.AR.A. 1991; I.F.S.A. 1992; E.S.I.F.Z. (1st and 2nd) N.J.C. 1993; S.I.F.E.P.Sp.FJ. WS.R.It.SA. 1994; E.S.I.J.I. 1995; It.E.S.I.F. 1996.

Lewis, E.J. *(Llandovery)* E. 81.

Lewis, Geraint *(Pontypridd)* SA*. 1998; It.*AR(2).C. 1999.

Lewis, G. Windsor *(Richmond)* E.S. 1960.

Lewis, Howell *(Swansea)* S.F.I. 1913; E. 1914.

Lewis, J. *(Llanelli)* I. 87.

Lewis, J.R. *(Cardiff and S. Glam. Inst.)* E.S.I.F. 1981; F.E.S. 1982.

Lewis, Mark *(Treorchy)* F. 1913.

Lewis, P.I. *(Llanelli)* A. 1984; S.I.F.E. 1985; E.S.I. 1986.

Lewis, Tom *(Cardiff)* E. 1926; E.S. 1927.

Lewis, W. *(Llanelli)* F. 1925.

Lewis, Windsor *(London Welsh, Maesteg and Cambridge)* I. 1926; E.F.I. 1927; NSW. 1927; F. 1928.

Llewellyn, David *(Ebbw Vale)* SA.* 1998; F.*It*. 1999.

Llewellyn, D.B. *(Newport and Llanelli)* SA.S.E.I.F. 1970; E.S.I.F. 1971; E.S.F. 1972; NZ. 1972.

Llewellyn, Gareth *(Neath and Harlequins)* NZ. 1989; E.S.I. 1990; E.S.A.* 1991; I.F.E.S.A. 1992; E.S.I.F.Z. (1st and 2nd) N.J.C. 1993; S.I.F.E.P.Sp.C.T. WS.R.It.SA. 1994; F.E.S.I.J.NZ.I. 1995; It.E.S.I.F.A. (1 and 2).B.F.It.A.SA. 1996; USA.S.I.F.E.USA (1 and 2).NZ. 1997; It. E. 1998; C*. 1999.

Llewellyn, Glyn *(Neath)* N. (1, 2),B. 1990; E.S.I.F.A.F. 1991.

Llewellyn, P.D. *(Swansea)* I.F.A. 1973; S.E. 1974.

Llewellyn, W. *(Llwynypia, London Welsh, Newport and Penygraig)* E.S.I. 99, 1900, 1901, 1902; I. 1903; E.S.I. 1904, 1905; NZ. 1905.

Loader, Christian *(Swansea)* SA.FJ. 1995; F.A. (1 and 2).B.F.It.A.SA. 1996; USA.S.I.F.E.USA. R.T.NZ. 1997.

Lloyd, D.J. *(Bridgend)* E.S.I.F. 1966; A. 1966; S.I.F.E. 1967; S.I.F. 1968; S.I.F.E.NZ.(1)A. 1969; F. 1970; E.S.F. 1972; E.S. 1973.

Lloyd, E. *(Llanelli)* S. 95.

Lloyd, G.L. *(Newport)* I. 96; S.I. 99; E.S. 1900; E.S. 1901; S.I. 1902; E.S.I. 1903.

Lloyd, P. *(Llanelli)* S.E. 90; E.I. 91.

Lloyd, R. *(Pontypool)* S.F.I. 1913; E.S.F.I. 1914.

Lloyd, T. *(Maesteg)* I.F. 1953.

Lloyd, T.C. *(Neath)* F. 1909; F.I. 1913; E.S.F.I. 1914.

Lockwood, T.W. *(Newport)* E.S.I. 87.

Long, E. *(Swansea)* E.S.I. 1936; E.S. 1937; S.I. 1939.

Lyne, H.S. *(Newport)* S. 83; E.S.I. 84; E. 85.

Maddock, H.T. *(London Welsh)* E.S.I. 1906; E.S. 1907; F. 1910.

Maddocks, K. *(Neath)* E. 1957.

Main, D.R. *(London Welsh)* E.S.I.F. 1959.

Mainwaring, H.J. *(Swansea)* F. 1961.

Mainwaring, W.T. *(Aberavon)* S.I.F.E. 1967; NZ. 1967; E. 1968.

Major, W. *(Maesteg)* F. 1949; S. 1950.

Male, B.O. *(Cross Keys Cardiff)* F. 1921; S. 1923; S.I. 1924; E.S.F.I. 1927; S.I.F. 1928.

Manfield, L. *(Mountain Ash and Cardiff)* S.I. 1939; A. 1947; E.S.F.I. 1948.

Mann, B.B. *(Cardiff)* E. 81.

Mantle, J. *(Loughborough College and Newport)* E.SA. 1964.

Margrave, F.L. *(Llanelli)* E.S. 84.

Martin, A.J. *(Aberavon)* A. 1973; S.I. 1974; F.E.S.I. 1975; A. 1975; E.S.I.F. 1976; I.F.E.S. 1977; E.S.I.F.A.(1 and 2)NZ. 1978; S.I.F.E. 1979; F.E.S.I.NZ. 1980; I.F. 1981.

Martin, W.J. *(Newport)* I.F. 1912; NZ. 1919.

Mason, J. *(Pontypridd)* NZ.* (2nd) 1988.

Mathias, R. *(Llanelli)* F. 1970.

Matthews, Rev. A.A. *(Lampeter)* S. 86.

Matthews, Chris *(Bridgend)* I. 1939.

Matthews, Jack *(Cardiff)* E.A. 1947; E.S.F. 1948; E.S.I.F. 1949, 1950, 1951.

May, P. *(Llanelli)* E.S.I.F.NZ.(1 and 2) 1988; WS. 1991.

McBryde, R. *(Swansea and Llanelli)* FJ. SA.* 1994; USA. 1997.

McCall, B.E.W. *(Welch Regt. and Newport)* E.S.I. 1936.

McCarley, A. *(Neath)* E.S.I. 1938.

McCutcheon, W. *(Swansea)* S. 91; E.S. 92; E.S.I. 93; E. 94.

McIntosh, Dale *(Pontypridd)* SA. 1996; E*. 1997.

Meek, N. *(Pontypool)* E.S.I. 1993.

Meredith, A. *(Devonport Services)* E.S.I. 1949.

Meredith, B.V. *(London Welsh and Newport)* I.F.S. 1954; E.S.I.F. 1955, 1956, 1957; A.E.S.I. 1958; E.S.I.F. 1959; E.S.F. 1960; SA. 1960; E.S.I. 1961; E.S.F. 1962; I. 1962.

Meredith, C.C. *(Neath)* S. 1953; NZ. 1953; E.I.F.S. 1954; E.S.I.F. 1955; E.I. 1956; E.S. 1957.

Meredith, J. *(Swansea)* S.I. 88; E.S. 90.

Merry, G.E. *(Pill Harriers)* I.F. 1912.

Michael, G. *(Swansea)* E.S.F. 1923.

Michaelson, R.C.B.*(Aberavon)* E. 1963.

Miller, F. *(Mountain Ash)* I. 96; E.S.I. 1900, 1901.

Mills, F. *(Swansea and Cardiff)* E.S.I. 92, 93, 94, 95; E. 96.

Moon, Rupert *(Llanelli)* F.Z. (1st and 2nd) N.J.C. 1993; S.I.F.E.Sp.C.FJ.WS.R.It.SA. 1994; E*. 1995.

Moore, Andrew *(Swansea)* *SA. FJ. 1995; S.I.F. Z.SA. 1998; C. 1999.

Moore, Andy *(Cardiff)* J.SA.FJ. 1995; It. 1996.

Moore, Steve *(Swansea and Moseley)* C*.R.T. 1997.

Moore, W.J. *(Bridgend)* I. 1933.

Morgan, C.H. *(Llanelli)* I.F. 1957.

Morgan, C.I *(Cardiff and Bective Rangers)* I.F. 1951; SA. 1951; E.S.I. 1952; S.I.F. 1953; NZ. 1953; E.I.S. 1954; E.S.I.F. 1955, 1956, 1957, 1958.

Morgan, D. *(Llanelli)* I. 95; E. 96.

Morgan, D. *(Swansea)* S. 85, E.S. 86; E.S.I. 87; I. 89.

Morgan, D.R. *(Llanelli)* E.S.F.I. 1962; E.S.I.F. 1963; NZ. 1963.

Morgan, E. *(Llanelli)* I. 1920; E.S.F. 1921.

Morgan, E. *(London Welsh)* E.S.I. 1902; I. 1903; E.S.I 1904, 1905; NZ. 1905; E.S.I.SA. 1906; F. 1908.

Morgan, E. *(Swansea)* E.S.I. 1938; E. 1939.

Morgan, Edgar *(Swansea)* E.S.F.I. 1914.

Morgan, F.L *(Llanelli)* E.S.I. 1938; E. 1939.

Morgan, H.J. *(Abertillery)* E.S.I.F. 1958; I.F. 1959; E. 1960; E.S.I.F. 1961; E.S.F.I. 1962; S.I.F. 1963; E.S.I.F. 1965; E.S.I.F. 1966; A. 1966.

Morgan, H.P. *(Newport)* E.S.I.F. 1956.

Morgan, Ivor *(Swansea)* A. 1908; E.S.F.I. 1909; F.E.S.I. 1910; E.F.I. 1911; S. 1912.

Morgan, J. *(Llanelli)* SA. 1912; E. 1913.

Morgan, Kevin *(Pontypridd)* USA (1 and 2).C.R. NZ. 1997; S.I.F. 1998.

Morgan, N. *(Newport)* S.I.F. 1960.

Morgan, P. *(Aberavon)* E.S.F. 1961.

Morgan, P. *(Llanelli)* S.*I.NZ.* 1980; I. 1981.

Morgan, R. *(Newport)* S. 1984.

Morgan, T. *(Llanelli)* I. 89.

Morgan, W. Guy *(Swansea and Guy's Hospital)* F.I. 1927; E.S.F.I. 1929; I.F. 1930.

Morgan, W.L. *(Cardiff)* S. 1910.

Moriarty, P. *(Swansea)* I.F.FJ.T.WS. 1986; F.E.S. I.I.T.C.E.NZ.A.USA. 1987; E.S.I.F.NZ(1). 1988.

Moriarty, R.D. *(Swansea)* A. 1981; I.F.E.S. 1982; E. 1983; S.I.F.E. 1984; S.I.F. 1985; FJ.T.WS. 1986; I.T.C.*E.NZ.A. 1987.

Morley, J.C. *(Newport)* E.S.F.I. 1929; E.I. 1930; E.S.F.I.SA. 1931; E.S.I. 1932.

Morris, Darren *(Neath, Swansea)* Z.SA*.SA*. 1998; S.I.It*. 1999.

Morris, G.L. *(Swansea)* I.E. 82; S. 83; E.S. 84.

Morris, H. *(Cardiff)* F. 1951; I.F. 1955.

Morris, Ivor *(Swansea)* E.S. 1924.

Morris, M. *(South Wales Police and Neath)* S.I.F. 1985; I.N.(1,2)B. 1990; I.F.WS. 1991; E. 1992.

Morris, R.R. *(Swansea and Bristol)* S. 1933, 1937.

Morris, S. *(Cross Keys)* E.S.F.I. 1920; E.S.I.F. 1922; E.S.F.I. 1923; E.S.F.NZ. 1924; E.S.F. 1925.

Morris, W. *(Abertillery)* NZ. 1919; F. 1920; I. 1921.

Morris, W.D. *(Neath)* F.E. 1967; E.S.I.F. 1968; S.I.F.E.NZ.(1 and 2)A. 1969; SA.S.E.I.F. 1970; E.S.I.F. 1971; E.S.F. 1972; NZ. 1972; E.S.I.A. 1973; S.I.F.E. 1974.

Morris, W.J. *(Newport)* S. 1965; F. 1966.

Morris, W.J. *(Pontypool)* S.I. 1963.

Morris, William *(Llanelli)* S.I. 96; E. 97.

Moseley, K. *(Pontypool and Newport)* NZ.(2nd). R. 1988; S.I. 1989; F. 1990; F.WS.AR.A. 1991.

Murphy, C. *(Cross Keys)* E.S.I. 1935.

Mustoe, L. *(Cardiff)* FJ. 1995; A. (1* and 2) 1996; USA (1 and 2).C.R*. 1997; E*.I*.F*. 1998.

Nash, D. *(Ebbw Vale)* SA. 1960; E.S.I.F. 1961; F. 1962.

Newman, C.H. *(Newport)* E. 81; I.E. 82; S. 83; E.S. 84, 85; E. 86, 87.

Nicholas, D. *(Llanelli)* E.S.I.F. 1981.

Nicholas, T.J. *(Cardiff)* NZ. 1919.

Nicholl, C.B. *(Llanelli)* I. 91; E.S.I. 92, 93; E.S. 94; E.S.I. 95, 96.

Nicholl, D.W. *(Llanelli)* I. 94.

Nicholls, E.G. *(Cardiff and Newport)* S.I. 96; E. 97; E.I. 98; E.S.I. 99; S.I. 1900; E.S.I. 1901, 1902; I. 1903; E. 1904; I.NZ. 1905; E.S.I.SA. 1906.

Nicholls, F.E. *(Cardiff Harlequins)* I. 92.

Nicholls, H. *(Cardiff)* I. 1958.

Nicholls, S.H. *(Cardiff)* M. 88; S.I. 89; S. 91.

Norris, H. *(Cardiff)* F. 1963; F. 1966.

Norster, R.L. *(Cardiff)* S. 1982; E.S.I.F. 1983; S.I.F.E.A. 1984; S.I.F.E.FJ. 1985; FJ.T.WS. 1986; F.E.S.I.I.C.E.USA. 1987; E.S.I.F.NZ(1) WS. 1988; F.E. 1989.

Norton, W.B. *(Cardiff)* I.F. 82; S. 83; E.S.I. 84.

O'Connor, A. *(Aberavon and Oxford Univ.)* SA. 1960; E.S. 1961; F.I. 1962.

O'Connor, R. *(Aberavon)* E. 1957.

O'Neil, W. *(Cardiff)* S.I. 1904; E.S.I. 1905; E.I. 1907; E.S.F.I. 1908.

O'Shea, J.P. *(Cardiff)* S.I. 1967; S.I.F. 1968.

Oliver, G. *(Pontypool)* E.S.F.I. 1920.

Osborne, W.T. *(Mountain Ash)* E.S.I. 1902, 1903.

Ould, W.J. *(Cardiff)* E.S. 1924.

Owen, Albert *(Swansea)* E. 1924.

Owen, G. *(Newport)* I.F. 1955; E.S.I.F. 1956.

Owen, R.M. *(Swansea)* I. 1901; E.S.I. 1902, 1903, 1904, 1905; NZ. 1905; E.S.I 1906; SA. 1906; E.S. 1907; F.I.A. 1908; E.S.F.I. 1909; F.E. 1910; E.S.F.I. 1911; E.S. 1912.

Packer, H. *(Newport)* E. 91; S.I. 95; E.S.I. 96; E. 97.

Palmer, Frank *(Swansea)* E.S.I. 1922.

Parfitt, F.C. *(Newport)* E.S.I. 93, 94; S. 95; S.I. 96.

Parfitt, S. *(Swansea)* N. 1*, B. 1990.

Parker, D. *(Swansea)* I.F.NZ. 1924; E.S.F.I. 1925; F.I. 1929; E. 1930.

Parker, T. *(Swansea)* NZ. 1919; E.S.I. 1920; E.S.F.I. 1921; E.S.I. 1922; E.S.F. 1923.

Parker, W. *(Swansea)* E.S. 99.

Parsons, G. *(Newport)* E. 1947.

Pascoe, D. *(Bridgend)* F.I. 1923.

Pask, A. *(Abertillery)* F. 1961; E.S.F.I. 1962; E.S.I.F. 1963; NZ. 1963; E.S.I.F.SA. 1964; E.S.I.F. 1965, 1966; A. 1966; S.I. 1967.

Payne, G.W. *(Army and Pontypridd)* E.S.I. 1960.

Payne, H. *(Swansea)* NZ. 1935.

Peacock, H. *(Newport)* S.F.I. 1929; S.I.F. 1930.

Peake, E. *(Chepstow)* E. 81.

Pearce, G. *(Bridgend)* I.F. 1981; I*. 1982.

Pearson, T.W. *(Cardiff and Newport)* E.I. 91; E.S. 92; S.I. 94; E.S.I. 95; E. 97; I.E. 98; E. 1903.

Pegge, E.V. *(Neath)* E. 91.

Perego, M. *(Llanelli)* S. 1990; F.Z.(1st)N*. 1993; S.I.F.E.Sp. 1994.

Perkins, S.J. *(Pontypool)* S.I.F.R. 1983; S.I.F.E.A. 1984; S.I.F.E.FJ. 1985; E.S.I.F. 1986.

Perrett, F. *(Neath)* SA. 1912; E.S.F.I. 1913.

Perrins, V.C. *(Newport)* SA.S. 1970.

Perry, W. *(Neath)* E. 1911.

Phillips, A. *(Cardiff)* E. 1979; F.E.S.I.NZ. 1980; E.S.I.F.A. 1981; I.F.E.S. 1982; C.E.A. 1987.

Phillips, B. *(Aberavon)* E.S.F.I. 1925; E. 1926.

Phillips, H. *(Newport)* E.S.F.I. 1927; NSW. 1927;E.S.I.F. 1928.

Phillips, H. *(Swansea)* F. 1952.

Phillips, K. *(Neath)* F.I.T.NZ.USA. 1987; E.NZ(1) 1988; NZ. 1989; F.E.S.I.N.(1, 2)B. 1990; E.S.I.F.A. 1991.

Phillips, L.A. *(Newport)* E.S.I. 1900; S. 1901.

Phillips, Percy *(Newport)* E. 92; E.S.I. 93; E.S. 94.

WRU National Coaches

1967-68	David Nash
1968-74	Clive Rowlands
1974-80	John Dawes
1980-82	John Lloyd
1982-85	John Bevan
1985-88	Tony Gray
1988-90	John Ryan
1990-91	Ron Waldron
1991-95	Alan Davies
(1995 Alex Evans, caretaker)	
1995-98	Kevin Bowring
(1998 Dennis John, caretaker)	
1998-	Graham Henry

Phillips, R. *(Neath)* USA. 1987; E.S.I.F.NZ. (1 and 2).WS. 1988; S.I. 1989.

Phillips, W.D. *(Cardiff)* E. 81; I. 82; E.S.I. 84.

Pickering, D.F. *(Llanelli)* E.S.I.F.R. 1983; S.I.F.E.A. 1984; S.I.F.E.FJ. 1985; E.S.I.F.FJ. 1986; F.E.S. 1987.

Plummer, R.C.S. *(Newport)* S.I.F. 1912; SA. 1912; E. 1913.

Pook, T. *(Newport)* S. 95.

Powell, G. *(Ebbw Vale)* I.F. 1957.

Powell, J. *(Cardiff)* I. 1906.

Powell, J. *(Cardiff)* I. 1923.

Powell, R.W. *(Newport)* S.I. 88.

Powell, W.C. *(London Welsh)* S.I.F. 1926; E.F.I. 1927; S.I.F. 1928; E.S.F.I. 1929; S.I.F. 1930; E.S.F.I.SA. 1931; E.S.I. 1932, 1935.

Powell, W.J. *(Cardiff)* E.S.F.I. 1920.

Price, B. *(Newport)* I.F. 1961; E.S. 1962; E.S.F. 1963; NZ. 1963; E.S.I.F.SA. 1964; E.S.I.F. 1965, 1966; A. 1966; S.I.F.E. 1967; S.I.F.NZ.(1 and 2)A. 1969.

Price, G. *(Pontypool)* F.E.S.I.A. 1975; E.S.I.F. 1976; I.F.E.S. 1977; E.I.S.F.A.(1 and 2)NZ. 1978; S.I.F.E. 1979; F.E.S.I.NZ. 1980; E.S.I.F.A. 1981; I.F.E.S. 1982; E.I.F. 1983.

Price, M. *(Pontypool and R.A.F.)* E.S.I.F. 1959; E.S.I.F. 1960; E. 1962.

Price, R.E. *(Weston)* S.I. 1939.

Price, T.G. *(Hendy, London Welsh and Llanelli)* E.S.I.F. 1965; E.A. 1966; S.F. 1967.

Priday, A.J. *(Cardiff)* I. 1958; I. 1961.

Pritchard, Cecil *(Pontypool)* E.S.I.F. 1928; E.S.F.I. 1929.

Pritchard, Cliff *(Newport and Pontypool)* S.I. 1904; NZ. 1905; E.S. 1906.

Pritchard, C.M. *(Newport)* I. 1904; E.S.NZ. 1905; E.S.I.SA. 1906; E.S.I. 1907; E. 1908; F.E. 1910.

Proctor, W.T. *(Llanelli)* A. 1992; E.S.Z.(1st and 2nd) N.C. 1993; I.C.FJ.WS.R.It.SA. 1994; S.I.NZ.FJ. 1995; It.E.S.I.A.(1 and 2).B.F.It.A. 1996; E*.USA (1 and 2).C.R. 1997; E*.S.I.F.Z. 1998.

Prosser, D.R. *(Neath)* S.I. 1935.

Prosser, Glyn *(Neath)* E.S.I. 1934; NZ. 1935.

Prosser, Greg *(Pontypridd)* NZ. 1995.

Prosser, J. *(Cardiff)* I. 1921.

Prosser, R. *(Pontypool)* S.F. 1956; E.S.I.F. 1957; A.E.S.I.F. 1958; E.S.I.F. 1959, 1960; SA. 1960; I.F. 1961.

Prothero, G.J. *(Bridgend)* S.I.F. 1964; E.S.I.F. 1965; E.S.I.F. 1966.

Pugh, C. *(Maesteg)* E.S.I.F.NZ. 1924; E.S. 1925.

Pugh, J. *(Neath)* USA. 1987; *S. 1988; S. 1990.

Pugh, Phil *(Neath)* NZ. 1989.

Pugsley, J. *(Cardiff)* E.S.I. 1910; E.S.I.F. 1911.

Pullman, J. *(Neath)* F. 1910.

Purdon, F. *(Newport)* E. 81; I.E. 82; S. 83.

Quinnell, Craig *(Llanelli, Richmond and Cardiff)* FJ. 1995;A*. 1996; USA*.S*.I*.E*. 1997; SA.AR. 1998; I.F.It.E.AR (1+2).SA.C.F. 1999.

Quinnell, D.L. *(Llanelli)* F.* 1972; NZ. 1972; E. S.A. 1973; S.F. 1974; E.* 1975; *I.F.E.S. 1977; E.S.I.F.A.(1)NZ. 1978; S.I.F.E. 1979; NZ. 1980.

Quinnell, Scott *(Llanelli and Richmond)* C. 1993; S.I.F.E.P.Sp.C.WS. 1994; USA.S.I.F.E. 1997; It.E.S*.Z. SA.AR. 1998; S.I.F.It.E.AR(1+2).SA.C.F. 1999.

Radford, W. *(Newport)* I. 1923.

Ralph, A.R. *(Newport)* F.I.S.A. 1931; E.S.I. 1932.

Ramsey, S.H. *(Treorchy)* E. 96; E. 1904.

Randell, R. *(Aberavon)* I.F. 1924.

Raybould, W.H. *(London Welsh, and Newport)* S.I.F.E. 1967; NZ. 1967; I.F. 1968; SA.E.I.F.* 1970.

Rayer, M.A. *(Cardiff)* WS.*AR.A.* 1991; E.*A. 1992; E.S.I.Z.(1st)N.J.* 1993; S.*I.*F.E.P.C.FJ. WS.R.It. 1994.

Rees, A. *(Maesteg)* E.S.F. 1962.

Rees, A.M. *(London Welsh)* E. 1934; E.S.I. 1935; NZ. 1935; E.S.I. 1936, 1937; E.S. 1938.

Rees, Aeron. *(Maesteg)* NZ. 1919.

Rees, B.I. *(London Welsh)* S.I.F. 1967.

Rees, C.F.W. *(London Welsh)* I. 1974; A. 1975; NZ. 1978; F.A. 1981; I.F.E.S. 1982; E.S.I.F. 1983.

Rees, D. *(Swansea)* S.I.F. 1968.

Rees, Dan *(Swansea)* E. 1900; E.S. 1903, 1905.

Rees, E.B. *(Swansea)* NZ. 1919.

Rees, H. *(Cardiff)* S.I. 1937; E.S.I. 1938.

Rees, H.E. *(Neath)* S.I.F.E. 1979; F.E.S.I.NZ. 1980; E.S.I.F. 1983.

Rees, J. Conway- *(Llanelli)* S. 92; E. 93, 94.

Rees, J. Idwal *(Swansea and Cambridge Univ.)* E.S.I. 1934; S.NZ. 1935; E.S.I. 1936, 1937, 1938.

Rees, Joe *(Swansea)* E.S.F.I. 1920; E.S.I. 1921; E. 1922; E.F.I. 1923; E. 1924.

Rees, L. *(Cardiff)* I. 1933.

Rees, Peter *(Llanelli)* F.I. 1947.

Rees, P.M. *(Newport)* E.S.I. 1961; I. 1964.

Rees, Richard *(Swansea)* Z. 1998.

Rees, T. *(Newport)* S.I. 1935; NZ. 1935; E.S.I. 1936; E.S. 1937.

Rees, T.A. *(Llandovery)* E. 81.

Rees, T.E. *(London Welsh)* I.F. 1926; NSW. 1927; E. 1928.

Reeves, F. *(Cross Keys)* F.I. 1920; E. 1921.

Reynolds, A. *(Swansea)* N. (1, 2*) 1990; A.* 1992.

Rhapps, J. *(Penygraig)* E. 97.

Richards, B. *(Swansea)* F. 1960.

Richards, Cliff *(Pontypool)* E.S.I.F. 1922; I. 1924.

Richards, D.S. *(Swansea)* F.E. 1979; F.E.S.I.NZ. 1980; E.S.I.F. 1981; I.F. 1982; E.S.I.R.* 1983.

Richards, E.S. *(Swansea)* E. 85; S. 87.

Richards, Gwyn *(Cardiff)* S. 1927.

Richards, H. *(Neath)* T.* 1986; T.E.NZ. 1987.

Richards, Idris *(Cardiff)* E.S.F. 1925.

Richards, K. *(Bridgend)* SA. 1960; E.S.I.F. 1961.

Richards, M.C.R. *(Cardiff)* I.F. 1968; S.I.F.E.N.Z. (1 and 2)A. 1969.

Richards, Rees *(Aberavon)* S.F.I. 1913.

Richards, Rex *(Cross Keys)* F. 1956.

Richards, T.L. *(Maesteg)* I. 1923.

Richardson, S.J. *(Aberavon)* A.(2)* 1978; E. 1979.

Rickard, A. *(Cardiff)* F. 1924.

Ring, J. *(Aberavon)* E. 1921.

Ring, M.G. *(Cardiff and Pontypool)* E. 1983; A. 1984; S.I.F. 1985; I.I.T.A.USA. 1987; E.S.I.F.NZ. (1 and 2) 1988; NZ. 1989; F.E.S.I.N. (1, 2)B. 1990; E.S.I.F.F.WS.AR.A. 1991.

Ringer, P *(Ebbw Vale and Llanelli)* NZ. 1978; S.I.F.E. 1979; F.E.NZ. 1980.

Roberts, C. *(Neath)* I.F. 1958.

Roberts, D.E.A. *(London Welsh)* E. 1930.

Roberts, E. *(Llanelli)* E. 86; I. 87.

Roberts, E.J. *(Llanelli)* S.I. 88; I. 89.

Roberts, G. *(Cardiff)* F.*E. 1985; I.T.C.E.A. 1987.

Roberts, H.M. *(Cardiff)* SA. 1960; E.S.I.F. 1961; S.F. 1962; I. 1963.

Roberts, J. *(Cardiff and Cambridge Univ.)* E.S.F.I. 1927; NSW, 1927; E.S.I.F. 1928; E.S.F.I. 1929.

Roberts, M.G. *(London Welsh)* E.S.I.F. 1971; I.F. 1973; S. 1975; E. 1979.

Roberts, T. *(Risca and Newport)* S.F.I. 1921; E.S.I.F. 1922; E.S. 1923.

Roberts, Willie *(Cardiff and Oxford Univ.)* E. 1929.

Robins, J.D. *(Birkenhead Park)* E.S.I.F. 1950, 1951; E.I.F. 1953.

Robins, R. *(Pontypridd)* S. 1953; F.S. 1954; E.S.I.F. 1955; E.F. 1956; E.S.I.F. 1957.

Robinson, I.R. *(Cardiff)* F.E. 1974.

Robinson, M. *(Swansea)* S.I.F.AR (1). 1999.

Roderick, W.B. *(Llanelli)* I. 84.

Rogers, Peter *(London Irish and Newport)* F.It.E. AR. (1+2).SA.C.F. 1999.

Rosser, M. *(Penarth)* S.F. 1924.

Rowland, C.F. *(Aberavon)* I. 1926.

Rowlands, D.C.T. *(Pontypool)* E.S.I.F. 1963; NZ. 1963; E.S.I.F.SA. 1964; E. S.I.F. 1965.

Rowlands, G. *(R.A.F. and Cardiff)* NZ. 1953; E.F. 1954; F. 1956.

Rowlands, J. *(Lampeter)* E. 85.

Rowlands, K.A. *(Cardiff)* F.I. 1962; I. 1963; I.F. 1965.

Rowles, G.R. *(Penarth)* E. 92.

Rowley, Mark *(Pontypridd)* SA. 1996; USA,S.I.F. R. 1997.

Roy, Stuart *(Cardiff)* J.* 1995.

Russell, S. *(London Welsh)* USA. 1987.

Samuel, D. *(Swansea)* I. 91, 93.

Samuel, F. *(Mountain Ash)* S.I.F. 1922.

Samuel, J. *(Swansea)* I. 91.

Scourfield, T. *(Torquay)* F. 1930.

Scrines, F. *(Swansea)* E.S. 99; I. 1901.

Shanklin, J.L. *(London Welsh)* F. 1970; NZ. 1972; I.F. 1973.

Shaw, G. *(Neath)* NZ. 1972; E.S.I.F.A. 1973; S.I.F.E. 1974; I.F. 1977.

Shaw, T. *(Newbridge)* R. 1983.

Shea, Jerry *(Newport)* NZ. 1919; E.S. 1920; E. 1921.

Shell, R.C. *(Aberavon)* A.* 1973.

Simpson, H.J. *(Cardiff)* E.S.I. 84.

Sinkinson, B. *(Neath)* F.It.E.AR (1+2).SA.F. 1999.

Skrimshire, R.T. *(Newport)* E.S.I. 99.

Skym, A. *(Llanelli and Cardiff)* E.S.I.F. 1928, 1930; E.S.F.I. 1931; SA. 1931; E.S.I. 1932, 1933; E. 1935.

Smith, J.S. *(Cardiff)* E.I. 84; E. 85.

Sparks, B. *(Neath)* I. 1954; E.F. 1955; E.S.I. 1956; S. 1957.

Spiller, W. *(Cardiff)* S.I. 1910; E.S.F.I. 1911; E.F. 1912; SA. 1912; E. 1913.

Squire, J. *(Newport and Pontypool)* I.F. 1977; E.S.I.F.A.(1)NZ. 1978; S.I.F.E. 1979; F.E.S.I.NZ. 1980; E.S.I.F.A. 1981; I.F.E. 1982; E.S.I.F. 1983.

Stadden, W.H. *(Cardiff)* I. 84; E.S. 86; I. 87; S.M. 88; S.E. 90.

Stephens, C.J. *(Llanelli)* I.F.E.A. 1992.

Stephens, Chris *(Bridgend)* E*. 1998.

Stephens, G. *(Neath)* E.S.I.F. 1912; SA. 1912; E.S.F.I. 1913; NZ. 1919.

Stephens, I. *(Bridgend)* E.S.I.F.A. 1981; I.F.E.S. 1982; I.F.E. 1984; A. 1984.

Stephens, Rev. J.G. *(Llanelli)* E.S.I.F. 1922.

Thomas, A. *(Newport)* NZ. 1963; E. 1964.

Thomas, Alun *(Cardiff and Llanelli)* E.S.I.F. 1952; S.I.F. 1953; E.I.F. 1954; S.I.F. 1955.

Thomas, Arwel *(Bristol and Swansea)* It.E.S.I. F*. SA. 1996; USA.S.I.F.USA.(1 and 2).C.R. NZ*. 1997; It.E.S*.Z.SA. 1998.

Thomas, B. *(Neath)* E.S.I.F. 1963; NZ. 1963; E.S.I.F.SA. 1964; E. 1965; E.S.I. 1966; NZ. 1967; S.I.F.E.NZ.(1 and 2) 1969.

Thomas, Bob *(Swansea)* E.S.I. 1900; E. 1901.

Thomas, C. *(Bridgend)* E.S. 1925.

Thomas, C.J. *(Newport)* I.M. 88; S.I. 89; S.E.I. 90; E.I. 91.

Thomas, D. *(Aberavon)* I. 1961.

Thomas, D. *(Swansea)* S.I. 1930; E.S.I. 1932; E.S. 1933; E. 1934; E.S.I. 1935.

Thomas, Denzil *(Llanelli)* I. 1954.

Thomas, Dick *(Mountain Ash)* SA. 1906; F.I. 1908; S. 1909.

Thomas, D.J. *(Swansea)* E. 1904; A. 1908; E.S.I. 1910; E.S.I.F. 1911; E. 1912.

Thomas, D.L. *(Neath)* E. 1937.

Thomas, E. *(Newport)* S.I. 1904; S.F.I. 1909; F. 1910.

OK Corral and Mr Richardson's Field 1881

Just after 2pm (kick-off early for TV!) on Wednesday, October 26, 1881 Wyatt Earp and his buddies set off along Fremont Street to the OK Corral in Tombstone, Arizona to walk into legend. In the same year, but eight months earlier, Wales had taken their step into history from the changing rooms on to Mr Richardson's Field at Blackheath for their shoot-out with England in the first Welsh international rugby match. Wales lost by seven goals, one dropped goal and six tries to nil. That would be 82 points by 1999 scoring values. Obviously, Wyatt Earp, Doc Holliday and Co would have appeared for England! Unless Graham Henry could find them Welsh ancestry! Wales had to wait until their seventh meeting before registering a first success.

Stephens, Rees *(Neath)* E.S.F.I. 1947; I. 1948; S.I.F. 1949; F. 1951; SA. 1951; E.S.I.F. 1952, 1953; NZ. 1953; E.I. 1954; E.S.I.F. 1955; S.I.F. 1956; E.S.I.F. 1957.

Stock, A. *(Newport)* F.NZ. 1924; E.S. 1926.

Stone, P. *(Llanelli)* F. 1949.

Summers, R.H.B. *(Haverfordwest)* E. 81.

Sutton, S. *(Pontypool)* F.E. 1982; F.E.S.I.C.NZ. *A. 1987.

Sweet-Escott, R.B. *(Cardiff)* S. 91; I. 94, 95.

Tamplin, W.E. *(Cardiff)* S.F.I.A. 1947; E.S.F. 1948.

Tanner, H. *(Swansea and Cardiff)* NZ. 1935; E.S.I. 1936, 1937, 1938, 1939; E.S.F.I. 1947, 1948; E.S.I.F. 1949.

Tarr, D.J. *(Swansea)* NZ. 1935.

Taylor, A.R. *(Cross Keys)* I. 1937, 1938; E. 1939.

Taylor, C.G. *(Blackheath and Ruabon)* E.S.I. 84; E.S. 85, 86; E.I. 87.

Taylor, Hemi *(Cardiff)* P.C.FJ.T.WS.*R.It.SA. 1994; E.S.J.NZ.I.SA.FJ. 1995; It.E.S.I.F.A.(1 and 2).It.A. 1996.

Taylor, J. *(London Welsh)* S.I.F.E. 1967; NZ. 1967; I.F. 1968; S.I.F.E.NZ.(1)A. 1969; F. 1970; E.S.I.F. 1971; E.S.F. 1972; NZ. 1972; E.S.I.F. 1973.

Taylor, Mark *(Pontypool and Swansea)* SA. 1994; F.E.SA.* 1995; Z.SA.SA.AR.1998; I.F.It.E.AR. (1+2). SA.F. 1999.

Thomas, G. *(Llanelli)* E.S.F.I. 1923.

Thomas, Gareth *(Bridgend and Cardiff)* J.NZ.I.SA.FJ. 1995; F.A.(1 and 2).B.F.It.A. 1996; USA.S.I.F.E.USA. (1 and 2).C.R.T.NZ. 1997; It.E.S.I.F.SA.AR. 1998; F*.It.E.AR(2).SA.F. 1999.

Thomas, Geo. *(Newport)* M. 88; I. 90; S. 91.

Thomas, H.W. *(Swansea)* SA. 1912; E. 1913.

Thomas, Harold *(Llanelli)* F. 1912.

Thomas, Harold *(Neath)* E.S.I. 1936, 1937.

Thomas, Ifor *(Bryncethin)* E. 1924.

Thomas, Justin *(Llanelli and Cardiff)* SA.FJ. 1995; It.E.S.I.F.B*. 1996; USA. 1997.

Thomas, L.C. *(Cardiff)* E.S. 85.

Thomas, L.I. *(Newport)* S. 94; E.I. 95.

Thomas, M.C. *(Newport and Devonport Services)* F. 1949; E.S.I.F. 1950, 1951; SA. 1951; E.S.I.F. 1952; E. 1953; E.S.I.F. 1956; E.S. 1957; E.S.I.F. 1958; I.F. 1959.

Thomas, Melbourne *(Bridgend and St. Bart's H.)* NZ. 1919; S.F.I. 1921; F. 1923; E. 1924.

Thomas, Nathan *(Bath)* SA*. 1996; USA (1* and 2). C*.R.T.NZ. 1997; Z.SA. 1998.

Thomas, R.C.C. *(Swansea and Cambridge Univ.)* F. 1949; I.F. 1952; S.I.F. 1953; NZ. 1953; E.I.F.S. 1954; S.I. 1955; E.S.I. 1956; E. 1957; A.E.S.I. 1958; E.S.I.F. 1959.

Thomas, Rees *(Pontypool)* F.I. 1909; S.F. 1911; E.S. 1912; SA. 1912; E. 1913.

Thomas, R.L. *(London Welsh and Llanelli)* S.I. 89; I. 90; E.S.I. 91; E. 92.

Thomas, S. *(Llanelli)* S.E. 90; I. 91.

Thomas, W.D. *(Llanelli)* A. 1966; S.I.F. 1968; E.NZ.(2)A. 1969; SA.S.E.I.F. 1970; E.S.I.F. 1971; E.S.F. 1972; NZ. 1972; E.S.I.F. 1973; E. 1974.

Thomas, W.H. *(Llanelli and London Welsh)* S. 85; E.S. 86, 87; S.I. 88; E.I. 90; S.I. 91.

Thomas, W.J. *(Cardiff)* F. 1961;F. 1963.

Thomas, W.T. *(Abertillery)* E. 1930.

Thomas, Watcyn *(Llanelli and Swansea)* E.S.F.I. 1927; E. 1929; E.S.SA. 1931; E.S.I. 1932, 1933.

Thompson, J. *(Cross Keys)* E. 1923.

Thorburn, P. *(Neath)* F.E.FJ. 1985; E.S.I.F. 1986; F.I.T.C.E.NZ.A.USA. 1987; S.I.F.WS.R(R). 1988; S.I.F.E.NZ. 1989; F.E.S.I.N.(1,2)B. 1990; E.S.I.F.A. 1991.

Titley, M.H. *(Bridgend)* R. 1983; S.I.F.E.A. 1984; S.I.FJ. 1985; F.FJ.T.WS. 1986; F.E. 1990.

Towers, W.H. *(Swansea)* I. 87; M. 88.

Travers, G. *(Pill Harriers and Newport)* E.S.I. 1903, 1905; NZ. 1905; E.S.I.SA. 1906; E.S.I. 1907; E.S.I.F.A. 1908; E.S.I. 1909; S.I.F. 1911.

Travers, W.H. *(Newport)* S.I. 1937; E.S.I. 1938, 1939; E.S.I.F. 1949.

Treharne, E. *(Pontypridd)* E. 81; E. 82.

Trew, W. *(Swansea)* E.S.I. 1900; E.S. 1901; S. 1903, 1905, 1906; E.S. 1907; E.S.I.A. 1908; E.S.F.I. 1909; F.E.S. 1910; E.S.F.I. 1911; S. 1912; S.F. 1913.

Trott, R.F. *(Cardiff)* E.S.F.I. 1948; E.S.I.F. 1949.

Truman, H. *(Llanelli)* E. 1934, 1935.

Trump, L. *(Newport)* E.S.I.F. 1912.

Turnbull, B.R. *(Cardiff and Cambridge Univ.)* I. 1925; E.S. 1927; E.F. 1928; S. 1930.

Turnbull, M.J. *(Cardiff)* E.I. 1933.

Turner, P. *(Newbridge)* I(R).F.E. 1989.

Uzzell, H. *(Newport)* E.S.I.F. 1912; S.F.I. 1913; E.S.F.I. 1914; E.S.F.I. 1920.

Uzzell, J. *(Newport)* NZ. 1963; E.S.I.F. 1965.

Vickery, W. *(Aberavon)* E.S.I.F. 1938; E. 1939.

Vile, T.H. *(Newport)* E.S. 1908; I. 1910; I.F. 1912; SA. 1912; E. 1913; S. 1921.

Vincent, J. *(Bangor)* I. 82.

Voyle, M. *(Newport and Llanelli)* A*.B. 1996; E.USA (1 and 2).C.T.NZ. 1997; It.E.S.I.F.AR*. 1998; S.*I.*It.*SA.* F*. 1999.

Wakeford, J. *(S.W.Police)* WS.R. 1988.

Waldron, R. *(Neath)* E.S.I.F. 1965.

Walker, N. *(Cardiff)* I.F.J. 1993; S.F.E.P.Sp. 1994; F.E. 1995; USA (1 and 2).C.R*.T.NZ. 1997; E. 1998.

Waller, P.D. *(Newport)* A. 1908; E.S.F.I. 1909; F. 1910.

Walne, Nick *(Richmond and Cardiff)* It.*E.C. 1999

Walters, D. *(Llanelli)* E. 1902.

Wanbon, R. *(Aberavon)* E. 1968.

Ward, W. *(Cross Keys)* S.I. 1934.

Warlow, J. *(Llanelli)* I. 1962.

Waters, D. *(Newport)* E.S.I.F. 1986.

Waters, K. *(Newbridge)* WS. 1991.

Watkins, D. *(Newport)* E.S.I.F. 1963; NZ. 1963; E.S.I.F.SA. 1964; E.S.I.F. 1965; 1966; I.F.E. 1967.

Watkins, E. *(Blaina)* S.I.F. 1926.

Watkins, E. *(Cardiff)* NZ. 1935; S.I. 1937; E.S.I. 1938; E.S. 1939.

Watkins, E. *(Neath)* E.S.I.F. 1924.

Watkins, H. *(Llanelli)* S.I. 1904; E.S.I. 1905; E. 1906.

Watkins, I. *(Ebbw Vale)* *E.S.I.F.NZ.(2nd).R. 1988; S.I.F.E. 1989.

Watkins, L. *(Llandaff)* E. 81.

Watkins, M.J. *(Newport)* I.F.E. 1984; A. 1984.

Watkins, S.J. *(Newport and Cardiff)* S.I.F. 1964; E.S.I.F. 1965; E.S.I.F.A. 1966; S.I.F.E. 1967; NZ. 1967; E.S. 1968; S.I.F.E.NZ.(1) 1969; E.I. 1970.

Watkins, W. *(Newport)* F. 1959.

Watt, W. *(Llanelli)* E. 1914.

Watts, D. *(Maesteg)* E.S.F.I. 1914.

Watts, J. *(Llanelli)* E.S.I. 1907; E.S.F.I.A. 1908; S.F.I. 1909.

Watts, Wallace *(Newport)* E.S.I. 92, 93, 94; E.I. 95; E. 96.

Weatherley, D. *(Swansea)* Z. 1998.

Weaver, D. *(Swansea)* E. 1964.

Webb, J. *(Abertillery)* S. 1907; E.S.F.I.A. 1908; E.S.F.I. 1909; F.E.S.I. 1910; E.S.F.I. 1911; E.S. 1912.

Webb, J.E. *(Newport)* M. 88; S. 89.

Webbe, G. *(Bridgend)* T.*WS. 1986; F.E.S.T.USA. 1987; *F.NZ(1).R. 1988.

Webster, R. *(Swansea)* A. 1987; B. 1990; AR.A. 1991; I.F.E.S.A. 1992; E.S.I.F. 1993.

Wells, G. *(Cardiff)* E.S. 1955; I.F. 1957; A.E.S. 1958.

Westacott, D. *(Cardiff)* I. 1906.

Wetter, H. *(Newport)* SA. 1912; E. 1913.

Wetter, J. *(Newport)* S.F.I. 1914; E.S.I. 1920; E. 1921; I.NZ. 1924.

Wheel, G.A.D. *(Swansea)* I.E.* 1974; F.E.I. 1975; A. 1975; E.S.I.F. 1976; I.E.S. 1977; E.S.I.F.A.(1 and 2)NZ. 1978; S.I. 1979; F.E.S.I. 1980; E.S.I.F.A. 1981; I. 1982.

Wheeler, P.J. *(Aberavon)* NZ. 1967; E. 1968.

Whitefoot, J. *(Cardiff)* A. 1984; S.I.F.E.FJ. 1985; E.S.I.F.FJ.T.WS. 1986; F.E.S.I.I.C. 1987.

Whitfield, J. *(Pill Harriers and Newport)* NZ. 1919; E.S.F.I. 1920; E. 1921; E.S.I.F. 1922; S.I. 1924.

Whitson, G. *(Newport)* F. 1956; S.I. 1960.

Wilkins, G. *(Bridgend)* T. 1994.

Williams, Aled *(Bridgend)* N.2* 1990; FJ.* 1995.

Williams, Barry *(Neath and Richmond)* F. 1996; R.T.NZ. 1997; It.E.Z*.SA.AR.* 1998; S.*I.It.* 1999.

Williams, Bleddyn *(Cardiff)* E.S.F.I.A. 1947; E.S.F.I. 1948; E.S.I. 1949; I. 1951; SA. 1951; S. 1952; E.S.I.F. 1953; NZ. 1953; S. 1954; E. 1955.

Williams, Brian *(Neath)* S.I.B. 1990; E.S. 1991.

Williams, Bryn *(Llanelli)* S.F.I. 1920.

Williams, C. *(Llanelli)* NZ. 1924; E. 1925.

Williams, C. *(Aberavon and Swansea)* E.S. 1977; F.E.S.I.NZ. 1980; E. 1983.

Williams, C.D. *(Cardiff and Neath)* F. 1955; F. 1956.

Williams, Darril *(Llanelli)* SA*. 1998.

Williams, D. *(Ebbw Vale)* E.S.I.F. 1963; E.S.I.F.SA. 1964; E.S.I.F. 1965; E.S.I. 1966; A. 1966; F.E. 1967; NZ. 1967; E. 1968; S.I.F.E.NZ. (1and 2)A. 1969; SA.S.E.I. 1970; E.S.I.F. 1971.

Williams, D.B. *(Newport and Swansea)* A.(1) 1978; E.S. 1981.

Williams, Eddie *(Neath)* NZ. 1924; F. 1925.

Williams, Evan *(Aberavon)* E.S. 1925.

Williams, Frank *(Cardiff)* S.F.I. 1929; E.S.I.F. 1930; F.I.SA. 1931; E.S.I. 1932; I. 1933.

Williams, G. *(London Welsh and Llanelli)* I.F. 1950; F.I.SA. 1931; E.S.I. 1932; I. 1933.

Williams, G.P. *(Bridgend)* NZ. 1980; E.S.A. 1981; I. 1982.

Williams, Gerald *(Bridgend)* I.F. 1981; E.*S. 1982.

Williams, Griff *(Aberavon)* E.S.I. 1936.

Williams, J. *(Blaina)* E.S.I.F. 1920; S.F.I. 1921.

Williams, J.F. *(London Welsh)* I.NZ. 1905; S. 1906; SA. 1906.

Williams, J.J. *(Llanelli)* F.*A. 1973; S.I.F.E. 1974; F.E.S.I. 1975; A. 1975; E.S.I. 1976; I.F.E.S. 1977; E.S.I.F.A.(1 and 2)NZ. 1978; S.I.F.E. 1979.

Williams, J.L. *(Cardiff)* SA. 1906; E.S.I. 1907, 1908; A. 1908; E.S.F.I. 1909; I. 1910; E.S.F.I. 1911.

Williams, J.P.R. *(London Welsh and Bridgend)* S.I.F.E.NZ.(1 and 2)A. 1969; SA.S.E.I.F. 1970; E.S.I.F. 1971; E.S.F. 1972; NZ. 1972; E.S.I.F.A. 1973; S.I.F. 1974; F.E.S.I. 1975; A. 1975; E.S.I.F. 1976; I.F.E.S. 1977; E.S.I.F.A.(1 and 2) NZ. 1978; S.I.F.E. 1979; NZ. 1980; E.S. 1981.

Williams, L. *(Cardiff)* S.I.F. 1957; E.S.I.F. 1958; E.S.I. 1959; F. 1961; E.S. 1962.

Williams, Les *(Llanelli and Cardiff)* E.S.F.I.A. 1947; I. 1948; E. 1949.

Williams, M. *(Newport)* F. 1923.

Williams, Martyn *(Pontypridd and Cardiff)* B.F.It*. 1996; It.E. Z.SA.AR. 1998; S.I.C. 1999.

Williams, Ossie *(Llanelli)* E.S.A. 1947; E.S.F.I. 1948.

Williams, Owain *(Bridgend)* N. 2 1990.

Williams, Ray *(Llanelli)* S. 1954; F. 1957; A. 1958.

Williams, R.D.G. *(Abercamlais)* E. 81.

Williams, R.F. *(Cardiff)* SA. 1912; E.S. 1913; I. 1914.

Williams, R.H. *(Llanelli)* I.F.S. 1954; S.I.F. 1955; E.S.I. 1956; E.S.I.F. 1957; A.E.S.I.F. 1958; E.S.I.F. 1959; E. 1960.

Williams, S. *(Llanelli)* E.S.F.I. 1947; S.F. 1948.

Williams, Sid *(Aberavon)* E.S.I. 1939.

Williams, Steve *(Neath and Cardiff)* T. 1994; *E.A.(1 and 2).B.F.It.A.SA.1996;USA.S.I.F.E. USA (1 and 2*).C.R*.T*.NZ*. 1997.

Williams, T. *(Pontypridd)* I. 82.

Williams, T. *(Swansea)* S.I. 88.

Williams, Tom *(Swansea)* I. 1912; F. 1913; E.S.F.I. 1914.

Williams, Trevor *(Cross Keys)* S.I. 1935; NZ. 1935; E.S.I. 1936; S.I. 1937.

Williams, Tudor *(Swansea)* F. 1921.

Williams, W. *(Crumlin)* E.S.F.I. 1927.

Williams, W.A. *(Newport)* I.F. 1952; E. 1953.

Williams, W.E.O. *(Cardiff)* S.I. 87; S. 89, S.E. 90.

Williams, W.H. *(Pontymister)* E.S.I. 1900; E. 1901.

Williams, W.O. *(Swansea)* F. 1951; SA. 1951; E.S.I.F. 1952, 1953; NZ. 1953; E.I.F.S. 1954; E.S.I.F. 1955; E.S.I. 1956.

Williams, W.P.J. *(Neath)* I.F. 1974.

Williams-Jones, H. *(S.W. Police and Llanelli)* S(R). 1989; F(R).I. 1990; A. 1991; S.A. 1992; E.S.I.F.Z.(1st)N. 1993; FJ.T.WS.*It.* 1994; E*. 1995.

Willis, R. *(Cardiff)* E.S.I.F. 1950, 1951; SA. 1951; E.S. 1952; S. 1953; NZ. 1953; E.I.F.S. 1954; E.S.I.F. 1955.

Wiltshire, M.L. *(Aberavon)* NZ. 1967; E.S.F. 1968.

Windsor, R.W. *(Pontypool)* A. 1973; S.I.F.E. 1974; F.E.S.I.A. 1975; E.S.I.F. 1976; I.F.E.S. 1977; E.S.I.F.A.(1 and 2)NZ. 1978; S.I.F. 1979.

Winfield, H.B. *(Cardiff)* I. 1903; E.S.I. 1904; NZ. 1905; E.S.I. 1906; S.I. 1907; E.S.I.F.A. 1908.

Winmill, S. *(Cross Keys)* E.S.F.I. 1921.

Wintle, Matthew *(Llanelli)* It. 1996.

Wintle, R. (London Welsh) WS.(R). 1988.

Wooller, W. *(Rydal School, Sale, Cambridge Univ. and Cardiff)* E.S.I. 1933, 1935; NZ. 1935; E.S.I. 1936, 1937; S.I. 1938; E.S.I. 1939.

Wyatt, Chris *(Llanelli)* Z*.SA*.SA.AR. 1998; S.I.F. It.E.AR (1+2).SA.C*.F. 1999.

Wyatt, Gareth *(Pontypridd)* T. 1997.

Wyatt, M. *(Swansea)* E.S.I.F. 1983; A. 1984, S.I. 1985; E.S.I. 1987.

Young, D. *(Swansea and Cardiff)* E.NZ.USA. 1987; E.S.I.F.NZ.(1 and 2)WS.R. 1988; S. 1989;A.SA. 1996; USA.S.I.F.E.R.NZ. 1997; It.E.S.I.F. 1998; I.E.*AR (1*+2*). SA.C*.F. 1999

Young, G.A. *(Cardiff)* E.S. 86.

Young, J. *(Harrogate, Bridgend and London Welsh)* S.I.F. 1968; S.I.F.E.NZ.(1) 1969; E.I.F. 1970; E.S.I.F. 1971; E.S.F. 1972; NZ. 1972; E.S.I.F. 1973.

Welsh victories over the South's Big Three

Wales defeated New Zealand in three of their first four meetings, a unique feat. The only game the 1905 All Blacks lost on their 33-match tour was to Wales at the Arms Park. They lost there again in 1935 and 1953 (after a 19-0 success at Swansea in 1924) and it was not until 1963 that they put the Cardiff bogy to rest.

WELSH VICTORIES

1905	New Zealand 3-0 (Cardiff)		1969	Australia 19-16 (Sydney)
1908	Australia 9-6 (Cardiff)		1973	Australia 24-0 (Cardiff)
1935	New Zealand 13-12 (Cardiff)		1975	Australia 28-3 (Cardiff)
1947	Australia 6-0 (Cardiff)		1981	Australia 18-13 (Cardiff)
1953	New Zealand 13-8 (Cardiff)		1987	Australia 22-21 (Rotorua)
1958	Australia 9-3 (Cardiff)		1999	South Africa 29-19 (Cardiff)

John Billot, former Sports Editor and chief rugby writer for *The Western Mail*, has been production editor and principal writer for the *Rugby Annual for Wales* for 31 years. He has brought up to date his definitive work on every match played by Wales, including many uncapped games. The *History of Welsh International Rugby* last appeared 27 years ago and, with the thrilling 1999 victories over France and England and then the historic first win against South Africa, the time is opportune to issue this revision of an essential reference work, printed and published in Wales. It is not intended to be overburdened with statistics, which often are outdated before a book is published; but the main ingredients are here. It is a book about men, matches and moments.

Opposite page: Master of the tap-down. Llanelli's Delme Thomas flips back for Wales against New Zealand in 1972. Glyn Shaw grimaces as he executes a crafty piece of lifting while Dai Morris, at the back, keeps an eagle eye on the ball.